I0093458

MATERIALIZING DEMOCRACY

NEW AMERICANISTS

A SERIES EDITED BY DONALD E. PEASE

MATERIALIZING DEMOCRACY

Toward a Revitalized Cultural Politics

Russ Castronovo and Dana D. Nelson, editors

DUKE UNIVERSITY PRESS   *Durham and London 2002*

©2002 Duke University Press
All rights reserved
Typeset in Minion by Keystone Typesetting, Inc.
Library of Congress Cataloging-in-Publication Data
appear on the last printed page of this book.
Wendy Brown's "Moralism As Antipolitics" originally appeared in
a slightly different form in her book *Politics Out of History*. Copy-
right 2001 by Princeton University Press. Reprinted by permission
of Princeton University Press.
Wai Chee Dimock's "Rethinking Space, Rethinking Rights: Literature, Law, and Science" originally appeared in a slightly different
form in *The Yale Journal of Law and the Humanities* 10 (1998):487–
504 reprinted here by permission.
An earlier version of Donald Pease's "Tocqueville's Democratic
Thing; or, Aristocracy in America" originally appeared in *boundary*
2 26.3 (1999) 87–114.
Lyrics to "Lida Rose" by Meredith Wilson © 1957 (renewed) Frank
Music Corp. and Meredith Wilson Music. Lyrics to "The Sadder
but Wiser Girl" by Meredith Wilson © 1957 (renewed) Frank Music Corp. and Meredith Wilson Music. All Rights Reserved.

CONTENTS

ACKNOWLEDGMENTS

Part of the problem of democracy is that it often represses the materiality and historicity of dialogue, hierarchy, production, and affect that factor into its ideals and daily operation. This volume, in contrast, does not pretend to stand free and clear. Its publication as a material artifact, as a fetish object with pages, brings us back to the colleagues who inspired us with their support and by their example.

Donald Pease encouraged this project in its infancy. Far beyond the essay to which he contributed to the volume, he lent us his guidance, friendship, and generosity. Wai Chee Dimock's enthusiasm at the panel where we launched the idea behind this collection gave us the nerve for the project. At key moments, Amy Kaplan and Chris Castiglia asked searching questions that helped us to refine our goals in collecting a variegated set of approaches to thinking through, about, beyond, and even against democracy. Bob Levine and Priscilla Wald ensured that our readings of democratic practice and thought never grew static. By debating our claims, conclusions, and methodologies, they imparted a rich and productive spirit of exchange to our efforts. Ken Wissoker has been an invaluable friend and editor to have in our corner: without his insight and dedication to this project, these pages would have come much harder, if at all. Katie Courtland and Christine Habermaas boosted our morale and helped us to get our ducks into something that usually resembles a row.

Finally: nothing without Tom Dillehay and Leslie Bow. What they offer us every day in the way of support amounts to far more than we can compensate with our thanks here.

MATERIALIZING DEMOCRACY

RUSS CASTRONOVO AND DANA D. NELSON

Introduction: Materializing Democracy and Other Political Fantasies

Democracy, for most U.S. Americans, is like the air we breathe: we live in it, we know it sustains us, we take it in out of reflex, and yet we give little thought to its shape, texture, or composition. Any appeal to democracy automatically assumes a political stance. But the appeal to democracy also takes form as an antipolitical gesture that closes down disagreement, contestation, and meaningful conflict. Attempts to deploy democracy in our political language, to activate it as a word and a concept in ways that gesture toward its symbolic depth, its historical complexity, and its open possibilities often only track across emptied-out clichés in a nationalist landscape. The short-circuiting of civic imagination about our supposedly most prized political ethic raises a question that undergirds the various theoretical and historicist aims of this volume: How might people define—let alone redefine—a political form that they know as intimately as the air that fills their lungs?

So familiar an ideal to citizens as to be *unfamiliar* in any "real" or specifically definitional sense—in short, so thoroughly naturalized as "common sense"— democracy in official as well as popular usage seems beyond contest or historical nuance. This inability to think critically about what is theoretically all around us—what we might consider the opacity of democracy—seems inherent to the first stirrings of popular government in the United States. Tom Paine's widely quoted (but seldom carefully studied) rendition of "common sense" democracy invokes a government that, in contrast to monarchical systems, is "formed on more natural principles."[1] Even as reliance on the "natural" suggests democracy's judicious authority, it also locates democracy outside history as though it were not the ongoing product of human effort, intervention, and contestation. Construed as a people's natural resource, democracy seems in need of conservation and protection. The question is, however, protection from what? Too often, the answer has assumed democracy not as a political process but as a sacred or reified thing to be safeguarded from popular usage, interpretation, and redefinition. Abraham Lincoln developed a parable to caution against this hypostatization of democracy, comparing democratic principles as given in the Declaration of Independence to a golden apple protected by the silver frame of the Constitution. "The picture was made, not to *conceal*, or *destroy* the apple; but to *adorn* and *preserve* it," explains Lincoln. "The picture was made for the apple—*not* the apple for the picture."[2] Yet Lincoln's formulation also aestheticizes the political, immuring democracy within stable structures that withstand the revisionary activities of the *demos*. Under the governmental structures and formal operations of the state, democracy has been confused with the walls that legislatively contain the people, a physical fact not the dynamic action created among the people themselves. Thus absented from the production of democracy, people have no sense that it is theirs to define. Rather, they worship at its walls. Formal procedures, legal institutions, and administrative frameworks corral democracy into predictable patterns. This reorganization of political possibility as political form seems, as Hannah Arendt puts it, "not the results of action but the products of [another's] making," not something people do but a structure that preexists them.[3]

Democracy itself is not something U.S. citizens argue much about. Instead, in the wake of Watergate, Irangate, and Monicagate what gets argued about is nonpolitical, moral categories: trust and privatized notions of ethics. In the most recent U.S. presidential election, candidates insisted on the importance of revitalizing the connection between democracy and trust.[4] In this popular debate, citizens and elected officials engage in a relation of faith rather than a negotiation of collective interests. In this way, democracy retreats to an exclusively moral category that is no longer interconnected with political, economic, or social categories.

The quality of civic trust is thus held open as a substitute for political debate as, for instance, when Robert Putnam laments an erosion of civic spirit in the United States. He looks beyond the usual data confirming a lack of voter interest to concentrate on a civic decline of another sort—the tendency of people to bowl alone apart from organized leagues: "Whether or not bowling beats balloting in the eyes of most Americans, bowling teams illustrate yet another vanishing form of social capital." Putnam both encourages more participation and speaks to a widespread anxiety that voluntary association and other modes of political life have become deadened. And people have been listening. The folksy research of this Harvard scholar has played well in chats at the White House, on radio talk shows, and in Internet interviews. For Putnam, the malaise of American democracy becomes evident in an "overall decrease in social trust."[5] But again, his diagnosis rests precisely on "common sense" notions of U.S. democracy that mystify the political through recourse to nonpolitical categories like "nature" and "trust." It corroborates a widespread belief that democracy should somehow rest outside the political—indeed, should be a reprieve from politics. Putnam's analysis deftly sidesteps the way "social capital," like all capital, is unequally distributed. We need to intervene in that problem politically, not trust that neighborliness will help us mind it less.

This book critiques a democracy that does not equate with politics. The problem we see is that democracy has become both an object of administrative technology and a subject of nationalism to the extent that its politicalness is either foreshortened or evacuated. To return democracy to the political is not to substitute democracy for the political, however. Fascism is also political. Instead, the task is to apprehend and analyze "democracy" as a historical range of practices, embedded in and managed by institutions and produced by material conditions. Thus while this methodological commitment to democracy is political, it is important to recognize that not all political modalities (even those operating in the "name" of democracy) invite open debate about their forms, practices, and goals.

NATURAL "DEMOCRACY"

In its highly assumed but vaguely articulated form at the start of the twenty-first century, then, commonsense democracy depends on antidemocratic moves that encourage our participation in a romantic ideal of civil life while discouraging our participation in gritty dialogues about the political (pre)conditions for community. It is good for neighbors to talk. But what socioeconomic requirements must first be satisfied and what phobias about race, immigration, sexuality, and class must be overcome before those neighborly conversations can even begin? As important, what kinds of neighborhoods never come into being?

These seldom-asked questions sustain the observation of a century ago that, when it comes to "equal laws" and "political equality," the native citizen "can neither feel nor understand" how U.S. institutions and traditions secure freedom and opportunity. This charge that Americans undertheorize and thus underappreciate democratic politics appears in a five-hundred-page overview of U.S.

history, population, geography, immigration, and economic fortunes, titled *Triumphant Democracy*, by Andrew Carnegie. With the claim that his status as a non–native-born citizen guarantees him an Archimedean vantage, Carnegie takes his place in the tradition of Alexis de Tocqueville, Francis Trollope, Domingo Faustino Sarmiento, Theodor Adorno, and Sacvan Bercovitch, all of whom with varying degrees of scorn and celebration evaluate the theory and practice of democracy in America. And what Carnegie perceives is that American democracy (and intellectual inquiry about democracy) is beyond politics. In this intellectual, patriotic, and familiar definition, American democracy triumphs over political democracy. Established as a space of consensus and registering time as a transhistory that obviates the need for historical analysis, the United States is "a land which has finally settled all fundamental political problems and now rests at peace upon the rock of the political equality of the citizen."[6] In this incarnation, democracy is lived out as some unquestioning reflex—that is, citizens meet state and national political expectations without pause *or* analysis—and Carnegie touts this as its principal virtue. Here democracy is neither a moral category nor a neighborly virtue: it is a physiological response like swallowing or like what one's leg does when the doctor taps the knee. Democracy is America's default reflex, its parameters and properties rarely subjected to a critical view that could suggest that political forms and rhetoric are other than the result of a natural course of events.

It is not hard from this vantage to peg Carnegie's theories about democracy-above-the-people as supplying their (fictionalized) assent to a philosophy of liberal individualism and industrial capitalism where the bosses inevitably know better than do regular citizens. To consent to that definition is to surrender democracy as though it were just a husk to be filled with apologies for—or an engine to be managed for the sake of—mass inequality, mass ignorance, mass apathy, or mass unsuitedness.[7] The contributors to this volume oppose that surrender as well as its correlatively false affirmation of a "freedom and opportunity" that many people neither experience nor know to miss in the first place. This unmourned lack of democratic actuality—how can we mourn what we never possessed?—nonetheless throbs at times with political sensation as though the commitment to economic justice, continuing and accessible public debate, and other democratic practices had become a phantom limb. As they question the right of men like Carnegie to define democracy for a putatively slack-jawed citizenry, the essays collected here aim toward recuperating public democratic sensibilities. But a project (such as this) of professional intellectuals proffering academic analyses may be structurally closer to Carnegie's position than to that of the "mass." In the context of a growing desire within humanities academia to be more public-minded, engaged, and relevant, some of the contributors to this volume turn a self-critical eye toward their own ongoing professional-managerial culture investments in "raising" public sensibility and "fixing" democracy rather than taking (an often far less grand) part in democracy's developing politicization.

Rather than being reluctant, cynical, or embarrassed about the possibilities of democracy, contributors to this volume insist on its often unrealized and even radical promises. The authors of these essays argue that any understanding of democracy will inevitably be an incomplete position in a much larger dialogue—in short, that democracy is a process and not a definition. Understanding democracy as simultaneously a debatable sociopolitical praxis and a theoretical horizon is central to repoliticizing its meaning and recuperating the idea of the political for all its practitioners.

If political theorist Sheldon Wolin's germinal formulation of politicalness—"our capacity for developing into beings who know and value what it means to participate in and be responsible for the care and improvement of our common and collective life"—was overly optimistic in its tacit idealization of the common, it has been helpfully supplemented by political theorists like Bonnie Honig and William Connolly, both of whom gesture toward the recuperation of democratic politicality as a practice of functional disunity.[8] Each critic differently highlights aspects of political practice and theorizing that idealize a system of action or inquiry that will effect some kind of national/communal unity, a unity that would mark the end of political work. Differently from Amy Gutmann and Dennis Thompson's supplemental formula of "democracy *and* disagreement," Honig and Connolly posit democracy *as* disagreement, a political process where "resolution" should only ever be conditional and temporary.[9] They thus reverse the negative valuation given to disagreement and politics in both political theory and public culture, insisting that what we have been trying to "solve" and even end on behalf of democracy is precisely its best and most vital aspect.

In Honig's and Connolly's arguments, the enabling condition for radical democracy is the ongoing cultivation of disagreement and difference, a reconceptualization of democracy as a more open-ended practice of, in theorist William Corlett's phrase, "community without unity."[10] Not aggregated around a single conceptual or consensual point, the cleavages of disunified community create multiple sites of address that do not feel compelled to speak *for* each other or speak *to* each other by sacrificing the historical accents of specific cultural idioms.

Not controlled by a single national consciousness, such a community *does not need* to repress the fractious materials that threaten the organization of community. Community without unity allows the uncanny citizens that Priscilla Wald sees inhabiting the United States to lay claim to representation.[11] Corlett thus urges, in a way that echoes Putnam's legitimate concerns, that we "use *community without teleology*" to create a life- and politics-enhancing commitment to what is not bound in our human relations by the rational and the instrumental, one that takes greater account of "accident and chance," play, unreason (*déraison*), and the human possibilities for extravagance together in a way that does not make a political or social "unity" its goal.[12]

OTHER POLITICAL FANTASIES

What falls outside the governing structure of reason may be our fantasies about what a materialized democracy would entail in terms of intellectual communication, pedagogy, familial and workplace structures, public space, sexual possibility, and identity practices. If we accept that the best energies of democracy are nonformal, the project of rethinking and reworking democracy seems difficult and scary. But it is possible to see that the terms of "difficulty" are generated by the formal rational system of law, procedure, and administration that manages political possibility, framing—perhaps falsely—what lies "inside" and "outside" democracy's purview. Rather than shy away from such supposed "inconvenience," "unruliness," and "unpredictability," a cohort of theorists have embraced concepts of democracy that refuse to take a preprogrammed shape as teleology. Instead, these theorists, working in interdisciplinary and international conjunctures, suggest that we might pattern democracy through the terms of affect, desire, unpredictability, and contingency.

C. Douglas Lummis in *Radical Democracy* seeks to correct critics, political thinkers, and policymakers who misrecognize democracy as the reasonable operation of the free market, nation-state allegiance, or other institutional affiliation. "Democracy is better described not as a 'system' or a set of institutions," writes Lummis, "but as a state of being and that the transition to it is not an institutional founding but a 'change of state.'"[13] This slippage between governmental state and metaphysical state, between state and state of being, opens up the subject of democracy itself, identifying democratic energies as questions of affect and feeling, unofficial contacts and random encounters, and episodic rituals and informal narratives—as well as traditionally recognized formal political practices.

Likewise, Chantal Mouffe dissociates democratic subjects from the narrowness of a legal status (such as citizenship) defined by the state. This reworking of the Tocquevillean formula so that all subjects are not exhausted by citizenship creates democracy as an open proposition always under construction where debate, dialogue, and contestation are continuous. "Radical democracy also means the radical impossibility of a fully achieved democracy," writes Mouffe.[14] If democracy is indeed under construction, it is best conceived as an undertaking that proceeds without a single set of blueprints. While an overarching vision would no doubt hasten completion of a "democratic" edifice, this project does not imagine politics as a single structure but as a host of habitats that combine, intersect, clash, and recombine in unexpected ways. Attending to structures of feeling and noninstitutional forms of political life reveals democracy as a messy prospect—the trick, as these various theorists suggest, is to resist the compulsion to clean up the mess by deadening the vibrancy or reducing the complexity of human political interactions.

Democracy can thus seemingly produce a bit of *mise-en-abyme:* in democracy, writes Claude Lefort, "the locus of power is an empty place, it cannot be occupied—it is such that no individual and no group can be consubstantial with it—and it cannot be represented."[15] The presumed risk, clearly, is that democracy tends to dematerialize under such accounts to the point where its real-world potential melts into air. At one moment, the unfocused aspect of power suggests democracy as a mirage, its appearance forever vanishing over the political horizon. At the next, democracy resists mediation or abstraction and can only be a direct experience that precedes the moment of representation. But what if our concern for form is the mirage? Even if its power is dispersed and its form remains open and indeterminate, democracy takes up space—psychically as well as politically and socially. As the authors in this volume argue, practices of democracy produce emotion and thought, inflict pain and healing, engender memory and amnesia, and organize and limit community as well as political action. And this sort of democracy has material effects on subjects and citizens.

A commitment to loosening the formalist rendition of democracy does not mean we are reaching for some impossible formlessness as utopian alternative. Even the mirage—the empty place of power—takes a certain form, however hazy. Form is inescapable, both in terms of the larger structures that support, administer, and hinder political action as well as the larger processes that create political actors. Indeed, it is this latter set of processes that target subjects in their most intimate recesses. One useful reading of democracy reminds us that, from its production of the citizen to its mobilization of collective power, any institutionalized practice of democracy serves as a technology that operates on, recognizes, legitimizes, and circumscribes—that is, forms—political actors. How does democracy organize politics into manageable or knowable formations? To what extent does democratic subjectivity require subjection? These questions concern political theorist Barbara Cruikshank: "Although I am deeply sympathetic to the project of radical or participatory democracy, I am skeptical that such a project presents an answer to questions of power, inequality, and political participation. Like any mode of government, democracy both enables and constrains the possibilities for political action." Citizenship functions as a technology that offers opportunities for participation in governance—provided that actors consent to occupy the calculable, governable space of citizen. Democracy-in-practice trades on various degrees of coercion and liberty. "The citizen is an effect and an instrument of political power rather than simply a participant in politics," writes Cruikshank.[16]

Insight into the effects of democracy, then, demands a material sensibility of power broader and more diverse than that implied by a materialist analysis of class. This introduction, like the essays that follow, stakes approaches that register the political as a multidisciplinary (even antidisciplinary), dense terrain of representation, psychology, aesthetics, sexuality, media, and so forth. Democracy, no matter how liberating a project, can never free itself of this terrain; democracy always remains impacted with antidemocratic residues, no matter how good citizens feel about their present or how effective amnesia has been.

DEMOCRATIC VISTAS

This is what *Materializing Democracy* will not do: we will not describe democracy in the terms of total freedom, good leadership, nationalist cant, protective institutionalism, rational rule, happy communitarianism, rigid formalism, transcendental formlessness, smug liberalism, or First Worldism. Instead, the contributors treat democracy as a constructed category in order to understand what conditions of thought and practice make it more and less possible, more and less livable, more and less emancipatory.

In reopening the question of democracy in this particular way, the essays in this book sidestep the temptation of formulating questions for the clean answer. Instead they pose a complex and open-ended investigation, which might be summarized as responding to what appears as a fairly simple question: *What makes democracy matter?* This volume adds to the conversation about radical democracy and its (forestalled) possibilities and, in particular, focuses for literary and cultural studies some critical convergences that interrogate the following:

—The tendency of democracy to become nonpolitical either by returning to foundations that are assumed to be beyond contestation and thus *pre*political or by searching for new consensual spaces that are emptied of debate and are thus *post*political

—The ambivalent relationship of democracy to formalism, especially in terms of legal apparatuses invested with the power to make citizens both appear and disappear (this does not mean, however, that democracy lies just over the horizon in zones of formlessness)

—The convergence of political and aesthetic apparatuses in popular representative praxis, engendering cultural practices that shape democratic memory and its loss

—The structures of enfranchisement that depoliticize citizens and install subjects as the investments of professional-managerial culture

—The relationship of affect and democracy, examining how forms of democracy are lived and felt with particular attention to the modes of feeling that enhance, sentimentalize, spiritualize, or block democratization

—The relationship of intellectuals to democracy and tensions between theoretical and practical approaches to democracy that emerge from this relationship

—The issue of what cultivates intellectual alienation and public disconnection from a sense of entitlement to political engagement

Two main lines of inquiry collate these concerns. In the first, the essays gathered here seek to understand the felt importance of democracy. This project entails examinations of the forces that make democracy matter to people in their day-to-day lives. Democracy is translated with varying degrees of success not just governmentally but also at more intimate levels of consciousness, feeling, and body. The idea (and ideal) of democracy transmutes into tangible (inter)personal effects and no less tangible dreams and nightmares. What histories and injustices make us want democracy? And at the same time, we need also to question the sources of prestige, privilege, and entitlement that dispose us to be indifferent toward the development of democracy. The critics in this volume, working from multiple and often colliding perspectives, problematize and pluralize democracy's histories and possibilities, its significance for politics and human freedom(s). The intent of this critical project is not to invalidate democracy. Quite the opposite: by making explicit and reexamining assumptions about equality and fairness that too often work toward opposite effects we hope to strengthen commitments to the messy, ongoing political work of democracy.

In its second line of inquiry, this volume gives shape and historical texture to the materials of democracy. It studies how democracy is made material—materially feasible and materially important and worth struggling for. This arena of examination insists on reading "matter" in a quasi-empirical way, as a sensuous category of thought, experience, and feeling or as an embodied practice. Political theorists have a well-developed critique of the relation of capital to democracy, but few have analyzed from a radical vantage how the cultural products of capital have or might work toward (re)building democracy. How central are materials such as public space, novels, advice manuals, celebrities, mass communication technology, classrooms, or prisons to the building of democracy? To think about the diverse ways that democracy matters and can matter is multiply to attend to the bodies, physical spaces, and lost memories that have witnessed the appearance and disappearance of democracy's manifestations.

Descriptions of democracy typically run along two different axes: one is plotted with specific reference points attentive to history and cultural difference and the other with more abstract, timeless coordinates. As this *demo*graphic storyline goes, material reality and empowering sociopolitical vision will converge at some future juncture that witnesses the earthly realization of an ideal political form. But these lines have yet to meet—and they never will—because of constitutive tensions between and within the material and the democratic. The essays in this volume stop trying to force that convergence, stop feeling sorry about its deferral, and turn to different ways of working at and thinking about democracy for the here and now. In counterpoising *materializing* democracy to *theorizing* democracy, then, we are not motivated by the hope that such a move will suture the unmatched edges between the ideal and the real, general and local, universal and particular, homogeneity and heterogeneity, equalization and equality, social harmony and dissensus, and cohesion and mess. Instead, these essays work to break apart the "self-evident" intelligibility of these binaries and agitate for new configurations of democratic possibility.

The project we are outlining here does not reject the customary aims of democracy theory but rather recoordinates them. Even before 1789 or 1776 broad declarations of general principles have been in vogue, and yet rarely have these historical expressions of theoretical equality translated into hard-and-fast policies that do the work of developing self-governance and generalizing political freedom. Indeed, the rhetoric of equality—"all men" or even "all persons"—has subtended theoretical dispositions to override the political identities of sub-groups and subalterns that compromise this "all." The vagueness of much democracy theory with regard to its human interactants is, in Bruce Robbins's view, a habit mined with political danger and pragmatic costs: "[We] do not know how to argue for the democracy we want without mobilizing an image of the public so hazy, idealized, and distant from the actual people, places, and institutions around us that it can easily serve purposes that are anything but democratic."[17] Too often in thinking about alternative democracies, theorizing means getting too much distance from both history and politics. Too often we appreciate the vox populi from the safe distance of a corrective schema that soothingly allows us to forget the dissonance, discordance, and disagreement that structures democratic polity.

We want to underscore without cynically giving up on radical democracy the ways that democracy is built out of direct *and* mediated uses of power and knowledge. Its various forms recognize and will not transcend historical conditions. Democracy's inability to exist outside of the concrete circumstances, events, and human particularity that cannot be subsumed under (or sanitized through) general accounts or descriptions literally disestablishes democracy *as* theoretical. Yet democracy's tenacious hold on the visceral and the contingent does not extend so far as to render it antitheoretical. Insofar as democracy describes a world that does not exist, it needs to take the form of theoretical narrative somewhat like a fantasy or counterfactual reality that we struggle to realize. But, as a material practice, democracy works toward actualizing the parameters and principles we theorize for it.

Democracy can't be imposed by model, and intellectuals shouldn't mistake their analytic "success" with the (antidemocratic) dream of fixing democracy for the rest of us. To confront this desire is to begin analyzing the psychopolitical dynamics and the repressed realities and histories of the "democracy" we live in. So familiar that the national collective body always already seems to know what it is, but so unfamiliar that America's desegregated bodies (women, queers, racial minorities, South American and Asian immigrants, the underclasses, etc.) dream more than encounter its realization, democracy takes on the structure of the uncanny. Framed by constructive histories we can't seem to remember, and by crimes we cannot forget, democracy involves cycles of repression and obsession. This is not a theoretical postulate but a real problem, because in order to begin acting on commitments to equality, fairness, justice, and freedom, this argument would suggest that we have to make conscious and work through our desires for and fears of democratic politics. And it is a problem of the real as well: on one hand notions of realpolitik, backed up by data and empirical estimates, limit citizens' understandings of democracy to what has been attempted before; on the other, members of the polity fail to face up to what really happened—"removal," internment, and slavery—in the past.

This volume thus gears itself toward understanding both the material effects of U.S. "democratic" political psychology and its dreamwork, the compensatory fantasies brought on by antidemocratic conditions that come to stand in as "democracy." How historically transparent and psychopolitically straightforward are desires for freedom and equality? In what ways do seemingly unrelated investments in familial and "private" practices alternately (or simultaneously) make possible and forestall wider democratic possibilities? How deeply attached are we to relationships of (our own) powerlessness within democracy?

The supposed futility of democratic critique is a specific malady of contemporary academic culture. So routine is this accusation that it is hard not to start wondering about the compulsive nature of the professoriate to bow its head, proclaim its worthlessness, and accept such allegations as true. To that end, the essays in this book mark a particular moment in humanities academic thinking on the subject of democracy, its radical possibilities for changing our worlds both inside and beyond our immediate work spaces. Interdisciplinary movements in academia have combined with the institutional entry and academic development of oppositional identity politics like race, ethnic and postcolonial studies, women's studies, and queer studies in ways that have radically changed the discourses, members, and operations of the university. Such changes, too often token in nature, are nonetheless susceptible to backlash and retrenchment. The contributors to this volume grew up as professionals in this institutional generation, and from it they respond to debates about the role of the humanities in articulating the duties and promoting the values of citizenship. In the decades leading up to the close of the twentieth century, polemics ranging from E. D. Hirsch's *Cultural Literacy* to Bill Readings's *The University in Ruins* have stressed the connection between the disciplines of the "liberal arts" and the discipline of the nation-state. From a host of materials ranging from popular icons and celebrities to "highbrow" texts of democratic theory, the essays gathered together here assemble an archive of democracy that coordinates readings of citizenship along different levels of culture (high, low, middling, and regional). Their scope implies an archive open to the public. Alexis de Tocqueville and Ralph Waldo Emerson appear in these pages, but Will Rogers, Monica Lewinsky, Princess Diana, and other figures who shape and are shaped by public imaginations are just as significant. These essays reconsider the academic and political arenas within which intellectual work takes place, and they look to other spaces for rethinking and reworking democratic possibility. Even as they ask what sort of material or practical approaches to politics are outlined and imagined by this cultural archive, they also ask if this cultural archive can provide, in Judith Butler's terms, a contingent foundation for democratic rearticulation.[18] That is, although we raise questions about the adequacy of this archive to help in actualizing radical democracy, we insist that the culture of democracy—which for the essays in this volume includes musicals, slave narratives, undergraduate classrooms, radio broadcasts, managerial practices—is indispensable to historicizing and mapping heterogeneous political possibilities.

Materializing Democracy asks how we can self-critically and critically regroup in ways that will help expand our own commitment to, ideas about, and tolerance for democracy. And there are some precise components to this critical project and our aim to make democracy matter more now. We are asking questions that address our inability to narrate democracy's shadow histories and speak forthrightly about our complex fantasies about it. Why can't we make democracy face up to the material? Why can't those of us dedicated to democracy risk having fantasies about the material without fearing this exercise of imagination as a disavowal of radical politics? That is, are projects that envision the equitable distribution of social resources (such as justice, decision making, claims to representation, and access to dialogue) anything more than fantasies? And if such projects are to remain unrealizable, what is the status of fantasy within the field of the political?

CROSS-CONVERSATIONS

In addressing the questions stated above, the essays gathered in this volume tell different sorts of stories. Some of these stories are more narratival than others; others assemble nonliterary archives; still others emerge from an intimate relation to experience. Yet they all share commitments to narrative as material practice. Neither a maneuver to retain aesthetic categories nor a bow to a postmodern world where anything goes, a methodological focus on narrative references politics as a complex set of stories that recuperates material that traditionally has been relegated to putatively nonpolitical spheres, housed under ideologies of the domestic, sentimental, spiritual, or personal. Narrative is, first of all, the stuff that too often gets left out of politics. Categories like citizenship, mechanisms like representation, and values like consensus often appear without any prehistory, as though there were no stories of power that stood behind such norms. We insist, however, that there is no way to engage democracy except through such categories, mechanisms, and values that stand in for a densely complex history of material relations that had to be first smoothed out, ignored, forgotten, or sorted and hierarchized in order to proclaim a particular version of democracy as a normative value.

In addition to recuperating excluded material, the understanding of democracy as narrative practice loosely implies a methodology that avoids routing all stories into metanarratives of liberal consensus or social contract. Instead, narrative is always provisional, never settling into ossified forms or incontrovertible precedents. For even as narrative suggests a fuller history than can be supplied by mere political categories, it also invites revision. Under these terms, stories—like a vibrant sense of the political—are constantly evolving and are subject to popular revision and rife with transformative potential. Stories represent, document, and, most important, reconstruct reality. Democratic politics hinge on this same attitude toward sociopolitical reality. Just as narrative reorders events and tinkers with and transforms circumstances, we need a politics that can think about the justice, equality, mutual respect, and all the other democratic prospects that in our current sociopolitical reality are "mere utopia."[19]

Donald Pease returns to one of the foundational narratives of American democracy. In his reading of Tocqueville, Pease finds that this originary pattern tends powerfully to devolve into antipolitical fantasy. Tocqueville's *Democracy in America*, he argues, is beset by "negative hallucinations" that induce Tocqueville and a host of contemporary political commentators *not* to see actually existing material conditions that compromise democracy, and thus also to miss more radical democratic energies. In this unreal but widely accepted reading of U.S. culture and political institutions, American democracy is retrofitted with an aristocratic sensibility for cohesion that mutes the importance of civic unpredictability and deep social cleavages.

Behind the ritualistic story of "democracy in America" lies a much less talked about story of unfreedom that routinely makes use of imprisonment, solitary confinement, and the death penalty. Joan Dayan confronts this contradiction head-on by examining the legal genealogy of slavery that remains in force today, stripping away the personhood of modern prisoners. Moving from medieval codes to contemporary legal decisions, Dayan pays close attention to what she calls the legal sorcery of the law—that is, the supernatural power of the state to make living citizens into civilly dead subjects—and its role in underpinning the formal operations of justice. This interest in rituals of exclusion also motivates Richard Flores's study of cultural imperialism along the Texas-Mexico border. U.S. democratic nationalism, Flores suggests, has long imagined Mexicans as prosthetic limbs ("wetbacks" and "braceros") to booster an anemic economy. Through readings of John Wayne's *The Alamo* and talk radio paranoia about the official currency of Spanish in El Cenizo, Texas, Flores reveals how the production of racial, linguistic, and cultural difference limits participation in democracy's public sphere.

As Dayan and Flores outline the gothic effects of democratic exclusions, Russ Castronovo starts by unpacking nineteenth-century fascination with the occult. He maps how constructions of "the soul" create a kind of political morbidity, setting depoliticized limits for the very political conditions in this world. Reading various manifestations of the occult from clairvoyance to slave superstition as activities of political theorizing, he reveals how heavenly visions of spiritual equality mask the inequalities of an abstract public sphere. The importance of the soul did not die out in the nineteenth century: contemporary defenses of higher education are haunted by notions of spirituality that threaten, as Castronovo contends, to erase the privilege and hierarchy reproduced by humanities discourse. Like Dayan, Flores, and Castronovo, Lauren Berlant suggests the dead as a point of political cathexis, but her point of connection is different from the socially dead or civilly dead persons of the previous essays. Interrogating the political forms that produce persons and non-persons, Berlant takes up two pedagogical mechanisms that have historically supported the liberal fantasy of a redemptive national future: the expansion of the vote (here specifically woman suffrage) and public fantasies that surround the dead-too-soon celebrity. Celebrity worship offers a model of citizenship fused to a popular death wish. Here, Berlant sees the triumph of women's politics, "the politics of a higher viscera" guiding what she terms "the new formalism of liberal citizenship."

If Berlant attacks the pacifying inclusive politics of liberalism for their deadening effects, Lisa Duggan exposes neoliberalism's growing addiction to exclusion in the name of liberalization. In the literature of the Independent Gay Forum (IGF), Duggan charts the emergence of centrist gay politics that seek to shrink rather than expand the public sphere. By locating the IGF proponents along a trajectory of gay activism from the 1950s to 1990s that has steadily flowed toward the mainstream, Duggan outlines serious possible consequences in the tendency of sexual political rhetoric to scale back its claims for equality and freedom to privatized spaces and nonpolitical forms. Chris Castiglia, somewhat differently, investigates the possibilities of private affect for reinvigorating persons left cynical by the U.S. government's false promises to and betrayals of its citizens. Turning to the musical's dramatization of interiority, such as the confession and the crush, he reevaluates and opens up scenes of sentimental privacy to public engagement. He looks to scorned citizens, notably Hester Prynne and Monica Lewinsky, as subjects who theatricalize emotion to ground a radically democratic impulse to replace heteronormative, abstract commitments with local, deeply felt forms of trust.

Whereas Castiglia's essay is concerned with the regenerative possibilities of the musical as political theater, Dana Nelson stresses the need to link democracy to counteraesthetic modes of representation. When we try to make democracy manageable or coherent, as she suggests Emerson does in *Representative Men,* we close down its capacity to produce disagreement and difference, which, however unpleasing or unsightly, are indispensable to real democratic vitality. Nelson instead argues that we take our cue from Rebecca Harding Davis's post–Civil War novel *Waiting for the Verdict,* which prefers open-ended conflicts to virtual forms of democracy. Democracy, in short, is difficult to represent, and may well not be amenable to representative substitution. Wai Chee Dimock's essay suggests that one reason for this difficulty is that it is hard to imagine a nonabsolute space in which rights, justice, and equality can materialize in ways that will allow for negotiation. By breaking down the idea of space to the level of its epistemological assumption and turning to Einstein's specific rejection of Kantian "absolute space," she opts for a relativist model of rights. As her essay explores the interstices of law, science, and local-color literature it visibly demonstrates that the ethical implications of the search for justice cannot be limited to the structural coordinates of a single formal domain.

Michael Moon invokes a different kind of attention to space in his case study of Will Rogers, the Cherokee cowboy philosopher who used his comedy and commentary routinely to contest the absolute spatiality of the western frontier. Moon examines how Rogers's apparently apolitical career moves from vaudeville and newspapers to the entertainment industry of radio, film, and television was in fact an improvisatory diplomacy, a subtle use of new media to carry on Native American diplomacy by other means. His essay combats the institutional amnesia that has depoliticized Rogers's legacy by turning him into a "unique" representative of the Cherokee, a representation that overshadows the collective politics that Rogers sought to further. Kevin Gaines helps place such concerns in internationalist context in his historicization of the democratic struggle advanced by black feminist politics. But this historicization is no easy task: a pathology of "black female belatedness" makes black women's political contributions to resistance and nationalism appear as a secondary effect of black militancy.[20] Examining the politics that gather in Toni Cade Bambara's germinal anthology *The Black Woman,* Gaines recovers a sense of revolution that interconnects diasporic contexts with everyday gender relations and ethical commitments to equality.

The value of rethinking legacies of the Left provides a broad focus for the final three essays in this volume. Chris Newfield turns to Bambara's provocative assertion that "revolution begins with the self, in the self," insisting that the Left has too often compromised on individual agency in its theorizing about democracy, and has for this reason too easily capitulated to neoliberalism's insistence that markets are the best providers for individual freedom. Newfield maintains that left critiques must develop around the ways that "democracy frees the self where markets do not." He urges left critics to notice the "widespread demoralization that accompanies procedural democracy in the United States," and he contends that we can better promote a full democratic project by focusing at the level of individual liberation not the individual as we liberally know it but a revolutionized subject conceptualized through the ideal of "unburdened agency." Jeffrey Goldfarb turns his focus toward the individual as intellectual in an essay on the role of liberal arts education by asking how intellectuals act in support of democracy, and how intellectual activity can work at cross-purposes with democracy. Applying lessons learned in the democratization of Eastern Europe, Goldfarb contends that too often intellectuals have substituted theories and ideology for democratic deliberation in our classrooms. This substitution closes debate, and in so doing it contributes to the narrowing of the very practices of openness and civility that characterize intellectual democratic work.

The legacy of a Left now discredited after the collapse of most existing socialist projects also haunts Wendy Brown's contribution to this volume. Refusing to be either paralyzed or entranced by the ghosts of the Left that still walk the halls of academia, Brown suggests a politics located beyond identity; that is, a post-identity politics that rejects the easy and quick condemnations of gender discrimination, censorship, homophobia, state-sponsored liberalism, and so forth and instead undertakes a "more serious project of transformation." To this end, she adduces distinctions between political morality and the political moralism that characterizes too often today what passes for radical politics.

This overview risks smoothing out the fault lines that crisscross this volume. That's not the aim of our work. Rather, we hope such fissures will rupture for the reader into the productive disagreements characteristic of democracy. For example, although Castiglia and Newfield turn to what we might think of Tocqueville's "habits of the heart" for the twenty-first century in examinations of radical affect and revamped individualism, Berlant and Castronovo differently argue that inwardness too often tends toward or results in a regressive, antipolitical position. Such tensions also characterize the very different kinds of positions that our contributors take on the roles of minorities within democracy. For instance, Flores and Dayan would seemingly agree that a white majoritarian bias functions as a structural block to full democratic realization, whereas Moon and Gaines would seem to insist that democracy's best energies and movements toward reformulation come from its outsiders. Or, to take another example, the level of hope for democracy varies from essay to essay (and from moment to moment within essays). Duggan fears that the public sphere is shrinking to a neoconservative rendition of sexual politics. Dayan concludes that the autonomous zone occupied by the individual is systematically being destroyed. Nelson seemingly records the vanishing of democratic energies within abstract systems of representation. But contrapuntal notes sound, for instance, in the essays by Dimock, Brown, and Goldfarb, which suggest a range of performances and performative sites from writing to teaching as interventions against the antidemocratic practices of state and professional institutions.

As we hope we have made clear, we've gathered these essays together not because they share some singular thematic focus on a particular vision of democracy but because they provoke argument and discussion.[21] Democracy is too rich and too freighted to be simply an idea to play variations on. Rather it is a type of knowledge, a structure of feeling, and a methodological problem. It is, moreover, an ethical engagement and a practice of recovery. And maybe it can be a historical destiny, if we keep working at it.

NOTES

1 Thomas Paine, *Common Sense and Other Political Writings*, ed. Nelson F. Adkins (Indianapolis: Bobbs-Merrill, 1953), 30. We see a difference between the way Paine is

used in the American "democratic" tradition and his own political/intellectual project. While nuggets from *Common Sense* have been picked up, the radical substance of his arguments has been left to languish much like George Washington left Paine himself to languish in a French prison for ten months. Here, Paine is clearly countering Hobbesian arguments that the state of nature is an antisocial state, and instead insists that the state of nature is a noninstitutionalized space of self-governance and of radical democracy.

2 Abraham Lincoln, "A Meditation on Proverbs 25:11" in *Collected Works of Abraham Lincoln*, ed. Roy P. Blaser, 9 vols. (New Brunswick: Rutgers University Press, 1953), 4:168.

3 Hannah Arendt, *The Human Condition*, 2nd ed. (1958; Chicago: University of Chicago Press, 1998), 194. Arendt's argument picks up on a thread from Aristotle's *Politics*, which considers the adequacy of defining the polis as a physical space: "It would be possible to surround the whole of the Peloponnese by a single wall [but would that make it a single polis?]." Or, perhaps it is better to define the polis in terms of a much more porous and changing notion of space, a space equivalent to "the dimensions of a people [*ethnos*] rather than those of a city" (*The Politics of Aristotle*, trans. Ernest Barker [New York: Oxford University Press, 1958], 98–99).

4 Here is an example from the 2000 presidential race. Bill Bradley: "The lifeblood of democracy and politics is trust"; Al Gore: "Democracy stands or falls on a mutual trust" between elected officials and voters (*www.billbradley.com/bin/article.pl?path= 210799/4; www.algore2000.com/speeches/harvard.html*). Bradley proposes specific voting and campaign finance election reform to remedy trust problems, while Gore urges voters to abandon their cynicism about elected officials and/or the United States.

5 Robert D. Putnam, "Bowling Alone: America's Declining Social Capital," *Journal of Democracy* 6, no. 1 (1995): 69, 72. Samuel R. Delany, an urban queer political theorist, describes a similar affective longing for community but provides a political-economic analysis, one that yields different agendas than Putnam's antipolitical/sentimental analysis. See Delany's *Times Square Red, Times Square Blue* (New York: New York University Press, 1999), especially part 2, ". . . Three, Two, One, Contact," where he outlines his arguments about the difference between networking and contact possibilities in urban democracy.

6 Andrew Carnegie, *Triumphant Democracy, or Fifty Years' March of the Republic* (New York: Charles Scribner's Sons, 1886), iii, 414.

7 But this assumption continues to supply one strong logic for U.S. practices of political representation, and some of our most passionate twentieth-century political theorists from Dewey to Dahl to Rawls seem almost inevitably to fall back on it in their analyses of possibilities for democratic revitalization. See John Dewey, *The Public and Its Problems* (1927; Chicago: Swallow Press, 1980); Robert Dahl, *Who Governs? Democracy and Power in an American City* (New Haven: Yale University Press, 1961); and John Rawls, *A Theory of Justice* (Cambridge: Harvard University Press, 1971).

8 Sheldon Wolin, "Contract and Birthright," in *The Presence of the Past: Essays on the*

State and the Constitution (Baltimore: Johns Hopkins University Press, 1989), 139; Bonnie Honig, *Political Theory and the Displacement of Politics* (Ithaca: Cornell University Press, 1993); and William Connolly, *The Ethos of Pluralization* (Minneapolis: University of Minnesota Press, 1995).

9 Amy Gutmann and Dennis Thompson, *Democracy and Disagreement: Why Moral Conflict Cannot Be Avoided in Politics and What Should Be Done about It* (Cambridge: The Belknap Press of Harvard University Press, 1996).

10 William Corlett, *Community without Unity: A Politics of Derridean Extravagance* (Durham: Duke University Press, 1993).

11 Priscilla Wald, *Constituting Americans: Cultural Anxiety and Narrative Form* (Durham: Duke University Press, 1995), 10.

12 Corlett, *Community without Unity*, 13, 213.

13 C. Douglas Lummis, *Radical Democracy* (Ithaca: Cornell University Press, 1996), 159.

14 Chantal Mouffe, "Preface: Democratic Politics Today" in *Dimensions of Radical Democracy: Pluralism, Citizenship, Community*, ed. Chantal Mouffe (London: Verso, 1992), 14. In this respect, Ernesto Laclau rightly undercuts the possibility of radical emancipation since an emancipated political order is necessarily tied—if only by way of opposition or priority—to an unfree society. Neither idealist despair nor worldly cynicism should be the fallout of this perspective. Laclau instead takes the impossibility of complete or radical emancipation as symptomatic of democracy. He writes: "Incompletion and provisionality belong to the essence of democracy" (*Emancipation(s)* [New York: Verso, 1996], 16).

15 Claude Lefort, *Democracy and Political Theory*, trans. David Macey (Minneapolis: University of Minnesota Press, 1988), 17.

16 Barbara Cruikshank, *The Will to Empower: Democratic Citizens and Other Subjects* (Ithaca: Cornell University Press, 1999), 2, 5.

17 Bruce Robbins, "Introduction: The Public as Phantom" in *The Phantom Public Sphere*, ed. Bruce Robbins (Minneapolis: University of Minnesota Press, 1993), xi.

18 Butler writes: "Although the political discourses that mobilize identity categories tend to cultivate identifications in the service of a political goal, it may be that the persistence of *dis*identification is equally crucial to the rearticulation of democratic contestation" (*Bodies That Matter: On the Discursive Limits of "Sex"* [New York: Routledge, 1993], 4). See also her "Contingent Foundations: Feminism and the Question of 'Postmodernism'" in *Feminists Theorize the Political*, ed. Judith Butler and Joan W. Scott (New York: Routledge, 1992).

19 This is Herbert Marcuse's phrase. He argues that "when truth cannot be realized within the established social order, it always appears . . . as mere utopia. This transcendence speaks not against, but for its truth." Marcuse identifies critical theory as the crucial agent in "utopian" social change: "Critical theory preserves obstinacy as a genuine quality of philosophical thought. . . . From the beginning it did more than simply register and systematize facts. Its impulse came from the force with which it spoke against the facts and confronted bad facticity with its better potentialities" (*Negations: Essays in Critical Theory*, trans. Jeremy J. Shapiro [Boston: Beacon Press,

1968], 143); thanks to Avery Gordon for drawing our attention to Marcuse, this passage in particular.

20 See Lora Romero, "Black Nationalist Housekeeping: Maria W. Stewart" in *Home Fronts: Domesticity and Its Critics in the Antebellum United States* (Durham: Duke University Press, 1997), 52–69.

21 Nor do the contributors share a disciplinary focus. Through their professional appointments in African American studies, American studies, anthropology, history, English, gender studies, politics, and social theory, the authors represent a variety of disciplines and fields.

DONALD E. PEASE

Tocqueville's Democratic Thing; or, Aristocracy in America

TOCQUEVILLE, THE MULLAH OF SURPLUS CONTAINMENT

In its February 2, 1998, issue the *New Republic* published an essay, titled "Tocqueville and the Mullah," in which the editors expressed their concern about an interview that CNN had broadcast with President Mohammed Khatami of Iran. They described the interview as posing a significant "threat" to the U.S. policy of "dual containment."[1] The dual containment policy operates on two separate but intertwined levels, which interconnect the national geography governed by state policymakers with the civil society inhabited by U.S. citizens. As an official foreign policy, dual containment implements the state's substitution of Iran and Iraq for Russia and China as the representatives, in the wake of the cold war, of the fundamental threats to the national security. In substituting Islamic terrorism for world communism as constituting a pervasive menace to the American way of life, the post–cold war policy conjoins the totalization of danger in the external realm with a reorganization of civil society internally.

"Tocqueville" and the "Mullah" act as condensed signifiers for the operations that produced both the threat and the territorial and civic spaces whereby the policy contained the threat. The enactors of containment as an official foreign policy invoked "Tocqueville's" description of the exceptional standing of the United States in the history of nations to authorize the securing of its territorial borders against threats posed by the "Mullah's" Islamic terrorists. Citizens found in "Tocqueville's" *Democracy in America* a representative account of U.S. civil society. "Tocqueville" described civil society as a social arena in which citizens can exercise their rights of voluntary association and free and open discussion as a consequence of the state's protection of its contours against the menace posed by the "Mullah's" civic violence and linguistic terrorism.[2]

But the threat that the editors characterized as posed by Khatami is neither that of the Muslim terrorist who justified the state's foreign policy nor that of the Islamic fundamentalist whose "incivility and irrationality" consolidated the contours of U.S. civil society. The greatest threat that Khatami posed to the editors grew out of his having declined to appear threatening. Khatami's carefully articulated refusal to identify either himself or Islam as a menace to U.S. democracy thereafter endangered both levels of the policy of containment which, as we have seen, depended on these negative representations of the Mullah for their effective operation.

Khatami gave expression to his refusal to ratify this negative representation in three separate but interconnected articulations: he refuted the claim that the Islamic Republic constitutes a threat to U.S. territorial borders; he proposed similarities between the religious cultures of the United States and Iran; and he declared the dual containment policy a violation of internationally agreed-on codes of civility and a threat to democratic cultures worldwide.[3]

While the editors found in the fact that the CNN interview with Khatami had taken place at all evidence of Iran's unwarranted reintegration within civil society, they were particularly vexed about Khatami's citations from Tocqueville's *Democracy in America* to justify Iran's change of status. Khatami had adapted his understanding of *Democracy in America* (a book he was "sure most Americans have read") to the task of formulating this complex repudiation of the dual containment policy. Proposing that the devotion to liberty of U.S. citizens was itself cultivated in the rites and traditions of what Tocqueville had described as a national civil religion, Khatami drew the conclusion that the U.S. civil religion was not altogether different from Iran's religious nationalism, which also "calls all humanity irrespective of religion and belief, to rationality and logic."

Khatami's deployment of Tocqueville's text to dismantle the containment policy should be understood as a reversal of the usages to which policymakers had previously put it. From the time of its initial publication in 1835, *Democracy in America* supplied the concepts, generalizations, and categories out of which U.S. citizens were encouraged to experience and make sense of U.S. democracy. Its system of representations anchored the presuppositions out of which citizens and politicians formulated their opinions. *Democracy in America* was reproduced, perpetuated, and transmitted through such discursive practices. Because it was reputed to have codified the governing norms and assumptions that undergirded U.S. democracy, political commentary on Tocqueville's *Democracy in America* elevated the text into a transhistorical representation of U.S. democracy's unchanging transcendental essence. It was as a consequence of the text's standing that the governmental officials responsible for the dual containment policy invoked the norms and rules informing Tocqueville's categorical understanding of U.S. democracy as politically authorized criteria for deciding that the United States and the Islamic Republic were absolutely opposed political formations.[4]

Insofar as Islam represented the political formation out of whose exclusion U.S. civil society had established its integrity, the political effectiveness of U.S. civil society might be described as having depended in part on Islam's ongoing negative valuation of its workings. Indeed, the "universal" value of the model of noncoercive communication underpinning U.S. civil society was produced out of its differential relation to its putatively negative valuation in Islamic countries.[5] Consequently, when President Khatami quoted from passages in *Democracy in America* as evidence of the similarities between Islamic nationalism and U.S. civic associations, he transgressed the borderline between the two political orders that "Tocqueville" had formerly delineated, and removed both cultures from the relationship of mutual exclusion in which they had been contained. When he constructed equivalences between the political aspirations of Iranian and U.S. citizens, however, Khatami accomplished more than the disruption of the policy's capacity to sustain the mutual antagonism between Americans and Iranians.

Khatami's invocation of *Democracy in America* to express his refusal to subject himself to its powers of containment transformed the policy itself into a matter for political deliberation. On materializing a common ground out of these homologies, Khatami deployed *Democracy in America* to open a place for Islamic fundamentalists *within* the U.S. democracy from which "Tocqueville" had prohibited them access. And in his CNN interview, President Khatami suggested that his heterodox reading of *Democracy in America* might become the basis for a free and open conversation between the two cultures.

When the editors subsequently quoted passages from the interview, however, they did not engage in a discussion of either the merits of President Khatami's reading of Tocqueville or the similarities between the two political cultures. The editors instead resorted to acts of verbal aggression and name calling that were apparently designed simply to annul Khatami's rights as an interlocutor within international civil society. The editors' symbolic violence involved the imposition of terms (e.g., "ayatollah," "mullah," "jihad") the connotations of which cohered around the signifier of Islam's unchanging equivalence with international terrorism, whose meaning Khatami had adamantly refused. Furthermore, when the editors did quote from the interview, they attributed to Khatami's statements significations that reversed their declared meanings and were designed to prove his colossal ignorance of democratic norms. After quoting Khatami's remark that "supporting peoples who fight for the liberation of their land is not, in my opinion, terrorism," for example, the editors interpreted this statement as evidence that Khatami had simply "resorted to the old semantics of revolutionary mischief." After thus substituting for Khatami's statement a signification that was precisely the reverse of the meaning that Khatami had declared, the editors proposed their substitution as proof of his failure to conceal his continued allegiance to Islamic terrorism.

The violence that the editors acted out in the process of removing President Khatami from the environs of the U.S. public sphere might be explained as a defensive reaction to his having proposed equivalences between the two orders. His production of this symbolic common ground trespassed the imaginary border that delineated each culture's totalized negation of the other. However, in aggressively projecting onto Khatami the identity of "menacing terrorist" that he had so adamantly repudiated, the editors also violated the norms of civility and noncoercive communication organizing the civic contract. Exactly why Khatami's interview should have provoked in the *New Republic*'s editors the threatening behavior and civil violence that the containment policy had formerly restricted to Islam requires some further consideration of the social work that the policy performed and the role of "Tocqueville and the Mullah" in its construction.

Claude Lefort has located one source of the editors' anxieties in what Tocqueville had called democracy's "limitless social power," a power that might be understood to underwrite the containment policy itself. Lefort draws the following descriptions of the immense dimensions of this power from the following passage from Tocqueville's *L'ancien regime et la revolution*: "It is the role of the State not merely to govern the Nation, but to shape it in a certain fashion; it is the task of the State to shape the minds of its citizens in accordance with the model that has been proposed in advance; its duty is to imbue their minds with certain ideas, and to inspire in their hearts such feelings as it judges necessary. In reality, no restrictions are placed upon its rights, and there are no limits as to what it can do; it does not simply reform men, it transforms them; and if need be, it will simply create other men."[6]

What Tocqueville discovers in this passage is that it is democracy's "limitless power" itself that constitutes the greatest threat to the democratic order. In the wake of the French Revolution, Tocqueville designated the centralized state and the people as the two agents that democracy had historically empowered to exercise this terrible power. In its recodification of the limitless powers that Tocqueville feared, the dual containment policy transformed the text through which Tocqueville had managed his fear into one of the instruments through which it produced an internal as well as an external limit to the exercise of this power.

The policy produced each of these limits out of a threefold operation. The policy alienated democracy's limitless power from its putative origins within the democratic people and the sovereign state, it divided this power into protective and aggressive manifestations, and then it externalized power's threatening aspects onto two substitute formations—the antidemocratic forces of foreign as well as domestic terrorists. After it displaced what Tocqueville had found threatening about the state's limitless power onto the menace posed by Islamic fundamentalism, the policy repositioned the source of the state's limitless power as a violence external to the nation. The policy's projection of the state's excess force onto the violence the "Mullah" directed against its citizenry produced a symbolic limit to the state's power. This imaginary boundary line between state violence and its externalization inscribed a limit that legitimated the state's use of force. This limit also enabled U.S. citizens to manage their fear that the state might direct its limitless power against them.

In addition to this external limit, the containment policy inscribed a limit to the democratic people's power that was internal to each individual citizen. The policy produced this internal limit out of the division of the citizen's potential expression of democracy's power into regulatory and menacing aspects. According to exponents of the containment policy, citizens exercised the regulatory aspect of their power when they redefined popular movements for democratic change as constituting threats to democratic governance akin to that of Muslim terrorists. The policy thereby managed the citizenry's own limitless power to effect democratic change when it recast collective democratic movements as themselves posing a threat to the democratic state.

"Tocqueville" and the "Mullah" thus named the condensed signifiers whereby the dual containment policy produced and managed the citizenry's fear of the limitless powers posed by the state and radical democratic movements. When President Khatami refused to identify with the position of the "Mullah" through which the policy had inscribed the external and internal limits to democracy's limitless powers, he quite literally brought the containment policy to its limits. Without containment's powers to externalize this threat, the editors of the essay came face to face with a quite literally unlimited democratic force. Unable to subsume Khatami within any of the already constituted positions *within* the containment policy, the editors performed the acts of civic violence that violated the distinction between "Tocqueville's" civility and the "Mullah" terrorism on which the dual containment policy had been founded.

Although the editors' aggressive actions may have seemed to violate the policy's founding prohibition of civic violence, these acts of incivility had in fact reestablished the distinction between "Tocqueville" and the "Mullah" on which the policy had been founded. In reestablishing the containment policy at the site of Khatami's annulment of its already constituted positions, the editors exercised what might be called the surplus power of containment.

By containment's surplus power I mean to indicate the excessive power required for the installation of the dual containment policy. As the tour de force that produced the founding distinction between "Tocqueville's" civility and the "Mullah's" terrorism, this inaugural event could not be sorted either within civil society or within the realm of Islamic terrorism out of whose ongoing negation the civic order achieved its coherence. The act that was responsible for the inscription of the policy, that is to say, could neither be subject to the rules and norms through which "Tocqueville" regulated the democratic order nor could it be represented within the system of representations through which the "Mullah" threatened that order.

Because this act was responsible for the production of the relation of mutual exclusion organizing the integrity and coherence of both realms, it necessarily surpassed the powers of containment of each. When the policy subsequently subsumed all acts of civic violence under the aegis of the "Mullah," it also tacitly proposed that the founding act of discrimination whereby the policy had irretrievably excluded Islamic fundamentalism from civil society had also designated itself as the single act of (civic) violence that constituted an exception to the "Mullah's" rule. As we have seen, President Khatami had compelled the editors to invoke this exception to the rule prohibiting them from performing acts of civic violence when he deployed "Tocqueville" to refuse the containment policy's suturing within the position of the "Mullah."

The editors enunciated the exception that overruled Khatami's refusal when they pronounced the phrase "Tocqueville was not all you needed to know." The "Tocqueville" whom the editors had invoked as the authorization for this pronouncement was the very same "Tocqueville" whom Khatami had cited as the authority for his refusal to acknowledge the oppositional relationship that the containment policy had erected between the two cultures. The exception that

"Tocqueville" appended to his own prohibition against civic violence targeted President Khatami as the "you" to whom this exception was addressed. The exception required "you" to know that "Tocqueville" was not all that "you" needed to know. What President Khatami also needed to know was that the position of the "Mullah" that the containment policy had mandated "you" to assume had been defined as lacking any politically legitimate knowledge of "Tocqueville." After the editors invoked "Tocqueville" to deauthorize the "Mullah's" knowledge of *Democracy in America,* they also reinstated the exclusion of the "Mullah" from the U.S. civic order.

"Tocqueville" thereby performed a double duty within the dual containment policy. "Tocqueville" materialized at once the internal limit to the limitless power of democracy and an exception to its rules and norms. But as the exception to his own rule prohibiting civic violence, "Tocqueville" was empowered to become the Mullah of the surplus powers required to recontain President Khatami within the position of "Mullah." The *New Republic*'s editors should thus be understood as having acted on the authority of "Tocqueville's" surplus powers of containment in their reinscription of the containment policy.

The fact that he provoked these extreme measures suggests that Khatami had also brought the editors face to face with the containment policy's inability fully to regulate the different kind of democratic politics that Khatami had employed Tocqueville to practice. In what follows, I shall try to explain the difference that Khatami's use of Tocqueville might entail for the prevailing understanding of democratic politics. In searching for that explanation, I shall briefly address a number of interrelated topics: the affective dimension of dual containment as a foundational fantasy of democratic governance; a critical genealogy of Tocqueville's role in the staging of this fantasy; an analysis of Tocqueville's trip to America in terms of this governing fantasy; a redescription of *Democracy in America* as Tocqueville's fantasy of French governance; and an account of the political rationale for C-SPAN's 1998 retracing of Tocqueville's 1831 itinerary.

THE DEMOCRATIC THING

Thus far I have analyzed the centrality of the Tocqueville project to the production of dual containment as a foreign policy and as a structure of domestic governance. But in doing so I have failed to distinguish between containment as a historically specific governmental policy and containment as a horizon of intelligibility that supported a collective fantasy of democratic governance. The *New*

Republic editors' anxiety over the loss of the power to project the political conflicts arising *within* democratic society onto the external threat posed by "Islamic terrorists" betrays a more profound anxiety. The anxiety arises from the editors' feared loss of the entitlement to manage U.S. democracy. As an expression of this anxiety, "Tocqueville and the Mullah" is symptomatic of a more pervasive fantasy about democratic governance.

Although the fantasy required the dual containment policy for support, it placed "Tocqueville" and the "Mullah" in the service of psychic as well as political processes. When taken up as a collective fantasy of democratic governance, dual containment hollowed out a space within the social order wherein citizens could imagine themselves the agents of the national will that expressed itself through that policy. When the fantasy depicted Iranians as terroristic religious nationalists who were contemptuous of the democratic norms underwriting U.S. civil societies, it effected an individual's identification with those norms as the agent responsible for the exclusion of the "fanatics."

Whereas the officials responsible for the regulation of the nation's territorial borders were government officeholders officially invested with the powers actually to practice containment as a state policy, the citizens who construed themselves having been empowered by this fantasy to participate in the governance of the social order had not been governmentally mandated to carry out this duty. The governance these citizens exercised resembled more closely the unofficial opinion-making powers of the *New Republic*'s editors. Like the editors, the citizens' imaginary participation in the nation's management did not result in material changes in the realm of realpolitik but entailed merely the feeling that they were entitled in the course of everyday life to make managerial statements about the nation's foreign policy.

Ghassan Haage has described citizens who share with the *New Republic*'s editors the belief that they possess the right to contribute personally to managing the nation's internal and external policies as enjoying a condition that he calls "governmental belonging." He distinguishes this mode of belonging from "passive belonging" in that those who imagine they belong governmentally to the democracy perceive themselves as agents and enactors of the national will whose purposes they believe themselves to inhabit. Their regulation of the democratic culture entails the fantasy that they inhabit American democracy at the level of its grounding norms and assumptions and that they enact those norms in their practice of governmental rule.[7]

Haage draws on Jacques Lacan's psychoanalytic explanation of fantasy to provide an understanding of the means whereby citizens transform themselves into the agents of the will responsible for the national governance. Haage differentiates the governance fantasy from daydreams in that the fantasy of national governance does not result in hallucinatory worlds that are external to the subject; rather, the fantasy reflexively produces the subject who thereby embodies the fantasy. Citizens who believe themselves empowered to act on the democratic norms and assumptions sedimented within the dual containment policy also believe themselves to be the authors and agents of the norms through which they "manage" U.S. democracy. These enactments materialize the fantasy spaces they inhabit and of which they recognize themselves to be a crucial part.

Before the fantasy could endow the citizens' lives with this raison d'être, however, the national will that supported and was supported by the fantasy had to be invested with a sense of meaning and purpose that could be communicated so as to be enacted by the subjects of the fantasy. "Tocqueville" and the "Mullah" named the psychic figures through whom the policy of dual containment was transposed into the fantasy that U.S. democracy was endowed with intrinsic values that made every citizen's life worth living. "Tocqueville" and the "Mullah" accomplished this transformation of dual containment into a collective national fantasy through "Tocqueville's" conversion of the process that the "Mullah" threatened into what might be called the "democratic thing." In referring to the democratic thing as the psychic product of the transaction between "Tocqueville" and the "Mullah," I mean "thing" in the Lacanian sense as what continues to bind the subject to the object of desire after the subject has finished desiring it.

In its office as a fantasy of democratic governance, dual containment would position the democratic thing as what necessarily exceeds the "Mullah's" efforts to appropriate it. As what persists in the form of an indissoluble remainder when Islam attempts to consume this object of national desire, the democratic thing names that specifically American form of democracy that supports the national uniqueness. Slavoj Žižek has described this aspect of the "thing" with admirable clarity:

> The element that holds together a given community cannot be reduced to the point of symbolic identification: the bond linking its members always implies a shared relationship toward a Thing, toward Enjoyment incarnated. This relationship toward the Thing, structured by means of fantasies, is what is at stake when we speak of the menace to our "way of life" presented by the Other. . . . National identification is by definition sustained

by a relationship toward the Nation qua Thing. This Nation-Thing is determined by a series of contradictory properties. It appears to us as "our Thing" (perhaps we could say *cosa nostra*), as something accessible only to us, as something "they," the others, cannot grasp, but which is nonetheless constantly menaced by "them."[8]

This passage describes the democratic thing as the outcome of contradictory processes. It names that aspect of the U.S. citizenry's collectively shared experience of democracy that is impossible for another nation to appropriate; yet it also proposes that the individual members of U.S. national culture can "enjoy" their democratic thing only by means of the collective fantasy of an Islamic menace to their democratic way of life. The fact that Žižek understands the second of these processes to constitute the precondition for the first discloses the centrality of the U.S. containment policy to the reproduction of the democratic thing.

U.S. citizens might be capable of enumerating the processes—liberty, egalitarianism, laissez-faire, individualism—constitutive of U.S. democracy. But, as we might plausibly infer from Žižek's theoretical fiction, it is only their shared fantasy of threats to those processes that secures the U.S. citizenry's connection to the democratic thing. In finding the "thing" threatened, the citizen-subject also undergoes a change in the condition of belonging to a national order. Following the threatened intervention of this Other order, national citizens experience their relation to the democratic objects of national desire as enjoyable restorations of the full significance of the democratic thing rather than alienating signs of its loss.

When mediated by the fantasy of the possible loss of the democratic thing, the entire symbolic order undergoes a doubling. The threat posed by Islamic fundamentalism recasts the citizen-subjects' relation to the democratic order. The threat to the survival of the democratic thing triggers a generalized process of transference whereby the citizenry cathect their fear over the loss of the "thing" into the need to *rescue* and protect the national uniqueness.

TOCQUEVILLE'S THING WITH AMERICAN DEMOCRACY

The quality of "uniqueness" that the "Mullah" threatened was not merely the outcome of democracy's negation of Islamic terrorism. It also included the value that Tocqueville had discerned in American democracy in 1831. Whereas the "Mullah" endowed the democratic thing with the values that pertain to a threatened national object, the value that "Tocqueville" invested in the democratic thing derived from the usage to which he wanted to put American democracy.

When "Tocqueville" traveled to the United States in 1831, he came in search of a form of democratic governance that would facilitate the restoration of order to French democracy. The forces of political change that the democratic revolution had effected in France had resulted in the removal of the liberties and privileges that had formerly signified the social standing of the French aristocracy of which Tocqueville's family had been prominent members. Having experienced the power of democratic change as the traumatic loss of the Tocqueville lineage's mandated social position, Tocqueville studied American democracy in order to discover the laws at work within a democracy that he found exceptional in lacking a revolutionary dimension.

Tocqueville wrote *Democracy in America* both as a scholarly analysis of the democratic institutions responsible for this unique form of governance and as a model for French democracy. It was the latter dimension of his project that would prove indispensable to the production of the fantasy of dual containment as well as the democratic thing on which it was grounded. In finding American democracy valuable in its possessing the property of meaningful order that other democracies lacked, "Tocqueville" endowed the U.S. democratic thing with the property of uniqueness that became the envy of other political cultures.

The democratic thing became the object cause of Tocqueville's desire—it named what Tocqueville desired and what caused him to exist as a desiring subject. In Tocqueville's case the democratic thing constituted his effort to overcome what French democracy was constitutively lacking. U.S. democracy became a "thing" when Tocqueville desired something more than the features comprising democracy in America. As this something more, the democratic thing named what gave plenitude and meaning and vitality to the national life. As the object cause of desire, the democratic thing also staged the fantasy space that caused Tocqueville to want to obtain it.

In *Democracy in America,* Tocqueville had transposed the democratic thing into the object of his political desire as well as the cause of subjectivity through which he desired to obtain it. When he wrote about U.S. democracy he wrote from the position of the aristocrat that democratic processes had completely removed from the French social order. His act of writing constituted an effort to identify with the will of the democratic powers that had accomplished the complete disinheritance of the position he had formerly enjoyed so that he might inherit from democracy the political will responsible for his social disinheritance.

Writing became for Tocqueville a means of identifying his will with the grounding rules and assumptions so that he might, on his return to France, exercise the will of democracy itself rather than subject himself to the unruly forms it might assume in an unruly French democratic culture. In place of the aristocratic body that French democratic processes had utterly destroyed, "Tocqueville" imagined himself to coincide with the aims and purposes of U.S. democracy, to inhabit its norms and rules and to be the agent of its will.

The fantasy through which citizens participated in the achievement of the containment policy's imperatives derived from their having imagined themselves as inhabiting the agency of the national will to which Tocqueville's *Democracy in America* had given them access. Like "Tocqueville" they imagined themselves inhabiting U.S. democracy at the level of its grounding norms and assumptions, and enacting those norms in their practice of managing democracy's conflicts.

When they exercised these powers of governance, U.S. citizens took up the privileged position that the French aristocrat imagined himself to occupy when he perceived himself as the enactor and agent of the national will. Instead of analyzing the text's significance, they turned to "Tocqueville" for the entitlement to assume the managerial role through which the French aristocrat had given expression to the tacit norms and rules regulative of democratic culture.

In "Tocqueville and the Mullah," the *New Republic*'s editors derived from Tocqueville the symbolic entitlement to exercise managerial control of the national contours and to make statements about its governance. When they exercised these ruling powers, the editors assumed the privileged position that the French aristocrat imagined himself to occupy when he perceived himself as the enactor and agent of the national will.

THE RETURN TO ALEXIS DE TOCQUEVILLE

In observing the role that "Tocqueville" has played in this fantasy, I do not mean to diminish his status in the scholarly archive. The part "Tocqueville" plays in the fantasy depends on the canonical value that the scholarly community has continued to invest in his work. Political scientists, literary theorists, philosophers, and citizens alike have invested Tocqueville's work with a metahistorical knowingness about U.S. democratic culture. As a consequence of this collective transference, *Democracy in America* has endowed U.S. democratic culture with a framework of intelligibility. Its categories, rules, and concepts have provided the metalanguage in which issues get identified, recognized, parsed, construed, ordered, and concatenated. Revered as the archive in which are preserved the United States's core metasocial significations, Tocqueville's *Democracy in America* was believed to possess the keys to the culture's purpose, and it has been invested with the authority to effect the culture's self-transformation.[9]

Tocqueville's work has released in commentators like the *New Republic*'s editors a kind of wishful thinking about its pertinence to the present historical conjuncture. That thinking has fostered the construction of a political mythology surrounding Tocqueville's project. Exempting it from the procedures of verification associated with other scholarly works, the mythology has elevated *Democracy in America* into a secular scripture. *Democracy in America* has supplied the concepts, generalizations, and categories out of which individuals were encouraged to experience and make sense of their historical conditions. Its system of representations anchored the presuppositions out of which individuals formulated their opinions. It was reproduced, perpetuated, and transmitted through such discursive practices. Because its terms were devoid of any necessary reference to the historical institutions Tocqueville had observed, they also outstripped the code-regulated relationship of signifier and signified. The mythology surrounding the book has construed it as containing instructions for bringing about what it described, thus entrusting the book with the task of facilitating a rite of passage from one order of cultural intelligibility to another.

Tocqueville's own prior usage of *Democracy in America* as a force crucial to achieving France's transition from a feudal monarchy to a democracy has encouraged the belief that his book could bring about the social conditions it also described. After returning to France, Tocqueville had reconceptualized problems specific to French national politics in terms of the compendium of precedents and examples he had recorded in *Democracy in America*. In so doing, he corroborated a belief that organized national aspirations throughout the cold war; namely, that a successful conclusion to it would enable nations throughout the world to adopt the U.S. model of liberal democracy.[10]

The fact that the end of the cold war did not result in a world of nations modeled after the U.S. example threatened to discredit the national narrative that had endowed antecedent events with significance. In place of corroborating them, the terminal events of the cold war—Russia's embrace of a market economy, the emergence of a globalized economy, the resurgence of ethnonationalisms— severely challenged the nation's core beliefs. With the demise of the Soviet Union, the United States had lost the antagonist whose efforts to impede its world historical mission had entrusted everyday events with a quasi-mythological standing. The sudden loss of the need to negate the Other's incursions against them threatened the nation's primary symbolic goods—the free market, democratic institutions, freedom of speech—with devaluation.[11]

Throughout the cold war, each of these symbolic goods had acquired their value in part from the desire to secure them against the Other's aggressively not desiring them. But because the ex-Other now desired the same things, this "undesirable desire" entered into such close proximity with the symbolic space of the national identity that it produced, in the words of Helga Geyer-Ryan, "regression into structures of the mirror stage (associated with memories of the disorganized body) or even farther back into psychotic dispositions." Anxieties over the feared loss of national distinctness and dissolution within an irreducibly alien universalism lay at the heart of a xenophobia "triggered by the collapse of the fantasy of the whole, unified, undamaged body in the space that is conceived of as metaphorically and metonymically as the body's extension or double."[12]

The nationalist anxieties released in the wake of the cold war should be construed as the basis for the quasi-mystical forces condensed in the phrase the "return of Alexis de Tocqueville." In its most encompassing sense, Tocqueville's "return" might be conceptualized as a symbolic compensation for the absence of an adequate conclusion to the cold war. As the personification of attitudes that had prevailed throughout the cold war, and as a resource for alternatives to them, Tocqueville returned to the symbolic space whose capacity to support the national identity had been severely jeopardized by the war's terminal events. Having previously turned U.S. democracy into the model for the future of France, Tocqueville had in fact already performed the action that would have provided the cold war with a felicitous ending. But his work had been no less crucial to the founding of the cold war settlement.

Although his work provided a model for U.S. democracy that could be emulated worldwide, neither Tocqueville nor his work were subject to its conditions of historicization. Because his work constituted the means of effecting these disparate historical dispositions yet had not become identical with any of them, the retrieval of it constituted a transhistorical resource for the production of a passage from one historical condition to another.

Within history, yet seemingly beyond it, "Tocqueville" produced historical continuity. Surviving as a living remnant, it performed the dual function of a part-object still connected to the cold war mentality and as a transitional object that permitted its separation. Having participated in founding the cold war epoch and yet surviving its termination, "Tocqueville" could be imagined as having returned to the foundational scene to inaugurate an alternative order. Resituated there, "Tocqueville" reduced the cold war past to the dimensions of the force it contributed to effect a historical transition.

After having prophesied the cold war, then, *Democracy in America* has re-emerged at its conclusion to add this magical scene of national transformation that the cold war's terminal events significantly lacked. In accomplishing this transition work, "Tocqueville" has shifted his core identity from that of the interpreter of U.S. exceptionality to that of the legislator who would subsume new cultural instances under more general regulative laws. In selecting "civic associations" as the new regulative ideal, Tocqueville's legislation has transferred U.S. citizens' cultural allegiances from actions on the scale of global Armageddon to the dimensions of the local town meeting.[13]

The Tocqueville revival has also reduced historical change to the selection of different passages from *Democracy in America.* After the shift of emphasis from Tocqueville on American exceptionalism to Tocqueville on civic associations, the "resurgence of Islamic fundamentalism" has replaced the threat of world communism as the repository for cultural processes that are intrinsically opposed to such initiatives. President Khatami's repudiation of the positioning of Iran as the signifier of negative civility disclosed his understanding of the role *Democracy in America* had played in the replacement of the nation with civil society as the space in which U.S. citizens consolidate their national belonging after the cold war.[14]

Among its pluralized contemporary manifestations, this intertextual terrain includes Newt Gingrich writing in support of a politics of law and order; William Connolly on the territorial rights of indigenous tribes; Arthur Schlesinger in opposition to a disunited nation; Anne Norton on feminism; David Campbell against the security state; Michael Sandel on communitarianism; Seymour Lipset in support of neoliberalism; and Cornel West in defense of a politics of difference.[15] This enchainment of argumentative positions is not governed by causal relations, and their means of association cannot be accounted for by a single explanatory principle. In fact there is no order of concatenation that binds these elements into a repertoire of examples except their appurtenance to a proper name.

In their introduction to their magisterial new translation of *Democracy in America,* Harvey Mansfield and Delba Winthrop have succinctly described Tocqueville's continued appeal to both the Right and Left:

On the Left he is the philosopher of community and civic engagement who warns against the appearance of an industrial aristocracy and against the bourgeois or commercial passion for material well-being: in sum, he is for democratic citizenship. On the Right he is quoted for his strictures on "Big Government" and his liking for decentralized administration as well as for celebrating individual energy and opposing egalitarian excess: he is a balanced liberal, defending both freedom and moderation. But for both of these parties he is welcome in an era when democracy has defeated totalitarianism and is no longer under challenge to its existence.[16]

The Tocqueville canon serves as the master signifier for the reconciliation of these apparently irreconcilable arguments.[17] Personifying its authority, Mansfield and Winthrop have exemplified the ways in which the Tocqueville canon controls the way these arguments are interpreted and received.[18] Articulating them to its framework of intelligibility, the Tocqueville canon nets the worth of their serial associations by describing the outcome as a representative civil society. "Tocqueville" thereafter reworks these arguments into terms that would appear to have achieved their reconciliation and designates civil society as the space in which such reconciliations have been transacted.

The pertinence of Tocqueville's nineteenth-century model of a civil society to the political imaginaries of the twenty-first century discloses the transhistorical value of his work. But in order to understand how Tocqueville's project has become transferable across history, we need briefly to examine the work to which Tocqueville had put this model in nineteenth-century France.

AFTER DEMOCRACY IN FRANCE

As a member of the French aristocracy that had been superseded with the revolutionary overthrow of the feudal order in France, Tocqueville characterized the emergence of democratic forces as a potential danger to the dominance of the French ruling elite. As a loyal French monarchist, Tocqueville owed his seat in the July monarchy to the votes of country landowners who counted him as a hereditary member of their territorial aristocracy. Prominent among his intended addresses, that class read *Democracy in America* as a defensive weapon useful in that historical moment's war of cultural positioning.

After Tocqueville had become a magistrate, he was commissioned to travel to America as an official of the French state. Tocqueville journeyed to America in order to ascertain the regulatory principles responsible for the construction of a people that "while all the nations of Europe have been devastated by war or torn by civil strife . . . remained at peace."[19] Tocqueville accepted temporary leave from his office as an assistant French magistrate with the understanding that the information he gathered during his trip to America concerning governmental rule in general and penitentiary reform in particular would become instrumental in regularizing democratic institutions in France. In *Democracy and Punishment: Disciplinary Origins of the United States* Thomas Dumm argues that the penitentiary system importantly contributed to Tocqueville's understanding of liberal democracy and deeply influenced the organizational matrix of *Democracy in America.*[20]

According to Dumm, *Democracy in America* and the U.S. penitentiary system constituted comparable yet autonomous symbolic practices that aspired to the rehabilitation of the persons who undertook them. The penitentiary system created the behavioral conditions responsible for shaping the political subjects required to internalize liberal and democratic values and fostered the creation of individuals who had learned how to rule themselves. Tocqueville's notion of civic associations resembled the penitentiary system in that the texture of attitudes embedded within both social formations would reproduce behavior so as to reform it.

Tocqueville addressed *Democracy in America* in the last instance to the governmental bureaucrats who granted him leave from his official duties. In fulfilling this mandate, Tocqueville accumulated a mass of details about democratic institutions in the United States that he painstakingly related to what he understood to be the central theme of *Democracy in America;* namely, the art of governmental rule. In his efforts to discover in the United States a form of democratic rule, Tocqueville devised a complex rhetorical strategy that enabled him to recover the persona of the French aristocrat as an analytic perspective required to formulate the differences between democracy in France and America.

In enunciating the social and cultural conditions surrounding America's distinctive form of democracy, Tocqueville habitually assumed an aristocratic attitude toward American democratic ideas and customs. Writing from this subjective standpoint authorized Tocqueville's signature detachment from the political phenomena that he described, and at key moments turned his exposition of the American political economy into a reflection on the generalized crisis that had emerged in France after it had undergone the loss of the institutions that had formerly legitimated the feudal order. By way of the masterful survey that Tocqueville had compiled of its customs and institutions, *Democracy in America* became the socially regulative ideal through which he displaced the violence of the French revolution from aristocratic memory.[21]

Writing thus became a kind of transferential process whereby Tocqueville translated the social position lost after the French revolution into the literary standpoint through which he practiced his historic movement throughout the United States. In codifying U.S. citizens' contradictory attitudes toward freedom and equality by way of formulaic phrases such as the "tyranny of the majority" and "salutary servitude" Tocqueville disclosed an anxious desire to recover the aristocratic tradition in the displaced form of the historical perspective from which he discerned what was significantly absent from American democracy.

As a representative of a superseded feudal tradition he construed American history as exceptional in lacking, Tocqueville also thereby added to Jacksonian America the class position that French democracy had replaced. This class supplementation was conveyed in the analytic distinctions Tocqueville adduced between political and civil society. The difference between civil society and political society was sustained, Tocqueville reflected, by the irresolvable conflict between "private interests" and "public liberty." Given this contrast and American individualists' "natural" predisposition to gratify their individual interests, political society depended on a residual feature of feudal society; namely, respect for liberty in its aristocratic aspect as a precondition necessary for its emergence.[22]

Paradoxical as it may seem, Tocqueville believed that the democratic individual's love of political liberty, in the words of George Lefebvre, "presupposed the presence of [a] kind of virtue of which the proud independence of feudalism was an anticipation."[23] Claude Lefort has traced Tocqueville's unworked-through attachments to the aristocratic tradition by examining the paradoxical status of American "individualism." American individualism, under Tocqueville's description, oscillated from an "abstract" subjectivity whose resolutely private interests alienated it from any meaningful political form to a social subjectivity so "lost in the crowd" of prevailing opinions as to be void of any subjective point of view. In Tocqueville's representations of his dilemma, the American individual had on the one hand "been released from the old networks of personal dependency and granted the freedom to think and act in accordance with his own norms," but on the other hand had been "isolated and impoverished and at the same time trapped by the image of his fellows, now that agglutination with them provides a means of escaping the threat of the dissolution of his identity."[24]

Writing thus became the means whereby Tocqueville translated the social position his family had lost after the French Revolution into the literary standpoint through which he practiced his historical movement across the United States. In writing about American political culture as if he were a living embodiment of aristocratic liberty, Tocqueville reconstituted the aristocratic psyche that had been debilitated in the democratic process. Tocqueville struggled thereby to recover, albeit in the displaced form of his literary style, from the loss of status the aristocracy had undergone in France.

Democracy in America performed the work of displacing the trauma of class conflict onto a place lacking the feudal tradition's sophistication. When he adapted its sociological generalizations and its temporally expansive claims to the work regulating the French social order, he also displaced the violence of the French Revolution from aristocratic memory. By "working through" residual class anxieties, Tocqueville turned the feudal tradition that he had associated with the displacement he feared into a backdrop against which he could project what he perceived American democracy to be lacking.

Claude Lefort has spelled out the dimensions of the trauma that he discerns at the very heart of Tocqueville's account of U.S. democracy. Upon encountering in the United States a democracy that had emerged voided of the feudal order's transcendental guarantees, Lefort believes that Tocqueville reexperienced the trauma of the French Revolution as the gap between a fully achieved civil society and the terror of civic violence:

> When social power is divorced from the person of the prince, freed from the transcendental agency which made the prince the guarantor of order and of the permanence of the body politic, and denied the nourishment of the duration which made it almost natural, this power appears to be the power society exercises over itself. When society no longer recognizes the existence of anything external to it, social power knows no bounds. It is a product of society, but at the same time it has the vocation to produce society; the boundaries of personal existence mean nothing to it because it purports to be the agent of all.[25]

Insofar as it closes around the exclusion of the traumatic violence that it aspires to control, Tocqueville's civil society constitutes a permanently incomplete task. It can never be fully achieved but only reconstituted through the externalization of the forces threatening its order. But its reconstitution required a shift in Tocqueville's persona from an interpreter of democratic culture in America into its legislator in France. The absence of class conflict and political turmoil that Tocqueville perceived in the U.S. political society contained what he had wished to be removed from French democracy. In his relentless depoliticiza-tion of U.S. political topography Tocqueville's *Democracy in America* produced a perceptual faculty that Freud has described as responsible for "negative halluci-nation"; that is, the capacity *not* to see what is actually there. In perceiving what he claimed was absent in U.S. democratic culture, Tocqueville accomplished a "democratic" desire to except those same elements from French democracy.

After returning to France, Tocqueville implemented his interpretation of U.S. democratic culture as if it comprised a legislative paradigm for the future of French democracy. Having already interpreted its accomplished formation in America, Tocqueville the legislator transferred onto *Democracy in America* the full amplitude of normative power required to manage the emergence of a demo-cratic culture in France. *Democracy in America* provided Tocqueville with a normative metalanguage from which he generated by negation the social forces that disallowed the condition of belonging to French democratic culture. Be-cause *Democracy in America* had predesignated residual feudal forces as what were lacking in democracy, Tocqueville thereafter deployed that designation as a warrant for the exclusion of class antagonisms and related manifestations of civic violence from French democracy.

DEMOCRACY IN FRANCE

In "Medusa's Head: Male Hysteria under Political Pressure" Neil Hertz borrowed the story of Perseus's encounter with Medusa to explain Alexis de Tocqueville's anxious reaction to the acts of civic violence that ensued after the fall of the second Empire.[26] Hertz includes an anecdote from Tocqueville's *Souvenirs* within a series of related examples of the Medusa fantasy drawn from Courbet, Hugo, and Burke. By way of the Medusa fantasy these authors experienced the threats that democratic changes posed to their position and property as castration anx-iety in which fear of female sexuality conflated and gave metaphorical expression to the losses they feared.

Hertz cites the following entry from Tocqueville's *Souvenirs* as a representative instance of a Tocquevillean Medusa fantasy. On June 24, 1848, the second day of street fighting that had broken out after attempts to overthrow Louis-Phillipe I had failed, Tocqueville was walking toward the Chamber of Deputies:

> When I was getting near and was already in the midst of the troops, an old
> woman with a vegetable cart stubbornly barred my way. I ended by telling

her rather sharply to make room. Instead of doing so, she left her cart and rushed at me with such sudden frenzy that I had trouble defending myself. I shuddered at the frightful and hideous expression on her face which reflected demagogic passions and the fury of civil war. I mention this minor fact because I saw it then and rightly, as a major symptom. At moments of violent crisis even actions that have nothing to do with politics take on a strange character of chaotic danger. These actions are not lost on the attentive eye and they provide a very reliable index of the general state of mind. It is as though these great public emotions create a burning atmosphere in which private feelings seethe and boil.[27]

The experience Tocqueville records in this anecdote would appear to confirm Hertz's classification—it entails Tocqueville's momentary loss of representational control and his attribution of the disempowerment to the peasant woman's unruly energies. Instead of following Tocqueville's order to get out of the way, the peasant stuns Tocqueville with the violence of a gaze that resembles Medusa's in that it threatens to reposition him within an antagonistic visual field. As a consequence of this encounter, Tocqueville temporarily experiences the loss of both his footing and the ground whereon he might take the succession of steps that would transport him from the public square to the assembly hall.

But the event Tocqueville records here is also important in that it vividly represents the democratic scenario of revolutionary violence he most feared and in the usage to which he puts the themes and categories of *Democracy in America* to manage this fear. The scene takes place at a border between antagonistic dispositions of the future of French democracy and under two different forms— as an event within Tocqueville's perceptual field and as an illustration of the themes that Tocqueville had recorded in *Democracy in America*.

Tocqueville's second mode of apprehending this event turns it into a *tableau vivant* of passages from *Democracy in America*. However, when he revisualizes the event's significance by way of the metalanguage inscribed in *Democracy in America*, Tocqueville does not perceive what is in fact taking place. He replaces the visual perception of the event with a reading of its significance. This substitution enables Tocqueville to transform the traumatic event into the occasion for visually recalling the themes from *Democracy in America*. Tocqueville's reading of the incident's significance has silently reinscribed *Democracy in America* into the visual field. By way of this re-vision, he turns this contemporary event that takes place in French democratic culture into a representation of the "demagogic passion" and the "fury of civil war" he had already thoroughly researched in his journey to the United States nearly two decades earlier.

But on recomposing this scene out of his already recorded observations about American democracy, those figures of memory transform what Tocqueville had earlier found frightening about the peasant woman's countenance into the orderly manifestation of the hidden laws of democracy. As the raw material for the transmutation of the scene, *Democracy in America* translates the terrifying event Tocqueville is the process of undergoing into what *Democracy in America* will have made of it. Its presuppositions and preconstituted representations thereafter become the means whereby he makes sense of the unfolding events. In the wake of this transposition, unfolding events cease to frighten him; instead they verify his understanding of the workings of democracy. His understanding of its themes transform Tocqueville from an individual who is subject to the vicissitudes of revolutionary democracy into the metasocial subject who can read events that illustrate the magisterial thesis of *Democracy in America*.

RE: *TRAVELING TOCQUEVILLE'S AMERICA*

As we have seen, Tocqueville could only imagine the United States as a totalized representation of civic order against the backdrop of the absented social forces that threatened to overwhelm that order in France. When he traveled to America, Tocqueville transferred onto its landscape the semblance of his desire for a fully realized democratic order. The Tocqueville revival might be construed as having performed a related transference at the present historical conjuncture. In returning to the Tocqueville who had validated the ideological assumptions of the sequence of events that had taken place during the cold war, interpreters of him at the present transition have effected a transposition of Tocqueville's function that is perhaps best understood in terms of the time-loop paradox familiar to lovers of science fiction. Understood in the logic of the time loop, the "return" of contemporary interpreters to an aspect of the Tocquevillean archive that was significantly different from the doctrine of U.S. exceptionalism that had "caused" the sequence of cold war events could trigger the cancellation of the entire sequence.

Turning now to what has replaced this canceled series, on May 9, 1997, C-SPAN launched a project they titled *Traveling Tocqueville's America*. This series did not merely draw on the astonishing renewal of interest in Tocqueville's *Democracy in America* but also elevated the Tocqueville revival into the basis for its spectacular restaging of the journey out of which Tocqueville had created the democratic imaginary. *Traveling Tocqueville's America* retraced the nine-month journey throughout the United States in 1831 that Alexis de Tocqueville had undertaken with his companion Gustave Beaumont. After a year of planning, c-span turned a forty-five-foot-long yellow bus into a high-tech network production vehicle from which they globally transmitted live reports from the fifty-five-stop tour through seventeen states.

In addition to the sixty-five hours of programming, c-span operatives distributed annotated road maps and set up an interactive Web site. They organized local town hall meetings and classroom teach-ins of the series, as well as scholarly conferences, week-long symposia, and a national essay contest on the subject of Tocqueville's *Democracy in America*. The tour guide c-span distributed along with the series included synopses of Tocqueville's and Beaumont's recorded impressions, sketches and folklore about the places and people Tocqueville visited, photographs and brief descriptions of famous local sights, and information about dining and accommodations.

Traveling Tocqueville's America installed Tocqueville's recorded memoirs of his initial trip through America as an intermediary between its television audience and America. It transformed the act of watching television into an interactive rereading of the themes and conceptual categories that Tocqueville described as having discerned within the U.S. landscape. But c-span's rendering of Tocqueville's text to the television audience's pluralized readings also legitimized as the final and true reading the one given by the socially authorized intellectuals whose understanding theatricalizes the dominance of its understanding.

Be describing it in metaphors borrowed from the mystery of the Incarnation, Jacques Rancière has invested this transferential process with a quasi-mystical dimension. Tocqueville had traveled to America, Rancière claims, in order to found a civil religion that borrowed its secular authority from the mystery of the Incarnation. Proposing that his travel narrative merges "the great mystery of the Word become flesh" with the "little scenes of everyday life," Rancière argues the importance of the transformation of the reader into a traveler who retraces the itinerary of these "little narratives of everyday life" to the accomplishment of the central mystery of Tocqueville's civil religion.[28]

Traveling Tocqueville's America overstepped the all-but-invisible boundary that, according to Rancière, distinguishes between the inside of Tocqueville's journal and the landscape that has enfleshed its words. In the very slight movement whereby reading becomes traveling, what is written undergoes a change of emplacement from the inside of the book into the thereness, or what Rancière calls the *ecceity,* of the landscape. Traveling thereby becomes the acquisition of a quasi-sacramental faculty: "the power of mapping together a discursive space and a territorial space, the capacity to make each concept correspond to a point in reality and each reality coincide with a point on the map."[29] When the traveler reencounters Tocqueville's descriptions in the sudden thereness of them within the living flesh of the landscape, the residual reader within the traveler becomes the vessel for the achievement of the coincidence of Tocqueville's words and the *ecceity* of their incarnation in and as the scenes so encountered. When *Traveling Tocqueville's America* lodged Tocqueville's journal in the popular consciousness it intermediated between places, scenes, and historical events and the viewers' perceptions, transforming the latter into revisualizations of Tocqueville's democratic culture.

But Tocqueville had not himself simply discovered the traces of his conceptual model already inscribed in American things. His model was not derived from nature, as Rancière suggests, so much as it was inscribed on it. He produced these inscriptions so that thereafter they could be written on the body politic of democratic societies as Tocqueville's means of regulating their representation of democracy. In keeping with this description, *Traveling Tocqueville's America* might be reconceptualized as the symbolic embodiment of a spatial practice. Tocqueville's text composed the America through which he journeyed into an itinerant yet regulated and progressive spatial practice. The categories, rules, and procedures into which he had transformed America could be operationalized either as reading or traveling. Both forms required the support of the flesh of the reader that the text changed into the bodies conforming to this regulated movement. *Traveling Tocqueville's America* constituted a symbolic action, an encoded behavior, for which the bodies of viewers and travelers were postulated as interchangeable agents.

After Tocqueville had collected and classified the exterior world into a system of representations, this system thereafter regulated his perceptions of American things. When c-span later aspired to adapt that model of democracy into a form of governance that would persuade its audience to conform to its rules, it accommodated Tocqueville's itinerant apparatus to the multiple and diverse resistances of the bodies to be conformed by fragmenting it into proverbs, sayings, retroactive dialogues, and other types of knowledge about the bodies that it would remap. Like the basic unit of symbolic exchange underwriting Tocqueville's treatise, c-span's Tocqueville tour animated a relationship with American democracy that was relentlessly circular and reciprocal. Tocqueville wanted to deliver to his readers a coherent image of America's national identity. Only metaleptically, however, and after a reading of America through the lens of Tocqueville's classic, could Americans reacquire a coherent self-image. Call-ins could append additional classifications to Tocqueville's discourse on democracy and specify more precisely their relationship to Tocqueville. *Traveling Tocqueville's America* situated Tocqueville's work within an expansive and interlocking set of intertextual relations that influenced how it might be used and how it was read.

What Tocqueville was looking for in America, as Jacques Rancière has remarked apropos of this intertextual process, was, in the words of Norman Birnbaum, "good democracy, reasonable democracy for he comes from the land of bad, unreasonable democracy."[30] America, in the post–cold war epoch, as we might plausibly extrapolate observation, had become a place that, in "having become opaque to itself" required Tocqueville's guidance to reclaim the transparency of its institutions. The Tocqueville tour by c-span entailed the reaffirmation of an essential Americanness by declaring the tour empowered to retrieve it. America's nineteenth-century past was restaged by c-span as a means of recovering from contemporary crises in the national identity. Each of the elements in the tour guide built on the collective wish to remake U.S. political culture in the image of Tocqueville's foundational text. The site from which Tocqueville returned would, according to this description, reconstitute the television viewer within the field of intelligibility regulated by Tocqueville's previous visualization of U.S. culture.

Understood as a response to the post–cold war dissociation of its conceptual mapping from the cultural terrain for which it had formerly provided an orientation, the tour might be described as a response to the desire to recover the cultural typology through which U.S. citizens had formerly taken conceptual possession of their surroundings. But the c-span tour may also have reintroduced television viewers to the challenges to its civic order that Tocqueville had not managed fully to exclude from his field of vision.

Remapping the nation as the object of the Tocquevillean gaze resituated its topography within what Benedict Anderson has described as the imagined national community. The experts that c-span invited to comment on Tocqueville's travels attempted to link his observations about women, African slaves, and Indians to the changes in the United States produced by multiculturalism in particular. But in the very act of positioning these changes in the political landscape within Tocqueville's 1831 gaze, the tour also released what Lisa Lowe has called "national anxieties about maintaining U.S. hegemony in an age of rapidly changing boundaries and territories."[31] In retracing Tocqueville's original travels through America, c-span also reengaged the anxieties that informed the original expedition. In reprojecting his conceptual schema and national mythology onto the U.S. landscape through which Tocqueville had once traveled, the c-span tour also acknowledged the fact that those places were now lacking that democratic topography.

Observing the importance of narratives to democratize places, Michel de Certeau has described the significance of their loss: "When stories disappear there results a widespread loss of place." The individual or the group regresses "as a result toward the disquieting experience of the formless, indistinct, deconsecrated states."[32]

THE RETURN OF THE POLITICAL

Earlier I proposed that Tocqueville's perception of the absence of political antagonisms in America produced a desire to remove them from French democracy. I have also claimed that c-span's restaging of the Tocqueville tour was in part complicit with Tocqueville's efforts to manage French democracy. But the c-span tour has also revealed within U.S. political culture a knowledge of the political antagonisms that the Tocqueville revival has failed to cover over. In rendering visible these class hierarchies and racial and economic inequalities and political antagonisms, c-span also produced an occasion for figures like President Khatami to invoke the Tocqueville tour for a visual lexicon with which to address the complexities that have replaced the wished-for certainties of Tocqueville and the national aristocracy that would naturalize his gaze.

When Khatami cited Tocqueville to describe the resemblance between America's embrace of religious freedom and Iranian religious nationalism, he refused efforts to exclude Tocqueville from the political terrain. Proposing that Tocqueville's devotion to liberty was itself cultivated in the rites and traditions of a national "civil religion," Khatami concluded that civil society could not be altogether distinguished from Iran's religious nationalism. In making this argument by way of the treatise that had been written to foreclose it, President Khatami introduced a conflict over the political significance of a democratic norm that Tocqueville had evacuated from his representation of U.S. democracy and that his heirs attempt to contain.

In ending this discussion of the Tocqueville revival with an observation of the usage to which President Khatami has put *Democracy in America*, I do not wish to conclude that democracy constitutes a nonviolable form of politics. On the contrary, I wish to elucidate the "knowledge" that Khatami had erected at the site where the *New Republic*'s editors had declared "Tocqueville is not all you need to know." This "knowledge" would propose a mutual inherence in the relation between identity and otherness that resists the desire to suture an identity at the site of the Other's exclusion. If the condition governing the formation of democratic "identity" entails the affirmation of self-alterity, its constitution involves the pluralization of democratic allegiances with which one can identify. The desire to resolve or disavow the articulation of liberalism's logic of differences to democracy's logic of equivalences can only lead to the destruction of democracy. It is only in the tension between the logic of antagonistic differences that Tocqueville left France to disavow and the logic of equivalence that Tocqueville wrote *Democracy in America* to embrace that democracy can materialize.[33]

NOTES

1 "Tocqueville and the Mullah," *New Republic* 333, no. 4 (February 2, 1998): 7 (all quotations are from this page).

2 Apropos of this imaginary geography, Edward Said has observed: "It can be argued that Islam (in the shape of the Muslim populations of North Africa, Turkey, and Indian sub-continent) is now the primary form in which the Third World presents itself to Europe, and that the North-South divide, in the European context, has been largely inscribed onto a pre-existing Christian-Muslim division" (*Orientalism* [London: Routledge, Kegan and Paul, 1978), 97. Following its exclusion from the precincts of western civilization Islam, as Aziz Al-Azmeh has observed, "appears indifferently among other things to name history, indicate a religion, ghettoize a community, describe a 'culture,' explain a despicable exoticism, and fully specify a political program" (*Islams and Modernities* [London: Verso, 1993], 24).

3 As Khatami explained, "Policies pursued by American politicians outside the United States over the past half a century, since World War II, are incompatible with the American civilization founded on democracy, freedom and human dignity" ("Tocqueville and the Mullah").

4 See Benjamin Barber, *Jihad vs. McWorld: How the Planet Is Both Falling Apart and Coming Together and What This Means for Democracy* (New York: Random House, 1995), 6. In positioning Iran within the new containment policy, Barber enlisted the following orientalist fantasy: "The apparent truth, which speaks to the paradox at the core of this book is that tendencies of both Jihad *and* McWorld are at work, both visible sometimes in the same country at the very same instant. Iranian zealots keep

one ear to the mullahs urging holy war and the other to Rupert Murdoch's Star television beaming in *Dynasty, Donahue,* and the *Simpsons* from hovering satellites" (5). Except for the fact that President Khatami was probably watching C-SPAN's *Traveling Tocqueville's America* rather than Rupert Murdoch's *Dynasty,* Barber's fantasy bears a family resemblance to the editorial perspective of the *New Republic.* His account of the official reaction of the Islamic state to Murdoch's Star TV describes what the editors of the *New Republic* might have expected to hear from President Khatami. About satellite programs being beamed into Tehran, Barber quotes an unidentified official of the Iranian Ministry of Culture and Islamic Guidance as having declared, "these programs, prepared by international imperialism, are part of an extensive plot to wipe out our religious and sacred values" (207).

5 Bobby Sayyid has described this process with remarkable cogency: "Muslims who use Islamic metaphors draw our attention to the fact that there is another way of doing politics which does not seem to rest upon the dominant language games of the last two hundred years. One of the main reasons why 'Islamic Fundamentalism' causes so much disquiet is because it seems to suggest that we may have confused the globalization of a political tradition with its universalization. By rejecting the dominant political discourses, 'Islamic Fundamentalists' make it difficult for us to describe them, since many of our theoretical tools are bound up with this dominant political tradition" ("Sign O'Times: Kaffirs and Infidels Fighting the Ninth Crusade," in *The Making of Political Identities,* ed. Ernesto Laclau [New York: Verso, 1994], 265).

6 Claude Lefort quotes this passage by Tocqueville in *Democracy and Political Theory,* trans. David Macey (Cambridge: Polity Press, 1988), 166.

7 See Ghassan Haage, *White Nation* (New York: Routledge, 2000), 70.

8 Slavoj Žižek, "Eastern Europe's Republics of Gilead," *New Left Review* 183 (September/October 1990), 51–52.

9 Useful accounts of the history of Tocqueville's reception can be found in A. Eisenstadt, ed., *Reconsidering Tocqueville's Democracy in America* (New Brunswick: Rutgers University Press, 1988); Seymour Drescher, *Dilemmas of Democracy: Tocqueville and Modernization* (Pittsburgh: University of Pittsburgh Press, 1968); Marvin Zetterbaum, *Tocqueville and the Problem of Democracy* (Stanford: Stanford University Press, 1967); Timothy Brennan, *At Home in the World: Cosmopolitanism Now* (Cambridge: Harvard University Press, 1997); Louis Hartz, *The Liberal Tradition in America: An Interpretation of American Political Thought since the Revolution* (New York: Harcourt Brace, 1955); Robert A. Nisbet, *The Sociological Tradition* (New York: Basic Books, 1966); and Larry Siedentop, *Tocqueville* (Oxford: Oxford University Press, 1994).

10 Slightly different genealogies of the discourse of U.S. exceptionalism can be found in Seymour Martin Lipset, *American Exceptionalism: A Double-Edged Sword* (New York: Norton, 1997); and Byron E. Shaffer, ed., *Is America Different? A New Look at American Exceptionalism* (London: Oxford University Press, 1991).

11 In his introduction to *Challenging Boundaries* Michael Shapiro has succinctly described the political implications of this national imaginary: "Because the United States had operated from a largely uncontested frame of reference, it, along with the

powerful political units that shaped first the colonial and then the postcolonial cold war world, functioned within a delusional political narrative. It imagined itself as part of a story in which its dominance in the world order is a historical destiny and a utopian end to global political forms" (*Challenging Boundaries*, ed. Michael Shapiro and Hayward R. Alker [Minneapolis: University of Minnesota Press, 1996], xvii). The role narrative closure plays in the maintenance of the authority of this paradigm can be found in Hayden White, "The Value of Narrativity in the Representation of Reality," *Critical Inquiry* 7 (1980): 5–27.

12 See Helga Geyer-Ryan, "Imagining Identity: Space, Gender, Nation," in *Vision in Context: Historical and Contemporary Perspectives on Sight*, ed. Teresa Brennan and Martin Jay (New York: Routledge, 1996), 121.

13 Vincent Ostrom has discerned civic associations as the core value of the Tocqueville project: "It is within families and other institutional arrangements characteristic of neighborhood, village, and community life that citizenship is learned and practiced for most people most of the time. The first order of priority in learning the craft of citizenship as applied to public affairs needs to focus on how to cope with problems in the context of family, neighborhood, village, and community" (*The Meaning of Democracy and the Vulnerability of Democracies* [Ann Arbor: University of Michigan Press, 1997], x).

14 In the following passage from *The Fragility of Freedom: Tocqueville on Religion, Democracy, and the American Future* (Chicago: University of Chicago Press, 1995), Joshua Mitchell has supplied the coda for the post–cold war mentality: "The real problem now that the cold war has receded and we fumble forward into the future is not, as it would appear, how to assure world-wide free markets; rather it is how, in America at least, to arrest the twin phenomena of a narrow egoism that would oversee only the world in its own purview and an overstepping fantasy that is forever unsatisfied with itself and the world" (42).

15 See Arthur M. Schlesinger Jr., *The Disuniting of America: Reflections on a Multicultural Society* (Knoxville: Whittle Direct Books, 1991); Newt Gingrich, *To Renew America* (New York: HarperCollins, 1995); Robert Bellah, "Civil Religion in America," *Daedalus* 96, no. 1 (winter 1967): 1–21; Lipset, *American Exceptionalism;* Anne Norton, "Engendering Another American Identity" and William E. Connolly, "Democracy and Territoriality," both in *Rhetorical Republic: Governing Representations in American Politics*, ed. Frederick M. Dolan and Thomas L. Dumm (Amherst: University of Massachusetts Press, 1993); Michael Sandel, *Democracy's Discontent: America in Search of a Public Philosophy* (Cambridge, MA: Harvard University Press, 1996); Michael Shapiro, "Introduction," and David Campbell, "Political Prosaics, Transversal Politics, and the Anarchical World," both in *Challenging Boundaries*, ed. Shapiro and Alker.

16 Harvey C. Mansfield and Delba Winthrop, "Introduction," in Alexis de Tocqueville, *Democracy in America*, ed. and trans. Harvey C. Mansfield and Delba Winthrop (Chicago: University of Chicago Press, 2000), xxiv.

17 According to Mansfield and Winthrop, Tocqueville accomplished this reconciliation through the invention of a political category that he called the *semblable*, which

rendered alike even the most irreconcilable of political positions: "Here there is no reconciliation between self and other in which one self finds itself in the other. Rather, that reconciliation is assumed from the beginning. The democrat considers others to be like himself, and if they are truly different he *sees* them to be like himself regardless. He ignores or flattens out any differences that might call equality into question" (*Democracy in America*, xlvii).

18 In his review of Mansfield and Winthrop's translation Gordon S. Wood has attributed to it the capacity to transcend and contain antagonisms that they discern in Tocqueville's masterwork. Wood distinguishes Mansfield and Winthrop's edition (which is the first English translation of *Democracy in America* since that by George Lawrence published a generation earlier) from its predecessor's in that it "tries to be as faithful as possible to Tocqueville's thought as he expressed it rather than restating his thought in modern terms. And it strives for the impartiality that Tocqueville himself desired" (*New York Review of Books* 48, no. 8 [May 17, 2001]: 46). Quoting Tocqueville's observation that a great democratic revolution is taking place among us, Wood proceeded to speak with comparable transhistorical force when he concluded that Tocqueville has articulated a democratic political theory whose capacity to transcend the specifically American example renders *Democracy in America* a universalizing political formation: "Indeed this revolution is continuing even today and accounts for much of present-day politics both in the United States and abroad" (48).

19 Alexis de Tocqueville, "Author's Preface to the Twelfth Edition," in *Democracy in America*, trans. George W. Lawrence, ed. J. P. Mayer (Garden City, N.Y.: Doubleday, 1969), xiv.

20 See Thomas L. Dumm, *Democracy and Punishment: Disciplinary Origins of the United States* (Madison: University of Wisconsin Press, 1987).

21 Linda Orr has remarked incisively concerning Tocqueville's politics of displacement: "It would be easy to say that the 'only essential difference' between the 'then' (Old Regime) and 'now' (Empire) of the text is the Revolution—and this would be true, except that the Revolution would be seen as an imperceptible step toward the Empire or the displacement between two historical objects (Old Regime and Empire) that are almost identical" (*Headless History: Nineteenth-Century French Historiography of the Revolution* [Ithaca: Cornell University Press, 1990], 100). Whereas Orr concentrates her analysis on the Old Regime and the French Revolution, I would argue that *Democracy in America* did the work of displacing the difference between the Old Regime and the Empire, thereby rendering the two events all but indistinguishable.

22 When Tocqueville claimed America as a French cultural possession, he was inaugurating a venerable cultural tradition whose legatees include Camus, Sartre, Malraux, and most recently Jean Baudrillard. Jean-Phillipe Mathy has provided an illuminating account of this tradition in *Extreme-Occident: French Intellectuals and America* (Chicago: University of Chicago Press, 1993).

23 Lefebvre cited by Blandine Kriegel in *The State and the Rule of Law* (Princeton: Princeton University Press, 1995), 157.

24 Claude Lefort formulated this dualism in *Democracy and Political Theory*, 180.

25 Ibid., 167.

26 Neil Hertz, *The End of the Line: Essays on Psychoanalysis and the Sublime* (New York: Columbia University Press, 1985).

27 Ibid., 174.

28 Jacques Rancière, "Discovering New Worlds: Politics of Travel and Metaphors of Space," in *Traveller's Tales: Narratives of Home and Displacement*, ed. George Robertson et al. (London: Routledge, 1994), 35.

29 Ibid., 33.

30 Norman Birnbaum has remarked that "de Tocqueville wrote about a preindustrial society: the recurrence of his thought may suggest something else than a commendable desire to go to the historical roots of our political culture. The nation has changed immensely since de Tocqueville's visit. The French thinker, a recalcitrant liberal (in the European sense) with deep doubts about democracy, [may have served to legitimate ambivalence about democracy.] He, or his ideas have also served to avert our gaze from problems presented by industrialization, by immigration, by the end of slavery and by empire" (*Radical Renewal: The Politics of Ideas in Modern America* [New York: Pantheon Books, 1988], 66).

31 See Lisa Lowe, *Critical Terrains: French and British Orientalisms* (Ithaca: Cornell University Press, 1991), 31.

32 See Michel de Certeau, *The Practice of Everyday Life* (Berkeley: University of California Press, 1988), 123.

33 For an illuminating discussion of this dynamic, see Chantal Mouffe, "For a Politics of Nomadic Identity," in *Traveller's Tales: Narratives of Home and Displacement*, ed. George Robertson et al., 105–13.

JOAN DAYAN

Legal Slaves and Civil Bodies

◆

I begin with a story, evidence of what some call the "supernatural," as entry into my discussion of the sorcery of law: most instrumental when most fantastic and most violent when most spectral.

> During my last visit to Haiti, I heard a story about a white dog. Reclaimed by a *oungan*, or priest, who "deals with both hands" practicing "bad" magic, the dog comes back to life in skin bloated with spirit. Starving, its eyes gone wild, it appears late at night with its tongue hanging out. A friend called it "the dog without skin," but this creature was not a dog. Instead when a person died, the spirit, once stolen by the *oungan*, awakened from what had seemed sure death into this new existence in canine disguise. We all agreed that no manhandled spirit would want to end up reborn in the skin of the dog. Being turned into a dog was bad enough, but to end up losing color, to turn white, seemed worse. In this metamorphosis, the skin of the dead person is left behind, like the skin discarded by a snake. But the person's spirit remains immured in the coarse envelope, locked in another form, trapped in something not her own.[1]

What was once condemned as unreal or magical, shunted aside or projected onto those peoples and places deemed "uncivilized," remains, though hidden, at the heart of the modern state. My inquiry concerns the metaphysical hub that gives law the power both to preserve and to manipulate the categories of spirit and body. This transformation of categories—the double movement and complex relations between the extremes of flesh and mind, external and internal, and what can be removed and what must remain—gives the juridical order the power to redefine persons.

By taking the story of the white dog as model and code for understanding the rituals of law, I intend to take spiritual belief as legal commentary and vice versa. In analyzing how the rhetoric of law both disables civil persons and invents legal slaves, I argue that the creation of an artificial entity, whether the civil body, the legal slave, or the felon rendered dead in law, takes place in a world where the supernatural serves as the unacknowledged mechanism of justice. From its beginnings, law traded on the lure of the spirit, banking on religion and the debate on matter and spirit, corporeal and incorporeal, in order to transfer the power of the deity and the dominion of the master to the corrective of the state. The rituals I examine not only became critical to the ideology of democracy and liberty but also shaped a genealogy of property and possession essential to America's social memory. Legal structures give flesh to past narratives and new life to the residue of old codes and penal sanctions.

The law materializes dispossession, and in far more corporeal ways than its abstract precepts might first suggest. How, then, do the terms of law legitimate containment and exclusion? What are the conditions under which categories of identity are legally reconstructed? Which words act as revenants, haunting the precincts of law? In the United States, the pure principle of democracy exacted the most extreme practices of oppression. This essay seeks to analyze, on one hand, how this domination proffered to a society of equals depended on rituals of expulsion and exclusion; and, on the other, how these practices took their consummate form in the penitentiary. Punishment and prisons not only became critical to the ideology of democracy and freedom but also shaped a genealogy of property and possession essential to the "American project."[2] Beaumont and Tocqueville's *On the Penitentiary System in the United States, and Its Application in France* (never reprinted since its publication in 1833) must thus be read as a dark gloss to Tocqueville's *Democracy in America*. Like the furies buried beneath Athens so that the ideal city can be born, the idea of freedom became coterminous with the necessities of containment. As Beaumont and Tocqueville confessed: "Whilst society in the United States gives the example of the most extended liberty, the prisons of the same country offer the spectacle of the most complete despotism."[3]

SACRIFICE

In his *Commentaries on the Laws of England*, William Blackstone, explaining how civil liberty arises on the ruins of the natural, set the ground for the creation of an artificial person in law: "But every man, when he enters society, gives up a part of his natural liberty, as the price of so valuable a purchase; and, in consideration of receiving the advantages of mutual commerce, obliges himself to conform to those laws, which the community has thought proper to establish. And this species of legal obedience and conformity is infinitely more desirable than that wild and savage liberty which is sacrificed to obtain it."[4] Unlike the Pauline admonition to relinquish the trappings of the physical to be raised a spiritual body, Blackstone's version of new life depends not on belief in Christ but in the civil order. The rebirth of the individual in society does not depend on dying through and to the law. Instead, the civil, once codified in the institution of law, demands the dual gestures of submission and repression of the natural. In these fictions of juridical obeisance, the old nature first takes on the skin of the civil, then pacts to contain itself within that skin. In this way, by the very terms of Blackstone's contract, the state of society never completely transcends that of nature. The natural person, who existed before the social contract, though reduced to a repressed spirit in civil skin, nonetheless haunts the margins of the formal community. Blackstone thus reminds his reader that in heralding the rituals of renunciation and repression as essential to the promotion of a coherent legal order, he means much more than a one-off exchange for the greater good. For the tradeoff is merely one instantiation of what must be a quasi-religious process, a ritual of citizenship to be staged again and again in order to keep the facade of the civil intact, the natural residuum in check, and thereby reassure the stability of civilization.

The image of the dog skin that encases the spirit of the dead person can be related figuratively both to the *civil body*, the artificial person who possesses self and property, and to the *legal slave*, the artificial person who exists as both human and property. In juxtaposing these two conditions of being, I suggest that the potent image of a servile body can be perpetually reinvented. In this ritual, both legal slave and civil body are sacrificed to the civil order. Although both entities are legally distinguished from natural persons, civil bodies are governed by one set of laws and legal slaves by another. Different as they are in position, in rights and duties, they cannot be the subjects of a common system of laws. The distinctions between them, however, remain shaky. The two conditions interrelate in crucial ways. I will suggest that certain images recur; and words like *blood, corruption,* and *death* have a remarkable staying power.

In reconstructing this narrative of human unfreedom, I need briefly to confront the problem of juxtaposing civil bodies and legal slaves. I begin with the equivalence of free person and slave because I want to analyze what happens to persons and progeny in two cases: the free person of property who commits a felony and undergoes civil death; and the enslaved person, whom I suggest is the carrier of "negative personhood," who has undergone social death. Although the person declared civilly dead had property to lose, in most instances the slave never had property and was in fact property and could never have any relation to property. The institution of slavery depended on embodying the black as merely material, what could be described as a philosophy of denaturalization that turned humans into things or mongrels. The fiction of the "citizen," however, summons a somewhat less certain transit between restraint and freedom, capacity and disability. In bringing what might first seem to be an unlikely conjunction to the fore, the lethal machinery of juridical value becomes clear. Slaves and criminals form the two extremes of this analysis, but these exceptions put the citizen who is nonslave or nonfelon in a constant and fearful zone of ambiguity.

Rather than focusing on social attitudes and relationships, in this essay I instead trace a developing logic in modern law. I explore how, by the eighteenth century, the appeal to Judeo-Christian antecedents and inchoate traditions of punishment would be redescribed and fully articulated as a rationale appropriate to the needs of emerging modernity. In this logic, the law covers the person with white skin and the law encases her in black, whether or not the colors can be seen. The law giveth and the law taketh away. The law kills and the law resurrects. Legal practice thus conflates symbolic control and the inscription of that control on real bodies. If the natural dies not to be reborn in the spirit but in the body of civil society, what kind of body is this?[5]

In *Slavery and Social Death*, Orlando Patterson makes two crucial points that suggest the troubling power of legal authority. In his section "Property and Slavery," he first draws our attention to the habitual definition of a slave as someone without a legal personality: "It is a fiction found only in western societies, and even there it has been taken seriously more by legal philosophers than by practicing lawyers. As a legal fact, there has never existed a slaveholding society, ancient or modern, that did not recognize the slave as a person in law."[6] Patterson proposes a theory of negative capability, while he remains silent about the disabling inherent in the very process of creating a legal personality that has been granted statutory life only to be enslaved. Then, discussing what he calls "liminal incorporation," while trying to come to terms with the socially dead slave who yet remains a part of society, he writes: "Religion explains how it is possible to relate to the dead who still live. It says little about how ordinary people should relate to the living who are dead" (45).

These two passages refer first to the actually dead though alive in spirit as opposed to the actually alive though dead in law; and, second, the supernatural relation of the believer to the dead who do not die, as opposed to the natural and daily relation of the living who are dead, who have undergone what Patterson, following Claude Messailloux, calls "social death" (38). Patterson's insistence that slaves in every legal code are treated as persons in law, urges upon us these questions: In what way and when were slaves allowed to be persons? When resurrected as legal personalities, what can they do, what are their possibilities? And if, finally, Patterson distinguishes between the ontology of civil life and the realm of myth or religion, what happens if we insist on bringing myth and legal practice together; or to be more precise, to juxtapose the "social death" of slaves with the "civil death" of felons in order to ask whether statute and case law could be more important than social custom in effecting rituals of exclusion, and, as I will emphasize, in maintaining the racial line. If we make slavery in the Americas our hypothetical still point, then we can consider what kinds of persons would end up being redefined as dead in law. It was as easy to deem the extinction of civil rights and legal capacities as punishment for, or the necessary consequence of, the crime of color as it was for the conviction of crime. For color, this appearance of moral essence or transmissible evil could stand in society as both a threat and a curse, or finally, as justification for the subjugation of those so tainted.

Using the legal fiction of "civil death" as anchor, I return to what has been deemed a remnant of obsolete jurisprudence: the state of a person who, though possessing *natural life* has lost all *civil rights.* Unnatural or artificial death as punishment for crime entailed a logic of alienation that could extend perpetually along constructed lines of racial kinship.[7] Its legal paradoxes, its gothic turns between tangible and intangible, life and death, became necessary to the racialized idiom of slavery in the American social order. The alternating moves between the idea of civil death and the meaning of servitude operated both forward and backward along a temporal continuum to exclude, subordinate, and annihilate. For what had been forfeiture of property and corruption of blood— those few circumstances in which civil death was coextensive with physical death and that were understood by Blackstone as caused by profession (as in a monk professed), abjuration from the realm (deportation for crime), and attainder and banishment (for treason)—became the terms for a specifically colonial rendition of legal incapacitation (1:128–29).

How did civil death affect rights of property and privilege at common law? There were three principle incidents consequent on an attainder for treason or felony: forfeiture, corruption of blood, and the *extincti* on of civil rights, more or less complete. Of Saxon origin, forfeiture was part of the punishment of crime by which the goods and chattels, lands and tenements, of the attainted felon were forfeited. According to the doctrine of corruption of blood, introduced after the Norman Conquest, the blood of the attainted person was held to be corrupt, so that he could not transmit his estate to his heirs, nor could they inherit. According to Blackstone, this inequitable and "peculiar hardship" meant that the "chanel" of "hereditary blood" would not only be "exhausted for the present, but totally dammed up and rendered impervious for the future" (2:256, 253).

I distinguish civil death from other legal sanctions because this concept and its attendant disabilities maintained both a strictly hierarchical order and the blood defilement on which that order depends. Corruption of blood operated practically as a severing of blood lines, thus cutting off inheritance, and metaphorically as an extension of the "sin" or "taint" of the father visited on his children. If we treat *blood* and *property* as metaphors crucial to defining *persons* in civil society, then it is easy to see how "corruption of blood" and "forfeiture of property" could become the operative components of divestment. By a negative kind of birthright, bad blood blocked inheritance, just as loss of property meant disenfranchisement. Yoked together as they are, these terms loosely but powerfully define types of slavery. Whether applied to the slave or the criminal, both are degraded below the rank of human beings, not only politically but also physically and morally.

In my pursuit of a conceptual framework for disabilities made indelible through time, I follow the call of *blood,* its meaning and effects, both literal and metaphoric, through three sites of disabling: from the feudal *attainder,* the essence of which became corruption of blood, as punishment for crime; to the transport of blood to the British colonies and its incarnation as the black taint that legally inscribed slavery; to the disabilities of the post–Civil War, when slaves were reborn as criminals and translated into "slaves of the state." I take this circuit of stigmatization as a *historical residue* that turns metaphoricity into a way of knowing; that is, acknowledging history. How this project of incapacitation has continued to threaten the weak and socially oppressed, how old rhetorical strategies initiate new forms of containment, is what matters here.

BLOOD

In rereading the claims of civil death into the genealogy of slavery and incarceration, I propose a continuum between being declared dead in law, being made a slave, and being judged a criminal. Blackstone referred to natural liberty as "residuum" (1:129), and he figured this residue of nature as a stain. The imprint of corruption becomes the legitimating metaphor for what I have described as the sacrificial formation of the civil person. In other words, for the figurative distinction of civil and natural to function in the realm of action, the metaphor of corruption must be grounded in would-be observable fact. Blackstone's language thus connected the figurative nature and the material body: "For when it is now clear beyond all dispute, that the criminal is no longer fit to live upon the earth, but is to be exterminated as a monster and a bane to society, the law sets a note of infamy upon him, puts him out of its protection, and takes no further care of him barely to see him executed. He is then called attaint, *attinctus,* stained or blackened" (4:380). The image of the "blackened" person, disabled but not necessarily dead, remained a more terrifying example of punishment than the executed body. Moreover, the deficiency of hereditary blood and its consequences for the felon's descendants became an alternative death penalty: not actually but civilly dead. Strict civil death, the blood "tainted" by crime, set the stage for blood "tainted" by natural inferiority. This discrimination would produce the nonexistence of the person not only in the West Indies but in the United States. The racialized fiction of blood, moreover, supplemented the metaphoric taint, not only defining property in slaves but fixing them and their progeny and descendants in status and location.

What is "corruption of blood"? According to legal doctrine, the blood of the attainted person was, as I have noted, judged to be corrupt, so that he could neither inherit nor transmit his estate to his heirs. As Thomas Blount explained in his 1670 *Nomo-lexicon, a law dictionary,* "Corruption of Blood [is] an infection growing to the State of a Man (attainted of Felony or Treason) and to his issue: For, as he loseth all to the Prince, or other Lord of the Fee, as his case is; so his issue cannot be heirs to him, or to any other Ancestor by him. And if he were Noble, or a Gentleman before, he and his children are thereby ignobled and ungentiled."[8] How was this degradation enacted? In exploring this terrain, I appeal to a history that emphasizes the paradox and reciprocity of disabling registered in both legal fictions and religious fantasies. For depersonalization took place in the marketplace as well as on the sacrificial altar, through commercial transactions as well as religious rites. Recall the general concept of corruption of blood in the curse of Psalm 109: "Let his posterity be cut off; and in the generation following let their name be blotted out. / Let the iniquity of his fathers be remembered with the Lord; and let not the sin of his mother be blotted out. /

Let them be before the Lord continually, that he may cut off the memory of them from the earth." In this banishing ritual, the enemy of David and his descendants lie under sentence of corruption of blood, turned base and ignoble and thus barred from inheritance into the remotest generation.

The term "corruption" itself must be considered cautiously. Although it meant "vile contamination," "infection," or "pollution" in early English as it does now, to the point of acquiring in Nathan Bailey's 1721 *An Universal Etymological English Dictionary: and An Interpreter of Hard Words,* the immediacy of stench and the visibility of blemish, its fundamental meaning remained in the semantic range of destruction, breaking up, dissolution, and decomposition.[9] That is, corruption of the convicted person's blood meant not just that it was tainted but that it legally ceased to flow in either direction, operating "*upwards and downwards,*" so that an attainted person could neither inherit lands or anything else from his ancestors, nor could he transmit property to his heirs.

What is most crucial to my mind about the definition of "attainder" is the way a probable mistake in philology became a useful means of exclusion. The similarity of "tainted" and "attaint(ed)," especially in their past-participial forms, would make their blending almost unavoidable. The OED, dating its lexical proof from 1563, focuses on what became the gist of attainder—corruption of blood— through this false derivation of attainder in "taint" or "stain": "L. *attingere* to touch upon, strike, etc.; subsequently warped in meaning by erroneous association with F. *taindre, teindre,* to dye, stain."[10] Beneath an apparently inadvertent, false, or at least loosely mixed-up terminology in late medieval England, exists an anatomy of disabling.[11]

Words, once repeated and recalled, are endowed with a resonance that tells the story of greed and racism operating over a long period of time. When did taint become allied with attainder? Can we trace the idea of tainted blood—that most critical mechanism for exclusion in the slave laws of the Caribbean and the American South—back to the metaphysics of metaphorical blood and biological destiny? The duplicity in meaning—the blending of hit, touch, or knock *and* tinge or tincture into stain, blemish, or contamination—suggests that this terminological history is one of cross-fertilization and not of sequentiality. "Corruption of blood" in English law probably never had anything to do with ethnicity or biology but everything to do with taking an attainted person's property to the exclusion of any otherwise rightful heirs. In the late 1450s, the truly harsh acts of attainder with the full legal force of corruption of blood came into frequent use. Who, one might ask, cared about the nil property had by the poor or unlanded, such as blacks, or by any other potential slaves later on? Nor would considering them and their progeny goods and chattels in themselves be legally relevant.

But as slavery in the colonies became profitable, requiring the justification of the depravity of those enslaved, color counted as presumption of servitude. Extensive English participation in the slave trade did not develop until well into the seventeenth century, but alternative experiments in unfreedom—the subjugation of the Gaelic Irish, the Vagrancy Act of 1547, indentured servitude, and the English galleys—had already provided a template for domination. As early as 1562 Sir John Hawkins introduced the practice of buying or kidnapping blacks in Africa and transporting and selling them for slaves in the West Indies. According to Winthrop Jordan, the sight of blackness had a powerful effect on the English as soon as they landed on the shores of Africa. In 1578 George Best decided that the blackness of Africans "proceedeth of some naturall infection of the first inhabitants of that country, and so all the whole progenie of them descended, are still polluted with the same blot of infection."[12]

The phantom language of colonial stigma would be literalized, especially in the eighteenth century, in juridical articulation. And although Blackstone denounced slavery, his description of the consequences of attainder promised a novel genealogical inscription of race that could be got from an old language of criminality and heredity. According to Blackstone, the king's pardon of an attainted felon made the offender "a new man" with renewed "credit and capacity." But Blackstone warned, "nothing can restore or purify the blood when once corrupted . . . but the high and transcendent power of parliament." Once pardoned by the king, however, the son of the person attainted might inherit, "because the father, being made a new man, might transmit new inheritable blood" (4:395). Law can make one dead in life, and even determine when and if one is to be resurrected. The restoration in blood, even when not possible for the attainted himself who remained dead in law, devolved on the son, who could receive the transmission of new blood and thus incarnate the privileges of birth and rank his father had lost.

Such transmission or pledge of purification would not apply to those who suffered the incapacitation by fiat, the perpetual decimation of personhood and property understood as domestic slavery. For what had been forfeiture of property and corruption of blood—those few circumstances in which civil death was coextensive with physical death—became the terms for a categorical redefinition of legal incapacity. Further, no longer under legal quarantine, tainted blood extends down through the generations. In this light, colonial legal history can be examined with a view to understanding how the construction of race (and racial stigmatization) served as the ideological fulcrum that allowed a penal society to produce a class of citizens who are dead in life: stripped of community, deprived of communication, and shorn of humanity.

GENEALOGIES

In the context of the eighteenth-century British West Indies, as in the southern United States, the significance of blood becomes clear if incredible. Blood penetrates into the inhabitants' bodies and racially marks them, granting them legal recognition according to degrees of mixture: either advancing toward white or regressing toward black. Emphasis on blood as conduit for the stain of black ancestry became more necessary as bodies of color began to merge and to lose the biological trait of blackness. The supremacy of whiteness now depended on a fiction threatened by what one could not always see but must always fear: the black blood that would not only pollute progeny but infect the very heart of the nation.[13]

The site of slavery in the colonies rendered material the conceptual, giving a body to what had been abstraction. Through the stigma of race, the spectral corruption of blood found bodies to inhabit and claim. An idea of lineage thus evolved and turned the rule of descent into the transfer of pigmentation, which fleshed out in law the terms necessary to maintain the curse of color. This brand of servility had the magical effect of dislocation, out of the civil and into the savage, because colonial slave law was "not the law of England, but the law of the plantations," according to the lawyers in *Somerset v. Stewart*. Although the argument smacks of the rather hypocritical shunting of impurity out from England's "pure air" (projecting dirt out from the "English garden" and onto the "West Indian hell," as Rochester put it to Jane in *Jane Eyre*), the fact remains that the local laws of the English colonies legalized extremes of dehumanization that harkened back to times Englishmen might well have judged barbarous, while they enjoyed the fruits of the labor that such treatment made possible.[14]

In *Democracy in America*, Alexis de Tocqueville compared the European's legally ordained inequality with what he found in the United States, drawing attention to the difference between "imagined inequality" (the "abstract and transient fact of slavery" among persons "evidently similar") and the "inferiority" that is "fatally united with the physical and permanent fact of color." He concluded by asking: "If it be so difficult to root out an inequality that originates solely in the law, how are those distinctions to be destroyed which seem to be based upon the immutable laws of Nature herself"? Yet Tocqueville also recognized that "nothing can be more fictitious than a purely legal inferiority."[15] The degraded essence flows, like blood itself, in and out of bodies either literally or figuratively stigmatized, through the enslaved and the freed, the legally dead and the metaphorically incarcerated. Racial markers, whether understood as those of lineage or descent or those specifically linked to the blackness of Africans and their progeny, mattered as they did because of the language of blood as inalienable inheritance.

By the 1660s, perpetual and hereditary servitude had been formalized in the British North American colonies. With independence, slave laws in the United States began to sanction permanent, lineal bondage as the system of chattel slavery evolved and expanded. The epistemology of whiteness depended on the detection of blackness: fantasies about hidden taints were then backed up by explicit legal codes; by what Virginia Dominguez in *White by Definition* has called "*de facto a classification by ancestry.*"[16] Unlike the Spaniards and French, who accounted for some 128 gradations of color from absolute black to absolute white and named combinations such as the French *quateron, metis, mamelouque, marabou, griffonne,* and *sacatra,* the most commonly observed distinctions in the British West Indies were sambo, mulatto, mustee, and octoroon.[17] Describing persons of "mixed blood," Bryan Edwards in his *The History, Civil and Commercial, of the British Colonies in the West Indies,* warned that although discriminations of color are not easily made, the civil law is clear: "In Jamaica, and I believe in the rest of our Sugar Islands, the descendants of Negroes by White people, entitled by birth to all the rights and liberties of White subjects in the full extent, are such as are above three steps removed in lineal digression from the Negro venter. All below this, whether called in common parlance Mestizes, Quadrons, or Mulattoes, are deemed by law Mulattoes."[18] In the *Journals of the Assembly of Jamaica* (1663–1826), the export of blood taint is made specific: " 'Corruption of blood' was visited upon 'not the sins of the fathers but the misfortunes of the mothers' unto the third and fourth generation of intermixture from the Negro ancestor exclusive."[19]

In the United States by the eighteenth century all persons presumed tinged with black blood were legally "mulatto," although the term was never as precisely defined as in the French colonies, where it meant not merely mixed blood (neither black nor white) but specifically the offspring of a white man and *négresse* on a geneological scale of minute gradations of blood and nuances of color. In the British West Indies, an octoroon was legally white and therefore automatically free in the British West Indies (permitted to the franchise and militia). Throughout the *Journals of the Assembly of Jamaica,* motions were made to present bills that would entitle free mulatto women and their children "to the rights and privileges of English subjects." Yet, unlike Jamaica, some southern states pushed the taint of negro ancestry from one-eighth to one-sixteenth part black blood, thus legally extending the stain to any product of intermixture. These degrees of blood, distinguished through the dubious means of observation, rumor, and reputation, reinforced the law's legitimation of whiteness.[20] After Emancipation, the ancestral taint took on renewed importance and left the body with amended blood at the mercy of a jury.[21] The concept of blackness ensured the racial subordination that made possible continued enslavement. The turn to blood was crucial to this strategy. As a metaphysical attribute, blood provided a pseudorational system for the distribution of a mythical essence: blood = race. Once the connection is made color can be referred to, but now it means blood. Like the word *blood, color* is fictitious, but the law—as in a colonial Second Coming—engineered the stigma that ordains deprivation.[22]

LEGAL PERSONALITIES

What was at stake inside England for the form that colonization would take? What laws became necessary for those who became masters and slaves? If Foucault's metropolitan world of public torture, what he described as "the liturgy of physical punishment," died out by the eighteenth and the beginning of the nineteenth century, the punitive spectacle and the requisite bodies were resurrected in the colonies.[23] In the English colonies, slaves, once reduced to a special kind of property, were to be governed as persons with wills of their own but fixed in their status as legal property, not, as with the Spaniards, an inferior kind of subject.[24] According to Jonathan Bush, nothing "remotely like a jurisprudence of slavery emerged in the English colonial world"; instead, "only one body of significant slave law exists in the English colonies: the incomplete and analytically inadequate colonial statutes."[25] Given the lack of precedents in English law, the speed with which the institution of slavery took shape in the United States and the severity of the laws that effected it are exceptional. The sources of the legal rules and principles of slavery in the American South are much debated. Depending on the source one reads on the origins of slavery in the United States, Roman civil law, the influences of colonial slave codes in the West Indies, the

French Antilles, and the Spanish and Portuguese possessions all contributed to the composite rhetoric of disabling and protection in the statute law of the slaveholding states.[26] Yet, as I have argued, strategies of divestment were already present in the rights of property and privilege at common law, which would later be tied to the definition of property in persons. Black slaves, regarded as outside the social order, reanimated legal precedent and gave new genetic capital to the principles of tainted blood, bondage, and servility.

Numerous eighteenth-century cases from Alabama to Mississippi to Virginia clarified the hybrid entity that could be both person and property. Thomas Cobb in his 1858 *Inquiry into the Law of Negro Slavery* described the birthing of that legal personality called "slave": "When the law, by providing for his proper nourishment and clothing, by enacting penalties against the cruel treatment of his master, by providing for his punishment for crimes, and other similar provisions, recognizes his existence as a person, he is as a child just born, brought for the first time within the pale of the law's protecting power; his existence as a person being recognized by the law, that existence is protected by the law."[27] The slave, once recognized as a person in law, becomes part of the process whereby the newborn person, wrought out of the loins of the white man's law—in a birth as monstrous as that of Frankenstein's creature—can then be nullified in the slave body. In superimposing Blackstone's reblooded heir onto the reborn slave, we begin to see how the law, invoking the double condition of the unborn and the undead, can eject certain beings from the circle of citizenry, even while offering the promise of beneficent protection.

The law, in recognizing the existence of the slave as person, confers no rights except to protect that existence. Yet that existence is rigidly curtailed and qualified. When protected from cruel treatment, what are the terms by which such dispensation is defined? What words in a statute extend to these individuals, and how do words change in meaning when applied to this legal creature? In *The State of Mississippi v. Issac Jones* (1821), slaves are first defined as both "chattels" and "men." They are deemed men when committing crimes. What happens to this trial of definition when crime is committed *against* a slave? Can murder be committed on a slave, the court asks; and if not, why not? Justice Joshua D. Clarke explains that "the taking away the life of a reasonable creature, under the king's peace, with malice aforethought, express or implied, is murder at common law."[28]

Reason is the crux here, but once attached to the slave, in what spirit is the word said? Justice Clarke's reasoning applies *only* to the anomaly the law has created. A series of questions undo the personhood of the slave even as they appear to retrieve it: "Is not the slave a reasonable creature, is he not a human being, for the killing a lunatic, an idiot, or even a child unborn, is murder, as much as killing a philosopher, and has not the slave as much reason as a lunatic, an idiot, or an unborn child?" (84–86). At the center of this rhetorical question lies the ostensibly uninhabited body, the cipher that waits to be filled by a cluster of beings who do not possess reason. Clarke claims that the law recognizes a powerlessness that actually exists, rather than effecting a removal of powers, as if the decision does not create incapacity but merely gives evidence of that incapacity. The apparent elevation of a piece of human property into the place of reason remains conditional. The dead slave gets the protection of positive law, but at great cost. In this ritual, the slave has been not only murdered but figuratively gutted: dispossessed of whatever autonomy had existed before the law recognized him. This radical qualification of legal identity is shored up by fictions of disability, which treat the figure of the slave as more or less human, not yet born and already dead.[29]

CIVIL DEATH

It can be argued that slavery in the United States resulted in a new understanding of the limits of human endurance, so that new, more refined cruelties could be invented. On the ruins of the rack, the thumbscrew, the wheel, and the iron boot, the atrocities of a more enlightened age came into being. In his *Commentaries*, Blackstone described how execution or confiscation of property without accusation or trial, although a sign of despotism so extreme as to herald "the alarm of tyranny throughout the whole kingdom," is not as serious an attack on personal liberties as "confinement of the person, by secretly hurrying him to gaol, where his sufferings are unknown or forgotten." For imprisonment, being "a less public" and "a less striking" punishment is "therefore a more dangerous engine of arbitrary government" (1:131). Civil death in the United States, although first affixed to the blood of a criminal capitally condemned, later was understood to be a result of life imprisonment, a consequence rare at common law.

Civil death and the consequent representation of the criminal imprisoned for life as being dead in law set the terms for a new understanding of punishment. Although slavery had ended, incarceration had not. Perpetual imprisonment, while promising humanitarian alternatives to physical torture, became a means of recreating an image of servility. How best could statutory law ensure that the "badges and incidents of slavery" might continue to exist under cover of civil death? How far could the legal fiction of civil death be carried? When definitions of law responded to the theological split between the spiritual and the natural body by dividing the body into the artificial and the natural, something happened to the idea of personal identity. Slaves, though legally not *civil persons,* yet remained *natural humans.* When committing a crime, however, slaves could be recognized as possessing a legal mind, a status for which they paid by being punished as criminals. During Reconstruction, with the advent of convict lease and the chain gang, the logic of subordination clarified the law of the New South. The felon inherited something like a double debt to society: not only figuring as the intermediate category between slaves and citizens but also as a synthetic or unnatural slave. An entity held between life and death, this body would then resurface in late-twentieth-century case law as the *human* who is no longer a *person.* From this perspective, it is possible to see how the shifting identity of the slave could be reborn in the body of the prisoner.

In New York the connection between civil death and slavery became critical. In the Act of March 29th, 1799, which changed the language of civil death from the common-law wording "shall thereafter be deemed civilly dead" to the more severe "be deemed dead to all intents and purposes in the law," the legislature set up a system of laws for the gradual abolition of slavery in New York. Thus, as the gradual abolition of slaves began, the revised statute revived disabilities in a new context. The civil death statute declared that a sentence of perpetual imprisonment entailed the loss of personal rights, including divesting the felon of property, and, further, dissolving his marriage so that his wife and children owed him nothing; while the gradual abolition statute provided that children born into slavery, after July 4th 1999, would henceforth be free, although still liable to be servants of the mother's proprietor.[30]

As set out in the U.S. Constitution, honors and crimes are no longer to be hereditary. Yet although acts of attainder and forfeiture are claimed to be unknown to American jurisprudence and prohibited by constitutional provisions, civil disabilities—and civil death more or less extreme—have continued to play a significant role in the treatment of criminals in the United States. In his dissent to the 1883 Civil Rights Cases, Justice John Marshall Harlan suggested how the "substance and spirit" of constitutional amendments had been "sacrificed by a subtle and ingenious verbal criticism" that connected the past prerogatives of the "white race" and the present presumption of the "state."[31] Words would continue to work wonders on the meaning of the Constitution, perhaps nowhere so boldly as in their inventive perpetuation of civil death. Although article 3 declares that "no attainder of treason shall work corruption of blood, or forfeiture, except during the life of the person attainted," and article 1 provides that "no bill of attainder or ex post facto law shall be passed," the numerous civil disabilities imposed on a convicted offender perpetuate the soul if not the letter of stigma. In some states, persons convicted of serious crimes are still declared civilly dead; and even if the words are not used, numerous civil disabilities sustain infamous status, sometimes even after release.[32]

A criminal punished with "civil death" became the "slave of the state," as so aptly put in *Ruffin v. Commonwealth* (1871), so that once incarcerated, the prisoner endured the substance and visible form of disability, as if imaginatively recolored, bound, and owned. Called on to define the condition of the convict and consider the implications of civil death for the applicability of the Bill of Rights, Justice Christian decided: "The bill of rights is a declaration of general principles to govern a society of freemen, and not of convicted felons and men civilly dead. Such men have some rights it is true, such as the law in its benignity accords them, but not the rights of freemen. They are the slaves of the State undergoing punishment for heinous crimes committed against the laws of the land."[33] The prison walls circumscribe the prisoner in a fiction that, in extending the bounds of servitude, became the basis for the negation of rights, thus reconciling constitutional strictures with slavery. It is not surprising that *Ruffin* acted as a memorial spot of time recalled by Justices Marshall, Brennan, and Stevens, as if exhuming for the Rehnquist Court the state-sanctioned bondage the Court will not name.[34]

What, then, is the status of inmates? Are they slaves of the state, wards of the state, or do they occupy some other status, perhaps "criminal aliens," in the words of the 1996 Antiterrorism and Effective Death Penalty Act?"[35] The prisoner's status remains the most neglected area of correctional law, in contrast to that of the slave, whose legal identity formed the crux of southern slave law. That the entity called "prisoner" has remained undefined in both district and Supreme Court cases means that ever more inventive deprivations can be justified. In the contemporary practices of punishment in the United States, singular and unparalleled not only in all the Western European countries but in most of the former Eastern European bloc of nations, including Russia, both *civil death* (the mandatory and permanent loss of a package of rights, privileges, and capabilities, once imprisoned) and *literal execution* join to give new meaning to "cruel and unusual punishment"; in the first case under cover of maintaining order and deterrence, and in the second under cover of decency and humane extinction of life.

Confinement of prisoners in the United States thus became an alternative to slavery, another kind of receptacle for imperfect creatures whose civil disease justified containment. I do not mean that slaves can be equated with criminals, as if slavery were the result of punishment. Rather, I am interested in how, once convicted of crime, the criminal can be reduced—not by a master but by the state—into a condition that is sustained under the sign of death. Justinian in his *Institutes* declared "slavery is death." He knew that death takes many forms, including loss of status beyond which life ceases to be politically relevant. How, then—and this is the crucial question—can corpses be legally fabricated?[36]

Imprisonment offers the opportunity to apprehend how the condition of being *civilter mortuus* or dead in law marks the *disabled citizen* as symptom of afflictive punishment. For unlike slaves, felons remain citizens: citizens who are restrained in their liberty. The "character" of prisoners, the alleged "danger" they pose to prison order, the need for them to be transformed all became part of the discourse of the restriction of rights. This legal curtailment resonates with the ways exslaves were effectively deprived of civil rights and reduced to the status of incomplete citizens after Emancipation. As far as those imprisoned for life were concerned, the idea was to emulate the results natural death would produce. Numerous nineteenth-century cases demonstrated the staying power of civil death, as well as the manipulation of property, possessed or lost, as crucial not only to legal status but to personal identity, and the sacrifice of that identity to punishment. Instead of explicitly abolishing the status of the person, civil death means rather the incapacity to exercise the rights attached to persons, what much later in *Trop v. Dulles* (1958) would be judged cruel and unusual punishment: "No physical mistreatment, no primitive torture," but "instead the total destruction of the individual's status in organized society," having "lost the right to have rights."[37]

Although this resurrection of slavery is often discussed in the turn to convict labor and the criminalization of blacks in the postbellum South,[38] I propose that the penitentiary, as zealously discussed and instituted in the North—especially "solitary," also known as "the discipline" or "the separate system"—offered an unsettling counter to servitude, an invention of criminality and prescriptions for treatment that turned humans into the living dead. Beaumont and Tocqueville in their study *On the Penitentiary System in the United States* contrasted corporeal punishment with "absolute isolation" a unique and severe punishment, warning that "this absolute solitude, if nothing interrupt it, is beyond the strength of man; it destroys the criminal without intermission and without pity; it does not reform, it kills." Depression, insanity, and suicide led Beaumont and Tocqueville to contrast the "punishment of death and stripes" for slaves with the "separate system" for criminals, implying that the unique deprivation fixed in the mind was far more cruel than corporeal discipline."[39] Although civil death might seem a more "decent" alternative than execution, the legal fiction molds the prisoner *as if dead* into the symbolically executed, a fate worse possibly than death, proving in the words of Elisha Bates that the penitentiary "where no light enters, where no sound is heard, where there is as little as possible to support nature that will vary the tediousness of life, by change" might come to "be regarded with more horror than the gallows."[40]

Before the abolition of slavery, William Crawford, reporting in 1834 on "the Penitentiaries of the United States" to the House of Commons, noted the great proportion of black crime to white, concluding that these "oppressed people" are even more "degraded" in the free than in the slave states: "A law has been recently passed, even in Connecticut, discouraging the instruction of coloured children introduced from other States; and in the course of the last year a lady, who had with this view established a school for such children, was prosecuted and committed to prison."[41] The Thirteenth Amendment to the Constitution (1865) marked the discursive link between the civilly dead felon and the slave or social nonperson, articulating the locus of redefinition where criminality could be racialized and race criminalized. Once readjusted to the demands of incarceration, the chiasmus that had previously made racial kinship a criminal affiliation resulted in a novel banishing and exile. This amendment, too often obscured by attention to the Fourteenth Amendment, is key to understanding how the burdens and disabilities that constituted the badges of slavery took powerful hold on the language of penal compulsion. Outlawing slavery and involuntary servitude "except as punishment of crime where of the party shall have been duly convicted," the exception in the amendment made explicit the doubling, back and forth transaction between prisoner and the ghosts of slaves past. Moreover, once the connection had been made, southern slavery, now extinct, could resurface under other names not only in the South but in the North.

The great and awesome symbol of solitary confinement was Eastern State Penitentiary in Philadelphia, popularly known as Cherry Hill, completed in 1829 and immortalized by Charles Dickens in his *American Notes*. More than solitary horrors, however, Dickens described the erosion of thought in terms that demonstrate how the prison had become the materialization, the shape and container, for what had been the language of civil death: "The system here, is rigid, strict and hopeless solitary confinement. I believe it in its effects to be cruel and wrong. . . . I hold this slow and daily tampering with the mysteries of the brain, to be immeasurably worse than any torture of the body." Once the black hood covered the face of the criminal condemned to Cherry Hill, the long process of executing the soul began, "and in this dark shroud, an emblem of the curtain dropped between him and the living world. . . . He is a man buried alive; to be dug out in the slow round of years; and in the meantime dead to everything but torturing anxieties and despair."[42]

The restraints of continuing solitude proved to be more corrective than corporeal punishment. Critics of the Pennsylvania "separate system," popularly known as "the discipline," called it inhuman and unnatural. William Roscoe, the noted English historian, penal reformer, and ardent abolitionist, considered the system as "destined to contain the epitome and concentration of human misery, of which the Bastille of France, and the Inquisition of Spain, were only prototypes and humble models."[43] But numerous reformers argued that criminality called for expiation and recognized that only secret punishment and ignominy could compel repentance. Roberts Vaux, chief spokesman for the Philadelphia Prison Society and later on the Board of Commissioners appointed by the governor to erect Eastern State Penitentiary, responded to Roscoe in his "Letter on the Penitentiary System" by insisting on separation and silence as the only cures for the polluting threat of those whose "unrestrained licentiousness renders them unfit for the enjoyment of liberty."[44]

The language of contagion thus sustained the common law definition of "corruption of blood" for the attainted felon, just as civil death maintained forfeiture of property and the degradation attached to that loss. As I noted earlier, although formally abolished in the Constitution, rituals of stigmatization never stopped, and the abolition of slavery summoned more devious means of exclusion and containment. Once systematized, the residue of past methods of punishment and the suggestive aura of taint ensured continued degradation but under cover of civil necessity. Francis Lieber in his preface and introduction to Beaumont and Tocqueville's *On the Penitentiary System in the United States* defended the penitentiary as fit container for the "poisonous infection of aggravated and confirmed crime" (xii), "contracted" bad habits (xviii), and "moral contagion" (xix). The diseased body must be extirpated from civil society; once removed, the convict became the visible record of the sacrifice on which civilization maintained itself. Not only did the gradual annihilation of the person, disabled but not dead, exemplify a punishment arguably more harrowing than execution, but solitary confinement became the unique site for the drama of law. Further, in a singular conjunction of bad faith and cunning, race seemingly dropped out of the intersection between civil and social.

CRUEL AND UNUSUAL

Solitary confinement and execution both mark the continuum between un-natural (civil or spiritual) death and natural (actual and physical) death. These two forms of death remind us of a peculiarly American preoccupation with bodies and spirits, matter and mind. I also suggest, and perhaps here lies the proving ground of my argument, that cases concerning the definition of cruel and unusual punishment give particular meaning to the status or identity of the prisoner. The Eighth Amendment to the U.S. Constitution reads: "Excessive bail shall not be required, nor excessive fines imposed, nor cruel and unusual punish-ments inflicted." Although brief, almost ghostly in its final clause as if punish-ment were an afterthought, the Eighth Amendment is the only provision of the Bill of Rights that is applicable by its own terms to prisoners. As a limit on the state's power to punish, the importance of this negative guaranty expands in the prison context. Because it includes nearly all parts of prison life that might be considered unconstitutional punishment, the Eighth Amendment remains the crucial ground for prisoners' rights. Words like *decency, humane,* and *dignity* jockey for preeminence in these cases, and alternate with less expansive, more constrictive phrases like *basic human needs* or *minimal civilized measure of life's necessities.*

Legal language has construed the alternating debates between abstract calls for dignity or decency and concrete examples of specific needs and quantifiable allowances in order to vacate the meaning of *human* when applied to prisoners. To understand how this double language or two-sided tactic works is to confront the unsettling possibility that the very notion of "evolving standards of decency" in *Weems v. United States* (1910) and the "dignity of man" in *Trop v. Dulles* narrowed the divide between the civilized and inhuman treatment of prisoners.[45] We must examine in this light the rite of punishment in *Trop* as contributing to what will become, due to the cynical logic of some contemporary justices, a ruse of beneficence. Recognizing the death penalty as an endpoint of abjection, "an index of the constitutional limit on punishment," the Court suggested that its validation as constitutional should not allow "the Government to devise any punishment short of death within the limit of its imagination" (597). What is essential here is the belief that the death penalty is exceptional, or "different," to recall Brennan's compelling argument in *Furman v. Georgia* (1972), the landmark case that declared capital punishment to be cruel and unusual, and therefore unconstitutional.[46] For once that rule is established, it becomes possible to accept (or imagine) abandoning prisoners to a range of other extraordinary sanctions: a fate less than death that can become quite ordinary in comparison. The Rehnquist Court's ability to define away the substance of an Eighth Amendment violation depends on establishing the *ordinariness* of prison conditions, once they are applied to criminals who remain outside the social compact. The verbal maneuvering of this current juridical order thus renames "cruel and unusual," even as it reclaims "human status" for its own uses. Out of an assumption of barbarism comes a new understanding of the limits of civilization.

The use of a dichotomy such as brutality or decency to allow ever more sophisticated torture to pass constitutional muster depends on manipulating language in such a way that the distinction between apparent opposites can be emptied of meaning. On a kind of sliding scale back and forth between extremes, difference is neutralized. Distinctions are offered the more effectively to be qualified out of existence. Perhaps this maneuver can better be understood by turning briefly to Errol Morris's documentary *Mr. Death: The Rise and Fall of Fred A. Leuchter, Jr.* Concerned about the "deplorable condition" of execution hardware in prisons, Leuchter explains how he designed an electric chair that would perform "humane" killings. State-sanctioned murder is never questioned, nor need it be, because the terms of the argument are designated as two extreme conditions, one of which must be preferable to the other. On one hand is "torture" if the chair malfunctions and too much voltage makes "the meat come off the executee like meat off a cooked chicken"; on the other is the "decency" of lethal injection and its promise of "more humane, painless executions." But even Leuchter wonders if the absence of smoke and burning flesh masks a more awful though unseen agony. For it is more difficult, he reflects, to take away than to give life.[47] At what point, we might ask, do executions become "humane" or "painless"? With whom does that ritual of definition lie?

Let us take the language of the law as a struggle between ways of thinking about what is human and what remains human even in instances of radical depersonalization. In *Louisiana Ex Rel. Francis v. Resweber* (1947), Willie Francis, "a colored citizen," was sentenced to death by a Louisiana court, and a warrant for his execution was issued on May 3, 1946.[48] The attempted electrocution failed, however, presumably due to mechanical difficulties, and Francis petitioned to the Supreme Court, arguing that a second attempt to execute him would be unconstitutionally cruel. Justice Reed, writing for the majority, ruled against Willie Francis. Even though Francis had already suffered the effects of an electrical current, that "does not," Reed explained, "make his subsequent execution any more cruel in the constitutional sense than any other execution. The cruelty against which the Constitution protects a convicted man is cruelty inherent in the method of punishment, not the necessary suffering involved in any method employed to extinguish life humanely" (464). How does punishment, no matter how insufferable, become legal? While acknowledging that the Eighth Amendment prohibited "the wanton infliction of pain," admitting that Francis had already endured the physical trauma associated with execution and would now be forced again to undergo the mental anguish of preparing for death, Reed concluded by shifting to the intentions of the one who pulls the switch: "There is no purpose to inflict unnecessary pain nor any unnecessary pain involved in the proposed execution. The situation of the unfortunate victim of this accident is just as though he had suffered the identical amount of mental anguish and physical pain in any other occurrence, such as, for example, a fire in the cell block" (464). The dissenting justices, understanding Francis's experience to be akin to "torture culminating in death," no matter the executioner's state of mind, distinguished between "instantaneous death and death by installments" (473), demanding finally, "How many deliberate and intentional reapplications of electric current does it take to produce a cruel, unusual and unconstitutional punishment? (476).

What, in this context, does the word "humane" mean? How does law use a specific history of punishment to authorize its decisions? Judges claim the ritual correctness of state-sanctioned execution by turning the Eighth Amendment against "cruel and unusual punishment" into assurances of *humane, clean,* and *painless* death. The unspeakable might well become possible wherever the legal or literal promise of humanitarian punishment is made. If the prohibitions of the 1689 English Bill of Rights are summoned as backdrop—disemboweling, decapitation, and drawing and quartering—then the ban on cruel and unusual punishments might well seem obsolete, aimed only at "barbarities" that have long since passed away.[49] Yet it is possible that this selective recollection necessarily implies a decision concerning the threshold beyond which punishment ceases to be legally relevant. In other words, excessive harm can be redefined in terms that put it outside the precincts of punishment, making it increasingly difficult to prove an Eighth Amendment violation. In *Louisiana Ex Rel. Francis v. Resweber,* Reed shaped the language that would become crucial in conditions of confinement cases: "unnecessary and wanton infliction of pain" as opposed to "inadvertence," "negligence," or "indifference." Coercive cruelty takes many forms other than the corporeal, but what is striking about contemporary Eighth Amendment cases, whether dealing with execution or confinement, is the legal acceptance of the corporeal punishment paradigm, attending to the body not the intangible qualities of the person (for example, psychological pain or fear) or the social and civil components of confinement.

In 1890, the Supreme Court decided two cases, both germane to my argument: the first, *In Re Kemmler,* pursued the cruel and unusual punishment standard in rites of execution; and the second, *In Re Medley,* applied that standard to solitary confinement.[50] The Court in *In Re Kemmler* held that a current of electricity scientifically applied to the body of a convict is a more "humane" even if "unusual" method of execution than hanging, since its use must result "in instantaneous, and consequently in painless, death" (443–44). Electrocution was thus held to be a reasonable and humane means of inflicting capital punishment, not in itself cruel and unusual. Although *Medley* did not ultimately argue that solitary confinement was unconstitutional, the Court commented on how its deterrent power resulted not from the immediacy of punishment but rather through extended suffering. Further, the Court admitted that the 1889 Colorado statute subjected the prisoner to "an additional punishment of the most important and painful character." The opinion emphasized the anguish that resulted when removing the convict from the place where his friends reside, where the sheriff and attendants may see him, and where his religious adviser and legal counsel may "often" visit him (169). What matters to the Court is the removal to "a place where imprisonment always implies disgrace," marking the prisoner as figure for "the worst crimes of the human race" and most of all, extending indefinitely the days in confinement before execution, resulting in "uncertainty and anguish" (168–71). Returning to the statutory history of solitary confinement in English law, to the early 1700s of King George II, the Court considered its "painful character" as "some further terror and peculiar mark of infamy," so harsh that in Great Britain the additional punishment of solitary confinement before execution was repealed.[51]

As in the perpetuation of civil death and execution, the United States has not only continued but refined the forms of solitary confinement, for the Supreme

Court has never judged that solitary confinement itself is an unconstitutional punishment.[52] In *Medley* the Court drew attention to the peculiar effects of total confinement, a gradual spiritual degradation as brutal as bodily destruction: "A considerable number of the prisoners fell, after even a short confinement, into a semi-fatuous condition, from which it was next to impossible to arouse them, and others became violently insane; others, still committed suicide; while those who stood the ordeal better were not generally reformed, and in most cases did not recover sufficient mental activity to be of any subsequent service to the community" (168). Decided nearly three months after *Medley, In Re Kemmler* reads almost as if suggesting the exceptional nature of separate confinement, affirming that "the punishment of death is not cruel, within the meaning of that word as used in the Constitution," for it "implies there something inhuman and barbarous, something more than the mere extinguishment of life" (933).

In summer 1997, death row inmates at the Arizona State Prison in Florence were moved from Cell Block 6 to Special Management Unit II (SMU II), the harshest of the segregation units in the Florence/Eyman Complex, reserved for the "worst of the worst." What had been judged too painful to be constitutional in *Medley* has now been reinstituted. This conjunction of natural and unnatural death permits the suffering of the soul before the death of the body. The spirit dies. The body awaits death. Or in the words of an inmate who once spoke words but now talks only in numbers: "If they only touch you when you're at the end of a chain, then they can't see you as anything but a dog. Now I can't see my face in the mirror. I've lost my skin. I can't feel my mind."[53]

TRIALS OF DEFINITION

How did the Court change over time, ultimately deciding that the anguish of solitary confinement, its slow but relentless assault on the mind of inmates, was no longer "cruel and unusual"? Further, how did the origins of solitary confinement in the belief in minds, which are, to paraphrase Jeremy Bentham, *subservient to reformation,* get recast as locales for *incapacitation* and *retribution*? Since the judicial involvement in prisons in the 1960s, both federal district courts and the Supreme Court have alternately extended and circumscribed the conditions deemed "humanly tolerable." The Rehnquist Court, in turning to the "subjective" expertise of prison administrators and "deference" to their special knowledge, has redefined the limits of pain through a language of fastidious distinctions and noncommittal formulas. The turn away from prisoners' enforceable rights and the language of rehabilitation was signaled with then Justice William Rehnquist's opinion in *Bell v. Wolfish* (1979).[54] The winnowing away of the substance of incarceration (what actually happens to the inmate) in favor of a vague if insistent pragmatics of forms, rules, and labels has allowed increasingly abnormal circumstances to be normalized once in prison. Further, the Court has turned to a different history of punishment, indeed a novel translation of *malice aforethought* for murderers into the *maliciously wanton* standard for prison officials.[55]

Contemporary terms and rules of judgment concerning punishment and victimization, as well as the assumptions about what constitutes the entity called "prisoner," thus mobilize a drama of redefinition, where what is harsh, brutal, or excessive turns into what is constitutional, customary, or just bearable. Moreover, the language constructs a person whose status—more precisely, whose very flesh and blood—must be distinct from the status of those outside the prison walls. The banishment and exile of feudal civil death are no longer necessary, for what Robert Cover has identified as "violence" operative on "a field of pain and death" is the terrain of law. What can be more violent than the conversion of the phrase "cruel and unusual" into "atypical but significant"; Chief Justice Rehnquist's turning of the often extraordinary rites of punishment after incarceration—disciplinary sanctions without due process or indefinite solitary confinement—into nothing more than "the ordinary incidents of prison life"?[56] Let us recall Rehnquist's order in *Atiyeh v. Capps* (1981), staying, pending appellate review, an injunction issued to alleviate prison crowding: "Nobody promised them a rose garden; and I know nothing in the Eighth Amendment which requires that they be housed in a manner most pleasing to them, or considered even by most knowledgeable penal authorities to be likely to avoid confrontation, psychological depression, and the like."[57]

In *Sandin v. Conner* (1995), for example, Rehnquist, writing for a majority of five, legitimated "solitary" (and refuted the plaintiff's due process claim) by adapting the vocabulary of decency to ever harsher conditions of confinement. Although Rehnquist chose trivial examples of prisoner due process cases, such as a claim to a tray instead of a sack lunch, DeMont Conner had raised a less trivial claim: he had been sentenced to thirty days lockdown in a special housing unit after a disciplinary proceeding that he claimed did not satisfy the procedural due process set forth in *Wolff v. McDonnell*.[58] First, Rehnquist juxtaposed "atypical and significant hardship" with "ordinary." Then he leveled the distinction between "disciplinary segregation" and "administrative segregation and protective custody": the conditions mirror each other, except for "insignificant exceptions." What does "atypical" or "significant" mean in the prison context? As the dissenters complained, the majority left "consumers of the Court's work at sea, unable to fathom what would constitute an 'atypical, significant deprivation' " (32).

Nowhere does the power of legality to ensure the extinction of civil rights and legal capacities become so evident as in the restricted settings of special security units. As we have seen, prisons in the United States have always contained harsh solitary punishment cells where prisoners are sent for breaking rules. But what distinguishes the new generation of super-maximum security facilities are the increasingly long terms that prisoners spend in them, their use as a management tool rather than just for disciplinary purposes, and their sophisticated technology for enforcing social isolation and control. Prisoners are locked alone in their cells for twenty-three hours a day. They eat alone. Their food is delivered through a food slot in the door of their eighty-square-foot cell. They stare at the unpainted, concrete, windowless walls onto which nothing can be posted. They look through doors of perforated steel. Except for the occasional touch of a guard's hand as they are handcuffed and chained to leave their cells, they have no contact with another human being.

The high-tech prison of the future, designed within the limits of the law, is a clean, well-lighted place. There is no decay, darkness, or dirt. There is, however, coerced isolation and enforced idleness. This is not the "hole" popularized in movies like *Murder in the First* or *Shawshank Redemption*. Instead, these locales are called—with that penchant for euphemism so prevalent in the prison surround—"special management," "special treatment," or "special housing units." The old term "solitary" has been vacated, leaving the benign and evasive terminology that allows public discourse to remain noncommital in the face of atrocity. By distorting the term's core meaning, the most severe of deprivations becomes "special care" for those with "special needs."

Because I believe that judicial attention to terminology and definition can undermine the obvious claims of brutal treatment, I want to consider briefly how the legal turn to meaning vacates the human. In the repeated attempts to decipher the meaning of Eighth Amendment language, interpretation makes possible the denial of inmate claims, while negating the humanity of the confined body. The legal demolition of personhood that began with slavery has been perfected in the logic of the courtroom. The qualifying practices of the Rehnquist Court, for example, make a history of deprivation matter only when "sufficiently serious," or punishment count only when involving "more than ordinary lack of due care," or conditions unconstitutional when they pose a "substantial risk of serious harm" or result in "grievous loss." Verbal qualifiers gut the substance of suffering in favor of increasingly rarified rituals of definition. What, after all, does the Court mean by *sufficiently, more than ordinary, substantial,* or *grievous?* Although apparently harmless, the imprecision of these terms neutralizes the obvious, making it impossible to rule on Eighth Amendment violations.

In the wake of the formulaic appeal to "evolving standards of human decency" and pursuit of the ever-elusive meaning of the phrase "cruel and unusual punishment," contemporary courts have repeatedly judged that solitary confinement does not constitute an Eighth Amendment violation. When Eastern State Penitentiary and Alcatraz closed, new control units continued to be built or added to existing high-security prisons. Under the sign of professionalism and advanced technology, idleness and deprivation constitute the "treatment" in these units. Although taking trauma to its extreme, these places are rationalized as "general population units": the general population of those judged to be the worst inmates who repeatedly offend (including gang members or "strategic threat groups," the mentally ill or "special needs groups," and protective custody). As William Bailey, the classification specialist at the Arizona Department of Corrections, explained: "They're not detention units, they're not punishment units, contrary to what inmates would like you to believe. They are general population units for the highest risk inmates. In a lot of respects, they're just regular places."[59] By turning away from *punishment* and concentrating on *procedures,* the administration of exceptional punishment itself becomes unexceptional. Thus, a rare and disciplinary condition once known as "solitary" can be redefined as a normal and general condition for those held under "close," "special," or "secure" management.

Isolation and lack of visual or intellectual stimulation do not matter to prisoners described by a deputy warden in SMU II in Arizona as "nothing but animals that we turn into senseless bums."[60] The nuances in naming mark the move from criminal to idler, from troublemaker to waste product. Such tags for negative personhood, giving substance and justification to those in lockdown, recall how proslavery apologists never tired of supplying reasons for enslaving those whose nature fit them for nothing else. Yet the argument of nature becomes more sinister when applied literally, not figuratively, to the prisoner. Whether deemed precious objects due to the trappings of romance (which often masked the extremity of violation) or evil agents insofar as they committed a crime, the slaves' legal status was continuously glossed. In the acuity and nuancing of these debates lay the success of slavery in the southern United States. Whereas there is ambiguity in the case of the slave—what could be termed "retractable person-hood" that accedes to the instrumental alternation between person and thing—it is striking that in contemporary case law the prisoner remains deprived of the moral, affective, and intellectual qualities sometimes granted to slaves.[61]

In contemporary cases, the old connection with slave status obscured and negative personhood assumed, the prisoner as dead in law is never discussed but simply assumed in a silence that assures that the actual habitats for incarceration—the technological nuts and bolts of brutalization—transform prisoners into a mass of not just servile but idle matter or waste product. In order to satisfy an Eighth Amendment violation, a condition of confinement must be shown to deprive the incarcerated of a basic human need, defined now as warmth, sanitation, food, or medical care. There is no place in these rock-bottom necessities for thought, feeling, or will; what an earlier court judged essential to "human dignity" or "intrinsic worth."

Just as southern case law was unique regarding slaves and their rights and disabilities, the current treatment of criminals in super-maximum security or control units and through state-sponsored execution remains singular in the so-called civilized world. In response to the federal judicial activism of the late 1960s and early 1970s, cases as diverse as *Rhodes v. Chapman* (1981) and *Wilson v. Seiter* (1991) laid the ground for a theory of punishment that implied that incapacitation and vengeance, as well as barbaric prison conditions, might no longer be Eighth Amendment violations.[62] The slave codes of the southern United States delimited the bodily punishment of slaves and commanded that they receive clothing, food, and lodging *sufficient to their basic needs*. In *Creswell's Executor v. Walker* (1861), for example, slaves, although dead to civil rights and responsibilities, retained their "value as human beings . . . endowed with intellect, conscience, and will."[63] Given this value, laws had to maintain slave lives. In other words, the subtext for these exercises in regulatory beneficence reads: "How much can you take away and still leave a 'human being'?" *Creswell's Executor* argues that they must have "a sufficiency of healthy food or necessary clothing . . . and the master cannot relieve himself of the legal obligation to supply the slave's necessary wants" (237).

This legal drive to ordain *what will suffice* bears an unsettling resemblance to the way U.S. courts have traditionally interpreted the cruel and unusual punishment clause in the Eighth Amendment. Yet, as I suggest, in recent conditions of confinement cases especially, the Supreme Court has, through a series of qualifications, adopted the corporeal punishment paradigm for the claims of convicted criminals: recognizing only *tangible harm, significant injury,* or *visible marks* as valid for an Eighth Amendment claim. In a penal system that has become instrumental in managing the dispossessed and dishonored, the delimitation in *Rhodes v. Chapman* of the "minimal civilized measure of life's necessities" or the "basic necessities of human life" (347) implies something unique about "lives" caught in the grip of legal procedures. Like the slave whose servile body had yet to be protected against *unnecessary* mutilation or torture, the criminal is reduced to nothing but a physical entity, suggesting that the term *human* in the phrase "a single, identifiable human need such as food, warmth, or exercise" in *Wilson v. Seiter* both suspends and redefines what we mean by human.

What are the terms of the dialogue between prison regulations and the law? In *Laaman v. Helgemoe* (1977), the federal district court held that confinement at New Hampshire State Prison constituted cruel and unusual punishment in violation of the Eighth Amendment.[64] The court's far-reaching relief order constituted the broadest application ever of the Eighth Amendment to prison conditions, condemning "the cold storage of human beings" (307) and "enforced idleness" as a "numbing violence against the spirit" (293). By the 1990s, however, as if in response to the *Laaman* court's focus on practices that made prisoner "degeneration probable and reform unlikely," conditions of confinement cases became the impetus for a new penology that emphasized incapacitation. Instead of determining that the closed, tightly controlled environment of prison might itself constitute punishment, especially if these conditions caused "degradation," "imposed dependency," "unnecessary suffering," or "degeneration" (to take words from *Laaman* that would never again be applied to that entity called "prisoner"), the stage was set for the allowable suffering paradigm of *Madrid v. Gomez* (1995).[65] This class action suit against Pelican Bay State Prison singled out the Special Housing Unit (SHU) as the locale for dehumanization.

Heard by the federal district court of California in 1993, prisoners incarcerated at Pelican Bay challenged the constitutionality of a broad range of conditions and practices to which they had been subjected. Chief Judge Thelton Henderson opened the case by announcing: "This is not a case about inadequate or deteriorating physical conditions. There are no rat-infested cells, antiquated buildings, or unsanitary supplies. Rather, plaintiffs contend that behind the newly-minted walls and shiny equipment lies a prison that is coldly indifferent to the limited, but basic and elemental, rights [of prisoners]" (1155). Although Henderson's decision offered partial relief to some inmates for some claims, he found generally that conditions do not violate "exacting Eighth Amendment standards." In the plaintiff's favor, he found that "defendants have unmistakably crossed the constitutional line with respect to some of the claims raised by this action" (1279), citing failure to provide adequate medical and mental health care and condoning a pattern of excessive force. Yet although he acknowledged that conditions in the SHU, the separate, self-contained super-maximum complex, "may well hover on the edge of what is humanly tolerable for those with normal resilience" (1280), such circumstances remain within the limits of permissible pain.

How restrictive can prison confinement be? Henderson responded fervently to the habit of caging inmates barely clothed or naked outdoors in freezing temperatures "like animals in a zoo"; to the unnecessary and sometimes lethal force used in cell extractions; to the habit of using lockdown in the SHU for treatment of the mentally ill; to the scalding of a mentally disabled inmate, burned so badly that "from just below the buttocks down, his skin peeled off" (1167). Yet Henderson's attention to excessive force on bodies distracts attention from the less visible effects of confinement in the SHU. Conceding "that many, if not most, inmates in the SHU experience some degree of psychological trauma in reaction to their extreme social isolation and reduced environmental stimulation" (1265), he then turned to constitutional minima. Although minimal necessities extend beyond "adequate food, clothing, shelter, medical care and personal safety" to include "mental health, just as much as physical health," Henderson nevertheless concluded that the SHU does not violate Eighth Amendment standards "vis-à-vis all inmates" (1260–61). Isolation and sensory deprivation are cruel and unusual punishment only for those who are already mentally ill or those at an unusually high risk of becoming mentally ill; those who "are at a particularly high risk for suffering very serious or severe injury to their mental health . . . such inmates consist of the already mentally ill, as well as persons with borderline personality disorders, brain damage or mental retardation, impulse-ridden personalities, or a history of prior psychiatric problems or chronic depression" (1235–36).

Who is to decide which prisoners are at a "particularly high risk" of suffering mental trauma? Henderson and the doctors who testified in the case provided ample evidence that any extended stay in SHU causes mental deterioration and psychological decompensation. Henderson admitted, when turning to the question of mental health, that "all humans are composed of more than flesh and bone—even those who, because of unlawful and deviant behavior, must be locked away not only from their fellow citizens, but from other inmates as well" (1261). Yet although Henderson prohibited punishment that will make the crazy crazier, he abandoned the sane to their fate. The court's decision suggests that inmates who become "insane" while in the SHU are doomed to remain there. Even though "conditions may be harsher than necessary," they're not "sufficiently serious," and the court must give "defendants the wide-ranging deference they are owed in these matters" (1263). The state, then, must exempt mentally ill inmates from confinement in the SHU if the inmates' illness stems from a previous occurrence or existed before incarceration. But if the state itself, through its methods of punishment, drives a prisoner insane, that imposition passes constitutional muster.

What kind of victimization is understandable? At what point can it be legally recognized? Even though Henderson referred to the prison setting as the cause of "senseless suffering and sometimes wretched misery," his real concern remains focused on abuse to the body or the already deficient mind. The intact person imprisoned in the SHU—who is not stripped naked, driven out of his mind, caged, mutilated, scalded, or beaten—disappears from these pages. Only the visible signs of stigma are recognized. If the slave could only legally become a person—possessing will and more than mere matter—when committing a crime, here the prisoner is legally recognized only insofar as he is either mentally impaired or physically damaged.[66]

Although it matters juridically if one is teetering on the brink of insanity or already gone over the edge, it matters not at all if one is only a little damaged; if, in Henderson's words, one's "loneliness, frustration, depression, or extreme boredom" has not yet crossed over into the realm of "psychological torture" (1264). What is at stake here? If it is true that loss of civil rights as a result of conviction for felony is punishment, the question becomes one of degree. In the prison context, there is a crucial difference between complete loss of civil rights, as in the case of civil death, and a "residue of rights" that remains even behind prison walls. The distinction, especially during the past fifteen years, hinges on the word *punishment*. And the strict meaning of legal punishment, for Justices Scalia and Thomas, especially, gets its charge from a peculiar turn to eighteenth-century criminal law.[67]

In *Wilson v. Seiter* (1991), Justice Scalia focused on the meaning and extent of punishment. Pearly Wilson, an inmate at the Hocking Correctional Facility in Ohio, brought a *pro se* lawsuit alleging that conditions in the prison, including overcrowding, excessive noise, inadequate heating and ventilation, and unsanitary dining facilities violated the Eighth Amendment. Adopting the "subjective component" standard of *Estelle v. Gamble* (1976), which concerned the "deliberate indifference to serious medical needs," Scalia went further. In this sharply divided decision, Scalia, writing for the five-member majority, defined "punishment" and elaborated Judge Richard Posner's return to the legal history of the term in *Duckworth v. Franzen* (1985) as "a deliberate act intended to chastise or deter."[68] The Supreme Court ultimately required not only an objective component ("was the deprivation sufficiently serious?") but also a separate subjective component for all Eighth Amendment challenges to prison practices and policies. The Court decided that if deprivations are not a specific part of a prisoner's sentence, they are not *really* punishment unless imposed by prison officials with "a sufficiently culpable state of mind" (5). In other words, no matter how much actual suffering is experienced by a prisoner, if the intent requirement is not met, then the effect on the prisoner is not a matter for judicial review. In Scalia's reasoning: "The source of the intent requirement is not the predilections of this Court, but the Eighth Amendment itself, which bans only cruel and unusual *punishment.* If the pain inflicted is not formally meted out *as punishment* by the statute of the sentencing judge, some mental element must be attributed to the inflicting officer before it can qualify" (9).

Punishment, outside of statutory or judicial decision, only counts *if* a prison official *knows* about conditions and remains indifferent. Cruelty in violation of the Constitution must depend on the intentions of those who punish and not on the physical act of punishment or its impact on the prisoner being punished. Obvious signs of violence disappear in quest of the unseen: What was the official thinking? Was he "deliberately indifferent"? Did he have a "sufficiently culpable state of mind"? Excess, then, is not a punishment, not an instrument of punitive power. Instead, the Supreme Court stages a drama of pursuit, seeking grounds and reasons after the fact. If the objective severity of conditions (a "sufficiently serious" deprivation) is only judged unconstitutional when the subjective intent of those controlling the conditions is present, Eighth Amendment violations are increasingly difficult if not impossible to prove. As Justice White noted in *Wilson v. Seiter:* "Not only is the majority's intent requirement a departure from precedent, it likely will prove impossible to apply in many cases. Inhumane prison conditions often are the result of cumulative actions and inactions by numerous officials inside and outside a prison, sometimes over a long period of time" (310).

The *Wilson* majority determined that "deliberate indifference" lay somewhere between the poles of "purpose or knowledge" on one hand and "negligence" on the other. Further, the personhood of the confined prisoner is caught between two extremes, held in the grip of two prongs of analysis: the punishment "formally meted out" by the sentencing judge and the "wanton" state of mind of the inflicting officer. What, then, is the legal personality of the criminal, once caught between these acknowledged acts of will or agency? If we limit the task of definition to *Wilson,* the intangible self, the *thinking thing* becomes detached from the criminal while the body comes forth as the focus: only the physical harm arising from conditions of confinement matters as evidence. What happens when a prisoner wants to claim psychological pain or mental suffering? If we follow the logic of this case, the full force of the mental (it gets to be wanton, malicious, obdurate, willful) is transferred to the person of the government official, while the mind, through the defining claims of legal reasoning, is literally sucked out of the prisoner. The Court's logic thus strips the victim of the right to experience suffering, to know fear and anguish. Legally, the plaintiff has become a nonreactive body, a defenseless object. Subjectivity is the privilege of those in control. In other words, the "objective component"—the severity of conditions of confinement—no longer matters once all the eggs of mental activity are in the basket of the perpetrator.

When does an emotional scar become visible? To make it visible is to stigmatize, yet only certain kinds of stigmatization are recognized: that which accords with the substandard or what prisoners are assumed to be. They are all bodies. Only some are granted minds: those who have already lost their minds or whose minds tend toward madness. And who is to decide? The same officers who punish? The mind is only recognized as worthy of saving if it has been lost, the body only worthy of saving if visibly harmed. The unspoken assumption remains: prisoners are not persons. Or, at best, they are a different kind of human: so dehumanized that the Eighth Amendment no longer applies. If prisoners happen to be normal, then harm must become ever more brutal to be considered "significant." Thus, the normal standards of human decency do not apply. If you happen to be a prisoner, without any status explicitly recognized in law, you possess rights only insofar as you have lost your skin or your mind.

THE CULT OF THE REMNANT

What remains after the soul has been damaged, when the mind confined to lockdown for twenty-three hours a day turns on itself? The Special Security Unit is a room in the smu I in Florence, Arizona. An inner sanctum, it is reserved for instruments of torture: lethal shanks made from bed frames or typewriter bars, darts made from paper clips and wrapped in paper rockets, razors melted onto toothbrushes, and pencils sharpened into pincers. The objects inmates use to mutilate themselves or others appear neatly displayed in rows on the contraband boards behind glass. "An amazing assortment of weaponry, isn't it?", the young correctional officer asked me. On the other wall near to the door through which I entered, to the left of the display of weapons, are photos commemorating the dead and the dying: inmates with slit wrists, first-degree burns, punctured faces, bodies smeared with feces, and eyes emptied of sight and pouring blood. Above this exhibit is a placard that reads "Idle minds make for busy hands."

Justice Brennan in his concurring opinion in *Furman v. Georgia* described what he later called (in *Gregg v. Georgia* [1976], which overturned *Furman*) the "fatal constitutional infirmity in the punishment of death": it treats "members of the human race as non-humans, as objects to be toyed with and discarded."[69] The savage effects of solitary confinement, offered to visitors as the material fragments, the leavings of the doomed, urge us to ask how the law can allow such torture. In the more than twenty years since Brennan's condemnation of the death penalty, the court has been instrumental in mobilizing the arena for mutilation by ensuring the legality of confinement that is beyond the limits of human endurance, and then by having allowed unbearable conditions (what might reasonably be expected in prison, to paraphrase Rehnquist), making the captives themselves responsible for, indeed deserving of, disfigurement.

How do we read not only the display in the Special Security Unit of SMU I, but the story told by the inmates through these objects and their uses? The room is filled with the concrete reminders of the effects of legal incapacitation. The inmates have reenacted the law's process of decreation on their own bodies, making visible what the law masks. And as if in a drama of historical revision these expressions of derangement recall the Quaker dream of spiritual rebirth through solitude, but instead the raw materials of legal authority, once turned on the prisoners' bodies, commemorate the death of the spirit. In *Ruffin v. Commonwealth*, Judge Christian created the "slave of the state," bereft of everything except "what the law in its humanity accords to him" (796). Here, in this room, we have the doubled figure of state and captive: the state that records, photographs, and collects the emblems of coercion, and the inmates who speak through the display, giving utterance to the inhuman face of the law. They also register an alternative history to the argument for "evolving standards of human decency" that ordained, or so it seemed, the journey out of darkness into enlightenment. In a lengthy digression in *Furman* on the meaning of the words "cruel and unusual,"

Judge Marshall confessed them to be "the most difficult to translate into legally manageable terms," lamenting that no adequate history exists "to give flesh to the words" (145) of the Eighth Amendment. In this severe rephysicalizing of civil death, inmates make the wounding of the body recall the tortures of the soul. They have returned to the drawing and quartering, disemboweling, and bloodletting of old in order to testify to their continuation in other forms.

A POSTSCRIPT: QUERYING THE SPIRIT OF LAW

How does the supernatural, the *dog without skin* that began my inquiry, urge us to reconsider what within the workings of the law might first appear all too natural? The image of persons locked down in cells, where the senses are deprived (nothing to see, no one to touch, nothing to do), can be said, in a specific but extremely real sense, to appear virtually as a *Cartesianism in extremis*. In his "Second Meditation," Descartes supposes: "I have no senses. Body, shape, extension, movement and place are chimeras. . . . I have no senses and no body. This is the sticking point: what follows from this?"[70] In the maddening solitude of the special cell, the inmate left alone with his mind, a thinking thing, does not have the luxury of ruminating on doubt, experimenting with the limits of thought thinking itself through. Although immured in lack, his incapacitation does not serve as source of identity but rather as cause of imbecility or proof of invalidity: the self become perishable and managed as waste.

I began with a story about a white dog, turned to the way a specter of corruption was embodied in the colonies as blood elided into racial categories, and, finally, moved to the mechanisms of disabling that turn prisoners into society's refuse. As I have argued, the fiction of civil death, shifted to varying locales when necessary, extended the logic of criminality and exclusion. Being dead in law thus sustained the image of the servile body necessary for the public endorsement of dispossession. That the juridical realm concerns itself now most with the inmate's body (whether beaten to a pulp or kept intact, treated brutally or decently) in considering Eighth Amendment violations becomes a cruel gloss on Descartes's method. For whereas he removes all that is bodily in order to confront the mind making personhood, the legal determination attends only to what is bodily in order to demolish personhood. Like the sorcery that chains the spirit to dog flesh, juridical reason defines a new legal body that buries the mind, recognizing only the corporeal husk emptied of thought. In their varying self-mutilations, then, inmates externalize their thought, making mind matter.

NOTES

Preliminary stages of this essay were first presented at the Barker Center at Harvard University on October 2, 1999; at the Clark Library at the University of California—Los Angeles on October 16, 1999; and as the John Hope Franklin Seminar lecture, cosponsored with the Atlantic Studies Group, at Duke University on February 25, 2000. For assistance in research I thank Catherine Vidler and Donald McNutt; for queries and inspiration I am grateful to Carl Berkhout, Ian Baucom, and members of the Duke Atlantic Studies Seminar. At the Princeton Program in Law and Public Affairs, discussions with Chris Eisgruber, Dirk Hartog, and Diane Orentlicher urged me to revisit points I had thought obvious.

1 Conversation (names withheld) Port-au-Prince, Haiti, June 1992.

2 Thomas Dumm, *Democracy and Punishment: Disciplinary Origins of the United States* (Madison: University of Wisconsin Press, 1987), 6. As I wrote in "Poe, Persons, and Property," *American Literary History* 11.3 (fall 1999): 406, Poe understood how the penitentiary, figured in tales such as "The Pit and the Pendulum" and "The Masque of the Red Death," became the material apparatus necessary to the ideal of a liberal republic.

3 Gustave de Beaumont and Alexis de Toqueville, *On the Penitentiary System in the United States, and Its Application in France,* trans. Francis Lieber (Philadelphia: Carey, Lea & Blanchard, 1833), 47.

4 William Blackstone, *Commentaries on the Laws of England,* 4 vols. (1769; Chicago: University of Chicago Press, 1979), 1:121. Subsequent citations are given parenthetically in the text.

5 For a rather different take on how the discursive construction of the legal body facilitates domination, see Alan Hyde, *Bodies of Law* (Princeton: Princeton University Press, 1997).

6 Orlando Patterson, *Slavery and Social Death: A Comparative Study* (Cambridge: Harvard University Press, 1982), 22.

7 See Blackstone, *Commentaries,* 2: 121, 4: 374–81; "Legislation: Civil Death Statutes—Medieval Fiction in a Modern World," *Harvard Law Review* 50 (1937): 968–77; and, especially, Kim Lane Scheppele, "Facing Facts in Legal Interpretation," *Representations* 30 (1990): 42–77.

8 Thomas Blount, *Nomo-lexikon, a Law Dictionary: Interpreting Such Difficult and Obscure Words and Terms As Are Found Either In Our Common or Statute, Ancient or Modern Lawes: With References to the Several Statutes, Records, Registers Law-books, Charters, Ancient Deeds, and Manuscripts, Wherein the Words Are Used: and Etymologies, Where They Properly Occur* (England: In the Savoy; Printed by Tho. Newcomb, for John Martin and Henry Herringman, 1670).

9 Nathan Bailey, *An Universal Etymological English Dictionary: and An Interpreter of Hard Words* (London: Printed for J. Buckland, J. Beecoft, J. Strahan, Hinton, 1773). Bailey defines "Taint" as "a Conviction, a Spot or Blemish in Reputation," links "to Taint" to the sequential mixing of "to corrupt, to spoil, to bribe, to attaint," then finds

another definition of "Taint" in "corrupted as meat, smelling rank," and, finally, he gives stench to the criminal, as he defines "Tainted" as "convicted of a Crime, having an ill Smell" (n.p.).

10 A. W. B. Simpson, writing about the doctrine of escheat following a felony, noted that "later, lawyers attributed the escheat in cases of felony to the biologically absurd notion that the felon's blood was 'corrupted,' whatever that may mean, so that inheritance was impossible through him" (*A History of the Land Law* [Oxford: Clarendon Press, 1986], 20).

11 "Attain" and "attainder" come through Norman French from Latin at *tingo, -tingere, -tigi, -tactum* (the base of which is the latin *tango*, etc., meaning to touch, strike, attack), which was then subsequently warped in its meaning by erroneous association with the French *taindre, teindre*, which has a different Latin etymology from "attain" and "attainder," from *tingo* (or *tinguo*), *tinger, tinxi, tinctum*, meaning to dye or to color (captured in the English *taint* and *tinge*). See John Cowell's singular exception in *The Interpreter: or Book Containing the Signification of Words.* (London: F. Leach, for distribution by Hen. Twyford, Tho. Dring, and Io. Place, 1658), where he recognizes the source of attainted (*attinctus*) in the French *teindre* or else of *attaindre*, with a further link to the French *estre attaint* and *vayncu en aucuncas*: "Which maketh me to think that it rather commeth from (*attaindre*) as we would say in English catched, overtaken, or plainly deprehended" (np).

12 Winthrop Jordan, *White over Black: American Attitudes toward the Negro, 1550–1812* (New York: Norton, 1977), 15.

13 See Thomas Cobb, *An Inquiry into the Law of Negro Slavery in the United States of America* (1858; New York: Negro Universities Press, 1968), for a discussion of the contagion of slavery in Europe long before subjection to Rome: "Frequently, the *status* of slavery attached to every inhabitant of a particular district, so that it became a maxim, 'Aer efficit servilem statum' [a servile status infects the air], a different atmosphere it must have been from that which fans the British shores, according to the boasts of some of their judges. It is a little curious that, by an ordinance of Philip, Landgrave of Hesse, the air of Wales was declared to be of the infected species."

14 In *The West Indian Slave Laws of the 18th Century* (London: Ginn and Company, Caribbean Universities Press, 1970), Elsa V. Goveia demystifies the "moral" of Somerset's case, while arguing that "police regulations lay at the very heart of the slave system." Stressing the way English law in the West Indies much reduced the possibility that the slave could ever be regarded as "an ordinary man," but must be legally reduced to "mere property," she argues that it was "the absence of laws providing sanctions for the enforcement of slavery" that enabled Somerset to win his freedom by refusing to serve any longer as a slave. See Somerset v. Stewart, 98 Eng Rep 499, KB 1772. Enforcement is the crux. Goveia claims that property in slaves "was as firmly accepted in the law of England as it was in that of the colonies," but what did not exist was "the superstructure raised on this basis," the "police laws" that governed slaves as "persons with wills of their own," but coerced these persons "to be kept in their fixed status as the legal property of their owners" (20–21).

15 Alexis de Tocqueville, *Democracy in America* (New York: Everyman's Library, 1994), 357–58.

16 Virginia Dominguez, *White by Definition: Social Classification in Creole Louisiana* (New Brunswick, NJ: Rutgers UP, 1986), italics mine.

17 For a discussion of the taxonomic intricacies and legal effects of French colonial mixing, see Jean-Luc Bonniol, *La couleur comme maléfice: Une illustration créole de la généalogie des Blancs et des Noirs* (Paris: Albin Michel, 1992); Joan Dayan, *Haiti, History, and the Gods* (Berkeley: University of California Press, 1995); and Yvan Debbasch, *Couleur et liberté: Le jeu du critere ethnique dans un ordre juridique esclavagiste* (Paris: Librairie Dalloz, 1967).

18 Bryan Edwards, *The History, Civil and Commercial, of the British Colonies in the West Indies*, 2 vols. (Dublin: Luke White, 1793–1794), 2: 17–18.

19 *Journals of the Assembly of Jamaica*, III, 124, of March 30, 1733, cited in Edward Brathwaite, *The Development of Creole Society in Jamaica, 1770–1820* (Oxford: Clarendon Press, 1971), 167–68.

20 James Kent, discussing the "Rights of Persons" in *Commentaries of American Law* (1826; Boston: Little, Brown, 1873), Vol. 2, Part 4, Lect. 25, considering the one-eighth rule in Louisiana, the French colonies, and South Carolina, reveals the illogical logic necessary to prove—without observable color—that one is part of the adulterated race: "A remote taint will not degrade a person to the class of persons of color; but a mere predominance of white blood is not sufficient to rescue a person from that class. It is held to be a question of fact for a jury, upon the evidence of features and complexion, and reputation as to parentage, and that a *distinct* and *visible* admixture of negro blood makes one a mulatto. If the admixture of African blood does not exceed the proportion of one eighth, the person is deemed white" (72–73).

21 In *Southern Slavery and the Law*, Thomas Morris explains how vague and sometimes capricious were definitions of the mulatto. Turning to the 1785 Virginia law (which would be copied in other jurisdictions), that "every person who shall have one-fourth part or more of negro blood, shall . . . be deemed a mulatto," he notes that the taint varied in other states on a scale from one-eighth to one-sixteenth, while other states "did not produce statutory definitions: it was a matter of observation in those jurisdictions" (Chapel Hill: University of North Carolina Press, 1996, p. 23).

22 See Cheryl L. Harris, "Whiteness as Property," *Harvard Law Review* 106, no. 8 (June 1993): 1707–91.

23 Michel Foucault, *Discipline & Punish: The Birth of the Prison*, trans. Alan Sheridan (New York: Vintage, 1979), 34.

24 In British colonial law, according to Goveia, a respect for the rights of private property resulted in harsher treatment of slaves, recognizing the slave as "a person in a sphere far more limited than that allowed him [in] either Spanish or French law" (*The West Indian Slave Laws*, 25).

25 Jonathan A. Bush, "Free to Enslave: The Foundations of Colonial American Slave Law," *Yale Journal of Law and Humanities* 5 (1993): 417–70.

26 See the brilliant early treatment of the quest for sources of the legal notions that helped to define American slave law: Thomas D. Morris, " 'Villeinage . . . as it existed in England, reflects but little light on our subject': The Problem of the 'Sources' of Southern Slave Law," *American Journal of Legal History* 32 (1988): 95–137.

27 Cobb, *An Inquiry into the Law of Negro Slavery*, 84.

28 *The State of Mississippi v. Issac Jones* 1 Miss 83, Mississippi 1821.

29 What Patterson in *Slavery and Social Death* called "the violent act of transforming free man into slave," is accomplished by law, I would argue, even more than by social relationships. Patterson knew how utterly crucial the legal slave became, for how could one have slaves without making them legal? If the law did not deal explicitly with the slave in terms of "personhood," then the natural, inalienable rights of persons would devolve onto the slave. The legal strategy worked first to recognize the slave as person only then to deprive her of what white persons (who do not need the law in order to exist or be recognized) are due by nature or under God. Slave law thus both creates and contains the subject, scrutinizes and redefines the person in law.

30 Kent, *Commentaries on American Law*, 256–57.

31 Civil Rights Cases 3 S. Ct. P. 18 US 1883: 26.

32 These disabilities include denial of such privileges as voting, holding public office, obtaining any jobs and occupational licenses, entering judicially enforceable agreements, maintaining family relationships, and obtaining insurance and pension benefits. In October 1998, Human Rights Watch and the Sentencing Project published *Losing the Vote: The Impact of Felony Disenfranchisement Laws in the United States* (Washington, D.C.: Human Rights Watch; New York: Sentencing Project, 1998), linking "slavery," "civil death," and contemporary legal disabilities "that may be unique in the world." "An estimated 3.9 million U.S. citizens are disenfranchised," concluded the report, "including over one million who have fully completed their sentences" (n.p.).

33 *Ruffin v. Commonwealth* 62 VA 790 (1871): 796.

34 See, for example, the dissents in *Jones v. North Carolina Prisoners Labor Union, Inc.*, 433 U.S. 119 (1977) (Marshall dissenting, joined by Brennan); *Meachum v. Fano*, 427 U.S. 215 (1976) (Stevens dissenting, joined by Brennan and Marshall); *Lewis v. Casey*, 518 U.S. 343 (1996) (Stevens dissenting).

35 104th Cong., 2d sess., S. 735, April 29, 1996. See Title IV, "Terrorist and Criminal Alien Removal and Exclusion," Sec. 440, 62.

36 In *Remnants of Auschwitz: The Witness and the Archive*, trans. Daniel Heller-Roazen (New York: Zone Books, 1999), see Agamben's compelling discussion of why Primo Levi, in dealing with the *Muselmänner*, states "one hesitates to call their death death," and his explanation of the "fabrication of corpses" as a way to understand those who, in Heidegger's words, do not die, but "decease. They are eliminated. They become pieces of the warehouse of the fabrication of corpses" (cited by Agamben on pp. 73–74).

37 *Trop v. Dulles*, 356 U.S. 86, 598 (1958).

38 For examinations of this inventive reenslaving, see David M. Oshinsky's argument in *"Worse than Slavery": Parchman Farm and the Ordeal of Jim Crow Justice* (New York:

Free Press, 1996) that the post-Emancipation criminal code was initiated as a vehicle of racial subordination. See also Alex Lichtenstein's study of convict lease and the subsequent public chain gang in *Twice the Work of Free Labor: The Political Economy of Convict Labor in the New South* (London: Verso, 1996); and the exhaustive chronicle of imprisonment as crucial to the American experience in Scott Christianson's *With Liberty for Some: Five Hundred Years of Imprisonment in America* (Boston: Northeastern University Press, 1998).

39 Beaumont and Tocqueville, *On the Penitentiary System in the United States,* 5, 15.

40 Elisha Bates, *The Moral Advocate: A Monthly Publication on War, Duelling, Capital Punishments, and Prison Discipline,* (Mt. Pleasant, OH: Printed by the Editor, 1821–1822), 1: 171.

41 William Crawford, "Report on the Penitentiaries of the United States, Addressed to His Majesty's Principal Secretary of State for the Home Department" (London: House of Commons, August 11, 1834, 26–27).

42 Charles Dickens, *American Notes and Pictures from Italy* (1842; New York: Oxford University Press, 1957), 99–100.

43 William Roscoe, *A Brief Statement of the Causes which have led to the Abandonment of the Celebrated System of Penitentiary Discipline in Some of the United States of America* (Liverpool: Harris and Co., 1827).

44 Roberts Vaux, "Letter on the Penitentiary System of Pennsylvania, addressed to William Roscoe, Esquire" (Philadelphia: Printed by Jesper Harding, 1827), 9.

45 *Weems v. United States* 217 U.S. 349 (1910).

46 *Sullivan v. State of Georgia* 194 U.S. 410 (1972).

47 *Mr. Death: The Rise and Fall of Fred A. Leuchter, Jr.,* dir. Errol Morris. Quotations from the film are my transcriptions.

48 *Louisiana Ex Rel. Francis v. Resweber,* 329 U.S. 459 (1947).

49 See Anthony F. Granucci, "'Nor Cruel and Unusual Punishments Inflicted': The Original Meaning," *California Law Review* 57 (1969): 839–65.

50 *In Re Kemmler,* 136 U.S. 436 (1890); *In Re Medley,* 134 U.S. 160 (1890).

51 "An Act for Preventing the Horrid Crime of Murder," Act 25, George II, c. 37, 1752, added solitary confinement as a special mark of infamy to capital punishment. In 1836, "An Act for Consolidating and Amending the Statutes in England Relative to Offences Against the Person," Act 6 and 7, William IV, c. 30, 1836, repealed the former statute by limiting the period of time before the execution and defining prison discipline: "Every Person convicted of Murder should be executed according to Law on the Day next but one after that on which the sentence should be passed." Note, however, that by the nineteenth century solitary confinement was no longer illegal in England. Further, after the Prison Act of 1865, the "solitary confinement" that had been repealed or, later, inflicted only for a limited amount of time, came under the new name of "separate confinement, inflicted in all cases as the regular and appointed mode of punishment" (Sir James Fitzjames Stephen, *A History of the Criminal Law of England* [London: Macmillan, 1883], 487). The source for the change and the renaming was the separate system in Philadelphia, news of which was reported to Parliament and to the Prison Commissioners on numerous occasions.

52 See Raymond H. Thoenig, "Solitary Confinement—Punishment within the Letter of the Law, or Psychological Torture?" *Wisconsin Law Review* 1 (1972): 233.

53 Conversation (name withheld). Port-au-Prince, Haiti, June 1992.

54 In *Bell v. Wolfish,* 441 U.S. 520 (1979), then Justice Rehnquist, writing for the Court, reversed the decision of the circuit court favoring the inmate-respondent. In the crucial passage that changed the brief period of advancing prisoner's rights, he insisted that "prison administrators . . . should be accorded wide-ranging deference in the adoption and execution of policies and practices that in their judgment are needed" (547).

55 The transfer of the criminal's requisite mental element (*mens rea*) to the prison official's state of mind (whether "sufficiently culpable," "unnecessary and wanton," "deliberately indifferent," or "malicious and sadistic") forms part of a chapter devoted to the subject of legal guilt and subjective blameworthiness in my book *Held in the Body of the State* (Princeton: Princeton University Press, forthcoming).

56 *Sandin v. Conner,* 515 U.S. 472 (1995). See Joan Dayan, "Held in the Body of the State: Prisons and the Law," in *History, Memory, and the Law,* ed. Austin Sarat and Thomas R. Kearns (Ann Arbor: University of Michigan Press, 1999), 202–14.

57 *Atiyeh v. Capps,* 449 U.S. 1312, 1315–16 (1981).

58 *Wolff v. McDonnell,* 418 U.S. 539 (1974).

59 Personal interview with William Bailey, Phoenix, Arizona (June 8, 1996). For an extended analysis of the Special Management Units in Florence, Arizona, and the strategic use of recent case law, see Dayan, "Held in the Body of the State."

60 Interview (name withheld), Arizona State Prison Complex, Tucson AZ, August 10, 1995.

61 Note especially the arguments of A. Leon Higginbotham Jr. and Barbara K. Kopytoff in "Property First, Humanity Second: The Recognition of the Slave's Human Nature in Virginia Civil Law," *Ohio Law Journal* 50, (1989) 511–40; and A. E. Keir Nash's remarkable and controversial analysis of the legal treatment of slaves, in "Reason of Slavery: Understanding the Judicial Role in the Peculiar Institution," *Vanderbilt Law Review* (January 1979): 7–218, which includes discussions of Robert Cover's *Justice Accused: Antislavery and the Judicial Process* (New Haven: Yale University Press, 1975); Mark Tushnet's *The American Law of Slavery 1810–1860: Considerations of Humanity and Interest* (Princeton, NJ: Princeton University Press, 1981); and Martin Hindus's "Black Justice under White Law: Criminal Prosecutions of Blacks in Antebellum South Carolina," *Journal of American Legal History* 63, (1976).

62 *Rhodes v. Chapman,* 101 S. Ct. 2392 (1981); *Wilson v. Seiter,* 501 U.S. 294 (1991).

63 *Creswell's Executor v. Walker,* 37 Ala. 233 (1861).

64 *Laaman v. Helgemoe,* 437 F. Supp. 269 (1977).

65 *Madrid v. Gomez,* 889 F. Supp. 1146 N. D. Cal. 1995.

66 Giorgio Agamben's *Homo Sacer: Sovereign Power and Bare Life,* trans. Daniel Heller-Rozzen (Stanford: Stanford University Press), came to my attention after my experiences in and writing about the Special Management Units in Florence, Arizona. His analyses of *bare life,* the "life that has been deadened and mortified into juridical rule," the "life which ceases to be politically relevant . . . and can as such be eliminated

without punishment" (139) are necessary reading if we are truly to understand the function of the prison and the criminal in the contemporary United States.

67 See Thomas and Scalia's dissents in *Hudson v. McMillian,* 503 U.S. 1, 112 S. Ct. 995 (1992) and *Helling v. McKinney,* 509 U.S. 25, 113 S. Ct. 2475 (1993). The majority opinion in both cases broke with the severe delimitation of cruel and unusual punishment (the "significant injury" requirement, e.g. leaving permanent marks or requiring medical attention) as argued in *Wilson v. Seiter.* These two cases also expanded the concept of "injury," and yet in *Hudson* Blackmun in his concurring opinion (aware of what the Court had left unsaid) felt he needed to make explicit the inclusion of the "psychological" as well as the "physical": "As the Court makes clear, the Eighth Amendment prohibits the unnecessary and wanton infliction of 'pain,' rather than 'injury.' 'Pain' in its ordinary meaning surely includes a notion of psychological harm" (16).

68 *Wilson v. Seiter,* 501 U.S. 294 (1991). See also: *Duckworth v. Franzen,* 780 F2d 645, 652 (C.A. 7 (Ill.) 1985).

69 *Gregg v. Georgia,* 210 S.E. 2d 659, GA 1974.

70 René Descartes, "Second Meditation," *Meditations on First Philosophy,* in *The Philosophical Writings of Descartes,* 2 vols., trans. John Cottingham, Robert Stoothoff, and Dugald Murdoch (Cambridge: Cambridge University Press, 1984), 2: 16.

RICHARD R. FLORES

Mexicans in a Material World:
From John Wayne's The Alamo to Stand-Up
Democracy on the Border

◆

Republic. I like the sound of the word.
Means people can live free, talk free, go or come, buy or sell.
—*John Wayne (as Davy Crockett),* The Alamo

DON: (dialing) (Here's) a story about a city in Texas, El Sneeze-O. Somebody threw pepper in my face. I have to El Sneeze-O. A tiny community 15 miles from Laredo . . . where they have made Spanish their official language. I cannot be more pissed off . . . (phone keeps ringing). Right there, right there, you've got your Mexican work ethic. They aren't answering the phone. (Using heavy accent) It's siesta time . . .
MIKE: I need a dreenk . . . I am obviously drunk . . . Make sure you leave the cellar open so we can come and sleep it off.—*The Don and Mike Radio Show,* August 17, 1999

Mexicans. Democracy. The public. In this essay I want to advance the notion of a generalized relationship between Mexicans, U.S. democracy, and the public through its crystallization in two events: John Wayne's film *The Alamo,* released in 1960 during the waning days of American high modernism, and a widely broadcast episode of *The Don and Mike Radio Show* from August 1999 when Don and Mike made a telephone call to the innocuous town of El Cenizo, Texas. These two examples are key markers in a generalized historical trajectory that demonstrates how U.S. democratic ideals of liberty and freedom continue to be forged on practices of cultural imperialism that advance a democratic nationalism founded on hierarchicalized and punitive practices of difference. We learn, I suggest, in anticipation of the full weight of my argument, how democracy in the United States—as a set of both practical and principled ideals—privileges not only wealth and property but more so the material relations of inequality that form the cornerstone of privilege and rank in our society. As such, the ideals of liberty, justice, and freedom serve as radical reminders of what democracy is not.

This is not to say that liberty, justice, and freedom are wholly absent in the U.S. democratic context but, rather, to underscore how these values exist as historically selective practices that limit, exclude, and negate in the very moment they are materially actualized.[1]

But my argument here must be mediated, allegorized if you will, with another event that both crystallizes a certain public understanding of "the Mexican" as well as shapes its future incarnation. This event is the official, bilateral, workers agreement between the United States and Mexico known as the Bracero Program, which was initiated during World War II and lasted into the early 1960s— roughly the same period Wayne was most active in his film career. In its inception, the program sought to address a labor shortage resulting from the vast conscriptions of World War II. But owing to a need for cheap labor after the war, corporate agriculture and other influences lobbied the government to maintain the program. Later, resistance by labor unions and other organizations led to the cancellation of the program in 1964.[2] The Bracero Program certainly fulfilled its mandate in alleviating the U.S. labor shortage, but its allegorical work—its role in shaping the American imagination concerning Mexicans—was even more effective as the Mexican "wetback" or undocumented worker became the primary icon of the Mexican Other. This image of the Mexican worker—not novel but certainly institutionalized and codified during this period—resonates with a deeper, more complicated figuration: that of the Mexican as prosthesis.[3] Both historically and figuratively (*bracero* is adjectively "an arm" or "a hand" as in "throwing a hand" or "giving an arm") Mexicans as cultural Others entered the public imagination as a social prosthesis to booster an anemic economy. I would even suggest that the notion of prosthesis itself serves as a narrative whose circulation advances, through culturally specific bodies, the need for such a figuration. That is, the need for cultural bodies that serve as a social prosthesis results from the material relations of inequality that are forged in the moment U.S. democracy appears. I am speaking here of the disastrous linking of democracy with capitalism that has become the defining feature of "liberal democracy."[4] I refer not only to the very concrete link between slavery and the founding of the United States in the liberal tradition of capitalist modernity, but also to the continued incorporation of cultural Others to serve as the arms and backs of U.S. imperial expansion.

The relationship between liberal democracy and the place of Mexicans has a long history. Although it begins in the early 1800s, and then specifically in 1848 when the United States signed the treaty ending the U.S.-Mexican War, it is primarily after the 1880s—as the forces of capitalism begin to erode various local social practices and economic arrangements and reorder them through a new socioeconomic rubric—that this relationship becomes one based on seeing the Mexican as outsider, Other, and a source of cheap labor. In this transformation, the social world of Mexicans in the U.S. Southwest was displaced and devalued as land was lost, stolen, and transformed from an inheritable family patrimony to a sharecropper wasteland. This chain of events is what I call the Texas Modern.[5]

The quotes by John Wayne and Don and Mike that begin this essay serve as critical markers of the relationship between Mexicans and the United States across a variety of public discourses in the United States. The interplay of these two narratives—separated by nearly four decades during which time the Civil Rights movement supposedly secured basic democratic rights for African Americans, Latinos, and other people of color on the periphery of American society— suggests a complex narrative about Mexicans and their place in American society.[6] This narrative reference is what many call the Mexican Question, and it bears a more complex analysis.

JOHN WAYNE AND *THE ALAMO*

My selection of Wayne's *The Alamo* is twofold.[7] First, Wayne has occupied such a visible role in American popular culture in the post–World War II era that he and his work have become synonymous with the rise of cold war nationalism of this period. Second, the Alamo for Wayne served as the quintessential American drama, one through which the basic democratic principles of freedom and liberty were expressed. If, as Garry Wills claims, John Wayne embodies an American myth, then I suggest that the Alamo serves as one of the primal scenes of an American national birth.[8] It has become a master symbol. Like all polysemous structures, the Alamo reached beyond its initial, but always present, historical text to inform other tales through its now classic narrative. And, while Wayne's particular rendition of this story went to great lengths to represent Mexicans in much better light than its predecessors, the tropological and binary structure of this film continues to inform issues of Mexicans and the public.

In content the film has little to do with the famous 1836 battle, but it uses this event as the idiom for Wayne's anticommunist nationalism.[9] His movie is best understood as if shot through a bifocal lens, a lens that allows Wayne to explore a number of issues removed from the putative events of the Battle of the Alamo, at the same time that it remains focused on the characters and social actors that appear on the Texas stage in 1836. This is possible because the Alamo story is by the late 1950s a formulaic narrative. Although Wayne claims to be highly concerned with reproducing an "authentic" version of the story, his film is forged from the ideological struggles of the post–World War II era.[10] The Alamo, for Wayne, is an American archetypal tale through which he preaches his views on patriotism and anticommunism.

According to Brian Huberman and Ed Hugetz, Wayne uses the Alamo story to express his understanding of freedom, responsibility, and the relationship of leaders to those who follow them.[11] Travis, the educated and sophisticated high-class southerner comports himself a step above the rest; he frowns upon his men and the citizens of the town, claiming "I am better than that rabble," and he is disgusted by Bowie's drunkenness in the early part of the film. Bowie, for his part, is the tough, hard-minded leader. Although serious like Travis, his leadership style depends on the rugged qualities of his persona. Crockett, on the other hand, is both the country populist who can out-punch and out-drink any of his followers and, in his city clothes, the street-wise, smart-thinking excongressman who can talk his way through any situation. He mediates between Travis's superior attitude and Bowie's stubbornness, seeking a common ground that can unite them. At various points in the film conflict erupts between Travis and Bowie, and each time Crockett intervenes. He is inevitably able to mediate their positions and values, while at the same time provide a perspective that underscores their commonality.

Through these figures Wayne addresses the tension between the freedom of the individual and the responsibility to the collective. This tension runs deep within Wayne's own autobiography. Wills claims that early on Wayne put his career ahead of patriotism and military service, only to rethink his exercise of individual "freedom" later through his ideologically driven war films, including *The Alamo.* We find, however, that freedom for Wayne remains both an idealized and individualistic experience. Like many during this period (and continuing into the present), freedom was an already realized state of affairs in the United States, and any discussion of "struggle" or "rights" for freedom was seen as a "communist" distraction and sentiment. Furthermore, any effort to actualize liberty through "praxis" or practical activity (spurious code words for marxism, it was thought) was interpreted as a threat to the already achieved, constitutionally granted freedom implicit in being "American." For Wayne and others of his generation and class, the threat to freedom was external, out there in the cold world waiting to infiltrate the nation; and that life in the United States could be anything but an experience of liberty and freedom was anathema. Hence, it was no secret that Wayne understood the true American patriot to be anticommunist. So deep were his convictions that when *The Alamo* failed to receive the critical praise he believed it merited, Wayne blamed the "commies." He interpreted any threat to freedom as a problem hoisted upon American democracy from the outside by tyrannous forces. This is why the Alamo—with Santa Anna as the consummate Mexican outsider—serves Wayne as a key vehicle through which to explore the relationship between freedom and the Other.[12]

Wayne's notion of freedom was deeply embedded in a singular subject: the common man. Freedom and liberty were important only insofar as they provided competitive individual access to the resources of the nation. From this viewpoint, being American meant having access to the common good (read: prosperity). Brian Huberman's documentary on the making of *The Alamo* puts it this way:

> The question of Wayne's capacity to be a leader coincides with the film's portrayal of Crockett as a man torn between the responsibility of leadership and the desire to be one of the men. Crockett's changing costume reflects this contradictory position. The frontier outfit suggests a belief in the rugged individual; the fancy city clothes are an expression of Crockett's social and political beliefs. Wayne's shifting position regarding the relationship of the people to their leaders reflects a major concern of Americans in the 1950s, of how big business and government might control their lives.[13]

Huberman is, I believe, mostly correct on this point. But what happens if we move from reading this film as an interpretation of leadership to one that explores the social location of its historical characters? What do we learn when we reinsert Wayne's omission of the social in this film? In place of understanding tyranny (a euphemism for communism in this film) as something beyond the limits of the American experience, I suggest we see it as the absent cause of the divisive class relations represented in this film.

Consider Travis. Although he claims to have come to Texas with just two uniforms, it is quite clear that he sees himself as a member of the elite class, better than the common "rabble" who serve under his rank (his finely starched and tailored uniforms, while perhaps limited to two, further illustrate his social position). His status and elite standing separate him from those around him. Bowie's class markings are equally visible. He is one of the landed elite and his comportment is much different from Travis's. In some ways one can sense the

conflict between Travis and Bowie as emerging from their different social locations. Travis, the consummate aristocrat and educated southerner, signifies a very
different relationship to wealth and land than the old ranching elite of Bowie.
Crockett, quite apart from Travis and Bowie, serves as the fast-thinking individual who has achieved a level of stature not from education or land but from his
own ingenuity. He is the idealized version of the common man who can, as he
claims, "make a buck or two," as well as maneuver his way to Congress. And when
the time arrives he moves on, ready to invent himself once again in another place.
Whatever challenges he meets, Crockett overcomes them by his own perseverance and self-confidence; he is the epitome of the pull-yourself-up-from-the-
bootstraps man. Together, Travis, Bowie, and Crockett serve as critical reminders
of dominant contemporary cold war U.S. ideology: the idea that personal initiative and liberty combined with private property allow for the fullest expression of
individual freedom. The united front of Travis, Bowie, and Crockett signifies
cherished equalitarian values of U.S. capitalist democracy.

But the irony is that in this archetypal tale of the American birth, not personal
initiative but class and social rank distinguish one "man" from another. Although
all the men in the Alamo may, according to Wayne's historically feeble rendering,
choose liberty and democracy over tyranny, some men are already imbued with
that indelible mark of freedom: class rank. The liberties and freedoms of democracy, according to this generalized understanding, bow before the materiality of
social rank.

Despite Wayne's contemporary concerns, *The Alamo* is a movie that must still
be shot through the lens of the 1836 battle. As such, the story of the Alamo can
never escape the Mexican Question, for Wayne's telling or any other. Wayne's film
is principally about liberty and nationalism, but the ambivalent projection of
Mexicans returns full-force through this film's narrative content. Although
Wayne's projection of Mexicans is perhaps the most neutral of all Alamo films, it
is a projection that equally captures the ambiguous social location of Mexicans,
Mexican Americans, and other ethnic groups during this period.

It is true that Wayne no longer portrays the Mexican army in general, and
Santa Anna in particular, through the racist imagery found in earlier films. Let
me even suggest that Mexicans fair better in this movie than in any other, at least
on initial reception. Don Graham suggests that by 1960 the cultural climate of the
United States had changed, making it unfashionable to "resort to the simple
racist contrasts" of earlier Alamo films, offering as evidence how the Mexican
army was portrayed as "a marching mass of choir boys." This avoidance of

blatant racist stereotypes is further evidenced when, in the midst of battle, the Gambler, one of Crockett's Tennesseans, turns to his compatriot and says: "I was proud of 'em [Mexican soldiers]. Speaks well for men that so many are ready to die for what they believe in." Paul Hutton, on this point, refers to Wayne's high regard for "Hispanic culture," including the fact that all three of his wives were Latinas. Wayne even portrays (although without developing the characters of) Mexicans fighting inside the Alamo alongside the Texans. And his depictions of Santa Anna as a "gallant gentleman" took some by surprise. But Mexicans and Mexico never leave one's ideological sight at the Alamo, despite Wayne's conciliatory portrait of them.[14]

Beginning with the Mexican forces we are indeed led to see that Mexicans are equal human actors. They act bravely, die with dignity, and comport themselves (especially Santa Anna) with utmost chivalry.[15] Their manners and practices, the exterior manifestations of culture, are likened to those of the Alamo defenders. Where, then, does difference lie? According to this film, the Mexican forces differ *ideologically*. As enforcers of Santa Anna's rule, they, like him, are aligned to a regime of "tyranny" that seeks to destroy freedom and liberty and to oppress the citizens of his country. Recall the opening text of the movie: "Generalissimo Santa Anna was sweeping north across Mexico toward them, crushing all who opposed his tyrannical rule. They now faced the decision that all men in all times must face . . . the eternal choice of men . . . to endure oppression or resist." According to Wayne, what separates Santa Anna and his men from the Texans, as well as what unites the Alamo defenders, is political ideology. This is significant because identifying a common "political" enemy in Santa Anna (or, for Wayne, in communism) works to obviate internal contradictory forces like those of social rank and class hierarchy.

But there are other differences that merit scrutiny, as witnessed in the character of Juan Seguín. The historical Seguín served with the Texas forces inside the Alamo until sent by Travis as a courier for reinforcements. Wayne depicts Seguín as a member of the Mexican landed elite—the Alcalde of San Antonio—and friend of Bowie.[16] Early in the film, when Seguín offers important details on the position of Santa Anna's forces, Travis explodes with suspicion:

TRAVIS: I'm sorry Señor Seguín, but as a civilian you cannot realize how worthless this sort of information is: some Indian told some *vaquero*. But, anyway, thank you sir and good day.

BOWIE: Travis, you know the Seguíns are absolutely reliable.

SEGUÍN (to Bowie): You'll excuse me.
TRAVIS: I make no personal affront, Señor Seguín. But I cannot make a plan
of action based on third-hand rumors.
SEGUÍN: I do not take personal affront Colonel Travis, else I should be
forced to act other than to just bid you good-day.
TRAVIS (later in his quarters, states to Lieutenant Dickenson): A true gentleman, Seguín. I dislike being rude to him.

There is historical precedence to this scene because the historical Travis was
mistrustful of Mexicans in town, but Wayne's idea to use Seguín, who historically
served under Travis, to portray this aspect of the narrative is troublesome. It is
only later when Seguín arrives with a group of volunteers from Gonzalez, both
Texan and Mexican, that Travis changes his views.

It is Seguín, I suggest, who manifests most clearly the ambiguous position of
Mexicans in this film: are they traitors or patriots, enemies or citizens, Others or
Americans? Besides their deep ideological differences, the Mexican army, even if
they demonstrate outward habits and practices of bravery, is still the "enemy."
Seguín, on the other hand, believes in the same political principles of Travis,
Crockett, and Bowie. He offers information against Santa Anna. He is, ideologically, one of the defenders (not to mention that the historical Seguín *was* a
defender). But, and herein lies his major mark of difference: he is a Mexican.
Racial difference, regardless of one's political views or everyday practice, serves to
differentiate, negatively in this case, more than allegiance to the same political
ideology. Seguín could pay with his life in the fight against Santa Anna but he
remains, distinctly, a Mexican Other.

The overall portrayal of Mexicans in *The Alamo* turns on differences between
culture and ideology. At one level Graham is correct: the features of radical
otherness found in earlier Alamo films are absent here. But in their place we find
an equally disturbing construction. At one level we can negate the depiction of
Santa Anna and his soldiers simply because there is no way of telling this narrative without scripting them as the "enemy." Seguín, on the other hand, is an issue.
His only measure of difference is his Mexican identity which, according to this
film, suffices to raise suspicion. Even when Seguín sacrifices his status as a Mexican citizen by opposing Santa Anna, he remains suspect. He may display the
values and ideas of the Texans but he remains Other. We learn from this film that
regardless of one's comportment and one's allegiance to the values of a democratic liberalism, cultural difference constitutes political otherness.

MEXICAN AS PROSTHESIS

On August 7, 1942, the *Los Angeles Times* reported the following: "Agreement Made to Import Labor—Undisclosed Number of Mexican Farm Hands Will Be Brought In to Maintain Food Output." In 1943, the *New York Times,* in similar fashion, stated: "California Needs 35,000 for Crops—Importing of 21,511 Mexicans Still Leaves Demand for City and School Workers" (June 27). These snippets from the 1940s echo through the comment of Salvador Silva sixty years later in this March 2000 report from the *New York Times:*

> "For the first time," [Salvador Silva] said, "I don't fear the raids." Such raids have all but stopped around the country over the last year. In a booming economy running short of labor, hundreds of thousands of illegal immigrants are increasingly tolerated in the nation's workplaces. The Immigration and Naturalization Service has made crossing the border harder than ever, stepping up patrols and prosecuting companies that smuggle in aliens or blatantly recruit them. . . . "It is just the market at work, drawing people to jobs, and the i.n.s. has chosen to concentrate its actions on aliens who are a danger to the community," said Robert L. Bach, the agency's associate commissioner for policy and planning. The new leniency helps explain why overall wage increases have been less than many economists and policy makers had expected, given an unemployment rate of only 4 percent and a strong demand for people to fill jobs that pay $8 an hour or less, which is 25 percent of all jobs. Immigrants—legal and illegal—have fed the pool of people available to take these lower-paying jobs. (*New York Times,* March 9, 2000)

Mexican as prosthesis runs deep in American cultural memory and practice. The Bracero Program of the 1940s codified the image, and its resonance carries even into the present. Most images of Mexican subjectivity, in popular representations, almost always turn on the Mexican as farm worker. It does not matter that Mexican farm workers constitute a very small percentage of this group's work force. The image endures. The Bracero Program and its formalization of the prosthetic Mexican did not happen by chance. Consider the following, one of the earliest essays on Mexicans in Texas written by John Gregory Bourke for a popular audience:

> In an official communication which I once made to the War Department . . .
> I compared the Rio Grande to the Nile, in the facts [*sic*] that, like its African prototype, the fierce River of the North had its origin in snow-clad sierras

far away in Colorado. . . . Through the centre of this unknown region, fully as large as New England, courses the Rio Grande, which can more correctly be compared to the Congo than to the Nile the moment that the degraded, turbulent, ignorant, and superstitious character of its population comes under examination. To the Congo, therefore, I compare it, and I am confident that all who peruse these lines to a conclusion will concur in the correctness of the comparison.[17]

Bourke equates the entire South Texas region with the Congo. His shift of geographic metaphor from the Nile to the Congo emphasizes the perception of Mexicans as closer to the "degraded" land of Southern Africa than to the Egyptian site of early civilization. This narrative displacement of Mexicans from the Nile to the Congo implicates Bourke in the task of colonial fashioning.[18] A military officer and ethnologist, Bourke is a critical actor in the drama of what I call the Texas Modern. By portraying the more exotic elements of Mexican expressive culture and discursively relocating them in the Congo, Bourke acts as the quintessential agent of modernity.

Bourke's modernizing discourse resonates with the shifting perceptions of Mexicans and their place in South Texas's social economy. The elements of these shifts are twofold. First, he dislocates Mexicans from their geographic lands by relocating them to the Congo. Second, he inscribes Mexicans as degenerate, ignorant, superstitious, and nomadic, constructing them as uncivilized and in need of colonial control. Here we find an instrumentalist "truth," a publicly rendered Mexican subjectivity that reads Mexicans not as subjects but as a social prosthesis: Mexicans are tools, as cheap labor they serve as a prosthetic aid to the state economy. For Bourke, and for other contributors to the public discourse on Mexicans during this period, the Mexican presence is a necessary brown blemish on America's destined domestic empire, an empire forged on the labor of border Mexicans as one of the many others Othered in the service of a capitalist democracy.

But what is this modernity and what relationship might it have for Wayne's late modern Alamo film, as well as for the more contemporary *Don and Mike Show?* Several critical changes affected the Texas economy between 1880 and 1900—namely, the closing of the range, the introduction of the railroad, and the beginning of commercial farming. Between 1900 and 1920 these changes accelerated, leading to increased social pressure and conflict. Overall, the period between 1880 and 1920 was one marked by the "working out" of new relationships, habits, and practices brought about by the rapid transitions of this period and resulting in the establishment of a social order segmented into various ethnic and class divisions.[19]

These eruptions are markers of a "cultural revolution": that unsettling and transitional period in which new practices and customs, forged from new relations of material and ideological production, are ascending to a position of dominance. The effects of the Texas Modern on the lives of the local Mexican and Mexican American population were severe: most experienced underemployment that meant a life lived in poverty; little access to public institutions, which was enforced by practices and policies of segregation; and loss of political power guaranteed through gerrymandering and the institutionalization of poll taxes. These tactics, reproduced through the political and social apparatuses of the state, produced a differential social body reproduced along racial, ethnic, and class lines.

I take the notion of the Mexican as prosthesis as both a metaphor and metonym for the larger public discourse on Mexicans in the United States. Beginning in the latter part of the nineteenth century, Mexicans (both foreign-born and Mexican American or U.S.-born) were socially inscribed into a burgeoning capitalist economy as cheap "labor hands."[20] Unable, unwilling, or both, members of the larger society recruited Mexican workers to undertake the backbreaking labor of a new industrializing state. As a prosthesis, however, Mexicans were incorporated, attached, or added on to the project of the nation, not as equal or even lesser subjects but as disembodied arms, backs, hands, and muscle. They were the raw, uncivilized, subjectless appendages whose presence, like a prosthetic wooden leg, supported but did not feel, carried but did not experience, the wealth of the nation. If, as David Wills claims, "prosthesis is inevitably about belonging," for Mexicans it has been a belonging without becoming, participation without membership, presence without visibility.[21] The public discourse on prosthetic Others undercuts the very legs they stand on, leaving them lame to the rights and liberties their subjectless bodies support. Like the phantom pains often experienced by those whose limbs have been lost, Mexicans remained a phantom presence in the public imagination: here but not seen, speaking but not heard, ethnic but not cultured or civilized. Even today, as the "browning" of the United States continues at rapid rates, concerns about civil and ethnic rights often take a black/white orientation, dismissing Latinos and Latinas with ghostly invisibility. They have remained subjectless participants, required to disembody their cultural selves. Like Wayne's portrayal of Seguín, cultural Mexicans remain suspect despite their commitment, participation, and allegiance to the values and principles of democratic ideals.

DON AND MIKE HYSTERIA

Now let's turn to the *Don and Mike Show*. First, I offer a rather lengthy transcription from an extraordinary 1999 broadcast from which to position my analysis below.

> DON: What took you so long to answer the phone? Were you having a siesta?
>
> BARTON [person who takes call in El Cenizo, Texas]: No. We're not having a siesta. We're in the City Hall.
>
> DON: Ha, ha. We ain't got no badges. You're in the United States of America. Speak English . . . I'm calling you because I am pissed that El Sneeze-o has made Spanish their official language. That's a disgrace. You're in America! You've got to speak American . . .
>
> BARTON: We speak Spanish to people that do not understand English.
>
> DON: Get on your burro, and go back to Mayheeco! . . . If those people do not understand my language, they should get on their burros and go back to Mayheeco.
>
> BARTON: You have to understand that if someone speaks Spanish, that does not make them un-American or any less of an American.
>
> DON: You people have your own country. Why are you trying to ruin our language?
>
> BARTON: No, we're not trying to ruin it . . . They are learning to speak English. . . .
>
> DON: I learned all right, let me give you a Spanish lesson right now. *Porque.* Let's listen to this. I got some Spanish here let's see
>
> BARTON: [inaudible]
>
> DON: —let's see if you know what they, what I'm saying here.
>
> BARTON: Okay.
>
> DON: Spanish lesson.
>
> VOICE [on Spanish language tape played by Don and Mike]: Spanish.
>
> DON: Spanish.
>
> VOICE: Spanish commands.
>
> DON: I'm going to give you some commands now, okay? Let's see. I'll show you how good I know Spanish. Listen to this.
>
> BARTON: That's not you talking.
>
> VOICE: Eat me.
>
> DON: All right. Eat.
>
> BARTON: That's not you talking.

MIKE: This is, this is our, our language tapes.

DON: Listen.

VOICE: Eat me. (In Spanish) *Come me!*

DON: (In Spanish) *Come me!* How you like that? (In Spanish) *Come me!*

BARTON: Go call the sheriff so they can listen to this please. They are out there.

DON: Yes, call the sheriff.

VOICE: Eat me. (In Spanish) *Come me!*

DON: (In Spanish). *Come me!* I'm just trying to learn your official language.

MIKE: These are our language tapes.

DON: I speak fourteen languages. You would be amazed at my many tongue techniques.

BARTON: Oh, really?

DON: Yes.

BARTON: No, because you, you have recorded.

MIKE: How many tongues do you speak right now?

DON: Fourteen, Mike.

BARTON: You have recorders, okay.

DON: Okay, listen to this.

BARTON: I'm going to find out where you originate.

VOICE: Eat sh——, and die.[22]

DON: Okay, listen to this now.

VOICE: (In Spanish) —— *y muerete.*

BARTON: I'm going to find out where you're really calling from.

DON: Pardon me?

BARTON: You're going to be in big trouble.

VOICE: Eat sh——, and die.

DON: How am I going to be in big trouble?

VOICE: (In Spanish) *Come me!* —— *y muerete.*

BARTON: I'm gonna, I'm gonna find out where you're calling from.

MIKE: This is a great country. This is the United States of America. It's a free country.

DON: Right. I'm telling you I don't like the fact that you made Spanish the official language.

BARTON: And how do you say it's a free country if you don't, you don't show it.

DON: It ain't that free, honey.

BARTON: You fellas, you're talking real ugly.

DON: I'm not talking ugly.

MIKE: We're not talking ugly.

BARTON: And this is a free country. You said it. So we can do what we want.

MIKE: That's right you can say anything to us. Go back to your country.

DON: Oh, I believe she's gone.

MIKE: And, she's gone. [Laughter]

DON: We'll never meet the sheriff now.[23]

Don and Mike's understanding of Mexicans as prosthetic workers to the U.S. economy has been challenged by the citizenry of El Cenizo who simply speak, as speaking subjects, in Spanish. Differently from the INS, who sees Mexicans as prosthetic extensions of the modern state economy, Don and Mike are traumatized by the events in El Cenizo because they, I suggest, are the true seers in this case. The El Cenizo community, Mexican and Anglo alike, is speaking not the language of the state but of their lived material reality. Speaking Spanish at city hall in this marginal town ruptures the fiction of the prosthetically rendered nonsubjectivity of the Mexican. It traumatizes Don and Mike just as it should. They sense that something has gone terrible awry, and in their hysterical reaction they fall back on their most basic and debasingly reductive notions of power: male dominance. Realizing Mexicans are no longer prosthetic limbs in the service of the state, Don and Mike refigure them as disembodied figures, an assemblage of objects, primarily oral, serving the whims of a male-fixated obsession.

Don and Mike's response, however crude, was not singular. Almost every major newspaper that covered this event, even those in Texas, reported it with surprise and suspicion. But the Don and Mike episode is particularly instructive. For a program broadcast in a number of major markets in approximately twenty-eight states at the time of this incident, its reach was formidable.[24] And, although complaints were lodged against them, only Albuquerque, New Mexico, staged a successful effort to remove their program from the local radio station. A formal complaint made against the show, its producers Infinity Broadcasting Corporation, and its licensee WJFK-FM in Manassas, Virginia, where the show is broadcast, was dismissed.[25] The distributors of the program, Westwood One, who also make available the G. Gordon Liddy program, targets a male audience between eighteen and forty-nine with *The Don and Mike Show*. Their strategy has been successful, indicated by the extension of the show's four-hour time slot each weekday afternoon. The hosts, Don Geronimo and Mike O'Meara, both in their early to mid-forties, have found a receptive audience for their particular style of commentary during their fifteen years of working together. Of course, the reaction by Don and Mike may not be the most representative response, at least in terms of its tone and baseness, but their indignation about the events in El Cenizo was shared quite broadly. It is this rather than the level of their creativity, I suggest, that warrants critical reflection.

If the Texas Modern shapes the frame through which Bourke reads the Rio Grande as the Congo, is there an equally salient Texas postmodern condition through which to understand how Don and Mike read the events in El Cenizo? Perhaps. But in place of writing the postmodern as the arrival of something like the flexible accumulation of capital, I would like to posit it as a kind of public accumulation of talk, as in the talk of talk radio.[26] Talk radio is the discourse of Don and Mike. It is the medium through which noise is accrued, sometimes as opinion, often times as commentary, but almost always in the postmodern rhetoric that flattens social commentary to private experience. Talk radio serves as a vehicle of expression, not for the masses but for the morass of public life where the ability to speak on air is mistaken for the ability to intervene or act socially. It is the junk bond of popular media, populated by those who speak for no social base beyond their own desire for an autonomous self; it is a technologically rendered medium that raises the personal to the public, bypassing the social. Here, in the public discourse of radio, we find a public traumatized by the Mexican-speaking subject, speaking Spanish in a public forum.

Does it matter to Don and Mike and their public that the inhabitants of El Cenizo did not pass a "Spanish only" law? Does it matter that the "facts" of this story were not represented correctly? Does it matter that no one has ever cared about the subjects who live in El Cenizo until the subjects began to speak publicly in Spanish? Not really.

All that matters is that the circulating, publicly produced discourses of prosthetically figured Mexicans are being challenged by a South Texas town whose presence has been mostly ignored. El Cenizo, which lies outside of Laredo, Texas, on the U.S.-Mexico border, was formed as a *colonia*, or border settlement, where utility and city services were absent in 1980. It was incorporated into a city in 1989. Don and Mike's assertions aside (along with a great many other newspaper and media sources), El Cenizo did not make Spanish the "official language of the city"; they simply passed an ordinance, through proper democratic means, stating that all city meetings will be held in the predominant language of the residents. This, for now, happens to be Spanish. As Patrick Train-Gutiérrez, a law clerk at the time of this incident, points out: "There is no official language in El Cenizo. Rather, there is a predominant language, and the ordinance says that business will be conducted in that language. Laws will still be written in English, and translations, which aren't legally binding, will be provided in Spanish. If, in the future, the predominant language ceases to be Spanish and becomes English or even some other language, this ordinance ensures that city business will be conducted in that language, whatever it will be."[27]

U.S. DEMOCRACY AND OTHER FREEDOMS

In his role as Davy Crockett in *The Alamo,* John Wayne states the following: "Some words give you a feeling. Republic is one of those words that makes me tight in the throat." Wayne's yearning for freedom can render democracy hollow and empty. If, as in the material lives of prosthetic users, phantom pains mediate between loss of limb and its mimetic substitute, do Mexicans, and various prosthetic others, serve the same presence in the United States? Do their pangs for justice serve as a ghostly reminder of the historical practices of American democracy that have rendered cultural Others as prosthetic devices in support of capitalist democracy? Imagining the arms, muscles, and backs of the backbreaking labor of Mexican braceros, African slaves, Chinese rail workers, along with a host of other historical Others, makes me gasp. Yes, Mr. Wayne, the word Republic does make me tight in the throat as well.

A defining feature of capitalism, found in Marx's theory of commodity fetishism and elsewhere, is the objectification of workers through the formation of wage labor. Briefly stated, the emergence of wage labor transforms a worker's labor into another commodity. This is accomplished as a worker's labor is objectified into labor power, which is then sold in return for a wage. If in fact wage labor serves to objectify both work and workers, do other forms of objectification coincide with wage labor to accomplish the same end? The answer is yes. Here let me offer the case of the cultural production of difference that results in marking others as Other.[28] By signifying Mexicans, among others, as radically different, they become marked as cultural Others in need of administration, surveillance, and control. Such a process, I offer, implicitly negates the principles of U.S. democratic freedoms by construing various subject positions as outside the realm of democratic participation. Full citizenship has been denied to women, certain people of color, and non-English speakers. The production of difference, therefore, serves as one of the significant means of limiting the participation, presence, and positionality of various subjects within democracy.[29] Or, as Don states so sharply when Ms. Barton queries him on American freedom: "It ain't that free, honey."

The exclusions of democracy, some historical, some operating in the present, reveal a deep gulf between members at the core of American society and those prosthetic Others, attached but serving only as an aid to the "real" subjects of the nation. What, then, might be the meaning of the principles of liberty and freedom, bedrock ideals of the U.S. democratic order, if they don't mean what they mean in practice? On this point, the congruent discursive meanings, circulating between and beyond Bourke, Wayne, and Don and Mike, are haunting reminders of what U.S. democracy is not. For Bourke, the Mexican is likened to the inhabitants of the Congo, those inhabiting the darkness of another continent; for Wayne, the Mexican, brave and loyal, remains a cultural outsider and socially suspect citizen; for Don and Mike, the embodied voices inflecting the American "middle-class" conservative values, the citizens of El Cenizo standing up and practicing democracy horrifies. Here are cultural Others—Spanish speakers, *colonia* dwellers, border inhabitants—not only espousing but utilizing their full democratic rights to achieve subjecthood and freedom as Others.[30] They are culturally rendered subjects speaking Spanish in the conduct of public, democratic, life. The horror for Don and Mike stems from the same beliefs we find in Wayne's film on the Alamo. They believe in an America of singular identity forged from ideological and cultural conformity. They have little room, if any, for the interpellation of difference; they have little room for dissenting Americans, cultured Americans and, need I say, Mexican Americans. Their social vision is rooted in conformity and acquiescence to a monolithic social order that requires the exclusion of cultural markers of difference for the privilege of inclusion in American democracy.

But the shock of Don and Mike, their encounter with the post-prosthetic Mexican as a speaking subject in El Cenizo, should not be entirely negative. It even could inspire some hope. If Richard Bernstein is correct when he states that "it is only by the serious encounter with what is other, different, and alien that we can hope to determine what is idiosyncratic, limited, and partial" then this culture shock serves a purpose.[31] For, I offer, it is only in engaging our various prosthetic objects of the state, those othered by the partial actualizations of democratic practices, that we recognize the limitations and partial subjects constituted in this process. We must recognize that the "all" in the phrase "and liberty and justice for all" is not a founding principle of democracy, it is not what comes before, but can only be the result, or in this case the goal, of a yet-materialized democratic state.

NOTES

1 Documentation on such negations is too numerous to list. For a general overview of how Mexicans and Mexican Americans have experienced such limitations and exclusions, see David Montejano, *Anglos and Mexicans in the Making of Texas, 1836–1986* (Austin: University of Texas Press, 1987). One key example of exclusion at the moment of (supposed) inclusion concerns land transfers after the war with Mexico and the Treaty of Guadalupe Hidalgo of 1848. Texas historian T. R. Fehrenbach, not known for his revisionist views, states: "There is some truth that many Mexican landowners, especially the small ones, were robbed in south Texas by force, intimidation, or chicanery. But what is usually ignored is the fact that the hacendado class, as a class, was stripped of property perfectly legally, according to the highest traditions of U.S. law" (*Lone Star: A History of Texas and the Texans* [New York: Macmillan, 1968], 510).

2 The history of the Bracero Program is long, complicated, and politically enlightening. See James Cockcroft, *Outlaws in the Promised Land* (New York: Grove Press, 1986), for his well-documented discussion of this program.

3 Kirby Farrell, *Post-Traumatic Culture: Injury and Interpretation in the Nineties* (Baltimore: Johns Hopkins University Press), 175.

4 C. B. Macpherson, *The Life and Times of Liberal Democracy* (Oxford: Oxford University Press, 1977), 21.

5 This critical period in Mexican American history has been well documented. For two accounts, see Montejano, *Anglos and Mexicans in the Making of Texas;* and Neil Foley, *The White Scourge* (Berkeley: University of California Press, 1996).

6 For further discussion on the Chicano/a movement, see Carlos Muñoz, *Youth, Identity, Power: The Chicano Movement* (New York: Verso, 1989); and Armando Navarro, *Mexican American Youth Organization: Avant-Garde of the Chicano Movement in Texas* (Austin: University of Texas Press, 1995), both of which offer overviews of the various facets of this important period.

7 *The Alamo,* dir. and prod. by John Wayne, Metro-Goldwyn-Mayer, 1960. All quotations from this film are my transcriptions.

8 Garry Wills, *John Wayne's America: The Politics of Celebrity* (New York: Simon and Schuster, 1997), 302. The idea of the Alamo as the scene of an American birth is not new. In 1915, just a few months after the classic film *The Birth of a Nation* was released by D. W. Griffith, the film *Martyrs of the Alamo; or the Birth of Texas* also came out. It was made by an associate of Griffith, Christy Cabanne, using some of the same actors found in Griffith's racist film. At least in the annals of popular culture, there is no doubt that the Alamo serves as a scene of American birth, as this film suggests. For more information, see my "Mexicans, Modernity, and *Martyrs of the*

Alamo" in *Reflexiones 1998: New Directions in Mexican American Studies,* ed. Yolanda Padilla (Austin: Center for Mexican American Studies; University of Texas Press, 1999).

9 Anticommunist activity kept Wayne in the news during his early career. In 1948 he served as president of the Motion Picture Alliance for the Preservation of American Ideals. It was the alliance that invited the House Committee on Un-American Activities to Hollywood in 1944, leading to the investigations of actors and writers. Moreover, his films like *Sands of Iwo Jima* (1949), *Flying Leathernecks* (1951), and *Big Jim McLain* (1952) cannot escape their propagandistic slant. But Garry Will's skepticism about Wayne's patriotism serves as an interesting counterpoint to Wayne's career. Wills claims that all the while Wayne was making his highly charged patriotic films in the 1940s and 1950s he was busy putting "careerism" ahead of his own military service. Wayne's patriotic, anticommunist role was, as Wills claims, "to emerge after the battle" to "shoot the wounded" (*John Wayne's America,* 197).

10 Wayne's goal was to make the most authentic film he could. And although the movie is better than most, it accomplished this goal in only one way—set design. The fictional liberties taken with the script, in particular the relationship between Bowie, Travis, and Crockett; the character of Flaca, the love-interest of Crockett; as well as several major blunders in terms of Texas history and geography (the Rio Bravo does not run through San Antonio de Béxar as the film states) resulted in one of the more fictionalized Alamo tellings. Regarding the set, the crew reconstructed, nearly in total, the Alamo mission compound. Alfred Ybarra, Wayne's art director, designed the mission church to scale and its surrounding buildings and walls to 75 percent of their size. It is estimated that the mission complex alone utilized nearly four hundred thousand adobe bricks, not including those used to construct the sets of the town. Such a task took the coordinated effort of the town of Brackettville, Texas, and, in a twist of fate quite consonant with my concerns here, required the importation of Mexican laborers to produce more bricks because American workers did not have the requisite skills to do so.

11 Brian Huberman and Ed Hugetz, "Fabled Facade: Filmic Treatments of the Battle of the Alamo," *Southwest Media Review* (spring 1985): 30–41.

12 Wills, *John Wayne's America,* 227.

13 *John Wayne's The Alamo,* dir. and prod. by Brian Huberman, MGM-United Artists, 1992 (videocassette).

14 Don Graham, "Remembering the Alamo: The Story of the Texas Revolution in Popular Culture," *Southwestern Historical Quarterly* 89, no. 1 (1985): 59. Paul Hutton, "The Celluloid Alamo" *Arizona and the West* 28, no. 1 (1986): 18.

15 According to Jim Crisp (personal communication) this portrait of the Mexican army was also reported by Ruben Potter, the writer of the first major historical account of the Alamo battle in a letter to Henry A. McArdle, the artist whose painting *Dawn at the Alamo* adorns the state capitol of Texas. For reasons that are not totally clear, by the time McArdle's painting was completed in 1905, his representation of Mexicans had totally changed. In place of representing them as upright and chivalrous, they

were portrayed more grotesquely and suspiciously, even cowardly. This, of course, fits in well with the interpretation we find in the film *Martyrs of the Alamo.*

16 Jesus de la Teja, *A Revolution Remembered: The Memoirs and Selected Correspondence of Juan N. Seguín* (Austin: State House Press, 1991), 79. It is correct that Seguín served as an early mayor of San Antonio, but this was not until the 1840s, some years after the Battle of the Alamo.

17 John Gregory Bourke, "The American Congo," *Scribner's Magazine,* May 15, 1894, 594.

18 I deal with Bourke and others at greater length in my "History, 'Los Pastores,' and the Shifting Poetics of Dislocation," *Journal of Historical Sociology* 6, no. 2 (1993): 164–85.

19 Although it is plotted in time, the Texas Modern is not so much a periodizing term as it is a social one. And while I use it to reference a complex series of events between 1880 and 1920, I would suggest it extends until 1960, thereby coming to a close about the time of Wayne's Alamo film.

20 See Marcelo Suárez-Orozco, *Crossings: Mexican Immigration in Interdisciplinary Perspectives* (Cambridge: David Rockefeller Center for Latin American Studies; Harvard University Press, 1998), for a cogent and nicely conceptualized overview of the social and economic issues related to Mexican immigration in the United States.

21 David Wills, *Prosthesis* (Stanford: Stanford University Press, 1995), 15.

22 Original transcriptions from the FCC came with these lines blank presumably because officials did not want to reproduce the language of Don and Mike. Although the intended reference can be surmised, I have decided to follow the FCC on this matter in place of wrongly attributing statements that were not spoken.

23 The transcription from the August 17, 1999, *Don and Mike Radio Show* is from the Latino Link news source, as well as from official documents from a press statement released by the Federal Communications Commission on May 18, 2000.

24 On May 18, 2000, the FCC dismissed an indecency complaint filed by Flora Barton, José Armas, and the National Latino Media Council, much to the chagrin and disagreement of FCC Commissioner Gloria Tristani.

25 To the best of my knowledge the list of cities that broadcast the *Don and Mike Show* in 1999 were Dothan and Mobile, Ala.; Little Rock, Ark.; Bakersfield, Port Hueneme, Sacramento, and Redding, Calif.; Denver, Colo.; Dover, Ocean View, and Seaford, Del.; Gainesville and Seffner (Tampa), Fla.; Honolulu, Hawaii; Burlington, Iowa City, and Le Mars (Sioux City), Iowa; Wichita, Kans.; Winchester, Ky.; Lafayette and Opelousas, La.; Portland, Maine; Baltimore and Hagerstown, Md.; Webster (Worcester), Mass.; Minneapolis/St. Paul, Minn.; Natchez, Miss.; Jacksonville, N.C.; Claremont, N.H.; Albuquerque, N.M.; Las Vegas and Sparks (Reno), Nev.; Plattsburgh and Rochester, N.Y.; Charleroi (Pittsburgh), Columbia, Elizabethtown, Philadelphia, Shamokin, and Williamsport, Pa.; Seneca (Clemson), S.C.; Lampasas (Austin), Tex.; Hudson, Wisc.; Barre, S. Burlington, Vergennes, White River, and Junction, Vt.; Manassas (Washington, D.C.), Va.; Spokane, Wash.; Charleston, W.V.

26 David Harvey, *The Condition of Postmodernity* (Cambridge, Mass.: Blackwell, 1990).

27 I am grateful to Angela Stuesse for sharing her deep knowledge of El Cenizo and this event with me. See her "Claiming Rights and Resources in El Cenizo, Texas" (masters thesis, Institute for Latin American Studies, University of Texas at Austin, 2001).

28 Akhil Gupta and James Ferguson, "Beyond 'Culture': Space, Identity, and the Politics of Difference," *Cultural Anthropology* 7, no. 1 (1992).

29 This point has been taken up by myself and others in our recent discussion of Latino cultural citizenship. See William Flores and Rina Benmayor, eds., *Latino Cultural Citizenship: Claiming Identity, Space, and Rights* (Boston: Beacon Press, 1997).

30 For a penetrating understanding of *colonias* and social policy on the U.S.-Mexico border, see Peter Ward, *Colonias and Public Policy: Urbanization by Stealth* (Austin: University of Texas Press, 1999). For a different but equally important look at the border through the recent militarization policies and tactics initiated by the United States, see Timothy Dunn, *The Militarization of the U.S.-Mexico Border, 1978–1992: Low-Intensity Conflict Doctrine Comes Home* (Austin: Center for Mexican American Studies; University of Texas Press, 1996).

31 Richard Bernstein, *The New Constellation: The Ethical-Political Horizons of Modernity/Postmodernity* (Cambridge: MIT Press, 1992), 328.

RUSS CASTRONOVO

Souls That Matter: Social Death and the
Pedagogy of Democratic Citizenship

The prominence of the body in contemporary cultural theory marks a democratic turn. Often a site of repression, exploitation, and violence, the body has been revalued within critical frameworks that examine how embodiment often equates to disempowerment and marginalization. But this examination of a contested corporeal terrain also legitimates another sort of exclusion: in its focus on the body, contemporary cultural theory fails to address regulatory norms transmitted along a less tangible register by the spiritual conditions that interpellate subjects with souls. Following a marxist cue that sees spiritual matters as so much false consciousness, many critics have pinned hopes of democratization on addressing the material conditions that disadvantage minority populations living in the U.S. nation-state as well as world populations living under transnational economies that cater to U.S. interests. But what determines hierarchies are not only the material conditions of the global marketplace or racial formations; what also sets political horizons and limits democratic possibility are constructions of inner life that are invoked to theorize the conditions of this world by making ultimately depoliticizing reference to a heavenly "other world."

Ours is not the first moment to contemplate embodiment. American democratic theorists of the nineteenth century also revalued—indeed, transvalued—both literal body and metaphoric body politic through an array of occult methodologies associated with mesmerism and spiritualism. Using somnambulism, hypnosis, trance, and other technologies that viewed the body as a conduit to ghostly communication, sleepwalkers and clairvoyants revealed a higher political order of perfect equality and justice. Social reformers, including abolitionists, women's rights activists, and communitarians, often formulated their calls for democracy with respect to "theories" of the afterlife that recalibrated the citizen's relation to the body politic by minimizing embodiment. An "*interior* government" of the soul fitted democracy for new heights as the subject "becomes his own legislator, his own executor, his own administrator. . . . In a word, he becomes, so far as government is concerned, an *individual,* an independent being, able, governmentally, to take care of himself," divined one spiritual medium.[1] This spectral but still political concern with interiority would seem to suggest that a democratic turn to the body leaves something out, that democracy is not a purely material enterprise. A measure of historical unconsciousness is needed to imagine embodied persons as abstract beings united by vague ideals and common interests. The soul—an epistemological formation that dispenses with historical accidents of the flesh—is a broad proposition that allows for the imagination of democratic commonality. Although the grim inequality that lies behind this fantasy is, if not well known, at least well documented, what remains less clear is the degree to which this fantasy reproduces privilege and hierarchy.

Democratic commitments privilege the autonomy of citizens' inner lives, but the capacity to have an inner life is itself an uninterrogated luxury. "Democratic politics," argues political theorist Barbara Cruikshank, "is not out there, in the public sphere or in a realm, but in here, at the very soul of subjectivity." Wrapped up in the constitution of the subject as citizen, democracy operates along an array of technologies that produce and govern interiority. For Cruikshank, democracy's production of the citizen packs "the twin possibilities of domination and freedom," revealing the soul and subjectivity as deeply political.[2] The soul is neither pre- nor nonpolitical; to be sure, putatively democratic statements of independence, self-reliance, and civil resistance recognize the political valence of the soul by claiming inner spiritual integrity as a component of natural law. Despite the frequency of such appeals, texts that politically theorize the soul are much less common. The slave narrative is one such text that understands how the privilege of interiority alternately fosters and restricts democratic discourses associated with the public sphere. Harriet Jacobs's slave narrative reevaluates the spiritual as a repressive force that converts embodied subjects into abstract beings that have transcendent access to the generic interests of democratic commonality. *Incidents in the Life of a Slave Girl* documents concrete prejudice as a function of race and gender in the United States, but her story also reveals how exploitation and forced amnesia emanate from an inclusive discourse of spirituality.[3] Her awareness that the soul is repressively constituted does not cause despair; rather it fuels a hope that spiritual matters can be reconstituted in ways that will rematerialize memories and revivify persons sentenced to the social death of slavery. Jacobs conducts an investigation into the spiritual preconditions of the nineteenth-century democratic subject, one that provides this essay with a critical vantage on late-twentieth-century theories of liberal education. But before we can read *Incidents* as political theory, a few examples of the spiritual workings of democracy are in order.

Democratic subjects are narrowed to a thin, historyless performance by dematerializing imperatives that assign a generic personhood to facilitate incorporation into national publics. As Jürgen Habermas explains, persons enter a public sphere in accordance with an "abstract universality" that recognizes individuals as equals by subsuming them "in an equally abstract fashion, as 'common human beings.' "[4] Whiteness and maleness—insofar as these attributes tend to be socially transparent—best allow a person to transcend the material processes that regulate the appearance and disappearance of race and gender (as well as class, region, and sexuality). A ghost gains admittance to the public sphere: what enters is a shadowy outline of the historically rich human actor, in short, a spectral citizen in which the texture of memory and particularistic identity are without substance and rendered historically dead. This experience of citizenship as a type of death unsettles our assumptions about democratic belonging because it is the social death of American slavery that also stigmatized people forever denied the generic personhood that received protection in both the state and the public sphere.

Democratic fantasies of commonality and equality have hinged on the disappearance of material differences. Even from within the security of cold war consensus, Walter Lippmann in 1955 diagnosed the undue prominence of the spiritual as a political malady: "For the radical error of the modern democratic gospel is that it promises, not the good life of this world, but the perfect life of heaven." Despite such political agnosticism, Lippmann still placed faith in a philosophy of the public that depends on dematerialized bodies. Devoted to curing a "functional derangement of the relationship between the mass of the people and the government," Lippmann offers a vision of liberal democracy that anticipates accounts of the public sphere. For Lippmann, as for Habermas, reason and abstraction rescue the polis from disorder by creating a generic space in which the force of particularity vanishes: "A large plural society cannot be governed without recognizing that, transcending its plural interest, there is a rational order with a superior common law."[5] In the face of the "plural" and unmanageable, singularity ensures "order." Democratic governance demands an overcoming of the social world's heterogeneity and unpredictability. Despite Lippmann's debunking of otherworldly politics, his ambivalence toward an unreflective and overembodied "mass" legitimates the operation of democracy in a transcendent mode. When democracy is attenuated to a matter of government and when it is asserted that "a mass cannot govern," individuals as social actors and political agents become immaterial.

The most trenchant critique of modern democratic gospel comes with Marx's rejection of bourgeois versions of reality, which operate in a phantasmatic mode by occluding the material sources of inequality. Foremost among such ghost stories is the state itself—what Marx early in his career calls "the *modern spiritualist democratic representative state*"—equipped with an ideology that makes actual community into a séance where citizens float above the conditions of the social world.⁶ So too the processes of commodity fetishism that mystify "the social character of men's labour" compare with the unexplained but ultimately contrived levitation of séance tables by disembodied spiritual forces. The commodity that transcendently hovers above the conditions that produced it seems "far more wonderful than 'table-turning' ever was."⁷ What are invocations of soul other than so much humbug? Recourse to the spirit in cultural analysis is often regarded as a gesture of bad faith that overlooks the prosaic and less lofty circumstances that sustain inequality in this world. As Marx wrote in 1852 just as spiritual mediums were ushering in a popular antiorthodox religious movement in the United States, history is a ghostly incarnation that leads people to "anxiously conjure up the spirits of the past" to frame revolutionary movements.⁸ But this making of history in terms of dead spirits from a past age is an unhistorical activity that, as Marx put it in an early work, "separates thinking from the senses, the soul from the body and itself from the world . . . and sees the origin of history not in coarse *material* production on the earth but in vaporous clouds in the heavens."⁹

Even as a national public sphere unequally distributes social and material resources, citizens frame their participation with respect to "vaporous clouds," establishing a transcendent politics of interiority that neglects the hard-and-fast circumstances that create inequality in the first place. Harriet Jacobs is no exception, and her attack on an oppressive American institution often looks for solace in the soul as a point beyond earthly regimes of law and prejudice. Recent critics of a very different institution—the university—also invoke the soul and interiority in their attacks on hierarchies of higher education that, in their view, relegate students and the love of learning to the bottom rungs. Like Jacobs, who provides a pedagogy for evading a system that would pinion body and spirit, commentators from both the Right and the Left, including Jane Tompkins, Page

Smith, and Roger Shattuck, turn to interiority as a means of outmaneuvering an educational system that they view as deadened and impersonal—in short, as soulless. Shattuck, for instance, writes about the "spiritual in art," an experience that leads to "moments of vision" and an "oceanic feeling," in an effort to recapture the humanities from theory, politics, and interdisciplinarity. But unlike Jacobs, who historicizes the soul that she invokes to reveal its potential for domination as well as liberation, these critics of higher education see spirituality only as a site of resistance.

This essay thus presents a double perspective that uneasily pairs readings of Jacobs and higher education's critics in order to think about how interiority both empowers and disempowers subjects. An aggressive democratic critique cannot simply dismiss spirituality as ideological mist. As the example of *Incidents* shows, the soul provides a regulatory apparatus that governs a public sphere based on formal principles of equality that identify subjects as citizens—even as this very identification depoliticizes human actors by trimming back subjectivity to the requirements of generic personhood. Souls matter to the construction of a public sphere that disembodies subjects.

SHADES OF THEORY

Yet it is the body that matters today in cultural criticism. In 1986, Sacvan Bercovitch announced that the demystification of American ideology demands a jaundiced view of the soul as a political space: "Ideological analysis begins on the other side of humanist absolutes, in a recognition of the material processes that the *rhetoric* of morality and the spirit seeks to conceal or disguise."[10] Although otherworldly cant is, as Bercovitch argues, an illusion, it is also more than smoke and mirrors. I contend that the shadowy stuff of spiritual rhetoric has very real effects in producing hierarchies and inequality. Concern in cultural theory for the material, especially in the guise of the body, has elided the extent to which the spiritual functions as a political apparatus.

"What about the materiality of the body, *Judy?*": Judith Butler's presentation of this question initiates one of the sharpest analyses of body in contemporary cultural theory. She concedes that this challenge, despite its infantilizing tone, offers a sort of primal scene for an investigation into "the normative conditions under which the materiality of the body is framed and formed." Butler works against notions of subjectivity as a fundamentally disembodied and noncontingent proposition. Examinations of such foundational categories contribute to an important political project in which questioning the very grounds of identity can lead to "the rearticulation of democratic contestation."[11] But this question also establishes a line of inquiry that skews descriptions of cultural hierarchies such that power appears to work its effects solely at the level where discourse becomes material. Not addressed by the question put to Butler are regulatory norms transmitted by airy, inexact discourses of the spirit.

The body's materiality is much more difficult for Jacobs to negotiate. Where Butler suspects that questions about materiality seek to reconstitute her "as an unruly child, one who needed to be brought to task, restored to . . . bodily being" (ix), Jacobs apprehends that any speculation about her body uncannily replays sentimental, scopic, and racist economies that fetishize and commodify black women.[12] Materiality returns Linda to overdetermined senses of embodiment, including the sexually harassed body of the "slave girl" and the debilitated body of the fugitive, which she cannot shake under the moral regime of abolitionism. In contrast to Butler's consideration of the body's materiality that paradoxically moves away from the body toward a reexamination of epistemological assumptions, Jacobs's considerations never escape the body—or the soul that it is presumed to degrade. As Jacobs reluctantly explores the body's materiality in a culture that castigated blacks and women precisely in terms of their embodiment, she returns to the soul as a site immune to paternalistic (de)valuation. Escape is short-lived, however, as she realizes that the spiritual itself constitutes a terrain colonized by white religious imperatives.

We can imagine the normative power of spirituality with a slight rephrasing of the question put to Butler: What about the materiality of the body, *Linda?* Here, Linda is Linda Brent, the pseudonymous heroine of *Incidents in the Life of a Slave Girl.* The substitution of "Linda" for "Judy" reveals the privilege involved in thinking about the body's materiality. Theorizing materiality affords Butler the opportunity of becoming disembodied at the textual site of public representation. For Jacobs, however, a focus on materiality reproduces her sexualization since, as her narrative silences make all too clear, to speak of the body is to overdetermine it. The point is not that Linda has no such privilege to underrepresent the body, nor is it that she has no access to metaphysical discourse as a way to veil her sexual history. Rather, even as Linda flees materiality, especially the conditions that commodify sexuality, she experiences regulations of the spirit in ways that Butler's argument cannot acknowledge. Linda refuses to see the soul as an alternative to the culturally bound and determined body because she never enjoys the luxury of having an unmarked and socially transparent public presence. To exist as a soul is to reap the rewards of generic personhood, but it is also to incur prohibitions that authorize the unequal distribution of disembodiment, abstract personhood, and other resources associated with the public sphere.

This privilege of not having a body emerges in Butler's reading of Western classical traditions that legitimate male disembodiment. Masculine reason achieves ascendancy by occupying a dematerialized position that also stigmatizes women and slaves as excessively embodied, inferior, and unqualified for rationality. As Butler makes this argument, she seemingly foregrounds her own body in a footnote that reads: "Donna Haraway, responding to an earlier draft of this paper in a hot tub in Santa Cruz, suggested that it is crucial to read Irigaray as reinforcing Plato as the origin of Western representation."[13] Despite the footnote's intimate setting, the body is here submerged under layers of privilege. The luxury of unwinding after a day of academic labor echoes the luxury of inviting speculation about the body. What are the material conditions of hot-tubbing in California? The issue is not only the status of Western philosophy but also the position of Western philosophers in the relaxed privacy of a hot tub. While mention of a hot tub invites speculation about the bodies of cultural theorists, this speculation leads away from materiality to dematerialized inquiry. The author's privileged invocation of the hot-tubbing body effaces the body; in parsing this footnote ("Donna Haraway, responding to an earlier draft of this paper in a hot tub in Santa Cruz") we see that Butler's body is *not* in the hot tub along with Haraway and, for that matter, neither is Haraway. Instead, what floats in the hot tub is "an earlier draft of this paper." Butler enjoys the privilege of syntactically not representing the body and is instead enabled to inhabit the philosophical space of the "origin of Western representation." For some, thinking about the body's materiality provides access to the privilege of disembodiment.

For Jacobs, disembodiment offers a means of evading racial and sexual exploitation only to install Linda Brent under yet another regulatory apparatus. This irony pits her against ghostly beliefs in spiritualism that underpinned discourses of nineteenth-century liberal reform communicating via mediums and séances, disembodied souls spoke in glorious tones of an afterlife beyond the body, of citizens freed from terrestrial injustice and worldly oppression. The dematerialized souls of slaves who visited clairvoyant séances in Mary Dana Shindler's *A Southerner among the Spirits* (1877), for instance, took pleasure in a sociocelestial sphere that, in contrast to the racial order of the South, placed them on equal footing with white spirits. In the plantation South, black access to literacy was strictly limited, but in the occult sphere the departed spirits of slaves knew enough of their letters to make use of early ouija boards and spell out messages for the living. Once painfully embodied slaves asked the *Banner of Light* and other spiritualist publications to "send word to Massa George Burgess . . . that twelve of us are in the spirit-land, happy and free."[14] The privilege of social transparency—of not having a stigmatized or an encumbered body—emanated from otherworldly citizenship. The spirits thus told a mediumistic circle in Nashville that perfect freedom attended the "soul when it is abstracted from the grosser elements of his body."[15] More than episodes of false consciousness, these encounters with spirits and spiritualism speak to a historical desire to achieve disembodied presence in the public sphere, a privileged opacity that would, theoretically, keep identity safe from the contingencies of institutional location and historical situatedness.

This desire constructs citizenship as a posthistorical identity. Dead white men who spoke to mediums relished disembodiment because it quieted anxieties about marketplace survival. As one departed citizen stated, "I feel that my knowledge, since I left my body, has greatly increased, for I now am free from much that used to claim my attention—that of providing for my own and my family's sustenance."[16] Disencumbered of the physical body, white middle-class men triumphed over rarely acknowledged contingencies to discover independence. According to this spectral politics, autonomy derived not from a masculinist fantasy of power and control but from an alienation that distanced subjects from palpable histories of the everyday. Many abolitionists found the spiritual especially attractive with its ordination of a vaporous public sphere whose disembodied contours resemble a Santa Cruz hot tub without bodies. For those seeking a liberatory agenda, emancipation of the spirit from a corporeal racial heritage seemed exactly the ticket. Even as they contributed to political critiques against slavery, antislavery activists including William Lloyd Garrison, Amy Post, William Nell, Lydia Maria Child, and Harriet Beecher Stowe attended mystic séances that provided an allaying shift from worrying about the unfree materiality of the black body to proclaiming the eternal immortality of the freed soul. But this immortality, rather than simply expressing a longing for everlasting freedom, intensifies the repression of the "slave girl."

This discursive milieu of the spirit bears down upon Jacobs. In the narrative of her body's trials she chats with her dead father, sees her children as ghosts, and longs for death as a final freedom. Instead of overcoming the institutional conditions that circumscribe her being, each of these spiritual encounters intensifies slavery's despair as "social death."[17] The final chapter of *Incidents*, titled "Free

at Last," invokes an African American spiritual as it moves beyond the compromised freedom of being "*sold* at last" toward an immaterial plane (200).[18]
The text concludes with two complementary—yet also mutually destabilizing—
images of spiritual liberation immune to earthly trammeling. Linda conjures up
"tender memories of my good old grandmother, like light, fleecy clouds floating
over a dark and troubled sea" in the last sentence of her autobiography (201). The
dead comfort the living in a world where an earthly past offers only a sadistic
institutional history. Amid "gloomy recollections" of the past, the dead speak of
an alternative world in which struggle has been laid to rest (201). The public
sphere here becomes indistinguishable from an occult sphere: whether as a generic political actor or as a socially dead ghost, the disembodied person rises
above discordant particularities that create inequality and political difference.
Spiritual discourse materially impacts the public sphere by idealizing citizenship
as abstract, posthistorical personhood. But it is not just that occult practices
come to substitute for rational processes of the public sphere; rather, the point is
that the public sphere always depends on a ghostly operation that dematerializes
uniquely embodied and specifically historical citizens in its production of the
liberal subject.

Against Linda's reveries of her deceased grandmother, however, comes a letter
communicating the death of her uncle Phillip. Instead of serene reflections that
transmogrify the earthly struggles of black embodiment, this obituary stirs up
sharp contradictions that deflate Linda's tendency to bury political struggle under a morbid sentimentality of death. Her uncle's eulogist writes that Phillip
receives posthumous enfranchisement in the columns of the town newspaper:
"Now that death had laid him low, they call him a good man and a useful citizen;
but what are eulogies to the black man, when the world has faded from his
vision? It does not require man's praise to obtain rest in God's kingdom" (201).
This honorific notice ironically incorporates "the black man" only when he lacks
the materiality of the body to put citizenship to use. Linda distances herself from
the state-authorized transubstantiation of bodily matter of black man into dead
citizen: "Strange they called a colored man a *citizen!* Strange words to be uttered
in that region!" (201). What is "strange" is that a community that so consistently
devalued black lives treasures reflections about a black man's death. Here lies a
political morbidity that rivals the peace Linda finds in her grandmother's spirit: a
spectral citizenship overshadows her uncle's body, his industrious efforts to work
toward his own and his family members' freedom forfeited to the town's official
memory. Her reflection signals the rupture caused when a racial body awkwardly

occupies the abstract designation of citizen. What remains unclear, however, is the precise locality of "that region." Contextually "that region" denotes the South, but syntactically it also refers to the logical antecedent of "God's kingdom" mentioned by her uncle's eulogist. This ambiguity suggests that the eternal—idealized as an egalitarian landscape where racial difference pales in light of the heavenly category of moral sameness—reproduces models of domination all too familiar in the sociopolitical world. The spiritual polices bodies even though a morbid sentimentality instructs her that hierarchies do not apply in death.

To transgress the corporeal and moral hierarchies that devalue her, Jacobs invokes spirits and the dead. Although her tactics create intimacy with the disembodied subject required by liberal politics, this spiritual relation exacts a price, namely by giving white citizens the privilege of thinking about the materiality of Linda's body against the virtues of their own dematerialized presence. Under the regime of nineteenth-century spiritualism, Jacobs's bid to emancipate subjectivity from enslaving material conditions falls short of democratic results. An alternative politics does not inhere in the region of the soul but instead represents an intensification of the same politics, of a regime that uses black embodiment to effect its own privileged opacity.

GHOSTS AND THE PUBLIC SPHERE

The history of Harriet Jacobs, specifically the conditions that precede her 1861 slave narrative, unveils the role of the soul in preparing a public sphere inhabited by abstract persons and other ghosts. Even as *Incidents* records her mental and physical sufferings, the specificity and particularity of black political expression at times disappears under a white spiritual discourse that surrounds her narrative. After Brent's narration is said and done, Amy Post appends a letter of reference to the slave autobiography. Because Jacobs's "sensitive spirit shrank from publicity," Post acts as a literary duenna for Jacobs's entry into public (203). The bulk of Post's letter testifies that Jacobs transcends her former status as slave and even her present status as exslave; she assures readers that the book's author has been successfully estranged from the indelicate corporeal history she relates. Jacobs's benefactress confides that deep within resides "her spirit—naturally virtuous" (203). Freedom does not lie in Jacobs's story, which too clearly dredges up a sexual past. Rather, a liberatory narrative comes in the endorsement of an abolitionist-spiritualist-feminist that frees the "slave girl" by exempting her from a moral economy of sin and guilt. Post never refers to bondage as material deprivation, and instead concentrates on the "mental agony" that renders memory of slavery "galling to a spirit" such as Jacobs's (204). She ignores Jacobs's corrupted body to rescue her soul. Abstraction of Brent's specific history into a general portrait of human suffering is not accomplished in one fell swoop of Post's letter, however. This spiritualization is the culmination of a process begun a decade earlier in Rochester.

When Kate, Margaret, and Leah Fox, the famous clairvoyant mediums who initiated and popularized spirit-rapping and séances, entered the public sphere by appearing before audiences at Rochester's Corinthian Hall, Post chaperoned the sisters on the stage. Not long after Post took an interest in spiritualism in the late 1840s, she and her husband, Isaac, invited Harriet Jacobs to share their domestic circle while Jacobs's brother traveled as an abolitionist lecturer.[19] Her residence in a household where tables tipped and spirits rapped set the stage for the "slave girl's" abstraction under which her sexual history prepares the Posts' liberal disembodiment. Her dematerialized corporeality and transcended blackness contribute to the paranormal domesticity of their home, and long before her autobiography was printed, Isaac Post published her story as a spiritualist narrative that veils Brent's sexuality, dematerializing her social identity as the "spirit" that Amy repeatedly mentions in the letter tacked on to *Incidents*. This pattern exemplifies the turbulent coexistence of the black body and white disembodiment: spiritualist messages borrow from African American narrative only to suppress the species-being of the black body as unsuitable for citizenship, even if that ideal first originates in the dematerialization of the "slave girl's" body.

When Jacobs entered the Posts' home in 1849, it was brimming with reformist energy. Amy Post had just attended the first Women's Rights Convention in Seneca Falls the previous year. Her awakened feminist consciousness readily fit with spiritualism, an occult devotion that Jacobs viewed with suspicion. Writing to Amy and her husband about the forthcoming British publication of her narrative as *The Deeper Wrong* (1862), Jacobs exclaimed that "we poor women has always been too meek," a thought that makes her "begin to think about poor Leah of the Bible, not Leah of the spirits."[20] Her letter alludes to the Posts' abiding interest in clairvoyants like "Leah of the spirits," the eldest Fox sister, for a mystic ability to provide higher confirmation of democratic social agendas. But this democracy threatens to make Jacobs—a historical person with an even more historical body—disappear as though she were a ghost. Her letter thus also documents—albeit less straightforwardly—her attempt to dissociate herself and her story from spiritualism. Jacobs's reluctance to entertain thoughts about a medium follows her refusal years earlier to invite someone to ghostwrite her slave narrative and accede to Cornelia Willis's recommendation that Stowe rework her story in *A Key to Uncle Tom's Cabin*. She rightly suspects that that spiritualism will dematerialize her history and experience.

As the energies of feminism, abolition, and spiritualism were animating Amy Post's social activism, Jacobs began a nine-month sojourn in this reformist household. At roughly the same time, Isaac Post happened on a technological innovation (of sorts) that greatly speeded transmission of messages across vast reaches of space. His discovery enabled the once inarticulate to write—a theme Amy Post and Jacobs would stress in the letters they exchanged. What Isaac developed was a new way of talking with the dead. Chatting with spirits had become a laborious process of asking yes-or-no questions and waiting for a specified number of knocks to signal either an affirmative or negative answer. But the spirits gained greater freedom of expression when Isaac suggested that the alphabet be read aloud so that disembodied souls could rap at letters to spell out words, sentences, and in many instances, entire books. On the cutting edge of spirit technology, Post was among the first to profit from his "invention," publishing *Voices from the Spirit World* in 1852.

Although he wrote it, Post did not claim authorship for this book. Rather, he claimed mediumship for a text produced "by the hand of Isaac Post" but narrated by the famous dead of American history. When departed statesmen such as Franklin, Calhoun, Penn, and Washington returned, they came to talk, not about the wonders of life after death, but about the iniquity of social death. In one séance, the father of his country guided the hand of Post to write: "Only reflect, that at the time I was in active bodily life, there was the great number of six hundred thousand slaves. Now there is no less than three millions. I cannot find words to express my abhorrence of this accursed system of slavery. I believe if the views here glanced at, were universally carried out, the National difficulties in regard to Slavery, would be ended, and the white and sable brother would live in harmony together, and blessings such as no one can imagine, would follow."[21] As Washington's soul addresses slavery, he ironically takes the same position as the unauthorized exslave who requires white mediation to narrate and authenticate his/her history. Marking the convergence of antislavery editor and clairvoyant medium, socially dead slave and dead person, and spiritualism and abolition, Washington prophesies a timeless era of homosocial accord where men without bodies promise to love one another.

Interrupting this ghostly procession of national bodies, a disembodied woman

contacts the medium in *Voices from the Spirit World.* Channeling her story
through Post, she conveys a tale of seduction, shame, and deathly impulses that
bears uncanny resemblance to the autobiography Linda Brent tells in *Incidents*.[22]
Not long after Jacobs departed the Posts' home, a departed spirit visits Isaac and
guides his hand in producing a narrative of sex, seduction, and lost womanly
virtue. Her story begins as does Brent's: just as Linda remains innocent of slaveholding culture's prurient interest in her body until she "entered on my fifteenth
year—a sad epoch in the life of a slave girl" (27), so for the spirit of Sarah Sharp,
"my life passed with nothing in particular to narrate, until I had grown to be a
woman" when men begin to show sexual interest in her womanhood.[23] Each
woman finds, however, that she has too much to tell when her body enters a
sexual traffic in which innocence affords little protection.

Linda Brent and Sarah Sharp narrate sexual incidents in the same way—by
suppressing lurid content. Each tells by not telling, employing narrative strategies
that refuse to exhibit the female body because such exhibition would inevitably
repeat their sexualization. The "metaphoric loopholes" that Valerie Smith identifies as key to the narrative logic of *Incidents* also appear in a section from Post's
Voices from the Spirit World titled "Communication from Sarah Sharp."[24] Brent
announces her second pregnancy out of the midst of one such ellipsis, referring
to premarital sexual activity only in passing as a subordinate clause: "When Dr.
Flint learned that I was again to be a mother, he was exasperated beyond measure" (77). Whereas her first liaison with Mr. Sands can be chalked up to girlish
indiscretion or a desperately conceived protective strategy, a second pregnancy
betrays her desire to return to what a sentimental reading public saw as im-
proprieties of the flesh. Because Brent argues that the slave girl should be judged
by a different moral standard than the one applied to bourgeois white women,
she at first may not be all that reluctant to acknowledge her sin, particularly since
her fall from virtue also indicts the impossible constraints of true womanhood
for slave women. But because her body is subject to controlling sexual scrutiny
from Dr. and Mrs. Flint as well as readers of *Incidents,* she refrains from discussing the body that commits "sin" more than once. The ghost voice of Sarah Sharp
employs exactly this evasive technique as she broaches her sexual history. Like
Brent, she mentions sexual activity only as a subordinated addendum in order to
avoid a strict accounting of her body's transgressions. Before her lover kills her,
Sharp asks him, "had you no pity for my daughter" to leave her motherless?[25] She
reveals the fact of her motherhood only after her lover has slit her throat; sexuality appears post facto when the body is no more. She confesses and enters the

public sphere only when her identity has become posthistorical. From the disembodied and sentimentalized space of a ghost story, Sharp speaks as a spirit to
Isaac in his capacity as medium: the conditions of her narrative alienate her from
the corporeality she has already disavowed. Like the socially dead "slave girl," the
literally dead white heroine employs a "loophole of retreat," deferring mention of
sexual activity until it comes under the auspices of disembodied motherhood.

Although the slave narrative hardly affords the same privileges of disembodiment found in spiritualism, these unwed mothers deploy gaps around the materiality of sex so that they can concentrate on their souls instead. Not so much the
loss of virginity but the loss of esteem is what each suffers. "My self-respect was
gone!" bemoans Linda just before her grandmother labels her a "disgrace" and
casts her out (56). Sarah also experiences rejection and desolation, realizing "that
I must lose my reputation among those whom I had been used to lovingly
associate" as the consequence of seduction. Her spirit laments to Isaac, "I felt the
need of a kind word, but in its stead, I met the cold repulse"[26]—a sentiment little
different from Linda's ineffective pleas to the grandmother who "had always been
so kind to me! *So* kind!" (57). Conveyed as similar stories, one to abolitionist-
spiritualist Amy Post and the other to spiritualist-abolitionist Isaac Post, *Incidents* and "Communication from Sarah Sharp" redeem the corrupted body as
the material occasion of the soul's trial.

Sympathy between disembodied soul sisters runs in the face of the expressly
nonsympathetic, antitranscendent, and historically specific chords of Brent's
autobiography. Appropriation of the slave girl's sexual harassment as the seduction of a ghostly white woman blunts *Incidents'* suspicion of white women
readers. Yes, the liberal assertion that Sarah Sharp and Linda Brent, or, for that
matter, northern white women and slave women, share the same emotional
distress and spiritual trials represents a progressive attitude at a time when biology, anthropology, phrenology, and scriptural interpretation insisted on the sep-
arateness of whites from other races. Even within a potentially radical sympathy
that aligns Post's white female spirit and the "slave girl" of Jacobs's title, however,
the black body and its historical experience merit no consideration. To narrate
the slave girl as the disembodied spirit of a fallen white woman is to assent to an
abstract moral standard that, at one moment, implies that unregulated sexuality
has no color and, at the next, insists that unregulated sexuality as a specific
practice must be "black." As Dana Nelson argues, "sympathy assumes *sameness* in
a way that can prevent understanding of the very real, material *differences* that
structure human experience in a society based upon unequal distribution of

power."[27] The propensity to read the black body as a revelation of white spirit recasts power-laden relations between mediums and ghosts and between blacks and whites as the power of sympathy.

Remaking the black body as a white spirit goes a long way in creating an abstract person qualified to enter the public sphere. Jacobs's story becomes public property once it behaves like the narrative of an unhistorical white woman, adhering only to the formal shadow of public personhood enacted by white female mediums who in spiritual demonstrations pretended that they were not right there on stage before an audience but elsewhere. In this occult public sphere, black women equate to white ghosts: it is an equality that depends on a rigid yet still spectral form that overrides the restrictive contents of historical difference. In place of a formal narrative of citizenship, however, *Incidents* suggests that political identity is a palimpsest of competing narratives erased and written over with multiple disavowals of embodiment, particularity, and memory.

GENERIC PERSONHOOD AND SOCIAL DEATH

But *Incidents* and "Communication from Sarah Sharp" are not the same story. Ironically, this divergence becomes most pronounced at the point where Jacobs adopts the ghostly, sentimental style of the Post household and Sarah Sharp's postmortem confession. She never accepts the morbid politics of liberal reform circles that idealize disconnection and disembodiment. But neither does she reject outright the spiritual, especially given nagging questions about the materiality of the "slave girl's" body. Instead Brent stages scenes of paranormal communication as material encounters in which the full force of repressed history comes to light. As with texts produced via séance, *Incidents* speaks obsessively of death with Linda Brent going so far as to imagine her children as spirits. In opposition to conventional wisdom that reads the spiritual as depoliticizing illusion, this slave narrative also provides a theoretical intervention that re-describes the spiritual as historical and political.

Ghosts are neither transcendent nor removed for Jacobs. The departed are densely historical for Jacobs who always places the dead in the context of slavery's social death. And by reevaluating the relationship of ghosts to history, by re-distributing material and spiritual resources, as it were, Jacobs seeks to democratize interiority. Rather than viewing the soul as a pre-given and uncontested category, she understands that any appeal to the spirit, especially constructions that authorize an autonomous inwardness or a transcendent generic identity for use in the public sphere, is the product of power and contestation. The immaterial dialectically engages with the material. She fuses body and spirit as a means of assessing the unequal and antidemocratic distribution of abstract personhood and disembodiment.

Linda Brent and Sarah Sharp still resemble one another in their morbid plans to redeem the sinful body. As she contemplates her degradation, Sarah longs for death: "My life became wretched. . . . Many times I craved that I might be taken from the evils with which I was surrounded."[28] Her lover grants this wish by murdering her, and now when she speaks to Isaac Post she seems close to a contentment she never knew in life. Linda similarly reveals, "I had often prayed for death" (61). But she backs away from this macabre antiactivism, perceiving how a postpolitical stance annihilates the specificity of the history that she and her children suffer. Brent's continuing concern is that others wish the resolution of death upon her. As her grandmother and a sympathetic white neighbor watch Linda's struggles, they jointly emplot the "slave girl's" life along the necrophilic lines of the story that Isaac Post tells for Sarah Sharp, a story that demurely concludes in death and overcomes the body's history. After Brent confesses her loss of virtue, her grandmother upbraids her, "O Linda! has it come to this? I had rather see you dead than to see you as you now are. You are a disgrace to your dead mother" (56). Her words are part accusation and part death wish that Brent inhabit a nonconditional world immune to the sexual complexities and racial hierarchies that beset sociohistorical life in Edenton, North Carolina, in the 1830s. Her grandmother's white tea partner, Miss Fanny, shares this postpolitical approach to the material conditions of historical struggle: "She wished that I and all my grandmother's family were at rest in our graves, for not until then should she feel any peace about us. The good old soul did not dream that I was planning to bestow peace upon her, with regard to myself and my children; not by death, but by securing our freedom" (89). Squeamish and judgmental about the physical immorality of the slave girl's body, these women prefer to ask: What about the immortality of the soul, *Linda?* It is a trap: Linda cannot safely respond to this question within the terms set by a culture that valorizes disembodiment. To answer is to take up their discourse of the spirit, which regulates subjects via a series of processes—abstraction and purification, redemption and regeneration, transcendence and disconnection—that deploy hierarchies beyond the body.

But *Incidents* stands neither as an out-and-out rejection of spectral politics nor as an absolute embrace of practical, embodied solutions to oppression. A thoroughly material politics excludes the soul that becomes "free at last" just as a

wholly material sensibility marginalizes the cultural heritage so difficult to preserve under slavery. Brent collapses the opposition between body and soul—an
opposition that demands her stigmatized embodiment in the public sphere—by
linking death both to the afterlife and to life under American slavery. Against the
maudlin sentimentality that privileges souls freed from the body, Jacobs con-
textualizes literal death with the social death that enslaves the body. For her, death
remains politically engaged with the material world, never reaching the calm of
the postpolitical. Brent's description of the fast-becoming anonymous graves of
her parents captures a ghostly legacy that is highly politicized but also too fleeting
to be detected by standard yardsticks of material politics: "The graveyard was in
the woods, and twilight was coming on. Nothing broke the death-like stillness
except the occasional twitter of a bird. My spirit was overawed by the solemnity
of the scene. . . . A black stump, at the head of my mother's grave, was all that
remained of a tree my father had planted. His grave was marked by a small
wooden board, bearing his name, the letters of which were nearly obliterated"
(90). What are the material conditions of a history that is being erased? Even
though the graphic markers of her parents' graves are crumbling into illegibility,
Brent hopes that what is *not there,* that what is as invisible as memory, can
provide foundations for resistance to institutional forces that circumscribe the
slave girl's body, sexuality, and family.

   Can a history that is not there have palpable consequences? If "the not there is
a seething presence," as Avery Gordon claims, then Brent reads her parents' vanishing graves as an imperative to reinvest the spiritual, the dead, the departed—in
short, all that is without historical substance—with the meaning of history.
Hounded by questions about the materiality of the body and immortality of the
soul, Brent returns to the "burying ground of the slaves." She offers a single
response to these questions that pull in opposite directions by embodying ghosts
and their history. Her interaction with spirits does not spell the death of political
thinking but rather rededicates her to radical democratic contexts. Entranced by
a ghostly connection with the no longer present, Linda realizes, in the words of
Gordon, that "to be haunted is to be tied to historical and social effects."[29] The
dead recall Brent to echoes of resistance: "As I passed the wreck of the old
meeting house, where, before Nat Turner's time, the slaves had been allowed to
meet for worship, I seemed to hear my father's voice coming from it, bidding me
not to tarry till I reached freedom or the grave. I rushed on with renovated
hopes" (91). The distant shadow of a slave meeting, this ruin recontextualizes
escape as collective action tied both to family and African American history. Im-

material conditions—a disembodied father, memories of communal gathering, a building that no longer stands—brace her decision to intervene in the institutional and legal identities that indifferently control the lives of her children.

Her allusion to Nat Turner suggests that ghostly thoughts, while often dematerializing and dispossessive, can also foment defiance. Her belief that the spiritual—if it can be rematerialized—carries liberatory potential pits her against one of the most cited authorities on revolutionary struggle, Frantz Fanon. Unlike Fanon's estimation of the occult as a backward tendency, Jacobs describes slavery's hauntings as tangible vestiges of a radical legacy that have been suppressed. Since the "occult sphere" deludes native inhabitants that "the zombies are more terrifying than the settlers," the concrete work of liberation is deferred when people participate in what Fanon views as ultimately misguided and empty rituals.[30] But in *Incidents,* the spiritual acquires a reality as palpable as Fanon's counterspiritual landscape of barbwire and guns. Her "father's voice" speaks of communal contexts and historical actors such as Nat Turner; the dead do not always retreat from the sociopolitical world and, instead in this case, encourage magnetic sympathy with a violent critic of the slave regime. Reference to the 1831 slave rebellion in Southhampton, Virginia, furnishes Jacobs with a potent precedent for actualizing an occult politics since Turner interpreted his visions as a divine go-ahead for revolutionary uprising against white rule. Decades before they rapped for the Fox sisters, the spirits offered a much more violent message to Turner. His discovery of "drops of blood on corn as though it were dew from heaven" along with visions of "white spirits and black spirits engaged in battle" impelled him and his comrades to contest social reality in murderous terms.[31] His trances tell him that a redistribution of social justice is at hand and, despite the millennial cast of such prophesizing, Turner sets about translating heavenly promise into historical event.

In pursuing a revolutionary memory as fragile as the ruin of a meeting house, *Incidents* recuperates black liberation theology from its subvention under white spiritualism. Although Linda's mystical memories would seem evidence of Jacobs's consent to white spiritual politics, *Incidents* rejects such dematerializing effects. Her aim is to historicize the eternal and the disembodied in terms of their specific material effects on the "slave girl" and her community. She treats the spiritual as a social, not paranormal, phenomenon. Troubled by thoughts of her children as dead or in the hands of a slave speculator, Brent is lulled by the mournful music of serenaders to suspend her burdened consciousness and forget an uncertain social world: "I listened till the sounds did not seem like music, but like the moaning of children. It seemed as if my heart would burst. I rose from my sitting posture, and knelt. A streak of moonlight was on the floor before me, and in the midst of it appeared the forms of my two children. They vanished; but I had seen them distinctly. Some will call it a dream, others a vision. I know not how to account for it, but it made a strong impression on my mind, and I felt certain something had happened to my little ones" (107–8). His vindictiveness backed by the force of southern law, Flint frustrates Brent's desires to shelter, nurture, and protect—in essence, to be a mother for—her children. In the dark about their whereabouts and legal fate, she only has imaginary access to them. "I had seen their spirits in my room" (108), she says, but the miraculous sight proves cold and unsatisfying since it fails to clarify their social identity or institutional location. Spirit communication confuses the serenity of death with the anguish of slavery's social death. Are her children at last beyond the slave power? Or, have they been purchased as chattel by their father to be freed? Does Flint retain possession of her son and daughter in order to exert control over Linda even in her fugitive status? Her trance is a phantasmatic yet still historical record of her anxiety "whether my children were dead, or whether they were sold" (108). Against a sentimental discourse of the afterlife, Brent wonders whether her children are socially dead or simply dead.

Even as she concedes that many will label Brent's experience a "dream" or "vision," Jacobs refuses to dismiss this manifestation of her children as otherworldly. In her mind, the spiritual does not represent an escape from history; the occult comes to her as a distressing echo of Flint's spite in particular and the slave system in general, both of which hold her hopes for Benny and Ellen hostage. Their spirits are not dead but full of historical life. Her trance is manifestation of an Africanist heritage, not an offshoot of popular spiritualism in vogue among her northern "sisters." Readers of *Incidents*, assumes Jacobs, will find that the description of her dematerialized children "illustrates the superstition of the slaves" (107). She goads readers to identify this paranormal episode as an element of slave culture and not as a version of occult disembodiment associated with a white, liberal public sphere. Slave superstition is not conducive to manifestations of generic personhood in which the vague contours of identity would seem to guarantee equality. Far from it: her trance invokes the specific persons of her children who suffer under a regime of inequality. In Jacobs's hands, the occult evasion of sociohistorical phenomena associated with the public sphere is revised as a confrontation that affirms ties to her displaced children and heritage.

If the master's property temporarily manifests itself as spirit, then Brent herself runs the risk of becoming a permanent absence in the lives of her children. Although freezing temperatures, insect bites, and atrophied muscles painfully remind the fugitive that she does have a body, Linda in the attic garret figuratively occupies the position of a maternal spirit hovering above the home made popular in white melodrama.[32] As a socially dead slave mother Linda Brent watches over her children's welfare, but she resists the saccharine pull of spiritualization that would idealize disembodiment at the expense of her own culturally specific maternity. She confesses to Ellen the historical conditions that dictate her ghostlike presence in her children's lives: "I took her in my arms and told her I was slave, and that was the reason she must never say she had seen me" (140). Mother teaches daughter how her fugitive status demands that they consent to a lack of presence. Significantly, however, Brent is careful to explain that this temporary dematerialization occurs as her daughter "nestled in my arms" (140). Ellen's touch confirms that her mother, who has been disappeared, does possess a social presence and belongs to a network of familial relations. Absent motherhood rests on tactics of repression mandated by slave law. The spiritual is not eternal; instead, disembodied mothers are a matter of historical necessity.

Amid collisions of abolitionism and spiritualism, Jacobs essays to withstand the interiorization of political reform that occurs in nineteenth-century occult public spheres. She writes with the possibility that the occult can foreground the often invisible hierarchies that extend the privileges of disembodiment only to a select few. Under the "black arts" of the occult, the spiritual is reinvested with political vibrancy much as socially dead slave children are reanimated in a moonlight vision.

VEILED HISTORY

Readers of Jacobs's slave narrative are also readers of a slave body, a fact that tends to deauthorize her intervention in spiritual matters. Fearful that readers will doubt her account of numbed joints and crippled limbs even as they give credence to sexual myths about black women, she admits to the dubiousness of Brent's story: "I hardly expect that the reader will credit me, when I affirm that I lived in that little dismal hole, almost deprived of light and air, and with no space to move my limbs, for nearly seven years. But is a fact; and to me a sad one, even now; for my body still suffers from the effects of that long imprisonment, to say nothing of my soul. Members of my family, now living in New York and Boston, can testify to the truth of what I say" (148). She invokes her body to exempt her soul. Using the language of an affidavit, Brent offers material evidence for her history while placing the spiritual beyond fuller discussion ("to say nothing of my soul"). She calls on "members of my family" to rescue her—this time from an unspecific history that would incorporate her into ritual displays of white liberal psychology. Deployed as living legal evidence, her body withstands sublimation. "To say nothing of my soul" amounts to a political stance in a sentimental culture that beseeches the oppressed to speak in spiritualist tones so that the enfranchised can forget the material nature of the ideological structures that secure their own privilege. Except that "to say nothing of my soul" is an apophasis that summons up the soul via understatement.[33] The magnitude of the soul's suffering is so great as to defy description. Her soul may exceed representation but not historicity.

In the doubleness of this expression that both foregrounds and veils the soul, Brent registers the contingency of black spiritual beliefs within a dominant culture that has shown itself all too disposed to adopt and abstract blackness to effect white disembodiment. To say "nothing" is to make a statement that documents repression; by speaking of the difficulty of talking about the soul Brent suggests the specific and conflicted discursive history, which shapes the ahistorical entities—ghosts, spirits, souls—that materialize and dematerialize in the pages of *Incidents*. She can say "nothing" of the soul because, according to the assumptions of white spiritualism, it has no social substance or historical texture. The soul that stands impervious to discussion memorializes the disappearance of history that attends the spiritual. Her simultaneously invoked and uninvoked soul serves as a figure of history, ambivalently marking the not there, the forgotten, the veiled as the very real stuff that predates history.

PEDAGOGY AND POLITICAL IDENTITY

Incidents tackles the soul as a deeply contested category invested with the double potential of democratic memory and the reproduction of privileged disembodiment. Jacobs's autobiography supplies lessons for unveiling the political valence of a putatively postpolitical sphere. Her pedagogy is important to keep in mind as the soul has made a comeback as a site of political commentary, especially in critiques of higher education in the United States. Jacobs provides an important caution to those who would seek to revitalize the humanities and its democratic commitments by appealing to spiritualized notions of interiority. Even though critics who invoke a discourse of the soul to intervene in debates about higher education, aesthetic value, and revisionist pedagogy are unabashedly political, their invocations fail to construe the soul as a historical category with material effects and thus ultimately tend to move beyond contestation by settling on a postpolitical orientation.

As a project for cultivating democratic citizenship, higher education has lost its way amid the production and maintenance of professional managerial culture, corporatization, overspecialization, arcane theoretical language, identity politics, and research at the expense of teaching. So charge its critics, many of whom offer the spirit as an emancipatory counterpoint for universities and colleges that, in their view, have been overrun by one or more of these factors. An emptiness haunts academia and, according to Robert Young, "spiritual well-being is a by-product instead of a main result of a public college education. When they look up to the stars, students in these colleges will not have heaven pointed out to them."[34]

Over and against an educational system that traffics in worldly affairs, both pundits and critics recall the foundational mission of guiding students through a process of internal discovery and personal transformation. In *Killing the Spirit: Higher Education in America,* for instance, Page Smith seeks to emancipate the university from the military-industrial complex and biotechnological corporations by recovering an image of the academy as unencumbered by federal grant money and corporate research dollars. His complaint charges that "universities sold their souls some time ago" and now are abandoned to the "spiritual aridity" and "spiritual illness of 'post-modernism.'"[35] Reference to the spirit comes as a tactic to defy the current material conditions that constrain imagination and free inquiry. But as a spiritual endeavor, the cultivation of democratic subjectivity attains a quasi-mystical status that removes identity, politics, and pedagogy beyond the ken of democratic contestation.

Echoing Smith's cosmic appeal to disentangle knowledge from the grips of capital and identity politics, Roger Shattuck highlights the spiritual as part of his "Nineteen Theses on Literature," a rambling manifesto that strives to deliver the arts and humanities from interdisciplinarity and identity politics. The path to human freedom lies in an admission that "there may be more than material nature and human nature."[36] In both Smith's leftist jeremiad and Shattuck's conservative polemic, the spiritual represents a calculated gambit to imagine an alternative political reality. Only by using a language that is not embarrassed to employ words like "spiritual" and "transcendent," argues Shattuck, can we overcome postmodern culture's degenerative path toward philistinism.

While refusing Shattuck's siege mentality, George Levine similarly suggests that as the aesthetic overwhelms us by contact with "what might be called the beautiful or the sublime" we approach its liberatory potential.[37] Levine's engagement with questions of art's ideological complicity and resistance nonetheless shares the postpolitical vision of Shattuck's ad hominem attack by identifying literature and art as irreducible domains that ultimately evade worldly limitations and surpass historical conditions. From Smith's liberal critique of the state's influence on university education to Shattuck's and Levine's recuperative aesthetics, the spiritual bears the promise of revitalizing democratic citizenship for an enlightened public sphere. Yet this pedagogy remains suffused by hierarchy: for those who invoke the soul and other putatively transcendent locations as sites of an alternative political epistemology, emancipation depends on minimizing a materialist focus on socioeconomic inequality or racial injustice while overdetermining a "higher" focus on spiritual equality. The question is not whether the spiritual is political; rather, we need to ask what sort of politics are deployed (and delayed) by invocations of the spirit. Does a liberatory pedagogy apply only to those subjects who consent to a dispossession of historical knowledge? Does the soul's emancipation depend on a barely visible regulatory apparatus that makes citizens equal by dematerializing—and forgetting—their unequal memories? In short, does a spiritual hierarchy constitute the prehistory of an abstract public sphere of supposedly open and equal access?

A similar concern with "hierarchical structure" leads Jane Tompkins to champion a pedagogy concerned with "students' emotional, physical, and spiritual lives."[38] Negotiating schismatic views of education as either an ethical concern for social justice or as an ethos for self-fulfillment, Tompkins's autobiographical *A Life in School* agitates for an educational system that will nourish "the whole human organism, emotions, body, and spirit, as well as mind."[39] The academy has had a hard time validating this New Age pedagogy. "Goofy," "lightweight," "laughable": these adjectives are used to describe Tompkins's book in a *Chronicle of Higher Education* article on scholars' reluctance to reflect on the spirit, to address questions beyond those of realpolitik. As one skeptical reader of *A Life in School* puts it, "I'm a Marxist and a materialist. . . . I'm uncomfortable with the language of spirituality. I don't know what it means."[40]

Rather than declare our ignorance before "spirituality" and render it a blank cipher, we need to assess how the discourse of the spirit produces a barrage of material conditions that make possible hierarchy as well as emancipation. It remains crucial to figure out how and what spirituality means: my approach here in reading *Incidents* as political critique informed by both historical materialism and historical spiritualism has been to examine how the soul and other pretensions to spiritual equality create a hierarchized public sphere that seems beyond either hierarchy or public contestation. Although Tompkins turns her attention to less material considerations, she seems unconcerned with how power is implicated in the rhetoric of spirituality. She examines neither the entitlement nor the institutional privilege that enables her to appeal to the spirit as a point of critique. What is the source of entitlement that allows her to occupy a disembodied position that dispenses with materialist considerations? Tompkins's sensitive curriculum imagines an alternative pedagogy, but as an epistemological claim her intervention is not subjected to an analysis that sees either inner life or spirituality as luxuries that are productive of power, as vocabularies that condition her own narrative of the university. We need to think not just about souls as Tompkins would have it, but about souls that matter to the construction of a public sphere that disembodies subjects.

Insofar as twenty-first-century democracy, like the ideal of a rational public sphere, is an illusion, it is one that depends on conditions that remain unrealized. This illusion is nonetheless vital because it offers citizens a counterimaginary that resists the social injustice and material inequity that have become all too real and accepted in our worlds. But if we are going to hold on to radical democratic prospects, we need to remember that not everyone has equal access to imagine them. The capacity to think of a better place—whether in the gritty terms of an alternative politics for this world or the sublime rhetoric of a ghostly otherworld—privileges persons who already enjoy the luxury of being more equal than others. The freedom to theorize democracy, like possession of an unmarked generic presence in public, remains opaque and unexamined. If allowed to stand beyond contestation, freedom appears as postpolitical and democracy becomes either an interior quest or a spiritual project. Rather than repeat familiar oppositions between body and soul or politics and the spiritual, we need to practice a pedagogy of citizenship, one suggested in part by *Incidents,* that remembers how disembodiment and other privileges are unequally distributed in the construction of political identities.

NOTES

1 A. E. Newton, *The Educator: Being Suggestions, Theoretical and Practical Designed to Promote Man-Culture and Integral Reform, with a View to the Ultimate Establishment of a Divine Social State on Earth. Comprised in a series of Revealments from Organized*

Associations in the Spirit-Life, through John Murray Spear vol. 1 (Boston: Office of Practical Spiritualists, 1857), 1: 394–95. The list of spiritualist and mesmerist tracts and books that make interventions in governmental policy and provide democratic commentary is both exhaustive and eclectic. From testimonies of Abraham Lincoln's participation in séances to transcripts of conversations with the departed soul of John Quincy Adams, the occult was politically charged. These sources are treated more thoroughly in my *Necro Citizenship: Death, Eroticism, and the Public Sphere in the Nineteenth-Century United States* (Durham: Duke University Press, 2001).

2 Barbara Cruikshank, *The Will to Empower: Democratic Citizens and Other Subjects* (Ithaca: Cornell University Press, 1999), 2, 124.

3 Harriet A. Jacobs, *Incidents in the Life of a Slave Girl*, ed. Jean Fagan Yellin (Cambridge: Harvard University Press, 1987). Subsequent citations are given parenthetically in the text.

4 Jürgen Habermas, *The Structural Transformation of the Public Sphere: An Inquiry into a Category of Bourgeois Society*, trans. Thomas Burger (Cambridge: MIT Press, 1989), 54.

5 Walter Lippmann, *Essays in the Public Philosophy* (Boston: Little, Brown, 1955), 14, 106, 142.

6 Karl Marx and Frederick Engels, *The Holy Family, or Critique of Critical Critique*, trans. R. Dixon (Moscow: Foreign Languages Publishing House, 1956), 164.

7 Karl Marx, *Capital, Volume 1*, in *The Marx-Engels Reader*, 2nd ed., ed. Robert C. Tucker (New York: Norton, 1972), 320.

8 Karl Marx, *The Eighteenth Brumaire of Louis Bonaparte* (New York: International Publishers, 1963), 15.

9 Marx and Engels, *The Holy Family*, 201.

10 Sacvan Bercovitch, "Afterword," in *Ideology and Classic American Literature*, ed. Sacvan Bercovitch and Myra Jehlen (Cambridge: Cambridge University Press, 1986), 432.

11 Judith Butler, *Bodies That Matter: On the Discursive Limits of "Sex"* (New York: Routledge, 1993), ix, 17, 4.

12 Critics attentive to the vexed placement of black women within white domestic traditions have mapped the narrow, cramped space allotted for representations of the materiality of the black female body within a northern sentimental discourse that privileged inner feeling over physical suffering. Once emphasized, the slave body becomes overemphasized, leading, as Mauri Skinful observes, to the "construction of black women as mere bodies" ("Nation and Miscegenation: *Incidents in the Life of a Slave Girl*," *Arizona Quarterly* 52 [summer 1995]: 71). Sandra Gunning notes that in dominant regimes of representation black women's bodies lapse into "the grossly physical," becoming "fetishized" as an indelicate corporeality against which white women imagine their own disembodied moral virtue ("Reading and Redemption in *Incidents in the Life of a Slave Girl*," in *Harriet Jacobs and Incidents in the Life of a Slave Girl: New Critical Essays*, ed. Deborah M. Garfield and Rafia Zafar [Cambridge: Cambridge University Press, 1996], 137, 135).

13 Butler, *Bodies That Matter*, 257 n.44.

14 "Message Department," *Banner of Light: A Weekly Journal of Literature and General Intelligence* 22 (August 27, 1864): 6. Shindler's text in part presents itself as a series of conversations between the medium and disembodied southerners. Confederate soldiers and plantation slaves equally visit the séances, seeking consolation from the spirit-rappers who they beseech to sing familiar tunes like "Dixie." The spiritual world convened by Shindler's clairvoyance seems dedicated not only to recuperating the voices of the dead but also the cultural forms of a dead social order.

15 J. B. Ferguson, *Spirit Communion: A Record of Communications from the Spirit-Spheres with Incontestable Evidence of Personal Identity, Presented to the Public, with Explanatory Observations* (Nashville: Union and American Steam Press, 1855), 51.

16 Isaac Post, *Voices from the Spirit World, Being Communications from Many Spirits. By the Hand of Isaac Post, Medium* (Rochester: Charles H. McDonnell, 1852), 168.

17 Orlando Patterson, *Slavery and Social Death: A Comparative Study* (Cambridge: Harvard University Press, 1982).

18 African American spirituals have to be distinguished from the rhetoric of white spiritualism. As several commentators have argued, African American spirituals are not solely concerned with the hereafter in ways that are dismissive of specific historical pressures. See Albert J. Raboteau, *Slave Religion: The "Invisible Institution" in the Antebellum South* (New York: Oxford University Press, 1978), 246; Lawrence W. Levine, *Black Culture and Black Consciousness: Afro-American Thought from Slavery to Freedom* (New York: Oxford University Press, 1977), 174; James H. Cone, "Black Theology as Liberation Theology," in *African American Religious Studies: An Interdisciplinary Anthology,* ed. Gayraud Wilmore, (Durham: Duke University Press, 1989), 177–207; and Eric J. Sundquist, *To Wake the Nations: Race in the Making of American Literature* (Cambridge: Harvard University Press, 1993), 458.

19 On Jacobs's residence in the Posts' home and Amy Post's political activities, see Jean Fagan Yellin, "Introduction," in *Incidents in the Life of a Slave Girl,* xvi–xvii.

20 Harriet Jacobs to Amy Post and Isaac Post, June 16, 1861, quoted in *Incidents,* 248. Although Jacobs does not give Leah's last name, she is almost certainly talking about Leah Fish, neé Fox, the elder sister of Kate and Margaret, who organized and managed the girls' public mediumship and later claimed clairvoyant powers herself.

21 Post, *Voices from the Spirit World,* 36, 39.

22 Although no evidence exists that Amy Post indiscreetly revealed to Isaac the details of her sisterly confidences with Jacobs, Linda Brent does suspect that her sexual history becomes a topic of conversation between at least one respectable married couple. On her arrival in Philadelphia, she divulges to Mr. Durham that she is a mother but not a wife, a confession that replays the moment when, as Jacobs said in a letter to Amy Post, "your purity of heart and kindly sympathies won me at one time to speak of my children" (Harriet Jacobs to Amy Post [1852?], quoted in *Incidents,* 232). The morning after Linda's disclosure, she takes leave of Durham's wife and wonders "whether her husband had repeated to her what I told him. I suppose he had" (162). Her doubts well apply to Amy and Isaac Post, especially since Isaac's mediumistic contact with a disembodied female soul echoes the narrative of gaps and silences found in *Incidents.*

23 Post, *Voices from the Spirit World*, 131. To suggest such parallels between the history of Harriet Jacobs and the ghost story in *Voices from the Spirit World* is not to ignore the fact that Post's spirit narrative is based on the historical events that befell a village girl named Sarah Sharp. For the sensationally rendered details of this story, see D. M. Dewey, *The History of Charles Edwards and Sarah Sharp: Being an Authentic Account of the Horrible Penfield Tragedy, Which Took Place January 26, 1851, together with the Particulars of the Causes Which Led to It, Including the Coroner's Inquest, in Full* (Rochester: D. M. Dewey, 1851). This history provides Post the content for his narrative of tragic female sexuality; in Harriet Jacobs's autobiography he found a form and style for representing and omitting problematic scenes of female embodiment.

24 Valerie Smith, " 'Loopholes of Retreat': Architecture and Ideology in Harriet Jacobs's *Incidents in the Life of a Slave Girl*," in *Reading Black, Reading Feminist: A Critical Anthology*, ed. Henry Louis Gates Jr. (New York: Meridian, 1990), 213.

25 Post, *Voices from the Spirit World*, 133.

26 Ibid., 132, 133.

27 Dana D. Nelson, *The Word in Black and White: Reading "Race" in American Literature, 1638–1867* (New York: Oxford University Press, 1993), 142.

28 Post, *Voices from the Spirit World*, 132.

29 Avery Gordon, *Ghostly Matters: Haunting and the Sociological Imagination* (Minneapolis: University of Minnesota Press, 1997), 195, 190. As Linda contemplates resistance, she seems haunted by spirits, specifically those of her mother and father, in ways that suggest the tangibility of her historical memory. "In many an hour of tribulation I had seemed to hear her [her mother's] voice, sometimes chiding me, and sometimes whispering loving words" (90). Later she hears her father's voice coming from Edenton's black graveyard.

30 Frantz Fanon, *The Wretched of the Earth*, trans. Constance Farrington (1961; New York: Grove Weidenfeld, 1963), 55–56.

31 Thomas R. Gray, *The Confessions of Nat Turner*, in *Nat Turner's Slave Rebellion. Together with the Full Text of the So-Called "Confessions" of Nat Turner Made in Prison in 1831*, ed. Herbert Aptheker (New York: Humanities Press, 1966), 136.

32 Without revealing her physical form, she watches her son and daughter from above. "As the 'disembodied' matron who must literally watch her children from above, Brent ridicules Northern white metaphoric self-construction (abolitionists supposedly watch over the slaves) as 'maternal' saviors," writes Gunning in "Reading and Redemption," 147.

33 Apophasis is a rhetorical device that denies an intention to speak of a subject which is at the same time specified or insinuated.

34 Robert B. Young, *No Neutral Ground: Standing by the Values We Prize in Higher Education* (San Francisco: Jossey-Bass, 1997), 141.

35 Page Smith, *Killing the Spirit: Higher Education in America* (New York: Viking, 1990), 13, 20, 5.

36 Roger Shattuck, *Candor and Perversion: Literature, Education, and the Arts* (New York: Norton, 1999), 4.

37 George Levine, "Introduction: Reclaiming the Aesthetic," in *Aesthetics and Ideology,*
ed. George Levine (New Brunswick: Rutgers University Press, 1994), 4; see also 22.

38 Jane Tompkins, *A Life in School: What the Teacher Learned* (Reading, Mass.: Addison-
Wesley, 1996), 215.

39 Ibid., xii.

40 Alison Schneider, "Jane Tompkins' Message to Academe: Nurture the Individual, Not
Just the Intellect" *Chronicle of Higher Education,* July 10, 1998. Tompkins's position is
more complex than such critiques suggest. "I wanted to never lose sight of the fleshy,
desiring selves who were engaged in discussing hegemony or ideology," she writes in
"Pedagogy of the Distressed," *College English* 52 (October 1990): 658.

LAUREN BERLANT

Uncle Sam Needs a Wife: Citizenship and Denegation

◆

At some level, presidents aren't supposed to have feelings.
—Bill Clinton, August 9, 2000

INTRODUCTION: BODIES POLITIC

"Body politic" suggests an indefinite mass, but it is more like a poster display of a steer already segmented into the commercial names of beef—with some cuts more valued than others. Embedded in its various parts are signs suggesting that these divisions and hierarchies of value emerge naturally from the beast's flesh. But in the imaginary register, the idea of the beast—the body politic—persists *without a body.* It is abstract and impersonal, a zone of humanity without humans. This is its promise and, indeed, its utopianism. It achieves shape only by association with particular state projects and kinds of person (the "cuts" of meat). From this perspective, political identity is a relation, not a thing: a relation not among things but among repetitions. What looks like "the people," "the citizenship form," or any type of politically identifiable person is really an aftereffect of reading events in a certain way. Thus the question, "What makes something an event or a nonevent?" is the counterpart of two other questions: "What makes someone a person or a nonperson?" and "What makes a norm into a form?"

Many scholars, including myself, have described this tripartite relation in terms of an antinomy between abstract universality and embodied particularity. These discussions tend to focus on the mirage of universality, so figured because the national subject legally protected as an abstract individual with human rights has had privileged material access to land and wealth precisely by virtue of his body, or should I say bodies—his hereditary body, his racial one, his masculine one, his heterofamilial one.[1] In contrast, the story goes, categorically embodied or particularized subjects, who are initially members not of the electorate but of what we might call the *particulate*, have long experienced having a legally zoned body that is an obstacle to the privilege of abstract valuation, whether in the form of full citizenship, social membership, or both. Recently, I have been rethinking this distinction between the universal and the particular in order to provide more heft to "particularity," a category that has been enumerated ad infinitum and yet whose swelling with detail has not amounted to its conceptualization except as the Other to the universal. Detail seems to be an obstacle to conceptualization, just as historically embodiments have organized the impediments to full citizenship.

In this essay I argue for a different understanding of political form, seeing it more as an outcome of repetition and convention than as an emanation from or projection onto things such as institutions and persons. My purpose is not to elevate the particular over the universal as a value; here I agree with Balibar and others that the content of the "human" of which liberal universalism is the theory must not be ceded to those who already benefit from it. Instead, I focus on the formalist pedagogies of liberal democracy, which train citizens to bargain for political optimism by consenting to read the details of national/democratic failure as evidence of successes said to be imminent in its political form.

I attend to the relationship between the normative affect of liberal optimism and ongoing structural violence, and tell some stories about a wish behind citizenship and other metacultural or nationally unifying forms that have long organized democratic will, struggle, and imagination. This desire (liberal formalism) is shaped by a phantom model of an unconflicted yet complex world, which heralds a good life that is yet to be made by law, by capital, or in social practice. In this liberal world of sovereign states and individualities, we witness the alchemical fantasy of concepts such as the "nation," "citizenship," "family," or the umbrella notion of "the good life" itself. Through these terms, opposing realities are supposed to find mechanisms for negotiating and neutralizing potentially threatening contradictions. National futurism grows from the promise of this overcoming. In this essay I focus on two such mechanisms. I track a broad shift from mass political investments in the juridical form of the vote to the current norm in which the collective witnessing of mass-mediated violence performs the body politic for itself. The first mechanism originates in the rule of liberal law, and is evidenced in the expansion of enfranchisement to include historically subordinated groups in the United States. The second taps into more archaic and more modern ways of experiencing national belonging, ways that neither enforce the equation of universality with the "human" as such nor locate material history in the codified qualities wrought by subjects' repeated encounters with power. Instead, I argue, national collectivity is now marked in a movement across the *sacro-political,* organized around a *sacred* iconicity of the political body, and the *sarco-political,* organized around the *flesh* of those deemed not to have the capacity to overcome their historic banishment from normative social membership. At the extreme, neither the sacro- nor the sarco-subject is deemed an ordinary human: yet in mass projections onto their destiny can be read concepts of ordinary personhood in the polis. Such a formalist genealogy will enable us to tell a conceptually quite different story about citizenship in the United States than the one that adjudicates universals and particulars. The analysis will link the long story of citizenship's privatization to the differential in scale that measures the consequences of bodily jeopardy for the overlapping but distinct populations of the U.S. body politic.

I am not concerned, then, with authoritarian regimes that admit violent hierarchy as a given in collective life but with forms of the liberal-hegemonic, those structures of consent that require ruling alliances to affix citizens to a political world that passes as worthy of optimism and self-idealization. Gramsci calls these consensual sites the machinery of "passive revolution," and one might add that formalism—the belief in the intelligibility of the liberal nation-state and promise/privilege of rights—is central to the reproduction of democratic sovereignty in the hegemonic mode.[2] The forms that are deemed indexical to an agreed-on standard of the good life might derive from popular memory, opinion, or the state: their proximity to the promise of protective and reparative law is central to the attractiveness of liberal hegemonic devices.

In the United States, juridical fetishism upholds the possibility of reparation for what look like the uninevitable harms of democratic culture—harms that are deemed not forms of repetitive injury but accidents of history, personal failures, and the like. Legal logic requires as well that harms be represented through "events," which means that particular instances of ordinary violence linked to structural subjection must be phrased as discontinuous from the political world in which these events take place. Even class action suits require individual participants to make and potentially benefit from a claim based on a particular unjust event. Likewise, the proactive or transformational effects of liberal law require citizens to encounter it one conscience at a time. From this perspective structural violence can appear only as a bad event in a domain of good theory. Just as the state has to be seen as being like a person who has good intentions, the good citizen appears as the subject who wants to rid the world of the bad, merging political viscera into political sense, which then seems like a true feeling or instinct.[3] The truth of the disciplined and educated political instinct, and its simultaneous equation with and superiority to rational self-reflection, is in this sense central to the optimistic affective norms of national-liberal hegemony.

What does it mean to argue that the formal guarantee of the liberal nation-state, with its assurance that the good life both has been achieved and is imminent in the sovereignty of just law, atrophies the critical desire to interfere with the reproduction of ordinary violence, violence that cannot be summarized but only symbolized in the discrete event? By ordinary violence I indicate actual and social death as well as the taken-for-granted negation of subordinate populations, those outcomes of social hierarchy that are a feature of capitalist democracies but that are rarely deemed a hardwired feature. Historically subordinated populations are always marked with the expectation that subordination is their destiny. Indeed, democratic fantasy—the thought that anyone in the United States can overcome a default (structural) adversity—presumes structural inequality. In part this has to do with the capitalist and monocultural terms in which "overcoming" is measured. Even if it is true in theory that class mobility and "minority" absorption into a general mass are possible, structural subordinations generally provide the content to the default story that one overcomes. But overcoming as a process of historical transformation—achieving a life beyond what is probable according to the event of identity—means something different at the scale of the individual rather than the social "detail." The relation between material, symbolic, and individual transformation is ever mutable and uneven in any case.

I open my archive with woman suffrage, a moment of tremendous optimism for the power of national culture to repair its own juridical errors. Particular states allowed women to vote in all but federal elections starting around the turn of the century. Not until 1916 were most women (whites and African Americans, not Asians, for example) deemed full citizens of nations and states and permitted to vote federally. *Uncle Sam Needs a Wife* (1925) is a citizenship training manual that was published almost a decade after women received the vote.[4] Its purpose was to reshape women's feelings about the privilege of their hard-won citizenship, not seeing the vote as citizenship achieved but as citizenship now possible. This manual, like so many produced during the century's first three decades, narrates incoherently the myriad ways that the entry of women into the body politic might transform both the nation and women. Incoherence itself does not invalidate the power of the franchise, though; political and social worlds are inevitably built across fault lines of contradiction and bad conceptualization that seem somehow not to threaten the general project. In the United States, the vote became the prize agreed on by a coalition of radicals, reformers, and social conservatives, even as they imagined a quite divergent range of social transformations to be the consequence.

In contrast, in the contemporary United States the political event of the vote and the citizenship form it expresses no longer organizes citizens' and national inhabitants' optimism for or sense of national belonging.[5] Instead, citizenship is now measured in the broader sense of social membership and is more likely to be enacted in responses to events in mass culture, especially those signifying evidence of democratic "accident" or ongoing violence—for example, Rodney King, the Thomas-Hill hearings, and O. J. Simpson. The centrality of sarco-political—racial and sexual—identities to this grouping is overdetermined but not haphazard. In these scenes universalist law is challenged to overcome itself, *to do the right thing.* At the same time the law is being judged by the entire body politic—which may disagree violently as to the terms of that judgment but which is seeing the same *scene*—as to whether the law can respond adequately to what can only be implied in the event, its exemplarity. This disjuncture enables broader discussion of the relation of structural violence to individual instance, and at the same time places pressure on conscience to generate the right opinion that might be obscure to the law. Does this mean that the body politic now "votes" for national continuity by investing in events of violence and death? What relation can we track between the democracy of death and the hierarchy of events that seems not, in the end, to verify universalism as abstraction but as the relative weight of the embodied detail made generally visible through suffering? In other words, what does the postpolitical citizenship form suggest about the destinies of the *particulate,* whose bodies now possess the franchise but not, as it were, its full promise of abstraction? Arguing that the contemporary subject becomes at its most collective postpolitically by reanimating the more archaic logic of sacred embodiment, this paper suggests that woman suffrage was a key switchpoint between an electoral model of legitimacy to the privatized sentimental one.

MAKING UP (WOMEN) CITIZENS

Between 1865 and 1920, the U.S. political public sphere was cracked open like a fresh egg whose purpose was to leak sovereignty onto the then formally excluded occupants of the United States; the model of political and social membership that dominated the formalist public imaginary was enfranchisement.⁶ To be enfranchised was to be free to vote, to self-alienate a political opinion; it was to be deemed a citizen who could self-represent autonomously and therefore be represented. Etymologically, suffrage indicates the capacity to express oneself in public; to receive suffrage was to be deemed competent to full participation in national culture as a holder of property and opinion. The capacity to hold and to alienate these private properties was what democracy seemed to secure. This is to say that the franchise was the *form* of alienable expression that confirmed a subject's political existence, like breath on a mirror. It established the citizen as evolved beyond the flesh—not dead, politically speaking.

The history of civil rights in the United States shows that gaining the franchise is both an event and a process, a zone of individualization that always crackles with contingency. Thus it is that the African American men who were enfranchised as abstract individuals by the Fourteenth Amendment struggled for another century until the "qualifications" to vote were no longer read right off of the body.⁷ Despite having the formal franchise, gays and lesbians remain excluded from many of the property protections allowed to American heterosexuals. Reproductive and labor safety laws formally speak to generic rights of citizens while actually designating women not of childbearing age, proletarian whites, and people of color as relatively disposable. Still, the franchise is the precise difference between zero and one for members of a historically excluded population: it changes the conditions of survival in relation to the domain of justice. No matter how small an event or gesture of agency, the vote not only signals something like full formal belonging to the body politic but registers a grounding that enables subjects to move across time and space, regardless of their particular or individual genealogies. I mean this concretely. The vote means that someone lives somewhere both local and national and that the experience of one's life matters in that sense, potentially reverberating within the expressed self-interest of "a constituency." It also provides a kind of paper identity, verifying for local, national, and international law the individual's distinguishing marks. Like the signature, the fingerprint, and the photographed right ear, the voter's registration confirms that someone was in fact at a jurisdictional place at a proper official time (at birth and at naturalization, for example).⁸

Since the 1840s, thousands of citizenship training manuals have been generated in the United States for the purpose of making both native-born and immigrant occupants literate in national culture and its various locales: states, townships, counties, school districts, villages, and so on.⁹ Produced by federal, state, and local governments for immigrants, students, and the military, and by private organizations for immigrants and new citizens like women and children, these manuals provide for us an image of the nation as it is imagined to be. What kinds of citizen subjectivity do these texts generate, and what images of a common culture are enfranchised by the vote?

A manual is a pragmatic pedagogic genre: a transformational environment in which abstract and bodily knowledge actually merge to change an object into something different and yet more itself—in this case, into a socially intelligible form of person whose politico-ethical sensorium is in the right order. The citizenship manual's technologies of the self are manifested through inculcated gestures and taken-for-granted repetitions that enable the emerging subject to seem continuous with her intention, her identity, her public qualities, and her agency, in the intelligible terms and values of civil society. Thus one might say that the law of the genre is to teach the subject how to pass as having always been a full citizen. Of course, the authors of these texts dedicated to women are as likely to argue that women's enfranchisement will change nothing socially as they are to envision an imminent feminine revolution in national morality and purity. But to work either of these scenarios the woman citizen must make her practice of mental and practical discipline so habitual that it will appear as the unity of her character and her essence.

The genre performs the desire to effect this appearance in a number of ways, rhetorically and ideologically speaking. Because it is a didactic form, the primer does not have to hide its pedagogy. But while focused on information communication, its pedagogy amalgamates many other normative associations as well.[10] For example, in terms of explicit tonality and address the manuals addressed to a generic citizen tend to conflate women, children, African Americans, and immigrants. They are all deemed to know nothing about the political world into which they are entering, presumably because such knowledge is inculcated only on a need-to-know basis. Rhetorically, these civics texts evoke a combination of baby talk and the image of an English speaker who, on encountering a foreigner, tries to communicate by yelling loudly and slowly in English. These are not merely metaphoric associations: just as immigration law placed pressure on the status of native-born enfranchisement at the turn of the century, so too was newly compulsory public education of previously excluded minorities and women cause and effect of constitutional change. Frequently, when the handbooks presuppose their utility as textbooks, they presume such multiple audiences, whose differences become nullified through the metacultural form of the nation and the juridical form of the vote. But the dehumanizing species associations among women, blacks, and the poor continue to emit a powerful vibe as well, as their ignorance and "inclination to measure everything in terms of the personal" suggests subcivilization, the negative reign of instinct over thought.[11]

At the same time, the citizen comes increasingly to be viewed as a psychological subject: especially the middle-class woman. The majority of the early-century citizenship manuals addressed to women come forth just as therapy culture begins to saturate the periodical culture addressed to "woman" as already expressing "her interests." Many suffrage manuals, plays, and novels, for example, associate the politically uninformed or disenfranchised woman with severe states of lethargy and depression, the turning inward of atrophied social energy.[12] "The social diseases and the economic diseases from which women are suffering are as distinctly women's diseases as are those of the physical body."[13] *Uncle Sam Needs a Wife* critiques women soundly for their political passivity, calling it narcissism: "See [women] plunging idly through superficial studies of superficial subjects under hypnotic headings while wars and strikes go on!"[14] It argues that as a result women become masochistic and bitter toward each other, refuse the challenges of difficult knowledge, and attach to trivial pursuits and other dissipation.

This is why education was deemed so central to the political cultivation of women's practical expertise. Women's *impractical* lack of knowledge engenders an image of what *Uncle Sam Needs a Wife* calls a political "moron" and an "idiot." In this hyperbole resonates a longer struggle within the movement about what it means to be constructing a citizen as someone who is formally educated. During the suffrage struggles of the late nineteenth century, the phrase "educated suffrage" marked a compromise developed by white middle-class suffrage activists. The purveyors of this model of suffrage meant to sacrifice working-class women of all races in order to gain patriarchal approval. It tapped into the hegemonic embrace of particularized universalism by admitting the presumption of "qualifications" to notions of the abstract individual with rights.[15] Despite this resonance, however, African American activists who refused such a compromise nonetheless lectured widely on the need to educate black women to the demands of citizenship. For some, education did not mean separation from the totality of black people but uplift for all; while for others, suffrage activism involved elevating black women over black men deemed incompetent to citizenship during the nightmare of reconstruction. In any case, all understood the importance of the deliberate dissemination of the tools that would promote African American social and political legitimacy.[16]

Across these different motives to teach women how to be citizens, then, there was the common thought that women are presumed to know nothing. It is astounding to read, over and over, elaborate definitions of the city, the state, the village, the school board, the ballot, the ballot box, the political party, and so on. The she-citizen is deluged by responsibility for the most minor details of bureaucratic process and public-sphere codes of behavior, such as how to write a letter to a congressman (the advice is: be polite). *Uncle Sam* archly notes that men never took classes in citizenship, but that citizenship training schools are being run for women and that women are wasting their time studying what men have taken for granted. At the same time as it hectors women, it elevates what they know. Female complaint rhetoric by women turned toward women, then, is ultimately sympathetic despite the shaming tone. *Uncle Sam* calls the bodily consequences of women's trivialization their mass "inferiority complex" and spends multiple chapters imagining its undoing.

This political development in the terms of therapy culture is itself a product of many forces. First, there were significant transformations in modes and norms of privacy and publicity in these early days of what I've called the "intimate public sphere." Among these would be the invention of national consumer markets in post–World War I culture, whose particular incitement to expertise is addressed—usually implicitly—to middle-class women and mothers. Deploying a distinction typical of the period but unusually explicitly defensive, one manual notes that: "In this connection it is an interesting fact that the woman most interested in voting appear to belong to the respectable middle class. Thus, in a fall election in 1912 the election commissioner of Denver found that in three small, prosperous or rich districts, 2,774, 2,496, and 909 women voted, respectively, while in the crowded 'Red Light' district of those days only 143 women voted and many of these were respectable wives of working men whom necessity forced to live in that section."[17]

Respectability was the key. Respectable women would produce a respectable world; as this example shows, respectability was evidenced more readily through proper sexuality than class location. But above all the therapeutic ghost in the citizenship machine emerges in its normative neutralization of what the structural transformation of women's political legitimacy might mean. "*It is up to every woman to get her ballot's worth,*" one manual writes. "And how do you get your ballot's worth? By application of the very principle you employ in the purchases you make . . . you are an experienced shopper; you are a recognized expert on values; you know quality and how to get quality; you can bargain skillfully; you know how to avoid being cheated. And I'll wager you did not learn to cook without a good cookbook at your elbow."[18] This author calls her text the *Fanny Farmer* of citizenship, a place where practical feminine knowledge is simply put to new use. It becomes a commonplace that woman's practical agency gives her both interest and expertise in engaging the political public sphere as mothers of the race, home economists, and managers of money, crisis, desire, and moral leadership. As a new citizen of the world she will be too busy adapting to the urgencies of consumer desire to have surplus or unwieldy desires that register beyond the normative machinery.

Indeed, the very existence of *Uncle Sam*—published in a panic that women had not sufficiently developed into full citizens even after the franchise was achieved—signals that other stories of sociocultural bargaining might be divined from the minor event of these pamphlets. One of these links the question of women's practical and visceral citizenship education to the pressure placed on U.S. cultural reproduction from the postwar influx of European immigrants, whose women were deemed to be in a better juridical situation than native-born women. Moreover, the return of underemployed military veterans, already decimated by the war's unprecedented brutality, conflicted with the transformation in the greater experience and expectations of the metropolitan women who had taken on greater public responsibility during the war, both in industrial and white-collar contexts. This latter element, usually associated with the post–World War II project of national remasculinization, actually played crucially in the formal political advancement of women, just as John D'Emilio has argued that it did for gay men and lesbians in less politically formal ways.[19]

In addition, at this moment woman suffrage became a part of a general expansion of the conditions of thinkable democratic form in the U.S. political public sphere. An intense education in a variety of potential U.S. socioeconomic destinies was made available. Mary Sumner Boyd's *The Woman Citizen* (1918) spends 50 of its 250 pages describing the platforms of the Socialist, Anti-Saloon, Prohibition, and National parties, along with the Democrats and the Republicans. Each platform is described with dignity, as though creative nonnormative political thought were deemed integral to patriotism itself. In addition, throughout this and many other manuals of the period, arguments for cross-segment alliances, especially around issues of class, are central to the reparative work woman suffrage was claiming it would do for industrialized worker populations, both in the United States and elsewhere. "We are the realists of the sexes," *A Political Handbook for Women* typically observes, explaining women's deeper understanding of more varieties of work.[20] The right of workers to tolerable work environments and adequate pay merged with the older sentimental rhetoric about women's essential and practical linkage to children and to the everyday. As often is the case, sentimentality returns here as a mode of realism that asserts women as best placed to ameliorate the harsh conditions of survival for the economically and politically subordinated. The rise of the international labor movement was crucial to the vitality of woman suffrage in this domain, as the depleted bodies of children and the poor were recognized as kindred symptoms of capitalist democracy's failure.

At the same time, the federal or state governments of Western democracies competitively took up championing the cause of woman suffrage, if not feminism.[21] A progressive stance on woman suffrage was seen to demonstrate a nation's moral and economic superiority to the nations and peoples they sought to dominate: "Woman suffrage is preeminently a war measure," one manual avers. It notes that "Great Britain and Canada have extended suffrage to women . . . [and that] France and Italy have virtually promised to do so," and even that Woodrow Wilson recognized it as crucial to any representation of democracy as the most humane and morally evolved political system.[22] As many historians have shown, and as Gayatri Spivak would have predicted, the tableau of white men saving brown women from brown men in the colonial context was a site for the enunciation of this strategy of U.S. imperial publicity.[23] In any case, by 1920 there is a general consensus that the emancipation of the oppressed woman into formal participation in U.S. democracy is crucial to the conversion what one manual calls women's unused "social capital," their knowledge and expertise, for the global advancement of national life.

These tropes sound rather patriotic. The citizenship manuals authored by and directed toward the white middle classes are critical of national/capitalist violence toward workers, children, and weaker countries. But they express little ambivalence toward the promise of the national, and at a moment where the trauma of world war could easily have made other positions plausible. To some degree, the ironies of strategic universalism were not lost on the white middle-class suffragettes. The author of *Uncle Sam Needs a Wife*, for example, self-mockingly appropriates a flirtatious mode of patriotic critique: "We love you Uncle Sam! Of course we do! Haven't we brought you into the world, and nursed you, and petted you, and spoiled you, and flattered you, and adored you? Haven't we taught you all you know? Haven't we lectured you and tried to reform you when you haven't turned out to be all that we expected you to be? . . . What better fate can befall a likely, promising, but unstable and spoiled young man than marriage to some wise, comprehending, intelligent, devoted woman!"[24] Jokes and lightness of speech are central rhetorical forms of female complaint. *Uncle Sam* is unusual in the lightness of its heavy-handed ridicule of men. But whether ironic or sincere, the citizenship manual directed to women inevitably muffles its critique with consoling references to the ongoing proprieties of married life. Heteronormativity remains the fundamental contradiction in the internally and externally directed pedagogy of the women's citizenship manuals. In the United States, heteronormativity should be understood to describe both white middle-class and "respectable" working-class aspirations to national universality. I do not mean by this that white and African American suffrage workers had no critique of the patriarchal family and capitalist inequalities: quite the contrary. But as a site of consent that secures the intelligibility of a particular image of a universalist national culture, the franchise is to citizenship what hetero-normativity is to social membership. They are particular means to an end that register as neutral, as taken for granted. Whereas the sovereignty of the individual is a central magnetizing figure for the generalized citizenship manuals, women's training in U.S. citizenship links their education to the production of more and better intimate normalcy in general as well as to a better "America."

Historians of suffrage love to point out that other historians of suffrage over-value the importance of the vote in telling the story of women's complex entry into the national/capitalist public sphere. They emphasize what I have empha-sized, that a wide range of reform movements—antipoverty, antiracist, anti-child labor, antiliquor, antiexploitation, antipatriarchal—were linked by the time woman suffrage turned into modern feminism. Still, in all accounts scholars argue that antifeminism was so strong in the United States that it was deemed necessary to articulate coalitions across vectors of difference around the form of the vote. The vote became the least common denominator in a variety of political struggles for greater racial, sexual, and economic equality. Alas, as it will, the least common denominator came to saturate the popular political imaginary, rather than becoming the basis on which a transformational politics could then be shaped. Focusing on the form stalled genuine institutional transformation.

For these reasons, women's vote came to be seen as a confirmation of U.S. political superiority. This additive model is as visible in the citizenship manual as it is in the title *Uncle Sam Needs a Wife*. Adopting a breezy tone of voice toward the vote's simple rationality, this political female complaint rhetoric stops at the heteronormative door, neutralizing the depth charge it might actually have deto-nated in the way it expresses its critique. Heteronormativity is offered up as a barrier not only to sexually heterodox movements but to economically and racially unorthodox ones as well. Such bargaining neutralized what so many activists actually knew about the centrality of the vote to the ongoing project of withdrawing consent from the hegemonic "promise" of national formalism, universalist humanism, and a politics of the future that ought to have been heard as a demand of the present.

SACRO-POLITICS

To the degree that they were ironic or *knowing,* the rhetorical registers of political bargaining during the women's enfranchisement struggles cannot be read entirely as motivated by expediency. The consoling image of an intimate sphere with strong but strongly differentiated men and women that enabled the victory of woman suffrage while minimizing what might be scary about it deployed a standard means of hegemonic persuasion. It is common to hold still a beloved social norm so that other changes can seem less threatening. Sexuality frequently plays this role, the role of the potentially anarchic force that must be bound conservatively so that additions might be made to the hegemonic field. Repeatedly during the twentieth century, political struggle around rights and practices not explicitly sexual have deployed the institutions and rhetoric of intimacy to threaten and promise citizens about the destiny of the good life for which they are aiming. The binding is achieved largely through the discourse I have called National Sentimentality, with its location of the ethical citizen less in his or her acts than in his or her proper feelings.[25] Sentimental politics risks the running out of control that sexuality also risks, but locates the problem of passion mainly in the subject's heart, addressing citizens as isolated subjects and charting their capacities for social membership through the manifestations in conscience of empathic identification and proper self-management. Where woman suffrage was concerned in particular, ideals of heterosexual difference preserved by the fetish of the vote required deprecating the political in the popular public sphere in favor of the high moral ground of right feeling. This expressed a long-term association of the political sphere with manliness, a paradoxical space in which men were deemed to act unfeelingly according to abstract principle and were deemed to act corruptly in terms of vulgar instrumentality and dissipation. What Ann Douglass called the "feminization" of American culture emerged from the paradox of women's response to this double view of political men. Both antiabstract and antivulgar, this feminized "culture" elevated a view that the capacity to feel pain and empathy is the central qualification for personhood and for citizenship. Pain is universal but not abstract; empathy is embodied but not undisciplined.

In the contemporary United States, the women's view—intimacy politics, the politics of the higher viscera—has at last become a cultural dominant/least common denominator, with mixed results, as we shall see. Let us take a recent event as our example of what we might call the new formalism of liberal citizenship. At the site where Princess Diana was killed in Paris, there is a statue that is now associated with her—an arm, perhaps the Statue of Liberty's arm, jutting out from a stone foundation.[26] Tourists come to this statue from all over the world, leaving offerings and writing graffiti on it that testify to Diana's ongoing significance, marking her death as a vibrant event that continues to teach something about something to someone. When John F. Kennedy Jr.'s plane crashed in 1999, the statue of Diana became a means for his secular deification: throughout the weeks following tourists left notes, signs, and other traces of homage to Kennedy on Diana's monumental body. The iconic proximity of these two figures creates a linked destiny for them. World citizens by accident of family, their lives ended tragically "before their time." They are joined somewhat like the famous picture of Elvis and Nixon shaking hands that made its way into Thomas Pynchon's *Vineland* or, more soberly, the photo of Malcolm X and Martin Luther King Jr. that Spike Lee features in *Do the Right Thing*. These startling images of public figures in figural intimacy circulate not only as evidence of lost personal futures but also as histories unfulfilled. But whose history, and how many? Capturing unlived potential, the imaged pressing of posthumous celebrity flesh comes to signal for a certain segment of its public a broken engagement with a better destiny. It is embodied, yet resonates impersonally; it is unreal and yet experienced emotionally.

These image/events are not official propaganda for a political good life circulated to enhance anyone's power. In part they are produced to generate reliance on media so that people come to define collective experience as a dense web of mediatized events. They can also be seen as evidence that in the United States celebrity attachments are preferable to a reality in which ordinary human relations seem less worth investing in, as intimate domestic and work situations become less likely to stretch over lifetimes. One could return, additionally, to Fredric Jameson's argument that celebrity or nonhuman icons like the shark in *Jaws* mark at least a collective sense of lack and longing for an underdefined *something*.[27] I want to focus here on the proximity of the mourned-for personage to the political world. Is the dead-too-soon celebrity citizen, like the shark, an event that calls out what would otherwise be political optimism, the form of the attachment that, at one time, would have circulated through the promise of universalism? What does it mean that an optimistic visceral politics seems most to resonate in this afterlife-laden affect world of postpolitical signs?

Kristin Ross argues that the post–World War II period in France (and, I think, generally in the West) was distinguished by a retreat from identification with national history, an emptying out of public memory as a suturing device.[28] What replaces it is a national-universalism organized by the privatized concerns of the everyday: homes, family, tactile experience, and an interest in augmenting hygiene everywhere. This shift in the domain of national identification, she argues, shaped the postwar critical interest in everyday life as well, serving the interests of nations and capital by distracting citizens and intellectuals from feeling accountable for the nation's ongoing imperial and capitalist relations. The events of 1968 were a direct challenge to this shift and yet also extended its new focus on the subject and experience as the site of history. If this is so, critical theory rooted in the subject and in modes of psychoanalysis and interpretation uncoupled with materialist politics must continue to carry the traces of the privatization of experience, the inculcated view that subjective cultures are the apolitical real that must be protected from the political surreal. In the United States, the continued emphasis on moral feeling as the center of political value continues the postwar pattern while also tapping into the longer tradition that elevates proper feeling as the ethico-political norm.

The maybe-future president and the quasi-princess were said to have touched "ordinary" people even though they were already in a space beyond that, even when they were living. Like the centaur that intermixes gods and humans, they seem, mainly after their deaths, to mediate alterity and intimacy, ordinariness and greatness, without fully embodying either. This is why they can represent mass futures along with tragic and farcical repetitions of power's chaos. But the collective investment in the strangely animated icons now hovering both beyond and within the political is not just an effect of postwar mass culture. As Claude Lefort, Michael Taussig, Louis Marin, Marina Warner, and most recently Giorgio Agamben have demonstrated, dense and radiant images of the politically saturated and especially the governing body have long been employed as vehicles for shaping a collective sense of social belonging.[29] It is as though an aesthetic of fascination or absorption by the image *is* the fulfillment of the promise of belonging that an icon holds out. Taussig tracks the posthumous cultural destiny of the state icon he calls "The Liberator": "But as we look at the fate of this body of the father stronger in death than when he was alive, we discern another body forming, not only of joy as well as of sorrow but of an underground grotesque as the body comes to be divided between the state and the people, interlocking entities hovering indeterminately between being and becoming in the glow of each other's otherness, irradiated by increasingly sacred remains."[30] In other words, attachment to a collectively held thing marks, among other things, a fantastic transpersonal intimacy, rendering a seam at the place where performativity and tautology almost meet. Marina Warner links this to ancient and Catholic assumptions that a god's human embodiment is not mimetic but representation plus, a scene of encounter with numina, not of masochism, anesthesia, or overreading. Agamben extends this story, arguing that it is wrong of Ernst Kanterowitz to compress the king into the two bodies human and political, a bifurcation dedicated to explaining how it can be that the sovereign is the law and yet does not take the law with "him" when he dies.[31] The political body becomes the sovereign's, Kanterowitz argues, when he comes to embody the articulation of the human to the transhistorical right of law. When the sovereign dies, however, the right of law does not die with him but transfers to whoever replaces him at that conjuncture.

Agamben argues that this model does not account for the element of the sacred that imbues the sovereign with something inhuman or impersonal that becomes his quality and not that of the formal office. For example, he points out that the murder of the sovereign is never deemed a homicide, because the sovereign is not an *homme*. His murder is not a sacrifice either, although the language of sacrifice might be deployed to distract from the fact that the law cannot be sacrificed to the law. Even when the modern representative politician transgresses, he cannot be laid bare to the law as such while he is in office, merely exposed to the pseudo law of, say, the impeachment trial, which can remove him from office. But even then he would only be human in a juridical sense, continuing to carry in his person the sacred illumination that derives from his embodiment of law as such. This is perhaps why the courts yielded to President Clinton's oft-asserted refusal to testify in real time; they were trying to preserve something of his inhumanity, his sacred superhumanity.

What difference does it make to think of the sacred aspect of contemporary mass iconicity, especially where it intersects with the political? Agamben's and my own main interest is in understanding the relation of democracy and state violence. He wants to shatter the paradigm that claims the law's rational sovereignty to itself according to the engines of interest that drive the Rousseauian general will. He uses the inhuman body of the sovereign who can be killed but not sacrificed to establish the performative consecration of law's absoluteness as in fact the "operative presupposition" of nations, democratic and otherwise.[32] This does not mean that there is no difference between sacred and secular states, or sovereign kings and representative presidents, but that the sovereignty of law in modern political worlds retains the traces of the logic of hallowed embodiment.

Agamben and Lefort associate the seduction of spectacular political embodiment with fascism and fascistic tendencies within capitalist democracies; whether or not one accedes to the ahistoricism of this bodily analogy, however, the analysis fortifies the mass cultural context of explanation for the phenomenon of overvaluation of the dead-too-soon icon whose popular appeal I have been tracking. It links them to the sublime and ridiculous ghostly representations of dead presidents, such as the now queerly supervalent nineteenth-century image of the heavenly George Washington taking Abraham Lincoln in his arms, and the ghostly homosocial utopia of the 1969 song "Abraham, Martin, and John."[33] Both of these scenes now can be read to show that the president has never been human, but circulates in a realm of principle, desire, and sacred autonomy that turns the democratic ideal of representation and representative democracy somewhat on its head. The sovereign, as embodied law, sublates the fallen flesh, taking it to something beyond ordinariness or the human. Diana and John F. Kennedy Jr., in turn, represent this hallowed aspect of publicness that citizens and subjects are trained to desire, but they go the politician one better as celebrities in the political sphere who possessed only symbolic power and so whose death is not accompanied by the ambivalence of the memory of their power over life and death. To love the law in this displaced yet sacred way is to ratify its irrationality, its auratic linkage to the beyond of history and humanity. This is one reason why the language of love is never out of place enough in the discussion of law; its fulfillment is also ultimately confirmed in a beyond of life in which it cannot be experienced.

These figures, then, at once human and superhuman, circulate as an achieved intimacy, a performative condensation of a collective desire to be possessed by a future that the ordinary person has no access to living, and the opportunity for which has now passed on. These figures displace attention to questions of the efficacy of social movements, politics engendered not around repetitions of spectacular failure and optimism but around political claims. In particular, the doubled ghost seems to speak of an attachment to public figures who move in undivided and undivisive realms beyond politics. It is as though these dead-too-soon personae represent a hole in the historical fabric through which the hierarchies of violence and alterity that we associate with the lawlessness of the law might, finally, *not* be reproduced. In their estrangement from sovereign normativity they might represent something like a lost revolutionary wrinkle in time, as the articulation of the sacred *against* the political, here seen not as sovereign but fallen law. In this way a postpolitical celebrity culture of mourning expresses a critical political position indeed. But it can only find negative articulation as personal loss and narcissistic wound, as well as a political *relation* not to the nation-state, but to other spectators of the failures enfigured by these dead-too-soon ciphers. What else does one make of the repetition of Diana-like mourning in the mass precipitation of flowers onto the New York City sidewalk right where Kennedy lived? Offerings like these constitute the mode of social participation du jour, for sure. But the gesture is a way of marking that one has been touched by the optimism of an attachment to the pre- and postpolitical, now made into the intimacy of belonging to an impersonal collectivity organized by loss that can serve as a topic for intimate conversation among strangers. Needless to say, this is a time of strange intensities, if vigils and flowers dedicated to celebrity deaths and big suffering are gestures toward salvaging civic optimism.

In short, America loves its dead objects, and why shouldn't it? Death and democracy are the two great levelers. By naming, marking, and marketing a fatal event, by making it big and of long duration, citizen-mourners meld, sharing feelings that confirm the very sense of cohesion promised but not delivered as experience by political form. Collective mourning means that there is a "we" who witness senseless not sacrificial death, confirming an unenumerated something in the common holding dear of a hard story. This is a scene of sentimental education; for, like sex, public death must be meaningful, engendering knowledge that in moving us beyond the finality of another ending performs and confirms a future in which we are not abandoned to the beyond or the beneath of history. The privileged and nightmarish anonymity of the mass subject is played out in the privileged and nightmarish hyperpublicity of the icon whose death makes him or her now a nonperson too, not anonymous but entirely figural.

This subject-forming, habit-forming aesthetics of attachment to disaster is what Michael Warner describes in his essay "The Mass Subject" and Mark Seltzer describes by the phrase "the pathological public sphere" in his book *Serial Killers.*[34] Warner and Seltzer hold that the U.S. mass subject becomes intimate impersonally with a larger world by virtue not of commonly held principles or desires but by the visceral experience of publicity organized by someone else's trauma. But trauma is a big word inappropriate for many species of negation. When the public adores the dead-too-soon political celebrity, the disaster form takes the measure of what might have been superhuman citizenship. But when the public invests in a noncelebrity tragedy as its own trauma, the logic of the inhuman plays itself out differently. Let me first distinguish fascination with disaster from the experience of trauma itself. Clinically speaking, one can experience trauma indirectly, which is to say through senses other than the skin, but it is fundamentally a negation—not a death and rebirth, exactly, but an experience in which a particular sense of continuity is lost forever to the traumatized subject. In contrast, the normative value of identification in mass society designates an empathic response as evidence that one is human in a way that animates others— it is evidence that you *belong.* This is quite the opposite of feeling isolated and overparticularized by trauma per se: mass cultural scandal or disaster engenders *publics* of opinion, identification, and social membership. This affective structure of collective identification permeates the U.S. public sphere to such a degree that one now reads about exhausted compassion, about the flattening out of a public capacity to take seriously the publicized pain with which it is also fascinated.[35]

Thirty years ago John Berger made the same argument about the exhaustion of authentic impersonal affect.[36] Then the referents were pictures of atrocity from the Vietnam War: the transmitted image of the generic traumatized body of the Vietnamese victim was all too easily consumed when published in a series of reports from elsewhere. The desensitizing effects of televisual seriality, he argued, lead to political irresponsibility, the refusal of the spectator to take on the trauma except as a kind of mirror on the wall of one's own desire to be morally worthy, if that. Susan Buck-Morss calls this response an aesthetic of moral anesthesia, and claims its centrality to the reproduction of fascism.[37] Such a distinction marks the sublime's difference from the beautiful: the sublime ejects you from the comfort of your sensibility, while the beautiful absorbs and confirms you, your sensitivity, your consciousness and conscience. Even if conscience links you to others by virtue of your recognition of their pain, to the degree that it remains a story of their pain and your compassion for it the prosthesis of the image keeps you and your world safe from risky transformation. This is to say that right feeling turns the repulsive into the beautiful. Such homeopathy through consumption of the wounded image is central to the liberal aesthetics of political experience, in which atrocity and the therapy culture that now subsumes politics redemptively draw out lessons from lesions, weaving gold out of straw.

Only the events that remain open, signifying beyond themselves, count as historic. This is also a quality of the traumatic narrative: it is traumatic because it cannot be stopped by the rational will, resonating much like a horror story. Yet liberal national culture has long hailed citizens through scenes of empathic identification with less fortunate others, risking the unending reverberations of publicized violence to deliver a sense of general moral propriety to the privileged. It is not that empathic rhetoric *has* to have this effect; I am talking about a pattern that has emerged from 150 years of events in the United States. As a result, the "less fortunate others" make claims for justice in the language of the harmed who need reparation, because this is a language in which a self-defined "good person" is emotionally literate. In this sense sentimental national culture educates the viscera so that citizens can meet across death and disaster in a way that is personal and impersonal. The feeling is personal and ethical: the structure of feeling remains impersonal, and the conditions of exemplarity for the event remain tacit. Publicity serves as a pseudo-neutral domain in which one's principles and one's affect are trained normatively, such that one takes one's responses as the expression of one's true capacity for attachment to other humans rather than as effects of pedagogy.

Foucault has called this belief and these practices around the affects of self in community "sexuality." In *The History of Sexuality* he argues that the cluster of feelings with which you identify the expression of your true self links you to a racial, sexual, religious, and political imaginary as well, giving you a blood-organized reproductive feeling of continuity over pasts and into futures.[38] Characterizing as "sexuality" the processes of impersonal but subjective attachment that I have been describing might feel like a stretch. But if we see the education of the viscera as central to the production of modern sexuality, the political world of feeling culture I am relating plays a central role in what constitutes not only erotically oriented meanings but the normativity of social attachment generally. I am claiming, then, that the heteronormativity of woman suffrage and the hegemony of intimacy politics that extends from it are just the beginnings of what we might rephrase as "sexuality." In the democratic culture of empathic identification there is a shadow politics of violent exemplification. Racism is displayed in spectacles of normative sexual difference, while the romance of class mobility links the working classes of all races and genders to images of disordered enfleshment. The bodies are *too much;* the people are *not enough.* Paradoxically, these structures of sexualization are dehumanizing, machines of the inhuman—that is, except where particular persons can be shown aspiring to the abstraction that would discipline, individuate, and privatize their drives, assuming a correct (sexual/class) orientation.

In short, no matter how empathic the privileged are to subordinated classes, as type the *particulate* remains absolutely inassimilable to liberal democratic ideology. Diana and John F. Kennedy Jr. put the optimistic face on this formation: mass empathy might express something optimistic about a political world that does not exist yet. In contrast, as I argue in *The Queen of America,* the notion that subordinated persons need to be given a "face" says it all about what they are otherwise presumed to be: all body.[39]

This is a complicated claim to rest on the shoulders of well-intentioned feeling, or national sexuality. We might turn here to Stjepan Meštrović's insistence that the United States is a postemotional society.[40] This counterintuitive observation makes a kind of uncanny sense, in that one so often sees performances of empathic attachment that can, one feels, barely resonate beyond the moment in which a confirming recognition happens. Meštrović dryly refers to President Clinton's capacity to "feel your pain"; but while he has no sympathy for the formal norms of collective intelligibility, I do, whether or not I deem them to be inauthentic, shallowly felt, or sadly not followed through. Who is to say that artifice is insincere, or when it is? In short, I do not mean to trivialize the democratic urge to pay attention to death by choosing Diana and Kennedy Jr. as cases of recent mass witnessing. Nor do I think that sentimental nationality is in itself false consciousness. I use these fresh examples to talk about technologies of feeling, the pedagogy of the viscera that organize a mass national experience of structural violence into a form that gets sensed as ordinariness. Historically viewed, national sentimentality has legitimated imperial and internal violence by linking opinion to right consciousness or feeling. It is not that empathic feeling is itself a bad thing, as the desire to feel inside of an intimate impersonal collectivity can have many different effects. It might ground resistance to political powerlessness; it might be a counterhegemonic drive that survives on small objects until the right one comes along; it might confirm what we already know, that publicity marks danger while private but collective spectatorship protects. One can spin a dozen optimistic and dark stories about the traffic in violence with which citizens of mass society are trained to identify: from *Schadenfreude,* pleasure at the suffering of others, to self-confirming pain, to an experience of the unlivable event that induces a will in someone or a public to take risks for change. But the repetition of empathic events does not in itself create change. Nor do all violent events take on an equivalent logic of importance. Different forms and scales of articulation are taken on by the formal events of public mourning. For the superhuman icon, special issues of paper and broadcast magazines generate a buzz and a memory of the excited feeling behind the frenzy of mournful attention. For those whose violent destinies also distinguish them from the ordinary human, other sites and practices of mourning mark the ongoing and painful life of what Elspeth Probyn would call *outside belonging*.[41] These spaces tend not to be capital intensive, and the events they commemorate are barely relevant to the almanac, the calendar, and the official time lines that are constantly reconstructed to provide national and global historical continuity. These minor forms are also authorless quasi monuments, but not made legitimate by mass cultural performance that absorbs much collective energy and value. Instead, they are irreducibly and painfully localized in zones of political anonymity not in the sacred beyond but the sordid beneath.

SARCO-POLITICS

Anyone paying attention during the last fifteen years will, no doubt, have seen the AIDS quilt, with its series of fabric tombstones that make portable and public lives otherwise anonymous. Many of us have also seen coverage of the Clothesline Project, which uses empty shirts on a line to designate women marked by domestic violence and rape.[42] Link these with the images of masses of empty shoe pairs that newspapers reproduce to illustrate popular protest against the traffic in guns.[43] Track the number of candlelight parades that erupt to witness any number of things, such as the burgeoning carceral culture of the United States, which now imprisons millions of the poorest and blackest occupants, or the proliferating number of hate crimes against gays and lesbians. In Point Richmond, California, where I run in a park next to the beautiful San Francisco Bay, two benches recently appeared, covered with cheerful ceramic squares. Each square is a message from an area youth to a sibling who was killed on the streets of Richmond, one of the poorest historically African American communities in the state.

This archive of precarious signs evokes Toni Morrison's *Song of Solomon*, which locates the import of its present moment in a catastrophic event: the "four little colored girls . . . blown out of a church" by anti–civil rights agitators on September 16, 1963.[44] Central to the novel is a struggle for the destiny of African American history and the congealed economic value of the African American labor on which that history is built. It places Milkman Dead at loggerheads with his exfriend Guitar. Milkman views and wants to possess history as his personal symbolic and economic property, while Guitar wants the money Milkman seeks so that he can fund a regime of counterviolence inspired by this haunting historic event: "Every night now Guitar was seeing little scraps of Sunday dresses—white and purple, powder blue, pink and white, lace and voile, velvet and silk, cotton and satin, eyelet and grosgrain. . . . The bits of Sunday dresses that he saw did not fly; they hung in the air quietly, like the whole notes in the last measure of an Easter hymn" (173). Small girls generate small monuments in memorial tatters. Like the anonymous ceramics of surviving siblings and the rotting flowers and melting candles of witnessing and protest, these tatters demonstrate the peculiar contingency of minor histories and lives. As we picture these squares and shreds of wasted personhood, we remember the promise that humans are to be protected as generic subjects within liberal democracies. So the question arises: Which kinds of life engender ordinary anonymity and which unhistoric lives are exemplary only as waste, uncanny in trauma, and perfected in death? A rupture with the dominant story leads to a momentary fold in space, and in a few hours the minor fold is reabsorbed into the concrete organizing signs of the built and more permanent world. Can the language of sacrifice, which presumes sacrifice *for,* actually be used when the dead are constituted by a prior negation? For whom is the rhetoric of sacrifice a call to arms, or a consolation rhetoric, or a sentimental form of mourning and self-confirmation?

This contrast between monumental styles of the mass public and scenes located in majority and subordinate publics, in big pieces and small scraps, and in iconic and hieroglyphic writing speaks volumes about the politics of anonymity or what Agamben calls "bare life" in a universalist culture that traffics in flesh. Here the privileged economy of the inhuman returns as social negativity, which marks its subjects out for a sensually violent destiny that is somehow made to seem almost random. There is nothing random about it. The populations that have been variously excluded from the U.S. franchise—African Americans, Asians, white women, criminals, and unnaturalized immigrants—have been negated in particular ways and at particular junctures. Yet they/we have had much in common too, linked to the gestures of denegation I list here and the ambiguities of social value they represent. Counterhegemonic activity like this measures the scale of negation any subordinated people negotiate, but many different vectors of subordination are measured therein. The contingent memorial is at once a gesture of internal affiliation and collective belonging, a performance of discontinuity with the privileged world, and a reaching out to the promise of democratic praxis and to alliances yet unmade. Engendering publicity about violence, suffering, and death, the makers of these memorial moments redeploy the technique of making publics through sentimental identification. Yet they also express not privilege but what is personal about impersonal and depersonalizing violence. Socially negated populations are marked definitionally by proximity to death and survival, by a sense of being too alive and not alive enough.[45] These survival subcultures are all associated with flesh, sexuality, and labor, and as such their gestures of denegation mark the impossibility of their absorption into the liberal machinery that also thrives on their availability to be negated, mourned for, regretted. No doubt other contradictory claims will be made about the conditions under which particular minoritized groups can survive in liberal democracies. What is at stake here is the status of a violent nonevent.

Can we also say that the liberal ideology of the additive population, of the capacity of the vote form to absorb economic and social antagonism and contradiction, is enabled by developments in the modernity of sexual culture? Woman suffrage offered a challenge to the structure of people's fantasies and intimacies, and everyone knew that. Insofar as it was organized by desires to change the rules of property in the self and in things, the new voting population's transformation into a nondangerous collectivity essentially required the sacrifice of the counterknowledge women of all classes and races knew they brought to the political public sphere. The least common denominator exnominated women from making their vote a new kind of political event.

I am suggesting that the mechanism for fashioning this impossible position is the sarco-political. By the turn of the century, the already immense imperial, capitalist, legal, and therapeutic investment in heteronormative institutions of intimacy and modes of regulation of labor value were faced with an overdetermined demand to change the mode of formal political membership referenced by the concept "legitimacy." At the same time the smaller the unit imagined the less likely were these structural expansions to engender greater instabilities. Heteronormativity kept the system stable through a species logic of social reproduction so that structural change could be experienced untraumatically, more like a deep breath than a surgical incision. When African American men were enfranchised, the abstracting ideology of free labor was appropriated to saturate the definition of freedom, muting out more radical critiques; meanwhile, the bodily mixing aversive to sarco-politics/heteronormativity was maintained by zoning and miscegenation laws that constrained black political participation until the civil rights moment of the mid-1960s. Thus although the *content* of the shift wrought by woman suffrage involved different semiotic elasticities—such as the deployment of sentimental realism and comic distraction to resolve the anxiety that women and men would become even more averse should women experience legal autonomy—the structure is much the same. Sarco-politics not only provides a way to read the hegemonic patterns of structural domination in the United States but is the heteronormative mechanism itself, using a racialized species logic to mark the dominated as both too alive and not fully human, therefore not relevant to notions of sovereign individuality—whether or not they have the vote.

Jacques Rancière points out that the *proletarii* are etymologically "those who do nothing but reproduce their own multiplicity and who, for this very reason, do not deserve to be counted."[46] This is why I have adapted philosopher Sue Golding's language of denegation to substitute for the democratic discourse of rights and legitimacy. In a universalist culture whose units of inclusion and exclusion are formally legal, the incommensurateness between legal standing and social membership (between formal inclusion in the law and informal domination by it, for example) militates against the citizenship of the sarco-subject.[47] He may become politically denegated but this has never yet erased the genealogy of inhumanity his body represents for its privileged others in so many symbolic, institutional, and economic contexts of production.

CONCLUSION: FLESH AND THE MAIDENS

This essay is the beginning of a thought about the scales and styles of domination that justify democratic violence, involving a productive contradiction between formal political inclusion and the relegation of entire populations to a dehumanized domain of liveness and violence.[48] The nation manages privilege according to a fantasy of privilege that involves merging into the ether of bodiless universality. In the United States dominant modes of universality have worked, by and large, according to three logics: the appearance of white maleness, the possession of property, and the capacity to feel pain. The abstracting effect of pain has been counterdeployed effectively as a universalist rhetoric of public seduction and demand by numerous countercultures since the early republic: this tactic seeks to affirm the deep identity of a humanity defined by its proximity to death and expiation. Yet we have seen that this tactic has not ameliorated the negation of the very people who adopt it as a sign of their actual humanity. When women sought the franchise, they wanted so many things. What they got instead was the formal vestibularity of the vote, which has spawned more than seventy years of further struggle to make claims on the modes of justice that got left behind when citizenship was reduced to the slightest possible event. It always seems like the generous thing to do, to find the smallest already available site of consensus and to organize the world around that site, promising that nothing will change except for the better life that can be already imagined. But we have seen that giving up the big claim on behalf of moderation moves the center to the right. We have seen that valuing pain as the only source of humanity that dissolves the specular and economic relays to citizenship splits the subaltern into ruined bodies and dismembered demanding voices. It has ended up reproducing the bodily logic of domination, which links the sarco-subject of citizenship to the body that is both too alive and too close to death to entrust with the future of history. Thus those associated with not the ownership of capital but the reproduction of life's material and tactile things are linked by the notion that one is reduced to the body, one becomes all surface, like flesh. Paradoxically, there is no homeopathic solution to this problem, either more body politics or less. The negated populations who cannot be absorbed into the normal without threatening to change its terms seem to increase their symbolic negativity, their association with subpersonhood, whenever they make a claim on the neutralizing structures of consent.

I recently saw the original version of *Island of Lost Souls*.[49] In this film animals are transformed into men in a room they call "the house of pain." "Take me to the house of pain," they plead, where through unanesthetized suffering and cutting they became more human. To be more human is to understand pain as the pedagogy that engenders respect for the law—it is an ethics of cruel optimism. Abstraction is held out as an ideal to which the men can aspire. Meanwhile, though, bodily pain is a burden the animal-men seek proudly to bear, as if submitting their bodies to the law, becoming cuts of meat for the body politic, were almost as good as enjoying the conceptual freedom of the law. Maybe it is. Nevertheless, the scientist cannot make more than one woman, and she cannot be a man before the law. The female animal is even more embodied than the animal-men by becoming a person; yet she is even less human than they are because she attracts the law, bringing it down to the shameful sensation of its own bodily particularity. Of course this is the standard critique of the embodied: they reduce the world to their level. Flesh begets flesh. This story about sexuality and its unshakable species logic cannot be dissolved, only sublimated, and barely that, within the liberal regime of juridical fetishism.

The "pacifying procedure"[50] of liberal inclusion, through the vote, gay marriage, and so on, works as a hegemonic lure only at the moment that it becomes an end in itself, not part of a larger world-changing project. The vote, for example, was not the opposite of the disenfranchisement of which it was a foundational part. Beyond the tactical embrace of liberal sovereignties it must become a democratic project to engender the flesh as the human, not as its opposite. This essay tries to demonstrate the complexity of such an aim. Subjects associated with the reproduction of life—with sexuality, manual labor, racial distinction—would then be imaginable within the intimate and economic imaginary of the social. The privileged individual, no longer optimistic, then, about the mobility made possible by normative universality, would also no longer feel confirmed while mourning the ongoing violence to women, people of color, queers, and workers whose bodies are deemed expendable. Finally, bodiliness, or *sexuality,* would no longer define the political value of the negated citizen.

NOTES

1 For a comparative argument that also links heterosocial kinship models to national ideologies of abstract universalism, see Jacqueline Stevens, *Reproducing the State* (Princeton: Princeton University Press, 1999).

2 Central to my thought about hegemony and formalism is Stuart Hall, "Gramsci's Relevance for the Study of Race and Ethnicity," in *Stuart Hall: Critical Dialogues in Cultural Studies,* ed. David Morley and Kuan-Hsing Chen (New York: Routledge, 1996), 411–40.

3 For the extended argument concerning U.S. pain culture, see my "The Subject of True Feeling: Pain, Privacy, and Politics" in *Cultural Pluralism, Identity, and the Law,* ed. Austin Sarat (Ann Arbor: University of Michigan Press, 1997), 49–84.

4 Ida Clyde Clarke, *Uncle Sam Needs a Wife* (Philadelphia: John C. Winston Co., 1925).

5 E. J. Dionne Jr., *Why Americans Hate Politics* (New York: Touchstone, 1992); Thomas J. Johnson, Carol E. Hayes, and Scott P. Hayes, eds., *Engaging the Public: How Government and the Media Can Reinvigorate American Democracy* (London: Sage, 1999); Albert H. Cantril and Susan Davis Cantril, *Reading Mixed Signals: Ambivalence in American Public Opinion about Government* (Baltimore: Johns Hopkins University Press, 1999).

6 Secondary texts on this topic that ballast my general representation of the period context and the contemporary historiography of it are Kristi Andersen, *After Suffrage: Women in Partisan and Electoral Politics before the New Deal* (Chicago: University of Chicago Press, 1996); Mary Jo Buhle, *Women and American Socialism, 1879–1920* (Urbana: University of Illinois Press, 1981); Nancy F. Cott, ed., *The History of Women in the United States,* vols. 19 and 20 (Munich: K. G. Saur, 1994); Nancy F. Cott, *The Grounding of Modern Feminism* (New Haven: Yale University Press, 1987); Janet M. Cramer, *Woman as Citizen: Race, Class, and the Discourse of Women's Citizenship, 1894–1909* (Columbia, SC: Association for Education in Journalism and Mass Communication, 1998); Ellen Carol DuBois, *Feminism and Suffrage: The Emergence of an Independent Women's Movement in America, 1848–1869* (Ithaca: Cornell University Press, 1978); J. Stanley Lemons, *The Woman Citizen: Social Feminism in the 1920s* (Urbana: University of Illinois Press, 1973); Sara Evans, *Born for Liberty* (New York:

Free Press, 1989); Barbara Green, *Spectacular Confessions: Autobiography, Performative Activism, and the Sites of Suffrage 1904–1938* (New York: St. Martin's Press, 1997); Aileen Kraditor, *The Ideas of the Woman Suffrage Movement, 1890–1920* (Garden City, N.Y.: Anchor, 1971); Janet Lewis, *Before the Vote Was Won: Arguments For and Against Woman's Suffrage* (New York: Routledge, 1987); Martha M. Solomon, ed., *A Voice of Their Own: The Woman Suffrage Press, 1840–1910* (Tuscaloosa: University of Alabama Press, 1991); Suzanne M. Marilley, *Woman Suffrage and the Origins of Liberal Feminism in the United States, 1820–1920* (Cambridge: Harvard University Press, 1996).

7 Taylor Branch, *Parting the Waters: America in the King Years, 1954–63* (New York: Simon and Schuster, 1988).

8 See Roger Rouse, "The Nightmare Paper," unpublished manuscript, n.d.

9 Among the myriad manuals read for this essay are Mary Austin, *The Young Woman Citizen* (New York: The Woman's Press, 1920); Hayes Baker-Crothers and Ruth A. Hudnut, *Problems of Citizenship* (New York: Henry Holt, 1924); Raymond F. Christ, *Teacher's Manual. Arranged for the Guidance of Public-School Teachers of the United States for Use with the Students Textbook to Create a Standard Course of Instruction for the Preparation of the Candidate for the Responsibilities of Citizenship* (Washington, D.C.: U.S. Bureau of Naturalization, 1918); *Citizenship Education and Naturalization Information* (Washington, D.C.: U.S. Department of Justice, 1997); *D.A.R. Manual for Citizenship* (Washington, D.C.: Daughters of the American Revolution, 1981); C. F. Dole, *The Young Citizen* (Boston: D. C. Heath, 1899); Eve Garrette, *A Political Handbook for Women* (Garden City, N.Y.: Doubleday, Doran, and Co., 1944); Shaler Mathews, ed., *The Woman Citizen's Library*, vols. 1–12 (Chicago: The Civics Library, 1914); Victor P. Morey and Fred T. Wilhelms, *Organizing and Conducting a Citizenship Class: A Guide for Use in the Public Schools by Teachers of Candidates for Naturalization* (Washington, D.C.: U.S. Government Printing Office, 1945); Joy Elmer Morgan, ed., *The American Citizen's Handbook* (1941; Washington, D.C.: National Council for Social Studies, 1968); William E. Mosher, ed., *Introduction to Responsible Citizenship* (New York: Henry Holt, 1941); Howard Washington Odum, *Community and Government: A Manual of Discussion and Study of the Newer Ideals of Citizenship* (Chapel Hill: University of North Carolina Extension Service, 1921); Elizabeth Fisher Read, *Citizenship and the Vote: A Statement for the Women Citizens of the State of New York* (New York: Americanization Committee of the New York State Woman Suffrage Party and the New York City Woman Suffrage Party, 1918); Benjamin D. Scott, *Citizenship Readers: Notable Events in the Making of America* (Philadelphia: Lippincott, 1930); Edwin DuBois Shurter, ed., *Woman Suffrage: Bibliography and Selected Arguments, June 1, 1912* (Austin: University of Texas, 1912); Edwin DuBois Shurter, *American Citizenship and Government* (Philadelphia: Lippincott, 1930); Justina Leavitt Wilson, *Woman Suffrage: A Study Outline* (White Plains, N.Y.: The H. W. Wilson Co., 1916); *U.S. Army Studies in Citizenship for Recruits* (Washington, D.C.: Government Printing Office, 1922).

10 Jean-François Lyotard, *The Inhuman: Reflections on Time*, trans. Rachel Bowlby and Geoffrey Bennington (Stanford: Stanford University Press, 1992).

11 Clarke, *Uncle Sam Needs a Wife*, 207.

12 See, for instance, the multiauthored novel *The Sturdy Oak*, which was serially published in *The Pictorial Review*, the same magazine from which *Uncle Sam Needs a Wife* was derived. One of the novel's authors, Mary Austin, was also the author of her own citizenship manual, *The Young Woman Citizen*. See also Elizabeth Jordan, ed., *The Sturdy Oak* (Columbus: Ohio University Press, 1998).

13 Clarke, *Uncle Sam Needs a Wife*, 185.

14 Ibid., 136.

15 See Rosalind Turborg-Penn, *African American Women in the Struggle for the Vote, 1850–1920* (Bloomington: Indiana University Press, 1998). For general discussions of the concept of an informed citizenry in the United States that address the relation of woman suffrage, see Richard D. Brown, *The Strength of a People: The Idea of an Informed Citizenry in America, 1650–1870* (Chapel Hill: University of North Carolina Press, 1996); and Robert Wiebe, *Self-Rule: A Cultural History of American Democracy* (Chicago: University of Chicago Press, 1995).

16 Turborg-Penn, *African American Women in the Struggle for the Vote*; Ann D. Gordon, ed., with Bettye Collier-Thomas, John H. Bracey, Arlene Voski Avakian, and Joyce Avrech Berkman, *African American Women and the Vote: 1937–1965* (Amherst: University of Massachusetts Press, 1997).

17 Mary Brown Summner Boyd, *The Woman Citizen: A General Handbook of Civics: With Special Consideration of Women's Citizenship* (New York: F. A. Stokes, 1918), 160.

18 Garrette, *A Political Handbook for Women*, 2–3. A consent-soliciting linkage between the vote and the commodity form suffused the twentieth-century suffrage and feminist movements, which made them look tactically more like mainstream politics than not. See also Andersen, *After Suffrage*.

19 John D'Emilio, *Sexual Politics, Sexual Communities: The Making of a Homosexual Minority in the United States, 1940–1970*, 2nd ed. (1983; Chicago: University of Chicago Press, 1998).

20 Garrette, *A Political Handbook for Women*, 2.

21 On the distinction between the suffragette and the feminist, see Cott, *The Grounding of Modern Feminism*. Cott argues that feminism, a more modern formation, was less focused on the vote and was more broadly based politically in terms both of class and sexual activism than was suffragism.

22 Austin, *The Young Woman Citizen*, 8, 3.

23 Gayatri Chakravorty Spivak, "Can the Subaltern Speak?" in *Marxism and the Interpretation of Culture*, ed. Cary Nelson and Lawrence Grossberg (Urbana: University of Illinois Press, 1988), 271–313.

24 Clarke, *Uncle Sam Needs a Wife*, 19.

25 For an expanded explication of national sentimentality see my "The Subject of True Feeling."

26 Many thanks to Marita Sturken for this information.

27 Fredric Jameson, "Reification and Ideology in Mass Culture," *Social Text* 1 (1979): 130–48.

28 Kristin Ross, *Fast Cars, Clean Bodies: Decolonization and the Reordering of French Culture* (Cambridge: MIT Press, 1995).

29 Giorgio Agamben, *Homo Sacer: Sovereign Power and Bare Life*, trans. Daniel Heller-Roazen (Stanford: Stanford University Press, 1998); Claude Lefort, *Democracy and Political Theory* trans. David Macey (Cambridge: Polity Press, 1988); Louis Marin, *Portrait of the King* (Minneapolis: University of Minnesota Press, 1988); Marina Warner, *Monuments and Maidens: The Allegory of the Female Form* (New York: Atheneum, 1985); and Michael Taussig, *The Magic of the State* (New York: Routledge, 1997).

30 Taussig, *Magic of the State*, 102.

31 Ernst H. Kantorowicz, with William Chester Jordan, *The King's Two Bodies: A Study in Mediaeval Political Theology* (Princeton: Princeton University Press, 1997).

32 Agamben, *Homo Sacer*, 106.

33 John Sartain, "Abraham Lincoln the Martyr" (1865); Dion DiMucci, "Abraham, Martin, and John" (1968). The latter song's remarkable staying power as a mnemonic for national desire can be verified in any Web search; thousands of hits register a vast number of usages from memories of 1968 to personal patriotic expression to a classroom tool for teaching history and citizenship.

34 Michael Warner, "The Mass Public and the Mass Subject," in *The Phantom Public Sphere*, ed. Bruce Robbins (Minneapolis: University of Minnesota Press, 1993), 234–56; Mark Seltzer, *Serial Killers* (New York: Routledge, 1998).

35 Susan D. Moeller, *Compassion Fatigue: How the Media Sell Disease, Famine, War, and Death* (New York: Routledge, 1999).

36 John Berger, "Pictures of Agony," in *About Looking* (New York: Pantheon Books, 1980), 37–40.

37 Susan Buck-Morss, "Aesthetics and Anaesthetics: Walter Benjamin's Artwork Essay Reconsidered" *October* 62 (fall 1992): 3–41.

38 Michel Foucault, *The History of Sexuality: An Introduction*, trans. Robert Hurley (New York: Pantheon Books, 1978).

39 Lauren Berlant, "The Face of America and the State of Emergency," in *The Queen of America Goes to Washington City: Essays on Sex and Citizenship* (Durham: Duke University Press, 1997), 175–220.

40 Stjepan G. Meštrović, *Postemotional Society* (London: Sage, 1997).

41 Elspeth Probyn, *Outside Belonging* (New York: Routledge, 1996).

42 "The Clothesline Project began in 1990 when members of the Cape Cod Women's Agenda hung a clothesline across the village green in Hyannis, Massachusetts with 31 shirts designed by survivors of assault, rape and incest. Women viewing the clothesline came forward to create shirts of their own and the line just kept growing. Since that first display the Project has grown to 300+ local Clothesline Projects nationally and internationally, with an estimated 35,000 shirts. The Clothesline Project has become a distinctive resource for healing from violence and creating social change. Lines have been displayed at schools, universities, State Houses, shopping malls, churches, and women's events. The first National Display took place April 8–9, 1995 in Washington D.C. in conjunction with NOW's Rally For Women's Lives. Similar to the AIDS quilt, the Clothesline Project puts a human face on the statistics of violence against women. The Project increases awareness of the impact of violence against women, celebrates a woman's strength to survive, and provides an avenue for her to

courageously break the silence. Families and friends of women who have died as a result of violence can make a shirt to express their deep loss" (from the Web site http://canes.gsw.peachnet.edu/~gswnow/clothesline.html).

43 "A Millennial March of Empty Shoes. Like the AIDS quilt, the Silent March is a deeply moving way of showing the human toll taken by the gun epidemic. In election year 2000, the Silent March will mobilize Americans to call for comprehensive federal regulation of firearms, just like cars, pharmaceuticals and other consumer products. Our fourth national campaign will again portray the terrible human toll taken by guns through a 'silent march'—rows and rows of silent, empty shoes, some with personal notes tucked inside sent by family members of victims. This sea of shoes represents the tens of thousands of Americans who lose their lives to guns every year" (from the Web site http://www.silentmarch.org/noguns/data/who.html).

44 Toni Morrison, *Song of Solomon* (New York: Plume, 1987). This segment extends the work on the aesthetic of representative fragments in minor literatures in my "'68 or Something," *Critical Inquiry* 21, no. 1 (fall 1994): 124–55.

45 See Lauren Berlant, "*Pax Americana:* The Case of *Show Boat,*" in *Institutions of the Novel,* ed. Deidre Lynch and William B. Warner (Durham: Duke University Press, 1997), 399–422.

46 Jacques Rancière, *Disagreement: Politics and Philosophy,* trans. Julie Rose (Minneapolis: University of Minnesota Press, 1998), 121.

47 Sue Golding, *The Eight Technologies of Otherness* (New York: Routledge, 1997).

48 Liveness describes a continually negotiated quality of sexuality and citizenship. See my "Live Sex Acts (Parental Advisory)," in *The Queen of America,* 55–81.

49 *Island of Lost Souls* (dir. Erle C. Kenton, 1933) is a remake of H. G. Wells's *The Island of Dr. Moreau.* I choose not to name the characters here because names humanize, and their subhumanity is the point both of the film and this anecdote.

50 Jacques Rancière, *On the Shores of Politics* (London: Verso, 1995), 11.

LISA DUGGAN

The New Homonormativity: The Sexual Politics of Neoliberalism

◆

At the 1999 "Liberty for All" Log Cabin National Leadership Conference in New York, gay Republicans assembled from across the United States heard a keynote address from New York City mayor Rudolph Guiliani along with a series of plenary lectures from Winnie Stachelberg of the Human Rights Campaign; Brian Bond of the Gay and Lesbian Victory Fund; Jonathan Rauch of the *National Journal;* and Urvashi Vaid, director of the National Gay and Lesbian Task Force Policy Institute. From her plenary platform, Vaid called for real dialogue, mutual respect, and even affinity between gay groups and gay leaders at serious political odds, against a backdrop of community unity.

But the conference sponsors were only superficially receptive to Vaid's call for respectful, inclusive dialogue. Rich Tafel, executive director of the Log Cabin Republicans, expressed a different notion of the basis for gay political unity—a transformed movement with a new center and definite exclusions: "The conference was the most important we've ever held, and its success solidified a clear shift that is taking place in the gay movement. There is a transformation going on across the country. . . . And [as] with any such transformation, those who had the most invested in the polarized status quo, notably extremists on the far left and far right, are beginning to resort to increasingly desperate tactics to stop it."[1] At the conference, Jonathan Rauch named this new center "libertarian radical independent," and pointed to the online writers' group, the Independent Gay Forum (IGF), as the "cutting edge" of a new gay movement.

Under the banner "Forging a Gay Mainstream," the IGF Web site proclaims the organization's principles:

—We support the full inclusion of gays and lesbians in civil society with legal equality and equal social respect. We argue that gays and lesbians, in turn, contribute to the creativity, robustness, and decency of our national life.

—We share a belief in the fundamental virtues of the American system and its traditions of individual liberty, personal moral autonomy and responsibility, and equality before the law. We believe those traditions depend on the institutions of a market economy, free discussion, and limited government.

—We deny "conservative" claims that gays and lesbians pose any threat to social morality or the political order.

—We equally oppose "progressive" claims that gays should support radical social change or restructuring of society.

—We share an approach, but we disagree on many particulars. We include libertarians, moderates, and classical liberals. We hold differing views on the role of government, personal morality, religious faith, and personal relationships. We share these disagreements openly: we hope that readers will find them interesting and thought provoking.[2]

This variety of "third way" rhetoric is now widespread in Western politics; it became familiar fare in the early 1990s, offered up by Western leaders ranging from Bill Clinton's New Democrats in the United States and Tony Blair's New Laborites in Great Britain to George W. Bush's "compassionate conservatism." It invokes a political mainstream described as reasonable, centrist and pragmatic—a mainstream constructed rhetorically through triangulation. The "new" center is contrasted with unacceptable poles of "extremism" or "old" politics on the Left and Right. The IGF follows this format, positioning itself against antigay conservatism and queer progressive politics—between which poles the "differing views" of its listed writers may range. Among the thirty men and three women named on the Web site (all white, with the exception of one African American man) are well-known writers such as Andrew Sullivan, author of *Virtually Normal: An Argument about Homosexuality,* and Bruce Bawer, author of *A Place at the Table: The Gay Individual in American Society,* as well as somewhat more obscure figures such as Walter Olson, a columnist for the magazine *Reason* and author of *The Excuse Factory: How Employment Law Is Paralyzing the American Workplace,* and David Boaz, executive vice president of the libertarian Cato Institute and author of *Libertarianism: A Primer.* Also included are a few popular writers with more murkily centrist views like Eric Marcus, coauthor with Greg Louganis of *Breaking the Surface,* and a handful of academically trained intellectuals, such as sociologist Stephen O. Murray, author of *American Gay.*

On the surface the IGF Web site's collection of downloadable articles is targeted on the one hand at conservative moralists, antigay church doctrine, and exgay propaganda (e.g., Paul Varnell's "Changing Churches" and "The Ex-Gay Pop-Gun"), and at queer cultural and intellectual radicalism on the other (e.g., Stephen O. Murray's "Why I Don't Take Queer Theory Seriously" and Jennifer Vanasco's "Queer Dominance Syndrome"). But surrounding and shaping the familiar political triangulation and the repeated assimilationist tirades against more flamboyant in-your-face gay activists is a broader agenda for the future of democracy. This highly visible and influential center-libertarian-conservative-classical liberal formation in gay politics aims to contest and displace the expansively democratic vision represented by progressive activists such as Urvashi Vaid, replacing it with a model of a narrowly constrained public life cordoned off from the "private" control and vast inequalities of economic life. This new formation is not merely a position on the spectrum of gay movement politics but is a crucial new part of the cultural front of neoliberalism in the United States.

Neoliberalism, the brand name for the form of procorporate, "free market," anti-"big government" rhetoric shaping U.S. policy and dominating international financial institutions since the early 1980s, is associated primarily with economic and trade policy. The cultural politics of neoliberalism are considered and debated relatively rarely in discussions of the economic and political mechanisms of U.S. cultural imperialism. In the domestic arena, the "culture wars" of the past twenty years are generally discussed separately from questions of monetary and fiscal policy, trade negotiations, and economic indicators—the recognized realm of neoliberal policy. But in a wide range of cultural policy territories—from public spending for culture and education to the "moral" foundations for welfare reform, from affirmative action to marriage and domestic partnership debates—neoliberalism's profoundly antidemocratic and antiegalitarian agenda has shaped public discussion. Neoliberalism in fact *has* a sexual politics, albeit a contradictory and contested sexual politics not unlike the equally contradictory and internally contested economic and trade politics that have defined the location "neoliberal" since the 1980s of Reagan and Thatcher.[3]

Neoliberalism is often presented not as a particular set of interests and political interventions but as a kind of nonpolitics—a way of being reasonable and of promoting universally desirable forms of economic expansion and democratic government globally. Who could be against greater wealth and more democracy? Especially since the fall of the Soviet empire at the end of the 1980s, neoliberals argue that all alternatives to the U.S. model have failed, including fascism, communism, socialism, and even the relatively mild forms of the welfare state advocated by social democrats, labor movements, and Keynesians. Not trumpeted are the sharply declining participation rates in the Western "democracies," and the rapidly expanding, vast economic inequalities that neoliberal policies have generated in the United States and Great Britain especially.[4]

The primary strategy of turn of the millennium neoliberalism is *privatization,* the term that describes the transfer of wealth and decision making from public, more-or-less accountable decision-making bodies to individual or corporate, unaccountable hands. Neoliberals advocate privatization of economic enterprises, which they consider fundamentally "private" and inappropriately placed in any "public" arena. They go further to advocate that many ostensibly public services and functions be placed in private profit-making hands, including education, garbage collection, prison building and operation, and cultural production.[5] All this privacy is rendered desirable by the recycling and updating of nineteenth-century liberalism's equation of economic activity with voluntary, uncoerced, private freedom and with productivity, efficiency, and wealth expansion. This private world appears as an imaginary construction not a historical reality—it operates as a phantom ideal that is then contrasted with coercive, plodding, incompetent, and intrusive post–World War II governments, from fallen totalitarian regimes to stagnant or bankrupt welfare states.[6]

Of course, this rhetorical universe in no way matches the "really existing" policies of neoliberal politicians, who often advocate government support for "private" industries, regulated economic competition to soften the effects of "free" market discipline, and a range of welfare state programs (especially those that benefit more affluent, voting populations). In actual policy debates, the project of coding the operative rhetorics of public and private can thus become quite complex. When the state acts to support "private" business interests, meaning the interests of business owners and corporations, that can be good. But when the state acts in the "public" interest, meaning in the interest of nonmarket forces or disadvantaged populations, that can be intrusive, coercive, and bad. The proper range for debate over government action is understood as relatively narrow, covering monetary, fiscal, and trade policies, infrastructure maintenance, and "nightwatchman" property protection and law and order measures. Thus neoliberalism shrinks the scope of democracy dramatically in all areas of material production and distribution.[7]

In the policy arenas of cultural and personal life, neoliberalism is currently more pointedly conflicted. Ranging from New Democrats to "compassionate conservatives," neoliberal politicians and organizations debate the relative merits of a more-or-less liberal, libertarian, or socially conservative agenda. Most flexibly combine apparently contradictory positions, in a kind of productive in-coherence designed to appeal and appease: Bill Clinton supported affirmative action and the death penalty, abortion rights and the Defense of Marriage Act. But the debate and continuing flexibility in these arenas, particularly in the United States, is working toward a "third way" rhetoric positioned between the moral conservatism of the religious Right and the perceived "multiculturalism" and "civil rights agenda" of the progressive Left. This is where the IGF with its "new gay politics" comes in. By producing gay equality rhetoric and lobbying for specific policies that work within the framework of neoliberal politics generally, the IGF and its affiliated writers hope first to shore up the strength of neoliberal-ism in relation to its critics on the Right and Left, but especially in relation to the gay Left; and, second, to push the neoliberal consensus in the direction of their brand of libertarian/moderate/conservative gay politics and away from politi-cally attractive antigay alternatives and compromises.

The beachhead established by the writers now posted on the IGF Web site has been remarkably effective in creating what Michael Warner has called "a virtual gay movement" in the mainstream and gay press since the mid 1990s.[8] By invok-ing a phantom mainstream public of "conventional" gays who represent the responsible center, these writers have worked to position "liberationists" and leftists as irresponsible "extremists" or as simply anachronistic. But this group has been much less successful in influencing national policy; they have failed to persuade many mainstream politicians to support their core issues of full access by gays to marriage and military service. But they are certainly not yet defeated on these issues or in their overall project of providing a new sexual politics for neoliberalism in the new millennium.

The new neoliberal sexual politics of the IGF might be termed the *new homo-normativity*—it is a politics that does not contest dominant heteronormative assumptions and institutions but upholds and sustains them while promising the possibility of a demobilized gay constituency and a privatized, depoliticized gay culture anchored in domesticity and consumption.[9] Writers in the IGF produce this politics through a double-voiced address to an imagined gay public, on the one hand, and to the national mainstream constructed by neoliberalism on the other.[10] This address works to bring the desired public into political salience as a perceived mainstream, primarily through a rhetorical remapping of public/pri-vate boundaries designed to shrink gay public spheres and redefine gay equality against the "civil rights agenda" and "liberationism," as access to the institutions of domestic privacy, the "free" market, and patriotism.

This remapping is a big job given the history of gay rights activism in the United States. Although the fight for gay equality has since the emergence of the homophile movement in the 1950s been rocked by internal conflict over assimilationist versus confrontational tactics, the overall goals and directions of change have been relatively consistent: the expansion of a right to sexual privacy against the intrusive, investigatory labeling powers of the state, and the simultaneous expansion of gay public life through institution building and publicity.[11]

During the 1950s and 1960s, homophile movement organizations entered a fraught rhetorical battlefield, riddled with intensely contradictory conflicts over public/private distinctions. The New Deal's expansion of public action into previously privatized bastions of economic power and cultural production, and the Civil Rights movement's struggle to further expand the arena of formal public equality from the state to "private" employment practices, civil institutions, and public accommodations, were under fierce attack by conservatives intent on reprivatizing as much of the common life of the nation as possible. However, in the kind of contradictory move that produced their constitutive hierarchies and exclusions, conservatives also worked to deny the protections of privacy against state interference in domestic and sexual life to all but the procreatively, intraracially married. Here they were countered by progressive efforts to eliminate laws against miscegenation, birth control, and sexually themed cultural expression.[12]

Thus, in the arena of economic and collective activities, conservatives coded the state as a bad, coercive, intrusive force against freedom, while New Deal and Keynesian liberals and many leftists invoked a democratically accountable "public" state interest in guaranteeing equality of access, if not always of distribution (here liberals and leftists often parted company). In the arena of personal, sexual, and domestic life, conservatives accorded "privacy" only to the favored form of family life, and supported state regulation of intimate relations in the name of social order for all others. Progressives ambivalently and unevenly, but increasingly, defended a right to sexual and domestic privacy for all, defined as autonomy or liberty from state interference.[13]

Homophile movement organizations, including the Mattachine Society, the Janus Society, and the Daughters of Bilitis, and homophile publications ranging from *One,* the *Mattachine Review,* and the *Ladder* to the *Homosexual Citizen* and *Drum,* served as platforms and forums for radicals like Mattachine founder and Communist Party member Harry Hay and well-known playwright Lorraine

Hansberry, cautious and assimilationist reformers including Daughters of Bilitis stalwarts Del Martin and Phyllis Lyon, and militant single-issue activists such as Franklin Kameny and Barbara Gittings. But despite internal disputes and significant political shifts over time, the homophile activists intervened in postwar conflicts by steadily expanding the notion of sexual or personal privacy to include not only sexual relations between consenting adults at home but freedom from surveillance and entrapment in public and collective settings. These activists worked in company with an expanding commercial sector serving gay and lesbian constituencies to attack the investigatory activities, in public settings including bars and parks as well as workplaces, of the local police, state liquor authorities, the FBI, and federal government employers. This complex maneuver involved not only defending the right to privacy of couples at home but defining a kind of right-to-privacy-in-public: a zone of immunity from state regulation, surveillance, and harassment. This project worked along with efforts to expand the allowable scope of sexual expression in public culture, both commercial and nonprofit/artistic, to complexly remap zones of collective autonomy in ways that displaced the conservative boundaries of corporate freedoms and personal/public moral constraints.[14]

In the 1970s, gay liberation exploded onto a rapidly shifting scene of contest over the meanings of public and private and the related meanings of democracy and autonomy in collective and personal life. Following the 1969 Stonewall rebellion and the subsequent emergence of new organizations and rhetorics, gay politics began to interact intensely with feminist, countercultural and antiracist rhetorics and strategies. The emphasis of political activism shifted away from arguments for privacy as autonomy, and toward public visibility and publicity. But the work of recombining rhetorics of public and private was not abandoned; the project of building an unmolested collective life required continuing remappings of a right-to-privacy-in-public and a right to publicize "private" matters considered offensive to the phantom "general public."

By the 1980s, antigay forces had retooled their strategies. They began slowly and unevenly to concede a right to privacy, but they defined privacy as a kind of confinement, a cordon sanitaire protecting "public" sensibilities. They attacked gay rhetorical claims for privacy-in-public and for publicizing the private, specifically, and worked to define the private sphere as an isolated, domestic site completely out of range of any public venue. Thus the strategy of state No Promo Homo referenda and attacks on public funding for homoerotic art: gay sex is fine in "private" but should not be "displayed" or "promoted" in public.

Meanwhile AIDS activism deepened and expanded the scope of gay politics, crucially supplementing a newly well-established gay rights movement focused on antidiscrimination and decriminalization. New activist energies organized in the face of the AIDS pandemic also helped to spawn a vigorous, emergent queer political front with visions of social and cultural transformation beyond the limits of identity politics.[15]

By the time of the 1992 presidential contest that elected Bill Clinton, neoliberal organizations and politicians had begun the task of separating themselves from the moral conservatism of the religious Right, as well as from the "failed" policies of "old" tax-and-spend liberals. And alongside radical and progressive AIDS activism a new strain of gay moralism appeared—attacks on "promiscuity" and the "gay lifestyle" accompanied advocacy of monogamous marriage as a responsible disease-prevention strategy.[16] In this fertile ground, the coterie of writers attached to the IGF began to spread the word about their new gay politics—a politics that offers a dramatically shrunken public sphere and a narrow zone of "responsible" domestic privacy, in terms arguably more broadly antidemocratic and antiegalitarian than the homophile movement at its most cautious and assimilationist.

The authors and articles collected on the IGF Web site are generally glib; the arguments assembled are characterized more by put-downs, pleas, and polemics than by sustained argument or analysis. One of the best-known writers on the site exemplifying this approach is Bruce Bawer, self-described elitist and monogamous churchgoing Christian, former writer for the right-wing *American Spectator;* editor of an anthology of articles by IGF colleagues, *Beyond Queer: Challenging Gay Left Orthodoxy;* and author of a long list of essays and reviews as well as of his own thoroughly humorless little homily, *A Place at the Table: The Gay Individual in American Society.* Bawer is practiced at the rhetorical techniques of triangulation, as well as the less-subtle joys of naked Left bashing. He invokes "most gay people" as a Nixonian "silent majority" of the conventional and opposed to Left "queerthink." He describes his own and his wished-for constituency's views as "postideological," and positions them in relation to the "anachronistic" multi-issue progressive politics of the Stonewall generation.[17] In two of his shorter screeds, he takes special aim at Urvashi Vaid, positioning her well outside the new center of the IGF's gay public by calling her an "ideological extremist" whose rhetoric is "old." He goes well beyond simple Left bashing, though, to set forth his alternative vision of the best sources of social change for gay equality, arguing that

In 1995, even as veteran activist Urvashi Vaid issued a call for a radical gay rights movement aligned with workers and other victim groups against the capitalist oppressor, mounting evidence suggested that major corporations may well do more to bring about gay equality than any other Establishment institution (or, for that matter, the National Gay and Lesbian Task Force). . . . More than ever, it seemed reasonable to suggest that much of gay America's hope resides not in working-class revolt but in its exact opposite—a trickling down of gay-positive sentiments from elite corporate boardrooms into shops, farms, and factories.[18]

Bawer looks unabashedly to a trickle-down vision of equality as corporate largess, and gleefully anticipates the Disneyfication of democracy as boardroom deal making.

As basic Left bashing, though, Bawer's attacks on Vaid have been mild and inconsequential compared with the efforts of IGF writer Rob Blanchard (now deceased) and his associates in San Antonio, Texas, who joined with Christian Right forces to attack the reputation and funding of the Esperanza Peace and Justice Center, the progressive arts and community organization led by lesbians of color. In 1997, Blanchard and five other white gay men claiming affiliation with the National Lesbian and Gay Journalists Association, the San Antonio Equal Rights Political Caucus, the Log Cabin Republicans, and the San Antonio Gay and Lesbian Community Center signed a letter to the city's mayor and city council members asking that Esperanza be denied city funding, arguing that "it is a political organization—obsessed with victimhood and using 'sexism, racism, classism, and homophobia' as rhetorical and political ploys to extract guilt money from individuals and organizations, including the City. Esperanza has made its battle for tax dollars a referendum on homosexuality and we resent this. But Esperanza's greatest damage to the gay and lesbian community is the divisiveness it creates within by repeatedly injecting issues of class, race and gender for self-serving purposes."[19] This attack attributes "divisiveness" to an inclusive agenda and locates unity in the unmarked centrality of prosperous white men, whose interests unproblematically define the interests of "the gay and lesbian community." It goes further to participate aggressively in the right-wing strategy of denying public funding for "political" arts projects, defining neoliberal advocacy by contrast as the nonpolitical exclusion of "issues of class, race, and gender."

Such attacks, while both ugly and revealing, do not clearly illuminate the underlying political logic of the IGF's new gay paradigm. The writer whose work most fully elaborates an overarching framework for the efforts of this group is former *New Republic* editor Andrew Sullivan, a prolific essayist with a Ph.D. in political science from Harvard and analytic aspirations somewhat higher than the level of earnest exhortation, vituperative attack, or clever polemics.

Well, Sullivan may aim higher, but in his most widely cited book, *Virtually Normal,* he falls well short of sustained, coherent analysis. He nonetheless sets the terms for neoliberal arguments about sexual politics, beginning with a triangulating framework that attacks the "extremes" of what he calls *prohibitionism* and *liberationism* and claims to reconcile the best arguments of contemporary conservatives and liberals to offer, in the "third way" mode, a new approach.

Sullivan's prohibitionism is the kind of social conservatism that would morally condemn and legally punish homosexuality. He distinguishes this view from bigotry, however, and argues respectfully that "in an appeal to 'nature,' the most persuasive form of this argument is rooted in one of the oldest traditions of thought in the West, a tradition that still carries a great deal of intuitive sense. It posits a norm—the heterosexual identity—that is undeniably valuable in any society and any culture, that seems to characterize the vast majority of humanity, and without which civilization would simply evaporate: and it attempts to judge homosexuality by the standards of that norm."[20] He follows this claim with an extended discussion of the published views of the Roman Catholic Church, from the writings of St. Thomas Aquinas to statements of church dogma published in 1975 and 1986 on homosexual relations. The centrality of Catholic doctrine to his analysis, rather than, say, the religious views of Baptists or the political opinions of the Republican Party, is not explained or justified—the fact that Sullivan is himself Catholic seems to be the motivation for this choice. He ultimately rejects the prohibitionist view, even in the respectfully distorted form in which he presents one variant of antigay discourse, as internally inconsistent (in a consistent approach nonprocreative heterosexuality would have to be condemned and punished as well as homosexuality) and just plain wrong in positing homosexuality as a threat to the predominance and prestige of the traditional heterosexual family. The core of Sullivan's argument here is also key to his entire framework— he argues that homosexuality is an involuntary condition (created by both nature and nurture at a very young age) in a small fixed minority of the population. In an analogy to natural variation he argues that "as albinos remind us of the brilliance of color; as redheads offer a startling contrast to the blandness of their peers; as genius teaches us, by contrast, of the virtue of moderation: so the homosexual person might be seen as a natural foil to the heterosexual norm, a variation that does not eclipse the theme, but resonates with it."[21] He implicitly concedes, here and throughout the book, that if homosexuality could be somehow chosen by more people than a very, very tiny percentage of "waverers," then antigay policies might make sense as discouragement of this choice. In his view it is only because homosexuality is involuntary, and therefore cannot threaten an equally involuntary heterosexual majority, that attacking it morally and legally does not make sense.

Sullivan inveighs against liberationism for a similar reason—its proponents' insistence that sexual identities are socially constructed rather than timelessly fixed within contemporary categories. On his side here he claims that "history itself" as uncovered by "contemporary historians" concurs with science and psychology in affirming the presence of homosexuals in all times and places. The fact that the overwhelming majority of historians of sexuality (several of whom he names or footnotes in other contexts) makes precisely the opposite argument is not mentioned.[22]

But it is not only his historical arguments that are unsupported; Sullivan's description of what he calls liberationism is completely confused and ultimately much more cartoonishly reductive than his description of prohibitionism. For the purpose of ridicule and dismissal, he collapses virtually all the political and intellectual approaches to sexual politics on the contemporary radical or progressive Left (approaches wildly at odds with each other analytically and strategically) into one big pot labeled "Foucauldean." He includes and collapses militant identity politics, such as Michelangelo Signorile's favored tactic of "outing" hypocritical closeted gays, or Larry Kramer's plans and pronouncements on AIDS politics, with anti-identity versions of queer coalition politics (which explicitly reject the parameters of narrow gay identity politics like Signorile's and Kramer's) and the writings of academics from social constructionist historians and sociologists to poststructuralist critics and philosophers, especially Judith Butler.

This hodgepodge of diverse and contentious activists and intellectuals is presented as a monolith of rigid orthodoxies. The strategy of "outing" is hilariously described as "a classic case of Foucauldean resistance," though no Foucauldian ever supported it (and its practitioners were generally nearly as hostile to Foucauldian academics as Sullivan himself). "Queer" is described as a uniform and compulsory identity "used to label . . . [and] to tell everyone that they have a single and particular identity," when "queer" has been used most often precisely to question the uniformity of sexual identities (like Sullivan's "gay" identity). And as a final summary and dismissal Sullivan proclaims that "the liberationists prefer to concentrate—for where else can they go?—on those instruments of power which require no broader conversation, no process of dialogue, no moment of compromise, no act of engagement. So they focus on outing, on speech codes, on punitive measures against opponents on campuses, on the enforcement of new forms of language, by censorship and intimidation."[23] This "authoritarian" project well describes the fantasied enemies of the right-wing front in the culture wars, but it bears no relation to the range of policies, projects, and arguments Sullivan tries to collect under the umbrella "liberationist." While some campus activists support speech codes and some liberal organizations fight for hate crime laws, many of the writers Sullivan names have opposed these specific proposals; his bête noire, Judith Butler, wrote *Excitable Speech* specifically to oppose efforts to regulate speech or belief.[24] But then, coherent analysis and engagement is less the point in Sullivan's discussion of so-called liberationists than it is in his discussion of the Catholic Church. Sullivan is not *addressing* the Left, he is caricaturing it.

Sullivan really gets down to business when he turns to classical liberalism in its contemporary liberal and conservative formations. These are the political perspectives he takes seriously; the ones he hopes to "marry" to derive a new politics of homosexuality. He defines liberalism as the commitment to a formally neutral state and to the foundational freedoms of action, speech, and choice—most fundamentally expressed in freedom of contract. By this definition, contemporary liberalism has deviated dangerously; in Sullivan's view, this has occurred particularly as a response to the politics of race in the United States.

Sullivan's account of the history of the state in the United States, and of the background and legacies of progressive liberalism, is severely stunted and distorted, leaving out, for instance, little details like the role of the turn-of-the-century women's movement, the labor movement, and the New Deal.[25] But his project is not to get history right, it is to set up his argument. He wants to position the "civil rights agenda" as *the* wrong road in contemporary liberal politics. And, although he vacillates about whether the historical injustices of race might have justified some departure from the tenets of classical liberalism, he ultimately critiques the Civil Rights movement's legacy of antidiscrimination law, particularly affirmative action, as veering too far away from the proper goals of state neutrality and private freedom of contract. If the politics of homosexuality continues to follow this model, he argues, the state and the law "will be forced into being a mixture of moral education, psychotherapy and absolution. Liberalism was invented specifically to oppose that use of the law."[26]

But when Sullivan turns his attention to contemporary conservatism, he suddenly alters his attitude toward the public inculcation of "values." He mostly endorses what he calls "conservative goods," with the exception of the hypocritical practice of private tolerance coupled with public disapproval of homosexuality. He believes that this conservative public/private pact of discretion is breaking down, even though it still underlies many state policies, including the logic behind the military's "don't ask, don't tell" policy. But he doesn't argue that in the face of such breakdown conservative family values should retreat to state neutrality, as he recommends for progressive values of equality and diversity. Instead, he claims to have a plan to offer a new public/private mapping that can combine conservative goods with classical liberal state neutrality.

Sullivan's plan is simple. It involves focusing primarily on two issues—gay access to marriage and the military—then demobilizing the gay population to a "prepolitical" condition. For Sullivan, the beauty of the debate over gays in the military is that even though it has temporarily been lost for the forces of gay inclusion, it garnered "the best of both worlds"; that is, it allows the conservative to "point to the virtues of a loyal and dedicated soldier, homosexual or heterosexual, and to celebrate his patriotism" with absolutely no abrogation of liberal principles. The marriage debate provides an even better opportunity. As the proclaimed centerpiece of Sullivan's new politics, "marriage is not simply a private contract; it is a social and public recognition of a private commitment. As such, it is the highest public recognition of personal integrity."[27]

But wait! Doesn't this role for marriage sound an awful lot like the dangerous mixture of "moral education, psychotherapy and absolution" that Sullivan warns progressive liberals against? According to Sullivan's account of liberal principles, should the state be in the business of recognizing one version of "personal integrity"? Apparently so. In comparing support for gay marriage to the currently available alternative government policy, specifically the passage of domestic partnership provisions for unmarried couples, Sullivan is the most explicit about the benefits of his plan:

> The conservative's worries start with the ease of the relationship. To be sure, domestic partners have to prove financial interdependence, shared living arrangements, and a commitment to mutual caring. But they don't need to have a sexual relationship or even closely mirror old-style marriage. In

principle, an elderly woman and her live-in nurse could qualify, or a pair of frat buddies. Left as it is, the concept of domestic partnership could open a Pandora's box of litigation and subjective judicial decision making about who qualifies. . . .

More important for conservatives, the concept of domestic partnership chips away at the prestige of traditional relationships and undermines the priority we give them. . . . Marriage provides an anchor, if an arbitrary and often weak one, in the maelstrom of sex and relationships to which we are all prone. It provides a mechanism for emotional stability and economic security. We rig the law in its favor not because we disparage all forms of relationship other than the nuclear family, but because we recognize that not to promote marriage would be to ask too much of human virtue.[28]

One might argue that domestic partnership as Sullivan describes it meets the criteria of state neutrality about "values" better than the marriages to which he advocates the state supply prestige. It certainly seems more democratic and less steeped in hierarchy and subjective judgment, as well as more egalitarian about how material and symbolic benefits might be allocated to households—not to mention a better approximation of his vaunted freedom of contract. But Sullivan upholds the most conventional and idealized form of marriage as lifetime monogamy (he says that he has tried to construct for himself the "mirror image of the happy heterosexuality I imagined around me") in utterly prefeminist terms (the operative word is *imagined,* and clearly from a husbandly point of view).[29]

But Sullivan's support for gay marriage is more than a conservative opinion on a hot issue—it is a linchpin for his broader political vision, one that overlaps considerably with most of the writers in the IGF panoply. Sullivan aims to construct a new public/private distinction that mobilizes gay equality rhetoric on behalf of a miniaturized state and constricted public life, confined to a very few policy decisions, coupled with a vast zone of "private" life dominated by "voluntary" economic and civic transactions, however conglomerated, oligarchic, and unaccountable. Marriage is a strategy for privatizing gay politics and culture for the new neoliberal world order. He explains:

It is, of course, not the least of the ironies of this politics—and of predominantly political argument—that, in the last resort, its objectives are in some sense not political at all. The family is prior to the state; the military is coincident with it. Heterosexuals would not conceive of such rights as things to be won, but as things that predate modern political discussion. But it says something about the unique status of homosexuals in our society that we now have to be political in order to be prepolitical. Our battle, after all, is not for political victory but for personal integrity. In the same way that many of us had to leave our families in order to join them again, so now as citizens, we have to embrace politics if only ultimately to be free of it.[30]

There is no vision of a collective, democratic public culture or of an ongoing engagement with contentious, cantankerous queer politics. Instead we have been administered a kind of political sedative—we get marriage and the military then we go home and cook dinner, forever.[31]

Sullivan is probably the single most influential writer among the neoliberal gang of gays published in a wide range of mainstream and gay newspapers and periodicals. But he is certainly not the sole voice along the range of moderate Democrats and Republicans to radical right-wing libertarians in the mix. Libertarians are particularly voluble; the IGF Web site probably adapted its name from the rightist, libertarian Independent Women's Forum and its brand of neoliberal "equality feminism."[32] We might imagine that in the more libertarian environs of such politics we might find more of a deregulating fervor in relation to intimate life. But no, opposition to state administration of marriage among gay libertarians, other than among the left-wing variety, is rare. But rare also is the kind of sentimentality and sanctimoniousness that is rife in discussions like Sullivan's. More typical of libertarian thinking is the hard-edged argumentation of David Boaz, vice president of the Cato Institute. Boaz argues, like Sullivan, that gay marriage is preferable to domestic partnership, because the latter undermines marriage's premium on commitment. But Boaz is much more explicit about the economic role of marriage and its relation to the "free" market—both impose discipline and privatize dependency among the poor. In "Reviving the Inner City," Boaz argues, in fine libertarian fashion, that drug laws as well as welfare state programs are "plantations" for blacks. But he makes clear that the problem is ultimately that welfare programs offer resources especially to poor women, who are thus enabled to make undesirable choices. The combination of market discipline, in the form of dependency on low-wage jobs, and family discipline, in the form of dependency on husbands, operates to create the best environment for Boaz's ideal world: "The stark truth is that as long as the welfare state makes it possible for young women to have children without a husband and to survive without a job, the inner city will continue to be marked by poverty, crime and despair."[33]

This kind of political vision ultimately displaces any belief that Urvashi Vaid or other progressive activists might have that "the gay movement" is one big tent of advocacy for generally democratic and egalitarian goals, with variation from single-issue focuses and assimilationist styles and strategies to multi-issue coalitionism and confrontational tactics. Arguably, such a description may accurately represent the organized gay movement from the homophile activism in the 1950s and 1960s through lesbian feminism and gay liberation in the 1970s to liberal gay rights advocacy in the 1980s. But since the 1990s, the influential new gay politics of the IGF writers have marked a decisive break from the centrist liberal/progressive to radical Left continuum generally invoked by the phrase "the gay movement."

This gay right wing, self-constituted as a new center, is definitively *not* a single-issue political lobby. The IGF's gay equality rhetoric is a proffered new window dressing for a broad multi-issue neoliberal politics. The privacy-in-public claims and publicizing strategies of "the gay movement" are rejected in favor of public recognition of a domesticated, depoliticized privacy. The democratic diversity of proliferating forms of sexual dissidence is rejected in favor of the naturalized variation of a fixed minority arrayed around a state-endorsed heterosexual primacy and prestige. This New Homonormativity comes equipped with a rhetorical recoding of key terms in the history of gay politics: "equality" becomes narrow, formal access to a few conservatizing institutions, "freedom" becomes impunity for bigotry and vast inequalities in commercial life and civil society, the "right to privacy" becomes domestic confinement, and democratic politics itself becomes something to be escaped. All of this adds up to a corporate culture managed by a minimal state, achieved by the neoliberal privatization of affective as well as economic and public life.

Welcome to the New World Order! Coming soon to a mainstream near you.

NOTES

1 Quoted in " 'Liberty for All' Conference Spotlights Political Transformation Under Way in Gay Movement," Log Cabin Republican press release, August 30, 1999. The kind of superficial inclusiveness that characterized this conference, coupled with a harshly elitist agenda, received national attention during the August 2000 Republican Convention at which George W. Bush's "compassionate conservatism" was deceptively and manipulatively sold on network television.
2 http://www.indegayforum.org.
3 See the special issue of *Public Culture*, "Millennial Capitalism and the Culture of

Neoliberalism," vol. 12, no. 2 (spring 2000), especially the introductory essay by volume editors Jean Comaroff and John L. Comaroff, "Millennial Capitalism: First Thoughts on a Second Coming," 291–343.

4 For an excellent discussion of the contours of neoliberal policies, see Andriana Vlachou, ed., *Contemporary Economic Theory: Radical Critiques of Neoliberalism* (New York: St. Martin's Press, 1999), especially the introduction to the volume by Vlachou and Georgios K. Christou.

5 Although many neoliberals would argue for the expansion of the institutions of civil society as alternatives to state action in the public interest, in practice this often means recommendations for corporate sponsorship (and thus corporate control of, for instance, arts institutions) or for the conversion of nonprofit to profit-making operations.

6 "Phantoms" of public and private spheres operate as highly productive rhetorics in the history of U.S. politics. The imaginary public/private boundary is invoked to support or contest a very broad array of cultural and political projects. For a sampling of discussions of this debate, see Bruce Robbins, ed., *The Phantom Public Sphere* (Minneapolis: University of Minnesota Press, 1993). See especially Robbins's "Introduction: The Public as Phantom," which takes off from Walter Lippmann's *The Phantom Public* (New York: Macmillan, 1927). An especially stark example of this kind of rhetoric as it is mobilized within contemporary neoliberalism can be found in a volume coedited by IGF contributor David Boaz and Edward H. Crane, *Market Liberalism: A Paradigm for the Twenty-First Century* (Washington, D.C.: Cato Institute, 1993). Boaz and Crane are officers of the rightist libertarian Cato Institute, which frequently advises the Republican "establishment" on issues of privatization, while maintaining its separate libertarian purity and sense of superiority.

7 See Noam Chomsky, *Profits over People: Neoliberalism and Global Order* (New York: Seven Stories Press, 1999). Chomsky clearly shows how "really existing free market capitalism" contrasts with the doctrines of neoliberalism by providing income supports and trade protections for politically powerful U.S. corporations while imposing "market discipline" on less-advantaged nations and businesses. Robert W. McChesney's introduction to the volume is a very lucid and helpful summary of the major tenets and historical effects of neoliberalism over the past two decades.

8 Michael Warner, "Media Gays: A New Stone Wall," *Nation*, July 14, 1997. Warner's article takes aim at a slightly different, though overlapping, target than the neoliberal writers I examine here. He analyzes the conservative sexual politics of a broader group including many who would not fall under the neoliberal rubric; for instance, Larry Kramer, Gabriel Rotello, and Michelangelo Signorile, none of whom would be included in the IGF's new gay paradigm.

9 I am riffing here on the term *heteronormativity*, introduced by Michael Warner. I don't mean the terms to be parallel; there is no structure for gay life, no matter how conservative or normalizing, that might compare with the institutions promoting and sustaining heterosexual coupling.

10 I use "gay" throughout my discussion here because it is the operative term for the

neoliberals. Although they occasionally gesture toward lesbian inclusion, women and gender issues are not substantively addressed in any of their policy recommendations. Terms such as *bisexual, transgender,* or *queer* occur only as targets of ridicule, and the presumptive whiteness of the audiences for these writers is unwavering.

11 The best description and analysis of the politics of the homophile movement remains John D'Emilio's classic *Sexual Politics, Sexual Communities: The Making of a Homosexual Minority in the United States, 1940–1970* (Chicago: University of Chicago Press, 1983).

12 I am using the terms *public* and *private* not as literally geographic spaces or social zones but as rhetorics employed in political debates. Moreover, I am necessarily compressing a very complex array of debates here. For a somewhat different account of the politics of public and private in relation to sexuality during this period, see David Allyn, "Private Acts/Public Policy: Alfred Kinsey, the American Law Institute, and the Privatization of American Sexual Morality," *Journal of American Studies* 30 (1996): 405–28.

13 The conservative version of family "privacy" amounted more to a kind of fathers' rights rhetoric than to an autonomy claim. Certainly in relation to women the "privacy" accorded was of a sequestering rather than protective sort. On the liberal/progressive side, the very slow and uneven expansion of claims to a right to privacy as autonomy is illustrated by the rocky course of the ACLU's policies; in 1957 the organization endorsed the constitutionality of statutes criminalizing homosexuality, but by 1967 it had adopted a broad gay rights position (see D'Emilio, *Sexual Politics,* 112, 213).

14 See D'Emilio, *Sexual Politics;* Rodger Streitmatter, *Unspeakable: The Rise of the Lesbian and Gay Rights Press in America* (Boston: Faber & Faber, 1995); Jim Kepner, *Rough News, Daring Views: 1950s Pioneer Gay Press Journalism* (New York: The Haworth Press, 1998); and Manuela Soares, "The Purloined *Ladder:* Its Place in Lesbian History," in *Gay and Lesbian Literature since World War II: History and Memory,* ed. Sonya Jones (New York: The Haworth Press, 1998), 27–49.

15 For an extended analysis of the 1980s antigay initiatives and the explosion of new queer activism in the face of AIDS, see Lisa Duggan and Nan Hunter, eds., *Sex Wars: Sexual Dissent and Political Culture* (New York: Routledge, 1995).

16 For a sharp analysis of this new gay moralism, see Michael Warner, *The Trouble with Normal: Sex, Politics, and the Ethics of Queer Life* (New York: The Free Press, 1999).

17 "Most gay people," "queerthink," and "post-ideological" are quoted from Bruce Bawer, ed., *Beyond Queer: Challenging Gay Left Orthodoxy* (New York: The Free Press, 1996), ix–xv. "Silent majority" is from *A Place at the Table: The Gay Individual in American Society* (New York: Simon and Schuster, 1993), 26. The reference to "anachronistic" Stonewall politics is in his "Notes on Stonewall: Is the Gay Rights Movement Living in the Past?" *New Republic,* June 13, 1994, 24.

18 Bruce Bawer, "Up (with) the Establishment," *Advocate,* January 23, 1996, 112. The accusation of ideological extremism is from Bawer's review of Vaid's book, *Virtual Equality: The Mainstreaming of Gay and Lesbian Liberation* (New York: Doubleday, 1995), which appeared as "Radically Different: Do Gay People Have a Responsibility to Be Revolutionaries?" in *New York Times Book Review,* November 5, 1995, 21.

19 The text of this letter, published in the *New York Times* on September 11, 1997, is included on a Web site with many other documents relating to this arts funding conflict: http://www.esperanzacenter.org. For an excellent, brief summary of events, see Alexandra Chasin, *Selling Out: The Gay and Lesbian Movement Goes to Market* (New York: St. Martin's Press, 2000), 228–33. Since 1997, the Esperanza Center has undergone repeated battles over the funding issue, and it is still involved in litigation as of this writing.

20 Andrew Sullivan, *Virtually Normal: An Argument about Homosexuality* (New York: Knopf, 1995), 21.

21 Ibid., 47.

22 Ibid., 69, 71. Sullivan cites U.S. social historian George Chauncey, historian and classicist David Halperin, and historical sociologist David Greenberg, so he cannot be unaware of the consensus against him on this point. As support for his version of "history itself" he names only John Boswell, a medieval Catholic Church historian who is nearly the lone voice on the issue of unvarying homosexual identity.

23 Sullivan, *Virtually Normal*, 85, 93.

24 Judith Butler, *Excitable Speech: A Politics of the Performative* (New York: Routledge, 1997).

25 For a restrained yet scathing review of Sullivan's historical account in *Virtually Normal,* see K. Anthony Appiah, "The Marrying Kind," *New York Review of Books,* June 20, 1996, 48–52.

26 Sullivan, *Virtually Normal*, p. 151.

27 Ibid., 176–79.

28 Ibid., 182.

29 Ibid., 192. In a hilarious critique of gay conservative idealizations of marriage, "Gay Marriage? Don't Say I Didn't Warn You" *Nation,* April 29, 1996, 9, Katha Pollitt writes: "When gay friends argue in favor of same-sex marriage, I always agree and offer them the one my husband and I are leaving. Why should straights be the only ones to have their unenforceable promise to love, honor and cherish trap them like houseflies in the web of law? Marriage will not only open up to gay men and lesbians whole new vistas of guilt, frustration, claustrophobia, bewilderment, declining self-esteem, unfairness and sorrow, it will offer them the opportunity to prolong this misery by tormenting each other in court."

30 Sullivan, *Virtually Normal*, 186–87.

31 In the epilogue to *Virtually Normal* Sullivan indulges a strange ambivalence, acknowledging that gay life, always and only white gay male life (his subject and audience are only ever presumptively white and male—for a perceptive exposure of the whiteness of Sullivan's "gays" see Phillip Brian Harper, "Gay Male Identities, Personal Privacy, and Relations of Public Exchange: Notes on Directions for Queer Critique" *Social Text* 52 (fall-winter 1997) 5–29, contains, in its differences, resources for the society at large. He points to the supportive role of friendship networks and to the admiral flexibility of many gay men who allow for "extramarital outlets" in their relationships. He was excoriated by the Right for the "extramarital outlets" reference, and retracted it in a new afterword to the paperback edition of the book. In a letter to the editor in

Commentary (November 1996)—a response to an attack by Norman Podhoretz on this issue—Sullivan clarified that "it is my view that, in same-sex marriage, adultery should be as anathema as it is in heterosexual marriage." One might ask, exactly how anathema is that?

32 An excellent discussion of the politics of right-wing libertarianism, including the activities of the Independent Women's Forum, is included in Jean Hardisty's "Libertarianism and Civil Society: The Romance of Free-Market Capitalism," in her *Mobilizing Resentment: Conservative Resurgence from the John Birch Society to the Promise Keepers* (Boston: Beacon Press, 1999), 162–88.

33 David Boaz, "Reviving the Inner City," in David Boaz and Edward Crane, eds., *Market Liberalism*, 189–203. Boaz expounds his position on marriage versus domestic partnership for gays in "Domestic Justice," *New York Times*, January 4, 1995. For a sharp and influential discussion of the relation of queer politics and the gender/race/class issues surrounding welfare politics, see Cathy Cohen, "Punks, Bulldaggers, and Welfare Queens," *GLQ* 3 (1997): 437–65.

CHRIS CASTIGLIA

The Genealogy of a Democratic Crush

◆

I had a full life in drama.
—*Monica Lewinsky, in Andrew Morton,* Monica's Story

All critical challenges to already existing democracy occur in the public sphere. Or so a good deal of Habermasian-inflected social theory would have us believe, contending that citizens speak from a realm detached from the state, from which they contest the assumptions of state-operated democracy.[1] By the same token, laments about collective exclusions from civil society—most notably those based on race, gender, sexuality, and class—for the most part take "exclusion" as a mendable shortcoming of public discourse, not as an argument for the location of revisionary democracy some "place" else.[2] In this sense, "exclusion" works for public debate in much the same way as "repression" in Foucault's famous critique of Freud works for sexual confession, inciting more articulations of citizens' desire to be in public, making the public, in effect, the sole location of democratic desire.[3]

Although theorizing (and, one would hope, mobilizing) against exclusions from public debate is urgently important, my concern in this essay is the framing of democratic citizens through discourses—often trivial and sentimental—constituted as "other" (and vastly inferior) to rational public debate. By this I don't mean to rehearse a tired distinction between public and private "spheres," but rather to assert the importance of democratic *interiority* to explorations of the sometimes dangerous, sometimes revisionary, interplay between the fantasies of citizens and their public utterances.[4] Extended analyses of democratic exchange in the public sphere often obscure how citizens are prepared—and prepare themselves—for their public performances, how the desire to debate in public arises, how certain constrictions of subjective interiority preclude the possibility of public voice, and how the state and its citizens debate, through enforced confession and fantastic resistance, in ways that bypass civil exchange altogether.

In making this claim, I am drawing a distinction between government and governance.[5] The "democracy" of government lies in the rights granted to citizens by the Constitution, which operate on the actions of citizens' bodies: how they act in public, where they assemble and with whom, what they can speak, and so forth. By "governance" I mean something akin to what Foucault describes as the generation, through coerced public confessions of nominally "private" emotions and "personal" acts, of an excess to the citizen's body—in the form of spirit, character, personality—that can be evaluated and reformed through the institutional knowledges of national subjectivity. Public institutions provide a range of *interiorizing discourses* that mediate between the nation-state and the citizen, prompting citizens to experience hierarchical systems of social power as emanations of their own interiority. Social order becomes, then, a function of individualized and self-regulated civil character, rather than (although always maintained in the potential presence of) state coercion. The nation-state's ability to read itself in the interiors of its citizens requires, however, the public confession of the citizen's interior states, confessions normatively regulated into shame or pride, fear or belligerence—whatever form of national affect the historical situation requires.

Sometimes, however, citizens deploy interiority to generate forms of support, communication, and pleasure for ends other than the fostering of national affect. Such moments of divergence require a citizen's willingness to struggle, through affective modes, with the sanctioned meanings of both interiority and democracy. In what follows, I locate such a struggle between two apparently trivial yet persistent analogies that have determined the shape of Monica Lewinsky's story. Many who have told that story have compared her to the heroine of Hawthorne's *The Scarlet Letter,* making Lewinsky into what Roger Chillingworth calls "a living sermon against sin."[6] In so doing, they invoke the image of a shamed woman, forced to confess her sexual secrets before a prurient public in order to reaffirm the shaky authority of a sanctimonious elite. Yet Lewinsky herself chose another narrative structure to tell her story. When FBI agents and Special Prosecutor Kenneth Starr's deputies apprehended Lewinsky on January 26, 1998, and brought her to a room in the Pentagon City Ritz Carleton for questioning, the usually loquacious Lewinsky refused to supply answers to the questions put to her. When, after several hours of interrogation, Lewinsky broke her silence, it was to tell the agents that, in high school, she had been involved in musical theater.[7] A trivial footnote in an already trivialized chapter of U.S. history, Lewinsky's ice-breaker offers a clue to how and why the intern used the sentimental logic of the musical to preserve her privacy and to demonstrate what was at stake for democratic interaction in her sentimental fantasies. By choosing the musical through which to frame her story, I will argue, Lewinsky turned her erotic interior from a site of shamed reform to one of democratic potentiality, centered on the particular emotional state known as a "crush." Through Lewinsky's story, then, I will trace a brief genealogy of what might be called a democratic crush; in so doing, I am arguing for the usefulness of affect, fantasy, and self-theatricalization deployed as a critical intervention in the operation of affective governance and hence as a radical alternative to the public commitments underlying democratic government itself.

ON MY OWN

Crushes, like democracy, are difficult to define. Nevertheless, I want to begin by suggesting some constitutive traits that distinguish crushes from, say, romances or infatuations. First, crushes, as they are dismissively conceived, are yoked first to shame and then to normalization (as expressed in the childhood chant, mandatory on the "discovery" of a crush: "first comes love, then comes marriage, then comes so and so with a baby carriage"). The person experiencing the crush, however, is enhancing the possibilities of affective exchange beyond the prescriptive social "realities" of courtship and marriage. Indeed, we might well ask: Is it simply children's wisdom that the crush's play of affection is more precious, because more contingent, than the adult sexuality that presumably lies on the other side of the crush? Is the tragedy of adulthood that it reduces crushes from a flexible if contingent bond to a restrictive certainty (first . . . then . . . then)?

Second, crushes are representational phenomena: it is very difficult—if indeed desirable—to confuse crushes with "reality" (or, looked at another way, crushes are the distilled representational bases of romantic "reality"). Crushes, moreover, are self-generating stories people tell themselves to know better who they are as desiring subjects; they are not strategic plans. Crushes don't translate well into social "reality" because they are predicated on unreciprocality; once one is "involved" with someone, the relationship would not be described as a crush. Although the crush is commonly given a negative interpretation along the lines of, "How desperate so and so is to have a crush on someone so beyond his reach," for the person engaged in the crush the unavailability of the object is frequently part of the pleasure; it affords a necessary safe distance, leaving the subject free to engage all the imaginative possibilities of self-generation.

Finally, crushes typically work up along a scale of power: one develops a crush on someone invested in a hierarchy (of gender, sexuality, class, appearance, social position) that makes romance unlikely. Rather than despairing in the face of that unlikelihood, or internalizing it as shame, the person with a crush appropriates qualities of the more powerful person into her or himself, inventing an affective world where power operates at the bidding of the person disempowered in the "real" world. The crush's self-generating representations are never purely private, then, but imagine a world where power dynamics alter long enough for the subject to imagine her or himself in more enabling ways.

Perhaps because of these qualities, crushes form the heart of the most popular (and populist) cultural forms (pop music, pulp fiction, Hollywood tearjerkers), all of which have flourished, in their inception, among peoples struggling to enter public enfranchisement. Following Lewinsky's lead, I want to focus on the deployment of crushes in one of the most discredited popular cultural forms, the musical theater. At the core of musical theater is a man or, more typically, a woman, who, faced with the seemingly hopeless confines of class or geography or convention, dreams herself into being by virtue of someone who is now gone or dead or—as is most typically and powerfully the case—has never been. Frequently, these musical crushes are efforts to bring into being not a romance but a more equitable social world.

In *Les Miserables*, for example, the waif Eponine, alone and forsaken, imagines herself through her fantasy of love for a man she can never have, at least not for long. Plaintively, but not without a degree of contagious pleasure, she starts out forlorn and abandoned, deprived of friends or even a stranger's kindness. Yet Eponine soon transforms her isolating solitude into a fantastic realm of imaginative satisfaction: walking "alone at night when everybody else is sleeping," she thinks "of him and then I'm happy with the company I'm keeping. / The city goes to bed / And I can live inside my head." This song, "On My Own," suggests a world of pleasure opened up for Eponine by the possibilities of desire "without him" (desires predicated on a "real" man, but a man pledged irredeemably to another woman). The crisis in Eponine's fantasy world comes from her interaction with the pedagogical lessons of the "real" social world, where she must articulate the self-delusions of her imagined romance:

> I love him, but when the night is over,
> He is gone; the river's just a river.

What is at stake in this crisis, however, what brings Eponine's pleasurable night-life to its pathetic end, is not the withdrawal of the man (his absence allows for pleasure in the first place) nor necessarily the sudden realization of how impossi-ble her desire is (an impossibility Eponine ostensibly knew when she began her nighttime strolls "on her own": "Without me, this world would go on turning").[8] What is lost when she loses her fantasy is *herself.* "Without him" is thus substi-tuted with "without *me,*" and while the first absence allows the world-generating pleasures of fantasy, the second loss—the loss of the self generated through the first fantasy—simply leaves the normative world of "realities" and "romances," where one is either happily married (and who gets to be that in a musical?) or one is alone (not quite "on one's own").

Significantly, Eponine's number, which sets the self-generating imaginings of the crush in opposition to the self-obliterating pedagogy of social wisdom, is preceded in the musical by the fantasy of political self-fulfillment, the roaring ensemble number "One Day More," which stages a collective desire for revolu-tion in the absence of democratic potentiality in the here and now. The score thus suggests a parallel between the collective fantasy of democratic justice and the self-generating fantasy of the crush.

When Monica Lewinsky entered a high school talent show, she chose to sing "On My Own" from *Les Miserables.* She not only won the competition, she was voted "Most likely to see her name in lights."

THAT WOMAN

Monica Lewinsky often felt deep connections to the literary productions of nineteenth-century America: her most cherished gift from the president was a volume of Whitman's *Leaves of Grass;* she placed a personal ad for Clinton in the *Washington Post* quoting Dickinson's "Wild Nights"; and her hairdresser was named Ishmael. And of course Lewinsky attended Hawthorne Elementary School, where one imagines she might have been a precocious and unusually invested reader of *The Scarlet Letter.* Not surprisingly, then, as the headline of Stephanie Salter's *San Francisco Examiner* column, "Monica's New Place in the U.S. of 'A,'" suggests, Lewinsky entered the national stage as Hawthorne's shamed heroine: "As surely as if she were wearing her own embroidered 'A' upon every blouse, jacket and dress in her closet," Salter comments, "Lewinsky is marked for life."[9] The parallels between Hester's story and Lewinsky's are strik-ing: both center on a secret romance with a leader who watches while his lover takes the heat for the affair made public and suffers the humiliation of his denial, until, persecuted by an overly zealous interrogator, the leader makes an eleventh-hour confession, leaving his lover alone, sewing for a living (Lewinsky went on to produce handbags with the trademark label "Made especially for you by Monica").

Lewinsky's casting as Hester redux is reinforced by her official biographer, Andrew Morton, whose *Monica's Story* narrates a latter-day allegory of shamed confession and reform. To note the parallels between Hester and Monica is to read the biography against its grain, for Morton, confidante to the late Princess of Wales, is no Puritan, condemning Special Prosecutor Kenneth Starr's "almost puritanical frustration and anger . . . , as if Lewinsky must be punished for her obstinacy, dating back to her refusal to wear a wire" (214). Morton further reports that "though Monica has been painted as a 'scarlet woman'—or worse—in the course of the whole Clinton scandal, she remains firm in her conviction that one's sexuality is nothing to be afraid of. 'I don't see sexuality as something to hide away in the dark or be ashamed of. I think our sexuality is something to be honored, cherished, and valued'" (51). More Queer Nationalist than the reclusive seamstress of Hawthorne's final pages, Lewinsky's defiant self-assertions thwart the shaming imperatives of civic scrutiny.

Despite his defense of Lewinsky, however, when Morton steps in, choruslike, to pronounce the moral of his tale he creates an image of Lewinsky drawn from the "family values" of Republican politics. Monica, he claims, always wanted a normal relationship (by which we are to read: with one, unmarried man, ready and willing to marry her and raise children in a monogamous union). When, after her affair with Clinton, Lewinsky becomes involved with filmmaker Jonathan Marshall, Morton reports, "For her, the friendship has been both a revelation and a reassurance, a first step into the real world of male-female relationships" (270). Not only is the "real world" defined for Morton in terms of heterosexual coupling, it is unembarrassedly conventional in terms of its attachment of gender and class roles to national identity. Thus, having discovered the "real world," Lewinsky becomes visible as an "essentially traditional, middle-class American girl" (271). The narrative supplies, as apparently satisfactory closure, heterosexual romance leading to the nuclear family, all despite the fact that Lewinsky—the child of divorce whose only lasting relationships are with women, and the recent participant in an extramarital affair with a man old enough to be her father—stands as a reminder of the pitfalls of that "real world" and of the pleasures of those supplemental desires (homosocial, incestuous, extrafamilial) that Morton forestalls in her name.

Although Morton defends Lewinsky against Starr's demands for confession, he simultaneously endorses the *content* of that demand when rendered as the voluntarily reformed desire of a sinner who "discovers" the hitherto obscured correspondence between the rules of civic order and the impulses of her heart. While Starr requires the confession of private transgression, Morton fantasizes the reform of that transgression in the image of public propriety, thus constructing an exact—and, more to the point, a *transparent*—correspondence between public and private "normalcy." In Morton's tale, no less than in Starr's, "privacy" is generated as "other" to public convention and is then eradicated to serve the best interests of the nation. If Starr's puritanical prosecution raises anxieties about the state's scopophilic movements into and out of the private lives of citizens, Morton's voluntary reformism makes Monica a generic emblem of *civic* desire. No longer possessed of anything that would taint her as a distinctive and unpredictable subject, Lewinsky, now an evacuated cipher, becomes an "essentially traditional, middle-class American girl" (271).

Hawthorne seems to place Hester in a similar position. In *The Scarlet Letter,* Hester appears, like Lewinsky, as both the embodiment of and "better than" her errant fantasies, just as she stands as a personification of and dire threat to Boston as a civic entity: " 'Do you see that woman with the embroidered badge?' they would say to strangers. 'It is our Hester,—the town's own Hester,—who is so kind to the poor, so helpful to the sick, so comfortable to the afflicted' " (181). Through identification with Hester ("our own Hester") the town is invited to imagine itself in the position of her transgression, only to transcend, with her, into a state of reformed normalcy, signaled not so much by a person (full of messy desires) but by a *pronoun* ("that woman") that turns the particular into a perpetually substitutable abstraction (a transformation Bill Clinton similarly performs on Lewinsky, claiming, "I did not have sexual relations with that woman"). Hester is the instrument, then, through which transgression is rendered as the condition of privacy, which in turn produces publicity as the confessed desire (always only partially achieved) of evacuated normalcy.

But *is* this where *The Scarlet Letter* leaves Hester? Or is it, rather, the result of a relentless pedagogy that has (mis)read the novel in order to justify using the possessive authority of the public sphere to coerce citizens into moments of confession and reform? In turning a blue dress stained gray into a gray dress stained scarlet, Morton draws on this pedagogy to assert the apparent transparency between public confession (what Monica now says she wants) and personal desires (what Monica may indeed want). I would argue, however, that *The*

Scarlet Letter shows how its heroine maintains interior opacity as a counterpublic performative that resists the normalizing incorporation that would leave Hester more of an abstract marker of publicized affect than the subject of her own fantastic desires. If such an abstraction (the pronouning of the citizenry), carried out through the public confession of a repentant interiority, introduces "strangers" to the proprietary civic knowledge (what Lauren Berlant calls a "national symbolic") that allows collectivity to emerge, the reckless inscrutability of Hester's interior reveals an insurgent countercitizenry that is a more likely basis for her association with the wayward intern.[10]

Let's take another look at "Another Look at Hester." In that chapter, Hawthorne initially presents Hester as fully conformed to public expectations: "She never battled with the public, but submitted uncomplainingly to its worst usage; she made no claims upon it, in requital for what she suffered; she did not weigh upon its sympathies" (179). At the same time, Hawthorne suggests not a transparent correspondence between inner and outer conformity, but their utter discrepancy, for despite Hester's public decorum, "The world's law was no law for her mind" (182). Hester, Hawthorne tells us, "assumed a freedom of speculation" that "our forefathers, had they known of it, would have held to be a deadlier crime than that stigmatized by the scarlet letter. In her lonesome cottage, by the sea-shore, thoughts visited her, such as dared to enter no other dwelling in New England; shadowy guests, that would have been as perilous as demons to their entertainer, could they have been seen so much as knocking at her door" (183). "It is remarkable," Hawthorne continues, "that persons who speculate the most boldly often conform with the most perfect quietude to the external regulations of society. The thought suffices them, without investing itself in the flesh and blood of action" (183). Hawthorne suggests, then, that Hester's "seclusion" is neither a punishment nor a destitute solitude, but rather a realm of fantasy where Hester is visited by spectral guests who bring her a previously unimagined freedom. This freedom arises from Hester's willful divorce of demeanor and desire in ways that render her inscrutable to "our forefathers," whose authority rests on their ability to make known the interior lives of citizens. Although this discrepancy would trouble the Puritan elite (of Arthur Dimmesdale, Hawthorne writes, "It may be, that his pathway through life was haunted thus, by a spectre that had stolen out from among his thoughts" [207]), Hester, with more to lose from certain visibility than from speculation, is comfortable with the "companionship of disembodied beings" (207). The more the Puritan elite insist, as Morton does, on the transparency of "public" and "private" through which the private can be inscribed and read as the always already public, the more Hester dwells in a fantasy world built on the opaque discrepancy between interior and exterior, between public conformity and the laws of her own mind.

If Monica Lewinsky bears a resemblance to Hawthorne's heroine it is arguably because, despite Lewinsky's claim that she sees no need to "hide away in the dark," both women use the discrepancy between fantasy and "reality" in order to resist the imperatives of civic normalcy. Another look at Monica might show that she, like Hester, operates by opaque "laws" of her own devising, thereby frustrating not only Starr's prosecurial scrutiny but Morton's voluntary reformism as well. "She yearned for a normal relationship," Morton acknowledges, "but when offered the chance of attaining her goal, she seemed to shrink back" (91). In the face of Lewinsky's refusal of normalcy, Morton can only pathologize his collaborator: "It is as though she felt unworthy of enjoying a typical romance." Lewinsky, like Hester, retreats to a place of her making, hinted at in her public actions but never fully named there: "So she clung to a romantic vision of love at once unattainable and unrealistic. . . . Better the anguished fairytale than the genuine but flawed reality" (91).

If we were to read Hester's story through Monica's, and not the other way around, we might engage in a moment of valuable speculation ourselves. Is it possible that, alone in her cottage late at night, Hester Prynne, forced by the clergy to forego the public enactment of her sexuality, "clung to a romantic vision" by inventing not just spectral visitors, but phantom lovers? While Hester's uncomplaining public conformity requires the apparent evacuation of her errant desires, is it possible that those desires thrive underground? Hawthorne suggests a continuum between the sexual crime "stigmatized by the scarlet letter" and Hester's inscrutable speculations, wherein resides the subterranean life of tenderness: "If she survive," Hawthorne conjectures, "the tenderness will either be crushed out of her, or—and the outward semblance is the same—crushed so deeply into her heart that it can never show itself more. The latter is perhaps the truest theory. She who has once been woman, and ceased to be so, might at any moment become a woman again, if there were only the magic touch to elicit the transformation" (182). This world of tenderness—a world that transforms the "crushed" into the "crush"—cannot be called forth by the already existing authorities of Boston, who are of so little use to Hester that, when she encounters her former lover, she seems disappointed at his flesh-and-blood existence, asking him, " 'And thou, Arthur Dimmesdale, dost thou yet live?' " (207). Disappointed with the limitations of his imagination, Hester asks him, almost scornfully, " 'Hast thou exhausted possibility in the failure of this one trial?' " (215).

But Hester keeps her possibilities open, preserved through her interior speculations, and transformed into a social realm governed, unlike the "reality" of Boston, by "truth, courage, and loyalty" (185). Dreaming in her cottage, Hester becomes the core of a distinctly un-Puritan counterpublic, comprised of those who, like Hester, understand shame and disgrace, but who likewise keep alive the possibility and yearn to share a narrative of longing and desire.[11] The collectivity formed from the vortex of Hester's crush(ed) tenderness rests not on public disclosure but on what Gordon Hutner has called secretive sympathy: an ability to share the phenomenon of nondisclosure without confessing its content.[12] Hester thus becomes, paradoxically, the secretive historian of a counterpublic, organized on a mutuality of respect, sympathy, and discretion, constructed from the affective waste materials of the Puritan public. We don't hear much in the novel about Hester "on her own," but it could be that that is where the real story begins, for in retiring from the world Hester Prynne becomes not only an erotic daydreamer but a democratic visionary as well.

THE SADDER BUT WISER GIRL

I smile, I grin
When the gal with the touch of sin walks in
I hope and I pray
For Hester to win just one more A
The sadder but wiser girl's the girl for me
The sadder but wiser girl for me
—Meredith Wilson, *The Music Man*

Musicals frequently feature heroines who yearn for fantasy figures who allow them to sing their hearts out or, rather, to sing their heart into being, giving rise to the sentimental scriptings that are the core of imaginative life and thereby pose alternatives to the mundane social conventions among which they otherwise live. Epitomizing this genre is Marian Paroo, heroine of Meredith Wilson's 1957 Broadway hit *The Music Man*. Marian is, famously, a librarian, outcast by the townspeople of River City, Iowa, because she encourages young peoples' taste for immoral literature ("Chaucer, Rabelais, Baaaaaaalzac!").[13] Scorned as an old maid, Marian devotes herself to private fantasies, expressed in such songs as "Goodnight, My Someone" and "My White Knight." Marian's mother worries that her daughter's stargazing makes her unfit for "real" romance because, as she tells Marian, no man could "hope to measure up / To that blend of Paul Bunyan,

Saint Pat and Noah Webster you've concocted for yourself" (45). Yet Marian purposefully blurs the distinctions between crushes and romances so as to keep the demands of River City propriety at bay. When, in the film version, her mother inquires, "Don't you ever think about being in love?" Marian replies that she has "been in love more than anybody else"; her fantasies move from the streetcar operator to a teacher with an impressive vocal range. Marian translates being "in love" into being "in crush," a relationship purely of her own making. How Marian manages to evade the town's label of outcast old maid while remaining a dreaming heroine is the story of *The Music Man*.

The answer to Marian's dreams arrives in the person of Harold Hill, a fast-talking traveling salesman set on swindling the citizens of River City by selling them the accouterments of a boy's band. Although initially skeptical of the salesman, Marian ultimately makes the townspeople believe that Hill's fake system of instruction—the "Think System"—is not fantasy but valuable and innovative pedagogy; or rather, she makes them see that the Think System is valuable pedagogy *because* it is based in fantasy. While Marian's turnabout seems an unexplained if necessary plot convention, her affections may be less fickle than they appear. When Marian finally declares her affections for Hill, she tells him not to fear, that he need not take responsibility for her girlish affection. After all, she doesn't expect a drummer, a traveling salesman, to settle down, especially in the likes of River City. She assures him she will "be grateful for what you will have left behind for *me!*" (139). Hill's attraction for Marian is apparently that he won't be around long; even before the romance has begun, Marian is speculating about what he "will have left." As someone inevitably loved-but-lost, Hill promises her only one thing—longing—and thus leaves her where he found her, the safe subject of the dream that she understands will pay off, not for River City's heteronormative propriety, but for *her*.

Finally, though, Marian's triumph is more than a lively lesson in the revisionist pedagogy of sentimental fantasy; it is a civic coup as well. The play stages several patriotic pageants that attempt to generate a collective belonging through a largely incoherent citation of national rhetoric. River City's Fourth of July exercises, for example, feature a rendition of "Columbia, the Gem of the Ocean" led by the mayor's wife, Eulalie Mackecknie Shinn, dressed as the Statue of Liberty. In a later scene, Mayor Shinn tries repeatedly to recite the Gettysburg Address while his wife and her cronies stage an Indian tableau, featuring Eulalie as "Heeawatha," all of which gets interrupted by an exploded firecracker. River City's patriotic dramas are dramatic flops, for under Shinn's leadership citizens' wills are

constantly thwarted, their desires crammed into predictable and ponderous patriotic channels. Nowhere is this more clear than in the mayor's own family.
Shinn repeatedly interrupts his daughter's flirtations with the town's bad boy and
continually silences Eulalie, a stage diva trapped in the body of Lady Liberty.
These small instances of corrective command, carried out in the name of self-
evident propriety, culminate in Shinn's desire to judge and punish Hill. Creative
energy, in the form of either erotic play or the erotics *of* plays, finds no place in
Shinn's democracy, repeatedly dismissed (like a musical itself) as a silly and
irrelevant hindrance to the serious work of patriotic profit. As a result, River City
initially prides itself on its lack of openness to new ideas, new ways of life, even
new people. One wonders whether Shinn might not be a stand-in for another
midwestern advocate of tar-and-feather, Joseph McCarthy, who died in 1957, the
year *The Music Man* opened on Broadway.

The old civic order of River City is quickly revised by Harold Hill. When Hill
first comes to town he seems even less in control of the symbolic vocabulary of
national history than Shinn, exhorting the townspeople to remember everything
from the pilgrims to the sinking of the Maine. Yet unlike Shinn, who operates by
dictate, Hill undergirds his incongruous yokings of history, militarism, and
bland Christianity with a new and cynical manipulation of fear and vanity. Hill's
success as a confidence man relies on his ability to discern and manipulate the
private vanities and insecurities of his victims; repeatedly, Hill reworks his victims' sentiments until they suit his sales pitch, and he encourages them to confess
the reworked sentiments, which they now believe were always their own. The
combination of disciplined desire and public confession convinces River City
citizens to participate in "voluntary" associations (the orchestra, the dance committee, a barbershop quartet) that counter the coercive dictates of the Shinn
government. Although Hill is apparently more democratic in fostering citizens'
emotions in the interests of volunteerism, both Hill and Shinn seek to redirect
desire into channels of consumption and self-governance that make their goals, if
not their means, similar. The only difference is that Hill makes citizens believe
they have chosen ("volunteered") where in fact they have been *managed*.

Ultimately, however, the drummer River City marches to is Marian. When
Shinn calls for Hill's tar-and-feathering, Marian comes forth to save the day,
reminding the townspeople how much better their lives are because of the illu-
sions Hill has brought them. Everyone has been made to see, thanks to Marian,
how much more pleasant it is to live in a world of fantasy than to live in a reality
cast as the dreary conventions of America's heart(land). Or maybe they have been

made to see how much more fun it is to live in a *musical*. For in the musical, the heroine can always have her crush, and now, in River City, so can Marian.

Contra Hill's encouragements of public confessions of disciplined desire, Marian is an advocate for holding one's cards close. Marian makes confessions only in the fantasy world of her own daydreams. As she sings, "Do I love you? / Oh yes, I love you / And I'll bravely tell you / But only when we dream again / . . . Will I ever tell you? / Oh no" (118). In this song, Marian frustrates the imperative, staged through the repeated questions, to confess her feelings, insisting instead on dreaming, which turns the committed and confessed category of "love" (i.e., coupled heterosexuality sanctioned by the state) into a state of private plenitude that answers to no one but the dreamer herself. Although "dreaming" might seem to lock the possibilities for change in the isolated space of the individual dreamer, closeted away from the spaces of public democracy, *The Music Man* suggests otherwise, depicting the transformation of River City into a place not of judgment but of forgiveness, not of convention but of play, not of closure but of expansion. That this democratic vision comes through the agency of the trivial—both Marian's crushes in the musical and the audience's enjoyment *of* the musical—is itself a commentary on the possibilities of resistance to the ponderous monumentalities of national life, which require the very hierarchies of high/low, serious/trivial, civic/sentimental that Marian, and the musical theater she represents, turn topsy-turvy.

The first musical Monica Lewinsky appeared in was, of course, *The Music Man,* in which she won a small part during her sophomore year at Beverly High. Through her participation, Morton reports, Lewinsky found a "sense of renewal" (33). If Lewinsky was renewed, did she find herself reborn as Marian? Not long after her appearance in *The Music Man,* Lewinsky became involved with a married theater technician, Andy Biedler, foreshadowing, as Morton and others suggest, her affairs with other married men, most notably Bill Clinton. Although most commentators have attributed Lewinsky's desire for unattainable men to her anger at her divorced father, I wonder if Lewinsky, like Marian, fell in love with men precisely because they were bound to move on, leaving her, like the dreaming librarian, all alone with her sentiments? Could Lewinsky have seen a parallel between Hill and her Handsome, a politician who, not unlike Hill, won the nation from his stodgy and often inarticulate predecessor by appearing on MTV to play, not a trombone, but a saxophone? And was Lewinsky's appropriation of the president of the United States into the most trivial of a citizen's activities—a crush—akin to Marian's renovation of democracy from a set of deadening commonplaces to one of imaginative renewals? If the FBI agents were more familiar with *The Music Man,* would they have been even more wary of the young intern than they were?

In his 1915 essay, "Thoughts for the Times on War and Death," Sigmund Freud wrote

> Life is impoverished, it loses in interest, when the highest stake in this game of living, life itself, may not be risked. It becomes as shallow and empty as, let us say, an American flirtation, in which it is understood from the first that nothing is to happen, as contrasted with a continental love-affair in which both parties must constantly bear its serious consequences in mind.[14]

No one in recent memory has gone further in popularizing American flirtations than Monica Lewinsky. Yet Lewinsky's flirtations test Freud's dismissal of what he considered our grossest national product, disproving his assumption that American flirtations take no risks. The most interesting risk of Lewinsky's flirtation with the president arises from its troubling of the apparently seamless yoking of trust and commitment implied in Freud's construction of the normative romance. In so doing, Lewinsky posed a significant challenge, not only to conventional romance but to the nationalist discourses of committed democracy as well.

Lewinsky has become known as the woman with hang-ups about commitment. Even her biographer professes bewilderment over Lewinsky's refusal to settle down: "For without a doubt one of her most endearing yet infuriating characteristics is that, while her head may tell her to take the course of action, her unruly heart will drag her in the opposite direction" (40). Lewinsky's "unruly heart" is particularly frustrating insofar as it bars her from the world of what Morton calls "genuine commitment." Despite her refusals to commit, however, Lewinsky remains "endearing" largely because of her unwavering loyalty, demonstrated by her refusal to wear a wire or to betray friends in the White House. Her unruly heart and her faithful heart: these are the Janus faces that make up the paradoxical public profile of Monica Lewinsky.

Lewinsky seems a paradox, however, only if one views as synonyms two features—trust and commitment—perhaps more profitably viewed as distinct, and distinctly productive, impulses. Lewinsky's apparently paradoxical character raises questions about the simultaneity of trust and commitment, questions with important implications for democratic theory. I want to suggest that if Lewinsky models what one might call a trusting lack of commitment (a trust *in* the lack of commitment), her story shows as well that the hetero- and national-normative relationships implied by the word "commitment" are actually based on a *lack* of trust. I want further to suggest that Lewinsky's deployments of crushes make legible exercises of trust that suggest modes of self-conception and democratic interaction that in turn trouble the commitments of the national-normative.[15]

First, commitment. In his imaginative study of psychoanalysis and pleasure, Adam Phillips argues for flirtation's relationship to contingency. The flirt, Phillips contends, is always at odds with commitments based on conventional convictions, which "conceal the sense in which we are continually making our minds up."[16] "Exploiting the ambiguities of promises—the difference, say, between someone being promising and someone making a promise—flirtation has always been the saboteur of a cherished vocabulary of commitment," of "reliability and the relatively predictable" (xvii). Flirtation's contingency is for Phillips an "often unconscious form of scepticism" (xii) directed particularly at conventional sexual subjectivity: "In our erotic lives—and not only there, of course—hierarchies and putative oppositions can be used to constrain the possibilities of difference, compelling us to make moral and erotic choices before we have been able to find out what there is to choose from (and whether the repertoire itself is sufficient)" (xxii). In finding a way around conviction, flirtation powerfully enacts what Foucault calls the care of the self, a return to a fluid moment of "becoming," which requires an active and ethical decision making about one's relation to bodies (one's own and others'), rather than the transfer of authority to the commitments and nominal protections sanctioned by science, religion, or law.

If flirtation opens a space for ethical becoming centered on erotic self-imaginings, it opens as well a realm of practical democracy. When Lewinsky flashed her thong at Bill Clinton she was not simply flirting with a man, after all; she was manifesting her crush on the president. At stake, therefore, were not simply the conventional commitments of heteronormative romance, although those certainly *were* at stake. By flirting with the president, Lewinsky also put into play—into *scepticism,* to use Phillips's term—the conventional commitments of the national symbolic. Here Phillips's comments on how flirtation transforms "promising" from a transitive verb to an indeterminate adjective is suggestive. The function of the president, the basis of his election to serve on behalf of the people, is to make—and, presumably, to keep—promises. The campaign "promise" is key to modern elections, placing presidential reliability not in the here-and-now of the candidate's political record or everyday actions but in the always deferred future. Political "promise" thus allows the perpetual state of deferred democracy that Dana Nelson calls "presidentialism": "Our constitutionally conditioned habit of looking to the President has trained us," Nelson writes, "to vest our desires in him for what we might otherwise see all around us. Or, to say this differently, people's ability to deal with a messier, open-ended, democratic heterogeneity is circulated through . . . presidentialism into constitutionally unhealthy longings for wholeness, unity, for 'democratic' homogeneity."[17] Presidentialism thus substitutes the impossible promise of a unified—and *reliable*—president, able to deliver on his (often contradictory) promises, for the realities of heterogeneous democracy, "compelling us," to use Phillips's words in a different but related context, "to make . . . choices before we have been able to find out what there is to choose from (and whether the repertoire itself is sufficient)" (xxii). Tellingly, as stated in Morton's book, Clinton often appears in Lewinsky's dreams, "ever present yet always elusive" (262).

And yet even while Lewinsky is condemned for her lack of commitment, she is known for her emotional resilience and for her loyalty. This brings me to the second term: trust. Lewinsky opened up a skeptical space within conventional commitments, I would argue, not because she is incapable of trust (a supposition derived from the common belief that commitments grow from and further foster trust); rather, it is Lewinsky's deep trustfulness that turns her against commitments (makes her "unruly"). To be more precise, trustfulness turns her away from those commitments that require that she—like the citizenry in general—surrender trust. The ultimate "scandal" of "Sexgate" is that everyone involved in the government in which we nominally place our trust proved all too willing to betray Lewinsky, while the intern remained steadfastly loyal. One conclusion we might draw from this is that conventional commitments, on which governmentality is built, deadens not only ethical self-becoming, as Phillips suggests, but trust itself. Conversely, Lewinsky's steadfast loyalty suggests that *lack* of commitment requires—even generates—trusting loyalty.

When trust comes loose from commitment, as Lewinsky's story insists it must, we can see the difference between what I think of as committed and uncommitted democracy. In the former (that is, democracy as it is currently practiced in the United States), when one commits, one places trust in structures outside one's own determination (law, religion, representational politics), which eventually erodes the responsibility for *making* trust, as an everyday and local practice and a primary civic responsibility. Citizens' sense of responsibility for other citizens erodes as civic "care" is increasingly ceded to the state, while at the same time we lose our pleasures in cultural differences that supposedly threaten the unity—and efficacy—of that state, now the primary guarantor of social harmony and well-being. In putting our trust in a government that promises us the unity and harmony that actual people challenge, we become increasingly willing to sacrifice our local loyalties to abstract national allegiances. Looked at in this way, commitments are the death not just of trust but of democracy.

Conversely, radical democracy requires the operation of trust on a local and contingent basis. By trusting in those in the White House as partners in locally made and maintained relationships, Lewinsky betrayed the White House's status as a symbolic marker of an abstract national relationship, refusing the imperative to invest trust in the symbolic functions of governmentality itself. In so doing, Lewinsky chose to treat those who abstractly represent the "country" as flesh-and-blood people toward whom she felt local rather than national affect (loyalty rather than patriotism).

And this ultimately leads me to the central question of this essay: How does one continue to believe—to trust—despite committed betrayal? Lewinsky's ability to maintain trust, and hence to revitalize the promise of radical democracy, goes hand in hand with her maintenance of crushes, even in her supposedly post-Clinton phase. Morton reports Lewinsky as saying, " 'There was a moment recently when I closed my eyes real tight and imagined myself back in my little office in the East Wing of the White House. The phone rang. I held my breath and sure enough, it was that voice, a voice so familiar to many but private to me, a voice suffused with longing, sadness and hunger' " (262). Lewinsky's daydreams remain a way to shift the balance of power, making public spaces private, abstract functionaries familiar, powerful men needy, and abject citizens possessed of the power to satisfy a national hunger.

Most important, however, Lewinsky's crushes remain a way to generate trust through and in herself. In this light, I would argue that Lewinsky's strength has surfaced not despite but because of the Clinton betrayal, of his ultimate "unavailability" (in his status as solve-all president as well as "committed" lover). For a crush ultimately takes a relationship of power (here a power constituted through the promise of presidential presence, turned by Lewinsky into the promise of presidential absence) and turns it into a relationship of self-generation in which one takes control and responsibility for one's own self-imaginings. One learns, that is, to trust in oneself before one sacrifices that trust in "commitments" to others. Lewinsky's presence as a trusting agent at the very heart of networks of *distrust*—the Pentagon, the White House, the State Department—makes her a remarkable emblem of democracy, not because she made visible the fault lines of presidential promise, but because of her sentimental trust, maintained through the appropriation of presidential promise to the private and self-generating stage directions of her crushes.

It is easy to dismiss Lewinsky as foolish and sentimental (foolish *because* sentimental), but one does so at one's peril. Starr's prosecutors puzzled over the so-called Talking Points (the list of answers to potential questions from the special prosecutor), refusing to believe that someone as obviously sentimental as Lewinsky could have written a document so intelligent and sensible (and so obviously alert to the prosecutor's "tricky" line of questioning). Her "crush," that is, canceled Lewinsky's intelligence. Ironically, when Hillary Clinton went on the air to declare her love for her husband, her testimony was discounted as cynical spin; Hillary and Monica are two sides of the same coin, both penalized because of the supposed incomparability of intelligence and sentiment.

It is not surprising that sentimentality should fall outside the comprehension of what Morton calls "professions defined by an adversarial rather than a conciliatory philosophy. Sentiment and romance," he rightly notes, "do not figure high on their agendas" (265). Predictably, Lewinsky angered those with a vested interest in the operations of a committed state (senators, special prosecutors, the president himself). Less predictably, Lewinsky became something of a citizens' hero: while pundits made Monica seem "the most humiliated woman in history" (247), she nevertheless ranked high in a December 1998 Gallop poll of Americans' most admired women (267). Could it be that Americans can identify with being humiliated in public by the broken promise(s) of the president? Could they have seen, in Lewinsky's flirtations, the potential for another relation to democracy? If the state was turned off by her flirtation, was the public turned on by her crush?

Political theorist C. Douglas Lummis, in describing his own affective state on beginning his investigation into radical democracy, reports: "It was an experience a little like falling in love with the girl (or boy) next door—the being you have always known suddenly appears so new, so fresh, so . . . unprecedented."[18] If discovering democracy is like developing a crush, couldn't it also be that developing a crush is like discovering democracy? Or, isn't sentimentality what keeps trust alive in a world that otherwise asks for its surrender? If Lewinsky risked anything, it was not commitment, but credibility, which is always at stake in professions of the utopian, the alternative, or the desired. But without those professions—not the confessions that tell our "true character" but professions of what the self is striving to bring into being—what is the hope of democracy and, more urgently, what is its point?

NOTES

I am grateful to audiences at Loyola University Chicago, the Narrative Conference (Atlanta), the Conference on Social Theory (Lexington), the Modern Language Association Conference (Washington, D.C.), the University of Pennsylvania, and Michigan State University for valuable responses to earlier versions of this essay. I owe special and heartfelt thanks to Russ Castronovo and Dana Nelson, whose insightful editing and generous encouragement made this essay much stronger, and to Ken Wissoker, who let me be part of an exciting project. My deepest and most affectionate debts are to Jeff Masten, who renewed in me an old love of musicals and showed me how to approach them with the mirthful seriousness they deserve; and to Chris Reed, who listened with tender and critical care to every thought and added many of his own.

1 See Jürgen Habermas, *The Structural Transformations of the Public Sphere: An Inquiry into a Category of Bourgeois Society* (Cambridge: MIT Press, 1989). See also Craig Calhoun, ed., *Habermas and the Public Sphere* (Cambridge: MIT Press, 1996); and Nancy Fraser, *Justice Interruptus: Critical Reflections on the "Postsocial" Condition* (New York: Routledge, 1997).
2 The most compelling corrective to Habermas's conception of bourgeois "publicity" takes the form of advocacy on behalf of plural "publics," a position endorsed by several contributors to *Habermas and the Public Sphere* (see, for example, Eley, Fraser, and Ryan). In "Sex in Public" (*Critical Inquiry* 24, no. 2 [winter 1998]: 547–66)], Lauren Berlant and Michael Warner contend for a sexual "counterpublic," in which nonnormative sexual practices would generate countervailing public discourses of sexual subjectivity. The most sustained argument for plural publics has been made by Nancy Fraser in *Justice Interruptus*. Critiquing Habermas's assumption that "a public sphere is or can be a space of zero-degree culture, so utterly bereft of any specific ethos as to accommodate with perfect neutrality and equal ease interventions expressive of any and every cultural ethos" (79), Fraser rightly notes that "unequally empowered social groups tend to develop unequally valued cultural styles" (79) that can, nevertheless, give rise to competing counterpublics. I agree with Fraser that "critical theory should expose ways in which the labeling of some issues and interests as 'private' limits the range of problems, and of approaches to problems, that can be widely contested in contemporary societies" (93); in part I am advocating that such "private" concerns might usefully be considered as theoretical speculations on public democracy, if they are taken seriously as they emerge in such discredited "counterpublics" as musical theater and fiction. My hesitation with Fraser's revision of Habermas, however, comes with her exclusive focus on "an orientation that is *publi-*

cist" (82). Establishing a counterpublic from the exclusionary practices of bourgeois publicity, however important to social theory, obscures the ways in which all publicities, bourgeois or otherwise, maintain an opposition between civil exchange and "interior" life, requiring the confession of privacy in order to enter a necessarily regulatory collective (it is striking how infrequently identity categories such as "gender," "sexuality," "race," or "class" are investigated in calls for revisionary plurality). Fraser's emphasis on public culture, as Judith Butler has noted ("Merely Cultural," *Social Text* 15, nos. 3–4 [1997] 265–77), obscures the structures of subject formation that allow the state to orchestrate itself in civil society one citizen at a time. More to the point for the purposes of my argument here, by ignoring the investments of the state, through the mechanisms of civil society, in shaping citizens' interiority, publicist social theory also tends to misrecognize forms of resistance (what de Certeau calls "tactics," forms of intervention that are explicitly resistant to locations in formal space or "publics") that arise from citizens' transformations in everyday practices of "private" affect. Rather than recasting interiority (whether imagined as privacy, personhood, fantasy, or emotion) in terms of "publicity," then, social theory might profitably recognize in interiority a potential site for the rich revisionary history of democracy that citizens, denied access to publicity (by their subaltern peers no less than by the bourgeoisie or the state) have developed.

3 See *The History of Sexuality, Volume 1* (New York: Vintage, 1990), in which Foucault argues that sexuality is not subject to systematic repression but to discursive incitement. Pressured to talk constantly about sex, citizens enter the disciplines that regulate sexuality through the productions of normalizing power knowledges constituted from the "data" of sexual confession and observation.

4 Important work by critics such as Richard Brodhead, Gillian Brown, Amy Kaplan, Lora Romero, Karen Sánchez-Eppler, and Laura Wexler, showing how "private" life, especially in the nineteenth century, "personalized" more public ideologies shaping class, gender, nationhood, and imperialism, should caution us against claiming a clear distinction between public/private life. However, as valuable as these critiques have been they have, perhaps, in critiquing the claims for the revisionary possibilities of domestic sentimentalism made by Jane Tompkins and others, thrown the baby out with the bathwater. Although it is undoubtedly true that the "home" was instrumental in developing and disseminating ideologies central to slavery, emergent industrialism, imperial expansion, and other threats to democratic collectivity, spaces defined as "other" to the national public lodged complaint as well as complicity, revision as well as reproduction. Such sites—which might be understood under the broad rubric of *interiority,* encompassing the rhetorical composition (through sentimentalism, benevolence, affection, mourning, etc.) of spaces "apart" from public life rather than the literal "sphere" of hearth and home—have recently received important critical attention in the work of critics such as Lauren Berlant, Joel Pfister, Nancy Schnog, Julia Stern, and others. I mean this study to extend that analysis in the direction of interiorly imagined democracy.

5 In distinguishing between government and governance, I am drawing on new work in

political theory that takes Foucault's insights from *Discipline and Punish* to a range of activities through which government purports to empower and protect citizens by regulating citizen subjectivity. See especially Barbara Cruikshank, who argues in *The Will to Empower: Democratic Citizens and Other Subjects* (Ithaca: Cornell University Press, 1999) that "the will to empower is a strategy of government, one that seeks solutions to political problems in the governmentalization of the everyday lives of citizen-subjects" (123); and Thomas Dumm, who, in *Michel Foucault and the Politics of Freedom* (Thousand Oaks, Calif.: Sage, 1996), traces the moves from disciplinarity to security, from the control of individual subjects to that of subject-populations, through modifications in popular conceptions of "freedom."

6 Nathaniel Hawthorne, *The Scarlet Letter* (New York: Penguin, 1983), 90. Subsequent citations are given parenthetically in the text.

7 Andrew Morton, *Monica's Story* (New York: St. Martin's Press, 1999), 185. Subsequent citations are given parenthetically in the text.

8 "On My Own" from *Les Miserables*. Broadway Cast Album, by Alain Boublil and Claude-Michel Schonberg. Lyrics by Herbert Kretzner. Geffen Records, 1986. The transcription is mine.

9 *San Francisco Examiner,* January 8, 2000 (⟨http://www.examiner.com/000109/0109salter.html⟩).

10 See Lauren Berlant, *The Anatomy of National Fantasy: Hawthorne, Utopia, and Everyday Life* (Chicago: University of Chicago Press, 1991).

11 Here I am building on Michael Warner's important insight, in *The Trouble with Normal: Sex, Politics, and the Ethics of Queer Life* (New York: The Free Press, 1999), about the revolutionary counterpublics that arise from shared experiences of sexual shame. The desire for normalcy gives rise, according to Warner, to an unethical drive to define oneself through negation, by putting other(s') sexual practices away from oneself. Although normalizing acts of (self)negation promise us "solidarity with the world," they in fact are isolating moments of communal dissolution that deprive us of "the very kind of active, public solidarity of which we are so acutely deprived" (70). Yet those defined outside the "norm" (which according to Warner includes virtually everyone) may evolve more ethical counterpublics, in which "the most heterogeneous people are brought into great intimacy by the shared experience of being despised and rejected in a world of norms that they now recognize as false morality" (36). "A relation to others, in these contexts, begins in an acknowledgment of all that is most abject and least reputable in oneself. Shame is bedrock," Warner writes, adding that the sexually shamed "can be abusive, insulting, and vile toward one another, but because abjection is understood to be the shared condition, they also know how to communicate through such camaraderie a moving and unexpected form of generosity" (35). Exactly this sort of counterpublic emerges, I am suggesting, around Hester Prynne in a remarkable communicative transformation of fearful normalcy into generous abjection.

12 In *Secrets and Sympathy: Forms of Disclosure in Hawthorne's Novels* (Athens: University of Georgia Press, 1988), Gordon Hutner argues that the revelation of a central

secret at the end of each novel is, in fact, only partial; the maintenance of secrets beyond the public (readerly) demand for disclosure is, Hutner rightly claims, the central feature of Hawthorne's works. Although Hawthorne frustrates full disclosure, he also encourages the sharing of knowledge through sympathy—an intuitive (and, for Hutner, apprehensive) state that allows "close, though not complete, identification with another. Through sympathy, the secret purposes of others can be discerned, corroborated, and met without being made explicit. In the less than perfect union it is supposed to create, sympathy allows neither party to risk a vacating of the self or of having the self violated" (14). Through the indirect communion of secretive sympathy, Hutner concludes, "readers can be led to apprehend their own secrets and to see how they share in the novel's community of guilt" (52). Hutner, who focuses primarily on the secrets associated with Arthur Dimmesdale, arrives at a community built on "guilt," whereas I am focusing more on the secrets surrounding Hester and therefore on communities based on shared "shame." For the reasons Michael Warner notes (see note 11 above), shame appears to be a more productive basis for counter-public communication than guilt. Yet we both are seeking to amplify, in the communal reformations generated around "secrecy," what Hutner identifies as the "lone note of optimism in Hawthorne's tragic romance" (63).

13 Meredith Wilson, *The Music Man* (New York: G. P. Putnam's Sons, 1958), 74. Subsequent citations are given parenthetically in the text.

14 Quoted in Phillips, xx–xxi.

15 An interesting contrast with *Monica's Story* can be found in George Stephanopoulos's memoir, *All Too Human: A Political Education* (Boston: Little, Brown, 1999), which oddly enough, given that Stephanopoulos is a presumably heterosexual man reporting on his career as a senior staffer in the Clinton White House, offers much more of a normatively romantic narrative. Stephanopoulos begins by narrating his decision not to work for the Greek American Paul Tsongas, "my intended," with whom his relationship felt like "an arranged marriage" (26). Even though Stephanopoulos acknowledges that Bill Clinton "wasn't my type" (26), he'd rather work for Bill than feel like he was "marrying the wrong girl" (31). The domestic bliss of heteronormative marriage finally comes to Stephanopoulos in a fantastic moment of identification and displacement. Meeting Clinton in the Arkansas governor's mansion, Stephanopoulos "followed him to his bedroom, where he started to change out of his jeans for a downtown lunch, then stopped to hand me an article from a pile on one of the night tables" (34). This oddly erotic moment—with Bill, now familiarly, with pants off and sequestered with a young staffer—requires Stephanopoulos to displace both his homosexual panic *and* his guilt at replacing Hillary by first identifying with Mrs. Clinton and then reimagining their relationship as an intellectual rather than a sexual one. "There were two of them [night tables]—one for him, one for her—both loaded down with novels, magazines, issue papers, and spiritual books. I hadn't yet met Hillary, but seeing the night table made me picture the two of them propped up late at night, passing the reading back and forth, arguing, laughing, educating each other, sharing a passion for ideas" (34). Translating his scopophilic relation to Bill for a "passion for

ideas," Stephanopoulos can safely displace Hillary, claiming "this was exactly what I wanted to be doing: building a presidential campaign—and exactly where I wanted to be: in its inner sanctum" (34).

Yet Stephanopoulos's narrative remains haunted by the erotic. He almost immediately feels like "Dustin Hoffman in the closing scene of *The Graduate*" (34) ("Mr. Clinton, are you trying to seduce me?"), and, being "smitten with Bill" (52), he uses the odd lingua franca of the homosexual underworld, becoming one of the "Friends of Bill" (35) (indeed, Stephanopoulos identifies himself with the ur-gender bender, noting that to the Washington Press Corps, he was "their boy George" [264]). With the normative marriage narrative, moreover, comes heterosexuality's discontents, most manifest in Stephanopoulos's persistent insecurity and jealous rage. After hearing the tapes of Clinton's lewd phone calls to Gennifer Flowers, for instance, Stephanopoulos admits that "hearing Clinton's unmistakably husky voice felt like picking up the phone to catch your girlfriend whispering with another man" (68). Visiting the White House after he has officially left Clinton's staff and sensing the president's near presence, Stephanopoulos reports, "My stomach floated with butterflies, the kind you get when you're walking down the street and spot a girl you lost but still love a couple of blocks ahead" (430). Above all, the book is suffused with rage at Hillary Clinton, who becomes the evil mother who must be done away with to make a clear path to the seductive daddy. While his faith in the hetero- and national-normative promises of the president leaves Stephanopoulos embittered and angry ("My heart was getting hard, partly from self-righteousness, partly as a shield against sadness and shame" [439]), Lewinsky, questioning those normative relationships (she doesn't really imagine herself propped up in bed with the president, working through their night-table readings), is much more resilient. Perhaps Stephanopoulos might have more carefully heeded the orphic Lewinsky when, encountering her one morning in a Dupont Circle (!) Starbucks, she asked him, " 'Does your president tell the truth?' " (433).

16 Adam Phillips, *On Flirtation* (Cambridge: Harvard University Press, 1994), xii.

17 Dana D. Nelson, *National Manhood: Capitalist Citizenship and the Imagined Fraternity of White Men* (Durham: Duke University Press, 1998), 204–5.

18 C. Douglas Lummis, *Radical Democracy* (Ithaca: Cornell University Press, 1996), 9.

DANA D. NELSON

Representative/Democracy: The Political Work of Countersymbolic Representation

◆

That political representation is a problem almost goes without saying, especially after Election 2000.[1] Aesthetic representation is a problem too; this we know after the past thirty years of poststructuralist theory and the political battles over NEH funding in the 1980s.[2] But in the midst of analyzing the problems of aesthetic and political representation, we seldom pause to ask questions about the relation of aesthetic representation to political affect, to the affect of citizenship. How does a particular mode of citizenship come to feel "normal"? In particular, how do people come to feel that they "want" to be politically represented, that they don't want to or cannot do that work themselves? It is worth insisting that representivity—the subjective internalization of particular norms of representation—does not come naturally for individuals or nations. It is important, then, to study closely what political and cultural practices of representation mean for the practice of democracy.

The history of U.S. citizenship reveals not just difficulties with representation but also with democracy itself. We love the word, but when it comes to arguments about extending its practice politically, economically, socially, and pedagogically we find people afraid of it, impatient with it, annoyed with it, or at least nervous about it ("would you *really* trust *them* to decide *anything?*"). As part of trying to understand that discomfort in ways that might take us outside of traditional explanations (that democracy needs to be "kept safe" from the mob mentality of the masses; that the people must "be saved" not only from corrupt rulers but from themselves), I'm interested in studying how representational models cultivate varying modes of comfort with democratic practices. In other words, rather than rehashing political theories for good or adequate representation, I am directing attention to questions about where political practice overlaps with and is reshaped or limited or enabled by particular aesthetic modes of representation.

Aesthetic modes condition not only our expectations for but also our feelings about both political representation and democracy. Here I am not suggesting that the problems of political representation can be fixed by aesthetics, nor am I disputing the necessity of representation to democratic political practice. I start my inquiries from F. R. Ankersmit's important argument that "political insight is not part of the realm of facts or of values, but of aesthetics,"[3] but before I begin I want to remind us, as Susanne Kappeler puts it, that "the aesthetic and the beautiful have their own histories."[4] Here I will explore those histories in the early United States, speculating along the way on what a countersymbolic mode of representation might contribute to democratic practice.[5]

This essay investigates sociopolitical, representational, and aesthetic tensions in, and artistic responses to, developing practices of representative democracy as they advance from the Constitutional reformulation of government (as national government) in 1789 and into the mid-nineteenth century. The patriotic unity-symbolics of Constitutional federalism, and the material conditions that surround its installation and maintenance, have ensured certain archival and historical amnesias around alternative representative and democratic practices, encouraging us to think of "our" democracy as singularly the best and most highly developed model.[6] It is, for instance, a widely regarded patriotic fact that the president of the United States "stands for" U.S. democracy, and in particular its national unity. But we should interrogate the democratic value of this national common sense. It assumes that democratic virtue is grounded in "the commitment to, knowledge of, and ability to stand for the whole."[7] This is the "strong logic" in the Constitutional model of representation, one that was receiving important aesthetic corroboration in transcendentalism, the dominant literary philosophy of the antebellum United States. In transcendentalism, as in constitutionalism, representivity is oriented toward spiritualized, virtual "wholeness," a symbolically aestheticizing relation where citizens cultivate their subjectivity with regard to the ideal "representative" and where the formfulness of representivity is offered *as* the subjectivity of citizenship. This aesthetic mode for sociopolitical being operates through formalistic and compensatory terms: it depends on the (false) ideal that peoples' particular *desires* for political participation and community can be satisfied through their identification with a singular, symbolic representative. Whose politics does this symbolics of wholeness in U.S. democratic practice serve?

This particular representative symbolic conjoins aesthetics and politics and offers unity and harmony as its goal. In doing so, it also prevents us from seeing and appreciating representational alternatives.[8] Our nation's presidentially conditioned representative symbolic awes and assuages us with the aesthetic satisfactions of form precisely as it teaches us to avoid and indeed disavow the more mundane satisfactions that come in daily contradictions of democratic political contact. It teaches us to regard those local and ephemeral interactions as intrusions in a rational political order: unnecessary and even dangerous for political or social good ("please don't talk about politics at *dinner;* it isn't *polite*"). At its least innocuous, this dominant representative symbolic is unable to register or value so much of what happens between people that can't be formally apprehended (e.g., democracy as something more than media polling, party conventions, and private voting booths); at its worst, it teaches us to regard social and political intersubjectivity as the diminishment of a higher good.

In order to open up questions about U.S. representative symbolics and possible alternatives, I contrast the strong, management-oriented symbolic representational model against a less culturally recognized countermodel, where citizens develop their social and political subjectivities in relation to multiple, local, and nonidealized relationships with others. This is a model that is hard to describe in terms of "aesthetic," because it is not really recognizable in the standard terms of beauty and regularity, of harmony and ideal. This model—we might call it "ugly democracy"—affirms not wholeness and symbolic consensus but the inevitable incompleteness of always dissensual community. I'm proposing that this alternative political aesthetic, situated within the context of human particularity and the open-endedness of regular human interaction, offers an important alternative representation for radical democratic praxis. This is a more social representation of democracy that opens its political imaginary to a fuller mode of human interaction—of interpersonal self-governance—at the level of the local.[9] I don't mean to supercede form with process (especially not a process that valorizes consensus) but I do want to call attention to how some representative modes vitiate its alternative or supplemental possibilities, leading us away from and indeed making us suspicious of democratic engagement, and leaving us with a simulacra of "democracy," a beautiful form without the satisfactions of (our) content.

Two nineteenth-century texts in particular caption the countervailing models that concern this essay: Emerson's *Representative Men* (1850) and Rebecca Harding Davis's *Waiting for the Verdict* (1867).[10] *Representative Men* exemplifies the developing cultural logic of the United States' dominant mode for symbol-driven representivity—its entailments both for the production of culture and for conceptualizing political ("democratic") practice. Emerson's symbolic relies on what

Hannah Arendt describes as poiesis, where a self-directed emphasis on form is substituted for the uncertainties of a more open-ended interpersonal praxis. This substitution produces an illusion of heroic singularity as the self-culture of the represented subject accomplishes his alignment with the Representative. Emerson's model concentrates on form, locating integrated democratic power in the Representative, where the power of the represented lies in their success at molding themselves to this larger, organically containing and representative power. Even taking seriously Emerson's own jabs at "Founding Fathers," we can see how this text corroborates the developing logic of a now-familiar political model: the United States's Constitutionally conditioned habit of looking to an idealized president simultaneously for "democratic" leadership and for his symbolic embodiment *of* democracy. This representivity trains citizens to vest democratic desires in a singular body—alternately the idealized Representative and the disciplined self. This representivity curtails interactive democratic power as it virtualizes democratic engagement, redirecting interpersonal action toward the containment work of self-culture.

In the context of my arguments about this mode of representivity's antidemocratic impulses, Davis's postwar historical romance, *Waiting for the Verdict*, counters Emerson's symbolics. It provides a counterpolitics, a countersymbolic aesthetic, a counteraffect. Davis's specific focus is on antiracist possibilities, in the face of the durability of white racism, in postbellum social and political Reconstruction. Her method for exploring this problem formulates a more open democratic aesthetic, a mode that emphasizes the imperfections, the always incomplete fit, or brokenness, of ordinary human interaction. Davis rejects Emerson's aestheticized relation between Representative and represented, picturing democratic relations through an aesthetic that foregrounds contiguity. Her representation of democracy looks less like management and more like engagement, more like what Hannah Arendt terms the " 'web' of human relationships," the intersubjective tangle of humanness where the desire for self-governance means ongoing negotiation with the complications, the complex inter- and intrapersonal contradictoriness and particularity of human desire.[11] Here, exchanges between people generate not a democratic symbol but democratic energy. This energy is precisely formless, seldom "unified" in intent, and for that reason unpredictable in outcome. Mixed unpredictability becomes a positive good in *Waiting for the Verdict*. Refusing logical binarism and tidy resolution, Davis develops a complicated political dialogue on the question of white racism by means of multiplying positions that are elaborated in various and often incompatible ways by questions of class, gender, and regional politics. Although this novel "fails" to present a unified, purified, or distilled vision by the kinds of aesthetic and political criteria that Emerson forwards (and that transcendentalism has helped institutionalize in literature and philosophy), it succeeds in processing a multiplex and dynamic representation of democratic interaction in all its messy, heterogeneous irreducibility. This social democratic model tries to take into account, rather than suppress, the desires produced precisely out of human incompleteness, where incompleteness generates disagreement and interconnection, disappointment and celebration, broken promises and forgiveness, and, in its optimal range, further engagement.

In the remainder of this essay, I briefly outline the historical development and the political/affective stakes of what I am describing as presidential or symbolic representivity. I consider at greater length the way Emerson corroborates the force and yet perhaps not unwittingly raises questions about the affective legacy of presidential representivity and its managerial entailments. Then I turn to Davis's alternative representation of democratic engagement, a text that helps us reopen questions about the value of representative form, the lack of alignment between representative form and democratic power, and the relative satisfaction of predictable and unpredictable democratic outcomes. I conclude with some reflections about the way representational models shape the democratic imaginary, delimiting the "practical" contours of its praxis and possibilities, arguing that the particular virtue of Davis's version is that it might help us productively to begin thinking, and perhaps even more importantly *feeling*, outside the box that Roberto Unger has described as "false necessity."[12]

REPRESENTATIVE PRESIDENTIALISM[13]

Some recent work in the early national period has helped us reformulate what we had long understood about the political disorders and mob actions of the early nation—what John Adams labeled "democratic despotism."[14] This was his phrase for describing local and radical reconceptualizations of democratic practice increasingly present throughout the United States,[15] where citizens of the states had begun more and more to insist on direct representation. This movement was expressed in a range of practices, including new, strict residency requirements for representatives, expanded suffrage definitions framed to ensure structures for electoral consent, and a model of equally weighted electoral districts that reflected the one-state one-vote rule of the Articles of Confederation. Beyond these restrictions for qualification, citizens began experimenting in self-representation, show-ing up at legislative sessions to deliver instructions to their delegates. Many put intensifying emphasis on the *local* as the best and most proper venue for demo-cratic practice. This growing insistence on local democratic involvement, on face-to-face, self-governing democracy, was amplified in the increasing phenomenon of the extragovernmental organization of people in county assemblies, watchdog committees, radical associations, and out-of-door actions.[16] Such democratic innovations were manifest in every major city and across the countryside. C. Douglas Lummis sees in such phenomenon fundamental evidence for radical democracy's gravitation toward the local: "Again and again, in the phase where revolution was still revolutionary, the polity has broken down naturally into units small enough that the people can confront one another in genuine communities, talk to one another, and choose and act collectively."[17]

Given the widespread outcroppings of and enthusiasm for these emergent democratic practices,[18] my study of the 1780s always returns me to this question: Why didn't the revolutionary democratic spirit, widely expressed in local, face-to-face practices, lead the people loudly to reject the virtualization of their de-mocracy under the Constitution for the way it displaced the relevance of local and direct self-governance?[19] If they were acting on chances to have more politi-cal self-management, why would they support a political form that anatomized and abstracted politics, that delegitimated peoples' efforts at self-government in the name of the people? The best answer I have been able to find comes in the way that proponents of the Constitution, most famously "Publius," hold out a refor-mulated ideal of "national manhood"—purified, vigorous, unified—as a coun-terphobic ideal for the kinds of social diversity and disruption foregrounded in emergently radical democratic practices. In other words, the conditional disunities and frictions of democratic negotiation entailed both by the more explicitly confraternal model of the Articles and by emergent local political practices is reassuringly covered over by an image of strong national unity, embodied in the national executive.[20] His unifying energy is representatively routed through male citizens, reassuring them about political discord along with other kinds of economic and familial dislocations.[21] The discomfiting actuality of fraternal *dis*agreement—a discomfort that always threatens but is entirely funda-mental to the possibilities for deliberative democratic self-governance—seem-ingly disappears in the representatively singular body of the president.[22]

Presidential historian Gary L. Gregg has recently reminded us that under the Articles of Confederation there was no single executive officer, and that "this lack of a central figure within the government was more important than most commentators and historians have noticed."[23] I'm arguing something a little different: that the transition *to* a governmental system headed by a president, a national union embodied in the single person of the president, is more symbolically important to our practice of democracy than we are in the habit of noticing. The OED tells us that "president" as a term designating the title of a person who "presides over the proceedings of a financial, commercial or industrial company" is an Americanism (the equivalent British usage is "governor"), and that its earliest usage is recorded as 1781, when the U.S. Congress granted a charter to and ordered the structure for the Bank of North America. This idea, to make the national executive somehow equivalent to the designated leader of an economic corporation precociously tapped the energy of corporatism's late-century expansion and economic reordering.[24] It made the nation analogous to a corporate body (treated by law as a single individual). The presidential reconstruction of national unity through representivity trains democratic energies into what we might loosely call corporately managed cites: through constitutional rationalization, democratic institutionalization, and market routinization. Presidentialism thus worked to reroute emergent radical democratic energies into structures of practical, political, and affective containment.

The president became one aspect of, but even more importantly the symbolic guarantor for, the Constitution's scientific system for national politics. The office of the president ostensibly transcends individual self-interest, specifically the local and contradictory self-interest of the people. Under the federal plan, the president would reflect a refined and rational version of "the sense of the people." The distance pyramidically installed between the people's general and "disorderly" interests and the president's judicious distillation of their (singular) interest delivers the president to the nation as a purified body, an entity who has risen above personal passions and factional interest, who presides democratically by transcending local investments and attending dispassionately to abstracted national interest. This is a structure that promises more representation for "the people": beyond their elected representatives in the House and Senate, now "the people" will find an even more concentrated and purified experience of representation in the executive body of the president.

We've been taught to regard this representation as good. But I'm arguing that presidential representivity is bad for democracy. It is bad because it reroutes the radical practice of democracy—the hard work of achieving plus-sum democratic dis/agreement—for a citizenry that learns from presidentialism to long for self-subordinating civic unity and national "wholeness," to desire power for our Representative ("the most powerful man in the world") instead of heeding the power we can generate between us. The presidential incarnation of representative democracy blocks an antisymbolic democracy imaginary of the political and cultural processes of multiple and diverse bodies, engaging their disagreements together in processes of self-governance.[25]

CENTRAL MAN; OR, (REPRESENTATIVE) SELF-CULTURE VERSUS (DEMOCRATIC) SELF-GOVERNANCE

Presidential representivity promises to manage democracy for the United States. But its satisfying symbolic coherence cannot affectively resolve what I take to be the central conundrum of presidentially representative democracy's double guarantee. This mode of representation holds out the assurance of safe management, of consensus, of political unity. Democracy's appeal lies in the cultivation of complex political difference, in the recognition of and protection for individual (political and nonpolitical) particularity, and in the earned satisfactions of political negotiation. Presidential representation offers protection; democracy offers contact.[26] These promises don't align structurally. Presidential representation's managerial comforts encourage us to avoid, disdain, even fear democracy's contact challenges, replacing with political poiesis—form building—the unpredictability, the discomfort, the "danger" of a more intersubjective and open mode of democratic praxis. Here I'm not advocating for anarchy against representative democracy (the familiar charge) or even saying that we should overturn a representative model for direct democracy. I am trying—perhaps polemically—to highlight the false assumptions of particular representative modes in order to think outside the usual representative/democratic "choices" (or "false necessities") that box us between, for instance, leadership and mobs or republican democracy and anarchy, so that we might think creatively about alternatives we can't see from inside the normative mode of U.S. representivity.

In this section, then, I briefly and schematically outline Emerson's struggle to make self-culture stand in for the more difficult and potentially more satisfying relationships required by democratic self-governance, a move he makes through a symbolic logic of representivity. This is a model that affirms the necessity of purifying the "common will" by isolating political actors one from another so that they can think separately and, as his model has it, more nobly for the common good in their isolation. This is a model that structures the primary

(political or cultural) symbolic as the self-disciplinary coordination of represented with the (imagined) Representative rather than as a representational negotiation between citizens, or between regular people.

It has long been convention to treat the political discourse of *Representative
Men* as "metaphorical" referent for a larger philosophy rather than as a direct
meditation on political systems. Political theorist Judith Shklar says flat out that
the text is "not about politics" but it seems worth it to me to treat it as though it
is.[27] The representative relationship has *never* been clearly resolved, and there is
no reason to read Emerson's text as though it uses a settled political practice as a
metaphor for an unfolding aesthetic one. It seems as arguable from my angle to
analyze how he is working to pull two fluid practices into a unifying, even
disciplinary, convergence.

We might read *Representative Men* as part of Emerson's ongoing argument
against Jacksonian era democratic culture, its party politics and passion for
"association." Here as elsewhere, he poses a version of "central man" as a corrective for the common man's "rude" politician.[28] Sacvan Bercovitch has argued that
Emerson's developing ideals for individualism were formulated in response to
"Jacksonian ideologues": "Jacksonians defended individualism as a social, economic and political system (as in fact the term then required). Individualism is
for them the natural condition of a new nation-state which is bringing to fru-
ition, institutionally, the 'great progressive movement' ascending from the 'state
of savage individualism to that of an individualism more elevated, moral and
refined.' For Emerson, on the contrary, individualism centers on the independent self. Progress is a function of self-reliance working against the ubiquitous
conspiracies of society."[29] Emerson counters what he sees as the mobbish tendencies, the banal, untidy and conformist orientation of association, with the higher,
symbolically directed exercise of self-culture. This is an argument that culminates
in "New England Reformers" (1844), when Emerson outlines his distrust of party
politics and reformist leagues:

> Concert is neither better nor worse, neither more nor less potent than
> individual force. All the men in the world cannot make a statue walk and
> speak, cannot make a drop of blood, or a blade of grass, any more than one
> man can. But let there be one man, let there be truth in two men, in ten
> men, then there is concert for the first time possible, because the force
> which moves the world is a new quality, and can never be furnished by
> adding whatever qualities of a different kind. What is the use of the con-
> cert of the false and disunited? There can be no concert in two where there

is no concert in one. . . . The union is only perfect, when all of the uniters
are isolated.³⁰

For Emerson, interaction compromises communal good more often than not: it
warps, distracts, and diverts civic actors.³¹ Emerson's spiritual good, "truth," is
unalloyed, an individual property guarded from "qualities of a different kind."
Political and spiritual good is *unity without community:* "The union must be
ideal in actual individualism" (*NE* 599).

If Emerson is taking aim at the growing associative and party power of the
"common man," we should notice that he features the antidemocratic architect
of the Republic as the first (and second) "Representative Man." In "Plato, or the
Reformer" he in fact lauds Plato as the Relationless Man, one who replaces
human relations with representation: "If he had lover, wife, or children, we hear
nothing of them. He ground them all into paint" (*RM* 635). This intellectual
provides Emerson his representational model, a model that would order human
relations. Hannah Arendt observes that Plato's Republic depends on a bodily
aesthetic, "his insistence that the city-state must be considered to be 'man writ
large.'" Even more, she argues, Plato builds a "psychological order" from that
analogy, an architecture she adduces from "the grandiose consistency with which
he introduced the principle of domination into the intercourse of man with
himself." For Plato as for Emerson, the "supreme criterion of fitness" for representivity is "the capacity to rule one's self."³² This capacity is figured, in *Representative Men,* as the ability of the soul to rule the body, of reason to rule passion, of
knowing to rule doing.

Emerson describes good political and social action consistently as self-
discipline. He values action, but only action oriented toward the self. He cherishes
not the interactions but the laws and theologies that delimit those interactions:
"Our theism is the purification of the human mind" (*RM* 616), he asserts, contrasting this purification to the "contagious" quality of interpersonal influence
("We must not be sacks and stomach. . . . Activity is contagious. Looking where
others look and conversing with the same things, we catch the charm which lured
them," [*RM* 620]). As he summarizes the lesson, the quality of representivity is
never interpersonal: greatness "never reminds us of others" (*RM* 617). If the two
great principles of being are action and thought, a balance the stakes of which
Emerson is at pains to detail, it is not a balance achieved with others, but one
entirely internal to the sovereign self, the "balanced soul" (cf. *RM* 639–41).

Where Plato generalizes the private sphere as model for the public, Emerson
makes a qualitatively different move. Here Anita Patterson's nuanced reading of

Emerson's articulation of race and rights provides a crucial insight. She suggests that in general Emerson does not attempt to avoid the public so much as he folds the public into the private, thereby proposing that "the truest form of participation in public life is a vanishing from that life, that publicity is best accomplished by sitting at home."[33] In this move, Emerson takes the political out of the realm of the interpersonal public, ennobling it by protecting it from the unpredictability of inter-action. He protects the form of the political from politicalness, the idea of the political from political interaction.[34]

In *Representative Men* we find an important corollary to the move Patterson analyzes that privatizes by internalizing the political. By Emerson's account, the concept of representation splices the aesthetic and the political at the site where representatives are "pictorial" (*RM* 618) making "unity" symbolically present where it did not before "exist." Indeed, by serving the Representative, we best advance our self: "We need not fear excessive influence. A more generous trust is permitted. Serve the great. Stick at no humiliation. Grudge no office thou canst render. Be the limb of their body, the breath of their mouth. Compromise thy egotism. Who cares for that, so thou gain aught wider and nobler?" (*RM* 629).[35] In such assertions he echoes Mason Locke Weems's pedagogical rationale for his biography of George Washington, and corroborates Weems's intensifying reversal of the (already conservative) Constitutional logic of representation. In Weems's lesson, the aim is not to see your own political desires represented in deliberative government but to model your personal desires on those of the representative: "Since it is the private virtues that lay the foundation of all human excellence . . . give us his private virtues! In these, every youth is interested, because in these every youth may become a Washington."[36]

Emerson's model for representation corroborates the Constitution's general suspicion of unmanaged interpersonal politicalness. Great men inspire us not to the challenge of deepened interaction but to active introspection. The virtue of this model for liberal/representative containment comes in the way that it relieves people of the necessity for "rude" interaction, it releases us "from too much conversation with mates" (*RM* 627). Thus democratic work is channeled symbolically and is self-directed. Democratic power entails not the generation, articulation, and negotiation of personal desires among others, but the determined, disciplined substitution of law-giving "Desire" in its stead. His is a model for inward rather than interpersonal democracy.

Arendt would argue that inasmuch as Emerson's representative remedy successfully displaces interaction from the action of representation, "it actually spoils the action itself, and its true result, the relationship it should have established."[37] His desire for an organizational Desire notwithstanding, Emerson actually has a passion for the possibilities of contact, and it's important to recognize this. Despite the insistent hierarchalization that structures how he thinks about manly interpersonal relations ("But bring to each an intelligent person of another experience, and it is as if you let off water from a lake, by cutting a lower basin" [*RM* 630]), he also points toward real egalitarian exchange. For instance, within the same paragraph that figures relations between men as a "drain," Emerson asserts: "As to what we call the masses, and common men;—there are no common men. All men are at last of a size; and true art is only possible on the conviction that every talent has its apotheosis somewhere. Fair play, and an open field, and freshest laurels to all who have won them!" (*RM* 630). In his analysis of *The Emerson Effect,* Chris Newfield comments on Emerson's ideal democratic sphere: "Emerson figures a type of consent that arises directly from relinquishing separatist individualism in favor of direct contact with the corporate body. This contact furnishes an idea of a democratic sphere in which one becomes individually powerful by relinquishing submission in favor of nonindividualist collaboration."[38] But as Newfield points out, Emerson's phobia about unmanaged interactions, his desire to purify the contact in advance of its occurrence, ultimately keeps him from figuring this collectivity's possibility as existing unmediated anywhere but in the virtual/spiritual realm of the individual's philosophical imagination. He imagines it for a cultured future, but he puts all kind of self-disciplining safeguards up for the route there.

Actually, the great or representative man was never a fully satisfactory substitute for democratic connection, no matter how much diversity Emerson attempted symbolically to load into his representative ideal. Consider this journal entry from 1846, a dream reverie where Emerson promises: "We shall one day talk with the central man, and see again in the varying play of his features all the features which have characterized our darlings." Like an alien morphing from one character to another in the *X-Files,* this "central man" lets us visit with Socrates, then Shakespeare, then Raffaelle who confronts us "with the visage of a girl." Faces "chas[e] each other like a rack of clouds."[39] But the dream "subsides," leaving Emerson "alone." This is a precise moment of democratic melancholy, the modus operandi of national manhood, which I have elsewhere described as an imagined fraternity that works best—and perhaps only—with absent or dead men.[40] National manhood functions in a state of melancholy, a false and unhealthy nostalgia for a uniform, brotherly state of unity and wholeness that never in fact did or even could exist. It misses constantly even as it renounces for the sake of its representative privilege the possibility of a richer and more profound mode of democratic human interaction.[41]

Emerson substitutes the symbolically organized Representative for the banal ordinariness of daily democracy. In his scheme, the representative makes "pictorial" ideal democracy, democracy as a unified, unbroken heroic mind/body. Central man provides a model for evading the real-life entailments of human difference: the desires, disappointments, and mixed possibilities manifested in these engagements are symbolically veiled, dressed as "unity."[42] This cloaking delivers aesthetic satisfaction and political/cultural strength. But it also produces loneliness and melancholy. Emerson's register of these unmet needs becomes the grounds for his sole critique of Plato, whom he finds lacking in "vital authority" because of his overreliance on intellect to the detriment of "passion . . . remorse . . . hope": "There is an interval; and to cohesion, contact is necessary" (*RM* 652).

I take seriously the "side effects" of Emerson's representative prescription because it is here that we can locate alternative possibilities for democratic relations. It is precisely these vestiges of unhappiness (which we might, as I've suggested above, think of as unmet needs for contact) for which Emerson faults Plato without being able to suggest a remedy, and that Davis's model for "ugly democracy" attempts to address. In the gap between desires and Desire lies the interaction, the workaday politicality, that her novel seeks to recover for alternative democratic imagining. Davis distances the formalizing drives of Emerson's representative aesthetic from her field of democratic practice, and she even suggests that democracy cannot be satisfactorily beautified. In fact, her countersymbolic novel implies that the danger in trying to make democracy singularly "representative" is that it brings one too close to the lure or longing of the symbolic, a beautiful, emotionally empty practice, a political unity with no human community.

DEMOCRACY AND DISAGREEMENT: DAVIS'S COUNTERSYMBOLIC

Waiting for the Verdict stages often irresolvable political dialogues between experientially incommensurable but—most important—characteriologically equal players. This novel's "social realism" attempts to imagine democracy socially, *as* disagreement between ordinary, limited, and frequently unsympathetic citizens.[43] In this world there is no possible "unity" exactly because no one person can "stand for" the "Good" of the whole. Instead, Davis offers us at least a gesture toward a different kind of democratic literature, an antiunity aesthetic that might outline a better representative political mode for democracy. This is a model that does not seek recourse in formalized unity, and as such offers a vision of what political theorist William Corlett calls "community without unity." This is a phrase he uses to describe a third option between liberal models of individualism and communitarian models that emphasize consensus and the goal of oneness. To get there, he provides a different etymology for the word "community": "*Com* stands for *with:* with what? is an important question. . . . If the final two syllables of *communis* are *unus,* one might combine them with *com* and say 'with oneness or unity.' This is how most so-called communitarian theorists answer the question, with what? But if *munus* follows *com,* one might say 'with gifts or service' instead. This is the everyday community most people take for granted."[44] It is this everyday community—a community that is not unified in strong consensus but built through a functional dissensus, one that depends on daily gifts and service from one person to another—that Davis's novel takes as its setting for exploring democratic possibility.

The backdrop for Davis's novel is, of course, the threatened breakdown of (imagined) community, the Civil War. Her plot relies on the model of historical romance, interweaving and intermarrying characters from Alabama, Kentucky, and Pennsylvania. In this nearly five-hundred-page novel there are dozens of characters whose lives rub up against each other's, impacting or failing to influence in more and less crucial ways. Conflicts and desire emerge around social difference: characters create and destroy relationships, seek each other out and disagree in ways that change lives on subjects of class, race, citizenship, and gender. Davis simultaneously uses and critiques the romance form, infusing it with a realist countersensibility.[45] Although numerous critics have traced Davis's rejection of romance and sympathy, it is important to this analysis to highlight how she uses both here and does not insist on choosing between the prioritization of order over chaos, of optimism over cynicism, of hope over despair. Not choosing between these forms facilitates her political critique of presidential or transcendentalist representation's "false necessities," the false choices that limit our imagination of political possibility.

The central plot turns around two sets of "mismatched" couples, who are together and whose stories occupy the bulk of the novel, and one well-matched couple (the married and enslaved Annie and Nathan), whose efforts to reunite forms much of the backdrop of the novel. We first meet Rosslyn ("Ross") Burley, the illegitimate daughter of Alabama planter James Strebling. Raised by her grandfather, Joe Burley (her mother dies the day after Ross is born, and her adoptive father, Robert Comly, dies shortly thereafter), Ross grows up as a market huckster on the streets of Philadelphia, with a developing sense of class solidarity and a (not always antiracist) commitment to abolition. In her wartime work for the underground railroad, Ross meets Kentucky native Garrick Randolph, who has romantically cast his lot with the Union cause, deciding impulsively to deliver the missive of a Union soldier he finds dead in Kentucky. In his romantic chivalry he is arrogant, paternalistic, and sexist; although he loves the proud Ross, he wants to put her in a much smaller box from the moment he begins loving her. His particular challenge comes in the form of a suspicious paternal legacy: it is rumored that Garrick's inheritance depends on the machinations of his father's personal slave, Hugh (who may also be his uncle: a family friend describes Hugh as his father's "foster brother"), who, as it turns out, did conceal the will that left everything not to the father, Coyle, but to James Strebling. Garrick sells the now-aged Hugh "down the river" in the middle of the war to suppress that truth, and then months later decides to try to redeem that act when confronted by Hugh's son (Garrick's cousin?), Nathan. This dynamic of character failure and growth complicates, jeopardizes, then moves toward redeeming the relationship between Ross and Garrick.

The other heteromantic plot centers on the mysterious Dr. John Broderip and Margaret Conrad, daughter of a blind, retired minister. Broderip is a renowned surgeon, educated in France, and is well admired among the social elite of Philadelphia, although his moodiness makes him socially remote. He falls in love with Margaret after she consults him about her father's blindness. Margaret (whose familial ancestry may include Native Americans, given the number of times the narrator refers to her "Indian" taciturnity, pride, and stoicism) is devoted to her father (or perhaps to duty) and is characterized by her absolute inflexibility of opinion. One of these options has to do with her belief—even in the context of her abolitionism—in an unbridgeable difference between blacks and whites, expressed as her absolute repulsion of blacks. The conflict between these two lovers emerges when Broderip painfully decides, late in the war, pub-licly to acknowledge the secret of his past: aided by white benefactors, he has been passing and is, "in reality," Nathan's brother and James Strebling's escaped slave, "Sip." Margaret renounces him immediately and absolutely; he enlists to lead a black regiment and dies at the end of the war from injuries sustained leading troops into Richmond, having just been released from a prisoner camp.

In its multiple plots, which work insistently to refuse the reader a central character, *Waiting for the Verdict* rebuts the symbolic-representative logic of Emerson's "central man." Indeed, the novel refuses to offer even a marginal but centrally wise character. If you begin expecting the Quaker Ann Yates to be that, you'd be wrong: the same woman who generously rescues a huckster girl from poverty and a dejected slave boy from slavery turns out in revealing moments to be wrong about the character of the people she is closest to and to be limited by a cynical racism. We can see Davis's strategy here not just in looseness of plot but also in her pictorialization of her key characters, none of whom are ever depicted as anything but average and even ugly—except in the eyes of those who love them best. In one key scene, Ann Yates misreads as "wretched" a lovingly painted scene from Ross's impoverished childhood: "Wretched?" exclaims Ross, "Did I make it that? I did not intend that. . . . These people were very kind to me—they're kinder to each other than any other class" (120). Every character in this novel operates fully as a multivalent, rich, *and* limited subject, where their multiplicity does not just emphasize "difference" but is escalated into a dogged insistence on *differences*. Davis denies power to the symbolic representative, depicting a democratic power that happens only in the "living together of people."[46]

Davis's argument is something other than a communitarian one, however, and indeed it gestures beyond our familiar individualist (competition)/communitarian (consensus) binary altogether. Davis pictures a democratic social power that generates in the ongoing dynamics of dis/unity, in the kinds of daily heroisms and generosities that can emerge between people who don't agree but keep making community together. Refusing to locate priority either in individual actors or in community consensus, Davis focuses on what happens in between, in the surplus space generated *between* people trying to forge varying levels of community—family, neighborhood, region, nation—across their many differences and ongoing disagreements.[47] In the particularity of human interactions, characters change and *effect change* in locally meaningful ways, as for instance when Margaret's relation with Broderip culminates in her beginning to school free blacks, or when Garrick, influenced by his love for Ross and the burdens of his own false pride in familial inheritance, volunteers to adopt the orphaned daughter of a southern antiracist educator murdered by the Klan. Both these characters continue with undeniable flaws. They don't become perfect, not even a whole lot better; it is the changing dynamic of their interactions that makes the difference. These actions neither redeem nor unify community. They just keep building it, in imperfect, open-ended ways.

As the complexly motivated characters interact, this novel stages a richly political discussion of white racism before, during, and in the aftermath of the Civil War. Thus the novel conceptualizes this deeply democratic question (can "we" admit, define, and practice a politics of equality?) by complicating the representative "we" at the outset. *Waiting for the Verdict* stages democracy *through* disagreement. In one key scene, for instance, the aged, working-class, and durably racist Burley has crossed through Confederate lines in an attempt to rescue the young, sympathetic fellow-Philadelphian Markle, who has not returned from a reconnaissance mission. Burley finds the injured Markle being sheltered by Nathan, a slave who is delaying his own escape in order to help this radical-abolitionist Union soldier. As the three men wait to escape, they debate racism and black potential. Even Markle is seen not fully to understand Nathan's human aspirations. None fully agrees with or understands the other two; the debate never achieves resolution. This is a pattern that repeats itself through the end of the novel, with the narrator repeatedly foregrounding how face-to-face democratic deliberation evokes "unease" in the interlocutors. Importantly, this unease, the brokenness of human interrelation, is shown neither to block nor fully to complete a unifying moment of "representative" understanding.

Davis's title, *Waiting for the Verdict* gestures toward an endpoint, a judgment on U.S. democracy. But it refuses to deliver one, preferring action to ending all the way. The novel makes its readers linger in unfinished process. It teaches that "waiting" is central to democratic engagement, not "the verdict." The novel ends with the interaction of Margaret Conrad, mourning for her now-dead lover Broderip, and Robert Markle (the most idealistic white abolitionist in the novel), who conveys the news of Broderip's death and who hopes, perhaps futilely, to woo Margaret to marry him. Working now to educate free blacks (and perhaps herself), Margaret seems on course to fulfill Broderip's prediction. Unable to love him fully in life, it seems she will be unable to forget him now that he is dead; in fact her mourning for this man and for her self-limiting refusal of their relationship may well redirect her life away from romance (with Markle) and toward other kinds of interactions with the exslaves.

The desire that propels Davis's emphasis on democratic contiguity elicits a certain consistent mournfulness in this novel, a mournfulness that might seem to mirror Emerson's melancholy. But I think this mournfulness is politically more productive than Emerson's representative melancholy, a productivity that comes precisely in the intersubjective, processual nature of mourning versus the lonely, stalled place of melancholy (this difference is discussed more fully below). Endpoints are *not* the point of this novel. Its emphasis is on the incompleteness of knowing. Waiting insists that we recognize and live productively with inevitable, difficult incompleteness of political, social, and affective engagement. Although representative symbolics offers us affective reassurance and the definite containment of beautiful form, Davis refuses to produce or invent such assurance. This novel insists that the local, negotiated, temporary intersubjective satisfactions are more productive of democratic movement, and it also insists on the extent to which political affect is produced by and modified within the social and private spheres.

The narrative, social, and political force of this novel derives from the quality of these intersubjective relations, from what Arendt describes generally as the "boundless . . . potentiality in being together."[48] For Davis, the most productive form of relation comes not through representivity but in contiguity, through the day-to-day forming of inter/subjectivity. John Broderip speaks directly to this when he affirms his commitment to abandon his worldly goods as he enters into the Union cause. A white friend, the Philadelphia lawyer Mr. Ottley comments on Broderip's decision to leave a particular engraving of Christ on the wall of his house, now donated as an orphan asylum. This is a portrait that is not idealized, but one that depicts a face "homely and strong, with a man's passion." Ottley complains about this: "there is more of the man than the God in it." And Broderip responds, "How to be a man—that's what we want to know—not how to be a God" (413). His response counters Emerson's abjection of man as a "god in ruins"—it is precisely that "ruin" that Davis's novel embraces. Broderip's recognition encapsulates the novel's affect, an inextricable mixture of regret *and* desire for the inevitability of human (and communal) incompleteness. For Davis, as for Arendt, power is what characters "keep alive through remaining together" and what they lose by withdrawing.[49] Rejecting intersubjectivity is not heroic, it is cowardly; it costs characters their human vitality. We see this death-in-life in Margaret after she decides to withdraw absolutely from her relationship with Broderip: "Her unlighted eyes vaguely wandered up and down the road as if the air that came to her had no living breath in it" (414).

The need for consensus, for unity, is demonstrated to be structurally "false," procedurally unnecessary. The complex and contradictory passions of the Civil War provide the backdrop to this false choice; Davis's characters carry on complexly in the interstices of this war. Unity is not what satisfies them either before or after the war: it is relationship that they seek, whose possibilities they grow in, whose failures they mourn. It is important to register the productivity of mourning in this novel. Mourning for Davis motivates at least movement if not always growth, functioning quite differently from Emersonian melancholia, which, she seemingly argues, blocks movement. Davis's antitranscendentalist argument about political affect can productively be mapped in psychoanalytic terms. Mourning is a productive process of incomplete incorporation. This incorporation, according to Freud's conception of it in his 1917 article, "Mourning and Melancholia," allows for the ego's partial identification with the lost object as it adjusts to its loss. Ultimately, this "incomplete" incorporation results not just in the ego's confrontation of the lost ideal of unity but also, as Nicolas Abraham and Maria Torak argue, ego expansion and growth.[50] Freud posits melancholia differently, as the stalled process of mourning where, fending off the painful process of ego reorganization, the subject attempts the "magical cure" of complete incorporation, refusing to confront ego incompletion by internalizing the lost beloved object whole, keeping it "alive" in a refusal to mourn. If we generalize this to a social model, we might say that melancholia produces celebrity and institution worship ("they stand for us"); mourning opens up the possibility of ongoing change by forcing a confrontation with de-idealized (incomplete) heroes, institutions, communities.

In these terms, we can better see the important contrast between Emerson's and Davis's political affect. To use Judith Butler's helpful terminology, melancholy is a "preemptive loss, a mourning for unlived possibilities."[51] Unity without community leaves Emerson alone, idealizing unity, and trying to "picture" its community by dreaming of a central man who can morph sequentially from one solitary man to another. The subject's growth in self-culture culminates in this melancholy, where intersubjectivity develops only in dreams and leaves the waking subject feeling "alone." Quite differently, community without unity allows Davis's characters to assist each other in the ongoing work of confronting and grieving for the possibilities they miss because of their own and others' human limitations, to live without the completion or closure they might sometimes desire.

Their ability productively to mourn—to integrate dis/unity—allows Davis's characters to build social if not necessarily political community *without* the consensus that presidentially representative—unified—political democracy craves.[52] They do this through their reliance not on unifying forms but on the always imperfect acts of forgiving and promise making. These are Arendt's categories for describing the redemption that can happen in the realm of human action, of human community. For Davis, these actions create redemption that is never complete, never fully unifies, and is never about the closure of consensus. For instance, early in the novel Ottley asks, as a favor, that Broderip use his prestige and social influence to help the newly arrived Garrick Randolph into a Union appointment. Ottley, because he believes Broderip to be a northern white and, hence, a fellow social elite, cannot know the irony of his request. Broderip struggles with the request for many hours. His first impulse is categorically to refuse. He explains vaguely to Ottley, "there is a class of men with whom it is better I should not come into contact. They—did not help me or mine in life as they might have done" (143). He later elaborates the issue for the white benefactress who stands as his mother in the north and who quarters in his house: "This man and his kin have made me what I am. Chance has so placed him in my power that I could put the bitter draught to his lips now, and make him drink it, drop by drop" (152). Finally, though, he decides that chivalry would demand that he write the letter. He promises Randolph when he next sees him, and he immediately executes the letter. Randolph never, of course, registers the irony or the quality of the gift. And when Ottley congratulates Broderip for conquering his "antipathy to the young fellow," Broderip returns, "Conquered it? . . . Conquered it?" (155).

Such moments of self-questioning ("Conquered it?" "Wretched?") are the heart of this book's argument about the political value of intersubjectivity. These moments defy the closure of symbolically driven representivity, and open up instead a space that requires characters to consider how they are understood by others. This *representational* negotiation destabilizes their self-perception, and it is precisely the interruption of their self-unity that allows for the intersubjective growth this novel values. It gestures toward that aspect of democracy that F. R. Ankersmit has described as its "honorable self-doubling": "Only this relation can ensure that in democracy the tensions, frictions and oppositions can be created that will illuminate and make visible the kind of political problems that we will have to address."[53] In these intermediate moments, characters are not heroic; they do not look monumentally unified like Emerson's poet or central man. They look disorganized, in process. In these disunified moments, characters grow. They grow in their ability to do the work of community, to make promises, to offer forgiveness, to engage in mutual service, without the assurances of representative unity, communal consensus, or what Wai Chee Dimock describes as "any notion of a redemptive universe."[54] *Waiting for the Verdict* suggests replacing the satisfaction of symbolic representivity with the broken and uneven representational satisfactions of the intersubjective, of contiguity. It illustrates that social community can go forward without strong unity and holds this model out as an approach to political questions. It urges that giving up the safeguards of form can open the way to something that could be more satisfying because it is less predictable.[55]

CONCLUSION

The structure of this essay has been one of contrast. I've highlighted strong differences between Emerson's and Davis's representational models for democracy, and tacitly, it seems, I've asked readers to choose between them. While schematically productive for sketching the stakes of my argument, it has not been a fair choice for a number of reasons, beginning with the nature of genre. Essays tend toward the abstract and philosophical, the thinking of the individual mind, but novels are built out of the social and interpersonal. And it is absolutely true, as I suggested by culling the passage about central man from his journals, that Emerson treats interpersonal questions more richly elsewhere.

It is also undeniable that Davis was influenced by transcendentalism and its symbolic ideals, as any reader of "Life in the Iron Mills" is likely to observe. But in fact, as I suggested above, "not choosing" seems to be a central component of her political representation and is perhaps our best lesson to draw at this point. Davis's "not choosing" recognizes the value of surplus difference, the difference suppressed by binary power models, the differences that, to borrow political theorist William Corlett's words, "cannot be reduced to opposition" and cannot be underestimated in their life-enhancing value. Davis does not seem finally to be advocating for, again to quote Corlett, "a reversal of the priority of [representative] order over [democratic] chaos."[56] Instead she seems to advocate the value of not choosing, not honoring those particular choices by confirming their inevitability, and it is on this wisdom that I want to draw for the remainder of this conclusion, even as I continue posing Emerson against Davis for the purposes of contrast.

Our fear of unknowable political outcome is legitimate and real. I'm not trying to deny (and I don't see Davis as denying) that we give up something significant if we work at reducing our desire for unified form and its more-or-less guaranteed outcomes for democracy. Arendt describes this fear of "the darkness of the human heart, that is, the basic unreliability of men who never can guarantee today who they will be tomorrow, and out of the impossibility of foretelling the consequences of an act within a community of equals where everybody has the same capacity to act."[57] But Arendt's (and Davis's) point is that accepting it and negotiating it daily, rather than warding it off with the protection of form (and of course consensus too is a form), is the central challenge and the central promise of democratic practice: "Man's inability to rely on himself or to have complete faith in himself (which is the same thing) is the price human beings pay for freedom; and the impossibility of remaining unique masters of what they do, of knowing its consequences and relying upon the future, is the price they pay for plurality and equality, for the joy of inhabiting together with others a world whose reality is guaranteed for each by the presence of all."[58] Faced with the fact of human incompleteness, Emerson projects completeness onto the ideal representative, and suggests we take our inspiration from him. Davis doesn't find a lot of inspiration in completeness. In her representational model, human incompleteness isn't a problem so much as a condition, the condition for growth. Accepting incompleteness opens us to the challenges of negotiating democratic representation, and that we do it differently from resigning or conforming our political aspirations to its symbolism.

Choosing "just" this model could mean, in the context of liberal normativity, a too easy privatization of politics, reducing political problems like the racism Davis's novel confronts to interpersonal moments and change-of-heart solutions.[59] That can't be any more adequate in dealing with unmet needs than the apparitional resolution of local disagreement in the unified body of a representative. The supplementary value of Davis's ugly democracy is that it opens a wider realm for extrainstitutional democracy and demands that we all be open to the possibility that democratic practice can change us profoundly, can change things between us. It demands that we work at mourning and releasing our vision of happy perfectibility in the future that liberal forms like Emerson's central man promise, and then keep working toward something more just, anyway. This in and of itself will never be sufficient to effect large-scale reforms or adequate protections against antidemocratic depredations of institutional racism, and we shouldn't kid ourselves that it will. But countering symbolic representivity with the cultivation of ugly democracy might facilitate a more practical comfort with the very difference and disagreement that white racism so viciously organizes, targets, and denies. It could cultivate the openness to expanding democracy through functional disagreement that antiracist politics more largely demand.

Davis's ugly democracy confirms Amy Gutman and Dennis Thompson's truism for deliberative democracy: "The politics of mutual respect is not always pretty."[60] Presidential representivity has encouraged us to look for aesthetically unified subjects—our political "betters"—to do the work of democracy, to make democracy "beautiful" for us and for the world. Davis challenges presidential representivity's narrow fantasies—fantasies that symbolically disguise democratic inadequacy as "plenitude"—with her story of ugly democracy, a narrative representation of what symbolically oriented representivity can neither manage nor contain. Her story insists that democracy is never adequately reducible to the containment of symbolic representation. She does not oppose her model to representivity so much as she uses it to open up the spaces closed by the demands of unity. Ugly democracy unhinges democracy from philosophical abstractions. It insists on the radical expansion democratic practice, bringing it out of voting booths, party conventions, and Congressional debates, and into all of the closest spaces between civic actors. This makes more room for democratic inchoateness and possibility, because here democracy is vested not within aesthetic abstractions like the people and their representatives, but in between particular, irregular folks.[61] She urges her readers to see that if democracy is to be made into anything more than a hollow and unsatisfactory formalism, it will and is already germinating there between us, in the interstices of daily living, and that it would be as useful to try to appreciate and cultivate it there as it would in the politics surrounding presidential elections.

NOTES

I owe thanks (and probably more!) to Dale Bauer, Chris Castiglia, Bob Levine, Debra Morris, Chris Newfield, Herb Reid, Betsy Taylor, and Chris Zurn, who variously commented on drafts, steered me to important sources, and offered a variety of inspirations. My most special thanks and gratitude go to Russ Castronovo for being a most fabulous coeditor, a source of theoretical inspiration, and a fun cowriter/thinker.

1 For the still-standard treatment of the political problem of representation, see Hanna Fenichel Pitkin's *The Concept of Representation* (Berkeley: University of California Press, 1967).

2 For an important collection of essays that treats the problem of representation in the context of poststructuralism, see Murray Krieger, ed., *The Aims of Representation: Subject, Text, History* (New York: Columbia University Press, 1987).

3 F. R. Ankersmit, *Aesthetic Politics: Political Philosophy beyond Fact and Value* (Stanford: Stanford University Press, 1996), 16.

4 Susanne Kappeler, *The Pornography of Representation* (Minneapolis: University of Minnesota Press, 1986), 45.

5 I'm drawing generally on Hal Foster's formulation of the "anti-aesthetic," which refers not to "the negation of art or representation as such" but works loosely as a "critique of Western representation(s) and modern 'supreme fictions; a desire to think in terms sensitive to difference . . .; a skepticism regarding autonomous 'spheres' of culture or separate 'fields' of experts; an imperative to go beyond formal filiations . . . to trace social affiliations" (Foster, "Introduction," in *The Anti-Aesthetic: Essays on Postmodern Culture*, ed. Hal Foster [Seattle: Bay Press, 1983], xv).

6 On this subject, see Sheldon Wolin's essay, "Tending and Intending a Constitution:

Bicentennial Misgivings," in *The Presence of the Past: Essays on the State and the Constitution* (Baltimore: Johns Hopkins University Press, 1989).

7 C. Douglas Lummis, *Radical Democracy* (Ithaca: Cornell University Press, 1996), 37.

8 For instance, I would argue that the persuasive force of presidentially conditioned representation has convinced the public that it best alone accomplishes democracy, overshadowing not just "other models" but even models that might combine modes of direct and representative democratic practice.

9 While there is every reason not to idealize locality as place—for the ways in which communities can constitute themselves through rigid, exclusionary, and antidemocratic practices of political and identity sameness—that in itself is no reason to surrender the value of the local for political *practice*. The value of the local for democracy is that it can work to invest us in our own politicalness (this is Sheldon Wolin's term, see *The Presence of the Past,* chapter 8). It is important to insist on the historical existence of nonuniformatized practices of democracy in the early United States, because it is only in so doing that we can understand the way the Constitution does not generate national identity and its political practices in a void so much as it seeks to subjugate local democratic practices, delegating the "local" to the far more manageable form of the state.

Here I want to be clear in my rejection of "Republicanism" as the originary politics of the U.S. political imaginary, where, the story goes, the logic of democracy was a later development. I'm insisting that in colonial localities, and then particularly during the course of revolution itself, Americans developed a variety of even occasionally radical democratic practices and commitments, and that Constitutional Republicanism understood itself to be in competition with those democratic logics and practices.

10 Ralph Waldo Emerson, *Representative Men.* In *Essays and Lectures.* Joel Porte, ed. New York: Library of America, 1983, 611–761. Subsequent citations are given parenthetically in the text with the abbreviation *RM*. Rebecca Harding Davis, *Waiting for the Verdict.* Donald Dingledine, ed. Albany, NY: NCUP, 1995. Subsequent citations are given parenthetically in the text.

11 See Hannah Arendt, *The Human Condition,* 2nd ed. (1958; Chicago: University of Chicago Press, 1998), 183.

12 See Roberto Unger, *False Necessity: Anti-Necessitarian Social Theory in the Service of Radical Democracy,* part 1 of *Politics: A Work in Constructive Social Theory* (Cambridge: Cambridge University Press, 1987); and his *Democracy Realized: The Progressive Alternative* (London: Verso, 1998), 20–27.

13 This section is drawn from my analysis of presidentialism in chapter 1 and the afterword of my *National Manhood: Capitalist Citizenship and the Imagined Fraternity of White Man* (Durham: Duke University Press, 1998). A version of this material is also included in my essay "Representative/Democracy: Presidents, Democratic Management, and the Unfinished Business of Male Sentimentalism," in *No More Separate Spheres!,* ed. Cathy Davidson (Durham: Duke University Press, 2002).

14 See for instance, Wolin, "Collective Identity and Constitutional Power," "Tending and Intending a Constitution," and "*E Pluribus* Unum," in his *The Presence of the Past;* Woody Holton, *Forced Founders: Indians, Debtors, Slaves, and the Making of the*

American Revolution in Virginia (Chapel Hill: University of North Carolina Press, 1999); Mark W. Kruman, *Between Authority and Liberty: State Constitution Making in Revolutionary America* (Chapel Hill: University of North Carolina Press, 1997); Saul Cornell, *The Other Founders: Anti-Federalism and the Dissenting Tradition in America, 1788–1828* (Chapel Hill: University of North Carolina Press, 1999); and Antonio Negri, *Insurgencies: Constituent Power and the Modern State*, trans. Mauriziz Boscagli (Minneapolis: University of Minnesota Press, 1999). See also chapter 1 in my *National Manhood*.

15 I want to register here that I'm fully persuaded by Gordon Wood's argument in *Creation of the American Republic, 1776–1787* (New York: Norton, 1981) that people across the states and across socioeconomic levels were registering the presence of some kind of crisis; I'm also fully persuaded by his move to locate the energy of the "crisis" in emerging political dissensus. Our difference lies in the relative values we attach to the notion of "dissensus," the ideal of "unity," and the Constitutional attempt to guarantee national unity. I'm interested here in pressuring "fragmentation" as a culturally dystopic framing of what might actually be regarded in the terms of *health*: of human and cultural diversity, of local political variety, and of what Christopher J. Newfield has described as the "disunited state of America" in his "What Was Political Correctness? Race, the Right, and Managerial Democracy in the Humanities," *Critical Inquiry* 19, no. 2 (1993): 336.

16 Wood notes that "more such groups sprang up in the dozen years after Independence than in the entire colonial period" (*Creation of the American Republic*, 325). Paul Gilje argues that "throughout most of the eighteenth century, mobs theoretically represented a united community acting to protect agreed-upon morals and customs" and were granted—even by the wealthy elite—a kind of "quasi-legitimacy." Such tolerance began to break down beginning in the 1780s, and although Federalists and Republicans continued to support their own out-of-doors actions, Gilje observes that they increasingly harshly condemned the actions of their opponents as a national danger (*The Road to Mobocracy: Popular Disorder in New York City, 1763–1834* [Chapel Hill: University of North Carolina Press, 1987], 118, 5; see especially chapter 4, "Political Popular Disturbances").

17 Lummis, *Radical Democracy*, 113.

18 I want to underscore that I'm not trying to present a romanticized tragedy of democratic declension here. I am trying to pay attention to democratic alternatives and to the specific ideological and discursive conditions through which those possibilities were narrowed in the United States.

19 I'm using the term "virtualization" to get at a fairly precise point (and one whose implications extend forward from this historical moment) about democracy, which is directed at the way the Constitution promised to "manage" democracy in order to make it "safe" for the people. To my mind, this constitutes a fundamental restraint on democracy energy and possibility. Constitutional order promises to eradicate the stresses of heterogeneity by distancing people from its "dangerous" expression. As it develops in practice, federal democratic order cleans up the messiness of radi-

cal democratic practice by virtualizing it, abstracting its face-to-face negotiations through the managed competition of private voting booths and the symbolically distancing and organizing mechanisms of party politics. Through the developing systematization of Constitutional presidentialism and the universalization of white male suffrage, "the people" would come to surrender the idea of locally negotiated, face-to-face democracy for the routine expression of their opinion on ballots and the embodiment of that "opinion" in the person of various elected officials, especially the president (see Lummis, *Radical Democracy*, 19 for a pithy summary of the relation of "allowing the people to have their say" to democracy). My term, "virtualization," plays on the logic of virtual representation as described by Edmund Burke (cf. Pitkin, *Concept of Representation*, 169–70) and as rejected by the American colonists (see Wood, *Creation of the American Republic*, 173–81) and on Baudrillard's evocative discussion of the operational simulation of the political economy. While it is interesting to see the way Baudrillard traces this logic into twentieth-century political economy, my claims for the purposes of this essay are more limited and specific: that Constitutional order takes away power (removes the impetus and redirects the structures for direct democracy) from the people in order to guarantee national order, all the while promising them recognition (the sovereignty of "the people") *as* (a substitute for) power. See Jean Baudrillard, *Symbolic Exchange and Death*, trans. Iain Hamilton Grant (London: Sage Publications, 1993).

For a very careful and informative analysis of where anti-Federalism goes after Constitutional ratification, see Saul Cornell's wonderful *The Other Founders*, which provides a rich account of how "middling democrats" and radical plebian democrats converged and diverged in their political purposes during and after the ratification.

20 There was little actual anti-Federalist opposition to the office of the president. As Jackson Turner Main notes, significant opposition focused on the issues of re-eligibility and scope of powers, but not on the fact of the office. See Main, *The Anti-Federalists: Critics of the Constitution, 1781–1788* (Chapel Hill: University of North Carolina Press, 1961).

21 This is an argument I map in greater detail in *National Manhood*, 29–34.

22 Importantly, his unifying energy is representatively routed through and supplied by male citizens in a way that can reassure individual men not only about political discord but about other kinds of cultural and economic dislocations. In the end, what might have most effectively garnered support for—or at least blunted resistance to—the Constitution was the way it convincingly and insistently circuited the ideal of political consensus through the similarly common ideal of a vigorous, strong, undivided manhood. The bribe of national manhood, a manhood that could be claimed through patriotic incorporation, effectively undercut the radicalizing energy of local democratic practices.

23 Gary L. Gregg, *The Presidential Republic: Executive Representation and Deliberative Democracy.* New York: Rowman and Littlefield, 1997, 23.

24 As Charles Sellers reminds us, in *The Market Revolution: Jacksonian America, 1815–*

1846 (New York: Oxford University Press, 1985), under British rule corporations could only be chartered as nonprofit agencies and only by legislative act. Seven such charters were organized in the colonial period. But after the Revolution, "the number climbed to forty in the first decade . . . and passed three hundred during the commercial boom of the 1790s" (44–45). Sellers details how these early corporations soon forged a link between the idea of public good and private profit, effectively convincing at least the courts that because corporate entrepreneurship was socially beneficial, large debtors like corporate officers should not be impeded from continuing their entrepreneurial work on behalf of such social good by, say, being imprisoned for debts and bankruptcy (47–90).

25 For a more concrete map of the way one version of such a process might work, see James S. Fishkin, *Voice of the People: Public Opinion and Democracy,* 2nd ed. (New Haven: Yale University Press, 1995). He argues for a system he calls "a democracy of civic engagement," which would protect four basic democratic conditions: political equality, deliberation, participation, and nontyranny (63, 34). His appeal is to "ideals without an ideal," a recognition that there "is not single ideal vision progressively to be realized" (63).

26 Samuel R. Delany, in *Times Square Red, Times Square Blue* (New York: New York University Press, 1999), outlines a luminous, pro-sex argument about the difference between the philosophy of "networking," the planned cultivation of strategic social, communal, and professional exchange, and what he calls "contact," a far more accidental, random, and occasionally serendipitous mode of encounter. His arguments center on urban planning and politics; his ideas about the boundary-crossing, life-enhancing, accidental qualities of "contact" inform and complement mine.

27 Judith N. Shklar, "Emerson and the Inhibitions of Democracy," *Political Theory* 18, no. 4 (November 1990): 612.

28 For a historical treatment of various developing postures within "the era of the common man," see Glenn C. Altschuler and Stuart M. Blumin, *Rude Republic: Americans and Their Politics in the Nineteenth Century* (Princeton: Princeton University Press, 2000), 10.

29 Sacvan Bercovitch, *Rites of Assent: Transformations in the Symbolic Construction of America* (New York: Routledge, 1993), 313.

30 Ralph Waldo Emerson, "New England Reformers," in *Essays and Lectures,* ed. Joel Porte (New York: Library of America, 1983), 598–99. Subsequent citations are given parenthetically in the text with the abbreviation NE.

31 Chris Newfield observes that "Emerson calls for resistance to a conformist social law the better to conform to a spiritual law" (*The Emerson Effect: Individualism and Submission in America* [Chicago: University of Chicago Press, 1996], 72).

32 Arendt, *The Human Condition,* 224.

33 Anita Patterson, *From Emerson to King: Democracy, Race, and the Politics of Protest* (New York: Oxford University Press, 1997), 186.

34 Political theorist Bonnie Honig describes a "virtue" theorist as a democratic analyst who believes "mistakenly that his own theory soothes or resolves the dissonances

other theories cause. Each yearns for closure and each looks to politics, rightly under-stood, to provide and replace it" (*Political Theory and the Displacement of Politics* [Ithaca: Cornell University Press, 1993], 3). Emerson's unifying symbolic, central man, provides this closure.

35 This argument evinces, as David M. Robinson puts it, Emerson's "aching desire to find the figure who makes the ideal and the real cohere," his labor to conceive of a self that could be legitimately, fully, and comprehensively constitutive of com-munity (*Emerson and the Conduct of Life* [New York: Cambridge University Press, 1993], 99).

36 Mason Locke Weems, *The Life of Washington,* ed. Marcus Cunliffe (Cambridge: The Belknap Press of Harvard University Press, 1962), 5.

37 Arendt, *Human Condition,* 196.

38 Newfield, *The Emerson Effect,* 77.

39 Ralph Waldo Emerson, *The Journals and Miscellaneous Notebooks of Ralph Waldo Emerson,* ed. William H. Gilman et al., 16 vols., (Cambridge: The Belknap Press of Harvard University Press, 1960–1982), 9:395.

40 See my *National Manhood;* see also my "Thoreau, Race, and Manhood: Quiet Desper-ation versus Representative Isolation" in *A Historical Guide to Henry David Thoreau,* ed. William Cain. (New York: Oxford University Press, 2000).

41 Russ Castronovo has proposed another term that could describe this Emersonian modality: "political necrophilia." Political necrophilia describes what Castronovo convincingly outlines as a long-standing, positive association in the United States of freedom with a state of (borrowing Orlando Patterson's phrase) "'social death'—a condition that severs self from kin and community. The staggering aspect of this conjunction," Castronovo observes, "is that for Patterson, alienation from family, tribe, or clan describes not freedom but slavery" ("Political Necrophilia," *boundary 2* 27, no. 2 [summer 2000]: 137).

42 Nancy Ruttenburg has argued something similar about Emerson and Fuller's second number of *The Dial,* where the "promise that a democratic literature, written by and for the people, would prove uniquely able to elide the gap between being and repre-sentation" (*Democratic Personality: Popular Voice and the Trial of American Authorship* [Stanford: Stanford University Press, 1998], 338).

43 Jean Pfaelzer, *Parlor Radical: Rebecca Harding Davis and the Origins of American Social Realism* (Pittsburgh: University of Pittsburgh Press, 1996), 157.

44 William Corlett, *Community without Unity: A Politics of Derridean Extravagance* (Durham: Duke University Press, 1993), 18.

45 On the subject of Davis's realism, see Sharon Harris, *Rebecca Harding Davis and American Realism* (Philadelphia: University of Pennsylvania Press, 1991); and Pfaelzer, *Parlor Radical.*

46 Arendt, *Human Condition,* 201.

47 Davis's model coordinates with an important recognition about democratic political process that Ankersmit describes thusly: "Power originates neither in the people . . . nor in the ruler . . . but *between* the people and the state" (*Aesthetic Politics,* 50).

48 Arendt, *Human Condition*, 201.

49 Ibid.

50 Nicolas Abraham and Maria Torak, "Mourning *or* Melancholia: Introjection *versus* Incorporation" in *The Shell and the Kernal: Renewals of Psychoanalysis,* ed. Nicolas T. Rand (Chicago: University of Chicago Press, 1994).

51 See Judith Butler, "Melancholy Gender, Refused Identification" in *Constructing Masculinity,* ed. Maurice Berger, Brian Wallis, and Simon Watson (New York: Routledge, 1995), 27. See also my *National Manhood,* chapter five, "The Melancholy of White Manhood," 176–203.

52 Davis's emphasis on disunity carries a lesson Chris Newfield summarizes for another context: "Our national 'disuniting' began with our inception and it's not too soon to get over our regret about this. Our 'pluralistic,' 'consensual' union, however one feels about it, has always rested on a divided, antagonistic multiplicity of cultures whose overlap has been sporadic, conflictual, or incomplete. The burden of providing a unified government has for too long interfered with our ability to understand cultural actuality. . . . Disunity is not a problem—in fact, it is usually preferable to more efficient resolutions. *Disunity* is another word for *democracy*" ("What Was Political Correctness?" 336).

53 Ankersmit, *Aesthetic Politics,* 347.

54 With reference to "Life in the Iron Mills," Wai Chee Dimock outlines Davis's commentary on "the phenomenon of loss in the routine of living, an involuntary attrition which, in making human agency porous in its effect, must render porous as well any notion of a recuperative universe. . . . In ways at once accidental and agonizing, the sum of the parts is always greater than the whole, is not so much an effect of our plenitude as an effect of our loss" (*Residues of Justice: Literature, Law, Philosophy* [Berkeley: University of California Press, 1996], 94–95).

55 Davis doesn't offer any guarantees. As Sharon Harris notes of her work more generally in a comparison with Hamlin Garland, "perhaps the greatest distinction between the two realists was that Garland believed the future *would* be democratized while Davis asserted it *could* be" (Harris, *Rebecca Harding Davis,* 11). I have been inspired to this aggressively political analysis of Davis's novel more generally by Harris's provocative introduction to *Redefining the Political Novel: American Women Writers, 1797–1901,* ed. Sharon Harris (Knoxville: University of Tennessee Press, 1995).

56 Corlett, *Community without Unity,* xvii, 14.

57 Arendt, *Human Condition,* 244.

58 Arendt, *Human Condition,* 244. Because Arendt has been such a help to me in sorting out the differences between Emerson's representivity and Davis's democracy, and especially because I have so fully seemed to align Davis with Arendt, it is important to flag Davis's challenge to Arendt. Where Arendt disallows the domestic as a political space, arguing that it is too closely tied to the enslaving demands of nature, because of the necessity of "having a body" (*Human Condition,* 68–73), Davis insists that it is precisely in this realm of necessity that we can best start developing democratic intersubjectivity. For a productive discussion of Arendt's problem with the domestic,

see Honig, *Political Theory*, 77–84. It also seems important to note that Davis is less confident of the "joy" that will come in the surrender of individualist mastery than is Arendt. As Dimock notes, Davis insists on "not only the incommensurability between the material and the immaterial, but also the incommensurability between self and world—a world that refuses to envelop us in reciprocity, to render back to us, in sonorous fullness, our need for attention, expression, conversation" (*Residues of Justice*, 95, see also 92).

59 For an extraordinary critique of this kind of sentimental "democracy," see Lauren Berlant, "Poor Eliza," *American Literature* 70, no. 3 (September 1998): 635–68.

60 Amy Gutmann and Dennis Thompson, *Democracy and Disagreement: Why Moral Conflict Cannot Be Avoided in Politics, and What Should Be Done About It* (Cambridge: The Belknap Press of Harvard University Press, 1996), 90.

61 With the term "irregular," I am referring to Russ Castronovo's extraordinarily useful elaboration on Wai Chee Dimock's discussion of how liberalism sustains a syntactic conception of political subjectivity. Castronovo explains that "liberalism sustains a syntactic subject, one whose being is 'generalizable,' recognizable to the social order only to the extent of his or her ability to exist abstractly. Structured by this political syntax, citizens adhere to a lexicon that governs without regard to 'irregular' conditions that particularize subjects such as institutional location or racial ancestry. . . . Such ecumenical thinking precludes the possibility that the subject instead might be semantic, understood only by the urges, remainders and details that diverge from the universal" ("Political Necrophilia," 116–17). See also Dimock, *Residues of Justice*, 119–20.

WAI CHEE DIMOCK

Rethinking Space, Rethinking Rights:
Literature, Law, and Science
◆

What exactly does it mean to "materialize democracy"? I want to put an unusual spin on this phrase, giving it two registers of meaning, one literal, the other less so. First, I take materialization to its lowest common denominator, linking it to physical space, the metrical coordinates of the world. From this literal register, I try to develop an argument—on a different dimensional plane—about space of a different sort, "material" not in the sense of being physically given but in the sense of being operationally nontrivial. This space, a grid defining the boundaries and limits of personhood, the boundaries and limits of entitlement, is crucial to any theory of democracy. It is especially crucial to one democratic practice, the practice of rights: the laying out of spheres of sanctity, and the corresponding need to adjudicate rival claims.

"Materialization," then, has one foot each in two domains of discourse: the discourse of science, and the discourse of law. In this essay I attempt to bring together these two domains; I attempt to put legal arguments in the context of a scientific debate, the debate about "absolute" versus "relative" space. This debate, a turning point in modern physics, issues a corresponding challenge to other domains of thought.[1] In what follows, I move across disciplines—going from law to science and pitting Einstein against Newton—in order to recover a genealogy of argument against the "absolute space" of rights. This movement across disciplines also brings into play another body of writing: a late-nineteenth-century genre usually associated with women and dubbed "New England local color." This literary genre, I argue, has something to say to law and science both. Separately formed and entirely ignorant of the other two, it is nonetheless part of a shared conceptual continuum. Extending for hundreds of years and articulated anew as literature, as law, and as science, this continuum bears directly on our democratic practice.

THE SPACE OF RIGHTS

I begin with a trenchant statement from Mary Ann Glendon's *Rights Talk* (1991). Glendon is critical of the dominant role of the judiciary in the United States, a nation she calls "the land of rights." According to her, this disproportionate centrality of the judiciary has led to a habit of speech likewise misguided, a speech so odd and so fiercely accented as to have the status of a dialect. This "rights dialect" "is set apart from rights discourse in other liberal democracies by its starkness and simplicity, its prodigality in bestowing the rights label, its legalistic character, its exaggerated absoluteness, its hyperindividualism, its insularity, and its silence with respect to personal, civic, and collective responsibilities."[2] For Glendon, the primacy of rights in the United States is most broadly registered in the linguistic practice of its citizens. American public life is dominated by a language that is anything but public-minded, a language fixated on the narrow meanings of personhood to the exclusion of other—more capacious, and perhaps more compelling—meanings. Rights are "insular." To map our being along the lines of that insularity is to imagine our humanness in discretely spatial terms; that is, in terms of what we can safeguard and defend against others. The assumption here is that there is a space of sanctity that ought not to be encroached. And, to make this space absolute, it is further assumed that any encroachment must result from someone overstepping a line, intruding into a place where he or she ought not to be.

In short, within the paradigm of individual rights, every moral dispute is spatially mappable, traceable to a territorial transgression. Given this logic, conflict resolution simply means a restoration of boundaries. This is something that can be done by going to court, by appealing to the verdicts of a juridical instrument. For that reason, Glendon argues that rights are the cornerstone of a legalistic culture, one that settles moral disputes by juridical force.[3] Litigation becomes the endpoint for ethical thinking, and its outcome is supposed to clear up all the perplexities, all the shadows and gray areas of that thinking. Because law has this alleged ability to cut through all dispute, "winning" and "losing" also become spatially segregable, each occupying an integral domain. One wins if one "has right," and one loses if one has "no right." The boundaries between these two can be juridically decided, can be mapped as inversions of each other. The space of sanctity goes only to one side; the other side comes away empty-handed.

According to Glendon, then, what the language of rights gives us is an ethical universe of undue clarity, a clarity issuing from the discrete spaces designated by the law. This judicial mapping breeds a kind of moral absolutism, fatal to the claims of others and to any hope for compromises, any hope for a "grammar of cooperative living."[4] Glendon's argument, I should also add, is not at all idiosyncratic. If anything, it is the summary of a line of thinking, a "critique of rights" that, in the past fifteen years, has emerged as one of the liveliest intellectual movements of our time. This movement is associated, most particularly, with critical legal studies in law, with the pragmatism of Richard Rorty, and with the civic republicanism of political theorists such as Michael Sandel.[5] Glendon's sweeping critique rests, of course, on many generalizations, some untenable.[6] Still, it has captured the prevailing spirit in what is surely the most divisive dispute of our time—namely, abortion. This dispute—especially when it is conducted outside the courtroom in the popular language Glendon calls the "rights dialect"—does indeed take the form of a clash of absolutes. Here, the fetus's absolute "right to life" is pitted against the woman's absolute "right to choose." Here, each claimant wants the space of sanctity only on one side; each tries to write its opponent completely out of the picture.

This essay is a dissent from such absolute claims. It is also an attempt to foreground—and to complicate—their spatial assumptions. What I hope to do, then, is to experiment with a twofold approach: a critique of rights that is also, in the same gesture, a reinvention of the concept.[7] I want to show that the adversarial language of rights can be subject to a more nuanced arbitration, that clean verdicts can be restored to a more humane fuzziness, and that the very concepts of "winning" and "losing" might also be more complexly imagined. They might be imagined, that is, not as binary opposites, categories defined by absolute inversion, but as overlapping domains, each putting pressure on the other, each affecting the shape of the other and being qualified by the other's constraints.

Eventually I want to show, as well, that this nondiscrete form of winning and losing, counterintuitive as it might seem, has actually been given a tentative expression in literature, especially in that late-nineteenth-century genre dedicated to confining and conflicted spaces: the genre called "local color."[8] This body of writing will be approached somewhat obliquely. I will first take my argument through what might seem a bizarrely unfamiliar context: Newton and Einstein. But it is only within this context that we can see spatial postulates in heightened relief: as the "ground" on which rights are posited as entities, with the property of being integral or not, permeable or not, discrete or overlapping. In short—and no doubt I am loading the dice here—I want to trace what Mary Ann Glendon calls the "exaggerated absoluteness" of rights to Newton's "absolute space," a concept long accepted as a truism in physics but singled out for critique, in the twentieth century, by Einstein's relativity.

NEWTON AND ABSOLUTE SPACE

Time and space, Newton said, are often seen from a contextual point of view, "from the relation they bear to sensible objects."[9] Such are the "prejudices" of "the common people" (6), and he is determined to set things right. Newton's magisterial treatise, the *Principia* (1686), thus stands as the founding text of the physical theory that has come to be known as "absolutism." In its pages, Newton takes it upon himself to distinguish, once and for all, between "absolute and relative, true and apparent, mathematical and common" space and time (6). "Absolute, true, and mathematical time," according to him, "flows equably without relation to anything external," just as "absolute space, in its own nature, without relation to anything external, remains always similar and immovable" (6). Absolute time and space are "absolute" because they are antecedently given and contextually invariant. They make up an a priori grid of the world. Only such an a priori grid would guarantee that there would always be true relations among things, relations neither circumstantial nor negotiable but that "from infinity to infinity, do all retain the same given position one to another" (9).

For Newton, then, a physics of absolute space was also, quite literally, the ground for a metaphysics: a metaphysics about what sort of entities were possible, what attributes constituted them, and what positions governed them. Because the natural order was a direct manifestation of the divine order, what was at stake in these postulates about the absolute relations among things was not only the physical underpinnings of the universe but also the moral underpinnings of human affairs. From the natural world, Steven Shapin notes, one could extrapolate "a set of ethical prescriptions about how one was to conduct oneself on earth."[10] These ethical prescriptives, disseminated by Anglican divines in, say, the Boyle Lectures,[11] quickly extended Newton's influence far beyond the technical spheres of science. The laws of physics seemed translatable into the laws of ethics; natural philosophy underwrote a civic religion. There was such a thing as "cultural Newtonianism."[12] Under its auspices, many began to hope that human society itself might prove to be rule-governed, harmonized by a prior design and running according to a fixed plan, as the natural world seemed to be. It was to this noble dream that Hume paid tribute when, in his *History of England,* he sang the praises of Newton on this uncharacteristically rhapsodic note: "In Newton this island may boast of having produced the greatest and rarest genius that ever arose for the ornament and instruction of the species."[13]

Nor was the worship of Newton limited only to the British Isles. Newton was the "demi-god" of the Enlightenment, Peter Gay points out, and, throughout the eighteenth century, his "deification" proceeded as briskly on the Continent as it did in England.[14] Voltaire spoke for an entire age when, in *Elemens de la philosophie de Neuton,* he proudly put his hero on the pinnacle of human achievement: "This philosopher gathered in during his lifetime all the glory he deserved; he aroused no envy because he could have no rival. The learned world were his disciples, the rest admired him without daring to claim that they understood him."[15] In France, in the Netherlands, and in Germany, Newton's authority was "unsurpassed and unsurpassable."[16] And so the abbé Jacques Delille surprised no one when, in the second half of the eighteenth century, nearly fifty years after Newton's death, he saw fit to adapt Pope's famous couplet for his French readers:

> O pouvoir d'un grand homme et d'une âme divine!
> Ce que Dieu seul a fait, Newton seul l'imagine,
> Et chaque astre répète en proclamant leur nom:
> Gloire à Dieu qui créa les mondes et Newton![17]

Such was the adulation from the religious-minded. Those more scientifically inclined did not lag behind. Indeed, for Enlightenment thinkers generally, Newtonian physics was nothing less than the pivot of all knowledge. But it was Kant, more than anyone else, who would try to graft a metaphysics onto the back of this physics, gathering the two into a formal ethical theory.

KANT AND ABSOLUTE RIGHTS

Like a good many Enlightenment thinkers, including d'Alembert and Condorcet, Kant had started out as a student of science before he turned to philosophy. He had done work in physics, astronomy, geology, and meteorology, and, as a lecturer at the University of Koningsberg, had taught not only ethics but also logic, mathematics, and the natural sciences, including the new subject of physical geography.[18] Newtonian physics for him was simply foundational. What he especially liked was the idea of absolute space. This Newtonian tenet he embraced almost wholesale in his early, precritical writings. In an essay titled "Concerning the Ultimate Foundations of the Differentiations of Regions in Space," Kant simply said, "absolute space has its own reality independently of the existence of matter," and "is itself the ultimate foundation of the possibility of its composition."[19] The statement had all the authority of Newton behind it; indeed, it could have come from Newton himself. Still, Kant is not one to move slavishly in another's orbit. Thirteen years later, in *The Critique of Pure Reason* (1781), he would amend his position, putting his own stamp on it.

Here, Kant once again insists on the "*a priori* necessity of space," but, departing from Newton, he now argues that for space to be truly a priori it cannot be taken as an observational datum. It cannot be a physical dimension of the world, "not an empirical concept at all."[20] Like Newton, Kant wants to think of space as a preassigned foundation. Unlike Newton, however, he doubts whether anything so foundational can come from the empirical world. Indeed, by his stricter reckoning, space must be formal rather than empirical; that is, it must be antecedently given rather than observationally derived. Kant thus insists that space is a form "exist[ing] in the mind" (71), "prior to any perception of an object" (70). This priority belongs to it, because it is the substrate of any cognitive process, the ground on which this process can claim to be self-adequating and self-validating. From this preassigned foundation we can affirm human "reason [as] the faculty which supplies the principles of *a priori* knowledge" (58).

As Kant himself makes clear, this a priori knowledge is not good enough for physics. He insists, however, that it is necessary for ethics. Natural science "may accept many propositions as universal on the evidence of experience," Kant says, "but it is otherwise with Moral Law. These, in contradistinction to Natural Laws, are only valid as Laws, in so far as they can be rationally established *a priori* and comprehended as necessary."[21] Kantian ethics, in short, distinguishes itself from physics by locating itself at a point prior to empirical constraints. It is this prior location that enables the *Critique of Practical Reason* to be bold, just as the *Critique of Pure Reason* has been cautious. The *Critique of Pure Reason* had begun with the premise that our empirical relation to the world is not transparent, but mediated. The *Critique of Practical Reason*, on the other hand, begins with the premise that our nonempirical relation to morality is not mediated, but transparent. Good and evil are concepts that we know in their absolute and eternal essence, in advance of their actual manifestations in the world. We can have direct access to a moral law that can be "unconditionally commanded as a law."[22]

Kant's ethics, in short, is an ethics that fancies itself to have transcended the limits of epistemology. It is prior to those limits, not mixed up with the other problems of human cognition. A space unto itself, it is free to dedicate itself to one unifying proposition: the "categorical imperative." This imperative, Kant says, "proclaims itself as originating law," and issues its commands as "a priori principles": "This principle of morality, on account of the universality of its legislation which makes it the formal supreme determining ground of the will regardless of any subjective differences among men, is declared by reason to be a law for all rational beings. . . . The moral law for them, therefore, is an imperative, commanding categorically because it is unconditioned" (32). Unconditionality, for Kant, turns out to be the very condition for morality. Kantian ethics is thus unconcerned with human disagreement, not only because the categorical imperative is supposed to be universal, but, perhaps even more basically, because the moral law is, by definition, not based on circumstances and not differentiated by circumstances. Its unity of expression overrides any morphological variation. Formalized outside the empirical world of human relations, Kant's ethics is also unaffected by those relations, untroubled by the chronic disputes that run through them. Morality thus entails a transaction between each of us and a preexisting moral law, rather than a transaction between human beings actually living side by side. The categorical imperative is "supremely self-sufficing" (33) in this sense, for the Kantian moral agent need only regulate himself in its image, his relations to actual human beings entering not at all into the picture.

This a priori conception of morality—its status as a given, not derived and not contingent—seems to me to be one of the most destructive legacies of Kant's ethics. And, to the extent that this Kantian tradition remains the dominant ethical tradition of the West, many of us are still in its shadow. The importance of Kant to John Rawls is a good measure, I think, of just how long that shadow is.[23] My critique of rights is a critique of this Kantian tradition. For while the concept of individual rights might indeed be traceable to antiquity, as Leo Strauss and Richard Tuck have argued, and while Hobbes and Locke were central to its seventeenth-century articulation, as Ian Shapiro has shown, there is something about its self-proclaimed antecedence that makes this concept recognizably Kantian.[24] It is only in an a priori moral universe that rights can be what they are and as they are: not only prior to any social relations, but, in their priority, also imagined to be discrete, to exist as absolute claims.

Rights, we might say, are the inhabitants of a moral "absolute space." Their ontology is "unconditioned." So it is perhaps not surprising that most of us, having rights, will now press forward our claims, will now insist on our due, without the slightest acknowledgment that there might be necessary constraints here, circumstances under which "our due" would have to be modified, truncated, perhaps even surrendered. The language of rights is a language burdened by little awareness of conflicting, overlapping, or incommensurate claims. For that reason, it also has no ability to predict its own limits, no provision for any sort of self-qualifying responsiveness. This moral absolutism seems to me to follow directly from the Kantian abstraction of Newtonian physics. To transform it, we need not only to undo its abstraction but also to revisit the physical theory that lies at its metaphysical foundation.

EINSTEIN'S RELATIVITY

It is helpful, then, to take a short detour across an intellectual landscape familiar to neither law nor literature, the mysterious world of modern physics. Here, we will find that Newton's theory is no longer the supreme theory it once was. It has been challenged, and to some degree superseded, by Einstein's theories of relativity. Einstein begins, in fact, with an explicit critique of Newton. "Absolute space" and "absolute time," he argues, are not meaningful concepts. It is not meaningful to talk about either distance or duration without specifying the states of motion from which that distance and that duration are being measured. Using the example of a moving train against the background of the embankment, Einstein shows that, given these two frames of reference, one moving and the other at rest, there can be no absolute agreement between the units of space and time measured from each. The time interval between two events will have a different measurement on the train from that on the embankment; so too will the space interval between two points. It is this variable distance and duration that Einstein calls the "relativity of space and time."[25]

The world summoned into being by Einstein is not a preassigned yardstick but an operational consequence. Here, a scientific account cannot proceed from a single frame of reference. Instead, it must engage the world conjunctively, in a kind of double description, recognizing the problem of noncoincidence between two frames. The self-sufficiency of a single object is replaced by the disagreement between two differently moving objects. This disagreement, in turn, points to a deep structure of constraints, a relational structure by which the description of any one term must be linked to its translation to a second term and must be conditioned by that second term. Einstein thus speaks not of space, a freestanding entity, but of "space-time," an interlocking continuum that we cannot cleanly dissect, cleanly chop up, or resolve into discrete units. And, as he moves from his special theory of relativity to his general theory, he also gives us the most dramatic account of just what sort of constraints this space-time continuum is subject to. In this expanded analytic universe, a universe governed by gravity, space-time is also compelled to respond to this added determinant. It is compelled, that is, to take the form of a "curvature" in the presence of a massive body, so much so that "the propositions of Euclidean geometry cannot hold exactly," and the very "idea of a straight line also loses its meaning."[26]

The conditionality of space-time is the single most intriguing image offered by Einstein. It is certainly tempting to turn that image into a lesson in ethics. Einstein, however, is the first to caution against such a move. In a short essay, "The Laws of Science and the Laws of Ethics," he explicitly says: "Scientific statements of facts and relations, indeed, cannot produce ethical directives."[27] Physics, in other words, is not even remotely translatable into ethics. It cannot serve as a foundation for our human affairs. And yet, in refusing to serve as a foundation it nonetheless issues a challenge that, Einstein says, ethics cannot afford to ignore.

And here, striking a distinctly un-Kantian note, Einstein suggests that the challenge of science to ethics is the challenge of *empiricism*. Ethics, like physics, cannot pretend to be a preassigned body of knowledge, cannot imagine itself to be spatially prior to the actual problems it confronts. No such priority inheres in any cognitive domain. Ethics is in the thick of things. Its axioms, for that reason, should be "tested not differently from the axioms of science"; that is, they should be tested as postulates whose domain of validity will have to be continually revised, subject to the pressures of expanding ranges of action. Ethics is empirical. Arising with new circumstances, it is meshed with those circumstances. Its very shape must derive from "the accumulated emotional reaction of individuals to the behavior of their neighbors."[28] There can be no antecedent moral law here, no axioms that precede the contexts of their usage. Einstein, who has been reading the *Critique of Pure Reason* since the tender age of thirteen, knows exactly what he is rejecting.[29] And he is emphatic in rejecting it: "I have never been able to understand the quest of the *a priori* in the Kantian sense."[30]

Understood as a challenge to a priori, Einstein's physics suggests that the absolute truths of formalism might never be ours. Empiricism is our fate. And, since fallibility is a likely outcome of empiricism, the shadow it casts is cast, without exception, on the full spectrum of cognitive endeavors. No space of the mind is prior to that. This new humility, taken in stride, has led to some spirited critiques of Kant within the philosophy of science, especially by Rudolf Carnap and Hans Reichenbach.[31] Among the American pragmatists, Charles Sanders Peirce has in fact anticipated Einstein in raising the same objection to Kant. Peirce, too, has immersed himself in the work of his adversary: "I devoted two hours a day to the study of Kant's *Critique of Pure Reason* for more than three years, until I almost knew the whole book by heart, and had critically examined every section of it."[32] His attention, again like Einstein's, is drawn to one specific point: Kant's commitment to the a priori. For Peirce, nothing can be more wrong-headed than this "confusion of *a priori* reason with conscience." Conscience so conceived, he says, "refuses to submit its dicta to experiment, and makes an absolute dual distinction between right and wrong."[33] Against this moralization of a priori reason, Peirce proposes the obverse: a radicalization of what he calls a "doctrine of fallibilism." This doctrine, as its name suggests, begins with human limits and stays with them: it refuses to posit a space beyond. Not positing such a space, it literally has no room for the sort of exemption Kant would like to claim. Ethics, like everything else, is mired in our cognitive shortcomings: its tenets cannot be antecedently cordoned off, cannot be located at a prior point of rightness.[34]

William James, following Peirce, thus defines pragmatism itself as a "radical empiricism," a philosophy that continually invalidates itself, shows that it is not entirely right, and departs from a "philosophy of the absolute" on just those grounds.[35] Radical empiricists, James says, begin with the idea that any truth-claim has its limits. For each claim can be enlarged, and unsettled in that enlargement: "Everything you can think of, however vast or inclusive, has on the pluralistic view a genuinely "external" environment of some sort or amount. Things are "with" one another in many ways, but nothing includes everything, or dominates over everything. The word 'and' trails along after every sentence. Something always escapes. 'Ever not quite' has to be said of the best attempts made anywhere in the universe at attaining all-inclusiveness."[36] Every truth-claim, however rigorously defined, carries with it a residuum, a trailing "and" that opens up its boundaries to the vexations of other claims and breaks down any assumption of an a priori, a logical space free from contextual specifications. Radical empiricism, understood in this sense, is a philosophy dedicated to the extending and dislodging of truths. John Dewey, inheriting this and fusing it with Einstein's relativity, is thus able to issue a challenge to the entire absolutist tradition: from the absolute space and time of Newton to the epistemology and ethics of Kant.[37]

More recently, in law, a skepticism toward the a priori has also led to some interesting arguments. In an essay titled "The Curvature of Constitutional Space: What Lawyers Can Learn from Modern Physics," Laurence Tribe directly invokes Einstein to argue for a legal paradigm forthright about its less than discrete, less than transcendent ontology. "Just as space cannot extricate itself from the unfolding story of physical reality," Tribe writes, "so also the law cannot extract itself from social structures."[38] The rule of law, in other words, does not emanate from anything that might be called "absolute space." Law does not stand "above" human conflict. It does not have the privilege of antecedence over what it adjudicates. Rather, it is a party to the grievances that come before it, a shaping force and an active contributor to that very fabric of relations that give rise to that grievance.

For Tribe, then, the crucial point here is that the law is not neutral. But his spatial language—his sense that the shape of the law might not coincide with the shape of human lives—also seems to suggest another line of inquiry. Indeed, what especially strikes me in this context is a question that leads directly back to the spatial dimension of rights; namely, the degree of coextension between our rights and our humanness, and, on a more pragmatic level, the degree of coextension between the domain of juridical action and the domain of human conflict. Are rights antecedently vested in us, grounded in our humanity? Or are they frame-dependent? What happens when the contours of the law correspond only imperfectly, and sometimes not at all, to the contours of our warring claims? How big and how central a part should the law play in our fabric of human relations? And, if it turns out that there is an entire spectrum of phenomena, an entire spectrum of conflict that is not resolvable through legal action, what are some other avenues of redress? What means of communication and of expression do we have beside litigation?

Any theory of democracy needs to ask these questions. And the answers are not easy, because an inveterate legalism does seem to go hand in hand with the "rights dialect" that is now our native tongue. Still, as Judith Shklar astutely points out, "the spirit of legalism is not now, and never has been, the only morality among men even in generally legalistic societies."[39] Law does not cover the field, nor does it exhaust the full spectrum of ethical possibilities. In the rest of this essay, I want to turn to one domain of thought not fully covered by the law, a domain informed by its spirit but not subsumable under it. This domain, not based on absolute space and not confident about the clean resolution of chronic disputes, points to the beginning of what we might call an empirical ethics. Featuring quarreling neighbors, it gives us a very different theory of democracy, one wary of the large claims of rights.

"LOCAL COLOR"

Something of that ethics is suggested by a New England literary genre called "local color," a genre mindful of space. It is especially mindful of contested space:

space described not through one reference frame but through the disagreement between frames. Early in the nineteenth century, the legal battles in this region over water rights—pitting the common law right of prior holding against the developmental right of mill owners—had dramatized "trespass" as a spatial conundrum.[40] By the late nineteenth century, the economic stagnation of rural New England and the disputed claims to finite sources turned that conundrum into an everyday battlefield.[41] In the very circumscription of its setting, the sheer proximity of the lives it delineates, the fictive world here is relational in quite a stifling sense: it is a web, a history of entanglement, a space-time continuum alternately registered as friction and kinship, endearment and encroachment. To my mind, this body of literature is one of the most compelling correctives to the fantasy of discreteness that so often accompanies the claim of rights. And, in renouncing that fantasy, it also renders vivid a democracy not mapped along the axis of winners and losers.

We can find an almost generic sense of this spatial mapping in the stories by Mary Wilkins Freeman, an author much read in the nineteenth century (and singled out for praise by William Dean Howells) but oddly neglected today. Born in Randolph, Massachusetts, in 1852, moving to Brattleboro, Vermont, in 1867, and returning to live in Randolph from 1883 to 1902, Freeman was especially alert to the narrow prospects, the involuntary nature of trespass, unavoidable in that environment. The central spatial paradigm in Freeman is thus the paradigm of overlap. Human association here turns out not to be a harmonious grid, not a grid of clean and pain-free adjacencies, for the commingling of lives is always a form of imposition. This is what happens in "A New England Nun," a story most often read with an emphasis on the last word of the title. In the context of this essay, we can also read it as a story about a woman not just giving up a man but, above all, being irritated by a man, irritated by the mere fact that he is a spatial entity. Louisa Ellis has waited fourteen years for her lover, Joe Dagget, to come back from Australia, and now she expects to marry him in a week. His very footsteps, however, fill her with dread: "He seemed to fill up the whole room. A little yellow canary that had been asleep in his green cage at the south window woke up and fluttered wildly, beating his little yellow wings against the wires. He always did so when Joe Dagget came into the room."[42] The very presence of Joe is an infringement, as far as Louisa is concerned. All during the visit, she is oppressed by the sense that he has left traces of himself everywhere, violating not only the neatness of the room but also the neatness of her life. When he is finally gone, Louisa set the lamp on the floor, and began sharply examining the carpet. She even rubbed her fingers over it, and looked at them.

"He's tracked in a good deal of dust," she murmured. "I thought he must have."

Louisa got a dust-pan and brush, and swept Joe Dagget's track carefully. (113)

It is possible to argue, I think, that the central character in "A New England Nun" is not really a human character, but an exacting ideal, a dream of absolute space so uncompromising that even specks of dust are taken as signs of trespass. This dream is not allowed to stand alone. It is qualified by a contrasting scene that unfolds outside Louisa's window, a world as crisscrossed as hers is self-contained. This space is multiply and interfusingly occupied, it is truly a continuum: "The air was filled with the sounds of the busy harvest of men and birds and bees; there were halloos, metallic clatterings, sweet calls, and long hummings" (125). Creatures human and nonhuman, noises animate and inanimate—all these are mixed up, permeated by one another, in an auditory arena in which nothing stands by itself.

Like a good many nineteenth-century American authors, including Edgar Allan Poe, Frederick Douglass, and Walt Whitman, Freeman is fascinated by the phenomenology of sound. In her case, that fascination is directly linked, I think, to the spatial attributes of sound: its attributes of permeability and mixability, its high degree of individuation, and its almost always contested character. For Freeman, these attributes are also the starting point for a democratic practice—an empirical ethics worked into an empirical epistemology—both issuing from the lack of harmony among human beings. It is that lack of harmony that makes up the central drama in "A Far-Away Melody," a story featuring a quarrel between two sisters occasioned by a bitter discrepancy in aural evidence: what one is able to hear and the other is not.

Priscilla and Mary Brown are twin sisters grown old together and looking almost exactly alike: the same face, the same height, the same "thick, white-stockinged ankles showing beneath their limp calicoes."[43] This perfect agreement breaks down one day, however, when, in the presence of Mary and a neighbor, Priscilla suddenly drops her work and whispers, "Hush!"

The other two stopped talking, and listened, staring at her wonderingly, but they could hear nothing.

"What is it, Miss Priscilla?" asked the neighbor, with round blue eyes. She was a pretty young thing, who had not been married long.

"Hush! Don't speak. Don't you hear that beautiful music?" Her ear was inclined towards the open window, her hand still raised warningly, and her eyes fixed on the opposite wall beyond them.

Mary turned visibly paler than her usual dull paleness, and shuddered. "I don't hear any music," she said. "Do you, Miss Moore?"

"No-o," replied the caller. . . .

Mary Brown rose and went to the door, and looked eagerly up and down the street. "There ain't no organ-man in sight anywhere," said she, returning, "an' I can't hear any music, an' Miss Moore can't, an' we're both sharp enough o'hearing. You're jest imaginin' it, sister." (213–14)

The dispute goes on for the rest of the day, with Mary sticking to a single refrain: "There ain't no music." That night, Priscilla dies. Grief-stricken, Mary is now the one to "sit at the kitchen window and listen day after day" (217). She hears nothing for a year. Finally, on her deathbed, a "cry of rapture" comes from her: "I've heard it! I've heard it! . . . A faint sound o' music, like the dyin' away of a bell" (218).

How are the claims of the two sisters to be adjudicated? Which of the two does truth side with? And does it make sense, in this case, to think of truth as "taking sides"—as segregable by a clean line and locatable within an absolute space? Freeman would seem to suggest not. For the individuation of sound is such as to open it perpetually to dispute, to the overlapping but nonidentical truth-claims of different hearers. This aural problem, an empirical problem in epistemology, calls for an ethics equally empirical: constrained by the fact of disagreement and living out its full implications. Many of Freeman's stories are ethically constrained in just this way, caught between dueling neighbors, moving between the truth-claims of each, using one to qualify the other. I conclude with a final story, one that, perhaps not accidentally, also begins with a quarrel, a dispute, a problem exacerbated (but eventually also redressed) by the frontal collision of sounds in space.

"A Village Singer" features an aging soprano, Candace Whitcomb, who has just been dropped by the church in which she has been singing for the past forty years. There have been complaints about her—some people think that her voice has "grown too cracked and uncertain on the upper notes"[44]—and now they have found someone else to replace her. Candace is not about to reconcile herself to this sort of treatment. And, as her house happens to be next door to the church, it is easy enough for her to take matters into her own hands. The first Sunday that the new soprano takes her place in the choir, Candace also takes her seat, in front of her own parlor organ, and sings as loudly as she can, "singing another hymn to another tune" (127), completely drowning out the voice of her rival.

When she is confronted by the minister, Candace has no apology. The fault is not hers; she is fully entitled to do what she does. "If I ain't got a right to play a psalm tune on my organ an' sing, I'd like to know. If you don't like it, you can move the meetin'-house" (136). It is not surprising that the language of rights should come gushing out at just this point, when Candace is most angry, most vulnerable, when she feels most keenly that she has been denied her due. She has, after all, given her whole life to the choir, and, by her reckoning, it would "be more to the credit of folks in a church to keep an old singer an' an old minister, if they didn't sing and an' hold forth quite so smart as they used to, ruther than turn 'em off an' hurt their feelin's" (134). That forbearance being denied her, she is determined, in her turn, to revert to an a priori claim of rights. Singing, she says, is something she is entitled to do in the privacy of her own house. She is not going to give up this preexisting right just to accommodate other people.

And yet, in the context of the story, it is also clear that this a priori language is literally put into quotation marks: it is coming out of the mouth of a woman whose claim is both deeply felt but also deeply unsustainable. The proverbial antecedence of rights is unsustainable, because the spatial property of sound is such that it will always spread outward, will impose itself upon other sounds, will sometimes drown them out. Taking this as a salient example of what it means to be alive, to be human, to have demands on the world and to be surrounded by other people who also have demands, "A Village Singer" comes very close, I think, to a conception of rights with a generic proviso for conditionality, a generic proviso for overlapping claims. Like so many other stories within the "local color" genre, this is a meditation on trespass, a phenomenon that arises, it seems, not only from the spatial needs so clamorous in all of us, but also from the lack of fit between that need and the world, the lack of fit between the discreteness of our claims and the failure of the world to honor that discreteness.

Mindful of this empirical fact, the story ends with Candace, on her deathbed, leaving her house to the new soprano (who happens to be engaged to her nephew). This goodwill gesture, however, is not an absolute concession, not even a sign that the battle is over. Cantankerous to the end, Candace does not hesitate to comment on the vocal performance of the recipient: "You flatted a little—on soul" (144). This is the only "triumph" she is allowed to have. It is not much, and perhaps that is the point. In this qualified happy ending, in the overlapping domains of "satisfaction" and "disappointment," Candace's triumph is also a triumph for her opponent. The story sides with neither one. Instead, it recognizes the irresolvable conflict between these two women; it gives full weight to their disagreement. Giving weight to that disagreement, it turns this unhappy fact into a structure of constraints: constraints on the claims of each woman, constraints on the physical and emotional space assigned to each. Compromises and concessions, rather than absolute victories, mark the endpoint of this theory of democracy.

Freeman's stories are not a refutation, not even a response, to Newton and Kant. Still, they do play out the consequences of a different set of spatial postulates, consequences that become legible only when seen against the more dominant tradition of Newtonian and Kantian space. Seen against that tradition, these stories point to a conceptual continuum, subtly interlocking but also variably inflected, generating echoes as well as dissonances across different domains of thought. Nonabsolute space, given mathematical expression by Einstein, has perhaps also been expressed in other idioms, other contexts. It invites us to rethink the meaning of democratic practice in law and literature both.

NOTES

1 Earlier this century, novelists, poets, and philosophers did draw inspiration from Einstein. The noncommunication between the humanities and the sciences is a relatively recent phenomenon. See Gerald Holton, "Einstein and the Shaping of Our Imagination," in *The Advancement of Science, and Its Burdens* (New York: Cambridge University Press, 1986), 105–22.

2 Mary Ann Glendon, *Rights Talk* (New York: The Free Press, 1991), x.

3 Ibid., 3–6.

4 Ibid., xii.

5 See, for example, the special issue "Symposium: A Critique of Rights," *Texas Law Review* 62 (1984): 1363–1617, especially Mark Tushnet, "An Essay on Rights," 1363–1403, and Allan C. Hutchinson and Patrick J. Monahan, "The 'Rights' Stuff: Roberto Unger and Beyond," 1477–1539. See also Morton J. Horwitz, "Rights," *Harvard Civil Rights–Civil Liberties Law Review* 23 (1988): 393–406. For Rorty's latest critique of rights, see "Fraternity Reigns," *New York Times Magazine*, September 29, 1996, 175–76; for Sandel's latest statement, see *Democracy's Discontent: America in Search of a Public Philosophy* (Cambridge: Harvard University Press, 1996).

6 The actual adjudicative process inside the courtroom is rarely the "winner take all" situation Glendon describes. The right to free speech, for example, has never been declared an absolute right by the Supreme Court; rather, it is always subject to restriction where the interests of the state (in maintaining order, in preserving communal well-being) outweigh the individual's freedom of speech. See, e.g., *Chaplinsky*

v. New Hampshire, 315 U.S. 568, 571 (1941): "It is well understood that the right of free speech is not absolute at all times and under the circumstance." The critique of rights, furthermore, fails to recognize the importance of civil rights for minorities. For a defense of rights in the context of race, see the forum "Minority Critiques of the Critical Legal Studies Movement," *Harvard Civil Rights–Civil Liberties Law Review* 22 (1987): 297–447, especially the essay by Patricia Williams, "Alchemical Notes: Reconstructing Ideals from Deconstructed Rights," 401–34.

7 Martha Minow suggests a parallel twofold approach. Taking rights as no more than "interpretive," she in effect constitutes them as prima facie. See Martha Minow, "Interpreting Rights: An Essay for Robert Cover," *Yale Law Journal* 96 (1987): 1860–1915.

8 My emphasis on the philosophical resonances of this genre is at odds with the current New Historicist approach. For an influential New Historicist reading, see Richard H. Brodhead, *Cultures of Letters: Scenes of Reading and Writing in Nineteenth-Century America* (Chicago: University of Chicago Press, 1993), 107–76. For a theoretical justification of the practice in this paper, see my "A Theory of Resonance," *PMLA* (October 1997): 1060–71.

9 Isaac Newton, *Philosophiae Naturalis Principia Mathematica* (1686), translated by Andrew Motte in 1729 as *Mathematical Principles of Natural Philosophy,* revised by Florian Cajori (Berkeley: University of California Press, 1934), 6. Subsequent citations are given parenthetically in the text.

10 Steven Shapin, "Of Gods and Kings: Natural Philosophy and Politics in the Leibniz-Clarke Disputes," *Isis* 72 (1981): 192. For High Church attacks on Newtonianism, see Larry Stewart, "Samuel Clarke, Newtonianism, and the Factions of Post-Revolutionary England," *Journal of the History of Ideas* 42 (1981): 53–72. For Newton's life in science and in politics, see Robert Westfall, *Never at Rest: A Biography of Isaac Newton* (New York: Cambridge University Press, 1980).

11 The Boyle Lectures were named after Robert Boyle, who left £350 in his will to endow lectures defending Christianity.

12 See Shapin, "Of Gods and Kings." For more general accounts, see Margaret Jacob, *Newtonians and the English Revolution, 1689–1720* (Ithaca: Cornell University Press, 1976); Betty Jo Teeter Dobbs and Margaret C. Jacob, *Newton and the Culture of Newtonianism* (Atlantic Highlands, N.J.: Humanities Press, 1995).

13 David Hume, *History of England*, 6 vols. (1688; Boston: Phillips, Sampson and Co., 1856), 6:374.

14 For a detailed account of Newton's centrality to the Enlightenment, see Peter Gay, *The Enlightenment: The Science of Freedom* (New York: Norton, 1977), 126–87.

15 Voltaire, *Elemens de la philosophie de Neuton*, in *Oeuvres* (1738), 22:402, quoted in Gay, *The Enlightenment*, 139.

16 Gay, *The Enlightenment*, 129.

17 Jacques Delille, *Oeuvres de J. Delille* (Paris: L. G. Michaud, 1824), quoted in Gay, *The Enlightenment*, 132. "Oh power of a great man and a soul divine! / That which God alone has made, Newton alone imagines, / And each star repeats and proclaims their name: / Glory to God who created the world and Newton!" (my translation).

18 Friedrich Paulsen, *Immanuel Kant: His Life and Doctrine,* trans. J. E. Creighton and Albert Lefevre (New York: F. Ungar, 1963), 35.

19 Immanuel Kant, "Concerning the Ultimate Foundation of the Differentiation of Regions in Space," in *Kant: Selected Pre-Critical Writings,* trans. G. B. Kerferd and D. E. Walford (Manchester: Manchester University Press, 1968), 37.

20 Immanuel Kant, *Critique of Pure Reason,* trans. Norman Kemp Smith (New York: St. Martin's Press, 1965), 68. Subsequent citations are given parenthetically in the text.

21 Immanuel Kant, *The Philosophy of Law,* trans. W. Hastie (Edinburgh: T. and T. Clark, 1887), 15–16. This is a translation of Kant's *Metaphysische Anfangsgrunde der Rechslehre* (1796), also translated as *The Metaphysical Elements of Justice.*

22 Immanuel Kant, *Critique of Practical Reason,* trans. Lewis White Beck (New York: Macmillan, 1993), 31. Subsequent citations are given parenthetically in the text.

23 Rawls's *A Theory of Justice* is a self-professed Kantian exercise. I should point out, however, that in *Political Liberalism* (New York: Columbia University Press, 1993), Rawls has put considerable distance between himself and Kant.

24 Leo Strauss, *Natural Rights and History* (Chicago: University of Chicago Press, 1953); Richard Tuck, *Natural Rights Theories* (Cambridge: Cambridge University Press, 1979); Ian Shapiro, *The Evolution of Rights in Liberal Theory* (Cambridge: Cambridge University Press, 1986), 82–89. For a discussion of the importance of the Lockean tradition in the American context, see Louis Henkin, *The Age of Rights* (New York: Columbia University Press, 1990), 83–108. For an analysis of the tension between the moral law and conflict resolution in Kant, see Leslie A. Mulholland, *Kant's System of Rights* (New York: Columbia University Press, 1990).

25 Albert Einstein, *Relativity: The Special and the General Theory,* 15th ed. (New York: Crown Books, 1961), 3–64.

26 Ibid., 91.

27 Albert Einstein, "The Laws of Science and the Laws of Ethics," preface to Philipp Frank, *Relativity: A Richer Truth* (Boston: Beacon Press, 1950), vi.

28 Ibid., vii.

29 As Gerald Holton reports, Einstein "at the tender age of thirteen was introduced to Immanuel Kant's philosophy, starting with the *Critique of Pure Reason,* through his contacts with a regular guest at the Einstein home, Max Talmey. He reread Kant's book at the age of sixteen and enrolled in a lecture course on Kant while at the Technical Institute in Zurich. . . . At the Institute in Princeton his favorite topic of discussion with his friend Kurt Gödel was, again, Kant." However, as Holton also points out, "All this, typically, did not make Einstein a Kantian at all," for "Einstein objected to the central point of Kant's transcendental idealism by denying the existence of the synthetic *a priori*" (Holton, "Einstein and the Cultural Roots of Modern Science," *Daedalus* 127 [1998]: 18–19).

30 Albert Einstein, "The Problem of Space, Ether, and the Field in Physics," in *Ideas and Opinions* (New York: Crown Brooks, 1982), 278.

31 See Rudolf Carnap, "Kant's Synthetic A Priori," in *An Introduction to the Philosophy of Science,* ed. Martin Gardner (New York: Dover, 1995), 177–83; Hans Reichenbach, *The Rise of Scientific Philosophy* (Berkeley: University of California Press, 1951), 39–49, 58–

67, 125–33; Hans Reichenbach, "The Philosophical Significance of the Theory of Relativity," in *Albert Einstein: Philosopher-Scientist,* ed. Paul Arthur Schlipp (La Salle, Ill.: Open Court, 1970), 287–311.

32 Charles Sanders Peirce, "Concerning the Author," in *Philosophical Writings of Peirce,* ed. Justus Buchler (1940; New York: Dover, 1955), 2.

33 Charles Sanders Peirce, "The Scientific Attitude and Fallibilism," in *Philosophical Writings of Peirce,* ed. Buchler, 42, 46.

34 Ibid., 58–59.

35 William James, *Essays in Radical Empiricism,* ed. Ralph Barton Perry (1912; Lincoln: University of Nebraska Press, 1996).

36 William James, *The Pluralistic Universe,*" in *William James: Writings 1902–1910,* ed. Bruce Kuklick (New York: Library of America, 1987), 776. The distinction between the monist and the pluralistic—between the philosophy of the absolute and radical empiricism—is central to James. See especially "The Types of Philosophic Thinking," lecture 1 of *The Pluralistic Universe,* 631–48.

37 John Dewey, *The Quest for Certainty,* vol. 4 (1929) of *The Later Works, 1925–1953,* ed. Jo Ann Boydston (Carbondale: Southern Illinois University Press, 1981), 47–50, 89–104, 113–17, 137–45.

38 Laurence Tribe, "The Curvature of Constitutional Space: What Lawyers Can Learn from Modern Physics," *Harvard Law Review* 103 (1989): 7.

39 Judith Shklar, *Legalism* (Cambridge: Harvard University Press, 1986, 1964), 2.

40 Morton Horwitz, *The Transformation of American Law, 1780–1860* (Cambridge: Harvard University Press, 1977), 47–54.

41 Rollin Lynde Hartt, "A New England Hill Town," *Atlantic Monthly* 83 (1899): 561–74, 712–20; Hal S. Barron, *Those Who Stayed Behind* (New York: Cambridge University Press, 1984), 31–50; Harold F. Wilson, *The Hill Country of Northern New England* (New York: Columbia University Press, 1936).

42 Mary E. Wilkins Freeman, "A New England Nun," in *Selected Stories of Mary E. Wilkins Freeman,* ed. Marjorie Pryse (New York: Norton, 1983), 111. Subsequent citations are given parenthetically in the text.

43 Mary E. Wilkins Freeman, "A Far-Away Melody," in *A Humble Romance and Other Stories* (New York: Harper & Bros., 1899), 208. Subsequent citations are given parenthetically in the text.

44 Mary E. Wilkins Freeman, "A Village Singer," in *Selected Stories,* ed. Pryse, 126. Subsequent citations are given parenthetically in the text.

MICHAEL MOON

A Long Foreground: Re-Materializing the History of Native American Relations to Mass Culture

◆

From the Romantic heyday of the figure of the "noble savage" to popular conceptions of deep ecology in our own time, it has been a long-standing habit on the
part of many white Americans to imagine Native Americans as being permanently located in the realms of the natural and the primitive, the rural and the
preindustrial. Yet anyone familiar with the history of the emergence of mass
culture in this country, from the time of the appearance of the first inexpensive
newspapers in the 1830s to the full development of the film industry and the
national broadcasting networks a century later, may be aware—in at least frag-
mentary fashion—of the manifold and formative contributions to the history of
Native American producers and performers, from George Guess/Sequoyah's invention of the Cherokee syllabary (the first Native American newspaper came
into being within a few years of this innovation) to Native American performers
in early western film to the spectacular careers of Maria Tallchief, Balanchine
prima ballerina and popularizer of American ballet, or of the celebrated humorist and pundit Will Rogers. For the project of "materializing democracy," in
which the essays in this volume are engaged, it is important to recognize the
intense and effectual involvement of large numbers of Native Americans in the
production of twentieth-century mass culture. As I shall detail in the pages that
follow, the career of Rogers, one of the most famous of these culture makers,
illuminates many of the ways in which such careers derive from the commitments and desires of much larger political, social, and cultural communities.

Will Rogers survives in public memory today in a fading photo or two, a
silently smiling embodiment of folksy bonhomie "American-style" in the period
between the world wars. But during his lifetime, Rogers's face was ubiquitous, his
running commentary on the political life of his times unquenchable. Millions
read his newspaper columns, saw him at the movies, and listened to his weekly

radio program. Born in Indian Territory in 1879, by the turn of the century he was playing cowboys, Indians, and blackface roles in Wild West shows that carried him as far afield as South Africa and New Zealand. After he returned from his travels, Rogers took his trick-roping act onto the American vaudeville circuit, where he gradually began to introduce homely wisecracks about current affairs. His frequent aside, "All I know's just what I read in the papers," became his mantra. By the end of World War I, he had become a star of the glamorous Ziegfeld Follies at the peak of their popularity, and the first entertainer to make American political life his primary topic. Rogers's film career was equally spectacular: he rapidly rose from playing "The Roping Fool" in a series of silent sagebrush two-reelers to become a leading box office star of the early talkies. Similarly, when he began delivering weekly talks on early radio programs, his popularity soon rivaled that of the medium's first megahit, the *Amos 'n' Andy* show. And throughout these years, Rogers remained one of the most prolific and widely syndicated newspaper columnists of the era.[1]

In the decades since his death in 1935, much of the extraordinary range of Rogers's career has become obscured by the compression of his remarkably productive professional life into the single alleged utterance, "I never met a man I didn't like." If Rogers is remembered for anything today, it is for having given to his fellow citizens through the rough and often bitter years of the Great Depression an emblematic performance of unfailing and universal (at least as far as the male gender goes) democratic affability.

Indeed, in popular memory his claim, "I never met a man I didn't like," has entirely replaced the other claim, "All I know's just what I read in the papers," which actually was his byword. Americans have largely forgotten the persona he fashioned through his countless performances across media of the mildly bewildered, basically unflappable, often bemused, and sometimes cranky respondent to the explosive social and political transformations of the 1920s and 1930s. Although he has become known to history by the vaguely anodyne title of "humorist," Rogers practiced a kind of humor that was reliably focused not on the foibles of individuals, real or invented, but on public and specifically political life. When annoyed readers wrote letters to the editor complaining that an avowed clown such as Rogers should stick to the business of humor and leave the serious matters of politics to those better qualified to comment, he would respond that his humor had always concerned itself with "national or international affairs." "Have you ever heard me tell a mother-in-law joke?" was his exasperated reply.[2]

Aside from his supposed universal amiability, Rogers's other characteristic that has not yet entirely faded from public memory is his often-expressed pride in his American Indian heritage.[3] He was born to parents of mixed ethnic heritage in Indian Territory. Both were, in the parlance of the time, "part Cherokee." His father had been an important leader of his people during the volatile period of transition from tribal rule to allotment, the U.S. government's parceling out of former commonly held lands as small individual holdings. At a time when, at least among white Americans, the recent "closing of the frontier" and its attendant myth of "the winning of the West" from the Indians by white settlers was *the* foundational narrative of national history, Rogers publicly and routinely expressed his satisfaction in being *both* cowboy and Indian. He also sometimes allowed himself to speak out sharply against the political betrayal of Native Americans.[4]

Native American scholar Jace Weaver has addressed the question of the relation of Rogers's politics to his Cherokee heritage. He writes:

> The homespun, commonsensical populism of Rogers may seem remote from a Native worldview, but it nevertheless has clear roots there. Rogers's father was prominent in the political affairs of Indian Territory, and Rogers never thought of himself as anything other than that oxymoron to Amer-European ears, an "Indian cowboy," a "half-breed" Cherokee ropesmith. He delighted in tracing his lineage, stating, "My ancestors didn't come over on the *Mayflower,* but they met the boat."[5]

During his lifetime Rogers was widely referred to in print as "the cowboy philosopher," with varying degrees of archness; in a 1934 review, a *New York Times* movie critic racheted the title up to "the cowboy Nietzsche." The joke registers a distance between the pat crackerbarrel wisdom that white readers and moviegoers expected Rogers to espouse and the attitudes with which he actually sometimes surprised and even disturbed them.[6]

If one were to choose a primary context for the career of the versatile Rogers, perhaps the most expansive category in which to consider his work would be one that combines writing and performance; one that, while recognizing the highly performative character of his writing (of humorous books, of newspaper columns and magazine articles), also registers the highly discursive character of the whole range of his performances—even those which might strike one on first thought as largely "nonverbal" ones, such as his trick-roping act (from which he was unable to suppress his wry comments), or his silent films (which continually weave his ironic asides through the action in the form of intertitles). One of the most remarkable characteristics of Rogers's performances is their highly improvisatory quality: directors as exacting as John Ford are said to have been content to rehearse the other performers in their films and then let Rogers walk through the final shoot inventing new material at every turn—after he had passed what had been rehearsal time for the rest of the cast just off the set, pounding out his newspaper column for the day, or napping if rehearsal went on that long.[7] Similarly, the voluble Rogers is said to have had a hard time adapting to the split-second time limits of national radio broadcasting, and after having run overtime he habitually set an alarm clock, audible at the end of many of his programs, to tell him when he had to relinquish the microphone to the announcer, even if he was in mid-story or mid-sentence.

In examining here the roots of Rogers's writing and performance styles in the context of the history of Native American performance of the time, I want to try to relate the improvisatory character of his work to what one might call its "diplomatic" quality or effects. Although Rogers's lack of a "diploma" for certified formal education was one of his favorite forms of self-gibing (he publicly declined several honorary degrees, claiming he did so to save otherwise unimpeachable educational institutions from hopelessly embarrassing themselves), he was frequently touted as the nation's leading "diplomat-without-portfolio," its highest-ranking, non–office-holding, improvising political agent. In his commitment to eschewing comedians' stock-in-trade ("Have you ever heard me tell a mother-in-law joke?") in favor of imbuing his performances with an edge of political mockery and critique, Rogers may be seen as a key participant in what critic Chadwick Allen has termed "treaty discourse"—the discursive field of relations between Native American and white Americans, and between Native Americans and the U.S. government, especially as this field has had to find new ways of extending and maintaining itself since the U.S. Congress permanently suspended the practice of treaty making in 1871. As Allen has demonstrated in his important article on interpreting *The Lone Ranger* (in its many forms across media, as radio and TV program, matinee serial, feature film, children's book series, etc.) "as treaty discourse," mass culture is one of the places (actually a place of innumerable sites) where treaty discourse has proliferated through the course of the twentieth century.[8] Similarly, I believe, Will Rogers's career across media provides a rich series of sites in which to examine the continuation of Native American diplomacy "by other means" than the formal treaty making process that had been in place for a couple of centuries before its termination by the U.S. government.

Invited by pop philosopher Will Durant to contribute to a volume of state-ments, *On the Meaning of Life,* written by leading public figures, Rogers obliged and published his contribution in one of his newspaper columns of the early 1930s. Those who know him only as an icon of amiability and "good-will ambas-sadorship" may be surprised at the homegrown nihilism with which he openly responded:

> What all of us know put together don't mean anything. Nothing don't mean anything. We are just here for a spell and pass on. Any man that thinks that Civilization has advanced you is an egotist. Fords and bathtubs have moved you and cleaned you, but you was just as ignorant when you got there. We know lots of things we used to dident know but we dont know any way to prevent 'em happening.[9]

In the first years of the Depression, when Progressivist rhetoric of the "let us now be up and doing" variety must have rung particularly hollow, the forthright cynicism of Rogers's little anticreed may have had the virtue of at least sounding honest, if somewhat grimly so. The only thing that Rogers allows to temper his pessimism is something he calls "satisfaction," which he attributes especially to his Indian ancestors, whom he sees as having enjoyed a lower level of social dependency than more supposedly "advanced" societies. Unlike many of his contemporaries, however—who, in the face of the catastrophe of the Depression, adopted some form of nostalgic primitivism as their working social theory—Rogers had long and intimate experience of some different kinds of social and political traditions from those European-derived white American ones that had brought so-called civilization to disaster. Again, unlike many of his contempo-raries, Rogers's dissatisfactions with the state of things in either its national or international forms were lifelong and were a product of political crises that long preceded the onset of the Depression.

In a weekly column that dates from the mid-1920s, at the height of the eco-nomic boom that underlay and enabled his own remarkable success across the burgeoning field of new media, Rogers projects himself backward into a place and time a generation before his actual birth, a place where he would have had little or no contact with white Americans or with American national life. As he does so, he also projects himself backward from the crucial political event that was actually happening in 1924—the imposition of U.S. citizenship on all Native Americans—to a moment when formal political treaty-making relations had not been abrogated by the U.S. government (Rogers extended "citizenship" in reverse in an offhand comment: "You know, Indians used to be the wards of the govern-ment, but now we all are. Everybody is an Indian").[10] Rogers imagines himself transported back to the first decades of Cherokee residence in the West: "I have always regretted that I didn't live about 30 or 40 years earlier, and in the same old country, the Indian Territory. I would have liked to have got there ahead of the 'Nestors,' the Bob wire fence, and so called civilization."[11] Although at first this may simply sound like nostalgia for the open range, Rogers's regretful desire is actually much more specific—and much more radical—than standard generic feeling. What fuels Rogers's regret is not any simple kind of nostalgia for the cowboy life but an enduring sense of the betrayal of his people and of others like them, of injustice visited on them by white Americans and their government, of unfinished political business that seemed to most white Americans to have con-veniently gone away but that never entirely receded from the shared memories of Native Americans.

In this essay I am interested in recovering some of the political significance of Rogers's career from the generally depoliticized legend that has grown up around his memory. The desire that impels this project for me is not so much to produce a corrective to our understanding of Rogers's career but to explore a set of broader questions about the emergence of that career from the matrix of Native American performance traditions of the late nineteenth and early twentieth centuries. Far from being the only Native American of his time to tour in vaude-ville, to appear in movies and on the radio, or to produce humorous political journalism on a regular basis, Rogers, in practicing these and other related modes of performance, can be seen as having participated in a long-established tradition that straddled many of the spaces in which Indians made and inhabited public space for themselves through their own political actions and cultural productions—often in ways that carried them into public space that was other-wise largely white dominated. This was particularly the case in popular enter-tainment, a series of booming industries in the first decades of the twentieth century that were relatively highly permeable by nonwhite performers and per-formance styles.

My overarching concern in this essay is to explore some of the ways in which the significance of a given people's history and traditions can be lost or obscured, at least temporarily, by being compressed into a narrative about the ostensibly unique genius or greatness of a single individual who is taken to be representative of—at the same time he (and only occasionally she) is somehow also unques-tionably superior to—the people from whom he emerges. Rather than attributing Rogers's remarkable success in achieving stardom across the whole spectrum of early-twentieth-century mass media only to some peculiarly personal combination of gifts of his own, I want rather to demonstrate how his career was enabled by the performances of hosts of his Native American predecessors and contemporaries working in a number of different fields cognate with those in which he achieved mass recognition. In looking at what Rogers's work has in common with that of other Native American performers across a broad range of media for the generation or two before his emergence, one may be able to recover a fuller sense of the kinds of energies and pressures that have been shaping Native Americans' participation in and exclusion from public life in this country from the late nineteenth century to the present. The four or five decades leading up to and including the years of Rogers's career are the very ones that followed on the U.S. government's decision to cease making treaties with native peoples in 1871. Many would point to these years as the nadir of American Indian history, but recent scholarship on the period suggests that it was also a time of tremendous political and cultural creativity. In this renaissance of politically charged Native American writing and performance, Rogers is certainly a significant but by no means a unique or isolated participant. Surely at least part of the reason that the highly significant contributions of Native Americans in general and Will Rogers in particular to modern mass-media culture has not yet been more adequately recognized or chronicled is because of the ways in which those very contributions elude and exceed the linear modes in which that history is usually presented. Many different aspects of Rogers's performances challenge our conventional notions of "history" and "time," from his commentary on "current events" that are inflected by his enduring memory of non-European social and political practices to his difficulty with adhering to the split-second time limits of national radio broadcasting. While it is easy to recognize how "up-to-the-minute" Rogers's humor was, it is also important to realize what a long foreground in Native American history his political attitudes and performance style had.[12]

A century of popular western narratives—novels, tales, films—has produced a widespread notion of the practice of treaty making that bears little relation to its actual history.[13] Of the hundreds of treaties with native peoples made by the United States and its colonial predecessor states, most completed before the third decade of the nineteenth century had as their primary purpose the regulation of trade between settlers and natives. In the 1820s and after, arrangements for "removal"—the forced yielding of their lands and the relocation of almost all native peoples to territories west of the Mississippi—became the chief concern of treaty making. In the ensuing century-plus since Congress's termination of treaty making with native peoples, the government has dealt with Indian groups unilaterally, by congressional or executive action. In the half-century before the government stopped making treaties with Indians, two quite contradictory versions of the political status of native peoples had emerged. One held that native peoples, insofar as they had the sovereign right to enter into treaty negotiations with the U.S. government, enjoyed the same kind of sovereignty that any autonomous foreign nation had. The other version of the political status of native peoples was a highly compromised one: according to it, Indians necessarily stood in the relation of wards dependent on the U.S. government's guardianship. The former understanding, that native peoples enjoyed a form of national sovereignty, has been a primary focus of native political activism for the past several decades. The strong discrepancy between the two statuses has been at the heart of native political struggle since the beginning of the removal period, when in the Supreme Court case *Cherokee Nation v. Georgia* (1831) John Marshall found that although the Cherokee Nation was a state in some sense of the term, it did not "constitute a foreign state in the sense of the constitution," and was, in fact, a "domestic dependent nation" that stood in a relation to the U.S. government of "ward to . . . guardian." As early as 1836, Pequot writer and native political leader William Apess rebutted, "From time immemorial the Cherokee Nation have composed a sovereign and independent state, and in this character have been recognized, and still stand recognized . . . in the various treaties subsisting between this nation and the United States."[14]

Recent scholarship suggests that crucially important aspects of the treaty-making process have become occluded by the common habit of using the term "treaty" to signify only the written document that was produced at the end of the process. It would be more accurate to refer to the entire process from its beginning as a "treaty," starting with the arrival of the various parties at the negotiations site and including the various rituals and ceremonies, speeches, debates, arguments, jests, translations, meetings official and unofficial, meals and conversations at meals that took place, as well as the production of some written account of the outcome of negotiations signed by representatives of the peoples involved. Published versions of treaties sometimes included some of these other aspects of the process; Benjamin Franklin published a number of treaties made in Pennsylvania in the 1730s and 1740s in folio format and sent many copies abroad to London for sale to readers interested in learning in some detail about the novel and exotic political procedures that settlers and indigenous people were developing in common in the colonies.

Considering the entire process, not just the written end-product, to constitute "the treaty" takes on special political significance when one considers that Indian peoples began to engage in alphabetic writing only around the last few decades of the treaty-making process—after the Cherokee began to use George Guess/Sequoyah's syllabary. It was at this point that treaties began sometimes to specify, at the behest of their white signers, that the document's binding force applied only to its English-language version and not to any translations of the treaty that might be made into the other language(s) of its signers. The frequent dissatisfaction expressed by native parties to treaties after the fact, and their frequent claim that the terms had not been made sufficiently clear to them during negotiations, suggests that in insisting that the legal and political effects of treaty making were necessarily monolingual white settlers were pressing an obvious legal and political advantage along with the linguistic one. Descriptions of the treaty-making process such as the one that historian James H. Merrell provides in his recent study of the figure of the "go-between" on the colonial Pennsylvania frontier—with its rich accounts of the complex interactions of interpreters and other participants, their conflicts over precedence, alleged misunderstandings on various sides, drinking rituals, music and dancing of a wide variety of kinds, Native condolence ceremonies, complaints about the quality of accommodations, scandalous exposures of would-be secret negotiations, sexual innuendo-making on several sides, and frequent drunkenness on all sides—restore to the reader some sense of the political and social density of the process of which only a trace at most is likely to find its way into the written treaty document.[15]

Seen in the context of the volatile, unpredictable, multifarious unfoldings of the treaty-making process as it was actually practiced, the spectacle of Will Rogers circa 1920 twirling a rope onstage and delivering hilarious and often deadly accurate political satire between elaborately staged review numbers featuring the statuesque and gauzily clad bodies of the reigning Ziegfeld girls is not as remote from the history of treaty making as it might initially appear to be. The uncanny power of the excessive energy of this process to persist in shared memory despite all attempts to exclude it from the official, legal written record has registered itself—albeit only with great intermittency—in academic literary and cultural scholarship of the past century. The leading cultural historian of American humor, Constance Rourke, with her usual arresting perspicacity, insisted in the 1930s about what we might call the performative qualities of Indian treaties: "These treaties were essentially plays—chronicle plays—recording what was said in the parleys, including bits of action, the exchange of gifts, of wampum, the smoking of pipes, the many ceremonials with dances, cries, and choral songs.

Even the printed form of the treaties was dramatic: the participants were listed like cast of characters, and precise notations were made as to ceremonial actions."[16] Rourke sees the primary influence of the high drama of treaty making at work in the formative period of the American theater in antebellum times, an arena in which a majority of the heroic figures were Indians: Pocahontas, Pontiac, Logan, Tammany, Tecumseh, Tenskwatawa, and so on. Many historians have pointed out the irony between white Americans' idealizations of these "noble savages" in their popular theater and literature during the very decades that genocidal intentions toward native peoples became clearly apparent to both sides. According to Rourke, the complex speech of Indian treaty-makers constituted a major resource for the development of early American drama: "Indian speech [as represented in treaty documents] was characteristically grave and rhythmic, but it attained a sharp and witty realism in the discussion of rum, trappers, traders, and white trickery. The Indian style of address was generally accepted and used by white men, even to the sly introduction of humor, and the Indians imposed their own rituals of procedure."[17] Here, Indian humor comes to the rescue of the potentially dehumanizing effects of the white imposition of cigar-store-Indian-style nobility on Native Americans, who instead bring to contact "a sharp and witty realism," imposing their own sometimes astringent humor on the false aspects of political relations. Given this enriched historical context, it is possible to see Will Rogers's celebrated drollery—his enactment of the role of the drawling, slow-witted backwoodsman whose supposedly naive comments on current affairs often carried a sting in their tail—as a reenactment of the roles of both the white settlers and the Indians as they confronted each other in the highly charged atmosphere of the treaty meeting.

It was Rogers's immediate ancestors, the generation of his parents and grandparents—the first generation of Cherokees to inhabit the western Cherokee lands of Indian Territory in the 1830s and after—who made explicit the issue of the white's linguistic domination of the treaty-making process. With George Guess/Sequoyah's development of a syllabary and the rapid spread of its use among his people in the late 1820s, Cherokee became the first native language that could be written in the English alphabet.[18] U.S. government authorities assented to the translation of treaties into Cherokee, but added codicils to such treaties stating that only the English-language version of the treaty was legally binding. The government's unwillingness to accord native languages a political and legal status on a par with English inadvertently contributed to the conditions that heightened the potential of such languages to serve as "codes of resistance" to this domination. Although the white mythology of Sequoyah's invention of a system of writing for Cherokees is that it gave his people immediate and direct access to "civilization," which has often been simply equated with a relatively high alphabetic literacy rate, Sequoyah appears to have had quite other kinds of practices and traditions in mind that this newly developed technology of writing might enable. White observers have tended to see his invention as having made it possible for the Cherokees better to imitate European settler culture, but as David Murray has shown, Sequoyah was actually an unbending traditionalist who seems to have seen his innovation as a practice that might enable his people to preserve their distinctive beliefs and learning *against* the encroachments of white "civilization." According to Murray, although Sequoyah's white contemporaries generally assumed that the introduction of writing would have the effect of maximizing the assimilation of his people to "white civilization," a few more informed observers discovered a quite different agenda among many Cherokees that seems to have been established by Sequoyah himself. Murray adduces the testimony of James Mooney, a collector of Native American writings for the Bureau of American Ethnology at the end of the nineteenth century. While Mooney found some of the kinds of writing that he had expected to find in the Cherokee archives, he professed himself astonished to discover how Sequoyah's syllabary had been "seized by the priests and conjurors of the conservative party for the purpose of preserving to their successors the ancient rituals and secret knowledge of the tribe, whole volumes of such literature in manuscript" having come to his attention.[19]

What Mooney observed, although he seems to have been unable to attach any positive value to the fact, is that there was a powerfully separatist impulse at work in Sequoyah's introduction of the syllabary and in its adoption by many of his fellow Cherokees. Judging from Murray's account of Sequoyah's literary performance in the broadest sense of the term, he may be taken to represent the limit case of the kind of witty and ironic gravity that Native Americans have brought to the treaty process: "Given his fame *and* his association with the written medium," Murray writes, "there is surprisingly little first-hand material on Sequoyah."[20] One way of understanding this "surprising" fact is the consequence of Sequoyah's having used writing as a complex means of sustaining his people's traditions *and* as a virtual vanishing point for himself. "It is as if in inventing writing he effaces rather than expresses himself," Murray concludes. Rogers, it seems to me, carried off a comparably successful—one might say triumphant—vanishing act in relation to the voluminous writings and other kinds of records of his performances that have survived him. American public memory has tended to turn both figures into vaguely beneficent "friends" of white civilization and "progress"— Sequoyah a supposed champion of white-style literacy and Rogers a kind of martyr to American expansionism through technology (he died in a plane crash in the process of publicizing American interests in aviation and Alaska). But the legacy of both still exerts potentially powerful Cherokee-separatist effects.

According to his biographer Ben Yagoda, Rogers's live radio broadcasts were the most "free-form" of all his performances; in contrast to the tightly scripted comedy of radio's other classic comedians, on his broadcasts Rogers "would throw away his notes and launch into a more or less free-form stream of consciousness."[21] On one of the first of these he bitterly lit into the government's record on treaty making:

> Our record with the Indians is going to go down in history. It is going to make us mighty proud of it in the future when our children of ten more generations read what we did to them. Every man in our history that killed the most Indians has got a statue built for him. . . .
>
> The Government, by statistics, shows they have got 456 treaties that they have broken with the Indians. That is why the Indians get a big kick out of reading the Government's usual remark when some big affair comes up, "Our honor is at stake."
>
> Every time the Indians move the Government will give them a treaty. They say, "You can have this ground as long as grass grows and water flows." On accounts of its being a grammatical error, the Government didn't have to live up to it. It didn't say "flown" or "flew" or something. Now they have moved the Indians and they settled the thing by putting them on land where the grass won't grow and the water won't flow, so now they have it all set.[22]

In one sense, of course, Rogers was merely joking when he attributed the government's general abrogation of its treaties to "grammatical error[s]," but in another sense the joke can be understood as precisely locating the main flaw in treaty making as it was historically practiced in the U.S. government's implicit domination of the process through linguistic means. Rogers's spontaneous projection of a future of "ten more generations" when the government's dishonorable role would become generally apparent suggests that, like many other Native Americans, he took the long view of the matter and by no means accepted the idea that the U.S. government's mode of suppressing Indian political autonomy was a permanent condition.

Although Yagoda does describe several of Rogers's public denunciations of the treatment of the Indians by the United States, he makes a statement in the introduction to his biography of Rogers that appears to contradict this important aspect of his presentation: "Other than a gag or two, and an occasional barbed reference to Jackson, Will Rogers did not make much of his Cherokee heritage. But the weight of that heritage, the sense that history can turn on you when you least expect it, surely helped forge in him an equanimity that colored everything he wrote or said."[23] While I agree with Yagoda that Rogers's awareness of Cherokee history "colored everything he wrote or said," I would demur from his suggestion that "equanimity" is necessarily the best term for the effect this awareness had on Rogers—unless we expand the meaning of the word to include the complex kinds of double-dealing in which Cherokee leaders had often been forced to engage under pressure of removal. If, as I have suggested, the self-effacing practice of Sequoyah was available to Rogers, so were the powerful counterexamples of a number of Cherokee leaders of Sequoyah's generation who made strong representations of their positions in writing (in the first Cherokee newspapers, as it happens) and faced the threat (and in some cases the fact) of imprisonment and assassination for doing so. Within a very short time after the introduction of Sequoyah's syllabary, Cherokee leader Elias Boudinot undertook to publish and distribute a newspaper, printed in both Cherokee and English, called the *Cherokee Phoenix*. Because he staunchly and openly opposed U.S. government policy that would force Cherokees from their southeastern homes, Boudinot was frequently harassed and threatened with public whipping by members of the white Georgia militia. During these years, he saw his closest allies jailed and sentenced to years of hard labor for expressing such beliefs. When removal began to seem inevitable to him and some other Cherokee leaders, he began to try to persuade other Cherokees to try to make the best of a bad deal that he and some of his associates had come to see as unavoidable. Since this was a minority sentiment, Boudinot felt obliged to resign his editorial position in August 1832. Ultimately, Boudinot was one of the leaders of the Cherokee minority—the so-called treaty party—who was assassinated (in 1839) by fellow Cherokees for his alleged complicity in the political circumstances that had produced the Trail of Tears. In the case of a figure such as Boudinot, who was executed for his role in assenting to a treaty that many of his fellow Cherokees found unacceptable, one can see another kind of limit case that contrasts with Sequoyah's example—one in which the gravity of the treaty process can be seen proceeding to the point of capital punishment and beyond. Here emerge the darkest sides of the treaty tradition. Like Plato's (and now Derrida's) term *phar-makos,* which is both poison and remedy at once, the word from which the English word "tradition" ultimately derives (the Latin verb *tradere*) can mean both "to hand down" and "to hand over," the latter in the sense of "to betray." One thing the Trail of Tears and its aftermath made unmistakably apparent was the intimate relation—an etymological one, but a truly political one as well—between the words (and actions) "to treat" and "to treaty" and the handing down and/or the handing over (in the sense of betraying) of traditions.

One tradition that the Cherokees—along with the Choctaws, Chickasaws, Creeks, and Seminoles—had taken over from their southern white neighbors was that of owning slaves (the irony has often been pointed out that slaveholding was one of the practices that earned from whites these five peoples the sobriquet of "the Five Civilized Tribes"). Unsurprisingly, given their historical participation in the formation of southern plantation society, the five tribes sided with the Confederacy during the Civil War. At the war's end, the U.S. government used the tribes' alleged disloyalty as a reason for substantially reducing their land holdings in Indian Territory. In response to these renewed political pressures on Indians in the decade after 1865, the Cherokees revived the newspaper-writing traditions that war had forced them to put aside.[24]

The diplomatic skills of native newspaper editors in post–Civil War Indian Territory were soon put to the test, when a victorious band of Sioux and Cheyennes overwhelmingly defeated Custer's U.S. army forces at the Battle of the Little Bighorn. Historian of native journalism John M. Coward writes of the "culturally complex task" that the editors of these papers had to perform: "Indian newspapers, after all, were founded to promote and defend Indian rights and their pages contained many stories documenting the education and advancement of particular tribes. The Sioux and Cheyenne victory over Custer threatened such ideas and put native editors in a precarious position. If they cheered too loudly for the Indian victors, they would risk the goodwill of many whites. If they condemned the Indian victory, they would risk the support of their Indian readers."[25] Coward describes with admirable thoroughness the intricate tactics whereby Boudinot and Ross negotiated the political minefield in which they found themselves. Of primary importance in the strategy they worked out was the widespread practice among nineteenth-century newspapers of reprinting large numbers of articles from "exchange papers"; that is, from other papers with which they exchanged copies with the shared understanding that material from one could be reprinted in any other participating paper. Coward demonstrates how Ross and Boudinot, using articles and editorials from other papers, as well as writing in their own respective voices, orchestrated a complex account of the significance of Little Bighorn. Boudinot suggests that Custer's fundamental tactical error had not been a specifically military one but, in fact, his own adoption of a pervasive white attitude: "He made the mistake so often made of confounding all Indians alike. The mistake cost him his life if not his reputation."[26] When some white defenders of Custer began to speak of the battle as an atrocious massacre and an indication of "red savagery," Ross reprinted an "exchange" article by one Rev. W. P. Nobles that made a firm distinction between the kind of pitched battle that Little Bighorn was and the maiming and killing of defenseless civilians that a massacre is.

Through these writers' intensive cultivation of an "exchange-paper" strategy for representing a wide range of political attitudes, they produced an alternative to both the vanishing act of Sequoyah and the fateful role that Elias Boudinot had ultimately felt constrained to assume during the decade of removal. Within the context of the history of this practice—whereby controversial opinions and attitudes could be defused of much of their inflammatory potential by being presented as part of a "mix" of opinion, much of it from "other" sources—Rogers's "All I know's just what I read in the papers," his ritual means of invoking new topics in current affairs, takes on a heightened resonance. Besides disarmingly asserting that he had no privileged access to knowledge or information about public life beyond the source he shared with everyone in his audience, Rogers's claim always to be discussing simply what he'd "read in the papers" effectively absolved him of promoting certain kinds of responses to "hot" (in the sense of both timely and controversial) topics; that is, he was merely engaging in the common activity of "exchanging" opinions not necessarily his own that were in wide circulation in the day's newspapers, in a manner that had been developed as a political strategy by Cherokee journalists during the decade of Rogers's birth.

Despite a fairly wide awareness of the Native American heritage of a number of successful media figures such as Rogers, many white Americans continue to associate Native Americans almost exclusively with rural and/or reservation life, with "natural" activities such as farming, herding, and handicrafts (weaving, beadwork, leatherwork), and other "traditional" practices such as herbal healing and ritual dancing and music making. In the Native American section of most large bookstores, volumes on Indian "mythology," oral traditions, and nature lore far outnumber those on Native American political history or professional accomplishments. Readers interested in learning about Native Americans are more likely to find books of "creation myths" and (often bogus) collections of "Indian eloquence" in the "noble savage" style that tend to dehistoricize and depoliticize their subjects than they are to find accounts of and writing by Indian journalists, political analysts, legal experts, literary critics, cultural theorists, and notable contributors to and innovators in mass and high culture (both as entrepreneurs and performers). If Will Rogers's accomplishments as a celebrated humorist, newspaper columnist, and movie and radio "personality" strike many white Americans as anomalous, that is because there is still so little awareness of the historical record of the very high level of participation and achievement of Native Americans in these fields.

In order to see Rogers more clearly as being thoroughly representative of, rather than a unique exception to, the strong presence of late-nineteenth- and twentieth-century Native Americans in the public life of the time and in the mass media, it may be helpful to consider briefly the case of Creek poet-journalist and political leader Alexander Posey, a contemporary of Rogers's who excelled in some of the same pursuits Rogers did. Posey had been born in the Creek Nation a half-dozen years before Rogers, in a settlement in Indian Territory about ninety miles due south of the Rogers's family home in the Cherokee Nation. After an early career as a Creek school superintendent, in 1902 Posey took over the editing of the *Indian Journal,* the intertribal paper that Cherokee William Potter Ross had founded in 1876.[27] Posey's most significant writing for the paper, and his signal contribution to the treaty/writing traditions I am tracing, was the "Fus Fixico Letters," a series of fictitious letters to the editor of the *Indian Journal* ostensibly written in heavily dialect accented English by a fullblood Creek character named Fus Fixico.[28] In the letters, Fus Fixico reports on the doings and conversations of Hotgun and Tookpafka Micco, two of his fellow fullblood Creeks who are "Snakes," or followers of Chitto Harjo (who was called "Crazy Snake" by whites). Repeatedly, in the first few years of the century, the Snakes attempted to resist the federal government's plan to dissolve the Creek Nation and allot individual land holdings to its members. Although Posey, in his capacity as an avowedly "progressive" newspaper editor, had consistently criticized the Snake faction as "holdback Indians" with a misguided attachment to the past, he nonetheless felt some strong admiration for their devotion to Creek traditions. Posey's mixed feelings about the political activities of the Snakes and the response of the larger community thereto—many members of the group were arrested and jailed for a time—may have influenced the public political turnabout he performed in May 1903, when he suddenly turned from an outspoken opponent to a leading proponent of separate statehood for Indian Territory. Having spilled much editorial ink in the months before his switch arguing that the development of the area depended on Native American residents doing their best to assimilate themselves to the coming communities of white farmers, Posey became a leading advocate of separate statehood for the eastern half of what would within a few years become Oklahoma. In tribute, perhaps, to the powerfully separatist politics that the dissemination of the syllabary had enabled, the "Indian state" was to be called "Sequoyah." When proponents of separate statehood met in 1905 to draft the Constitution of the State of Sequoyah, Posey served as secretary of the convention.[29] Posey advocated for the cause through his fullblood personae, having Fus Fixico report the eloquent speech of Hotgun on the constitutional proceedings: "Long time ago he ['the Indian'] give a war whoop and go on warpath; this time he call a convention and go on record. Instead a making medicine he make history; instead of chasing the pioneers with a tomahawk, he preside in convention and use the tomahawk for a gavel and call the pioneers to order; and instead a swearing vengeance against the pale face, he get up and make a big talk on how to make a state. The Injin is civilized and aint extinct no more than a rabbit."[30] Here, Posey tellingly juxtaposes the white stereotype of the savage Indian on the warpath, bent on taking revenge with his tomahawk, with the constitution-making, political-conventioneering body who, rather than waiting for white settlers to determine the political character of the territory, "call the pioneers to order." For a brief time in 1905 it was possible to imagine that the continuing political struggles of the native peoples inhabiting the Indian Territory might expect the full support of the U.S. government; Posey's Hotgun continues, "The United States was bound by treaty and Christian duty to back the Injin up in the struggle for his rights."

But as little as six months later it was clear that the movement for Indian statehood was doomed. Although the Constitution of the State of Sequoyah had been ratified and taken to Washington for presentation to Congress, by early 1906 it was clear that Congress strongly favored the admission of a single state politically dominated by its white residents. In March of that year, Fus Fixico reported that Tookpafka Micco had instructed his wife "she mus' quit huntin' wild onions in the creek bottom an' gather gossip in the womens' literary club, an' stop poundin' sofky corn an' subscribe for the Ladies' Home Journal, an' go shoppin' in a buggy with red runnin' gears an' a high seat 'stead of on a three hundred pound filly."[31] This time the satirical political edge of the details cuts in a different direction from the Hotgun's speech of a few months before; rather than transforming the tomahawk into a gavel to call other Indians *and* whites "to order" at a constitutional convention, the Creek wife is advised to lay aside traditional life entirely for a new, extremely attenuated political order of gossiping, shopping, and magazine reading (or at least subscribing). Her husband's relation to the new order is doubly attenuated because he is dependent on her participation in consumer "civilization" for any connection to it. This is the very moment when the young Will Rogers left Indian Territory behind him for good and initiated his remarkable career as a performer in mass media. Within the next few decades, as Tookpafka Micco's wife continued to pursue the new consumerist "lifestyle" that had immediately succeeded the defeat of the movement for political and cultural separatism among her people, she may have been unsurprisedly pleased to keep encountering a near-"homeboy" in the figure of Rogers as she took in the latest in magazine and newspaper humor and "personality profiles," comic western movies, and phonograph-record and radio comedy. Alexander Posey himself, who as a journalist and political leader was committed strictly to local issues, enjoyed a short-lived national celebrity when the *New York Times* and many other papers briefly championed him as the latest American master of political satire in dialect. The radically localist Posey suddenly found himself fielding offers of syndication and a prominent position on national lecture circuits. Sadly and ironically, he survived his first fame by only a couple of years and Oklahoma's admission as a state in 1907 by only one year: he drowned at the age of thirty-four in a flash flood. His admirers eulogized him as another young literary genius who had been snatched away before he could fulfill his great promise. Some of his fellow Creeks believed the legendary Creek figure of the water-dwelling "tiesnake" had dragged Posey to his untimely death as a punishment for the work he had done for the Dawes Commission to advance the task of allotment.[32]

Where Posey and the forces for separate statehood had failed, Will Rogers's father and the single-state party triumphed a few years later. Clement Vann Rogers served as a key delegate to the constitutional convention for the proposed state of Oklahoma in 1906–7; it was the culmination of a long career in Cherokee and Indian Territory politics that had begun in the conflagration of the Civil War.[33] Will's relation to his father during the time of the latter's greatest prominence in regional politics took the form of the younger man's sending large checks home as an inarguable sign of his early successes on the vaudeville circuit. Rather than participating directly in the dissolution of the Indian nations of the Territory, as his father and Posey were doing, Will Rogers turned all his attention and drive to the task of establishing himself as a major player in the new "media nation" that was forming at the same time. Although his behavior may have looked like political indifference, or worse, back home, it is possible to understand Rogers's quiet but relentless drive toward succeeding in every arena of mass-mediated public life available to him in his time as a complex act not only of protest against his people's political betrayal but also of an iron determination to carry on treaty discourse "by other means" than those through which it had previously been transacted. As Muskogee Creek and Cherokee scholar Craig S. Womack has recently pointed out in the conclusion to his own discussion of the legacy of the "Fus Fixico Letters," "Will Rogers, influenced by Creek and Cherokee newspapers, is the next link after Posey in developing a unique brand of Indian humor, and Rogers succeeded in bringing it into the American mainstream."[34] In order to do so, Rogers would take the droll but politically acute humor practiced by Posey and others back to the newspapers, as well as to places on the new map of the mass media where it was about to be heard for the first time.

It was in the last years of his life, when he was the most popular comic star of early sound film, that the complex racial politics of Rogers's career came to manifest themselves most strikingly. The issue of whites' "playing Indians" versus Indians "playing themselves" in dramatic representations of the American West had been playing itself out in relation to the prevalence of blackface as a popular comic mode in the white-dominated nineteenth-century American theater for a couple of generations before Rogers came on the scene.[35] When artist George Catlin took his gallery of paintings and Indian artifacts to London for exhibit in 1840, he supplemented his lectures with *tableaux vivants* of "stirring scenes of Indian life"—performed by twenty Cockney men and boy actors. Several years later, when he brought the show back to New York City, where it had enjoyed only a middling success a few years earlier, Catlin's use of "real Indians"—first a group of Ojibways and then one of Iowas—made it a sensation.[36] Various Native American groups had been "performing themselves" ("Indians playing Indians") for paying audiences since around the time of removal: an Iroquois band had danced and demonstrated ambush-and-scalping techniques at Peale's Museum in New York City in 1827, and, twenty years after Catlin and his company had come and gone, groups of western Indians appeared at P. T. Barnum's American Museum.[37]

These early Native American performers were the prototypes of the "Show Indians" who would become increasingly numerous for a couple of generations after William F. "Buffalo Bill" Cody opened the first Wild West show in 1883.[38]

Indian performers danced and reenacted famous battles in Wild West shows all over the world during their heyday from around the turn of the century to 1917 or so—and, as we know from the example of Will Rogers, while some seem always to have "played Indians," others versatilely adopted blackface and whiteface as well. Bands of "Show Indians" were major attractions at the Columbian Exposition in Chicago in 1893 and at the similarly mammoth Louisiana Purchase Exposition in St. Louis in 1904.[39] At the latter, Will Rogers, aged twenty-four, performed as one of Colonel Zack Mulhall's "Congress of Rough Riders and Ropers"—ironically cast as the last soldier to die in a reenactment of Custer's Last Stand. He also did trick-roping, and colleagues later said that it was in St. Louis that Rogers gave the first demonstrations of the professional abilities and star quality he had developed in his Wild West show tours of South Africa and New Zealand during the previous several years.[40]

These were the years when the Wild West show began to be superseded by the early movie western, which first emerged as a recognizable and very popular film genre after director Edwin S. Porter released *The Great Train Robbery* in 1903. Although Porter's classic western had been shot in rural New Jersey, the film industry as a whole soon began moving westward. During its first years of statehood, Oklahoma itself temporarily became a center for filming westerns; characteristically, given the wild-and-woolly reputation of the first whites who had come to Indian Territory, the peculiar western subgenre that developed there was the cowboy-gang narrative produced and performed by the ex-gangsters themselves: reformed train robber Al Jennings played himself in *The Bank Robbery* (1914), and Emmett Dalton (last survivor of the notorious Dalton gang) played himself in *The Last Stand of the Dalton Boys* (1912) and *Beyond the Law* (1918).[41] The center of filmmaking in the new state was the famous Miller Brothers' 101 Ranch, a vast spread near Ponca City that the entrepreneurial Miller family used both as a working ranch and as a kind of laboratory for developing new methods of selling the Wild West to the new mass culture; westerns were being filmed there as early as 1909. The young Will Rogers found life on the 101 Ranch so appealing that as a young man he more than once served as an unpaid cowhand there (it was only about sixty miles west of his family's home).[42]

But the Territory's reign as a center of filmmaking was short-lived. In the years following, directors newly arrived in Hollywood decided that the flat, grassy plains of Oklahoma could not compete for visual drama with the canyons around still-rural Santa Monica, and the Miller Brothers' Wild West show found themselves in their winter quarters in southern California being recruited to do more westerns by leading early director Thomas Ince. Unlike many early westerns that featured only cowboys, Ince's films employed large numbers of Indian performers, a feature that appears to have made them particularly popular. Given the clear edge that their participation was giving Ince's westerns, it is unsurprising that some of Ince's Native American performers pressed the director to feature them in leading roles. Ince appears to have given major roles to at least a few of these players—such as William Eagleshirt, an Oglala—but the experiment was short-lived; the racist convention whereby "pretend Indians" starred and "real Indians" worked as extras established itself in Hollywood very early on.[43]

The resultingly wooden Indians who appeared in the foreground of cowboy-and-Indian pictures soon became a predictable object of burlesque in the movies and beyond them. By the time Will Rogers's fellow star-comedians Fanny Brice and Eddie Cantor joined him to headline the *Ziegfeld Follies of 1917,* both were old hands at burlesquing Indian performance: Brice had sung "I'm an Indian" in Yiddish in vaudeville, and Cantor had gotten his start in a review called *Indian Maidens.*[44] In his first starring film role, Cantor appeared in the ultimate Indian burlesque film, *Whoopee!* (1930), in the self-parodying role of a Jewish "pansy" who is "captured" by Indians. The role derived from Cantor's trademark character of the young "negro pansy" he had played in blackface, in a father-son act he had performed with the great African American comedian Bert Williams in the 1917 edition of the *Ziegfeld Follies.*[45]

In *Blackface, White Noise,* Michael Rogin has meticulously analyzed the history of the use of blackface by Jewish performers such as Brice, Cantor, and Al Jolson to consolidate their appeal to white audiences and to enable their ascent to leading positions in the American entertainment industry in the transition from vaudeville to motion pictures in the decades between the world wars. In passing, Rogin also makes some astute remarks on the impersonation of Native Americans by non-Indian performers. As a non-Jew, Will Rogers is only marginal to Rogin's account, yet Rogers's performance in the title role of John Ford's 1934 film *Judge Priest* is important enough to the story told in Rogin's book to merit extensive discussion in it.[46] Technically, Rogin writes, the film is not a blackface film but a notable variation thereon: what Rogers does in his role as Judge Priest is not to wear literal blackface but, in a crucial scene, to ventriloquize the speech of a black servant named Jeff Poindexter and played by Stepin Fetchit (Rogers apparently donned actual blackface again, in the 1935 film *In Old Kentucky*).[47] In his last films, Rogers costarred with three of the most celebrated (and in Fetchit's case, derided) African American performers of the time—with Stepin Fetchit in four films of 1934 and 1935, with Hattie McDaniel in *Judge Priest,* and with Bill "Bojangles" Robinson in *In Old Kentucky.* For Rogin, *Judge Priest* is essentially a transitional film, pointing the way into the blackface musical of the 1930s and 1940s, but he gives the reader enough information to perceive (a perception completely confirmed by viewing the film) that it is also quite a significant link in the white-supremacist, neo-Confederate-nationalist impulse centrally instanti-ated in American film history by Griffith's *The Birth of a Nation* (1915). Rogin mentions that the climactic dramatic monologue in the film is performed by actor Henry Walthall, who had worn Klan robes to lead the charge in *The Birth of a Nation,* but he does not mention that alone of the throng of listeners to Walthall's character's supposedly heartrending tale of Confederate war heroism, Will Rogers's character Judge Priest responds not with tears and groans but with a strikingly noncommital grin and a barely perceptible roll of the eyes—an echo of a moment earlier in the film when he walks by a Confederate veteran narrating his own supposed-to-be gripping tale of wartime derring-do and remarks, "Put-tin' them gunboats in there is new, isn't it? That's a nice touch!"

Although it is true that Rogers was the son of a former slaveowner, the particu-lar difficulties that Cherokees and other residents of Indian Territory had experi-enced during the Civil War, and the particular modes that several of the native peoples developed for politically and socially incorporating their former slaves into their numbers after the end of the war, significantly distinguished their relation to the legacy of the war and of slavery from that of their white southern neighbors. Although many white filmgoers may have perceived him simply as white or perhaps as "part-Indian," Rogers saw himself as a person and as a performer as having emerged from an at least partly shared space between the Native American and African American worlds of his childhood. When a public outcry arose on one occasion after he referred to a popular song as a "nigger spiritual," Rogers countered charges of racism by insisting that back in Indian Territory he had been a grown child before he ever realized that there were white people.[48] Rogers also claimed to have learned his first performance skill, trick-roping, from Bill Pickett, the legendary African American/Cherokee cowboy who invented the rodeo sport of "bulldogging."[49] When Rogers joined the *Zieg-feld Follies* as a star-comedian in 1916, he had been preceded in that position by Bert Williams, who had been starring in the *Follies* since 1910. Williams was celebrated for the character he performed, a poor black man who exhibited some of the signs of minstrelsy—he was sad and shuffled—but whom Williams invested with a kind of philosophical dignity and pathos that deeply moved many specta-tors.[50] One can readily imagine the newspaper-reading Cherokee comedian Rogers standing in the wings observing the rich, affective burden Williams pro-jected through his character and thoroughly absorbing the lesson that a black or

Indian "clown" could perform truths about their respective—and sometimes shared—histories that far exceeded the discursive "content" of their acts.

Rogin refers to Rogers as "part-Cherokee" at one point and as "part-Indian" at another.[51] Although within Native American groups there appears to have been a general awareness of who was a "fullblood" and who a "mixedblood," what is often hardest for whites to understand is that neither "fullbloods" nor "mixedbloods" considered "mixeds" to be proportionately "less" Indian if only a half or a quarter (or whatever) of their ancestors were Indians. Although it is true that some mixedbloods have led assimilationist movements and some fullbloods have led traditionalist ones, such assertions are routinely contradicted throughout the history of Indian-white contact, as in the crucial case of the development of the syllabary by the mixedblood Sequoyah/George Guess that allowed his fellow Cherokees to preserve traditional aspects of their culture that would otherwise most likely have been lost (but also to participate in certain kinds of institutions—publishing a newspaper, writing letters—that some would see as assimilationist). While he was far from being a Cherokee nationalist or traditionalist, Rogers referred to himself as a "Cherokee" and an "Indian" and never as being "part-Cherokee" or "part-Indian." When he claimed that "All [he] knew's just what [he] read in the papers," the implicit but by no means secret irony of the statement was that unlike the great majority of his (American, national) audience, the papers Rogers had grown up reading included the *Cherokee Phoenix* and the *Indian Journal,* as well as the *New York Times* (which Rogers's father had delivered to his ranch in Indian Territory so that he could keep up with his investments beyond home). Implicit in Rogers's claim to know nothing but what he "read in the papers" was a powerful assertion that also informed the performances of Bert Williams: that their respective performance styles carried some of the extraordinary burdens and manifested some of the powers still latent in their people's histories. The rich and volatile political history transmitted down to the present through the remarkable creativity of nonwhite journalists, vaudevillians, movie stars, and movie extras continues to unfold; its promise, at the beginning of another century, is still unresolved, still in many ways unfulfilled.

NOTES

Thanks to Jonathan Goldberg for his attentions to this piece, and to Russ Castronovo and Dana Nelson for their editorial expertise.

1 Ben Yagoda's *Will Rogers: A Biography* (New York: Knopf, 1993), with its judicious and richly detailed accounts of Rogers's elaborate career across media, has been invaluable

to me in thinking about the relations of that career to its various antecedents in Native American history.

2 Ibid., 291.

3 Only as I was making final revisions to this essay was I able to read Lary May's chapter "Will Rogers and the Radicalism of Tradition" in his *The Big Tomorrow: Hollywood and the Politics of the American Way* (Chicago: University of Chicago Press, 2000), 11–53. May argues, as I do, that Rogers's Native American heritage crucially informed his politics, but he does so in quite different terms from the ones I invoke, pointing out what he sees as Rogers's participation in a Native American "trickster" tradition and in a "multicultural" politics.

4 On one occasion when Rogers found himself performing before a large group of his fellow Cherokees, a journalist reports that the comedian unexpectedly strayed onto the topic of Andrew Jackson, who had forced the Cherokees and their southeastern neighbors off their lands and onto the Trail of Tears in the 1830s. At that point, the reporter writes, "suddenly, he became furious. His transformation was terrifying, and for three minutes his astonished audience was treated to a demonstration of what primitive, instinctive hatred could be." In response, someone in the audience emitted a piercing "war cry," and Rogers for once appears to have found himself at a loss for words, as he stood "trembling and actually aghast" at the intensity of his own out-pouring of rage (Yagoda, *Will Rogers,* 281). But by no means did Rogers limit his critical observations about white Americans to Indian audiences; for a representative compendium of such remarks, see, for example, "Indians," in Bryan B. Sterling, *The Best of Will Rogers* (New York: Crown, 1979), 179–83.

5 Jace Weaver, *That the People Might Live: Native American Literatures and Native American Community* (New York: Oxford University Press, 1997), 198–99 n.10.

6 *New York Times* review of John Ford's *Judge Priest,* October 12, 1934; quoted in Bryan B. Sterling and Frances N. Sterling, *Will Rogers in Hollywood* (New York: Crown, 1984), 147.

7 See the interview with director John Ford in Bryan B. Sterling, ed., *The Will Rogers Scrapbook* (New York: Grosset & Dunlap, 1976), 175. See also the comments by director Frank Borzage and fellow actor Joel McCrea on Rogers's improvisations in Sterling and Sterling, *Will Rogers in Hollywood,* 105 and 111, respectively.

8 Chadwick Allen, "Hero with Two Faces: The Lone Ranger as Treaty Discourse," *American Literature* 68, no. 3 (September 1996): 609–38.

9 Will Rogers, *Will Rogers's Weekly Articles: The Hoover Years, 1931–33,* vol. 5 (Norman: University of Oklahoma Press, 1982). Yagoda discusses the passage in his *Will Rogers,* 281–82.

10 Quoted in Sterling, *The Best of Will Rogers,* 181.

11 Will Rogers, *Weekly Articles* (vol. 2), 160–61.

12 The phrase "a long foreground" is, of course, the one Ralph Waldo Emerson used in writing to Walt Whitman to thank him for the gift of the first (1855) *Leaves of Grass.* While recognizing Whitman's great originality, Emerson also recognized that such a beginning, as he put it, "must have had a long foreground somewhere."

13 For an illuminating and thorough history of Native American treaty making, see

Francis Paul Prucha, *American Indian Treaties: The History of a Political Anomaly* (Berkeley: University of California Press, 1994). For acute political analysis of that history, see Vine Deloria Jr. and David E. Wilkins, *Tribes, Treaties, and Constitutional Tribulations* (Austin: University of Texas Press, 1999), especially chapter 5, "The Historical Development of Constitutional Clauses," 58–70.

14 Quoted by Maureen Konkle, "Indian Literacy, U.S. Colonialism, and Literary Criticism," *American Literature* 69, no. 3 (September 1997): 466–67.

15 James H. Merrell, *Into the American Woods: Negotiators on the Pennsylvania Frontier* (New York: Norton, 1999). Merrell writes: "Revisiting treaties with the go-between messes up the simplified, sanitized view of these extraordinary occasions. A negotiator knew treaty culture better than anyone, knew it from the council ground at midday to an Indian camp late at night to a governor's chamber at sunup, knew it as high pageantry and (sometimes) low comedy, short tempers and frayed nerves, perilous moments when people forgot, rewrote, or discarded the script and magical moments when those people found communion" (255).

16 Constance Rourke, "The Rise of Theatricals," in *The Roots of American Culture and Other Essays*, ed. Van Wyck Brooks (New York: Harcourt, Brace, 1942), 61–62.

17 Ibid., 62, 63.

18 The standard academic history/biography of Sequoyah/George Guess and his development of the Cherokee syllabary is still Grant Foreman's *Sequoyah* (Norman: University of Oklahoma Press, 1938).

19 David Murray, *Forked Tongues: Speech, Writing, and Representation in North American Indian Texts* (London: Pinter, 1991), 27.

20 Ibid.

21 Yagoda, *Will Rogers*, 308.

22 Steven V. Gragert, ed., *Radio Broadcasts of Will Rogers* (Stillwater: Oklahoma State University Press, 1983), 18. Yagoda discusses the passage in *Will Rogers*, 308–9.

23 Yagoda, *Will Rogers*, xii.

24 The *Cherokee Advocate* was directly descended from the Cherokee's earlier newspaper, the *Cherokee Phoenix*, and was in fact edited by William Penn Boudinot, son of Elias Boudinot, editor of the *Phoenix*. An intertribal paper called the *Indian Journal* was established at the same time (1876), and was edited by William Potter Ross, a nephew of Cherokee chief John Ross, who had remained staunch in his opposal to removal and had led the majority antitreaty party. Both publications appear to have been read both by natives residing in Indian Territory and by white readers interested in Indian affairs; early in its run, the *Indian Journal* boasted of having subscribers in seventeen states, as far away as New York and Pennsylvania. For the most detailed accounts of these and other early Native American publications, see Daniel F. Littlefield Jr. and James W. Parins, *American Indian and Alaska Native Newspapers and Periodicals, 1826–1924* (Westport, Conn.: Greenwood, 1984). For an important analysis of the propagandistic effects of the *Phoenix*, see the essay of prominent historian of the Cherokees Theda Perdue, "Rising from the Ashes: The *Cherokee Phoenix* as an Ethnohistorical Source," *Ethnohistory* 24 (summer 1977): 207–18.

25 John M. Coward, "Explaining the Little Bighorn," in Frankie Hutton and Barbara

Straus Reed, eds., *Outsiders in Nineteenth-Century Press History: Multicultural Per-spectives* (Bowling Green, Ohio: Bowling Green University Popular Press, 1995), 145–57. The quotation is from 145–46.

26 Quoted by John M. Coward, "Explaining the Little Bighorn," 153.

27 Daniel F. Littlefield Jr. has done invaluable scholarship on Posey and his political and cultural contexts in *Alex Posey: Creek Poet, Journalist, and Humorist* (Lincoln: University of Nebraska Press, 1992).

28 Daniel F. Littlefield Jr. and Carol A. Petty Hunter, eds., have produced an exemplary edition of Alexander Posey's *The Fus Fixico Letters* (Lincoln: University of Nebraska Press, 1993).

29 Littlefield, *Alex Posey,* 214–15.

30 Ibid., 213–14.

31 Posey, *The Fus Fixico Letters,* 238–39.

32 Littlefield, *Alex Posey,* 254–55.

33 Yagoda, *Will Rogers,* 120–21.

34 Craig S. Womack, *Red on Red: Native American Literary Separatism* (Minneapolis: University of Minnesota Press, 1999), 172.

35 For a highly suggestive account of the significance of whites impersonating Native Americans "from the Boston Tea Party to the present," see Philip J. Deloria, *Playing Indian* (New Haven: Yale University Press, 1998).

36 L. G. Moses, *Wild West Shows and the Images of American Indians, 1883–1933* (Albuquerque: University of New Mexico Press, 1996), 16.

37 Bunny McBride, *Molly Spotted Elk: A Penobscot in Paris* (Norman: University of Oklahoma Press, 1995), 43–44. McBride's account of Spotted Elk's international career as a dancer and showgirl, based on Spotted Elk's extensive personal diaries, provides an interesting comparison with Rogers's own complex performance career—as it does with that of others of Spotted Elk's contemporaries, such as leading modernist ballerina Maria Tallchief and the other Native American women chronicled in Lili Cockerille Livingston, *American Indian Ballerinas* (Norman: University of Oklahoma Press, 1997). See also Maria Tallchief, with Larry Kaplan, *Maria Tallchief: America's Prima Ballerina* (New York: Holt, 1997).

38 L. G. Moses gives a brief history of the use of the term "Show Indians" in his *Wild West Shows,* 138–39.

39 On the performances of Native Americans in Wild West shows during their heyday, as well as at the world's fairs in Chicago and St. Louis at the turn of the century, see chapters 7–9 of L. G. Moses, *Wild West Shows.*

40 Yagoda, *Will Rogers,* 71.

41 For a good summary of extensive filmmaking activities in the early days of Oklahoma, see Michael Wallis, *The Real Wild West: The 101 Ranch and the Creation of the American West* (New York: St. Martin's Press, 1999), 377–85. Wallis describes the cinematic self-exploitation of ex-criminals Jennings and Dalton on pp. 378 and 382.

42 Wallis, *The Real Wild West,* 241.

43 Michael Wallis asserts that Ince never honored any of his Native American actors'

suggestions for featuring them in larger roles (*The Real Wild West,* 375). L. G. Moses credits Ince with at least experimenting with Indians in larger roles (*Wild West Shows,* 227) but also quotes film historian Jon Tuska to the effect that none of these larger roles was actually a starring one; see Tuska's *The Filming of the West* (Garden City, N.Y.: Doubleday, 1976), 25.

44 Michael Rogin provides a brief history of the burlesquing of Indians from popular Yiddish theater to vaudeville to Broadway and Hollywood musicals in his *Blackface, White Noise: Jewish Immigrants in the Hollywood Melting Pot* (Berkeley: University of California, 1996), 151.

45 Cantor describes the skit in some detail in *As I Remember Them* (New York: Duell, Sloan & Pearce, 1963), 48–49.

46 Rogin, *Black Face, White Noise,* 153–55.

47 This is according to the *Philadelphia Record* review quoted in Sterling and Sterling, eds., *Will Rogers in Hollywood,* 169.

48 Yagoda, *Will Rogers,* 309.

49 Pickett and Rogers performed together at the 1904 St. Louis World's Fair. See Bailey C. Hanes, *Bill Pickett, Bulldogger* (Norman: University of Oklahoma Press, 1977), 143.

50 Mel Watkins gives an illuminating account of the careers of both Bert Williams and Stepin Fetchit in his excellent *On the Real Side: A History of African American Comedy* (New York: Simon & Schuster, 1994), on pp. 175–79 and 247–62, respectively. For more on Williams, see Eric Ledell Smith, *Bert Williams: A Biography of the Pioneer Black Comedian* (Jefferson, N.C.: McFarland, 1992); and Ann Charters, *Nobody: The Story of Bert Williams* (New York: Macmillan, 1970).

51 Rogin, *Blackface, White Noise,* 150, 174.

KEVIN GAINES

From Center to Margin: Internationalism
and the Origins of Black Feminism

◆

I want to make two arguments in this essay, each as part of the elucidation of two distinct moments in a genealogy of black feminism. My first contention is that the most democratic and enduring legacy of the African American freedom movement was the intellectual intervention of black feminism against the masculinist posturing endemic within the Black Power movement of the late 1960s. Black Power advocates generally posited the self-determination and control of black communities and their institutions as the objective of democratic struggle. But black feminist writers and activists emphasized gender egalitarianism as the decisive terrain of democratic practice, without which community remained an unrealized ideal. My second argument is that this black feminist critique of Black Power can be traced to antecedents in progressive political and cultural trends of the post–World War II period. In other words, what might retrospectively be considered the origins of black feminism existed in a symbiotic relationship to a black radical culture of internationalism, largely based in northern black urban centers such as Harlem and Chicago, which, ironically enough, were major sites of what would eventually be called Black Power. This internationalism was shaped by the convergence of African independence and Civil Rights movement activism in the United States. I will also consider here the significance of African American expatriates in Ghana as a manifestation of this internationalism that enabled black feminism. The expatriate experience suggests that within this progressive black culture of internationalism, an expansive, democratic diaspora identity could flourish. It was this enabling sense of diaspora identity within black urban and expatriate communities that animated their commitment to forging transnational solidarities and the linkage of democratic movements. That diaspora sensibility and the internationalism that provided the framework for a critique of American racism constituted the thread linking the two moments of black feminism discussed here.

While other scholars have noted the feminist intervention made by black women writers against misogynist tendencies in the Black Power and Black Arts movements and, subsequently, have contributed important intellectual interventions that have laid the groundwork for black feminist studies,[1] my discussion of black feminism focuses on the period predating the gender disputes and controversies of 1960s militancy. For the radical democratic significance and potential of black feminism to be fully appreciated, that intervention so familiar to scholars of the Black Arts movement must be seen in the context of an earlier moment that was far less defined by gender conflict. There was, in fact, a synthesis between incipient literary, artistic, and political expressions of black women's subjectivity and black struggles for equality since the postwar period, if not before. Reclaiming this synthesis between black feminism and movements for black cultural and political emancipation stands as a corrective to the historical amnesia that represses or distorts the memory of progressive black struggles. The exclusion of black women and black feminism from African American struggles for equality is a primary example of such amnesia. Such disregard for the centrality of black women in these struggles has disastrous consequences not only for democratic activism but also for the prospects facing black lives and communities.

My objective in arguing that well before Black Power a black feminist vision was an integral part of black opposition and solidarity is to help lay to rest the popular fallacy that black feminism is an externally imposed construct that is alien and antagonistic to black communities. In what follows, I am equally concerned with exploring the affinities between incipient black feminist and black studies discourses as I am with discussing the vision of radical democracy contained in the black feminist critique of the excesses of Black Power militancy.

What do I mean here by black feminism? The meaning of the term is inherently elusive and inevitably contested. To begin, the meaning of black feminism is contingent on the historical moment it occupies. Although it is tempting to regard black feminism as the highest stage of black radicalism, there is, in fact, no place in my argument for any teleological notion of black feminism that sees it evolving (or devolving) over time toward (or away from) some normative statement or agenda. Moreover, I would urge caution lest we impose contemporary, presentist criteria that might hinder historical understanding of antecedents of what might be called black feminism. In other words, not all the issues and objectives presently identified with feminism, (e.g., reproductive rights or ending violence against women) can be located in black feminism before the Black Power era. Unlike those who have been troubled by the term "feminism" out of an understandable desire to distinguish their own gender consciousness from that established by the white, middle-class U.S. women's movement,[2] I prefer "black feminism" because not only does it predate the women's movement it is also independently "black" in origin and by definition. In other words, it has constituted a political perspective defined by women's struggles for self-consciousness and autonomy that were integral parts of a black radical democratic movement. Finally, my understanding of black feminism, as best articulated in the anthology *The Black Woman* (1970), edited by Toni Cade Bambara, regards it as a comprehensive, democratic perspective that grounds its critique of patriarchy within radical critiques of racism, capitalist exploitation, and empire.[3]

To explore the roots of black feminism is to complicate the narrative of the emergence of Black Power radicalism from the collapse of the liberal consensus for civil rights reforms. Such a narrative renders prior black radicalism invisible. It is critical, then, to emphasize that the roots of black feminism lay not simply in a critique of the patriarchal gender politics of the Black Power movement. Instead, a black feminist foresight, seen in the work of such writers as Gwendolyn Brooks, Alice Childress, and Lorraine Hansberry, was integral to what is now understood as the black studies project from its inception. Here, I understand black studies to be the intellectual extension of African American and African freedom movements. It is simply a matter of historical amnesia that affinities between these writers and the black studies project have often gone unrecognized. In all likelihood the nonrecognition of these contributions stemmed from the concern of Black Power militants to confine black women's role in nation-building to motherhood and child rearing. In any case, it was the attempt within the Black Power phase of the movement to marginalize black women's role that called forth an explicit statement of black feminism, epitomized in Bambara's *The Black Woman.* In this volume, which amounted to a collective black feminist manifesto, the critique of sexism in the movement sought to redirect the struggle in a more democratic direction.

Although linked to the groundbreaking work of Brooks, Hansberry, Childress, and others, the black feminist critique of sexism in the Black Power movement represented a major shift from the black progressive political culture of the 1950s that preceded it. First and foremost, that earlier phase of northern urban black radicalism lacked the overt gender polarization of Black Power. In concert with a rising autonomy in black consciousness and political agency, mediated and enabled by internationalism, there existed a space for black women writers to pursue issues of gender within their depictions of urban black social milieu. This is not to exaggerate the gender egalitarianism of postwar black radicalism: I wouldn't go so far as to claim that a commitment to gender equality extended to the everyday lives and relationships of black men and women, nor was any belief in gender fairness shared by the era's predominantly male literary critics, who often marginalized or ignored black women's writing. But while the everyday dimension of gender relationships remained shaped by patriarchy and homophobia, the progressive human rights consciousness of black radicalism made overt demands of women's subservience for the good of the racial community unthinkable, at least until the advent of Black Power.

What, then, was the relationship of black feminism to black cultural expression? I would suggest that one can find evidence of nascent black feminist perspectives in black literature, as well as the arts and political activism. Trade unionist and civil rights activist Ella Baker coauthored with Marvel Cooke a pathbreaking analysis of the plight of black women domestic workers in northern urban labor markets.[4] In the visual arts, Faith Ringgold has been noted as an artist whose work has expressed, in the words of Richard Powell, "a visual black nationalism—prescribed by a feminist stance that constantly negotiated between a personal identity and a political one."[5] No doubt other examples can be found in these and other fields, but here the focus will be on postwar African American women writers, who were at the forefront of bringing to light the struggles and perspectives of black women against their marginalization and silencing. Gwendolyn Brooks's novel *Maud Martha* (1953) is, in retrospect, a founding black feminist text and a groundbreaking work from the standpoint of an evolving black studies discourse.[6] Moreover, when it appeared, its feminist vision was inseparable from its project of cultural commentary. Through the perceptions and experiences of Maud, a working-class black woman reared and residing in the predominantly black south side of Chicago, Brooks gives a devastating account of the gulf between Maud's youthful dreams of romance and material comfort and her joyless marriage and the destitution of her family's poorly furnished kitchenette flat. In doing so, Brooks also provides a powerful and far more compassionate critique of black middle-class ideology, with its underlying desperation and conformity, than that advanced several years later by E. Franklin Frazier. Brooks's critique of intraracial class divisions illuminates the unspoken yet central functioning of patriarchy within the black bourgeoisie, namely through white-defined standards of ornamental female beauty as prerequisites for the acquisition and maintenance of middle-class status.

Her disappointments notwithstanding, Maud searches for the meaning of her life and, Brooks suggests, its significance for the African American community around her. "What she wanted," rather than fame, or greatness through the creation of works of art, "was to donate to the world a good Maud Martha. That was the offering, the bit of art, that could not come from any other" (22). Despite the narrative's focus on Maud's interior life, it would be erroneous to relegate the novel's purview to domesticity and the private realm. For *Maud Martha* engages the deeply public matter of fashioning healthy selfhood in a racist society, amidst the black community's ambiguous negotiations of racism.[7] When Maud confronts her beautician after a white saleslady has resorted to the epithet "nigger," Maud represses her anger at the beautician's flimsy explanation for letting the slight pass: "Maud Martha stared steadily into Sonia Johnson's irises. She said nothing. She kept on staring into Sonia Johnson's irises" (142). Mary Helen Washington observes that the literature of black women "takes the trouble to record the thoughts, words, feelings and deeds of black women, experiences that make the realities of being black in America look very different from what men have written." Washington's discussion of black women's writing is framed by her reading of *Maud Martha*, which, "though it perfectly expresse[d] the race alienation of the 1950s," was neglected and eclipsed by Ralph Ellison's *Invisible Man*, which also appeared in 1953.[8] The neglect of *Maud Martha* suggests that although spaces for black women's literary creativity existed, the politics of canonization often operated to obscure the contributions of these writers. However unremarked in its day, Brooks's text presented an incipient black feminist perspective, an offering written, to paraphrase one of the reviewers of her poetry, "in the confidence and momentum of a tradition that intends to be established."[9]

What can now be discerned as a tradition of writing linking black women's subjectivity to racial solidarity includes the novel *Like One of the Family* (1956) by Alice Childress.[10] The novel is structured by brief vignettes consisting of conversations between Mildred, a domestic worker who resides in Harlem, and her friend Marge. Throughout, Mildred regales her friend with tales of her struggles and confrontations with her employers, the outcome of which is usually their enhanced respect for Mildred. The "conversations" between Mildred and Marge, which are actually dominated by Mildred, the novel's protagonist (Marge's responses are wordlessly signified by ellipses), originally appeared as newspaper columns in the black press, including Paul Robeson's *Freedom* newspaper, based in Harlem. The columns reached far many more readers than did the novel, which sold little after going virtually unnoticed by critics. Indeed, the purely fictive, fantasy aspect of Childress's trickster heroine was cruelly underscored by the fact that the small Brooklyn firm that published the novel failed to pay the author any royalties.[11] Nevertheless, the novel exudes a spirit of protest and perseverance against such inequities, as Mildred deploys her considerable resources of mother wit, intelligence, and charm to maintain control over her working conditions and to foil the exploitative and insulting schemes of her employers. She is also a dedicated race woman, with strong opinions on the current desegregation crisis in the South. In one sketch, Mildred confessed being so angered by cold war liberals' studious reluctance to acknowledge the brutality of Jim Crow that she took it out on an exacting employer: "Have you ever heard any of these politician speakers say 'Jim Crow'? No, they will say the race *situation* or the *problem* of minorities or race *tensions* or somethin' like that. . . . Nobody comes down to the nitty gritty when it calls for namin' things for what they are. . . . You right, we always some 'problem' and people takin' potshots at us is always called 'tension' and why you and me who have been citizens for generations should be called 'minorities' is more than I can see" (82). Mildred's insistence on dignity and equality in her dealings with her employers is consistent with her democratic perspective, which encompasses the status of African Americans. Childress's text also shares the concerns of black studies discourse by virtue of its incisive analyses of, for example, African liberation, racism in U.S. popular culture, the self-deception of black middle-class injunctions that the race's members prove themselves the equal of whites, and the unconscious racism of white liberals.

Mildred is a subaltern who speaks with forceful and persuasive vernacular eloquence, and significantly, through her, it is from the black working-class position that Childress locates her critiques of cold war America. Some may contend that Mildred does not explicitly articulate a feminist perspective. But I would argue that Mildred's feminism is defined by her complete insistence on dignity and honor irrespective of her gender and class position. Mildred's democratic conception of equal rights explicitly includes black women. As Trudier Harris observes, through Mildred "Childress lets us hear the many women in Afro-American history whose occupations have silenced them" (xxix). Noting that Mildred is a major precedent for post-1950s fictional creations of black women, Harris finds in her the realization of unified selfhood that several other black female characters in black women's fiction struggle vainly to achieve: "Mildred is a black woman who knows that black women, even when they have been domestic servants, have had dignity and a degree of self-determination to sustain and define themselves against frightful odds" (xxi).

Like Childress, playwright Lorraine Hansberry served her literary apprenticeship among Harlem's black radical intellectual community. Both writers were associated with Robeson's *Freedom* and the left-wing journal *Masses and Mainstream*. Both shared the black Left's abiding concern with internationalism as a crucial perspective from which to challenge the institutionalized racism and exceptionalist claims of American nationhood. Hansberry's classic *A Raisin in the Sun* (1959) echoes many of the concerns of *Maud Martha,* as well as sharing its setting in the south side of Chicago.[12] But unlike the previous works discussed, Hansberry's play achieved critical and commercial success despite its meditation on unrequited African American aspirations, reflecting the black experience of an exclusionary American dream. The theme of feminism dwells comfortably within the play's well-known plot of a working-class black family's struggle to leave their rundown apartment and purchase a home in an all-white suburb, despite the likelihood of white vigilante attacks.

The play's feminist content, as well as its internationalism, is represented in the daughter, Beneatha, who is in college and plans to attend medical school. Indeed, her ambition challenges what may well have been her family's expectations of female deference, as implied by her first name. Beneatha's struggle for an autonomous identity as a young black woman, however earnest and self-indulgent at times, reflects the impact of African independence on black diaspora consciousness. Beneatha enacts not only the author's feminism but also serves as the vehicle for Hansberry's criticism of the shallow materialism and assimilationism of the black bourgeoisie. Beneatha's prospects for realizing her professional ambitions, as well as her desire to be taken seriously as an independent-minded woman, are rendered all the more uncertain by the lackluster choice she must make between her two suitors. Despite the contrast between her suitors—one is an affluent, black middle-class college student of predictably hidebound views; the other is a progressive and worldly African exchange student from Nigeria—there is no assurance that either would be receptive to Beneatha's career aspirations.

Ironically, Hansberry was posthumously attacked by militants (she died of leukemia in 1965) for, among other things, having written what they denounced as an "integrationist" play, and for seeming to have played into the hands of antiblack stereotypes of matriarchy by pitting the formidable Mama Younger's dream of homeownership against her oldest son's desire to support his own family with an ultimately disastrous plan to invest in a liquor store. These misguided attacks on Hansberry's reputation were part of the erasure of postwar black radical antecedents in what amounted to a tacit collusion between black nationalist extremism and cold war repression. The rise of black militancy and its attendant sexism further marginalized this inchoate genealogy of emergent black feminism that joined Brooks, Childress, and Hansberry. In self-defense against this overt challenge, advocates of black feminism would assert themselves more explicitly as such. Obscured in that blinding moment of polarization that shaped the volume's reception was any sense of continuity between Bambara's anthology, *The Black Woman,* and the prior generation of black women writers. Unlike its antecedents, which can only be read retrospectively as black feminist texts, *The Black Woman* was a black feminist manifesto shaped by political urgency. It crystallized the idea of black feminism as a means of interrogating the rhetoric of revolution and liberation, rhetoric that at that time both masked and underwrote profound gender conflicts and contradictions both in the movement and within black public culture.

Interestingly, Bambara's anthology contained writing that issued from that earlier period in which black feminist writing was, notwithstanding a sexist critical discourse, at home, so to speak, within black literary circles. Bambara's inclusion of Paule Marshall's 1962 story "Reena" is instructive for understanding this aspect of the emergence of black feminism as a genealogy of writing that, as much as anything else, nurtured and inspired other black women writers.[13] "Reena" strongly reflects the impact of African independence on the diaspora identities of northern blacks. As the freedom movement gained momentum in the South, with masses of African Americans willing to endure jail terms and confront white mobs, black radicals in northern cities took inspiration from African independence movements. Without minimizing their solidarity with the struggles of southern blacks, struggles for African independence lent a new substance and urgency to black nationalist sentiment. For diaspora Africans, the prospect of African statehood and global influence constituted *their* movement, providing a psychic and, for a few, physical refuge from the alienation of northern ghettos.

It was the rise of Africa on the world stage and in the consciousness of diaspora Africans that provided Marshall the context for the story's formulation of black feminism. The plot of "Reena" hinges on the reunion of childhood friends separated by twenty years; their conversation provides an occasion for reflection and self-knowledge. Once neighbors in Brooklyn, both Reena and her friend Paulie, a writer, are of West Indian background. Brought together again by the death of Paulie's godmother, Reena's Aunt Vi, the women abandon the post-funeral gathering for the quiet of Aunt Vi's upstairs bedroom. Paulie remembered being intimidated by Reena's brilliance and intensity: "She ruthlessly analyzed herself, sparing herself nothing. Her honesty was so absolute it was a kind of cruelty" (21). Reena's conversation that night brought home to Paulie "what is perhaps the critical fact of my existence—that definition of me, of her and millions like us, formulated by others to serve out their fantasies, a definition we have to combat at an unconscionable cost to the self and even use, at times, in order to survive; the cause of so much rage, as well as, oddly enough, a source of pride: simply, what it has meant, what it means, to be a Black woman in America" (21).

Reena's analysis of her experiences is thus presented as emblematic of black women's struggle for self-consciousness. Paulie and Reena commiserate over loneliness and the problems of male-female relationships, the dearth of eligible black men, and the seeming profusion of relationships between white women and black men. Reena described her failed marriage to a black man, a struggling photographer who came to resent Reena's ambition for him, and her own career aspirations. Having gained custody of their three children, she looked forward to working in journalism, instilling in her children pride in their blackness, and engaging in local politics to improve the public schools. But uppermost in Reena's plans was to live and work in Africa for an extended period, if not permanently: "All I know is that I have to. For myself and my children. It is important that they see Black people who have truly a place and history of their own and who are building for a new, and hopefully, more sensible world. And I must see it, get close to it, because I can never lose the sense of being a displaced person here in the United States because of my color" (28).

Marshall's "Reena" explores aspects of black feminism, including the struggle for autonomy, economic independence, and personal fulfillment, and the elusiveness of sisterhood and community among themselves. Both the subject matter and setting of "Reena," as well as its inclusion in Bambara's anthology, support my argument that black feminism initially emerged as an organic part of postwar black struggles for equality. When "Reena" was first published, black feminism as subject matter for black women writers lacked the controversy it would have eventually in the wake of Black Power. Why this was the case is an intriguing question. Early black feminist writing helped define a solidarity characterized by both a rejection of an unquestionably pernicious American racism and an embrace of an affirming black diaspora identification with the promise of a liberated Africa. It was the optimism and unity imposed by this righteous struggle against the manifest evils of Jim Crow and colonialism that for the most part kept quotidian sexism within the realm of "private" behavior (without, of course, eliminating it from public culture), or, indeed, lent legitimacy to women activists' efforts to challenge it in a forthright manner. Later, with Black Power, and with the struggle to redefine the movement's goals and tactics further exacerbated by state repression, gender recrimination would overwhelm solidarity. Black feminism would be increasingly defined by militants as antagonistic to the struggle. It was only then, that, of necessity, black feminism adopted a stance of internal dissent and self-defense. Black feminists argue throughout Bambara's anthology that they had been committed all along to the struggle. Unfortunately, the myth of black feminism as antagonistic to the so-called black community and its interests is an enduring legacy of those violent and confusing times.

What is also striking about "Reena" is that it suggests a scenario for the genesis of black feminism that complicates the familiar narrative of its having evolved out of gender and racial inequalities within the Civil Rights and women's movements, respectively. Marshall's story, along with the work of Brooks, Childress, and Hansberry, suggests that the elaboration of a worldview through the eyes of urban black women resided on fairly egalitarian terms within a black public culture democratized by struggle. To be sure, this is not to idealize a usable past of normative gender relations among black peoples, for an autonomous black feminism implied at the very least a critique of patriarchy, as well as the gendered dimensions of racial oppression. What Marshall's story demonstrates, along with many of the contributors to Bambara's anthology, is that the urban North of the 1950s was a principal setting for black feminist consciousness-raising and activism.

It was in the urban North, particularly Harlem, that internationalism and the image of renascent Africa lent a tremendous cultural vitality to black diaspora consciousness. Hence Reena's aspiration to relocate her family to Africa. Viewing Bambara's anthology as a product of location, one can discern internationalism as a thread linking the early voicings of black feminist discourse with the intervention against overt male chauvinism in black movement politics, the latter of which displayed a deep engagement with the rhetoric of Third World revolution. Bambara and other contributors to *The Black Woman* recast internationalism in an ideological struggle against the domestic U.S. fusion of patriarchal racism with black nationalism—namely, the misguided embrace of the myth of black matriarchy by many black militants in the wake of the Moynihan report. In its new guise, running the gamut from intimate relationships to transnational revolutionary movements, internationalism provided a language by which black feminists contested black male militants' attempts to circumscribe the role of women within activist groups. As a case in point, I turn to the African American expatriate community in Ghana as a concrete example of this symbiotic relationship between radicalism, internationalism, and black feminism.

As we have seen, Africa's struggles against European colonial rule exerted a powerful hold over the imaginations of blacks in the diaspora. After the McCarthy-era prosecution of black radicals' support for anticolonialism, the well-publicized independence of Ghana in 1957, coinciding with violent racial unrest in the South, sparked a resurgence in black protest and solidarities. The close of the decade even witnessed cooperation between northern and southern movement activists around the armed self-defense movement of Robert Williams, the North Carolina NAACP leader.[14] Foremost among intellectual developments was the founding of the American Society for African Culture (AMSAC) by the political scientist and civil rights activist John A. Davis. Under Davis AMSAC sought to promote cultural exchange, collaboration, and heightened mutual understanding between African American and African intellectuals. The group facilitated the efforts of black musicians, artists, and writers of varying political involvements to independently enact their international visions of solidarity.

This fascination with Africa was gender diverse. Women writers like Marshall, Audre Lorde (also anthologized in *The Black Woman*), Maya Angelou, and Rosa Guy shared an enthusiasm for African independence movements with male colleagues in the radical Harlem Writers' Group, including John Oliver Killens, Julian Mayfield, and John Henrik Clarke. Women exercised editorial leadership and were contributors to the black left-wing journal *Freedomways*. Shirley Graham Du Bois, Esther Jackson, Lorraine Hansberry, Gwendolyn Brooks, Jean Carey Bond, and other women joined Mayfield, Clarke, and James Baldwin as leading contributors to *Freedomways*. Indeed, as we have seen, Hansberry and Childress, along with Graham Du Bois, Eslanda Robeson, and the trade unionist Vickie Garvin were all frequent contributors to the precursor of *Freedomways*, the short-lived radical Harlem newspaper, *Freedom*. In 1966, Freedomways would anticipate the Bambara anthology with a symposium by Childress, Marshall, and novelist Sarah E. Wright on "The Negro Woman in American Literature." The contributors criticized the pervasiveness of stereotyped images of black women in U.S. popular culture, protested black male militants' accusations of matriarchal domination, and regarded such misrepresentation as a stimulus to literary production by and for black women.[15] As members of the Cultural Association for Women of African Heritage, the jazz vocalist Abbey Lincoln, Maya Angelou, and Rosa Guy participated with others, including men, in the demonstration at the United Nations against its role in the assassination of

Patrice Lumumba, the revolutionary pan-Africanist and deposed prime minister of the independent Congo.[16]

One important, though neglected, aspect of the transformative significance of Ghana and African liberation movements for black identity is the extent to which black feminist consciousness was shaped by the expatriate experience. During the early 1960s, Ghana and Mali hosted international conferences on the status of women of Africa and African descent. It was axiomatic for many of the expatriate women in Ghana and their radical counterparts back in the United States that gender equality was integral to their revolutionary agenda. Such ideology was tested, and ultimately reinforced, by the profoundly gendered nature of the expatriate experience in Africa, which provided something of an answer to the speculative interest evidenced in Hansberry and Marshall's writings. In Africa, solidarity between black men and women of the diaspora was put to the test by the contrasting experiences of male sexual adventurism and obstacles to Western women's expectations of independence rooted in African custom and tradition. This confrontation between feminist ideals and patriarchal realities contributed in part to several women expatriates' early formulations of black feminist critique by the decade's end. Indeed, black women's engagement with these questions compelled African American male expatriates to reflect on the implications of these differently gendered experiences. Actor and novelist Julian Mayfield, who lived in Ghana from 1961 to 1965, noted in an unpublished memoir that African American women enjoyed an advantage in gaining access to the higher echelons of Ghanaian politics, an access unavailable to most African American men. He also confessed that men like himself would visit the residence shared by women expatriates Angelou, Garvin, and Alice Windom for home cooking, which invariably would be served with a scathing critique of their sexual exploitation of Ghanaian women.[17]

In a lengthy analysis of the Ghana coup of February 1966, contained in a letter to Mayfield, Sylvia Ardyn Boone identified sexism and the exclusion of black women from leadership as the downfall of black progressive movements. Interestingly, Boone exempted the late Malcolm X from her indictment, identifying him as the only leader who in her view granted black women equal status in his fledgling Organization of Afro-American Unity.[18] The Ghana expatriates were unique for their gender diversity and egalitarianism, which emerged out of their vision of racial solidarity. In 1970, having returned to the United States after extensive field research throughout West Africa, Boone, later a professor of art history and the first black woman tenured at Yale, convened a pathbreaking conference at Yale on "The Black Woman," at which fellow Ghana expatriates Angelou and Graham Du Bois spoke, along with John Henrik Clarke. Gwendolyn Brooks participated as well by reading from her work, as well as from the works of several other young black women poets. Further illustrating the inseparability of black feminism from the movement, the conference included declarations of support for Angela Davis, then imprisoned on conspiracy charges of which she would eventually be acquitted.[19]

Boone's conference at Yale was no isolated phenomenon. Toni Cade Bambara described numerous workshops and study groups among black women in the late 1960s, many of them based in the New York area, at which black feminist working papers were circulated and discussed. The journals *Liberator* and *The Black Scholar,* both dedicated to radical internationalism, had begun publishing articles by black women intellectuals addressing gender politics. Alice Walker had attracted notice with her story "Diary of an African Nun," which appeared in *Freedomways* in 1968. *Essence* magazine appeared in the early 1970s in the wake of several failed magazine ventures focusing on black women's concerns. Women writers and poets, including Angelou, Audre Lorde, Sonia Sanchez, Nikki Giovanni, June Jordan, Jayne Cortez, and others were prominent within the Black Arts movement. Indeed, given the continuities discernable in the genealogy of black feminism, despite the rupture in black consciousness asserted and imposed by Black Power, one might argue that these writers were as integral to the Black Arts movement as their antecedents Brooks, Hansberry, Marshall, and Childress were to their literary context and the discourse of black studies.[20] There were also institutions at which an extraordinary confluence of intellectuals had a generative impact. In 1967, for example, June Jordan, Bambara, Barbara Christian, Addison Gayle, Audre Lorde, and Adrienne Rich taught together at City College of New York. Finally, the feminist journal *Conditions* devoted an entire issue to black lesbian writing in 1975.[21]

Although primarily devoted to nonfiction essays, Bambara's *The Black Woman* documents this moment of black women's intellectual production, as well as its antecedents. Bambara had conceived of the volume as an inexpensive, mass market paperback edition, with the clear intention that it serve as contribution to the struggle and prove to the publishing industry that a market for such work existed.[22] The commercial success and wide distribution of the anthology complicates the belief that black feminism occupied a marginal or sectarian relationship to the black movement. The volume collected essays by Student Nonviolent Coordinating Committee (SNCC) activists (including an essay by Joanne Grant on SNCC's unsung leader, Ella Baker), graduates of City College, and several members of an outreach program devised by Mina Shaughnessy of City College to prepare working-class students of color to pass the City University system's entrance exams. Under Bambara's editorial guidance (she also contributed an introduction and three essays to the volume), *The Black Woman* contains pointed critiques of patriarchal articulations of black militancy. But in retrospect it was also part of that vast literature of the Black Power era whose purpose was to define the future objectives, strategies, and agendas of the black freedom movement. As such, Bambara's *The Black Woman* is an enduring work that can be read alongside Martin Luther King Jr.'s aptly titled *Where Do We Go from Here: Chaos or Community?* (1966). Indeed, in revolutionary commitment and analytical rigor, *The Black Woman* surpasses such influential texts as Harold Cruse's *Crisis of the Negro Intellectual* (1968) and Stokely Carmichael's (Kwame Turé's) *Black Power* (1967).

The black feminism generally on view in Bambara's essays and throughout the volume is informed by the revolutionary nationalism that looked to Third World liberation movements for inspiration. Bambara noted that members of black women's study groups "have begun correspondence with sisters in Vietnam, Guatemala, Algeria, [and] Ghana on the Liberation struggle and the Woman plank."[23] This radical internationalism represented the commitment on the part of Bambara and many of her contributors to frame their analyses of patriarchy within their anti-imperialist, antiracist, and anticapitalist arguments. In fact, several contributors produced critiques of the romantic, adventurist version of internationalism deployed by black male militants who sought to restrict the role of black women to "having babies for the revolution," in the parlance of that era. As if to anticipate a wider audience than movement activists, the volume includes essays that, as Farah Griffin has observed, convey a more traditional gender politics of protection and respectability.[24] There is even an essay, "The Black Revolution in America," by Grace Lee Boggs, the Detroit-based Chinese American (though black by persuasion) activist, which takes an exclusive focus on the black movement, with virtually nothing to say of gender politics.[25]

Ideological diversity notwithstanding, Bambara's project seeks to redefine internationalism, as well as "the struggle," in more egalitarian democratic terms. Like most revolutionary nationalists of the period, Bambara and others drew on Fanon, but for the specific purpose of demonstrating how revolutionary movements fostered the abandonment of traditional gender roles for more equitable gender relations. In her characteristically witty and streetwise prose (reminiscent of the vernacular eloquence of Childress, Langston Hughes, or Malcolm X) Bambara posed a challenge to self-styled black militants:

> We'd better take the time to fashion revolutionary selves, revolutionary lives, revolutionary relationships. Mouth don't win the war. It don't even win the people. Neither does haste . . . Not all speed is movement. Running off to mimeograph a fuck whitey leaflet, leaving your mate to brood, is not revolutionary. Hopping a plane to rap to someone else's "community" while your son struggles with the Junior Scholastic assignment on the "Dark Continent" is not revolutionary. Sitting around murder-mouthing incorrect niggers while your father goes upside your mother's head is not revolutionary. Mapping out a building takeover when your term paper is overdue and your scholarship is under review is not revolutionary. . . . If your house ain't in order, you ain't in order. It is so much easier to be out there than right here. The revolution ain't out there. Yet. But it is here. Should be.[26]

In a similar vein, Francee Covington's essay "Are the Revolutionary Techniques Employed in the Battle of Algiers Applicable to Harlem?" was a critique of the then fashionable concept of armed struggle. For Covington, the answer to the question posed by the title of her essay was emphatically negative. Reading Mao and Fanon on violence did not make one a revolutionary, and it did not take much reflection to realize that the application of urban guerilla tactics to U.S. cities was suicidally unfeasible.[27] Elsewhere, in a sophisticated analysis of the commodification of militancy, Joyce Green pointed out the limitations of the hypermasculinity of some black men as merely so much posturing. "The reality is that the 'man, the honkie, the pig' cannot be destroyed by quoting Mao or by a Harlem riot. In fact, these steps are insurance policies for the status quo."[28] Not only did such black macho grandstanding titilate white television audiences, it aggravated tensions between black men and women in its refusal to tolerate much-needed internal criticism.

But while *The Black Woman* sought to cool the revolutionary ardor of some militants (and in this connection the absence of members of the Black Panther Party as contributors is telling), many of its contributors pursued an analysis that linked local and global issues. This was in keeping with Bambara's concept of revolution encompassing, if not originating with, one's intimate relationships. The activist Maude White Katz prefaced her critique of institutional racism in New York public schools by identifying herself as part of a "revolutionary change [that] has taken place in the minds of Black parents." Rejecting resignation and accommodation to the status quo, these politicized black parents "may not know all the facts about their history, but since Lumumba, Nkrumah, and others, they know they have a history."[29] In what has become a classic essay, Frances Beal linked the economic exploitation of black and Puerto Rican women workers to imperialist oppression overseas, condemning the ILGWU for its investments in apartheid South Africa. Beal also decried the forced sterilization of Third World women justified as a means of population control.[30]

While Black Power advocates espoused a regressive domestic (U.S.-based) nationalism that prescribed patriarchy as the solution to the supposed problems of "emasculation" and "black matriarchy," contributors to *The Black Woman* offered both a critique of this false militancy and a substantive revolutionary vision like Katz's, whose internationalism was enacted through the work of strengthening local black communities. This project included an exploration of the ethics of human interaction among black people, as seen in "The Kitchen Crisis," Verta Mae Smart-Grosvenor's humorous but deadly serious meditation on the decline of the cultural tradition of kitchen hospitality among African Americans and other ostensibly progressive people: "In most other cultures when you enter a persons home you and the host share a moment together by partaking of something. rapscallions love to talk about culture but their actions prove they ain't got none. they don't understand that it is about more than the coffee tea or drink of water. its about extending yourself. So watch out for rapscallions. they'll mess up your kitchen vibes. PROTECT YOUR KITCHEN."[31] By exhorting her readers to protect their kitchens from ungracious and selfish "rap-scallions" who refuse offers of hospitality because they themselves don't want to incur the obligation to reciprocate, Smart-Grosvenor refigures the proverbially domestic space of the kitchen as a site of community, affirmation, and solidarity. In doing so, she reinforces the anthology's theme of revolution as a way of being in the world, an approach to everyday life, and an ethical ideal governing inter-personal relationships.

Black feminist writing, as presented in *The Black Woman,* was undoubtedly a reaction to the masculinist cultural nationalism of Black Power. But it is also important to regard it as an autonomous project that predates Black Power and is continuous with the writings of Brooks, Childress, Hansberry, and others. Certainly black feminist writing was autonomous as it involved the creative writer's inevitable quest for inspiration, technique, and original subject matter. But these black women writers were part of intellectual and activist communities whose radical democratic projects also provided a haven for their early formulations of black feminist discourse. Audre Lorde acknowledged the impact of the Harlem Writers' Group on her artistic development in a letter to fellow writer Julian Mayfield: "Because my [contact] with the Harlem Writers' in 1949–1951 was the first hint for me as a writer that I was not alone, . . . I owe more than I can say here, as Black woman and writer, to the encouragement, stimulation and insights gathered in those meetings through the lean years; I shall always feel a debt of gratitude and appreciation to you, . . . to Rosa Guy, and to John Henrik Clarke."[32] Later, black feminism was certainly shaped by gender conflict within the black freedom movement and racial tensions within the women's liberation movement. That said, black feminism does not owe its existence to these conflicts. There is ample evidence that black women writers were refining their craft long before the appearance of the Moynihan report and the rise of Black Power. The institutional contexts for black women writers' literary production were varied, but their common thread was a political culture of black radicalism informed by an internationalism that conjoined the democratic aspirations of black Americans to the liberation movements of African and Third World peoples. This internationalism provided the context for an explicit black feminism that sought to cool the angry, inflammatory, and divisive militancy of the late 1960s with its commitment to critical reflection. This version of black feminism promoted an ideal of egalitarian interpersonal relationships as the core element of democratic practice—of what it meant, ultimately, to be a revolutionary. As historians continue to assess the legacy of Black Power, Toni Cade Bambara's *The Black Woman* will be recognized as being among the most valuable and influential contributions of that period.

NOTES

I wish to thank the editors of this volume, as well as Barbara Ransby, Diana Linden, Mary Helen Washington, and Penny Von Eschen, for their criticisms, suggestions, and encouragement.

1 See, for example, You-Me Park and Gayle Wald, "Native Daughters in the Promised Land," *American Literature* 70, no. 3 (September 1998): 607–33; E. Frances White, "Africa on My Mind: Gender, Counter Discourse, and African-American Nationalism," *Journal of Women's History* 2 (1990): 73–97; Ann du Cille, *Skin Trade* (Cambridge: Harvard University Press, 1996); Gloria T. Hull, ed., *All the Women Are White, All the Blacks Are Men, but Some of Us Are Brave* (Old Westbury, Conn.: Feminist Press, 1982); Rosalyn Terborg-Penn, Sharon Harley, and Andrea Benton-Rushing, eds., *Women in Africa and the African Diaspora* (Washington, D.C.: Howard Univer-

sity Press, 1987); and Patricia Hill Collins, *Black Feminist Thought: Knowledge, Consciousness, and the Politics of Empowerment* (Boston: Unwin & Hyman, 1990). One of the outcomes of this intervention has been the increased attention to gender and sexuality within the field of African American history. See Michele Mitchell, "Silences Broken, Silences Kept: Gender and Sexuality in African American History," *Gender and History* 11, no. 3 (November 1999): 433–44.

2 The term "womanist" as an alternative to "feminist" was popularized by Alice Walker in *In Search of Our Mothers' Gardens: Womanist Prose* (San Diego: Harcourt Brace Jovanovich, 1983). For recent discussion of this question, see Patricia Hill Collins, "What's in a Name? Womanism, Black Feminism, and Beyond," *Black Scholar* 26, no. 1 (1996): 9–17.

3 Toni Cade Bambara, *The Black Woman: An Anthology* (New York: Signet Books, 1970).

4 Ella Baker and Marvel Cooke, "The Bronx Slave Market," *The Crisis* (November 1935): 330.

5 Richard Powell, *Black Art and Culture in the Twentieth Century* (New York: Thames and Hudson, 1997), 148.

6 Gwendolyn Brooks, *Maud Martha: A Novel* (Chicago: Third World Press, 1993). Subsequent citations are given parenthetically in the text.

7 In this, Brooks's text exemplifies what Deborah E. McDowell has described as "a consistent preoccupation of black female novelists" with the construction of selfhood. See McDowell, " 'The Changing Same': Generational Connections and Black Women Novelists," in Henry Louis Gates, ed., *Reading Black, Reading Feminist: A Critical Anthology* (New York: Meridian, 1990), 94.

8 Mary Helen Washington, "The Darkened Eye Restored: Notes Toward a Literary History of Black Women," in Henry Louis Gates, ed. (New York: Meridian, 1990), 35.

9 The quote comes from a review of *In the Mecca*. See William Stafford, "Books That Look Out, Books That Look In," in *On Gwendolyn Brooks: Reliant Contemplation,* ed. Stephen Caldwell Wright (Ann Arbor: University of Michigan Press, 1996), 26.

10 Alice Childress, *Like One of the Family: Conversations from a Domestic's Life* (Boston: Beacon Press, 1986). Subsequent citations are given parenthetically in the text.

11 Trudier Harris notes that the novel received only one review, in *Masses and Mainstream.* See her introduction to the novel, xxvii–xxviii.

12 Lorraine Hansberry, *A Raisin in the Sun: A Drama in Three Acts* (New York: Random House, 1959).

13 Paule Marshall, "Reena," in *The Black Woman,* ed. Bambara, 21. Subsequent citations are given parenthetically in the text.

14 Tim Tyson, *Radio Free Dixie: Robert Williams and the Roots of Black Power* (Chapel Hill: University of North Carolina Press, 1999).

15 Alice Childress, Paule Marshall, and Sarah E. Wright, "The Negro Woman in American Literature," *Freedomways,* no. 1 (1966); reprinted in Esther Cooper Jackson, ed., *The Freedomways Reader* (Boulder: Westview Press, 2000), 291–98.

16 On the Harlem Writers' Group and the Cultural Association for Women of African Descent, see Maya Angelou, *The Heart of a Woman* (New York: Vintage Books, 1996).

A brief account of AMSAC, including its demise on the disclosure that it received covert funding from the CIA, is in John A. Davis, "Black Americans and United States Policy Toward Africa," *Journal of International Affairs* (1970): 236–49.

17 These issues will be further explored in my forthcoming book, *Black Expatriates in Nkrumah's Ghana* (Chapel Hill: University of North Carolina Press, forthcoming).

18 Sylvia Ardyn Boone to Julian Mayfield, March 26, 1966, Julian Mayfield papers, Schomburg Center for Research in Black Culture, New York Public Library.

19 Thomas A. Johnson, "Yale Conference Studies Role of Black Woman," *New York Times,* December 14, 1970; Bettina Aptheker, *The Morning Breaks: The Trial of Angela Davis* (Ithaca: Cornell University Press, 1999). See also Angela Davis, *Angela Davis: An Autobiography* (New York: Random House, 1974).

20 Indeed, Houston A. Baker Jr. makes a convincing case for Sonia Sanchez as an exemplary poet of what he calls the Black Renaissance, a mode of expression rooted in the black vernacular and liberated from the assimilationist assumptions of the so-called Harlem Renaissance. The point here is that Baker regards Sanchez as central to the Black Arts movement rather than occupying a quite different position of internal dissent. See Baker, "Our Lady: Sonia Sanchez and the Writing of a Black Renaissance," in *Reading Black, Reading Feminist,* ed. Gates, 318–47.

21 June Jordan describes the intellectual and political circles at City College in the interview with Peter Erickson, "After Identity: A Conversation with June Jordan," *Transition* 63 (1994): 140.

22 Farah Jasmine Griffin, "Conflict and Chorus: Reconsidering Toni Cade's *The Black Woman: An Anthology,*" in *Is It Nation Time? Critical Essays on Black Power and Black Nationalism,* ed. Eddie Glaude Jr. (Chicago: University of Chicago Press, 2002).

23 Bambara, *The Black Woman,* 10.

24 Griffin, "Conflict and Chorus." See also Farah Jasmine Griffin, "Toni Cade Bambara: Free to Be Anywhere in the Universe," *Callaloo* 19, no. 2 (spring 1996): 228–31.

25 Grace Lee Boggs, "The Black Revolution in America," in *The Black Woman,* ed. Bambara, 211–23.

26 Toni Cade Bambara, "On the Issue of Roles," in *The Black Woman,* ed. Bambara, 110.

27 Francee Covington, "Are the Revolutionary Techniques Employed in the Battle of Algiers Applicable to Harlem?" in *The Black Woman,* ed. Bambara, 244–51.

28 Joyce Green, "Black Romanticism," in *The Black Woman,* ed. Bambara, 137–42.

29 Maude White Katz, "End Racism in Education: A Concerned Parent Speaks," in *The Black Woman,* ed. Bambara, 124.

30 Frances Beal, "Double Jeopardy: To Be Black and Female," in *The Black Woman,* ed. Bambara, 94–95. See also Angela Davis, "Racism, Birth Control, and Reproductive Rights," in *Women, Race, and Class* (New York: Vintage Press, 1983), 202–21.

31 Verta Mae Smart-Grosvenor, "The Kitchen Crisis," in *The Black Woman,* ed. Bambara, 123.

32 Audre Lorde to Julian Mayfield, August 25, 1968, in the John Henrik Clarke Papers, folder marked "Julian Mayfield Correspondence," Schomburg Center for Research in Black Culture, New York Public Library. Lorde would remember the black literary

ferment of the 1960s with much more ambivalence: "If we talk about black poetry in the '60s, there was no room for black lesbian and gay poets. The very people who were running around raving about James Baldwin were calling him a 'skinny faggot.' And they didn't want to hear things he had to say" (Kevin Powell, "A Dialogue with Audre Lorde," *Emerge* (November 1992): 23–24.

CHRISTOPHER NEWFIELD

Democratic Passions: Reconstructing
Individual Agency

◆

U.S. democracy has been driven by neoliberal economics for the past thirty years, and any discussion of democratic possibilities must begin there. Neoliberalism was spearheaded by American conservatives, but it is also the basic philosophy of the New Democrats who continue to control the Democratic party.[1] The term "neoliberalism" crosses the wandering U.S. boundary between liberal and conservative and illuminates an underlying consensus on political economy that has dominated electoral politics under both major parties. This consensus has persuaded many people that market-based economic transactions can subordinate and in many cases replace political democracy. This is because they allegedly offer the freest forms of choice in their everyday activity, where choice is defined as essentially economic.

THE MARKET IDEAL

There is almost nothing new about neoliberalism. It carries on a classical liberalism whose core features have remained stable for about two centuries. One of these core features is the ideal of the "self-regulating market." This term has been fully analyzed by economic historian Karl Polanyi. "A market economy," he wrote, "is an economic system controlled, regulated, and directed by market prices; order in the production and distribution of goods is entrusted to this self-regulating mechanism." Economic liberalism's second core feature follows directly from this, and that is that the market must remain autonomous from society and its politics: "Nothing must be allowed to inhibit the formation of markets, nor must incomes be permitted to be formed otherwise than through sales. Neither must there be any interference with the adjustment of prices to changed market conditions. . . . Neither price, nor supply, nor demand must be fixed or regulated" by government action. Polanyi noted that, for economic liberals, the state could intervene in markets only to help markets supersede the state: "Only such policies and measures are in order which help to ensure the self-regulation of the market by creating conditions which make the market the only organizing power in the economic sphere."[2]

Polanyi was describing the ideology that supported nineteenth-century industrialization in England, but it should sound familiar to anyone who has been following U.S. economic policy discussions or the globalization debates. Globalization is regularly used as a euphemism for emancipating economic activity from the societies and populations that conduct it. Again, there is nothing new about this. Polanyi claimed that the fundamental economic revolution was not an industrial but a market revolution. The market revolution meant that markets, which had been "embedded" in society for all of prior human history, had revolted against society and declared their independence. Polanyi called this a utopian project, and it is a third feature of market economies: they cannot *in fact* transcend their embeddedness in society, but instead continually aspire to this transcendence. They tirelessly arouse the population against any infringement on market self-regulation. Polanyi also elaborated a fourth core feature of market economies: they cause levels of suffering, injustice, and inequality that produce a popular backlash, whose major form in Polanyi's time was fascism.

With this background in mind, we can understand why American neoliberals have worked so hard for so long to construct their enormous and expensive apparatus for installing the market ideal in society.[3] The work is simply never done, and it is always on the verge of coming undone.[4] Self-regulating markets do not exist, cannot exist, have not existed, and will not exist. Self-regulating markets are more openly managed by concentrated corporate power than ever before. And yet the effort to get entire societies to aspire to "free markets" has dramatically shifted power from governments to markets, most triumphantly in the United States.

I agree with Polanyi and many others that the ideal of self-regulating markets is impossible, undesirable, and socially destructive. But if we are right, why is the market ideal, though slain any number of times, so undead? Why is the self-regulating market so powerful while the Left's ideal—markets embedded in democratic social relations—seems so weak?

Part of the answer is that the popularity of the market ideal is an illusion created by promarket spin control: polling data actually suggests weak public support when the "market" is described as "business" or "big companies" or "corporate money" and the like.[5] A further explanation of the power of market ideals would have many other dimensions, including the obvious wealth and related political power of the business institutions that benefit from it.

I'm going to devote this essay to looking at still another, central part of the explanation. The past and present of market ideology suggests that its popularity hinges on its ability to represent freedom. Demonstrations that markets damage social justice unless society's interests are protected through democratic intervention, although true in my view, simply fail to address the market appeal to freedom. The Left has generally (though with important exceptions) neglected to construct nonmarket models of *individual* freedom, models that work with the systems of democracy and social justice that the Left rightly cares about.[6]

I am motivated by my concern that the glaring absence of equality in U.S. life, coupled with the widespread claim that the market has delivered freedom, has muted demands for expanded forms of *social* freedom. I am interested in the widespread demoralization that accompanies procedural democracy in the United States. I am interested in the everyday feeling of powerlessness in people who are formally and technically empowered. I am interested in this experience of weak or pointless personal agency both because it feels bad, thereby limiting individual capacity, and because it prevents full "participation," thereby gutting democracy and leaving its forms. I am alarmed that democracy continues to feel and act like a burden on individuality. Most political theory accepts this as inevitable. But this means accepting the continuing decline of democracy.

In response, I am going to make two arguments. First, I will suggest how self-regulating markets damage the individual autonomy and agency they claim to protect. Second, I'll describe forms of *social* autonomy that are both the prerequisite to a fully democratic society and suppressed by self-regulating markets.

THE MARKET CLAIM TO FREEDOM

Liberal theorists have never sought democracy through the political system alone. They have regarded even the U.S. Constitution as by itself unequal to the task of sustaining a social order. Liberalism has not settled for the "constituted" power of the state, or for the "constituent" strength of the democratic masses, or for some combination of the two.[7] It has also invoked the market as a necessary arena of democratic self-regulation and of freedom. The success of liberal thought in Western societies can be measured by the currency of the belief that political activity sustains social order through its interaction with market activity.

In keeping with the tradition of economic liberalism, neoliberalism formulates the centrality of markets through a pair of equations. The first equates deregulated commercial markets with political democracy. For example, Francis Fukuyama's emblematic essay, "The End of History and the Last Man," attributed the end of the cold war to the spreading belief that "free markets" were the same as "representative democracy."[8] Fukuyama was consolidating an already common view of market deregulation as enhancing the economic power of ordinary people. For example, airline deregulation has long been credited with lowering prices and increasing the access of ordinary Americans to air travel; its main architect, Cornell economist Alfred Kahn, has been described as a latter-day Jefferson—"the father of cheap airfares."[9] Such views build on at least a century of developments in marketing, advertizing, and kindred fields that have defined the United States as the world's most advanced "consumer society." Consumption is widely regarded as something like democratic choice. Business's devotion to sales is seen as devotion to popular demand. Economic policy is one long "kitchen debate" that defines development much like Richard Nixon's praise of American capitalism to Nikita Khrushchev on the grounds of its labor-saving household appliances. The United States is not a social democracy but rather a market democracy and a consumer democracy. As a result, most U.S. political leaders now assume that markets are better than government at perceiving demand, better at designing the service, better at building the product, better at customer delivery, and better at responding to feedback.[10] Under neoliberalism, markets have successfully put this question to governments: What aspect of democracy—meaning responding to the everyday needs of ordinary citizens—can *you* do better than *we* do?

Neoliberalism's second equation claims that markets promote individual freedom. It defines the "freedom to choose" as market choice—the choice of goods to consume, the choice of means of production. Individual agency may be small in market practice, but it is a giant in market theory. Thirty years of conservative calls to "get the government off our backs" have forged powerful associations between the ideal of self-regulating markets and the always popular vision of individual liberty. Neoliberalism borrows a language of popular economic revolt against political tyranny, a language that in the United States harkens back at least to the Boston Tea Party, in which ordinary, enterprising citizens fight the economic coercion of a regulative government. In the 1990s, conservatives were joined by market liberals like Bill Clinton, Tom Peters, and most of the mainstream media in accepting the view that markets were both the most efficient medium of transmitting economic information *and* the natural ally of human creativity.[11]

Although its causes are complex, the outcome is clear: by the early 1990s the market had become the friend not of the plutocrat and monopolist but of the citizen and employee. Peters confessed, "I love markets. I admit it. I love radical decentralization. I am an enemy of elaborate plans. An ally of hasty action. An enemy of excessive order. A friend of disorderly trial and error—especially error."[12] What kind of an economy encourages professional consultants to confess *love* for markets? One that has managed to equate markets with freedom, with the feeling of one's own unlimited possibilities, with a belief in action without government's fixed determinations. This market liberates individuals from capitalist discipline, the better to liberate capitalism itself. Mediterranean societies, Peters continued, "were the first, according to Hayek, to accept 'a person's rights to dispose [of property], thus allowing individuals to develop a dense network of commercial relations.' . . . The right to dispose of one's assets provides the basis for dealing with—or not dealing with—others of one's choosing."[13] For neoliberalism, markets transform the raw material of private property into the material and spiritual reality of personal freedom. Hayek's history rests on the same idealization that produces Peters's love, but that only enhances its psychological appeal.

Liberty has always been liberalism's ace in the hole, and neoliberal arguments have carried on the tradition. Ideological success always depends on laying out a positive ideal effect that will draw people in spite of their misgivings about your program. People are more likely to accept your cuts in Medicare payments, for example, if you tie them to expanding the freedom to choose physicians. Another ingredient of ideological success is removing your ideal from the zone of debate. You will have trouble if your enemy attacks your ideal in the name of their better version of it. It is better for you if you can get your enemy to ignore your ideal and fail to claim it for themselves.

Neoliberalism owes some of its success to the Left's tendency to make this tactical mistake. Market critics have tended to target neoliberalism's first equation and have found that markets are often undemocratic and damage basic equity and equality. These arguments are extremely important, but they are simply beside the point of the second equation of markets with freedom. Showing that markets damage equality and direct political participation, the classical components of democratic states, does not amount to showing that markets damage liberty. To make matters worse, market critics actually *reinforce* the massively popular neoliberal equation of markets and liberty when they criticize individualism as a market ideal or equate individual rights with neoliberalism.[14]

An example of how the Left tacitly enforces the link between personal freedom and markets is its polarization of the positions of sociologists Anthony Giddens and Pierre Bourdieu. At one time they adhered to similar versions of democratic socialism. Giddens now celebrates "the new individualism," the stress on "self-fulfillment, the fulfillment of potential," as part of his "Third Way" acceptance of market mechanisms. Bourdieu, by contrast, rejects market-based governance. He calls instead for "a social order which would not have as its sole law the pursuit of egoistical interests and the individual lust for profit, and which will find a place for collectives oriented towards the *rational pursuit of collectively elaborated and approved goals.*"[15] Bourdieu's rejection of market governance involves the rejection of individualism as irrational selfishness that destroys social justice.

But must Bourdieu yoke the term "individual" to the term "lust for profit"? Is self-fulfillment really dependent on egoistical interests and exploitation? Aren't there ways of fulfilling individual potential that are democratic rather than market-based, that in fact make democracy possible and meaningful? Don't we in fact need self-fulfilled citizens to do valid collective planning, and valid collective planning to support self-fulfillment? Perhaps Bourdieu would say yes to these, but I can't find any evidence in his attacks on neoliberalism. I find myself in the apparently awkward position of agreeing with Bourdieu on the value of social planning and with Giddens on the value of self-fulfillment.

Neoliberal theory has worked hard to produce this polarity, which is enormously convenient for the ideal of the self-regulating market. The polarity says that liberty and democracy are fundamentally at odds. States that incline toward democracy incline toward restricting liberty, for liberty inherently leads toward antisocial egoism. That means, in a common American theme, that the defense of liberty requires the suppression of states. The most desirable default becomes the marketplace, which is said to deliver both democracy and liberty through a mechanism inherently superior to state and anarchy. If you seek Bourdieu-like control of bad market outcomes, then you must side with the state against liberty; if you seek liberty with Giddens, then you must oppose the justice-seeking state. The only winner in this argument is the ideal of the self-regulating market.

Neoliberalism has used this theme to move far down the road to political ascendancy. But it has also achieved something more. By inducing the liberal tension between liberty and equality in the heart of left-wing antimarket argumentation, it has pulled the Left off of its highest ground. The crux of leftist political insight during these recent liberal centuries has been that liberty and equality and democracy go hand in hand. You cannot have genuine liberty without equality, or equality without liberty.[16] This conceptual truth appears clearly in moments of revolution in which the masses demand democracy in the name of their own liberation. Democracy, and the equality that enables it, is sought for the sake of freedom and not order. It is only later, as Antonio Negri points out, that the masses' "constituent power," having formed a state, finds itself reduced to the form of a law.[17] In its own proper form and desire it seeks its own freedom, including the freedom to make and remake its own law. The task of a fully democratic society is to preserve the "constituent power" that seeks its own freedom. There is no genuine democracy, in other words, that does not express this collective freedom.

The market ideal succeeds for at least two reasons of strategy: it claims to represent individual liberty, and it induces its left-wing opponents to encourage this view. By installing the conflict between liberty and equality as national common sense, neoliberalism immeasurably strengthens the market ideal while discrediting the Left's vision of democracy as in conflict with freedom. Radical democrats lose political power and, all too often, commit the huge intellectual error of repressing their defining attachment to individual liberty.

MARKET DETERMINISM

It would be easier to see the connection between democracy and individual liberty if we could specify the limits of market liberty. As part of the process of forging the link between markets and freedom, neoliberalism has had to ignore or discredit the possibility that a common feature of markets is coercion or determinism. Market determinism is a version of what Raymond Williams once called "abstract determinism." By this Williams meant the experience that the economy is run by forces outside of anyone's and everyone's control.[18] "The strongest single reason for the development of abstract determinism," he wrote, "is the historical experience of large-scale capitalist economy, in which many more people than marxists concluded that control of the process was beyond them, that it was at least in practice external to their wills and desires, and that it had therefore to be seen as governed by its own 'laws.' "[19] Free choice was not, for Williams, the general experience of people in markets.

In the wake of market triumph, how do we now talk about the way markets produce this loss of control? Categorical rejection of markets as such is ineffective and wrong. "Markets," as exchanges among people, are inevitable and valuable. On the level of everyday exchange, markets provide freedom largely in the form of consumer choice. Markets make goods available by linking producers and consumers through price signals and other forms of information that keep the entire economic system in motion. Market critics can accept such propositions without feeling that they weaken our case. But choice and information are only two features of markets; they are also hierarchical and regulated structures. The freedom of the isolated purchase is a popular icon of market behavior but it does not accurately represent the overall operation of a market system.

When we assess freedom within a system it is most useful to see freedom as a function of *complexity.* For psychologist Sylvan Tomkins, complexity means "the number of independently variable states of a system. . . . The end points of degrees of freedom, or complexity, are complete redundancy in which no change is possible and complete randomness in which any change is possible."[20] Freedom does not mean the absence of prior causality, which does not exist. Freedom is not, therefore, unconditioned human intentionality. Freedom instead refers to relatively greater degrees of "independently variable states." In this account, independence is as important as variability. Freedom is directly proportional to the degree of both variability and independence within a given system.[21]

Variability is a common feature of capitalist markets, but it is not an essential feature. Variability is not the primary goal of producer behavior in capitalist markets. Profit is the primary goal. If producers can make money by reducing variability they will reduce variability. This is a frequent occurrence in business, where excessively complicated product lines get trimmed back to lower costs, or where intricate management structures are dismantled when they make decisions too hard, or where multidivisional corporations sell business units to focus on their "core competencies." Variability is also not *unique* to capitalist markets. Given the contingency that inhabits every system, variability cannot ever be avoided. Every system has some degree of variability, and this is true of planned economies. Variability can in fact be planned. There's nothing about the ignorance or disorganization of an unplanned economy that in itself increases variability; to the contrary, most actors cope with disorganization by reducing variability as much as they can. The supposedly self-regulating market should not be allowed to present itself as the unique or privileged vehicle of maximum variability.

Capitalist markets have an even harder time laying claim to independence.

This may seem counterintuitive, but that is because we inhabitants of neoliberal cultures are taught to confuse independence with competition, variability of goods, and consumer choice. Competition is usually an obligation rather than a free choice, and it takes place under specific rules and relentless pressure. Competitive performance, even when fun, rarely expresses relative independence from the system's conditions.

As for consumer choice, it is the most expensively choreographed social act in the United States. Any firm in any industry spends as much of its cash flow as it can afford to narrowing the consumer's conscious range of possibility to its own product. Recent advances in niche marketing have focused the address of particular campaigns on demographic groups as small as one person. The flashing ad in the margin of your Web browser may be seen only by you, having been generated by the cookie-trail of your previous computer purchases. The obvious goal is to hook you and not to free you up. Marketing never succeeds at eliminating independent choice, but dependence on one firm is its Platonic ideal. Market competition requires that firms seek the reduction of consumer independence. Markets cannot not present themselves as independence's special patron.

The same goes for virtually every other aspect of business life, where success requires maximum control of your environment's independent variables. The uncertain, the unknown, the uncontrolled, the truly independent are your enemies. They will steal your employees, your customers, your suppliers, your regular revenues, your profits, everything you care about. Your job is to reduce everyone's power except your own. Reduce labor's bargaining power so you can keep wages down. Increase your supplier's dependence on your business so you can control their pricing. Damage your competitor's leverage with a new product by flooding the market with your imitation. Reduce the visibility of their brand by saturating the airwaves with yours. Increase the price of electricity by artificially reducing its supply; time your reductions for maximum effect by, for example, taking a plant offline in the middle of a heat wave.[22] Such lists could go on for hundreds of pages. They illustrate ordinary, everyday market calculation. The general goal of this calculation is to protect your position by minimizing the independence of everyone and everything else.

A similar pattern dominates the life cycle of firms. Apostles of the "new economy" trumpet a "free agent nation" and the creative small companies that markets fertilize like weeds. In reality, these companies exist to be mown down. Few independent companies can survive on their own, and the ones that do are generally in quieter, lower-margin industries. The general rule of industry is consolidation. The small are squeezed by the large in every category—supplier relations, marketing, economies of scale, distribution networks, you name it. The small are bought, or grow big, or die. There's little room for small-scale independence. "Be first or second in every industry," said influential General Electric chairman Jack Welch, who forced his divisions into the forefront or sold them off.

An identical pattern marks globalization, in which "free trade" produces increasing levels of dependence on foreign capital in "developing nations." Wealthy nations make market rules from their position of superior market power, and these relations often amount to a neocolonial authority over the poorer region or country. Again, this restriction on the poorer country's options is not an accident but is the deliberate aim of neoliberal policy. When the policy is thwarted, Western wrath is instantaneous. In 1998, Malaysian Prime Minister Mahathir Mohamad responded to capital flight by instituting, among other things, a tax on investment returns that favored investors who left their money in place for at least one year. "Essentially, you've got a Government that makes its own rules," one fund manager exclaimed indignantly.[23] Investors earn far more money by making rules for others, rules that may be procedurally fair but clearly favor one party or position. Market success routinely involves reducing the independence of variables, which means relentless and effective attacks on others' independence.

Markets, of course, do not *intrinsically* require dependence any more than they guarantee freedom: like any system, they offer a mixture of both. The mixture is what the strong defense of markets denies.[24] It is certainly true that markets offer freedom to people in the right market position. The right position is usually a compound of access to capital, brand visibility, social status, product advantage, good timing, and other network effects of competitive advantage. Freedom follows from a superior position. It is not a *general* ability of people in markets but is contingent on unusual wealth or institutional power—on executive status in a large corporation, on distinctive professional status, on banking connections from a previous job, on unique product design, and so on. Markets offer certain individuals *contingent* freedom: the individual's effective freedom is contingent on her advantageous position in the market.[25]

For both firms and individuals, the struggle for market success is the struggle to be the *exception* to market norms of dependence on general determinants. The weakness or absence of popular economic control is the heart of the neoliberal defense of markets over governments. Government, they say, introduces distortion into market mechanisms because it reflects the attempts of various actors to steer markets their way. Neoliberals praise markets precisely for ignoring the will of individuals as expressed through government; this is the basis of their supposed impartiality. Neoliberals trace wealth to the market's indifference to individual will and poverty to the "political" control of markets. The next step on this road is also familiar: neoliberals define unregulated markets as equivalent to democratization. This is a startling claim, but it is professional economic orthodoxy that can be read every day in major newspapers.[26] Markets deliver "economic democracy" by keeping political democracy out of economics. The absence of popular power over market mechanisms is, for neoliberals, what makes markets work.

Although market deregulation proceeds in the name of more individual opportunity, it in fact turns previously guaranteed choices into contingent ones. For example, many firms have replaced "defined benefit" pensions, which pay out according to a set formula, with "defined contribution" pensions, in which individuals pay into a fund whose outputs depend on its fortunes in the market. This increases the freedom of movement of one's pension's market value but it decreases one's own autonomy from market movements. Deregulation increases the market's deterministic power over individuals, whether or not the individual benefits financially. Fixed, formulaic pensions sheltered the individual from the market, which meant shelter from the wills of vastly more powerful market actors like corporate boards and pension fund managers. Fixed pensions offered an increasingly rare freedom of choice within the pension's limits. Deregulation has meant that many benefits of citizenship, assured in the political sphere, have been redefined as returns on competitive investment, won in the economic sphere. An "entitlement," after all, offered an individual right, and that right defined a scope of free operation. Markets eliminate these rights and their contractual freedoms.

Market freedom is contingent on market position; different positions offer their inhabitants very different possibilities for controlling markets. The *majority* experiences their contingent freedom as insufficient power to control markets, as weak and fitful freedom, as market determinism. Although market movements are shaped by elaborate webs of law and policy, and although these laws can be changed, market theory withholds the power of change from ordinary actors. The minority possibility of changing markets by pulling strings in remote, invisible, and superior locations does not ease the majority experience of determinism on the ground. Once again, this is not an unfortunate by-product of self-regulating markets, but rather is their stated goal: market ideals reject mass control of economies, which must take place in the political realm, and revere minority control of economies by those who, having passed "market tests," have acquired concentrated power.

Neoliberal market theory is hostile to economic democracy, so much so that it overrides a central liberal political value. Liberalism has always opposed contingent freedom in the political sphere on the grounds that freedom is an individual right held by the individual regardless of her particular social situation (wealth, race, creed, color, sexual orientation, national origin). Such guarantees actually increase the complexity of the political system by increasing independence and potential variability. Yet liberals routinely defend contingent freedom in markets, where one's capacity is directly dependent on one's market situation. Although countless stories and studies show that people with different economic resources have very different life chances, neoliberals still claim that individual freedom is either unaffected by one's market position or is affected only in justifiable ways. Neoliberals, in short, are in the conflicted position of advocating uniform freedom in law and politics while defending contingent freedom in the economy.

Given these features of markets, there's no reason why the Left should concede any part of the neoliberal claim that markets generally sponsor a freedom that states and publics do not. To the contrary, the market, unmodified by society, reduces the systemic complexity and suppresses the personal agency that underlines liberty and democracy alike.

COMPROMISED AGENCY

The current state of democratic theory offers further evidence that the market ideal has damaged our models of strong individual agency. Market critics generally insist that markets are embedded in society and must respond to its patterns and needs. But they proceed with a notion of weak agency that keeps the market in a dominant place.

A lucid example of this thinking appears in the work of political theorist Michael Walzer. Liberalism means at least two things for Walzer. First, the market would be more fair were it "to be set firmly within civil society, politically constrained, open to communal as well as private initiatives."[27] In a move destined to appall market conservatives, Walzer declares the need "to socialize the economy so that there is a greater diversity of market agents, communal as well as private."[28] Having reconnected liberalism to its twentieth-century alliance with social democracy, Walzer suggests that liberalism means a second thing: these social and political constraints cannot act as straightforward controls. Rather than *explicitly* weakening the political constraints he has just placed on the market, Walzer describes the weakening as the inevitable multiplicity of complex systems. Liberalism, in its second and fundamental meaning, involves the advocacy of multiple determinations against the allegedly singleminded claims of politics, labor, nations, and even markets (as interpreted by conservatives).

Walzer is right about the inevitability of multiple determinations, and he is also right about the need for political constraints on markets. Like markets, "civil society, left to itself, generates radically unequal power relationships, which only state power can challenge." The continuous danger of inequality means that "across the entire range of association, individual men and women need to be protected against the power of officials, employers, experts, party bosses, factory supervisors, directors, priests, parents, patrons; and small and weak groups need to be protected against large and powerful ones." "Only a democratic state," Walzer concludes, "can create a democratic civil society."[29] Walzer adds that "only a democratic civil society can sustain a democratic state." Civil society can keep the state democratic only if it is democratic itself. "A democratic civil society," he writes, "is one controlled by its members, not through a single process of self-determination but through a large number of different and uncoordinated processes."[30]

Democracy means control, control exercised by a state but held by society's members. But since this control must operate in complex systems, it cannot be thought of in traditional ways. The sheer fact of multiplicity, Walzer writes, requires that we give up "Rousseauian self-determination" and "creativity in the Marxist sense," for each rests on monistic demands that are no longer viable.[31] Direct self-governance, "political community," and "cooperative economy" have been made impossible not by bad political choices or deregulated capitalism or timid liberalism but by the sheer complexity of modern societies. The complexity of modern society means that we must give up the standpoints that have historically sought to control multiply determined outcomes. Walzer proposes that we replace these with "critical associationism," which stresses inclusiveness rather than individual heroism. "Associational engagement" involves a "large number of different and uncoordinated processes. These need not all be democratic. . . . Civil society is sufficiently democratic when in some, at least, of its parts we are able to recognize ourselves as authoritative and responsible participants."[32]

By this point, Walzer has gotten himself into an awkward spot. He rightly insists that democracy involves collective political control via multiple processes. Yet the normal individual experience is to have little or no control at all. It is especially likely that the citizen will lack control in the exact moments when she really needs it—when control has been amassed elsewhere and against her interests. Since citizen control gets overwhelmed by the "large number of different and uncoordinated processes," it is also likely that control will migrate to the state, a state that, in Walzer's model, continues to stand apart from and—implicitly—above civil society. In their associations, citizens will not experience control so much as "inclusion" or "participation"—the latter being the biggest fudge word in political theory because it can mean anything from direct control to representative democracy to being consulted on a decision one cannot affect. In effect, Walzer argues that democracy means retaining control *and* giving up control. He uses the fact of complexity to redefine democracy as the retention of a control over marketlike systems that citizens in fact do not retain.

One response to this objection is "so what?" Walzer seems to be describing the mixture of freedom and determinism that marks every system and every experience of agency. Democratic control within a complex system would plausibly involve this mixture. All this means is the truism that everyone has agency sometimes and some places and not others, and in a complex system we can't expect more. Just because we don't control final outcomes doesn't mean we lack power and agency, this argument goes. It is childish to confuse limited agency with agency's destruction. This follows from the fact that we cannot define individual agency as the direct, linear, absolute control of outcomes in a group or polity.

This last claim is correct, but it ignores an important thing that the child knows. His interests are damaged by the context of low expectations for direct agency. In this context, *any* concession to multiple or shared agency is likely to lead to his *loss* of agency. The child would like his agency *transmitted* or relayed to the next step in decision making. The child would like at least partial control over the outcome of the process—perhaps some kind of power sharing or turn-taking. The parent chooses to interpret the child as wanting everything his way. The parent, in other words, interprets the demand for direct—and shared—control as a demand for complete control. This interpretation is convenient for the parent because it helps him rule unilaterally. The child's insistence is intensified from previous experiences of having his complaints about insufficient power rejected as excessive, illegitimate, even dictatorial. He knows he has much less power than the parent, for he lives as a small person in a land of giants. He knows that the parental system has the power to define his desire for power-sharing as a desire for everything, a desire that can safely be righteously denied.

The citizen is usually in a similar situation. She is generally as aware as Walzer of the multiplicity and complexity of the social systems in which she finds herself. Her interest is to acknowledge real complexity *and* preserve her agency within it. Preserving agency does not mean single-step processes or single-handed authority over the outcome. The citizen *does* ask that her agency be transmitted rather than contained. She will experience herself as having agency to the extent that it enters the collective domain intact—that is, without being rewritten, denied, or turned back. She does accept the dilution of her agency that results from the numbers of her collaborators and the intricacy of their relations. She may get frustrated, but *complexity* in itself does not in itself lead to the feelings she wants to avoid, the feelings of having her agency negated or overridden. These feelings of powerlessness come when her inputs are rejected, deformed, and blocked on their way through the complex process.

The citizen experiences this blockage as the result of the interplay of two elements. The first is inequality. The citizen of a complex system, like the child, also lives in a land of giants: her sphere is not simply local, for it is also smaller and politically inferior to those that make the final decisions. Sheer multiplicity does not erode individual agency; *inequality* does. Multiply determined complex systems spoil agency when they take hierarchical forms in which some domains count more than others. Liberal and Left thinkers—Walzer included—try to be sensitive to the problem of inequality. They note that markets and corporations each perpetuate radically unequal microsystems and that the market language reciprocity and fluidity should not be allowed to veil the unequal status of market actors.

Agency is also impaired by a subjective factor—the experience of individual powerlessness. Various schemes to equalize parts of a system may help, as in Walzer's plan for the state monitoring of markets. But they will help only if they try to address individual feelings of blocked agency. Remedies work only if they take this experience seriously, if they take seriously the desire that one's agency not be blocked *either* by inequality *or* by sheer complexity. Whatever the cause, the citizen's capacity is diminished by the experience of blockage. Procedures and domains can approach equality but will not be democratic unless the individual citizen is in the psychological position to take advantage of them. That means that the citizen has a consistent experience of unblocked agency as the basis for his or her public action.

Walzer is aware of the damage inequality can do. But he also tries to reconcile citizens to the fitful, partial, and short-range agency that was inequality's bad outcome in the first place. Walzer sidesteps the real issue, which is not *only* to choose multiple over single determinations, and not *only* to choose egalitarian over hierarchical types of multiply determined systems, but to choose transmitted over dispersed individual agency *within* complex systems.

The stakes here are large. If Walzer's form of short-range, intermittent agency is good enough liberty and democracy, then we can get all we need of both from market systems partially stabilized by the state. Market governance has been advanced through the ideal of the self-regulating market, but is also advanced by liberalism's melancholic sense that modern complexity means citizens must give up the desire for control. It is fairly easy to suggest that complexity makes individual agency difficult. It is much harder to address the questions on the table for those who are not content with market governance. How does individual agency survive and thrive in group complexity? If we can't come up with good answers to these questions, democracy will continue to lose out to markets.

UNBURDENED AGENCY

Nonmarket democracy is democracy that operates independently of self-regulated (stratified, heavily managed) markets. This democracy has at least two major elements. The first is procedural equality across the whole mix of social terrains. I plan to talk about a psychological measure of nonmarket democracy that I believe is more basic, but procedural equality is important. Great benefits follow from the real implementation of the liberal ideals of due process and equality under the law. The ideal of procedural equality appears under a variety of names: in addition to due process in the law, market actors seek "transparency" of information when they make investments; markets rest their claims for efficiency on the basis of every actor making his or her decisions on the basis of identical knowledge. Allegedly efficient markets are themselves dependent on state-sponsored forms of procedural equality, and so is virtually every form of justice. It should also be noted that procedural equality depends on good bureaucratic administration.[33] The subjective elements I am more interested in cannot "scale up" to a municipal or national level without the dense networks of regulations that often affront individuality while being crucial to any kind of equal treatment.

One of liberalism's historical weaknesses is its tendency to describe certain inconsistencies in its ideal of due process as tolerable and necessary. Walzer follows in these footsteps by asking us to accept many undemocratic steps in complex governance. An even more serious liberal flaw is its elevation of equal treatment over equal outcomes. When the two are in conflict liberals generally side with regularized process rather than equitable impact. For example, liberals have generally been unwilling to defend affirmative action as a "quota system" that produces racial proportions settled by democratic deliberation. They speak instead of outreach programs, admission by class percentile, and so on as removing barriers to equal opportunity. In contrast, I understand Left democratic traditions as seeking equality of outcome in any arena that affects life chances. I favor differentiated equality of outcome, but the questions that always arise are what do we mean by equal outcomes and how are we going to measure it?

In my view, the most profound measure of equal outcomes is subjective. Do the affected individuals feel outcomes are equal enough to allow their own freedom? In other words, are outcomes equal enough to allow them to feel their *unburdened agency*?

I am interpreting democratic theory as requiring three things. Individuals must (1) control the whole, (2) in collaboration with the whole society, and (3) without the impairment or burdening of their individual powers. The first two phrases reiterate Walzer's and nearly every other definition of mass democracy. The third phrase is the crucial one. It must be noted that I do not mean that an individual has direct control over all outcomes. One *cannot* say one's powers are impaired because one's unilateral goal is blocked. The term "unburdened agency" means that the individual's wish or position is present in and is transmitted through the entire decision chain without rejection or repudiation.[34]

Traditional notions of democratic citizenship have always involved some version of unburdened powers. They tend to measure these in the quasi-quantitative terms of equivalence. The concept of equal protection, for example, means that no one's treatment—and no one's agency—will be the same across social positions. This tradition of citizenship insists that one's placement, specialization, connections, access, or *office* in society will not affect one's substantive powers. The system can be highly differentiated without becoming *inequitably* differential. I agree that equity and equality must be evaluated in terms of due process, as traditional notions insist, *and* also in terms of the individual experience of agency. This means, to satisfy due process, that one's agency is unburdened if one's experience of it is not diminished by *any special fact of one's position*. Democracy depends on this experience of unburdened agency in the sense of an experience of having one's identity, passions, and interests recognized and then passed on into a larger collaborative system. Complex systems, in order to be democratic, cannot simply point out the burden of complexity. They must find ways of preserving the agency of each member in the course of complex contact.

In defining equal outcomes through unburdened agency, I am not dismissing the more objective and quantifiable measures of interpersonal equality that include analysis of personal income, access to health care and education, and equal numbers of minutes waiting for women's and men's restrooms. Those measures are important, but they have unfortunately eclipsed the deeper level of equality's impact on subjective experience, in particular the experience of freedom. Burdened agency is agency that has little or no effect on the outcome of processes that it addresses. Only part of this burden can be measured quantitatively. It is intensely subjective and interpretive. It consists of the *feeling* of blockage, of futility, of helplessness, of lacking power, of not being recognized, of not being respected, of not being properly counted. We are used to demanding objective measures of burdens and sufferings, and while those forms of accounting must continue and must improve, they encourage us to ignore or downplay personal testimonials to agency's condition. Individuals routinely provide their own data on the extent of their burdens, and some of the process of democratization consists of learning to take this personal data seriously. In spite of our enormous cynicism about people's self-descriptions, self-descriptions of one's burdens (and other conditions) are simply irreplaceable—they are not reducible to accounts provided by others, be they sociologists, policy analysts, police, social workers, family members, lovers, or friends.[35] Descriptions of the burden on agency must come finally from the agent him or herself. It is in fact one of the greatest burdens on agency that we have become so unable to trust the accounts of it coming from the agents themselves.

These reflections lead to some straightforward additional principles, following on the numbering of the series above. Democracy means (4) the coordination of differentiated and even conflicting subsystems across boundaries such as class and race. This coordination is democratic to the extent that its various subsystems or local cultures are (5) permeable and (6) of *equal* status such that (7) individual agency from any domain can be equitably transmitted through to any other, thus (8) offering individual members the experience of an agency unburdened by the collective process.

Complications are of course unavoidable.[36] But for too long the Left has let its brilliant grasp of the complications deter it from developing models for unburdening individual agency within complex democracies.

THE PRACTICE OF CONTACT

A superb portrait of freedom in groups appears in *Times Square Red, Times Square Blue,* a book about contemporary New York City by novelist Samuel R.

Delany.[37] Delany's topic is the Guiliani administration's "redevelopment" of Times Square, and he cuts between the larger social forces at work and his personal experience of the changes they have wrought. Redevelopment destroyed a range of low-cost venues for public interaction, many of them illegal and most regarded as antisocial by the powers that be. Delany describes the codified and yet spontaneous, pleasure-based social lives that passed in the bars, clubs, and porn theaters of the old Times Square area, where he conducted an important part of his own sexual and social life over several decades. He contrasts this with the large-scale redevelopment, which rests on a much more restrictive idea of desirable public conduct. To show that redevelopment was unnecessary and repressive, Delany describes how the former citizens of Times Square had found ways to combine personal and public life that made external controls invasive and unnecessary.

How can Delany make this case, especially given his candor about the local scourges of addiction, illness, and crime? First, Times Square society is *not* a self-regulating market, for it is regulated by the directed activity of its members. Transactions are face-to-face and resemble precapitalist market exchanges of goods and services that avoid commodification and higher management. Some participants pay for sex but most do not, giving and receiving according to mutual arrangements. Although there is nothing anarchistic about public sex, which Delany describes as highly choreographed, its practitioners make and change most of their own rules.[38]

The sign of this power of rule making is what the more regulated market terms sexual perversity. Perversity designates the unmanaged range of practices that includes oral sex, mutual masturbation, and open voyeurism; in short, sex across every imaginable body type, functionality, and above all social class. Perversity is a name for this very unusual range of choices, an epithet commonly applied to self-authorized personal decisions. In the market ideal, markets operate according to impersonal laws. Delany shows that everyday users operate on principles so different from those that have redeveloped Times Square that they comprise an alternative kind of market behavior. No cash is exchanged, no accumulation takes place, no class inequalities occur: in the *capitalist* sense, it is not market behavior at all.

Sexual exchange generally expresses some kind of interest and some anticipated benefit. Delany's own interests are remarkably nonphobic and varied, and include interest in normally "undesirable" people—the mentally and physically disabled, malformed, or ill. Delany specifies the core of sexual interest in terms that are especially relevant to our discussion:

There are as many different styles, intensities, and timbres to sex as there are people. The variety of nuance and attitude blends into the variety of techniques and actions employed, which finally segues, as seamlessly, into the variety of sexual objects the range of humankind desires. . . . We do a little better when we sexualize our own manner of having sex—learn to find our own way of having sex sexy. Call it a healthy narcissism, if you like. This alone allows us to relax with our own sexuality. Paradoxically, this also allows us to vary it and accommodate it, as far as we wish, to other people. I don't see how this can be accomplished without a statistically significant variety of partners and a fair amount of communication with them, at that, about what their sexual reactions to us are. . . . When Lacan says, "One desires the desire of the other," self-confidence is, generally speaking, the aspect of it desired.[39]

Unlike a self-regulating market, sexual exchange works through ranges restricted only by the practitioners. Desire is variable within one person, is changeable, is nonlinear, is not exactly predictable. Delany insists on the nonmonogamous and polymorphous nature of interest; interest is fundamentally polymorphous wherever it is not controlled, as it usually is, by the great intrapsychic manager, shame.[40] The still more basic point is that the most satisfying form of exchange depends on what I've been calling unburdened agency. "Healthy narcissism" is the state of feeling no limit on one's basic capacity. It is also the thing we desire in others and that triggers our desire—their self-confidence, their own refusal to experience social life as a burden. Sex is the meeting of two temporarily and partially unburdened agents, whose social ties support the unburdening. This condition of strong agency, so often derided as wishful and naive by professionals and theorists, lies at the core of human pleasure. This is also the extraordinary, the charmed core of a just society, where relationships express the freedom and agency of their members.

The crucial question is how to find the kind of social system that supports healthy narcissism, pleasure, and self-confidence. Delany takes for granted that it will involve addressing unequal power relations within the complex systems that support such phenomena as Times Square redevelopment. Society is always a net situation, and "in a net situation," Delany writes, "information comes from several directions and crosses various power boundaries, so that various processes— modulating, revisionary, additive, recursive, and corrective (all of them critical, each of them highlighting different aspects) can compensate for the inevitable reductions that occur along the constitutive [linear] chains."[41] But Delany also thinks that "networking" is only one of the ways to exist in social nets. People in net situations might be networking, or, on the other hand, they might be engaging in "contact."[42]

Some oversimplified contrasts will help here. Networking is formally structured. Contact is not. "Contact is the conversation that starts in the line at the grocery counter with the person behind you while the clerk is changing the paper roll in the cash register. It is the pleasantries exchanged with a neighbor who has brought her chair out to take some air on the stoop. It is the discussion that begins with the person next to you at the bar. . . . It can be two men watching each other masturbating together in adjacent urinals of a public john—an encounter that, later, may or may not become a conversation."[43] Networking occurs in professional societies where, for example, a senior member of your field likes a paper she hears you present and helps you get it published. Contact occurs when you, a struggling writer, start a conversation with the man standing next to you at the remainder table in your local bookstore, continue by complaining about the treatment your genre receives from reviewers, and end by discovering your new acquaintance is one of those reviewers who winds up praising your book in his next column.[44] "Networking tends to be professional and motive-driven. Contact tends to be more broadly social and appears random. . . . Networking is heavily dependent on institutions to promote the necessary propinquity. . . . Contact is associated with public space and the architecture and commerce that depend on and promote it."[45]

Although networking and contact interact and overlap, they part company on the issues of scarcity, loss, and agency. Networks are devices for managing scarcity. Networks are similar to self-regulating markets in which everyone competes for goods distributed according to general laws. Delany tells the story of his own early experience of getting enormous positive attention and a big career push from a writer's conference. No one else got much of anything. Networking is good at enriching a handful of people, he notes, while offering deprivation to the rest. "The *amount* of need present in the networking situation," he writes, "is too high for the comparatively few individuals in a position to supply the much needed boons and favors to *distribute them in any equitable manner.*"[46] Networks offer opportunity along with the spectacle of continuous and massive failure.

Individuals manage network scarcity in familiar ways. Most blame themselves *and* see their failure as outside their control. They come to experience themselves as in need of defense against further loss, which encourages them to impose various restrictions on their interest and desire.[47] And yet they feel dependent on the same network against which they defend themselves. Individuals look to superiors rather than to peers for meaningful help. They largely cede to superiors their power to make general rules for the disposition of people and things. They become small branch offices of self-policing. The network in this way shapes and reduces individual autonomy without overt coercion. The resulting states of reduced capacity are so common we rarely notice them, and yet we cope by abandoning whatever agency doesn't fit. As small-scale markets, networks manage scarcity in a way that generates the routine experience of absent control. The member's habituation to noncontrol is a primary burden on their agency.

The experience of contact offers a different structure. Whether in line at the grocery, trying lipsticks at the cosmetics counter, sitting down with a new person in the factory lunchroom, or drinking in a sports bar, a person sustains contact through direct and continuing effort. The processes of contact are not determined by the net in which they occur. Although contact is governed by a local set of implicit rules, these rules do not in themselves keep the contact going or determine its outcome. In networking situations the individual is dwarfed by the structures and procedures of the governing institution. In contact, individuals hold not the sole but the decisive power over inputs and outcome. Although the individuals who encounter each other remain within their complex social relations, these relations are indeterminate in regard to their specific encounter, which turns on a contingent range of environmental factors. The experience of contact is the experience of the system's contingency and indeterminacy, which allows agency to feel unburdened.

Contact's contingency, indeterminacy, intimacy, and open interest allow each person to face the other as an approximate and provisional peer. The parties may come from quite various social positions—one guy in the bookstore reviews for national newspapers and the other is a twenty-year-old nobody—but they are peers for the duration of the contact. They are two people looking for dollar books, and they are as close or remote, equal or unequal, as their conversation. The twenty year old may get something he wants from the contact because of the other's network, but he does not approach him as he would in a network, where he would be a junior person approaching a senior, the one who lacks approaching the one who has. The relationship is not controlled by the dominant party, and it doesn't require general management to regulate the effects of inequality. The partial relief from domination allows a partial lowering of defenses. While individuals never fully escape negative affects like fear and shame that inhibit interest, contact is a situation in which the individual feels a reduced need to defend herself against her own interest. Contact allows the individual to experience herself as one who creates the interaction through her own agency. Contact offers unburdened agency, and offers it not simply to the winners in marketlike competition but to everybody.

The freedom experienced in contact is social. Contact offers individuals the experience of public relations in which their autonomy is not sacrificed. It is any ordinary experience of small-scale linkages to others that we can make and unmake as we go through the day. Contact is generally local because it involves someone on the same bus bench or gym pool, but it contains the experience of unrepressed interaction that serves as the positive benchmark for social experience. Having experienced freedom in public, most of us are reluctant to sacrifice it for better regulation or even equity. Apparently democratic procedures that block the circulation of our interest no longer feel democratic. Delany is particularly emphatic that contact must and does take place across social barriers, class barriers above all.[48] Ordinary contact offers the experience not only of unburdened agency but of agency unburdened by barriers of unequal power and conflicting interests.

Contact encourages the individual to measure her agency by its capacity to transmit itself through social spaces normally charged by polarity and stratification. With the temporary, provisional, and partial lifting of immediate barriers, her baseline standard for wider society is that it furnish unburdened interest. This experience goes by many names, and one is Delany's idea of "pleasantness." The individual moves from one interest to the next without barriers signaled by blockage and deprivation. Contact focuses the self on the enjoyment it takes from the continuous coexistence of irreducible differences in a democratic mass. Contact offers an experience in which the liberal opposition between liberty and equality does not exist. Contact is the repeated revelation that, contrary to much current democratic theory, strong agency can thrive on complexity.

THE AGENCY PROJECT

I started by suggesting that market critics have erred when they have assumed that individual agency is alive and well and/or an effect of the market ideal. Neoliberalism has done so well in large part by championing liberty while quietly tailoring it to a highly managed corporate economy. In the current contest, I've said, the Left must insist on personal, individual agency, one as radical as we can imagine. I have in mind an agency that, without naively seeking atomistic escapes from discourse and organizations, and while seeking better collective action, can first imagine itself acting without these. It would be an agency that is not shame based, that is not only in the service of a defensive ego, that can act in collectives with a sense of its own freedom, that does not seek mastery at the expense of relations, that will not restrict these collectives because of the freedom it has not received.

I contrasted Delany's view of public life with Walzer's because Delany's offers a way of talking about how democracy frees the self where markets do not. Although American discussions routinely use terms like "free market," markets restrict complex determinism's actual possibilities. Contact is a way of talking about complex and decentralized social relations that are not subject to markets even as they interact with them. Contact is temporary, but it sets a standard of pleasure in social encounters. It helps to give us our sense of *social* freedom as such. It is only on the basis of that freedom that we will get the viable collective agency that democracies promise.

I will end with a few pushy imperatives. I'd like to see a democratic agency project, one that builds on identity politics and our current ambivalent pursuit of philosophically adequate political agency. This will mean attracting others with our openly delighted embrace of the material practices of "self-composition." This will need to be a theme for which we never apologize—it means self-creation as something like a U.N.-sanctioned human right, hardly mentioned in the current process of globalization. We will need to endorse what allows this unshamed self-creation: the centrality of identity and identity politics in individual life. We will need to explain why Toni Cade Bambara was right to say "Revolution begins with the self, in the self."[49] We will need to rearticulate important moments of radical humanism, as when Jean-Paul Sartre wrote "we must militate in our writings in favor of the freedom of the person *and* the socialist revolution. It is our job to show tirelessly that they imply each other."[50] We will of course need to maintain our grasp of systemic forces, coercion, contradiction, and negative affect while nonetheless stressing what Alaine Touraine has called "offensive identity"—not "an appeal to a mode of being but the claim to a capacity for action and for change."[51] We will need to rework some New Left / social movement themes to counter an age of corporate liberation—themes like alienation as a major problem, identity-based subordination as a destructive injustice, difference as basic and wonderful, self-management as a key to happiness. The result will be, once again, to show how market freedom—individual agency always mediated by corporations—is not as good as democratic freedom; that without the latter justice and life are lost. The democratic version of freedom means individual agency for all. Elaborating this is a crucial part of moving toward the postcorporate world for which artists and writers and cultural academics have so often stood.

NOTES

1 It is interesting to remember the different position of Jerry Brown, one of Clinton's competitors for the 1992 Democratic presidential nomination: "I believe that the enshrining of the market beyond its competence is the central fallacy affecting America. It turns the marketplace into a closet dictator so that if a market says close down your automobile plant in Flint, MI and go to Mexico . . . you must do it" ("Interview with Jerry Brown," *Los Angeles Times*, June 1, 1992, M3). It's also worth remembering that "neoliberalism" has been used to describe Democratic Party members who rejected their party's New Deal liberalism: "Neo-liberalism emerged as a major political tendency out of the midterm elections of 1974. In this Watergate-dominated election, the Democrats swept dozens of largely affluent, previously Republican congressional districts that were conservative on economic issues but liberal on social issues. Three of neo-liberalism's defining figures won major offices—Jerry Brown became California governor; Michael Dukakis, Massachusetts governor; and Gary Hart, Colorado senator. The fourth defining figure was Jimmy Carter, who became president two years later.

"The neos were liberal on process, not dollars and cents. While enacting campaign-finance reform and environmental legislation, they disparaged the major economic programs and public works that their Democratic predecessors had advanced. . . . Four years later . . . Carter 'failed to deliver on the very parts of the liberal agenda that were broadly *popular:* national health insurance, full employment, fairer taxes for the people in the middle of the income structure' " (Harold Meyerson, "Memo: Class and Country—the 1992 Campaign and Beyond," *L.A. Weekly*, September 20–26, 1991, 16–17; Meyerson is citing E. J. Dionne). Neoliberal Democrats overlap with southern Democrats, as in the cases of Carter, Clinton, and Gore, and continue parts of the latter's paternalistic, trickle-down laissez-faire on economic policy, which has always been more acceptable on the national scene than its longtime partner, racial segregation, but which, like segregation, placed public resources and decision making in the hands of local business oligarchies (as in the early "Friends of Bill").

2 Karl Polanyi, *The Great Transformation: The Political and Economic Origins of Our Time*, 2nd ed. (1944; Boston: Beacon Press, 2001), 71–72.

3 I am using the term "market ideal" as shorthand for the "ideal of the self-regulating market."

4 One example is the Indonesian riots following the Asian financial crisis of 1997, when the International Monetary Fund forced the population to cut further into basic necessities like food and shelter to pay foreign creditors for loans that they would have lost in what was looking like a large number of ordinary bankruptcies.

5 A *Business Week*/Harris poll conducted in August 2000 found that 73 percent think executives are paid too much, 74 percent think big companies have too much political influence, 87 percent think "entertainment and popular culture are dominated by corporate money which seeks mass appeal over quality," and 95 percent think companies "owe something to their workers" and communities and not just to shareholders (Aaron Bernstein, "Too Much Corporate Power?" *Business Week* 11 [September 2000]: 144–58). Sometimes the mass media takes note of this widely held economic populism. In September 2000, Paul Krugman observed that "ordinary people, when push comes to shove, feel that sometimes the market just isn't fair—and have sympathy for those who protest that unfairness" (Paul Krugman, "Britain's Stormy Petrol," *New York Times*, September 17, 2000, sec. 4, p. 19). Local resistance to corporate behavior is fairly common, and includes fighting new Wal-Mart stores, forcing Starbucks to increase the price at which it buys its coffee, antisweatshop protests against Nike and other clothing manufacturers, anti-WTO protests in various cities—the list continues to grow. This is more evidence for the view that neoliberalism must maintain itself through constant intervention in public discourse.

6 I use the term "nonmarket" to refer to exchanges that are not exclusively subject to the principles and management of capitalist economic institutions. Nonmarket exchanges interact with market forces but are not determined by them. They may work on a smaller scale and involve "face-to-face" relationships among individuals, but the crucial feature is that they are not primarily controlled by financial criteria.

7 For definitions of constituted and constituent power, a discussion of the many theories of their interrelation, and a passionate, comprehensive defense of constituent strength as authentic democracy, see Antonio Negri, *Insurgencies: Constituent Power and the Modern State*, trans. Maurizia Boscagli (1992; Minneapolis: University of Minnesota Press, 1999).

8 Francis Fukuyama, "The End of History and the Last Man," *The National Interest* (summer, 1989): 3–18. Arguments like Fukuyama's build on Frederick Hayek's World War II era argument that markets are always faster, more refined, and more accurate conveyers of information than state-run organizations. Hayek's influence on market theory rests in part on his translation of political into epistemological issues: he helps U.S. economists ignore questions of power relations within markets in favor of the transmission of price signals.

9 Jon E. Hilsenrath: "The Outlook: The Pros and Cons of Power Price Caps," *Wall Street Journal*, June 4, 2001, A1. This article reiterates the standard argument: "By allowing airlines to set their own prices and pick their own routes, practices previously regulated by the government, competition among airlines drove ticket prices lower on many popular routes. By some accounts, deregulation has saved travelers about $19 billion a year. Letting the market dictate prices 'is the best way of bringing customers low prices and improved service,' Mr. Kahn says."

10 As I write, outright market failure has not dented market dogma. Commenting on California state government's efforts to intervene in the "deregulated" electricity markets that produced exponential wholesale price increases and rolling blackouts, businessman and former Democratic gubernatorial candidate Al Checchi asserted

that "California politicians and bureaucrats cannot reasonably expect to purchase, finance, transmit, or generate electricity more efficiently than their private-sector counterparts" ("Deeper and Deeper We Get in Risky World of Power," *Los Angeles Times,* February 16, 2000, B9).

11 Here one usually sees a citation to master guru F. A. Hayek, from his mid-century arguments against Soviet state planning such as *The Road to Serfdom* (Chicago: University of Chicago Press, 1956), to his exploration of the market as a discovery process in *The Fatal Conceit: The Errors of Socialism,* ed. W. W. Bartley (Chicago: University of Chicago Press, 1989).

12 Tom Peters, *Liberation Management: Necessary Disorganization for the Nanosecond Nineties* (New York: Knopf, 1992), 484.

13 Ibid., 499. Markets and personal choice meet around "decentralization," which Peters associates with a good kind of chaos and unknowability, because these force experimentalism and thwart the tyranny of planning.

14 This trend is certainly not universal: liberals and radicals have sometimes objected to the claim that individual freedom interferes with democracy and justice. For example, Will Kymlicka writes, "Various critics of liberalism—including some Marxists, communitarians, and feminists—have argued that the liberal focus on individual rights reflects an atomistic, materialistic, instrumental, or conflictual view of human relationships. I believe that this criticism is profoundly mistaken, and that individual rights can be and typically are used to sustain a wide range of social relationships. Indeed, the most basic liberal right—freedom of conscience—is primarily valuable for the protection it gives to intrinsically social (and noninstrumental) activities" (Kymlicka, *Multicultural Citizenship* [Oxford: Oxford University Press, 1995], 26). The radical feminist Ellen Willis makes a similar point: "In a way it's true that feminism is bourgeois. Women's demand for self-determination is rooted in the idea of the autonomous individual, and it is the institution of wage labor that made it possible for women to conceive of independence from men. . . . There is a common theme in leftists' reductive view of bourgeois liberties, their contempt for mass culture, and their dismissal of sexual politics. I think all these antipathies reflect a puritanical discomfort with the urge—whatever form it takes—to gratification now, an assumption that social concern is synonymous with altruism and self-sacrifice" (Willis, *Beginning to See the Light: Sex, Hope, and Rock-and-Roll,* 2nd ed. [Hanover, N.H.: Wesleyan University Press, 1992], xix, xx). But the Left can dismiss thinkers like Kymlicka as liberals and Willis as a second-wave feminist, thus failing to engage with their important claims for the individual.

15 Anthony Giddens, *The Third Way: The Renewal of Social Democracy* (Cambridge: Polity Press, 1998), 37; Pierre Bourdieu, *Contre-feux: Propos pour servir à la résistance contre l'invasion néo-liberale* (Paris: Editions Raisons d'Agir, 1998), 117–18. Both texts are cited in Alex Callinicos, "Social Theory Put to the Test of Politics: Pierre Bourdieu and Anthony Giddens, *New Left Review* 236 (July/August 1999): 82, 91.

16 This is the point of what Etienne Balibar called "egalliberty," an "impossible" but necessary term. "If it is absolutely true that equality is *practically* identical with

freedom, this means that it is materially impossible for it to be otherwise, in other words, it means that they are necessarily always *contradicted together*. . . . There is no example of conditions that suppress or repress freedom that do not suppress or limit—that is, do not abolish—equality, and vice versa" (Balibar, " 'Rights of Man' and 'Rights of the Citizen': The Modern Dialectic of Equality and Freedom," in *Masses, Classes, Ideas: Studies on Politics and Philosophy Before and After Marx*, trans. James Swenson [New York: Routledge, 1994], 48).

17 Antonio Negri, *Insurgencies*, 3.

18 The abstract determinist holds that "some power (God or Nature or History [or markets]) controls or decides the outcome of an action or process, beyond or irrespective of the wills or desires of its agents" (Raymond Williams, *Marxism and Literature* [Oxford: Oxford University Press, 1977], 84).

19 Ibid., 86.

20 Silvan S. Tomkins, *The Positive Affects*, vol. 1 of *Affect, Imagery, Consciousness* (New York: Springer Publishing Company, 1962), 109–10. Tomkins continues with an example: "A computer which can scan all the potentially relevant information, select what is most relevant and decide which computations to carry out is far more free than an adding machine which can perform only addition on whatever numbers are fed to it. Both systems are determined, but one is freer, more complex and more competent than the other" (110).

21 Freedom of consciousness is "a conjoint function of its complexity and the complexity of its surround." This means that freedom can be measured as "the product of the complexity of its 'aims' and the frequency of their attainment (Tomkins, *Affect, Imagery, Consciousness*, 111).

22 For example, see Doug Smith, Carl Ingram, Rich Connell, "Duke Shaped Power Market, Three Tell Panel, *Los Angeles Times*, June 23, 2001, A1.

23 Mark Landler, "The Ostrich that Roared," *New York Times*, September 4, 1999, B2, quoting Henry Lee, the managing director of Hendale Asia, based in Hong Kong.

24 The weaker claim, that deregulated markets are better than socialism, blocks discussion of mixed economies only when it imports the strong, untenable version.

25 For example, people are free to go to college in the United States, but their actual access to a particular college is contingent not simply on their own efforts (measured imperfectly by such measures as their grades in high school) but on where they live, parental income, racial and other identity factors, and so on. The problem is not that people lack *identical* opportunities: it is impossible to put everyone in a differentiated system in the equivalent position. Rather, the problem is that most people lack agency that is on par with that of the market—an equivalent *agency* that would allow them to control their position.

26 See Thomas I. Friedman, *The Lexus and the Olive Tree: Understanding Globalization* (New York: Farrar, Strauss, Giroux, 1999). In his review, David Moberg notes: "This is a pernicious abuse of the idea of 'democracy.' If democracy means that the people have power to govern their society, globalization is more often the antithesis of democracy than its promoter" (Moberg, "Electronic Herd Mentality," *In These Times*,

May 16, 1999, 20). Economist Burton G. Malkiel notes that "the efficient market theory has been the mantra of my generation" ("Are Markets Efficient?" *Wall Street Journal* 28 December 2000: A18).

27 Michael Walzer, "The Civil Society Argument," in *Dimensions of Radical Democracy: Pluralism, Citizenship, Community,* ed. Chantal Mouffe (New York: Verso, 1992), 100.

28 Walzer, "Civil Society," 106.

29 Walzer, "Civil Society," 104.

30 Walzer, "Civil Society," 105.

31 Walzer, "Civil Society," 99.

32 Ibid., 105. Walzer continues: "States are tested by their capacity to sustain this kind of participation—which is very different from the heroic intensity of Rousseauian citizenship. And civil society is tested by its capacity to produce citizens whose interests, at least sometimes, reach further than themselves and their comrades, who look after the political community that fosters and protects the associational networks."

33 All complex systems require some version of bureaucratic administration. For a strong defense of its democratic value, see Paul du Gay, *In Praise of Bureaucracy: Weber, Organization, Ethics* (London: Sage, 2000). Du Gay is particularly eloquent on Weber's insistence that bureaucracy be separated from politics.

34 I use the term "unburdened agency" because I don't think individual agency has a positive content that can be applied in a general way. I do not use the term "free agency," for example, because I don't think individual agency can be unrestricted, open, unconditioned, or undetermined within the systems in which it inevitably operates.

35 Policy makers, professionals, pundits, and sometimes the general population have an extremely hard time taking individual self-descriptions at face value. One of the major jobs of expert knowledge is to distrust personal statements and provide allegedly more public and objective languages to describe it. Expert knowledge systematically burdens individuality as it enters public systems, forcing this individuality to express itself in reductive languages. We support this process by assuming that people are so biased in favor of themselves that we can trust little that they say about themselves. Workplace performance reviews generally come from supervisors and not candidates, because the supervisor is thought to be more objective about the candidate's performance than the candidate. Psychotherapy has a hard time taking the client's self-descriptions at face value, or deepening their insight without showing they mean something like the opposite of what their user thought. The "client-centered" therapy of Carl Rogers and others has little credence among theorists. In the academic humanities, critical theory is equally cynical about individual self-description, given its legitimate and illuminating concerns with the subject's entrenched narcissism, the workings of the unconscious, the operations of aggression and power, and the treachery of language, among many others.

36 All persons have an unconscious. Their motives and desires will be opaque and confusing even to them. All signals have noise. Interpretation will always be necessary, and interpretation will not be "rational" or generalizable. Transparency and linear

control will *never* take place. The unburdened agent will never have the feeling of unconditioned sovereignty. But these are the inevitable features of complexity and translation; they are already the conditions of all transmitted agency.

37 Samuel R. Delany, *Times Square Red, Times Square Blue* (New York: New York University Press, 1999). For a parallel treatment of redevelopment and sexual repression, see Michael Warner, *The Trouble with Normal: Sex, Politics, and the Ethics of Queer Life* (New York: The Free Press, 1999), especially chapter 4. Warner's advocacy of "sexual autonomy," his calls for sex's public elaboration, his sense of the value of variation, and his analysis of shame as a repressive force overlap with Delany's perspective.

38 "Another point that people lose track of: Public sex situations are not Dionysian and uncontrolled but are rather some of the most highly socialized and conventionalized behavior human beings can take part in" (Delany, *Times Square Red*, 158).

39 Delany, *Times Square Red*, 45–46.

40 Here I am following psychologist Silvan Tomkins, who defines interest as a positive affect whose orientation is "track, look, listen." Interest is a fundamental reflex—prior, for Tomkins, to drives—that opens the self to the world and enables all intellectual and perceptual development. "The function of this very general positive affect," he writes, "is to 'interest' the human being in what is *necessary* and in what it is *possible* for him to be interested in" (*Affect, Imagery, Consciousness*, 1:337, 342). Tomkins continues: "For some time now, both Psychoanalysis and Behaviorism have regarded interest as a secondary phenomenon, a derivative of the drives, as though one could be interested only in what gave or promised drive satisfaction. We have turned this argument upside down. It is interest or excitement . . . which is primary, and the drives are secondary. . . . Excitement, rather than being a derivative of drives, is the major source of drive amplification" (1:342). (See also *Shame and Its Sisters: A Silvan Tomkins Reader*, ed. Eve Kosofsky Sedgwick and Adam Frank (Durham: Duke University Press, 1995), 75–76.

41 Delany, *Times Square Red*, 122.

42 As I discuss these terms, I'm going to contrast them in a way that Delany explicitly warns against. I heed his warning that "we must not let [their] opposition sediment onto some absolute, transcendent, or ontological level that it cannot command" (*Times Square Red*, 129). Contact and networking coexist, overlap, and regularly work together, and there are times when they cannot be told apart. My goal is not to replace networking with contact, but to help make visible the features of contact in a society in which it tends to be absorbed or trivialized by networking.

43 Delany, *Times Square Red*, 123.

44 Delany is recounting a bit of "SF folklore" about Ray Bradbury's random encounter with Christopher Isherwood in a bookstore, who then helped launch Bradbury's career (*Times Square Red* 134–35).

45 Delany, *Times Square Red*, 129.

46 Delany, *Times Square Red*, 136.

47 One common form of loss is the loss of autonomy. Delany borrows an example from Jane Jacobs's classic *The Death and Life of Great American Cities* (New York: Random

House, 1961): "A park with no public eating spaces, restaurants, or small item shopping on its borders forces mothers who live adjacent to it and who thus use it the most to 'share everything or nothing' in terms of offering facilities of bathroom use and the occasional cup of coffee to other mothers and their children who use the park but do not live so near. Because the local mothers feel they must offer these favors to whomever they are even civil with (since such services are not publicly available), they soon become extremely choosy and cliquish about whom they will even speak to. . . . Similarly, if *every* sexual encounter involves bringing someone back to your house, the general sexual activity in a city becomes anxiety-filled, class-bound, and choosy. This is precisely *why* public rest rooms, peep shows, sex movies, bars with grope rooms, and parks with enough greenery are necessary for a relaxed and friendly sexual atmosphere in a democratic metropolis" (Delany, *Times Square Red*, 126–27).

48 Delany begins the book's second essay, " . . . Three, Two, One, Contact: Times Square Red," in this way: "The primary thesis underlying my several arguments here is that, given the mode of capitalism under which we live, life is at its most rewarding, productive, and pleasant when large numbers of people understand, appreciate, and seek out interclass contact and communication conducted in a mode of general good will" (*Times Square Red*, 111).

49 Toni Cade Bambara, "On the Issue of Roles," *The Black Woman: An Anthology*, ed. Toni Cade Bambara (New York: New American Library, 1970), 109.

50 Jean-Paul Sartre, "Introduction," *Les Temps Modernes* 1 (October 1945); cited in Arthur Hirsh, *The French New Left: A History and Overview* (Montréal: Black Rose Books, 1982), 42.

51 Alaine Touraine, *Return of the Actor: Social Theory in Postindustrial Society*, trans. Myrna Godzich (Minneapolis: University of Minnesota Press, 1988), 81.

JEFFREY C. GOLDFARB

Anti-Ideology: Education and Politics as Democratic Practices

Learning and teaching constitute the free public space in education, and these practices have a very difficult relationship to politics. Although education may be about politics, it should be free from politics. In fact, politics compromises education, and education compromises politics in crucial ways. Reflecting on this suggests that we distance ourselves from both sides of the American cultural wars of the past decades. We should understand what conservatives and radicals contribute to the project of education while we distance ourselves from their partisan positions (even those we share beyond the classroom). In the classroom, the positions should be understood as they exist in dialogue, without easy pre-fabricated conclusions. I make these assertions informed by the experiences of modern tyranny, (i.e., totalitarianism) and its opposition.[1]

As a problem in politics: Note that the modern tyrant tries to educate the population; to build "Soviet Man," as was the case in previously existing social-ism; or to prepare the nation for democracy, as was the case in Pinochet's Chile and other authoritarian political orders. Hannah Arendt observes the general principle that "education can play no part in [free] politics, because in politics we always have to deal with those who are already educated. Whoever wants to educate adults really wants to act as their guardian and prevent them from political activity."[2] Confusing education with politics substitutes the authorita-tive relationship between teacher and students for the democratic relationship among citizens.

As a problem of education: On the other hand, the substitution of a citizen's relationship for the relationship between teacher and student is also a problem. It undermines the educational endeavor. Students have to be prepared to take part in the world, but they are not yet equipped. The educator's first responsibility to her or his students is to present them with the world as she or he knows it, so that they can later act on it using their own judgments. The student must be protected from immediate political and economic concerns and pressures so that he or she can be prepared to take part in public life as a mature, responsible, equal citizen. Along these lines, Michael Oakeshott observes that "education in its most general significance may be recognized as a specific transaction which may go on between generations of human beings in which newcomers to the scene are initiated into the world they are to inhabit."[3] He goes on to explain that a liberal education involves "the invitation to disentangle oneself, for a time, from the urgencies of the here and now and to listen to the conversation in which human beings forever seek to understand themselves."[4] Oakeshott succinctly tells us what education is in its most basic sense, a transaction between one generation and the next, and specifies the particulars of a liberal education.[5] It is free and about understanding the human condition. The dynamic key word in this basic approach to education is "conversation." Oakeshott understands conversation to be the operative element of liberal education, underscoring that it must be conducted freely, unconstrained by the powers that be or by their critics. I agree. Education is a special kind of free public activity.

The teacher reveals to students the world in all its complexity without a specific political or economic agenda in mind, not so that the world will be preserved as is, nor to promote a particular program for change, but so that the student, when ready, can act independently in the world. I want to be clear on this. I think that education, properly pursued, is not an ideological activity. Indeed, it should be anti-ideological. I am going to say more about how I define ideology in order to explain why, as I have argued elsewhere, that ideological practices are among the chief causes of the major political tragedies of the twentieth century, the gulag and the holocaust. Here I want to underscore that I think that the same sort of practices can be the ruin of education. When intellectuals and education are free of ideology, their democratic contribution is possible.

Before we proceed, I must make clear what I mean by ideology. Conventionally, ideology is considered in a variety of related ways. One position views ideology as a kind of socially induced cognitive distortion. It was in this sense that Marx wrote *The German Ideology.* The young Hegelians were dismissed because theirs was a bourgeois philosophy: "The ruling ideas of the time are the ideas of the ruling class."[6] Ideology is distinguished from science in the name of class-based critique. The science of the ascending, purportedly universal, class is contrasted to the ideology of the dominant one. But a funny thing happened in the history of the term: Lenin initiated a second meaning. In his classic piece justifying party censorship of the press, he called for party ideology in the party press.[7] The party press is to present working-class ideology exclusively. Here a second meaning appears, which was later personified in the history of Marxist Leninism in the Communist Party "Ideologist." Ideology is no longer contrasted with truth, but with other ideologies. Ideology is an idea weapon of a particular political and social position. Working-class ideology confronts bourgeois ideology; feminist ideology confronts patriarchal ideology; black ideology confronts white ideology.

Outside the marxist tradition, Karl Mannheim synthesized these two meanings of ideology and contrasted them with science, in the form of particular ideology and total ideologies versus the sociology of knowledge.[8] Particular ideologies were understood as being the intentional tendentious forms of knowledge defending a class interest, while total ideologies were understood as distortions of cognitive realities formed by the conditions of their creation; that is, formed by historical and social structural specificity. The only truth available was through (what Mannheim problematically imagined) the relational truth made available by free-floating intellectuals.[9]

These conceptualizations, ideology as class distortion versus a class-based truth, ideology as a class weapon, and ideology as a social and historical determination of truth, and the many alternative positions that are formulated as syntheses of these positions, all are engaged in a similar activity. As Foucault has put it, they understand "thought in general by sensation."[10] Foucault, fully aware that this turn toward a sociology of knowledge is a historical development, shows how it, along with the Kantian quest to ground knowledge in universals, is engaged in the struggle with the limits of representation. Yet, it should also be recognized that the generality of the observations, from those of Marx, Lenin, Mannheim, and Foucault, among many others, overlooks the specific history of ideology as a political force of remarkable power in the twentieth century. This is my concern. They overlook the centrality of a special kind of thinking implicated in the major tragedies of our recent past.[11]

Common to the political ideologies that have prevailed in the modern era is a kind of magical mono-causal explanation of history and the human condition. The complexity of the social world is reduced to some underlying idea and deductions from that idea, archetypically in the case of the totalitarian ideologies of our century: to the ideas of race and class. The ideas are linked to power, and the consequences have been tragic.[12] Now is not a time when such explanations are fashionable. Ordinary people are suspicious because they have suffered from the false promises of these ideologies, as they have rationalized modern barbarism, from the killing fields of Europe to the killing fields of Cambodia. In more sophisticated circles, we all "know" that the age of the grand narrative is over; our faith in progress has been severely tested.[13] Yet, one very important and negative legacy of ideological thinking is the notion that behind the world of appearances is an underlying reality, explained by some master concept, be it of race, class, or gender, or some other *key* to history and its problems. Only the foolish take ideas and ideals at face value. Ideas and ideals are matters of one form of false consciousness or another. They are all "ideologies." Observing this legacy, and analyzing how it permeates American society, was the goal of my book *The Cynical Society.* Here we should note that those who have fought against ideology in its totalitarian form can instruct those who are faced with the cynical consequences of ideological thinking, remembering that when I refer to ideology I am not referring to the understanding that social ideas and political ideals are socially constructed, shaped, or determined, but to *the historical specificity of ideology in modern politics.* Politics in the modern era has become a battle among politicians with distinctive ideologies that are varieties of "isms." This was a distinctive development with a distinctive beginning and perhaps an end. We will consider the possibility of an ending in the contributions of anti-ideological political agents who helped democratically to overturn totalitarianism so that we may appreciate the role of the anti-ideological education. The key figure in this is the intellectual.

Intellectuals matter. That they can matter, and support democracy, was wonderfully revealed in our recent past by the heroic activities of the democratic anti-ideological opposition to previously existing socialism. Democratic intellectuals in Poland, Czechoslovakia, and Hungary, such as Adam Michnik, Vaclav Havel, and Georg Konrad, through their written and spoken words and through their actions, revealed "the power of the powerless," as Havel put it.[14] They contributed to the peaceful collapse of the Soviet empire and to the emergence of democracy in Central Europe, a part of the world where democracy has been the rare exception to authoritarian rule. They did this not by being prophets nor by being philosopher kings nor by being members of a political vanguard; rather, they provided striking alternatives to the totalitarian models and ideological practices both in the form and the content of their actions. And the way they did this changes and challenges not only what their world once was but also what our world is. There are many dimensions to their challenge. Here we concentrate on how their way of being intellectuals can inform our way of doing the liberal arts. We will move across a wide political and historical terrain. I will attempt to demonstrate how the extraordinary actions of democratic oppositionists to previously existing socialism points to a distinctive approach to liberal arts education. The oppositionists underscore the importance of a free public life and suggest the important, and threatening, role that education plays in its constitution.

Intellectuals, such as those of Central Europe, are capable of being key democratic agents by providing the means for a society to talk and deliberate about its problems, not by providing easy singular answers. They do this in two ways: first, they provide the means by which people *civilize* their differences, so that enemies become opponents who disagree and compromise, convince and tolerate, rather than wage war against each other. Second, intellectuals *subvert* the limitations of the often quite civil conventional wisdom, so that hidden social ills and injustices are revealed and can be discussed and acted on. These two ways of being a democratic intellectual played a key role in the development of a democratic alternative in the "other Europe," demonstrated in the works of Michnik and Havel. Their writings and actions stand in stark contrast to ideological practices.

Adam Michnik was probably the most important democratic oppositionist in Poland. In 1968, he became known as a student leader to a general public, Poland's equivalent of Danny the Red or Tom Hayden, although he was a proponent of liberal freedoms while they were radical critics. He led demonstrations demanding greater academic freedom at Warsaw University, linking this demand to a general call for greater political freedom in socialist Poland. As a result of these actions, Michnik spent the first of his many sojourns in a Polish prison. After his release in the 1970s he became known officially as one of Poland's leading "antisocialist elements," sometimes labeled a Trotskyist (a clear anti-Semitic allusion), sometimes simply "anti-Polish." Yet, he really was one of the leading opponents of totalitarianism of our times. He and his Czech colleague, Vaclav Havel, had clear ideas about what was wrong with the world of previously existing socialism, as well as straightforward ideas about how to begin the process of correcting it. Two essays written in the mid-1970s, Havel's "The Power of the Powerless" and Michnik's "The New Evolutionism," reveal the nature of their insights and their identities as democratic intellectuals, demonstrating the civil and subversive roles of democratic intellectuals as alternatives to ideological practices.

At that time, Havel was primarily known internationally as an interesting dramatist, an avant-gardist whose work revealed the absurdities of modern times. Today, he is president of the Czech Republic. In my view his greatest achievements lie between these two points of his international fame. He is an unsurpassed political essayist, a heroic subversive. In his greatest essay, he critically revealed the vulnerability of the totalitarian order. In "The Power of the Powerless," Havel tells the story of a green grocer, who every morning puts in the window of his shop with the fruits and vegetables a sign with the slogan "Workers of the World Unite!"[15] Havel asks what the grocer is thinking when he puts out the sign. Answer: not much, it is an automatic activity, which has little or nothing to do with the toiling masses around the globe. He speculates about what would happen if the grocer decided to "live in truth" and no longer put up the sign. Answer: his life would be ruined. He would lose his job, his prospects for a nice summer vacation in Bulgaria, and his children's chances for higher education, as he would lose his friends and colleagues, who would learn that his friendship is dangerous. In this way, Havel revealed the social constitution of late totalitarianism, along with its vulnerability. He demonstrated how the ordinary citizen was deeply implicated in the continuation of the totalitarian order, and how it was within his or her power to challenge that order. He subverted the commonsense notion that totalitarianism in Czechoslovakia was enforced by the Soviet troops who invaded the country in 1968, and showed how the most ordinary of citizens enforced the hated order of things. He showed how the power of the authorities was significantly supported by everyday activities. The social order was legitimated by little acts of tribute to the powers, and the system was sustained by these acts even when they were not believed. As long as people appeared to be engaged in building the "bright and happy future," they were so engaged, whether they believed in the official ideology or not.

Havel's essay has wonderful ironic turns and moments of illumination, but its great significance is that it was tied to practical action. Havel goes on to wonder what would happen if the green grocer along with his friends began to "live in truth." And in real life he acted, along with many colleagues, and answered his queries. What was distinctive about "Charter 77," the great Czechoslovak dissident movement of the late 1970s and 1980s, was that it openly questioned the legitimacy of the communist order. It distinguished itself not through clandestine action, nor by proposing one "ism" as a replacement of another, but as an open opposition to specific acts of repression by the communist authorities, initially as a protest against the repression of a rock group, Plastic People of the Universe. Its activities were open, consisting of little more than the simple act of not putting a sign in the window. It acted on principle, not on an elaborated scientific view of the world linked to organized power; that is, not on the basis of an ideology. By such acts it, along with comparable groups in Central Europe, frontally challenged the previously existing socialist order.

At about the same time, but independently, Michnik proposed a theory of social change that more or less employed Havel's strategy. In his "Letters from Prison" he called his a theory of the "new evolutionism."[16] Under this title, Michnik reflected on the available and closed avenues of social change. The available repertoire for social change seemed to be exhausted in the Soviet bloc: revolution from below proved to be impossible in Hungary in the events of 1956, and reform from above was ruled out in Prague in the events of 1968. Michnik reasoned that this suggested a new "long march," reform from below: essentially a societal secession from the party-state order. People should act as if they live in a free society and take back zones of freedom from the ruling order. He was counseling that the green grocers of the world unite and work for a more decent alternative social order. Michnik was, in fact, reflecting on the little successes that people did build into their lives, essentially arguing for the expansion of the zones of private freedom, known to exist among friends and family and centered in the kitchens throughout the old bloc. And this was the strategy of the democratic oppositions in East and Central Europe: culminating in the creation of Solidarnosc, as a free and independent but "nonpolitical" labor union (in their self-understanding, nonpolitical in the sense that it did not challenge the "leading role of the Party"). Michnik named and in a sense codified Havel's subversion, highlighting the path activists did indeed take, leading to the collapse of the communist orders of Central and Eastern Europe.

In Michnik's major book of the 1970s, *The Church and the Left*, he went further and showed how the people who could agree to meet in these new evolutionary activities could come from distinct and even opposing political and cultural traditions.[17] In this volume he examined how the secular Left and the Church could act together as if they lived in a free democratic society, despite their fundamental differences. They could come together in free common public space, created by their commitment to live apart from official lies, and help constitute a free society on the basis of their differences. It is interesting to note that Michnik has repeated this approach throughout his career as a public intellectual, both as an oppositionist and as a political commentator in postcommunist Poland. Michnik has taken the narratives of the Church and the Left, of the independent Polish socialists (of Pilsudski) and the National Democrats (of Dmowski), as well as of the post-Communist and post-Solidarity parties, and attempted at different times to make possible a coherent politics among those who differ: before the fall of communism, a democratic opposition; after the fall of communism, a non-authoritarian alternative to the totalitarian Left and to the newly emerging nationalist Right.[18] He has not tried to eradicate the identity of the societal actors whose stories he appreciates, but he has tried to tell their different stories in ways that they come to be seen as compatible, at least for a period of time. The secular Left and the Catholic Church are different, but for a time their concern for human rights and dignity in opposition to communism made enough sense so that they were able to act in concert. The Polish nationalists and the Polish liberals and socialists tell their histories in opposition to each other, but the integrity of their opposing stories constituted a political pluralism in the opposition that prefigured the idea of pluralism in an open society. Former communists and former oppositionists have faced each other as jailers and jailed, but they now have a common interest in the rule of law and sound economic policies in the postcommunist period. Michnik has helped turn fundamental and incompatible differences among political enemies into civilized differences among political opponents, and in the process, along with his subversive notions, he has very significantly contributed to the formation of a democratic culture in a world where such a cultural approach is essentially unprecedented.

Although the power of anti-ideological intellectuals was most apparent in our recent past in the former Soviet bloc, in the activities and writings of figures like Michnik and Havel the need for such power is very great in our society, where cynicism has become the preferred mode of explanation for problems in our private and public life, and where the commercial mass media have become the primary educators. For very different reasons, the people of the formerly existing "evil empire" and its allies, and the people of what used to be called the "free world," have lived with a deliberation deficit: there because of the workings of totalitarianism; here as a consequence of the fact that we have been "amusing ourselves to death," as Neal Postman has put it.[19]

We have a great deal of difficulty in deliberately considering our problems, exchanging alternative judgments and deciding on agreed-on courses of action. Incoherence characterizes public life. Our need for civil and subversive intellectuals is no less than that which the societies of East and Central Europe experienced, if the reality of democratic practices is to have a resemblance to the democratic ideal of self-governance by the people. As we learn to distrust the grand narratives of classical intellectuals and their totalized calls to the barricades, we need to appreciate that this is not the end of the intellectuals in public life and in fact it is the moment when their democratic contribution becomes clear.

It is here where the link between the liberal arts and Central European opposi-tional intellectuals becomes apparent: what the intellectuals of Central Europe achieved as a result of their heroic actions is what a liberal arts education should, and often does, provide citizens in the normal course of their lives. This is what Bruce Kimball in his history of the idea of liberal education has called the oratory tradition of the liberal arts, which he contrasts with the philosophical tradition and traces back to antiquity.[20] A liberal education prepares students and teachers to be life-long intellectuals and the informed audiences of intellectual discus-sions. It is not only concerned with the search for truth, as Kimball highlights in the legacy of Plato, but also with the development of the free citizen prepared to take part in public life, which Kimball highlights in the legacy of Cicero. The preparation is for free participation. It is not participation connected to one or another partisan position, neither necessarily for or against particular political arrangements. A liberal education prepares us to take part as citizens in the great conversation about the values of a good society, providing the means to judge and realize these values: learning and questioning inherited wisdoms, being capable of engaging in civil conversation about ideas that matter and capable of subverting civility when it masks things that matter. What connects the extraor-dinary actions of the Central European dissidents and the ordinary action of liberal arts education is the centrality of public space for open deliberation. This is the great alternative to ideology in politics and education. Keeping this in mind, a distinctive approach to the liberal arts is called for.

Contrary to the neo- (and not so neo-) conservatives, the point is not to provide students with an understanding of the great achievements of "our" civilization. And contrary to progressives of various sorts, the point is not simply to provide critiques of this civilization nor simply to reveal the evils of Western hegemony. A liberal arts education, like the intellectuals of our century, fails when it provides easy answers or when it uses ideological formulas. Please note that I am not just advocating "teaching the conflicts," as does Gerald Graff.[21] In fact, in a sense I am advocating ignoring the conflicts, the specific cultural ideologies of the academic tribe. Instead of advocating one educational ideology or another, I am suggesting that we attempt to avoid them so that we can teach students what we know about the world so they can develop their own judgment and act in the world as independent agents. Teach what can be learned in alternative positions as they exist in dialogue with each other in pursuit of understanding, not as true believers conflict in their parochial battles. Michnik and Havel didn't propose some bright and certain future to their compatriots and they didn't teach the conflicts between the bright and certain futures of communism and anticommunism. They provoked their fellow citizens to act by giving them new ways to talk about their problems. Liberal education should prepare students for such activities.

The competing approaches of the conservatives and the progressives, it seems to me, are implicated in the tragedy of intellectuals in this century. The approach to education that I am advocating is informed by my guarded appreciation of the democratic role of intellectuals. I am fully aware that intellectuals have often been very undemocratic agents. Intellectuals, as ideologists of the Left and Right, are implicated in the horrors of racism and fascism, stalinism and nazism. The point is that intellectuals make their special contribution to democracy when they contribute to public deliberation, not when they act as politicians or gurus or vanguardists. And a liberal arts education serves education, and not ideology, when it provides students with the knowledge and the critical capacity to fully engage in a special kind of informed discussion. This claim will seem less remote if we consider briefly the emergence of such public space within a totalitarian landscape, and the relationship between this space and our own activities. What follows is my birds-eye view, along with the implications for liberal arts in America.

Since the early 1970s, I have investigated independent public life in a Central European society: when the communist order still appeared to be quite stable; when the order was in disarray, leading to collapse; and after the fall of the communist regime. There was nothing automatic about this progression, but the power of the public and of civil society was most clearly revealed and pushed forward by it.

As part of my dissertation research I studied officially tolerated independent public expression in the student theaters of Poland.[22] I observed how these theaters created an alternative world for themselves and their audiences, with unorthodox reflections on questions such as the roles of the church, nationalism, and the Romantic tradition in Polish society. They independently approached problems of daily life and boldly confronted the official party-state ideology. Although they created politically challenging theater, theirs was primarily a concern with new ways of communicating through theater. These theaters introduced to the Polish audience for the first time the great theatrical experiments of the twentieth century, including the remarkable works of Stanislaw Witkiewicz and Witold Gombrowicz, the great interwar avant-gardists. They employed critically the newest tradition of Grotowski, challenging the limits of theatrical expression. This was a free public life within a totalitarian context. The makers of the theater interacted with their audiences on their own terms, drawing on their theatrical inheritance and set apart from the constraints of the communist system.

Although the accomplishments of these theaters and of other arts that were officially tolerated were great indeed (their very existence changed the order of things), they were, nonetheless, limited by the need to receive official approval. From the mid-1970s onward an alternative emerged: a completely independent, but also illegal, public life was created in Poland. Its beginnings were modest and political, an information bulletin concerning the fate of the victims of "socialist" justice following strikes in 1976. But when this bulletin survived, despite repression, an alternative, clandestine cultural system was formed in the late 1970s, and throughout the 1980s, including a wide range of alternative publications, performances, university classes, and even clandestine radio and TV broadcasting. The first of the literary journals was the primitively produced *Zapis*, where previously censored fiction and nonfiction were published. Later, in this and many other journals of ever-greater sophistication, works were created free of the censor, including the self-censor. These works were conceived for and constituted an independent public life. The principle of independent public action included the artists, who experienced a world free of official ideology, as well as union activists, who wished to create a social movement free of party-state control to defend their interests. There was a direct connection between the officially tolerated independent art, the free oppositional culture, and the development of Solidarity and its victory. People who first spent their lives gaming with the censor were among those who created the public space of democratic opposition.[23]

I think of Stanislaw Baranczak, the Polish poet and literary critic, now professor of Slavic languages at Harvard. In 1970, it was his poetry that inspired the greatest of the student theaters of Poland—Theater of the Eighth Day of Poznan—which combined Baranczak's concern with the poetry of daily life and Grotowski's new language of theatrical expression. But by 1976, Baranczak was an editor of *Zapis*, a contributor to other underground cultural journals, and a founding member of the Committee to Defend Workers, the key organization of the Polish democratic opposition. It was in reflection on the emergence of this group that Michnik wrote his essay "The New Evolutionism," and it was in the context of this activity that Havel wrote "The Power of the Powerless" and

Charter 77 was formed. These activities laid the groundwork for Solidarnosc and the democratic revolutions of 1989.

Open, free discussion, broadly understood, and the possibility of common action based on the discussion, is what the various forms of Polish resistance to modern tyranny had in common. The democratic opposition provided Polish society the possibility to discuss its situation and potentially to act on that discussion, in ways that were set apart from the definitions and dictates of the official ideology. And it was this willingness to secede from the ruling order that empowered Solidarity. Open discussion, freely constituted, led a labor movement to challenge the communist order, not by being an anticommunist force, at least manifestly, but as a force for open self-definition, defense, and determination. And it is the same sort of discussion that is at the center of the university and the tradition of liberal education.

There are, of course, important differences. The Polish theater people sought to develop their art, which incidentally had political implications. They never confused with political action their engagement in a challenging theater. Writing about another art form, Milan Kundera aptly describes what is the content of the public space opened by independent art, whether it is that of the theater or the novel: "The novelist," Kundera declares, "needs to answer to no one but Cervantes."[24] Following the same sort of insight, the Polish theater artists knew their work was theater, answering, in their own terms, the questions posed by the theatrical tradition.

When in places like student theater the world of the independent public emerged in the margins of the official cultural world, and when this world at the margins worked its way to the center, in the democratic opposition, in Solidarity, and now in an openly liberal society, a free public life, a civil society, was replacing the world of adult political education, in Arendt's pejorative sense. Polish citizens were developing their capacities to act freely, in interaction with each other, independent of the political education of official guardians and the party-state ideology. And educational institutions too had to cease being institutions of political education and become institutions of education as such. The point was not to replace a liberal ideology for the previously existing ideology of Marxism-Leninism; the point was to help form a university on a nonideological basis. And this point is ours as well as theirs.

It is with a sense of this that I embarked a few years ago on my study of the role of the intellectual in democratic society. The study started with the paradox to which I have already alluded. On the one hand, many of the horrors of the twentieth century implicate intellectuals. Modern tyrannies of the Left and the Right have sprung from the imaginations of major intellectuals. In terms of the task at hand, intellectuals have taken upon themselves to be political educators, and gulags and concentration camps have been the result. But, on the other hand, the key opponents to these tyrannies have included intellectuals: such people as the ones I came to know in the alternative world of Polish theater and in the opposition circles of Poland, Hungary, Czechoslovakia, and beyond. What do intellectuals do when they support democracy? And what do they do when they are among its primary opponents? These are the central normative questions posed in my book *Civility and Subversion.*[25] Here, I ask the additional question, how can the answers to the first two questions inform an approach to the liberal arts?

Concerning the political role of intellectuals: I present the conclusions of my study and consider their implications. Intellectuals are different from ordinary people. They are special kind of strangers (not foreigners). As strangers, they are both of the communities to which they belong and from elsewhere. The stranger, as Georg Simmel classically observed, is both present and absent, and has special insights and a special role to play.[26] And, I observe, this is also the case with intellectuals. They differ from the archetypical strangers, the tradesmen, in that their elsewhere is not of markets but of knowledge, of theories, literatures, and histories, that reach beyond the local. Intellectuals are special kinds of strangers, who pay special attention to their critical faculties. To the degree to which they are independent and not just servants of one prince or another, they act autonomously of the centers of power and address a general public.

And, crucially, the way these strangers address their public determines whether they support or undermine democracy. If they address the public to promote discussion and common action, they play the specialized democratic role. They enable the people to speak with each other and act in concert. This is what happened in the recent past of Central Europe. It is, for example, what Vaclav Havel and Adam Michnik did by revealing how intellectuals can help bring into being new democracies. But if intellectuals dogmatically assert the answers and use power to enforce the answers, if they act as ideologists as did Marx and Lenin and all the lesser Marxist-Leninists, they serve tyranny, or, at the very least, undermine democratic practices.

Intellectuals serve democracy by opening and encouraging discussion about things that matter, and they undermine democracy when they substitute their theories and ideologies for democratic political deliberation, judgment, and decision. The major democratic role of intellectuals, then, is to cultivate and provoke informed public discussion. I identify two ways by which this is accomplished: first, by making discussion possible between those who do not understand each other, who view each other as enemies. This is the project of civility. The second way that intellectuals open discussion is by revealing how some common sense, some prevailing view, hides or represses matters that are in need of public attention and discussion. This is the project of subversion. In *Civility and Subversion* I consider a number of different civil and subversive intellectuals, including John Dewey, Walter Lippmann, C. Wright Mills, Edward Said, Martin Luther King Jr., and Malcolm X. I attempt to show that intellectuals are as important in the United States in the support of democracy as they have been in Central Europe. I argue that this is because intellectuals enhance our society's capacity to deliberate, and that this is sorely needed. It is here that we see liberal arts education performing the equivalent of the extraordinary activities of Central European oppositions. Such an education works to enhance the quality and capacity to deliberate, as a normal course of action.

The actions of democratic intellectuals and the democratic contribution of a liberal arts education are not ideological. They are, in fact, anti-ideological. They do not serve a particular political program or self-consciously serve particular political interests, rather they open their audiences—the general public in the case of intellectuals, students in the case of a liberal education—to informed discussion. When I assert this, it does not mean that I am unaware of the fact that all the intellectuals I have mentioned, from Dewey to Michnik to Malcolm X, have strong political opinions, nor am I unaware that even teachers in the most esoteric of liberal arts seminars also have political commitments. Yet, the democratic intellectual and the successful teacher do not impose a political view, rather they open problems to alternative views that interact with each other.

The key question centers on the quality of the conversation that is liberal education, not its ideological position. The greatness of the American university, the fact that it is a sort of miracle (something that Edward Said observed in a public lecture[27]), is not that it is a center of progressive political politics, to the Left of the political consensus of the American society. This is incidental, something that may or may not conform to the horrified imaginations of conservative critics of the American academy. Its distinction is not derived from the fact that we pass on a political prejudice to our students but rather because we are part of an institution that has opened American discourse and public life. My pride in being a member of the New School for Social Research, for example, is connected to the fact that since 1919 that university has distinguished itself by the clarity of its commitment to academic freedom and innovation. Whether it has been a matter of World War I dissidents, or exiles from nazi Europe, or the dissidents from the former Soviet bloc, we have broadened American academic discussion by including the politically marginal. We subverted the common sense of American academia, as we made it possible for broader perspectives to civilly engage each other. I think of Alfred Schutz's attempts to make European phenomenology and American pragmatism talk to each other, of Hannah Arendt presenting a conversation between German political theory and American political history, of my colleagues today at the graduate faculty who specialize in broadening the American academy and making it more cosmopolitan. We are special agents in what I like to think of as an international cosmopolitan conspiracy. Then and now, the special contribution of the university is not only that an alternative is being presented to the prevailing view (the task of subversion), but also a dialogue is being established with prevailing views (the task of civility).

Let's observe, then, how the liberal arts work to undermine the cynicism. A liberal education provides an understanding of the importance of our inheritance of culture. Culture, that is, as a taste-judging activity that supports the capacity to reflect and the ability to take part in critical discourse as an end in itself. Teaching culture, in this sense, has always been the concern of a minority and an important part of the liberal arts. In that it has always supported and been supported by the class system, it is in danger of disappearing in mass democracies. Quantitative calculations are replacing qualitative judgments. An image-making elite is replacing a cultural elite. Culture is a noninstrumental activity, not required for the growth of modern technological order. But the uselessness of culture, nonetheless, does have a place in democracy as an alien force that provides the possibility of renewal and critical examination. This is the reason why my colleague Agnes Heller, in a recent public presentation, underscored the importance of culture when she answered her own question, "Does democracy require a cultural elite?" in the affirmative.[28] Culture, and the elite that defends it, presents quality in a sea of quantity, an outpost and an independent public zone, which Heller hopes is a part of liberal education, providing an alternative to the young during their time of prolonged adolescence. This cultural enterprise, as a significant part of the liberal arts, helps educators and students to confront the world in a complexity that is overlooked by the normal instrumental logic of modern times. It provides alternatives. By being organized around the non-instrumental activity of judging quality, it subverts the logic of quantity. In my terms, the critical study of the cultural inheritance, as Heller understands it, contributes to the subversive role of the intellectual and the liberal arts. It makes it possible to discuss problems that, from the dominant perspective of market calculation, are invisible.

But a liberal education should not stop here. There is great promise in critically considering how our cultural inheritance is limited and in working on its expansion. The elitism that Heller defends poses problems. The critical insights and understandings of the world of vast parts of humanity have not been considered as part of the liberal arts project, as educators such as Michael Oakeshott have taught students about the great conversation of what it means to be human. In another recent public presentation, my colleague Heidi Krueger reflected on this issue. What we pass on to the next generation about the world they are to inherit is highly problematic, given the plurality of the human experience. Liberal education is challenged by the knowledge at the margins, both because a discreet kind of knowledge is added and because this addition changes the conversation and transforms the terms of critical cultural discourse, makes it difficult for people to understand one another, confuses what it means to be human. I think this is where civility, and our discussion of the importance of the free public space and its relationship with the liberal arts, comes in. It is in the dialogue between the previously included and the previously excluded (Krueger highlights Faulkner and Morrison), and in the conversation with students about such problematic dialogue, that the liberal arts civility project can be found. If we understand that a liberal education is about preparing students to take part in the conversation about what it means to be human, a broader range of human experiences, much of which has been excluded from the prevailing cultural practices of liberal arts colleges and universities, has to be confronted. But this is not to come to a new conception of truth or a competition among a wide array of knowledges, it seems to me. It is so that a wider, enriched, and more broadly informed conversation can develop. This implies an education in competing perspectives, with a broadened understanding of the plurality of human experiences, but it also suggests the need to cultivate and pass on the cultural project of civility. It makes it possible for those who disagree, who do not understand each other, or who do not even recognize each other to converse with each other and with students of the next generation.

Considering the subversive project of culture and the civil project of confronting the Other has its problems. If culture is taken out of the special liberal arts space of conversing about what it means to be human, if it is taken out of its dialogic framework and is dogmatically asserted and taught, as many of the defenders of the Western tradition would have it, then it becomes a justification of the privilege, of the educated from certain places with certain characteristics both social and biological. Then the critiques of the knowledge of dead white men, and the like, come to make some sense. The notion that cultural refinement is but an instrument for class distinction, as the distinguished French sociologist Pierre Bourdieu infamously (in my judgment) implies, would be confirmed.[29] And there is a danger that the cultural activities of the marginal, or of the less formally educated, will not be appreciated.

But if the insights of the marginal, of the multicultural, are taken out of the dialogical context that is liberal education, the result is no better. There is a danger of confusing context for content, for engaging in cynical dismissal of content by revealing context. We are confronted here with the problems of reductionism and relativism. There is in the present cultural environment a real threat that liberal arts educators may contribute to an unthinking cynicism rather than offer an alternative. I fear that when I hear students preface their comments with such expressions as "as a white woman, I think . . ." or "as an Asian American, I believe . . ." they think that knowledge and truth have been accounted for, have been confronted. As a sociologist, I know that the opinions the students have, and the courses I teach, are very much shaped by our iden-tities and by our position in society and history (i.e., they are ideological in the conventional sense I referred to above). Yet, the idea that we thus have different "knowledges," as some theorists would suggest—or worse, that we have different truths, as suggested by some students—is deeply troubling. This is the sociology of knowledge run rampant, where knowledge itself apart from sociol-ogy does not seem to have an independent existence. Such judgment exists in the shadows of ideology. It confuses cynicism for critical understanding, making it seem that if you identify the source of a theoretical proposition or a piece of art, you have understood it. Liberal arts educators must not contribute to this problem. We must attempt to show how the different positions, in themselves, may not be conflicting positions in opposition to each other but in potential dialogue with each other: a dialogue that we must help foster, a dialogue that has no easy conclusions.

And then there are questions about the practical side of the matter: how do the liberal arts relate to vocational training? How do they engage political realities?

As I have already indicated, I agree with Oakeshott, Arendt, and Heller on general principle: a liberal arts education must be distinguished from the realm of practical affairs. It cannot be understood merely as a practical instrument; rather it needs to be cultural, in Heller's sense. Yet, some qualification of this position is necessary. Reflecting on what it means to be human requires an understanding of how the world works, and this may be most soundly informed by reflecting on the experiences derived from political and economic engagements. Further, it should be recognized that the divide between the reflective and practical engagement is especially hard to discern in technology- and knowledge-driven societies. And the divide between vocational and liberal education is not something that can or should absolutely be sustained.

In part, of course, this is a practical matter. Students go to colleges and universities to get a good job. They expect to be prepared. But for this to work with rather than against the pursuit of a liberal education, this very motivation and its particular qualities should be used to serve the purpose of taking part in the liberal arts conversation. Thus, for example, when Randy Swearer, dean of Parsons School of Design, seeks to revitalize his institution by advocating that design itself should become a vital species of the "liberal arts of a technological society," he is revealing an understanding that design contributes to the discussion about what it means to be human. If we reflect on the meaning of design in our society and in history, we will understand the human condition more accurately. Design problems are linked with discussions about the true, the beautiful, and the good. Swearer tellingly addressed this when he considered the dark side of modernism and the activities of designers and architects during the Nazi era. Considering the problematic relationships between politics and design is important to the training of designers in a knowledge-driven society, an immediate practical concern of Swearer, and also to the education of citizens of such a society, as a contribution to a liberal education.

The link between liberal education and citizenship used to come naturally to the liberal arts colleges of America. The relationship between the community and the liberal arts colleges was once something that occurred quite routinely. Political engagement followed a normal course; much of it deeply implicated in class, gender, and racial privileges. The colleges' prestige and the elite status of the students prepared them to be leaders in their communities, and this led to broader political commitments. More recently, the relationship has come to be one of what Eugene Lang calls "random initiatives of volunteerism." While civic concerns and pressing social issues "permeate the humanities and social sciences," Lang observes, they are strangely disconnected to how these concerns and issues confront the greater community outside the academic setting. In order to keep liberal arts colleges and their privileged students honest, or at least to enable them to serve democracy, they must be engaged with the wider community. Community engagement and political activism thus can serve as a part of the liberal arts experience. It informs liberal education through the experience in the outside world. Lang advocates one specific area of activity, support of public education, as an example of the sort of concerted engagement he has in mind. He cogently argues that liberal arts colleges are well configured to help address major problems of our primary and secondary school systems. Liberal arts students can help solve a major social problem as they learn the tools of citizenship and community involvement. The ideal of citizenship can be learned as it is realized in the practical action of community involvement. But, it seems to me, this good practical and theoretical purpose must be committed to opening and sustaining the liberal arts conversation in order for the liberal arts to maintain their special cultural purpose.

There still is danger when the liberal arts are conflated with practical political and economic activity. When liberal education, vocational education, and citizenship involvement are not separated, the fundamental character of liberal learning may be lost. It may be cynically reduced as a means to economic or political ends. Liberal education loses its identity when it becomes indistinguishable from vocation and citizenship. This can only be avoided when vocational concerns and political engagement are committed to opening and sustaining the liberal arts conversation. Ultimately, this is a commitment to free conversation and free public interaction of the sort that I observed in the theaters of Eastern Europe and that we have all observed in the grand changes in that part of the world, as they have changed their world and ours. It also is the sort of conversation that characterizes educational interaction, especially in that rare thing, a successful liberal arts seminar.

I am reminded of one such seminar, which I hope will help me successfully to sustain my argument. A quick analysis of the seminar's proceedings will tie together and qualify a bit what I have been trying to argue here. In fact, the seminar, titled "The Post Totalitarian Mind," was the inspiration for this chapter.

We had in this particular first-year seminar a respectful transgenerational conversation about what it means to be human. We worked on how the experiences of the totalitarian past and its opposition spoke to the students' concerns, particularly concerning political responsibility. They began to learn what it means to have lived in the twentieth century. Their common sense was challenged, subverted in fact; for example, they came to appreciate political authority in ways they did not expect. But they also came to understand the difficult task of civility, as it has existed through time—what it means to have a mutually respectful conversation with someone with whom you have fundamental disagreements. They were introduced to and appreciated the task of culture and the importance of considering the Other. They connected their reflections to their imagined vocational ambitions, and they did it in a way that reached beyond the narrow confines of the usual college discussion.

One of the high points of the seminar was a meeting with someone who is a master of civility and subversion, Adam Michnik, and who for them, as a result of our seminar, was not just a famous and clever intellectual celebrity but a thinker and political actor who took responsibility by acting in the most difficult of circumstances, the author of texts that repeatedly return to the project of respecting and learning from one's political and cultural Other. For the students, after reading Hannah Arendt on Eichmann and the origins of totalitarianism, the great importance of such action and civility was something they appreciated.

In the seminar, the students came to understand the importance of public space, as they, themselves, constituted the public space of the seminar. I was their teacher, in that the books we read and our central themes were predetermined by me, but the actual intellectual transaction that is the liberal arts existed among the equal members of the seminar; this is the paradox of my strong insistence on the distinction between politics and education and the need to keep out the world of immediate economic and political considerations so that education can proceed.

I served as a guide to the students in moving them from the insulated world of the American high school to the intellectually vibrant world of higher education, but once the step into serious reflection was made, our interaction was not that of hierarchy but of equality. I used my authority to prepare them to practice intellectual equality, with each other and with me. I demonstrated by self-consciously practicing equality with them. Liberal arts education starts with the authority of the teacher but proceeds with the equality of inquirers. This is, I think, where we find the link between the liberal arts mission of universities and their advanced research mission. Ideally, the only things that distinguish participants in a seminar, and distinguish the participants in scholarly inquiry of the most advanced sort, are the knowledge and quality of mind that go into the seminar and scholarly contributions. It is this equality, and the fact that the teacher learns as much from the students as they do from him or her, that reveals the active preparation for the world that is higher education. A liberal arts education, such as the one my class and I experienced, challenges the students (including the teacher) to question common sense and prepares them for civil discussion with those who are different, or who think and act differently. Utilizing civility and subversion, the liberal arts should, and often do, challenge cynicism, because they teach students and professors to constitute a common field of mutually respectful conversation that is the basis of democracy in a civil society.

Thus, when we try to support democracy through practical action, it is necessary to go beyond misleading academic truisms, as well as self-satisfied ideological positions. It is clear to the critical academician that the university is part of the "state ideological apparatus." Whether she or he uses the clumsy Althusserian language or not, the truth it seeks to name is overwhelming. Education is a means by which the prevailing order reproduces itself. Cultural works that glorify the powers are enshrined in canons, and technical training prepares the young for a niche in society, from skilled workers to engineers to medical doctors to the masters of the financial world. It is equally clear to the critics of the "tenured radicals" that the adversary culture, the culture of the intellectual elite, does not properly support common values while it indoctrinates into the culture of the politically correct. There is no doubt some truth to these positions: education does prepare students for niches in the existing social formation, and American educators in institutions of higher learning are significantly to the Left of the general societal consensus. And yet, both the radical and the conservative critics confuse politics with education and overlook the most significant action in the educational domain: its special qualities as a distinctively free and open public domain. It is liberal in that it is free from and escapes the political demands of critics from the Left and the Right. Even as it is influenced by various powers, it persists as something else, with a strong family resemblance to the anti-ideological heroes of our recent past.

NOTES

1 The appreciation of totalitarianism as a distinctively modern form of tyranny is one of the major contributions of Hannah Arendt in her classic *The Origins of Totalitarianism* (New York: Harcourt, Brace, 1951). Hers is an account of the deformation of the

project of modernity yielding a truly new form of tyranny. For the present inquiry, crucial to the deformation are the distortion of critical scientific inquiry into scientistic ideology and the loss of public space in politics and in educational practices. For the latter, see Arendt's "Crisis in Education," in her *Between Past and Future* (New York: Penguin, 1980). I analyze systematically the notion of a radical alternative to totalitarian thought in my *Beyond Glasnost: The Post-Totalitarian Mind* (Chicago: University of Chicago Press, 1989).

2 Arendt, "Crisis," 177.
3 Michael Oakeshott, *The Voice of Liberal Learning* (New Haven, Yale University Press, 1989), 63.
4 Ibid., 41.
5 Liberalism (as a political doctrine and type of political regime) and liberal education are different. Although liberal political orders are relatively friendly places for liberal education (i.e., states that are formally restricted in their interventions in cultural life do tend to leave liberal arts educational institutions alone), liberal education is not only constituted in this negative fashion but also is a positive cultural endeavor, where the educational transaction between generations is linked to the question of what it means to be human. It is also a problematic cultural endeavor; on the problematic relationship between liberal orders and cultural freedom, see my *On Cultural Freedom: An Exploration of Public Life in Poland and America* (Chicago: University of Chicago Press, 1982).
6 Karl Marx, *The German Ideology,* in *The Marx-Engels Reader,* ed. Robert Tucker (New York, Norton, 1972), 136–37.
7 Vladimir Ilyich Lenin, "Party Organization and Party Literature" (1905), in *Marxism and Art,* ed. Maynard Solomon (New York: Vintage Books, 1972), 179–83.
8 Karl Mannheim, *Ideology and Utopia* (New York: Harcourt, Brace and World, 1963).
9 Paul Ricoeur provides us with a critical appreciation of Mannheim's position as it is informed by a reading of Clifford Geertz's approach to ideology. See Ricoeur, *Lectures on Ideology and Utopia* (New York: Columbia University Press, 1986).
10 Michel Foucault, *The Order of Things: An Archaeology of Human Sciences* (New York: Vintage Books, 1973), 241.
11 See Francois Furet, *The Passing of Illusion* (Chicago: University of Chicago Press, 1999).
12 Arendt, *Origins;* see especially chapter 13, "Ideology and Terror."
13 The classic development of this position is Lyotard's. See Jean-François Lyotard, *The Postmodern Condition: A Report on Knowledge* (Minneapolis: University of Minnesota Press, 1985). My favorite account can be found in Milan Kundera's novel, *The Unbearable Lightness of Being* (New York: HarperCollins, 1999).
14 See Jan Vladislav, ed., *Vaclav Havel, or Living in Truth* (Boston: Faber & Faber, 1986); Adam Michnik, *Letters from Prison and Other Essays* (Los Angeles: University of California Press, 1985); and George Konrad, *Antipolitics* (New York: Harcourt, Brace, Jovanovich, 1984). For a more complete analysis of their position see my *Beyond Glasnost.*

15 Havel, "The Power of the Powerless," in *Vaclav Havel,* 23–96.

16 Michnik, "The New Evolutionism" in *Letters from Prison and Other Essays,* 135–148.

17 Adam Michnik, *The Church and the Left* (Chicago: University of Chicago Press, 1993).

18 For a complete sampling in English, see Michnik, *Letters from Prison,* and *Letters from Freedom: Post Cold War Realities and Perspectives* (Los Angeles: University of California Press, 1998).

19 Neal Postman, *Amusing Ourselves to Death: Public Discourse in the Age of Show Business* (New York: Penguin, 1986).

20 Bruce Kimball, *Orators and Philosophers: A History of the Idea of the Liberal Education* (New York: Henry Holt, 1985).

21 Gerald Graff, *Beyond the Cultural Wars: How Teaching the Conflicts Can Revitalize American Education* (New York: Norton, 1993).

22 See Goldfarb, *The Persistence of Freedom: The Sociological Implications of Polish Student Theater* (Boulder: Westview Press, 1980).

23 See Timothy Garton Ash, *The Polish Revolution: Solidarity* (New York: Vintage Books, 1985); Lawrence Weschler, *Solidarity: Poland in the Season of Its Passions* (New York: Simon and Schuster, 1982); and David Ost, *Solidarity and the Politics of Anti-Politics: Opposition and Reform since 1968* (Philadelphia: Temple University Press, 1990).

24 Milan Kundera, *The Art of the Novel* (New York: HarperCollins, 1989), 144.

25 Jeffrey C. Goldfarb, *Civility and Subversion: The Pursuit of Democracy in Central Europe* (New York: Basic Books, 1992).

26 Donald Levine, ed., *Georg Simmel on Individuality and Social Forms* (Chicago: University of Chicago Press, 1985).

27 In a lecture given at New York University on the obligations of intellectuals, connected to his book *Representations of the Intellectual* (New York: Pantheon, 1994), Said modified his criticism of American public life, recognizing the extraordinary openness to critical voices of the American academy. I maintain that this openness is a definitive quality of education.

28 In the following pages, I am reflecting on a public discussion and seminar series in 1999 on the liberal arts at the New School for Social Research. The papers included Agnes Heller, "Does Democracy Require a Cultural Elite?"; Heidi Kreiger, "What Did Herpyliss Know?"; Randy Swearer, "Design and the Liberal Arts"; and a published paper by Eugene Lang, "Distinctively American: The Liberal Arts College," *Daedalus* (winter 1999): 133–50. In the discussion, the major competing approaches to the liberal arts were confronted. This paper is a continuation of that confrontation.

29 Pierre Bourdieu, *Distinction: A Social Critique of the Judgment of Taste,* trans. Richard Nice (Cambridge: Harvard University Press, 1984).

WENDY BROWN

Moralism as Antipolitics

◆

The Left has traditionally distinguished itself from liberal reformers by its object—critique—as well as by the drama and scope of its political vision. Rather than attend to what it regarded as contingent injustices in the social order, it criticized more fundamental dynamics of injustice or domination as inherent to the regime. While reformers addressed particular inequities or cruelties within the fabric of capitalism or liberalism, the Left located sources of suffering in what it conceived as the constitutive premises and hence the totality of these arrangements. And it called for the replacement of this totality with a radically more humane and egalitarian order of economic life, to which would correspond a less individualistic, alienated, and socially irresponsible organization of political life.

What becomes of such distinctions when the traditional objects of left critique—liberalism, capitalism, and the state—emerge as the apparently ubiquitous institutions of the present and future? What happens when these objects no longer seem eligible for replacement by alternative economic and political forms but assume only a variety of cultural and historical shapes around the globe? What becomes of the desires animating left critique and fueling left political projects when not only the historical ground but also the political and philosophical foundations of that critique and that project have been compromised beyond recognition?

This condition, in which promising alternatives to liberalism and capitalism have largely vanished, has not emerged only since the fall of the Berlin Wall and the disintegration of the Soviet Union—it has been unfolding for almost half a century. Periodically accented by events such as Khrushchev's 1956 speech detailing what the world's unconscious already knew about Stalin's atrocities, and similar revelations twenty years later about the nightmare of China's "cultural revolution," the period has been marked as well by various failed Third World

experiments in socialist autonomy and by the history of an economically impoverished, as well as culturally and politically repressed, Eastern Europe. This
history was consummated in the 1980s by the virtual disappearance of the Left in
the United States, the strikingly nonsocialist reign of François Mitterand in
France, the dramatic shrinking of Communist Parties in Western Europe, and,
finally, the crumbling of the Soviet bloc. The Reagan-Thatcher decade, characterized by Stuart Hall as one in which the Left utterly lost its way (while the Right
forged a new hegemony out of "the remaking of common sense"), is probably
best explained as part of a longer history of the unraveling of the Left: marxism
proved unable to address critical issues of need, desire, and identity formation in
late modernity, and marxist projects failed by almost all economic, political, and
eudaemonistic measures.[1] In short, in the second half of the twentieth century,
liberalism and capitalism have been quietly consolidating their gains less because
they were intrinsically successful than because their alternatives collapsed. Now
both appear fat and happy, indeed triumphant, even as they are not always able,
in Herbert Marcuse's words, "to deliver the goods"[2] either by providing stable,
just, pluralistic orders or by alleviating poverty, economic deracination, a vac-
uum in social and political meaning, and the largely unsatisfying work done by
those in almost every economic stratum.

If the viability of democratic alternatives to liberal democracy and the metaphysical grounds of the standard left critiques of liberalism both eroded significantly in the last quarter of the twentieth century, from where might the Left
draw its inspiration and its instruments of critique? And if those drawn to a left
weltanschauung have traditionally found compelling its claims to apprehend a
social totality and meaning in history, as well as its promise of a redemptive
future, where does this desire live now and, markedly unfulfilled, what form of
social expression might it take?

We are well schooled in one answer to this question. What today travels under
the name of cultural politics, identity politics, the politics of cultural diversity,
new social movement politics, or the politics of new social antagonisms is widely
considered to have taken over the ground formerly occupied by a socialist Left.
Where there was once the movement, there are now multiple sites and modalities
of emancipatory struggle and egalitarian protest. Similarly, where there was once
a millenarian, redemptive, or utopian project around which to organize the
various strategies of the political present, such projects have splintered politically
at the same time that they have been quite thoroughly discredited by cultural and
philosophical critique. Yet this description of a shift in political formations,

political analysis, and correlative theoretical articulations does not address the fate of the *desire* for total critique and total transformation, the impulse to wholly indict the structures of the present and stake all on the absolute justice of a radically transformed future. What shape does this desire take when diffused into local, issue-oriented, or identity-based struggles that generally lack a strong alternative vision and strong moral project? In the work of contemporary political activists and thinkers, what has replaced the passionate attachment to a dream of another political, social, and economic world? What are the psychic consequences for political life when total critique is abandoned and the aspirations for total transformation are shattered?[3]

In formulating these questions in terms of the fates of a left sensibility and project, I do not mean to obscure the extent to which they grip some liberals as well. Notwithstanding liberalism's sustained hegemony in the West, key premises underpinning the legitimacy and optimism of the liberal project have been shaken profoundly in recent decades. Liberal universalist and progressive principles have been challenged by the antiassimilationist claims of many current formations of politicized "differences," including those marked by ethnicity, sexuality, gender, and race; by a political ethos promulgating *agonistic* social relations associated with these cultural differences, as opposed to a model of pluralistic conflicting interests on the one hand, or of general social harmony on the other; and by the patently mythical nature of a progressive political worldview that presumes steady improvement in the general wealth, felicity, egalitarianism, and peacefulness of liberal societies. Undermined by historical as well as intellectual events in the late twentieth century, the seamlessly egalitarian social whole constituting liberalism's vision of the future now appears problematic both theoretically and practically.

Just as leftists are not free of attachment to total critique and total transformation, so liberals are not free of attachment to ontological and political universalism and hence to assimilationist politics. Neither leftists nor liberals are free of the idea of progress in history. Neither can conceive freedom or equality without rights, sovereignty, and the state, and hence without the figures of a sovereign subject and a neutral state. The consequence of living these attachments as ungrievable losses—ungrievable because they are not fully avowed as attachments and hence are unable to be claimed as losses—is theoretical as well as political impotence and rage, which is often expressed as a reproachful political moralism. Put differently, the righteous moralism that so many have registered as the characteristic political discourse of our time—as the tiresome tonality and uninspiring spirit of Right, Center, and Left—I see as a *symptom* of a certain kind of loss. Yet insofar as politics is a nonorganic domain in which symptoms transmogrify into forms of action and thence into political formation—nothing is ever *merely* a symptom—this phenomenon also must be understood as constituting a pervasive political and intellectual way of life in contemporary North America.

When genealogy replaces totalizing and dialectical history, and contests for hegemony replace progressivist formulations of change, when the future thus becomes relatively continuous with the present so that radical political discontent can no longer make a home in an analysis of a powerfully determining history and a transformed future, where does it then live? What form does this radical discontent take within the emotional substructure of political expressions and political formations? If, as Nietzsche recognized, impotent rage inevitably yields a moralizing (re)action, how might we succeed in rereading contemporary political life through this recognition? Might it help us understand, for example, the contemporary tendency to personify oppression in the figure of individuals and to reify it in particular acts and utterances, the tendency to render individuals and acts intensely culpable—indeed prosecutable—for history and for social relations? Might it help us understand the paradoxical tendency toward a politics of hypersovereignty and literalism within an ostensibly postsovereign and postliteral theoretical regime; that is, in a discursive epoch when both sovereignty and literalism have been called into question because of the models of the subject, power, and language that they embody? An inquiry along these lines also permits questions about the relationship of moralizing discourse to democratic political possibility and to the kind of free-ranging intellectual inquiry required for the nourishment of a democratic polity. What does the pervasiveness of moralizing discourse *do* to political life, to intellectual life, and, most important, to their complex claims on—and needs for—each other? Why has moralizing discourse become particularly intense in left activist and academic life, and what makes "cultural politics" particularly susceptible to this discourse ultimately subversive of the putatively emancipatory aims of such politics?

Although both morality and moralism take their bearings from and constitute their identity by distancing themselves from what they take to be power, and therefore both lodge uneasily in political life, morality and moralism are not equivalents. Thus, we might begin by distinguishing the problem I am calling political moralism from the older, more familiar problem of morality in politics. Such a distinction is not meant to suggest that morality's place in politics was ever unproblematic, that morality does not persistently risk devolving into moralism, or that morality is a straightforward political good while moralism is a political evil. But I have written elsewhere against moral truths as a substitute for political struggle, relying mainly on adaptations of Nietzsche's genealogical study of (Judeo-Christian) morality; and I now want to rethink an aspect of my critique, and Nietzsche's too, by paying closer attention to the difference between a galvanizing moral vision and a reproachful moralizing sensibility. Previously I argued that certain contemporary moral claims in politics issue from a combination of attachments—both to Truth (as opposed to power) in a postfoundational era and to identity as injury in a political domain of competing survivor stories.[4] Here, I reconsider moralizing politics as marking a crisis in political teleology. I propose to read such politics not only as a sign of stubborn clinging to a certain equation of truth with powerlessness, or as the acting out of an injured will, but as a symptom of a broken historical narrative to which we have not yet forged alternatives.

The *Oxford English Dictionary* offers an unremarkable set of definitions for *morality:* "Ethical wisdom; knowledge of moral science . . . moral qualities or endowments . . . moral discourse or instruction . . . doctrine or system concerned with conduct or duty . . . moral conduct." However, the same dictionary defines *moralism* as "addiction to moralizing . . . religion consisting of or reduced to merely moral practice; morality not spiritualized." Indeed, one citation suggests that *moralistic* is the opposite of *moral,* as the nineteenth-century theologian Boyd Carpenter discriminates between the two: "Such an action is moralistic rather than moral for it has not been prompted by the sentiment of goodness."[5]

From this account, moralism would appear to be a kind of temporal trace, a remnant of a discourse whose heritage and legitimacy it claims while in fact inverting that discourse's sense and sensibility. At the extreme, moralism may be seen as a kind of posture or pose taken up in the ruins of morality by its faithful adherents; it is thus at once a "fall" from morality, a "reversal" of morality, and an impoverished substitute for, or reaction to, the evisceration of a sustaining moral vision. As an "addiction," the compulsive quality of moralism stands opposed to measured, difficult, and deliberate action that implicates rather than simply enacts the self; as "religion reduced to merely moral practice," it consists of precepts and remonstrances whose spiritual incitation and inflection is lost to history, and whose secular enactment becomes ritualistic—and, not incidentally, often punitive. The element of punishment arises because moralism appears to be, in the Nietzschean sense, a reaction (or, more precisely, a compulsive re-proach) to a certain kind of action or power and thus a recrimination against the life force that action or power represents. To continue briefly in a Nietzschean vein, moralism, considered as an effect or consequence of weakened life forces, strikes at what appears to subordinate or humiliate it (but which has actually produced it): expressions of life forces or power. As a codification of disappoint-ment or disenthrallment, it seeks to make a world in its own self-image and thus reproves everything tainted with power. In this way, a strange breed of nihilism—opposition to life itself—disguises itself in the clothing of its opposite: righteous political principle.

But while the distinction between moralism and morality is rendered sharply in dictionaries, in politics the two have a closer relationship. There is, of course, a long tradition of inquiry into the place of morality in politics. In the West, it could be said to extend from Thucydides, the Sophists, and Aristotle's critique of Plato through Machiavelli, Kant, Croce, E. H. Carr, Hans Morgenthau, Martin Luther King Jr., and Gandhi. These last four names remind us that in the twen-tieth century, the question of morality's place in politics has mostly been cast as setting "realpolitik" against "moral or religious principle," although this formu-lation is not, as Machiavelli made clear in his relentless exposé of the papacy as both an instrument and culture of power, without a certain analytic duplicity. Even in its least philosophical modality, the problematic of morality in politics is usually thought to center on the complex relation between principle and power, or on the important intervals between aim, strategy, action, and effect. Conven-tional inquiries into morality and politics almost always assume the relationship between principle and power to be fully antagonistic, whether through the no-tion that "power corrupts" or through its mirror, that "principle is averse to power"; in either case the potential for absolute goodness is conferred on princi-ple and absolute evil on power. It is this assumption that Machiavelli most boldly and Nietzsche most ingeniously reversed. Refusing principle's ruse of represent-ing its aim as indifferent to power—and thereby exposing the will to power in principle and especially, for Machiavelli, in Christian principle—both thinkers sought to depict the power that could play under the name of moral principle disguising itself as unarmed.[6]

Notwithstanding this critique and its more recent embellishments by Fou-cault, a formulation of the relationship of politics and morality that reduces to "power versus principle" has persisted into the present, especially when violence is at issue. Consider the kind of conundrums generally posed to students contemplating the place of morality in politics: According to what criteria can economic sanctions be said to be more humane than other forms of international aggression? Is nuclear warfare uniquely immoral in the history of humankind? Is property damage in the course of civil disobedience consistent with principles of nonviolent protest? When is war as such justified; when is pacifism or non-intervention immoral? Do women have the moral right to determine the fate of fetal life carried in their own bodies? Do humans have the moral right to kill animals? What is common, and commonly irritating, about these questions is that they formulate a moral problem abstracted from the specific context in which such questions arise, and disavow as well the discursive framing through which they are proffered. Precisely for this reason morality often has been regarded by critical political thinkers as not simply a naive but a depoliticizing form of political discourse: consider how different the "moral" question of abortion appears when emphasis is placed on women's near-total responsibility for children in a historically produced context of relative lack of control over the terms of sexual, economic, and political life—that is, in a context of the powers that make and organize gender.

Yet the play of morality in politics is not entirely confined to relatively abstract dilemmas about right action or moral limits to the exercise of power. Whole political formations have taken their bearings from their moral opposition to a historically specific "immoral" regime. The founding and sustaining principle of the Civil Rights movement in the United States was the immorality of racial segregation in a liberal democratic nation; substantively and tactically, the movement staked everything on opposing the differential treatment of citizens in an ostensibly egalitarian order as a moral wrong. It explicitly posed—as did Gandhi's campaigns against British colonial rule and the Indian caste system—moral right *against* power. But these movements also turned principle into an explicit and self-conscious form of power that worked by distinguishing itself in style, bearing, and tactics from the power and interests of the regime it decried.

To be sure, a theological pathos is operative when a rhetorical opposition is established between the virtuous position of the disenfranchised and the iniquity of dominance. This is the pathos Nietzsche denounced as slave morality for its general objection to power as such. But here, Nietzsche may have failed to distinguish adequately between active moral struggles against subordination and the reproaches and nay-saying of what he called slave morality. Certainly, the movements led by King and Gandhi would seem to be instances of the former insofar as they affirmed the capacity of the subjugated to *overcome* their injury, their socially structured subordination, and to assume a place in the world, rather than as Nietzsche insisted slave morality always does—to distribute their suffering in the world, "to make others suffer as the sufferer does."[7]

The shared features of these affirmative moral struggles also distinguish them from projects animated by political moralism: their relatively open, democratic character; their tendency not to vest the evil they are fighting in persons or even in social positions but rather in social arrangements and institutions; and the relative abstractness of their motivating principle—its lack of cultural specificity or attachment to a particular people. While these movements did not wholly eschew the phenomenon of identity produced through oppression, neither did they build solidarity on the basis of that production; rather, solidarity was rooted in shared beliefs. They did not make a cultural or political fetish out of subordinated identities, out of the *effects* of subordination. Moreover, these movements were fueled by opposition to specifically articulated political systems or social arrangements—segregation, colonialism, or caste society—rather than by opprobrium toward persons (whites or the British) or by amorphous campaigns against racism. In a word, these were movements that took shape within the humanist tradition of universal principles, particularly the principles of universal human value and universal human rights.

But if these movements differed markedly from what today often travels under the sign of cultural politics, especially insofar as they eschewed cultivation of identity-bound difference claims, they might be critically interrogated precisely for their unreflexive traffic with humanism—their embrace of universal and even essentialized personhood, their inattention to cultural difference, their relative neglect of the historically contingent and contextual character of political life. Here one would ask both when a movement for inclusion is problematically assimilationist, because indifferent to the norms regulating that assimilation, and also when a movement animated by moral principle can be fouled by the contextually specific political constraints and content with which it must deal. To the extent that the classical invocation of morality in politics entails subscription to universalism, it is not only contemporary antihumanist or posthumanist critics but also those in the "realist" tradition of Machiavelli and Morgenthau who are dubious about the fit between such universals and the contingencies of politics. Indeed, Machiavelli's sharpest criticism of a moral politics pertained not to its naïveté about human motives or human nature but to naïveté about the dynamics of power and fluidity of context in which actions motivated by the finest of intentions produce effects of incalculable tragedy and suffering. Hence Machiavelli's disturbing rumination: "If a prince has [only virtues] and always practices them, they are harmful; and if he appears to have them, they are useful."[8] Because the realm of politics cannot be ordered by will and intention, but is a complex domain of unintended consequences that follow the unpredictable collisions of human, historical, and natural forces, a politics of abstract principle risks missing its aim and indeed producing the opposite of the wished-for result. "Therefore, [a prince] must have a mind ready to turn in any direction as Fortune's winds and the variability of affairs require[;] . . . he holds to what is right when he can but knows how to do wrong when he must."[9] And it may be precisely when the limitations of a politics of morality reveal itself to highly invested players that a moral politics inevitably begins to acquire some of the trappings of a moralizing one. Those who are no longer able to *act* in good-faith accord with their moral vision strike out angrily against the world that affords their adherence only mockery. Life-affirming moral passion in this way converts to life-negating moralizing rancor, an effect that Nietzsche memorably characterized as "this *instinct for freedom* forcibly made latent . . . pushed back and repressed, incarcerated within and finally able to discharge and vent itself only on itself: that, and that alone, is what the *bad conscience* is in its beginnings."[10]

Neither a pure politics of morality nor of realpolitik describes the political or theoretical register in which we are primarily ensconced today. With the exception of a relatively marginal order of religious activists, cultural feminists, and nonviolent peace workers, most leftists and liberals do not subscribe to the opposition between Truth and Power on which both a politics of morality and a politics of realism depend. The conventional (Platonic, Christian, marxist, and liberal) equation of truth and goodness on one side and power and oppression on the other has been disrupted both by the late modern decentering, multiplication, and politicization of Truth and by critiques of modernist formulations of power as repressive, commoditylike in form, or independent of hegemonic truth claims. Even where these critiques are either unacknowledged or explicitly rejected—where the morality- and truth-bearing capacities of powerlessness are fiercely reasserted against all that has discredited the partnership—the attempt of powerlessness to claim truth is shaken by the crumbling of utopian or millennial political visions: with little hope and no precise architecture for a radically different order, the martyred in *this* world have a sharply attenuated moral-epistemological status. While martyrdom may retain an element of rhetorical force, it is moralistic rather than moral insofar as it no longer can draw on any larger cosmology.[11]

But the loss of conventional epistemological ground for a strong moral position, and even for morality as such, does not quash the moral impulse itself. Here we return along a different path to the question with which we began: what form does this impulse take when it has lost its lodging in an abstract principle and vision of the good . . . when moral claims reduce to moralizing complaint? It is when the telos of the good vanishes but the yearning for it remains that morality appears to devolve into moralism in politics. It is at this point that one finds moralizers standing against much but for very little, adopting a voice of moral judgment in the absence of a full-fledged moral apparatus and vision. Alternatively, the moralizer refuses the loss of the teleological and becomes reactionary: clinging without logical ground to the last comforting frame in the unraveling narrative—pluralism, the working class, universal values, the movement, standpoint epistemology, a melting pot America, woman's essential nature—whatever it was that secured the status of the true, the status of the good, and their unbroken relationship. This, too, is a form of moralizing, but it takes the especially peculiar shape of reproaching history by personifying and reifying its effects in particular individuals, social formations, theories, or belief structures. Thus, for example, some leftists have recently called for the resuscitation of universal political identity and a universal progressive political aim, while blaming something they name "postmodernism" or "identity politics" for the loss of these goods and for the promulgation of highly fractured (and fractious) political claims and aims. In a similar vein, many denounce as morally or politically bankrupt those theoretical formations that call into question the privileged ontological and epistemological status of the oppressed or that do not prescribe the nature of the good. "If poststructuralist theory cannot tell us what to value and what to fight for," a colleague of mine recently queried a graduate student in a qualifying examination, "what can possibly be its worth for political thinking?" But dubiously grounded political *doctrine,* rather than political thinking, would seem to be what my marxist colleague was really mourning. And democratically contestable, partial, provisional political judgments appeared to be what he was moralizing against.

Despite its righteous insistence on knowing what is True, Valuable, or Important, moralism as a hegemonic form of political expression, a dominant political sensibility, actually marks both analytic impotence and political aimlessness—a misrecognition of the political logics now organizing the world, a concomitant failure to discern any direction for action, and the loss of a clear object of political desire.[12] In particular, the moralizing injunction to act, the contemporary academic formulation of political action as an imperative, might be read as a symptom of political paralysis in the face of radical political disorientation and as a kind of hysterical mask for the despair that attends such paralysis. This is the very dynamic Nietzsche denoted as issuing from the "instinct for freedom forcibly made latent." However tendentious the language of instinct, what remains compelling in Nietzsche's understanding of the dynamic in which a desire for freedom or the will to power is turned back on itself is the idea that a life force flattened into a passive or paralyzed stance toward the world turns against life as it turns against itself; it turns against that which incites the subject to overcome itself. Indeed, paralysis of this sort leads to far more than an experience of mere frustration: it paradoxically evinces precisely the nihilism, the antilife bearing, that it moralizes against in its nemesis—whether that nemesis is called conservatism, the forces of reaction, racism, postmodernism, or theory.

While moralizing discourse symptomizes impotence and aimlessness with regard to making a future, it also marks a peculiar relationship to history, one that holds history responsible, even morally culpable, at the same time as it evinces a disbelief in history as a teleological force. When belief in the continuity and forward movement of historical forces is shaken, even as those forces appear so powerful as to be very nearly determining, the passionate political will is frustrated in all attempts to gain satisfaction at history's threshold: it can acquire neither an account of the present nor any future there. The perverse triple consequence is a kind of moralizing *against* history in the form of condemning particular events or utterances, personifying history in individuals, and disavowing history as a productive or transformative force. This triple effect, and the limits it imposes on a substantive emancipatory politics, is captured in the often overburdened significance ascribed to "subject position"—one's own and others'—in our time. Having lost our faith in history, we reify and prosecute its *effects* in one another, even as we reduce our own complexity and agency to those misnamed effects.

Morality stands in an uneasy relationship to the political insofar as it is always mistrustful of power; and it bears a slightly truncated relationship to the intellectual insofar as it is rarely willing to explore the seamy underside of righteousness or goodness in politics. Moralism is much less ambivalent: it tends to be intensely antagonistic toward a richly agonistic political or intellectual life. Moralism so loathes overt manifestations of power—its ontological and epistemological premises are so endangered by signs of action and agency—that the moralist inevitably feels antipathy toward politics as a domain of open contestation for power and hegemony. But the identity of the moralist is also staked against intellectual questioning that might dismantle the foundations of its own premises; its survival is imperiled by the very practice of open-ended intellectual inquiry. It is thus in a moralistic mode that the most expansive revolutionary doctrines—liberalism, Maoism, or multiculturalism—so often transmogrify into their opposite, into brittle, defensive, and finally conservative institutions and practices. Here I offer an example from within the academy.

At a workshop on the present and future of "cultural studies"—where this amorphous academic entity was taken to include women's studies, sexuality (queer) studies, ethnic studies, and certain types of American and other area studies—I reflected aloud on worries I have been harboring for some time about the institutionalization of political identities as academic programs. My focus was women's studies, which I know best, and the first part of my presentation went as follows:

> I have had a number of conversations in the last few years that may bear kinship with some that American Communist Party members had with each other in the fifties. Here is the prototype: I meet someone whose name has long been familiar to me as both a feminist scholar and trenchworker in the field of women's studies. She helped build women's studies at her institution and for years has defended it against onslaughts—political, financial, and internal—threatening its survival. She is possibly on the editorial board of one or more feminist journals, and is prominent in various feminist professional and political associations. She bears the scars and the pride of years of feminist work, both inside and outside the academy.
>
> Because we have not met before but, like members of the Old Left, we have fundamental work and commitments in common, we begin getting to know each other by talking about that work. And then—the shift is always imperceptible—we begin to connect through another bond, a complexly traitorous bond, as it becomes evident that we are both taking distance from women's studies. We may chair programs in it, publicly defend it, teach courses in it, have part or all of our faculty appointment in it, and know that it not only once gave us life but perhaps now butters our bread. But we don't identify with it anymore, or we don't need it anymore, or our work isn't located there anymore, or perhaps most devastating of all, we don't believe in it anymore.

Why are these conversations happening and how might they usefully go public? Why are certain established feminist scholars having such senti-ments, and why are younger scholars notably not drawn to women's stud-ies? What has it meant to institutionalize a program rooted in contingent social identity, how has our own scholarship imploded this identity and exposed the many facets of its contingency, and what is the consequently fraught or conservative nature of the intellectual position women's studies now finds itself having to occupy in order to persist?

Here is a second way into this problem. The women's studies program at my university recently undertook that frightening project of self-scrutiny known as curriculum revision. What brought us to this point is itself inter-esting. For a number of years, we limped along with a set of requirements consisting of an odd mix of the generic and the political. *The generic:* students were required to take a three-term sequence consisting of "Intro-duction to Feminism," "Feminist Theory," and "Methodological Perspec-tives in Feminism," a sequence marked by distinctions scandalously at odds with the expansive understanding of theory and the critique of methodism putatively fundamental to feminist inquiry. *The political:* the only other content-specific requirement for the major was a course called "Women of Color in the United States." This strange combination of genres in the curricular requirements underscored for students the isolated intellectual (and putatively nonracialized) character of something called theory, the isolated (and putatively nontheoretical) political mandate of race, and the illusion that there was something called method (applied theory?) that unified all feminist research and thinking. It also meant that most women's studies students regarded the requirements as something to be borne, and the major as having its rewards elsewhere. Finally, and most disturbing, the limited and incoherent nature of these requirements as a course of study meant that some of our students were obtaining BAs on the basis of very poor educations, something women have had too much of for too long.

But what happened when we finally sat down to revise the curriculum is even more interesting than what the previous curriculum symptomized. We found ourselves absolutely stumped over the question of what a women's studies curriculum should contain. Since, in addition to trying to provide curricular integrity, we were also trying to address faculty frustration about students not being well enough trained in anything to ever provide reward-ing classroom exchange in the faculty's areas of expertise, we focused in-tently on the question of what would constitute an intellectually rigorous program as well as an intellectually coherent one. We speculatively explored a number of different possibilities—a thematically organized curriculum, pathways that roughly followed the disciplines—but each possibility collapsed under close analysis. We also found ourselves repeatedly mired in a strange chasm between faculty and students in the program: Most of our 200-plus majors were interested in some variant of feminist sociological or psychological analysis—experientially, empirically, and practically oriented. Not one of our core faculty worked in sociology, psychology, or ahistorical empirical studies.

If the practical project we set for ourselves was running aground, certainly we were in the grip of an important historical-political problem. Why, when we looked closely at this thing so hard fought for and now academically institutionalized, could we find no there there? We were up against more than the oft-discussed divide between women's studies and feminist theory, the political insidiousness of the institutional division between ethnic studies and women's studies, a similarly disturbing division between queer theory and feminist work, or the way that the ostensibly less identitarian rubric of cultural studies promises to relieve these troubling distinctions. And we were up against more than the paradox that the disciplines which have been so denatured in recent years are also apparently that which we cannot do without, if only to position ourselves against them within them. We were also up against more than the dramatic fracturing of women's studies as a domain of inquiry during the 1980s—the fact that contemporary feminist scholarship is not in mass group conversation but is, rather, engaged with respective disciplines, or bodies of theory, that are themselves infrequently engaged with each other. And we were up against more than the ways that this decade's theoretical challenges to the stability of the category of gender, and political challenges to a discourse of gender apart from race, class, and other severe markers of identity, constituted very nearly overwhelming challenges to women's studies as a coherent endeavor. We were up against more than the fact that the impulses which had fomented women's studies have now disseminated themselves—appropriately, productively, and in ways that profoundly challenged the turf women's studies had claimed as its own.

We were up against more than any one of these challenges because we were up against all of them. But rather than considering them in their specificity, I want to suggest that together, they call us to account for our effort to *institutionalize* as curriculum, method, field, major, or bachelor of arts what was a profoundly important *political* moment in the academy, the moment at which the women's movement challenged the ubiquitous misogyny, masculinism, and sexism establishing norms and exclusions in academic research, curricula, canons, and pedagogies. Indisputably, Women's Studies as a critique of such practices was politically important and intellectually creative. Women's Studies as contemporary institution, however, may be politically and theoretically incoherent, and tacitly conservative. It is incoherent because by definition it circumscribes uncircumscribable "women" as an object of study, and it is conservative because it must, finally, resist all objections to such circumscription: hence the persistent theory wars, and race wars, and sex wars, notoriously ravaging women's studies. Theory that destabilizes the category of women, racial formations that disrupt the unity or primacy of the category, and sexualities that similarly blur the solidarity of the category—each of these must be resisted, or worse, colonized, to preserve the realm. Each, therefore, will be compelled to go elsewhere; and women's studies will consolidate itself in the remains, impoverished by the lack of challenges from within, bewildered by its new ghettoization in the academy, a ghettoization produced this time by feminists themselves. There is no such thing as women's studies. Now what?[13]

The overwhelming response to these reflections, from my cultural studies colleagues ostensibly gathered for a day of critical self-reflection, was glowering silence later broken by sotto voce hallway denunciations of my presentation as "reactionary" and "collaborationist with the enemy." While attempting to articulate what I took to be something approximating a crisis in women's studies, I had broken the taboo against calling into question the institutionalization of critical political moments inside and outside the academy. The punishment for this breach was moralism at its finest: to reproach the questioning *and* the questioner as politically heinous, hence also intellectually unworthy.

"Speech codes kill critique," Henry Louis Gates remarked in a 1993 essay on hate speech.[14] Although Gates was referring to what happens when hate speech regulations, and the debates about them, usurp the discursive space in which one might have offered a substantive *political* response to bigoted epithets, his point also applies to prohibitions against questioning from within selected political practices or institutions. But turning political questions into moralistic ones—as speech codes of any sort do—not only prohibits certain questions and mandates certain genuflections, it also expresses a profound hostility toward political life insofar as it seeks to preempt argument with a legislated and enforced truth. And the realization of that patently undemocratic desire can only and always convert emancipatory aspirations into reactionary ones. Indeed, it insulates those aspirations from questioning at the very moment that Weberian forces of rationalization and bureaucratization are quite likely to be domesticating them from another direction. Here we greet a persistent political paradox: the moralistic defense of critical practices, or of any besieged identity, weakens what it strives to fortify precisely by sequestering those practices from the kind of critical inquiry out of which they were born. Thus Gates might have said, "Speech codes, born of social critique, kill critique." And, we might add, contemporary identity-based institutions, born of social critique, invariably become conservative as they are forced to essentialize the identity and naturalize the boundaries of what they once grasped as a contingent effect of historically specific social powers.

But moralistic reproaches to certain kinds of speech or argument kill critique not only by displacing it with arguments about abstract rights versus identity-bound injuries, but also by configuring political injustice and political righteousness as a problem of remarks, attitude, and speech rather than as a matter of historical, political-economic, and cultural formations of power. Rather than offering analytically substantive accounts of the forces of injustice or injury, they condemn the manifestation of these forces in particular remarks or events. There is, in the inclination to ban (formally or informally) certain utterances and to mandate others, a politics of rhetoric and gesture that itself symptomizes despair over effecting change at more significant levels. As vast quantities of left and liberal attention go to determining what socially marked individuals say, how they are represented, and how many of each kind appear in certain institutions or are appointed to various commissions, the sources that generate racism, poverty, violence against women, and other elements of social injustice remain relatively unarticulated and unaddressed. We are lost as how to address those sources; but rather than examine this loss or disorientation, rather than bear the humiliation of our impotence, we posture as if we were still fighting the big and good fight in our clamor over words and names. Don't mourn, moralize.

But here the problem goes well beyond superficiality of political analysis or compensatory gestures in the face of felt impotence. A moralistic, gestural politics often inadvertently becomes a regressive politics. Moralizing condemnation of the National Endowment for the Arts for not funding politically radical art, of the U.S. military or the White House for not embracing open homosexuality or sanctioning gay marriage, or even of the National Institutes of Health for not treating as a political priority the lives of HIV target populations (gay men, prostitutes, and drug addicts) is a politics that conveys at best naive political expectations—and at worst, patently confused ones. For this condemnation implicitly figures the state (and other mainstream institutions) as if it did not have specific political and economic investments, as if it were not the codification of various dominant social powers, but was, rather, a momentarily misguided parent who forgot her promise to treat all her children the same way. These expressions of moral outrage implicitly cast the state as if it were or could be a deeply democratic and nonviolent institution; conversely, it renders radical art, radical social movements, and various fringe populations as if they were not potentially subversive, representing a significant political challenge to the norms of the regime, but rather were benign entities and populations entirely appropriate for the state to equally protect, fund, and promote. Here, moralism's objection to politics as a domain of power and history rather than principle is not simply irritating: it results in a troubling and confused politics. It misleads about the nature of power, the state, and capitalism; it misleads about the nature of oppressive social forces, and about the scope of the project of transformation required by serious ambitions for justice. Such obfuscation is not the aim of the moralists but falls within that more general package of displaced effects consequent to a felt yet unacknowledged impotence. It signals disavowed despair over the prospects for more far-reaching transformations.

What of moralism in intellectual life, represented by what has often been termed "political correctness" inside and outside the academy—a high level of righteousness, defensiveness, and concomitant refusal of the very intellectual and political agonism that one expects to find celebrated in left and liberal thinking? How have commitments to knowledge, questioning, and intellectual depth been overtaken by the kind of fundamentalism historically associated with conservatives?[15] To what extent is moralism within intellectual life a displaced response to political paralysis outside the academy, a paralysis guiltily taken up by and turned back against intellectual life in self-flagellating fashion? Does this anti-intellectual self-flagellation itself substitute for action in the face of despair about action? Or is this moralism a response to an aimlessness within contemporary intellectual life—a feeling of political irrelevance and purposelessness that redoubles some intellectuals' sense of impotence, now experienced both in the political and in the intellectual domains? Precisely what does the moralism specific to contemporary intellectual life symptomize?

A return to the contrast between a substantive moral bearing and its redacted and transmogrified moralistic cousin may help us develop these questions. A richly configured political or intellectual morality bears an openly contestable character insofar as it must be willing to give an account of itself and be tested against other accounts of the good.[16] And it cannot encode itself as law, or in law, without losing its philosophical and spiritual depths—precisely the evisceration that has befallen both liberal and socialist moral doctrine when codified as absolute truth. Moralism, however, is animated by a tacitly antidemocratic sentiment: it does not want to talk or argue but rather seeks to abort conversation with its prohibitions and reproaches. Put another way, while political morality at its best aims to incite a particular political formation and seeks to unite a people under the auspices of the understanding it tenders, moralism takes up and rebukes isolated "positions." In this regard, moralism can be understood as a historically specific effect of quite isolated and vulnerable subjects—subjects who claim membership in an abstract identity-based community but rarely experience themselves as concretely sustained or protected by actual communities of solidarity. Similarly, while any particular moral system derives its validity from the possibility that any person might adopt and inhabit it, contemporary political moralism tends to conflate persons with beliefs in completely nonvolunteristic fashion: persons are equated with subject positions, which are equated with identities, which are equated with certain perspectives and values. To be a white woman is thus equated with speaking or thinking *as* a white woman, just as to include a "diversity of perspectives" is equated with populating a panel or a syllabus or an anthology with those who are formally—or, more precisely, phenotypically, physiologically, or behaviorally—marked as "diverse."

Inadvertently, it seems, I have now raised the question of the relationship between moralizing discourse and contemporary cultural or multicultural politics. What makes such politics especially susceptible to a moralizing didacticism? I want to venture four brief and highly speculative answers. First, as counterhegemonic cultural and political formations, they transpire outside the domain of the officially political realm, and in some discursive contrast to that realm's preoccupation with power and interest. Thus, these political formations often understand themselves as truer, as less bound to the corrupting forces of power and interest—in short, as occupying higher moral ground than that of either their putative opposition or their interest-group cousins. At the same time, their discursive exclusion by and from the conventional political order constitutes an incessantly repeated injury (thereby redoubling the social injury constitutive of their original formation) that provides the perfect breeding ground for moralism.

Second, notwithstanding the Right's view of them as a monolith, these political formations are so fragmented, are such small elements of movement often so tenuously linked with each other (when they are linked at all), that they invariably assume a siege mentality and see almost all forms of power as a threat to their existence. They are thus susceptible to growing rigidly defensive and brittle out of a sense of their imperiled existence; this defensiveness also tends to preclude their addressing deep sources of injustice and to incite instead a politics that acts at the largely symbolic and gestural level, the level at which moralism runs rampant.

Third, to the extent that identity politics are institutionalized—in academic programs and in political caucuses or other political organizations—they are susceptible to the profoundly depoliticizing logic of liberal institutions: historical conflicts are rendered as essential ones, effect becomes cause, and "culture," "religion," "ethnicity," or "sexuality" become entrenched differences with entrenched interests. But precisely because effects of power have been discursively converted to essentialized entities, their interests cannot be addressed within that discourse. To put this problem another way: identitarian political projects are very real effects of late modern modalities of power, but as effects they do not fully express its character and so do not adequately articulate their own condition; they are symptoms of a certain fragmentation of suffering, and of suffering lived as identity rather than as general injustice or domination—but suffering that cannot be resolved at the identitarian level. It may be easier to see this dynamic in discourses that essentialize conflict in places such as Northern Ireland, the Middle East, or South Africa. To formulate the problem in those regions as one of Catholics versus Protestants, Arabs versus Jews, or blacks versus whites, rather than understanding the oppositional character of these identities as in part produced and naturalized by historical operations of power (settler colonialism, capitalism, etc.), is a patently dehistoricizing and depoliticizing move—precisely the sort of move that leads to moralizing lament or blame, to personifying the historical conflict in individuals, castes, religions, or tribes, rather than to potent political analysis and strategies. The mechanism is relatively easy to see in cases remote from North American shores; but largely because of the essentializing logic of liberal institutions, such a perspective is much more difficult to sustain when one considers the politics of "cultural diversity"—the depoliticization is in the very appellation—in the United States.

Fourth, and related to the previous point, what travels under the sign of cultural or identity politics often has very little in the way of what neo-Gramscians call a new hegemonic project. By this, I do not meant that "multicultural politics" lacks a proper sense of patriotism, as Richard Rorty has argued,[17] but that it often has no vision of emancipation from racism, homophobia, or sexism (nor a serious analysis of the relationship of these ills to capitalism, and hence to class). Put another way, the problem with a politics of "difference" is that it lacks a vision of the future that overcomes the political significance of such differences, and thus lacks an affirmative collective project. Perhaps it is for this reason that such political formations at times appear more invested in amassing and citing continued evidence of the injury justifying their existence than in figuring alternatives to these conditions.[18] Indeed, where would programs in women's studies or ethnic studies be without the nightmare of gender and ethnic subordination and violation, on the one hand, and the conceit of the analytically isolatable character of these injuries, on the other? Yet these kinds of negative political investments (which themselves signify a form of political paralysis), combined with the bad conscience they foment over the injuries and sufferings of other groups, are sure recipes for moralizing politics. It is as if moralizing filled in the painful and embarrassing blank drawn by so many over the "think globally" side of the postmarxist imperative to "think globally, act locally." As our global analyses lead us to appreciate the powers constitutive of our current predicament as overwhelming, and as this appreciation stands denuded of the faith that God or Progress will lead us out of this predicament, our local actions reduce to moralistic reproaches—rarely transformations—of the traces of these powers coursing through our immediate environs.

If moralistic discourse always harbors a certain anxiety about "practice," it also operates as a strange substitute for action; it is what Nietzsche called "reaction" posing as action. Moralizing is aimed either at prohibiting certain things, words, or deeds or at compelling a very narrow set of words and deeds—and the latter, of course, is also a form of prohibition. Its function is to limit rather than to open, to discipline rather than to incite. This recalls again the anti-intellectual force of moralism, a turn against the intrinsic riches of intellectual life as well as against its particular value for radically democratic practices.

Stuart Hall once characterized the distinction between theory and politics as that between a domain in which meaning is opened up, potentially infinitely, and one in which it is intentionally and strategically arrested.[19] It is the task of theory, he insists, to "make meaning slide," while the lifeblood of politics is made up of bids for hegemonic representation that by nature seek to arrest this movement, to fix meaning at the point of the particular political truth—the nonfluid and nonnegotiable representation—that one wishes to prevail. With due concern for all that such a rough distinction elides, let us ask what happens when intellectual inquiry is sacrificed to an intensely politicized moment, whether inside or outside an academic institution. What happens when we, out of good and earnest intentions, seek to collapse the distinction between politics and theory, between political bids for hegemonic truth and intellectual inquiry? We do no favor, I think, to politics or to intellectual life by eliminating a productive tension—the way in which politics and theory effectively interrupt each other—in order to consolidate certain political claims as the premise of a program of intellectual inquiry. Indeed, we usurp the increasingly scarce space allocated today to thinking, to making meaning slide, as we politicize a space that must in turn guard its borders and mount the barricades to defend the identity it protects. In codifying such a politics as the basis of intellectual life, we ultimately reproduce the reaction of our ostensible opposition as we fix our position, thereby becoming reactionary ourselves. If consolidated representations of identity are the necessary premise of certain democratic political claims, they also necessarily destroy the openness on which the intellectual life required by rich formulations of democracy depends. Can we live with this paradox?

In a remarkable little essay titled *Politics and Morals* (1930), Benedetto Croce formulated the problematic of politicized theoretical inquiry this way:

> Why have I insisted on pointing out, with the greatest care, the distinction between theory and practice, between the philosophy of politics and politics? To urge the philosophers to be modest and not to confuse political life, already sufficiently confused, with inopportune and feebly argued philosophy? Yes of course. . . . But I confess that I was moved, above all, by the opposite desire, namely, to save historical judgment from contamination with practical politics, a contamination which deprives historical judgment of tolerance and fairness. This desire is also, in its own way, politics, profound politics, if what Aristotle, the father of political science, used to say is true, about the contrast between the active and the contemplative life—that not only the actions which turn towards the facts are practical, but even more practical are the contemplations and reflections which have their origin and end in themselves and which, by educating the mind, prepare for good deeds.[20]

Croce here assists us in making an intriguing return to the problematic of morality whose trace I have argued we now experience painfully as the antilife, antipolitical, and anti-intellectual force of political moralism. Yet our return is not a simple recuperation, precisely because we are today forced to openly *invent* our political projects and their moral content, without relying on either teleological or redemptive history, without having recourse to moral or other ontological systems rooted in nature, fetishized reason, the dialectic, or the divine. We are confronted today with the fact of history—and so also with political futures and the actions that would produce and configure them—as a sheer problem of power. This is what is brought into view at the moment that historical meta-narratives are fully exposed as fictions.

Put another way, Croce's argument for a literal and figural separation between political life and intellectual inquiry suggests possibilities both for the rejuvenation of a rich moral political vision and for an abatement of the moralizing by which contemporary intellectual and political formations currently infect each other. To imagine what this stance might look like for intellectuals, consider Foucault's response to an interviewer who asked whether he wrote *The Use of Pleasure* and *Techniques of the Self* "for the liberation movement." "Not for," replied Foucault steadily, "but *in terms of*, a contemporary situation."[21] The difference between "for" and "in terms of" is critical: it indicates whether intellectual life will be submitted to existing political discourses and the formulation of immediate political needs those discourses pronouns, or will be allowed the air of independence that it must have in order to be of value *as* intellectual work for political life. Foucault does not position his work with indifference to an existing political movement, nor does he argue that his thinking is unconditioned by it. Rather, he distinguishes the value of critical thinking from position taking or policy formulation.

Maurice Merleau-Ponty makes a similar argument while quarreling with Jean-Paul Sartre about the relevant level of engagement with politics by philosophers.

> I have in no way renounced writing about politics. . . . With the Korean War, I made the decision—and this is something entirely different—to stop writing about events as they occur. . . . In times of tension, taking a stand on each event becomes a system of "bad faith." . . . That is why on several occasions I suggested in this journal [*Les Temps Modernes*] that we present comprehensive studies rather than hastily taken positions. . . . This method is closer to politics than your method of continuous engagement. That in itself makes it more philosophical, as it creates a distance between the event and our judgment of it, defusing the trap of the event.[22]

The trap of the event, to which we might today add the "trap of existing discourses," is precisely that which intellectuals who aim to be thoughtful and useful to political life need to spring open; Foucault similarly calls for a critique of the political rationalities organizing existing events and political claims, a critique that can occur neither inside the terms of "the event" nor inside an existing array of political and subject positions. Yet both Foucault and Merleau-Ponty also insist that to argue for a separation between intellectual and political life is not to detach the two. The point instead is to cultivate among political intellectuals an appreciation of the productive, even agonistic, interlocution made possible between intellectual life and political life when they maintain a dynamic distance and tension. By itself a political act at a time when universities are increasingly underwritten by "interested" corporate, private, and state funds, such cultivation is also quite possibly a route to freeing political life from its current moralizing despair and intellectual life from the grip of bad conscience. In the effort to revitalize left politics with rich genealogies, discerning institutional analyses, and compelling political visions, intellectuals who are deeply learned, imaginative, and independent can be of enormous value. But to the extent that critical thinkers in the academy are caught in the dehistoricizing, depoliticizing, and intellectually stifling political moralism spurred by the political disorientations of our time, we will not be available for this work. To the extent that we do not come to terms with the losses generating this moralism, we will remain captive to a melancholy that rehearses it. We will thus be of little help in forging alternatives to those bankrupt trajectories in whose ghostly orbit contemporary political life spins.

NOTES

1 Stuart Hall, *The Hard Road to Renewal: Thatcherism and the Crisis of the Left* (London: Verso, 1988), 8.

2 Herbert Marcuse, *One Dimensional Man: Studies in the Ideology of Advanced Industrial Society* (Boston: Beacon Press, 1964), xiv.

3 These questions assume that however much a left project was epistemologically and ontologically *legitimated* by Enlightenment scientific discourse, it was politically *animated* by a moral vision about the truly just society.

4 See my *States of Injury: Power and Freedom in Late Modernity* (Princeton: Princeton University Press, 1995), chapters 1–3.

5 The citation from W. Boyd Carpenter is extracted from *The Permanent Elements of Religion: Eight Lectures Preached before the University of Oxford in the Year 1887* (Lon-

don: Macmillan, 1889), 211. Boyd continues: "Thus, where inward sympathy with good is lacking, though there may be outward moralism, there can be no true morality" (212).

6 I draw these general characterizations of Machiavelli's and Nietzsche's thought from Niccolò Machiavelli's *The Prince* and *Discourses on Livy* in *The Chief Works and Others*, 3 vols. trans. Allan Gilbert (Durham: Duke University Press, 1965); and from Friedrich Nietzsche's *On the Genealogy of Morals*, trans. Walter Kaufmann and R. J. Hollingdale (New York: Vintage, 1969).

7 Nietzsche, *On the Genealogy of Morals*, 65.

8 Machiavelli, *The Prince*, 1:66.

9 Ibid.

10 Nietzsche, *On the Genealogy of Morals*, 87.

11 One might use this distinction between the moralistic and moral to read various attempts to render the figure of Rodney King in a discourse of martyrdom. Unquestionably an icon of late-twentieth-century racist police violence, in terms of what imaginary struggle or radically transformed future could this King be drawn as a martyr rather than a victim?

12 Stuart Hall makes a similar point: "We find it easier to be righteously moralistic about Thatcherism ('isn't she a cow?'): harder to grasp its logic as a political strategy. . . . Our sectarianism is often a product of fear—the changing world is seen as a strange and threatening place without signposts. It is also symptomatic of the way our [left] thinking has become stuck in a particular historic groove" (*The Hard Road to Renewal*, 273).

13 The talk from which these remarks are excerpted has now been published as a longer essay titled "The Impossibility of Women's Studies" in a special issue of *Differences* (9, no. 3 [1997]: 79–101) on the future of women's studies, edited by Joan Wallach Scott.

14 Henry Louis Gates Jr., "Truth or Consequences: Putting Limits on Limits," in *The Limits of Power in American Intellectual Life* (New York: American Council of Learned Societies, 1993), 19.

15 For an insightful discussion of this intellectual fundamentalism, see William Connolly's *Ethos of Pluralization* (Minneapolis: University of Minnesota Press, 1995), especially chapter 1.

16 William Connolly has articulated this claim regarding the contestable in intellectual morality in much of his recent work. See especially *The Ethos of Pluralization* and *Why I Am Not a Secularist* (Minneapolis: University of Minnesota Press, 1999).

17 Richard Rorty, *Achieving Our Country: Leftist Thought in Twentieth-Century America* (Cambridge: Harvard University Press, 1998).

18 This investment is explored in greater detail in chapter three of my *Politics Out of History* (Princeton, NJ: Princeton University Press, 2002).

19 Stuart Hall, "Identity in Question," a public lecture at the University of California, Santa Cruz, March 21, 1991.

20 Benedetto Croce, *Politics and Morals*, trans. Salvatore J. Castiglione (London: Allen and Unwin, 1946), 43.

21 Michel Foucault, "The Concern for Truth," interview by François Ewald, trans. Alan Sheridan, in *Politics, Philosophy, Culture: Interviews and Other Writings, 1977–1984*, ed. Lawrence D. Kritzman (New York: Routledge, 1988), 263.
22 Maurice Merleau-Ponty, "Sartre, Merleau-Ponty: Les lettres d'une rupture," *Magazine Littéraire*, no. 320 (April 1994): 74–76.

WORKS CITED

Abraham, Nicolas, and Maria Torak. *The Shell and the Kernal: Renewals of Psychoanalysis.* Ed. Nicolas T. Rand. Chicago: University of Chicago Press, 1994.

Agamben, Giorgio. *Homo Sacer: Sovereign Power and Bare Life.* Trans. Daniel Heller-Roazen. Stanford: Stanford University Press, 1998.

———. *Remnants of Auschwitz: The Witness and the Archive.* Trans. Daniel Heller-Roazen. New York: Zone Books, 1999.

Al-Azmeh, Aziz. *Islams and Modernities.* London: Verso, 1993.

Allen, Chadwick. "Hero with Two Faces: The Lone Ranger as Treaty Discourse." *American Literature* 68, no. 3 (September 1996): 609–38.

Allyn, David. "Private Acts/Public Policy: Alfred Kinsey, the American Law Institute and the Privatization of American Sexual Morality." *Journal of American Studies* 30 (1996): 405–28.

Altschuler, Glen C., and Stuart M. Blumin. *Rude Republic: Americans and Their Politics in the Nineteenth Century.* Princeton: Princeton University Press, 2000.

Andersen, Kristi. *After Suffrage: Women in Partisan and Electoral Politics before the New Deal.* Chicago: University of Chicago Press, 1996.

Angelou, Maya. *The Heart of a Woman.* New York: Vintage Books, 1996.

Ankersmit, F. R. *Aesthetic Politics: Political Philosophy beyond Fact and Value.* Stanford: Stanford University Press, 1996.

Appiah, K. Anthony. "The Marrying Kind." *New York Review of Books,* June 20, 1996, 48–52.

Aptheker, Bettina. *The Morning Breaks: The Trial of Angela Davis.* Ithaca: Cornell University Press, 1999.

Arendt, Hannah. *Between Past and Future.* New York: Penguin, 1980.

———. *The Human Condition,* 2nd ed. 1958; Chicago: University of Chicago Press, 1998.

———. *The Origins of Totalitarianism.* New York: Harcourt, Brace, 1951.

Aristotle. *The Politics of Aristotle.* Trans. Ernest Barker. New York: Oxford University Press, 1958.

Ash, Timothy Garton. *The Polish Revolution: Solidarity.* New York: Vintage Books, 1985.

Austin, Mary. *The Young Woman Citizen.* New York: The Woman's Press, 1920.

Bailey, Nathan. *An Universal Etymological English Dictionary: and An Interpreter of Hard Words.* London: Printed for J. Buckland, J. Beecoft, W. Strahan, Hinton, 1773.

Baker, Ella, and Marvel Cooke. "The Bronx Slave Market." *The Crisis* (November 1935): 330.

Baker, Houston A. Jr. "Our Lady: Sonia Sanchez and the Writing of a Black Renaissance." In *Reading Black, Reading Feminist: A Critical Anthology,* ed. Henry Louis Gates Jr. New York: Meridian, 1990. 318–47.

Baker-Crothers, Hayes, and Ruth A. Hudnut. *Problems of Citizenship.* New York: Henry Holt, 1924.

Balibar, Etienne. *Masses, Classes, Ideas: Studies on Politics and Philosophy Before and After Marx.* Trans. James Swenson. New York, Routledge, 1994.

Bambara, Toni Cade, ed. *The Black Woman: An Anthology.* New York: New American Library, 1970.

Barber, Benjamin. *Jihad vs. McWorld: How the Planet Is both Falling Apart and Coming Together and What This Means for Democracy.* New York: Random House, 1995.

Barron, Hal S. *Those Who Stayed Behind.* New York: Cambridge University Press, 1984.

Bates, Elisha. *The Moral Advocate: A Monthly Publication on War, Duelling, Capital Punishments, and Prison Discipline.* 3 Vols. Mt. Pleasant, O.: Printed by the Editor, 1821–1822.

Baudrillard, Jean. *Symbolic Exchange and Death.* Trans. Iain Hamilton Grant. London: Sage Publications, 1993.

Bawer, Bruce. "Introduction." In *Beyond Queer: Challenging Gay Left Orthodoxy,* ed. Bruce Bawer. New York: The Free Press, 1996.

——. "Notes on Stonewall: Is the Gay Rights Movement Living in the Past?" *New Republic,* June 13, 1994.

——. *A Place at the Table: The Gay Individual in American Society.* New York: Simon and Schuster, 1993.

——. "Radically Different: Do Gay People Have a Responsibility to Be Revolutionaries?" *New York Times Book Review,* November 5, 1995.

——. "Up (with) the Establishment." *The Advocate,* January 23, 1996.

Beaumont, Gustave de, and Alexis de Tocqueville. *On the Penitentiary System in the United States, and Its Application in France; with an Appendix on Penal Colonies, and also, Statistical Notes.* Trans. Francis Lieber. Philadelphia: Carey, Lea & Blanchard, 1833.

Bellah, Robert. "Civil Religion in America." *Daedalus* 96, no. 1 (winter 1967): 1–21.

Bercovitch, Sacvan. "Afterword." In *Ideology and Classic American Literature,* ed. Sacvan Bercovitch and Myra Jehlen. Cambridge: Cambridge University Press, 1986.

——. *Rites of Assent: Transformations in the Symbolic Construction of America.* New York: Routledge, 1993.

Berger, John. *About Looking.* New York: Pantheon Books, 1980.

Berlant, Lauren. " '68 or Something." *Critical Inquiry* 21, no. 1 (fall 1994): 124–55.

——. *The Anatomy of National Fantasy: Hawthorne, Utopia, and Everyday Life.* Chicago: University of Chicago Press, 1991.

——. "Poor Eliza." *American Literature* 70, no. 3 (September 1998): 635–68.

——. *The Queen of America Goes to Washington City: Essays on Sex and Citizenship.* Durham: Duke University Press, 1997.

——. "Pax Americana: The Case of *Show Boat.*" In *Cultural Institutions of the Novel.* Ed. Deidre Lynch and William B. Warner. Durham: Duke University Press, 1996. 399–422.

——. "The Subject of True Feeling: Pain, Privacy, and Politics." In *Cultural Pluralism, Identity, and the Law,* ed. Austin Sarat. Ann Arbor: University of Michigan Press, 1997. 49–84.

Berlant, Lauren, and Michael Warner. "Sex in Public." *Critical Inquiry* 24, no. 2 (winter 1998): 547–66.

Bernstein, Aaron. "Too Much Corporate Power?" *Business Week* 11 (September 2000): 144–58.

Bernstein, Richard. *The New Constellation: The Ethical-Political Horizons of Modernity/ Postmodernity.* Cambridge: MIT Press, 1992.

Birnbaum, Norman. *Radical Renewal: The Politics of Ideas in Modern America.* New York: Pantheon Books, 1988.

Blackstone, William. *Commentaries on the Laws of England.* 4 vols. 1769; Chicago: University of Chicago Press, 1979.

Blount, Thomas. *Nomo-lexikon, a law dictionary: interpreting such difficult and obscure words and terms as are found either in our common or statute, ancient or modern lawes: with references to the several statutes, records, registers law-books, charters, ancient deeds, and manuscripts, wherein the words are used: and etymologies, where they properly occur.* England: In the Savoy: Printed by Tho. Newcomb, for John Martin and Henry Herringman, 1670.

Boaz, David. "Domestic Justice." *New York Times,* January 4, 1995. A15.

——. "Reviving the Inner City." In *Market Liberalism: A Paradigm for the Twenty-First Century.* Ed. David Boaz and Edward H. Crane. Washington, D.C.: Cato Institute, 1993.

Boaz, David, and Edward H. Crane, eds. *Market Liberalism: A Paradigm for the Twenty-First Century.* Washington, D.C.: Cato Institute, 1993.

Boggs, Grace Lee. "The Black Revolution in America." In *The Black Woman: An Anthology,* ed. Toni Cade Bambara. New York: New American Library, 1970. 211–23.

Bonniol, Jean-Luc. *La couleur comme maléfice: Une illustration créole de la généalogie des Blancs et des Noirs.* Paris: Albin Michel, 1992.

Bourdieu, Pierre. *Contre-feux: Propos pour servir à la résistance contre l'invasion néo-liberale.* Paris: Editions Raisons d'Agir, 1998.

——. *Distinction: A Social Critique of the Judgment of Taste.* Trans. Richard Nice. Cambridge: Harvard University Press, 1984.

Bourke, John Gregory. "The American Congo." *Scribner's Magazine,* May 15, 1894.

Boyd, Mary Brown Summner. *The Woman Citizen a General Handbook of Civics: With Special Consideration of Women's Citizenship.* New York: F. A. Stokes, 1918.

Branch, Taylor. *Parting the Waters: America in the King Years, 1954–63.* New York: Simon and Schuster, 1988.

Brathwaite, Edward. *The Development of Creole Society in Jamaica, 1770–1820.* Oxford: Clarendon Press, 1971.

Brennan, Timothy. *At Home in the World: Cosmopolitanism Now.* Cambridge: Harvard University Press, 1997.

Brodhead, Richard H. *Cultures of Letters: Scenes of Reading and Writing in Nineteenth-Century America.* Chicago: University of Chicago Press, 1993.

Brooks, Gwendolyn. *Maud Martha: A Novel.* Chicago: Third World Press, 1993.

Brown, Richard D. *The Strength of a People: The Idea of an Informed Citizenry in America, 1650–1870.* Chapel Hill: University of North Carolina Press, 1996.

Brown, Wendy. "The Impossibility of Women's Studies." *Differences* 9, no. 3 (1997): 79–101.

———. *States of Injury: Power and Freedom in Late Modernity.* Princeton: Princeton University Press, 1995.

Buck-Morss, Susan. "Aesthetics and Anaesthetics: Walter Benjamin's Artwork Essay Reconsidered." *October* 62 (fall 1992): 3–41.

Buhle, Mary Jo. *Women and American Socialism, 1879–1920.* Urbana: University of Illinois Press, 1981.

Bush, Jonathan A. "Free to Enslave: The Foundations of Colonial American Slave Law." *Yale Journal of Law and Humanities* 5 (1993): 417–70.

Butler, Judith. *Bodies That Matter: On the Discursive Limits of "Sex."* New York: Routledge, 1993.

———. "Contingent Foundations: Feminism and the Question of 'Postmodernism.'" In *Feminists Theorize the Political,* ed. Judith Butler and Joan W. Scott. New York: Routledge, 1992.

———. *Excitable Speech: A Politics of the Performative.* New York: Routledge, 1997.

———. "Melancholy Gender, Refused Identification." In *Constructing Masculinity,* ed. Maurice Berger, Brian Wallis, and Simon Watson. New York: Routledge, 1995.

———. "Merely Cultural." *Social Text* 15, no. 3–4 (1997): 265–77.

Craig Calhoun, ed. *Habermas and the Public Sphere.* Cambridge: MIT Press, 1996.

Callinicos, Alex. "Social Theory Put to the Test of Politics: Pierre Bourdieu and Anthony Giddens." *New Left Review* 236 (July/August 1999): 77–102.

Campbell, David. "Political Prosaics, Transversal Politics, and the Anarchical World." In *Challenging Boundaries,* ed. Michael Shapiro and Hayward R. Alker. Minneapolis: University of Minnesota Press, 1996.

Cantor, Eddie. *As I Remember Them.* New York: Duell, Sloan & Pearce, 1963.

Cantril, Albert H., and Susan Davis Cantril. *Reading Mixed Signals: Ambivalence in American Public Opinion about Government.* Baltimore: Johns Hopkins University Press, 1999.

Carnap, Rudolf. "Kant's Synthetic A Priori." In *An Introduction to the Philosophy of Science,* ed. Martin Gardner. New York: Dover, 1995. 177–83.

Carnegie, Andrew. *Triumphant Democracy, or Fifty Years' March of the Republic.* New York: Charles Scribner's Sons, 1886.

Carpenter, W. Boyd. *The Permanent Elements of Religion: Eight Lectures Preached before the University of Oxford in the Year 1887.* London: Macmillan, 1889.

Castronovo, Russ. *Necro Citizenship: Death, Eroticism, and the Public Sphere in the Nineteenth-Century United States.* Durham: Duke University Press, 2001.

———. "Political Necrophilia." *boundary 2* 27, no. 2 (summer 2000): 13–48.

Certeau, Michel de. *The Practice of Everyday Life.* Berkeley: University of California Press, 1988.

Charters, Ann. *Nobody: The Story of Bert Williams.* New York: Macmillan, 1970.

Chasin, Alexandra. *Selling Out: The Gay and Lesbian Movement Goes to Market.* New York: St. Martin's Press, 2000.

Childress, Alice. *Like One of the Family: Conversations from a Domestic's Life.* Boston: Beacon Press, 1986.

Childress, Alice, Paule Marshall, and Sarah E. Wright. "The Negro Woman in American Literature." *Freedomways,* no. 1 (1966). Rpt. in Esther Cooper Jackson, ed. *The Freedomways Reader.* Boulder: Westview Press, 2000. 291–98.

Chomsky, Noam. *Profits over People: Neoliberalism and Global Order.* New York: Seven Stories Press, 1999.

Christ, Raymond F. *Teacher's Manual. Arranged for the Guidance of Public-School Teachers of the United States for Use with the Students Textbook to Create a Standard Course of Instruction for the Preparation of the Candidate for the Responsibilities of Citizenship.* Washington, D.C.: U.S. Bureau of Naturalization, 1918.

Christianson, Scott. *With Liberty for Some: Five Hundred Years of Imprisonment in America.* Boston: Northeastern University Press, 1998.

Citizenship Education and Naturalization Information. Washington, D.C.: U.S. Department of Justice, 1997.

Clarke, Ida Clyde. *Uncle Sam Needs a Wife.* Philadelphia: John C. Winston Co., 1925.

Cobb, Thomas. *An Inquiry into the Law of Negro Slavery in the United States of America.* 1858; New York: Negro Universities Press, 1968.

Cockcroft, James. *Outlaws in the Promised Land.* New York: Grove Press, 1986.

Cohen, Cathy. "Punks, Bulldaggers, and Welfare Queens," *GLQ* 3 (1997): 437–65.

Collins, Patricia Hill. *Black Feminist Thought: Knowledge, Consciousness, and the Politics of Empowerment.* Boston: Unwin & Hyman, 1990.

———. "What's in a Name? Womanism, Black Feminism, and Beyond." *Black Scholar* 26, no. 1 (1996): 9–17.

Comaroff, Jean, and John L. Comaroff. "Millennial Capitalism: First Thoughts on a Second Coming." *Public Culture* 12, no. 2 (spring 2000): 291–343.

Cone, James H. "Black Theology as Liberation Theology." In *African American Religious Studies: An Interdisciplinary Anthology,* ed. Gayraud Wilmore. Durham: Duke University Press, 1989.

Connolly, William. "Democracy and Territoriality." In *Rhetorical Republic: Governing Representations in American Politics,* ed. Frederick M. Dolan and Thomas L. Dumm. Amherst: University of Massachusetts Press, 1993.

———. *The Ethos of Pluralization.* Minneapolis: University of Minnesota Press, 1995.

———. *Why I Am Not a Secularist.* Minneapolis: University of Minnesota Press, 1999.

Corlett, William. *Community without Unity: A Politics of Derridean Extravagance.* Durham: Duke University Press, 1993.

Cornell, Saul. *The Other Founders: Anti-Federalism and the Dissenting Tradition in America, 1788–1828.* Chapel Hill: University of North Carolina Press, 1999.

Cott, Nancy F. *The Grounding of Modern Feminism.* New Haven: Yale University Press, 1987.

———, ed. *The History of Women in the United States.* 8 vols. Munich: K. G. Saur, 1994.

Cover, Robert M. *Justice Accused: Antislavery and the Judicial Process.* New Haven: Yale University Press, 1975.

Covington, Francee. "Are the Revolutionary Techniques Employed in the Battle of Algiers Applicable to Harlem?" In *The Black Woman: An Anthology,* ed. Toni Cade Bambara. New York: New American Library, 1970. 244–51.

Coward, John M. "Explaining the Little Bighorn." In *Outsiders in Nineteenth-Century Press History: Multicultural Perspectives,* ed. Frankie Hutton and Barbara Straus Reed. Bowling Green, Ohio: Bowling Green University Popular Press, 1995. 145–57.

Cowell, John. *The Interpreter: or Book Containing the Signification of Words.* London: F. Leach for distribution by Hen. Twyford, Tho. Dring, and Io. Place. 1658.

Cramer, Janet M. *Woman as Citizen: Race, Class, and the Discourse of Women's Citizenship, 1894–1909.* Columbia, SC: Association for Education in Journalism and Press Communication, 1998.

Crawford, William. "Report on the Penitentiaries of the United States, Addressed to His Majesty's Principal Secretary of State for the Home Department." London: House of Commons, August 11, 1834.

Croce, Benedetto. *Politics and Morals.* Trans. Salvatore J. Castiglione. London: Allen and Unwin, 1946.

Cruikshank, Barbara. *The Will to Empower: Democratic Citizens and Other Subjects.* Ithaca: Cornell University Press, 1999.

Dahl, Robert. *Who Governs? Democracy and Power in an American City.* New Haven: Yale University Press, 1961.

D.A.R. Manual for Citizenship. (Washington, D.C.: Daughters of the American Revolution, 1981).

Davis, Angela. *Angela Davis: An Autobiography.* New York: Random House, 1974.

———. "Racism, Birth Control, and Reproductive Rights." In *Women, Race, and Class.* New York: Vintage Press, 1983. 202–21.

Davis, John A. "Black Americans and United States Policy Toward Africa." *Journal of International Affairs* (1970): 236–49.

Davis, Rebecca Harding. *Waiting for the Verdict.* Donald Dingledine, ed. New Albany, NY: NCUP, 1995.

Dayan, Joan. *Haiti, History, and the Gods.* Berkeley: University of California Press, 1995.

———. "Held in the Body of the State: Prisons and the Law." In *History, Memory, and the Law,* ed. Austin Sarat and Thomas R. Kearns. Ann Arbor: University of Michigan Press, 1999.

———. "Poe, Persons, and Property." *American Literary History* 11.3 (Fall 1999): 405–25.

Debbasch, Yvan. *Couleur et liberte: Le jeu du critere ethnique dans un ordre juridique esclavagiste.* Paris: Libraire Dalloz, 1967.

"Deeper and Deeper We Get in Risky World of Power." *Los Angeles Times,* February 16, 2000, B9.

Delany, Samuel R. *Times Square Red, Times Square Blue.* New York: New York University Press, 1999.

Deloria, Philip J. *Playing Indian.* New Haven: Yale University Press, 1998.

Deloria, Vine Jr., and David E. Wilkins. *Tribes, Treaties, and Constitutional Tribulations.* Austin: University of Texas Press, 1999.

D'Emilio, John. *Sexual Politics, Sexual Communities: The Making of a Homosexual Minority in the United States, 1940–1970.* 2nd ed. 1983; Chicago: University of Chicago Press, 1998.

Descartes, René. *Meditations on First Philosophy.* In *The Philosophical Writings of Descartes.* 2 vols. Trans. John Cottingham, Robert Stoothoff, and Dugald Murdoch. Cambridge: Cambridge University Press, 1984.

Dewey, D. M. *The History of Charles Edwards and Sarah Sharp: Being an Authentic Account of the Horrible Penfield Tragedy, Which Took Place January 26, 1851, together with the Particulars of the Causes Which Led to It, Including the Coroner's Inquest, in Full.* Rochester: D. M. Dewey, 1851.

Dewey, John. *The Public and Its Problems.* 1927; Chicago: Swallow Press, 1980.

——. *The Quest for Certainty* (1929), vol. 4 of *The Later Works, 1925–1953.* Ed. Jo Ann Boydston. Carbondale: Southern Illinois University Press, 1981.

Dickens, Charles. *American Notes and Pictures from Italy.* 1842; New York: Oxford University Press, 1957.

Dimock, Wai Chee. *Residues of Justice: Literature, Law, and Philosophy.* Berkeley: University of California Press, 1990.

——. "A Theory of Resonance." *PMLA* (October 1997): 1060–71.

Dionne, E. J. Jr. *Why Americans Hate Politics.* New York: Touchstone, 1992.

Dobbs, Betty Jo Teeter, and Margaret C. Jacob. *Newton and the Culture of Newtonianism.* Atlantic Highlands, N.J.: Humanities Press, 1995.

Dole, C. F. *The Young Citizen.* Boston: D. C. Heath, 1899.

Dominguez, Virginia. *White By Definition: Social Classification in Creole Louisiana.* New Brunswick, NJ: Rutgers University Press, 1986.

Drescher, Seymour. *Dilemmas of Democracy: Tocqueville and Modernization.* Pittsburgh: University of Pittsburgh Press, 1968.

DuBois, Ellen Carol. *Feminism and Suffrage: The Emergence of an Independent Women's Movement in America, 1848–1869.* Ithaca: Cornell University Press, 1978.

du Cille, Ann. *Skin Trade.* Cambridge: Harvard University Press, 1996.

du Gay, Paul. *In Praise of Bureaucracy: Weber, Organization, Ethics.* London: Sage, 2000.

Duggan, Lisa, and Nan Hunter, eds. *Sex Wars: Sexual Dissent and Political Culture.* New York: Routledge, 1995.

Dumm, Thomas. *Democracy and Punishment: Disciplinary Origins of the United States.* Madison: University of Wisconsin Press, 1987.

——. *Michel Foucault and the Politics of Freedom.* Thousand Oaks, Calif.: Sage, 1996.

Dunn, Timothy. *The Militarization of the U.S.-Mexico Border, 1978–1992: Low-Intensity*

Conflict Doctrine Comes Home. Austin: Center for Mexican American Studies Books; University of Texas Press, 1996.

Edwards, Bryan. *The History, Civil and Commercial, of the British Colonies in the West Indies.* 2 vols. Dublin: Luke White, 1793–1794.

Einstein, Albert. "The Laws of Science and the Laws of Ethics." Preface to Philipp Frank, *Relativity: A Richer Truth.* Boston: Beacon Press, 1950.

——. "The Problem of Space, Ether, and the Field in Physics." In *Ideas and Opinions.* New York: Crown Books, 1982.

——. *Relativity: The Special and the General Theory.* 15th ed. New York: Crown Books, 1961.

Eisenstadt, A., ed. *Reconsidering Tocqueville's Democracy in America.* New Brunswick: Rutgers University Press, 1988.

Emerson, Ralph Waldo. *Essays and Lectures.* Ed. Joel Porte. New York: Library of America, 1983.

——. *The Journals and Miscellaneous Notebooks of Ralph Waldo Emerson.* Ed., William H. Gilman et al. 16 vols. Cambridge: The Belknap Press of Harvard University Press, 1960–1982.

Erickson, Peter. "After Identity: A Conversation with June Jordan." *Transition* 63 (1994): 132–149.

Evans, Sara. *Born for Liberty.* New York: The Free Press, 1989.

Fanon, Frantz. *The Wretched of the Earth.* Trans. Constance Farrington. New York: Grove Weidenfeld, 1963.

Farrell, Kirby. *Post-Traumatic Culture: Injury and Interpretation in the Nineties.* Baltimore: Johns Hopkins University Press, 1998.

Fehrenbach, T. R. *Lone Star: A History of Texas and the Texans.* New York: Macmillan, 1968.

Ferguson, J. B. *Spirit Communion: A Record of Communications from the Spirit-Spheres with Incontestable Evidence of Personal Identity, Presented to the Public, with Explanatory Observations.* Nashville: Union and American Steam Press, 1855.

Fishkin, James S. *Voice of the People: Public Opinion and Democracy.* 2nd ed. New Haven: Yale University Press, 1995.

Flores, Richard R. "History, 'Los Pastores,' and the Shifting Poetics of Dislocation." *Journal of Historical Sociology* 6, no. 2 (1993): 164–85.

——. "Mexicans, Modernity, and *Martyrs of the Alamo.*" In *Reflexiones 1998: New Directions in Mexican American Studies,* ed. Yolanda Padilla. Austin: Center for Mexican American Studies Books; University of Texas Press, 1999. 1–19.

——. "Wayne's World: Latinos and Latinas in the Duke's Post-War Imaginary." Presented at the Conference on Latinos in World War II, University of Texas at Austin, May 2000.

Flores, William, and Rina Benmayor, eds. *Latino Cultural Citizenship: Claiming Identity, Space, and Rights.* Boston: Beacon Press, 1997.

Foley, Neil. *The White Scourge.* Berkeley: University of California Press, 1996.

Foreman, Grant. *Sequoyah.* Norman: University of Oklahoma Press, 1938.

Foster, Hal. "Introduction." In *The Anti-Aesthetic: Essays on Postmodern Culture,* ed. Hal Foster. Seattle: Bay Press, 1983.

Foucault, Michel. "The Concern for Truth." Interview by François Ewald. Trans. Alan Sheridan. In *Politics, Philosophy, Culture: Interviews and Other Writings, 1977–1984,* ed. Lawrence D. Kritzman. New York: Routledge, 1988.

——. *Discipline and Punish: The Birth of a Prison.* Alan Sheridan, trans. New York: Vintage, 1979.

——. *The History of Sexuality: An Introduction.* Trans. Robert Hurley. New York: Pantheon Books, 1978.

——. *The Order of Things: An Archaeology of Human Sciences.* New York: Vintage Books, 1973.

Fraser, Nancy. *Justice Interruptus: Critical Reflections on the "Postsocial" Condition.* New York: Routledge, 1997.

Freeman, Mary E. Wilkins. "A Far-Away Melody." In *A Humble Romance and Other Stories.* New York: Harper & Bros., 1899.

——. *Selected Stories of Mary E. Wilkins Freeman.* Ed. Marjorie Pryse. New York: Norton, 1983.

Friedman, Thomas L. *The Lexus and the Olive Tree: Understanding Globalization.* New York: Farrar, Strauss, Giroux, 1999.

Fukuyama, Francis. "The End of History and the Last Man." *The National Interest* (summer, 1989): 3–18.

Furet, Francois. *The Passing of Illusion.* Chicago: University of Chicago Press, 1999.

Garrette, Eve. *A Political Handbook for Women.* Garden City, N.Y.: Doubleday, Doran, and Co., 1944.

Gates, Henry Louis Jr., ed. *Reading Black, Reading Feminist.* New York: Meridian, 1990.

——. "Truth or Consequences: Putting Limits on Limits." In *The Limits of Power in American Intellectual Life.* New York: American Council of Learned Societies, 1993.

Gay, Peter. *The Enlightenment: The Science of Freedom.* New York: Norton, 1977.

Geyer-Ryan, Helga. "Imaginary Identity: Space, Gender, Nation." In *Vision in Context: Historical and Contemporary Perspectives on Sight.* Ed. Teresa Brennan and Martin Jay. New York: Routledge, 1996.

Giddens, Anthony. *The Third Way: The Renewal of Social Democracy.* Cambridge: Polity Press, 1998.

Gilje, Paul. *The Road to Mobocracy: Popular Disorder in New York City, 1763–1834.* Chapel Hill: University of North Carolina Press, 1987.

Gingrich, Newt. *To Renew America.* New York: HarperCollins, 1995.

Glendon, Mary Ann. *Rights Talk.* New York: The Free Press, 1991.

Goldfarb, Jeffrey C. *Beyond Glasnost: The Post Totalitarian Mind.* University of Chicago Press, 1989.

——. *Civility and Subversion: The Intellectual in Democratic Society.* New York: Cambridge University Press, 1998.

——. *On Cultural Freedom: An Exploration of Public Life in Poland and America.* Chicago: University of Chicago Press, 1982.

——. *The Persistence of Freedom: The Sociological Implications of Polish Student Theater.* Boulder: Westview Press, 1980.

Golding, Sue. *The Eight Technologies of Otherness.* New York: Routledge, 1997.

Gordon, Ann D., with Bettye Collier-Thomas, John H. Bracey, Arlene Voski Avakian, and Joyce Avrech Berkman, eds. *African American Women and the Vote: 1937–1965.* Amherst: University of Massachusetts Press, 1997.

Gordon, Avery. *Ghostly Matters: Haunting and the Sociological Imagination.* Minneapolis: University of Minnesota Press, 1997.

Goveia, Elsa V. *The West Indian Slave Laws of the 18th Century.* London: Ginn and Company Limited; Caribbean Universities Press, 1970.

Graff, Gerald. *Beyond the Cultural Wars: How Teaching the Conflicts Can Revitalize American Education.* New York: Norton, 1993.

Gragert, Steven V., ed. *Radio Broadcasts of Will Rogers.* Stillwater: Oklahoma State University Press, 1983.

Graham, Don. "Remembering the Alamo: The Story of the Texas Revolution in Popular Culture." *Southwestern Historical Quarterly* 89, no. 1 (1985): 35–66.

Granucci, Anthony F. " 'Nor Cruel and Unusual Punishments Inflicted': The Original Meaning." *California Law Review* 57 (1969): 839–65.

Gray, Thomas R. *The Confessions of Nat Turner.* In *Nat Turner's Slave Rebellion. Together with the Full Text of the So-Called "Confessions" of Nat Turner Made in Prison in 1831.* Ed. Herbert Aptheker. New York: Humanities Press, 1966.

Green, Barbara. *Spectacular Confessions: Autobiography, Performative Activism, and the Sites of Suffrage 1904–1938.* New York: St. Martin's Press, 1997.

Green, Joyce. "Black Romanticism." In *The Black Woman: An Anthology,* ed. Toni Cade Bambara. New York: New American Library, 1970. 137–42.

Gregg, Gary L. *The Presidential Republic: Executive Representation and Deliberative Democracy.* New York: Rowman and Littlefield, 1997.

Griffin, Farah Jasmine. "Conflict and Chorus: Reconsidering Toni Cade's *The Black Woman: An Anthology.*" In *Is It Nation Time? Critical Essays on Black Power and Black Nationalism,* ed. Eddie Glaude, Jr. Chicago: University of Chicago Press, 2002.

——. "Toni Cade Bambara: Free to Be Anywhere in the Universe." *Callaloo* 19, no. 2 (spring 1996): 228–31.

Gunning, Sandra. "Reading and Redemption in *Incidents in the Life of a Slave Girl.*" In *Harriet Jacobs and Incidents in the Life of a Slave Girl: New Critical Essays,* ed. Deborah M. Garfield and Rafia Zafar. Cambridge: Cambridge University Press, 1996.

Gupta, Akhil, and James Ferguson. "Beyond 'Culture': Space, Identity, and the Politics of Difference." *Cultural Anthropology* 7, no. 1 (February 1992): 6–23.

Gutmann, Amy, and Dennis Thompson. *Democracy and Disagreement: Why Moral Conflict Cannot Be Avoided in Politics and What Should Be Done about It.* Cambridge: The Belknap Press of Harvard University Press, 1996.

Haage, Ghassan. *White Nation.* New York: Routledge, 2000.

Habermas, Jürgen. *The Structural Transformation of the Public Sphere: An Inquiry into a Category of Bourgeois Society.* Trans. Thomas Burger. Cambridge: MIT Press, 1989.

Hall, Stuart. "Gramsci's Relevance for the Study of Race and Ethnicity." In *Stuart Hall: Critical Dialogues in Cultural Studies,* ed. David Morley and Kuan-Hsing Chen. New York: Routledge, 1996. 411–40.

——. *The Hard Road to Renewal: Thatcherism and the Crisis of the Left.* London: Verso, 1988.

——. "Identity in Question." Public lecture at the University of California, Santa Cruz, March 21, 1991.

Hanes, Bailey C. *Bill Pickett, Bulldogger.* Norman: University of Oklahoma Press, 1977.

Hardisty, Jean. *Mobilizing Resentment: Conservative Resurgence from the John Birch Society to the Promise Keepers.* Boston: Beacon Press, 1999.

Harper, Phillip Brian. "Gay Male Identities, Personal Privacy, and Relations of Public Exchange: Notes on Directions for Queer Critique." *Social Text* 52 (Fall-Winter 1997): 5–29.

Harris, Cheryl L. "Whiteness as Property." *Harvard Law Review* 106, no. 8 (June 1993): 1707–91.

Harris, Sharon. *Rebecca Harding Davis and American Realism.* Philadelphia: University of Pennsylvania Press, 1991.

——, ed. *Redefining the Political Novel: American Women Writers, 1797–1901.* Knoxville: University of Tennessee Press, 1995.

Harris, Trudier. "Introduction." In Alice Childress, *Like One of the Family: Conversations from a Domestic's Life.* Boston: Beacon Press, 1986.

Hartt, Rollin Lynde. "A New England Hill Town." *Atlantic Monthly* 83 (1899): 561–74.

Hartz, Louis. *The Liberal Tradition in America: An Interpretation of American Political Thought since the Revolution.* New York: Harcourt Brace, 1955.

Harvey, David. *The Condition of Postmodernity.* Cambridge, Mass.: Blackwell, 1990.

Hawthorne, Nathaniel. *The Scarlet Letter.* New York: Penguin, 1983.

Hayek, F. A. *The Fatal Conceit: The Errors of Socialism.* Ed. W. W. Bartley. Chicago: University of Chicago Press, 1989.

——. *The Road to Serfdom.* Chicago: University of Chicago Press, 1956.

Henkin, Louis. *The Age of Rights.* New York: Columbia University Press, 1990.

Hertz, Neil. *The End of the Line: Essays on Psychoanalysis and the Sublime.* New York: Columbia University Press, 1985.

Higginbotham, A. Leon Jr., and Kopytoff, "Property First, Humanity Second: The Recognition of the Slave's Human Nature in Virginia Civil Law." *Ohio Law Journal* 50, no. 3 (1989): 511–40.

Hilsenrath, Jon E. "The Outlook: The Pros and Cons of Power Price Caps." *Wall Street Journal,* June 4, 2001, A1.

Hindus, Martin. "Black Justice under White Law: Criminal Prosecutions of Blacks in Antebellum South Carolina." *Journal of American Legal History* 63 (1976): 575.

Hirsh, Arthur. *The French New Left: A History and Overview.* Montréal: Black Rose Books, 1982.

Holton, Gerald. "Einstein and the Cultural Roots of Modern Science." *Daedalus* 127 (1998): 1–44.

——. "Einstein and the Shaping of Our Imagination." In *The Advancement of Science, and Its Burdens*. New York: Cambridge University Press, 1986.

Holton, Woody. *Forced Founders: Indians, Debtors, Slaves, and the Making of the American Revolution in Virginia*. Chapel Hill: University of North Carolina Press, 1999.

Honig, Bonnie. *Political Theory and the Displacement of Politics*. Ithaca: Cornell University Press, 1993.

Horwitz, Morton J. "Rights." *Harvard Civil Rights–Civil Liberties Law Review* 23 (1988): 393–406.

——. *The Transformation of American Law, 1780–1860*. Cambridge: Harvard University Press, 1977.

Huberman, Brian, and Ed Hugetz. "Fabled Facade: Filmic Treatments of the Battle of the Alamo." *Southwest Media Review* (spring 1985): 30–41.

Hull, Gloria T., ed. *All the Women Are White, All the Blacks Are Men, but Some of Us Are Brave*. Old Westbury, Conn.: Feminist Press, 1982.

Human Rights Watch and the Sentencing Project. *Losing the Vote: The Impact of Felony Disenfranchisement Laws in the United States*. 1998.

Hume, David. *History of England*. 1688; Boston: Phillips, Sampson & Co., 1856.

Hutchinson, Allan C., and Patrick J. Monahan. "The 'Rights' Stuff: Roberto Unger and Beyond." *Texas Law Review* 62 (1984): 1477–1539.

Hutner, Gordon. *Secrets and Sympathy: Forms of Disclosure in Hawthorne's Novels*. Athens: University of Georgia Press, 1988.

Hutton, Paul. "The Celluloid Alamo." *Arizona and the West* 28, no. 1 (1986): 5–22.

Hyde, Alan. *Bodies of Law*. Princeton: Princeton University Press, 1997.

Jacob, Margaret. *Newtonians and the English Revolution, 1689–1720*. Ithaca: Cornell University Press, 1976.

Jacobs, Harriet A. *Incidents in the Life of a Slave Girl*. Ed. Jean Fagan Yellin. Cambridge: Harvard University Press, 1987.

Jacobs, Jane. *The Death and Life of Great American Cities*. New York: Random House, 1961.

James, William. *Essays in Radical Empiricism*. Ed. Ralph Barton Perry. 1912; Lincoln: University of Nebraska Press, 1996.

——. "The Pluralistic Universe." In *William James: Writings 1902–1910*, ed. Bruce Kuklick. New York: Library of America, 1987.

Jameson, Fredric. "Reification and Ideology in Mass Culture." *Social Text* 1 (1979): 130–48.

Johnson, Thomas A. "Yale Conference Studies Role of Black Woman." *New York Times*, December 14, 1970, 45.

Johnson, Thomas J., Carol E. Hayes, and Scott P. Hayes, eds. *Engaging the Public: How Government and the Media Can Reinvigorate American Democracy*. London: Sage, 1999.

Jordan, Elizabeth, ed. *The Sturdy Oak*. Columbus: Ohio University Press, 1998.

Jordan, Winthrop. *White over Black: American Attitudes toward the Negro, 1550–1812*. New York: Norton, 1977.

Kant, Immanuel. "Concerning the Ultimate Foundation of the Differentiation of Regions in Space." In *Kant: Selected Pre-Critical Writings,* trans. G. B. Kerferd and D. E. Walford. Manchester: Manchester University Press, 1968.

——. *Critique of Practical Reason.* Trans. Lewis White Beck. New York: Macmillan, 1993.

——. *Critique of Pure Reason.* Trans. Norman Kemp Smith. New York: St. Martin's Press, 1965.

——. *The Philosophy of Law.* Trans. W. Hastie. Edinburgh: T. and T. Clark, 1887.

Kantorowicz, Ernst H., with William Chester Jordan. *The King's Two Bodies: A Study in Mediaeval Political Theology.* Princeton: Princeton University Press, 1997.

Kappeler, Susanne. *The Pornography of Representation.* Minneapolis: University of Minnesota Press, 1986.

Katz, Maude White. "End Racism in Education: A Concerned Parent Speaks." In *The Black Woman: An Anthology,* ed. Toni Cade Bambara. New York: New American Library, 1970. 124–31.

Kent, James. "Rights of Persons." In *Commentaries of American Law.* 1826; Boston: Little, Brown, 1873.

Kepner, Jim. *Rough News, Daring Views: 1950s Pioneer Gay Press Journalism.* New York: The Haworth Press, 1998.

Kimball, Bruce. *Orators and Philosophers: A History of the Idea of the Liberal Education.* New York: Henry Holt, 1985.

Konkle, Maureen. "Indian Literacy, U.S. Colonialism, and Literary Criticism." *American Literature* 69, no. 3 (September 1997): 466–67.

Konrad, George. *Antipolitics.* New York: Harcourt, Brace, Jovanovich, 1984.

Kraditor, Aileen. *The Ideas of the Woman Suffrage Movement, 1890–1920.* Garden City, N.Y.: Anchor, 1971.

Kriegel, Blandine. *The State and the Rule of Law.* Princeton: Princeton University Press, 1995.

Krieger, Murray, ed. *The Aims of Representation: Subject, Text, History.* New York: Columbia University Press, 1987.

Krugman, Paul. "Britain's Stormy Petrol." *New York Times,* September 17, 2000, sec. 4, p. 19.

Kruman, Mark W. *Between Authority and Liberty: State Constitution Making in Revolutionary America.* Chapel Hill: University of North Carolina Press, 1997.

Kundera, Milan. *The Art of the Novel.* New York: HarperCollins, 1989.

——. *The Unbearable Lightness of Being.* New York: HarperCollins, 1999.

Kymlicka, Will. *Multicultural Citizenship.* Oxford: Clarendon Press, 1995.

Laclau, Ernesto. *Emancipation(s).* New York: Verso, 1996.

Landler, Mark. "The Ostrich that Roared." *New York Times,* September 4, 1999, B2.

Lang, Eugene. "Distinctively American: The Liberal Arts College." *Daedalus* (winter 1999): 133–50.

Lefort, Claude. *Democracy and Political Theory.* Trans. David Macey. Minneapolis: University of Minnesota Press; Cambridge, Eng.: Polity Press, 1988.

Lemons, J. Stanley. *The Woman Citizen: Social Feminism in the 1920s.* Urbana: University of Illinois Press, 1973.

Lenin, Vladimir Ilyich. "Party Organization and Party Literature" (1905). In *Marxism and Art,* ed. Maynard Solomon. New York: Vintage Books, 1972. 179–83.

Levine, Donald, ed. *Georg Simmel on Individuality and Social Forms.* Chicago: University of Chicago Press, 1985.

Levine, George. "Introduction: Reclaiming the Aesthetic." In *Aesthetics and Ideology,* ed. George Levine. New Brunswick: Rutgers University Press, 1994.

Levine, Lawrence. *Black Culture and Black Consciousness: Afro-American Thought from Slavery to Freedom.* New York: Oxford University Press, 1977.

Lewis, Janet. *Before the Vote Was Won: Arguments For and Against Woman's Suffrage.* New York: Routledge, 1987.

Lichtenstein, Alex. *Twice the Work of Free Labor: The Political Economy of Convict Labor in the New South.* London: Verso, 1996.

Lincoln, Abraham. "A Meditation on Proverbs 25:11." In *Collected Works of Abraham Lincoln,* ed. Roy P. Blaser. 9 vols. New Brunswick: Rutgers University Press, 1953.

Lippmann, Walter. *Essays in the Public Philosophy.* Boston: Little, Brown, 1955.

——. *The Phantom Public.* New York: Macmillan, 1927.

Lipset, Seymour Martin. *American Exceptionalism: A Double-Edged Sword.* New York: Norton, 1997.

Littlefield, Daniel F. Jr. *Alex Posey: Creek Poet, Journalist, and Humorist.* Lincoln: University of Nebraska Press, 1992.

Littlefield, Daniel F. Jr., and James W. Parins. *American Indian and Alaska Native Newspapers and Periodicals, 1826–1924.* Westport, Conn.: Greenwood, 1984.

Livingston, Lili Cockerille. *American Indian Ballerinas.* Norman: University of Oklahoma Press, 1997.

Lowe, Lisa. *Critical Terrains: French and British Orientalisms.* Ithaca: Cornell University Press, 1991.

Lummis, C. Douglas. *Radical Democracy.* Ithaca: Cornell University Press, 1996.

Lynch, Deidre, and William B. Warner, eds. *Cultural Institutions of the Novel.* Durham: Duke University Press, 1996.

Lyotard, Jean-François. *The Inhuman: Reflections on Time.* Trans. Rachel Bowlby and Geoffrey Bennington. Stanford: Stanford University Press, 1992.

——. *The Postmodern Condition: A Report on Knowledge.* Minneapolis: University of Minnesota Press, 1985.

Machiavelli, Niccolò. *The Prince.* In *The Chief Works and Others.* Trans. Allan Gilbert. Durham: Duke University Press, 1965.

Macpherson, C. B. *The Life and Times of Liberal Democracy.* Oxford: Oxford University Press, 1977.

Main, Jackson Turner. *The Anti-Federalists: Critics of the Constitution, 1781–1788.* Chapel Hill: University of North Carolina Press, 1961.

Mannheim, Karl. *Ideology and Utopia.* New York: Harcourt, Brace and World, 1963.

Marcuse, Herbert. *Negations: Essays in Critical Theory.* Trans. Jeremy J. Shapiro. Boston: Beacon Press, 1968.

——. *One Dimensional Man: Studies in the Ideology of Advanced Industrial Society.* Boston: Beacon Press, 1964.

Marilley, Suzanne M. *Woman Suffrage and the Origins of Liberal Feminism in the United States, 1820–1920.* Cambridge: Harvard University Press, 1996.

Marin, Louis. *Portrait of the King.* Minneapolis: University of Minnesota Press, 1988.

Marshall, Paule. "Reena." In *The Black Woman: An Anthology,* ed. Toni Cade Bambara. New York: New American Library, 1970. 20–37.

Marx, Karl. *Capital, Volume 1.* In *The Marx-Engels Reader,* 2nd ed. Ed. Robert C. Tucker. New York: Norton, 1972.

——. *The Eighteenth Brumaire of Louis Bonaparte.* New York: International Publishers, 1963.

Marx, Karl, and Fredrick Engels. *The Holy Family, or Critique of Critical Critique.* Trans. R. Dixon. Moscow: Foreign Languages Publishing House, 1956.

Mathy, Jean-Phillipe. *Extreme-Occident: French Intellectuals and America.* Chicago: University of Chicago Press, 1993.

Mathews, Shaler, ed. *The Woman Citizen's Library.* 12 vols. Chicago: The Civics Library, 1914.

May, Lary. *The Big Tomorrow: Hollywood and the Politics of the American Way.* Chicago: University of Chicago Press, 2000.

McBride, Bunny. *Molly Spotted Elk: A Penobscot in Paris.* Norman: University of Oklahoma Press, 1995.

McChesney Chomsky, Robert W. "Introduction." In Noam Chomsky, *Profits over People: Neoliberalism and Global Order.* New York: Seven Stories Press, 1999.

McDowell, Deborah. "'The Changing Same': Generational Connections and Black Women Novelists." In *Reading Black Reading Feminist: A Critical Anthology,* ed. Henry Louis Gates Jr. New York: Meridian, 1990. 91–115.

Merleau-Ponty, Maurice. "Sartre, Merleau-Ponty: Les lettres d'une rupture." *Magazine Littéraire,* no. 320 (April 1994): 74–76.

Merrell, James H. *Into the American Woods: Negotiators on the Pennsylvania Frontier.* New York: Norton, 1999.

Meštrović, Stjepan G. *Postemotional Society.* London: Sage, 1997.

Meyerson, Harold. "Memo: Class and Country—The 1992 Campaign and Beyond." *L.A. Weekly,* September 20–26, 1991, 16–17.

Michnik, Adam. *The Church and the Left.* Chicago: University of Chicago Press, 1993.

——. *Letters from Freedom: Post Cold War Realities and Perspectives.* Los Angeles: University of California Press, 1998.

——. *Letters from Prison and Other Essays.* Los Angeles: University of California Press, 1985.

"Minority Critiques of the Critical Legal Studies Movement: A Forum." *Harvard Civil Rights–Civil Liberties Law Review* 22 (1987): 297–447.

Minow, Martha. "Interpreting Rights: An Essay for Robert Cover." *Yale Law Journal* 96 (1987): 1860–1915.

Mitchell, Joshua. *The Fragility of Freedom: Tocqueville on Religion, Democracy, and the American Future.* Chicago: University of Chicago Press, 1995.

Mitchell, Michele. "Silences Broken, Silences Kept: Gender and Sexuality in African American History." *Gender and History* 11, no. 3 (November 1999): 433–44.

Moberg, David. "Electronic Herd Mentality." *In These Times,* May 16, 1999, 20.

Moeller, Susan D. *Compassion Fatigue: How the Media Sell Disease, Famine, War, and Death.* New York: Routledge, 1999.

Montejano, David. *Anglos and Mexicans in the Making of Texas, 1836–1986.* Austin: University of Texas Press, 1987.

Morey, Victor P., and Fred T. Wilhelms. *Organizing and Conducting a Citizenship Class: A Guide for Use in the Public Schools by Teachers of Candidates for Naturalization.* Washington, D.C.: U.S. Government Printing Office, 1945.

Morgan, Joy Elmer, ed. *The American Citizen's Handbook,* 1941; Washington D.C.: National Council for Social Studies, 1968.

Morley, David, and Kuan-Hsing Chen, eds. *Stuart Hall: Critical Dialogues in Cultural Studies.* New York: Routledge, 1996.

Morris, Thomas D. "The Problem of the 'Sources' of Southern Slave Law." *The American Journal of Legal History* 32 (1988): 95–137.

———. *Southern Slavery and the Law.* Chapel Hill: University of North Carolina Press, 1996.

Morrison, Toni. *Song of Solomon.* New York: Plume, 1987.

Morton, Andrew. *Monica's Story.* New York: St. Martin's Press, 1999.

Moses, L. G. *Wild West Shows and the Images of American Indians 1883–1933.* Albuquerque: University of New Mexico Press, 1996.

Mosher, William E., ed. *Introduction to Responsible Citizenship.* New York: Henry Holt, 1941.

Mouffe, Chantal. "For a Politics of Nomadic Identity." In *Travellers' Tales: Narratives of Home and Displacement.* Ed. George Robertson et al. London: Routledge, 1994.

———. "Preface: Democratic Politics Today." In *Dimensions of Radical Democracy: Pluralism, Citizenship, Community,* ed. Chantal Mouffe. London: Verso, 1992.

Mulholland, Leslie A. *Kant's System of Rights.* New York: Columbia University Press, 1990.

Muñoz, Carlos. *Youth, Identity, Power: The Chicano Movement.* New York: Verso, 1989.

Murray, David. *Forked Tongues: Speech, Writing, and Representation in North American Indian Texts.* London: Pinter, 1991.

Nash, A. E. Keir. "Reason of Slavery: Understanding the Judicial Role in the Peculiar Institution." *Vanderbilt Law Review* (January 1979): 7–218.

Navarro, Armando. *Mexican American Youth Organization: Avant-Garde of the Chicano Movement in Texas.* Austin: University of Texas Press, 1995.

Negri, Antonio. *Insurgencies: Constituent Power and the Modern State.* Trans. Maurizia Boscagli. 1992; Minneapolis: University of Minnesota Press, 1999.

Nelson, Dana D. *National Manhood: Capitalist Citizenship and the Imagined Fraternity of White Men.* Durham: Duke University Press, 1998.

———. "Representative/Democracy: Presidents, Democratic Management, and the Unfinished Business of Male Sentimentalism." In *No More Separate Spheres!,* ed. Cathy N. Davidson. Durham: Duke University Press, 2002.

———. "Thoreau, Race, and Manhood: Quiet Desperation versus Representative Isolation." In *A Historical Guide to Henry David Thoreau,* ed. William Cain. New York: Oxford University Press, 2000. 61–93.

——. *The Word in Black and White: Reading "Race" in American Literature, 1638–1867.* New York: Oxford University Press, 1993.

Newfield, Christopher J. *The Emerson Effect: Individualism and Submission in America.* Chicago: University of Chicago Press, 1996.

——. "What Was Political Correctness? Race, the Right, and Managerial Democracy in the Humanities." *Critical Inquiry* 19, no. 2 (1993): 308–36.

Newton, A. E., ed. *The Educator: Being Suggestions, Theoretical and Practical Designed to Promote Man-Culture and Integral Reform, with a View to the Ultimate Establishment of a Divine Social State on Earth. Comprised in a series of Revealments from Organized Associations in the Spirit-Life, through John Murray Spear.* Vol. 1. Boston: Office of Practical Spiritualists, 1857.

Newton, Isaac. *Philosophiae Naturalis Principia Mathematica* (1686). Trans. by Andrew Motte in 1729 as *Mathematical Principles of Natural Philosophy.* Revised by Florian Cajori. Berkeley: University of California Press, 1934.

Nietzsche, Friedrich. *On the Genealogy of Morals.* Trans. Walter Kaufmann and R. J. Hollingdale. New York: Vintage, 1969.

Nisbet, Robert A. *The Sociological Tradition.* New York: Basic Books, 1966.

Norton, Anne. "Engendering Another American Identity." In *Rhetorical Republic: Governing Representations in American Politics,* ed. Frederick M. Dolan and Thomas L. Dumm. Amherst: University of Massachusetts Press, 1993.

Oakeshott, Michael. *The Voice of Liberal Learning.* New Haven: Yale University Press, 1989.

Odum, Howard Washington. *Community and Government: A Manual of Discussion and Study of the Newer Ideals of Citizenship.* Chapel Hill: University of North Carolina Extension Service, 1921.

Orr, Linda. *Headless History: Nineteenth-Century French Historiography of the Revolution.* Ithaca: Cornell University Press, 1990.

Oshinsky, David M. *"Worse Than Slavery": Parchman Farm and the Ordeal of Jim Crow Justice.* New York: The Free Press, 1996.

Ost, David. *Solidarity and the Politics of Anti-Politics: Opposition and Reform since 1968.* Philadelphia: Temple University Press, 1990.

Ostrom, Vincent. *The Meaning of Democracy and the Vulnerability of Democracies.* Ann Arbor: University of Michigan Press, 1997.

Paine, Thomas. *Common Sense and Other Political Writings.* Ed. Nelson F. Adkins. Indianapolis: Bobbs-Merrill, 1953.

Park, You-Me, and Gayle Wald. "Native Daughters in the Promised Land." *American Literature* 70, no. 3 (September 1998): 607–33.

Patterson, Anita. *From Emerson to King: Democracy, Race, and the Politics of Protest.* New York: Oxford University Press, 1997.

Patterson, Orlando. *Slavery and Social Death: A Comparative Study.* Cambridge: Harvard University Press, 1982.

Paulsen, Friedrich. *Immanuel Kant: His Life and Doctrine.* Trans. J. E. Creighton and Albert Lefevre. 1902; New York: Charles Scribner's Sons, 1963.

Peirce, Charles Sanders. "Concerning the Author." In *Philosophical Writings of Peirce,* ed. Justus Buchler. 1940; New York: Dover, 1955.

——. "The Scientific Attitude and Fallibilism." In *Philosophical Writings of Peirce,* ed. Justus Buchler. New York: Dover, 1955.

Perdue, Theda. "Rising from the Ashes: The *Cherokee Phoenix* as an Ethnohistorical Source." *Ethnohistory* 24 (summer 1977): 207–18.

Peters, Tom. *Liberation Management: Necessary Disorganization for the Nanosecond Nineties.* New York: Knopf, 1992.

Pfaelzer, Jean. *Parlor Radical: Rebecca Harding Davis and the Origins of American Social Realism.* Pittsburgh: University of Pittsburgh Press, 1996.

Phillips, Adam. *On Flirtation.* Cambridge: Harvard University Press, 1994.

Pitkin, Hanna Fenichel. *The Concept of Representation.* Berkeley: University of California Press, 1967.

Polanyi, Karl. *The Great Transformation: The Political and Economic Origins of Our Time.* 2nd ed. 1944; Boston: Beacon Press, 2001.

Pollitt, Katha. "Gay Marriage? Don't Say I Didn't Warn You." *Nation,* April 29, 1996, 9.

Posey, Alexander. *Alexander Posey's* The Fus Fixico Letters. Littlefield, Jr., Daniel F., and Carol A. Petty Hunter, eds. Lincoln: University of Nebraska, 1993.

Post, Isaac. *Voices from the Spirit World, Being Communications from Many Spirits. By the Hand of Isaac Post, Medium.* Rochester: Charles H. McDonnell, 1852.

Postman, Neal. *Amusing Ourselves to Death: Public Discourse in the Age of Show Business.* New York: Penguin Books, 1986.

Powell, Kevin. "A Dialogue with Audre Lorde." *Emerge* (November 1992): 23–24.

Powell, Richard. *Black Art and Culture in the Twentieth Century.* New York: Thames and Hudson, 1997.

Probyn, Elspeth. *Outside Belonging.* New York: Routledge, 1996.

Prucha, Francis Paul. *American Indian Treaties: The History of a Political Anomaly.* Berkeley: University of California Press, 1994.

Putnam, Robert D. "Bowling Alone: America's Declining Social Capital." *Journal of Democracy* 6, no. 1 (1995): 65–77.

Raboteau, Albert. *Slave Religion: The "Invisible Institution" in the Antebellum South.* New York: Oxford University Press, 1978.

Rancière, Jacques. *Dis-agreement: Politics and Philosophy.* Trans. Julie Rose. Minneapolis: University of Minnesota Press, 1999.

——. "Discovering New Worlds: Politics of Travel and Metaphors of Space." In *Travellers' Tales: Narratives of Home and Displacement,* ed. George Robertson et al. London: Routledge, 1994.

——. *On the Shores of Politics.* London: Verso, 1995.

Rawls, John. *Political Liberalism.* New York: Columbia University Press, 1993.

——. *A Theory of Justice.* Cambridge: Harvard University Press, 1971.

Read, Elizabeth Fisher. *Citizenship and the Vote: A Statement for the Women Citizens of the State of New York.* Published by the Americanization Committee of the New York State Woman Suffrage Party and the New York City Woman Suffrage Party, 1918.

Reichenbach, Hans. "The Philosophical Significance of the Theory of Relativity." In *Albert Einstein: Philosopher-Scientist*, ed. Paul Arthur Schlipp. La Salle: Open Court, 1970. 287–311.

——. *The Rise of Scientific Philosophy*. Berkeley: University of California Press, 1951.

Ricoeur, Paul. *Lectures on Ideology and Utopia*. New York: Columbia University Press, 1986.

Robbins, Bruce. "Introduction: The Public as Phantom." In *The Phantom Public Sphere*, ed. Bruce Robbins. Minneapolis: University of Minnesota Press, 1993.

Robinson, David M. *Emerson and the Conduct of Life*. New York: Cambridge University Press, 1993.

Rogers, Will. *Will Roger's Weekly Articles: The Coolidge Years, 1925–27*. 5 vols. Norman: University of Oklahoma Press, 1981.

——. *Will Roger's Weekly Articles: The Hoover Years, 1931–33*. 5 vols. Norman: University of Oklahoma Press, 1982.

Rogin, Michael Paul. *Blackface, White Noise: Jewish Immigrants in the Hollywood Melting Pot*. Berkeley: University of California Press, 1996.

Romero, Lora. *Home Fronts: Domesticity and Its Critics in the Antebellum United States*. Durham: Duke University Press, 1997.

Rorty, Richard. *Achieving Our Country: Leftist Thought in Twentieth-Century America*. Cambridge: Harvard University Press, 1998.

——. "Fraternity Reigns." *New York Times Magazine*, September 29, 1996, 175–76.

Roscoe, William. *A Brief Statement of the Causes which have led to the Abandonment of the Celebrated System of Penitentiary Discipline in Some of the United States of America*. Liverpool: Harris and Co., 1827.

Ross, Kristin. *Fast Cars, Clean Bodies: Decolonization and the Reordering of French Culture*. Cambridge: MIT Press, 1995.

Rourke, Constance. *The Roots of American Culture and Other Essays*. Ed. Van Wyck Brooks. New York: Harcourt, Brace, 1942.

Rouse, Roger. "The Nightmare Paper," unpublished manuscript.

Ruttenberg, Nancy. *Democratic Personality: Popular Voice and the Trial of American Authorship*. Stanford: Standford University Press, 1998.

Said, Edward. *Orientalism*. London: Routledge, Kegan and Paul, 1978.

——. *Representations of the Intellectual*. New York: Pantheon, 1994.

Sandel, Michael. *Democracy's Discontent: America in Search of a Public Philosophy*. Cambridge: Harvard University Press, 1996.

Sayyid, Bobby. "Sign o' Times: Kaffirs and Infidels Fighting the Ninth Crusade." In *The Making of Political Identities*, ed. Ernesto Laclau. New York: Verso, 1994.

Scheppele, Kim Lane. "Facing Facts in Legal Interpretation." *Representations* 30 (1990): 42–77.

Schlesinger, Arthur M. Jr. *The Disuniting of America: Reflections on a Multicultural Society*. Knoxville: Whittle Direct Books, 1991.

Schneider, Alison. "Jane Tompkins' Message to Academe: Nurture the Individual, Not Just the Intellect." *Chronicle of Higher Education*, July 10, 1998, A8.

Scott, Benjamin D. *Citizenship Readers: Notable Events in the Making of America.* Philadelphia: Lippincott, 1930.

Sellers, Charles Grier. *The Market Revolution: Jacksonian America, 1815–1846.* New York: Oxford University Press, 1991.

Seltzer, Mark. *Serial Killers.* New York: Routledge, 1998.

Shaffer, Byron E., ed. *Is America Different? A New Look at American Exceptionalism.* London: Oxford University Press, 1991.

Shapin, Steven. "Of Gods and Kings: Natural Philosophy and Politics in the Leibniz-Clarke Disputes." *Isis* 72 (1981): 187–215.

Shapiro, Ian. *The Evolution of Rights in Liberal Theory.* Cambridge: Cambridge University Press, 1986.

Shapiro, Michael. "Introduction." In *Challenging Boundaries,* ed. Michael Shapiro and Hayward R. Alker. Minneapolis: University of Minnesota Press, 1996.

Shattuck, Roger. *Candor and Perversion: Literature, Education, and the Arts.* New York: Norton, 1999.

Shklar, Judith N. "Emerson and the Inhibitions of Democracy," *Political Theory* 18, no. 4 (November 1990): 601–14.

——. *Legalism.* Cambridge: Harvard University Press, 1986, 1964.

Shurter, Edwin DuBois. *American Citizenship and Government.* Philadelphia: Lippincott, 1930.

——. *Legalism.* Cambridge: Harvard University Press, 1986.

——, ed. *Woman Suffrage: Bibliography and Selected Arguments June 1, 1912.* Austin: University of Texas, 1912.

Siedentop, Larry. *Tocqueville.* Oxford: Oxford University Press, 1994.

Simpson, A. W. B. *A History of the Land Law.* Oxford: Clarendon Press, 1986.

Skinful, Mauri. "Nation and Miscegenation: *Incidents in the Life of a Slave Girl.*" *Arizona Quarterly* 52 (summer 1995): 63–79.

Smart-Grosvenor, Verta Mae. "The Kitchen Crisis." *The Black Woman: An Anthology,* ed. Toni Cade Bambara. New York: New American Library, 1970. 119–23.

Smith, Doug, Carl Ingram, and Rich Connell. "Duke Shaped Power Market, Three Tell Panel." *Los Angeles Times,* June 23, 2001, A1.

Smith, Eric Ledell. *Bert Williams: A Biography of the Pioneer Black Comedian.* Jefferson, N.C.: McFarland, 1992.

Smith, Page. *Killing the Spirit: Higher Education in America.* New York: Viking, 1990.

Smith, Valerie. "'Loopholes of Retreat': Architecture and Ideology in Harriet Jacobs's *Incidents in the Life of a Slave Girl.*" In *Reading Black, Reading Feminist: A Critical Anthology,* ed. Henry Louis Gates Jr. New York: Meridian, 1990. 212–26.

Soares, Manuela. "The Purloined *Ladder:* Its Place in Lesbian History." In *Gay and Lesbian Literature since World War II: History and Memory,* ed. Sonya Jones. New York: The Haworth Press, 1998. 27–49.

Solomon, Martha M., ed. *A Voice of Their Own: The Woman Suffrage Press, 1840–1910.* Tuscaloosa: University of Alabama Press, 1991.

Spivak, Gayatri Chakravorty. "Can the Subaltern Speak?" In *Marxism and the Interpreta-*

tion of Culture, ed. Cary Nelson and Lawrence Grossberg. Urbana: University of Illinois Press, 1988. 271–313.

Stafford, William. "Books That Look Out, Books That Look In." In *On Gwendolyn Brooks: Reliant Contemplation,* ed. Stephen Caldwell Wright. Ann Arbor: University of Michigan Press, 1996.

Stephanopoulos, George. *All Too Human: A Political Education.* Boston: Little, Brown, 1999.

Stephen, Sir James Fitzjames. *A History of the Criminal Law of England.* London: Macmillan, 1883.

Sterling, Bryan B. *The Best of Will Rogers.* New York: Crown, 1979.

——, ed. *The Will Rogers Scrapbook.* New York: Grosset & Dunlap, 1976.

Sterling, Bryan B., and Frances N. Sterling. *Will Rogers in Hollywood.* New York: Crown, 1984.

Stevens, Jacqueline. *Reproducing the State.* Princeton: Princeton University Press, 1999.

Stewart, Larry. "Samuel Clarke, Newtonianism, and the Factions of Post-Revolutionary England." *Journal of the History of Ideas* 42 (1981): 53–72.

Strauss, Leo. *Natural Rights and History.* Chicago: University of Chicago Press, 1953.

Streitmatter, Rodger. *Unspeakable: The Rise of the Lesbian and Gay Rights Press in America.* Boston: Faber & Faber, 1995.

Stuesse, Angela. *Claiming Rights and Resources in El Cenizo, Texas.* Masters thesis, Institute for Latin American Studies, University of Texas at Austin, 2001.

Suárez-Orozco, Marcelo. *Crossings: Mexican Immigration in Interdisciplinary Perspectives.* Cambridge: David Rockefeller Center for Latin American Studies; Harvard University Press, 1998.

Sullivan, Andrew. *Virtually Normal: An Argument About Homosexuality.* New York: Knopf, 1995.

Sundquist, Eric J. *To Wake the Nations: Race in the Making of American Literature.* Cambridge: Harvard University Press, 1993.

"Symposium: A Critique of Rights." *Texas Law Review* 62 (1984): 1363–1617.

Tallchief, Maria, with Larry Kaplan. *Maria Tallchief: America's Prima Ballerina.* New York: Holt, 1997.

Taussig, Michael. *The Magic of the State.* New York: Routledge, 1997.

Teja, Jesus de la. *A Revolution Remembered: The Memoirs and Selected Correspondence of Juan N. Seguín.* Austin: State House Press, 1991.

Terborg-Penn, Rosalyn, Sharon Harley, and Andrea Benton-Rushing, eds. *Women in Africa and the African Diaspora.* Washington, D.C.: Howard University Press, 1987.

Thoenig, Raymond H. "Solitary Confinement—Punishment Within the Letter of the Law, or Psychological Torture?" *Wisconsin Law Review* 1 (1972): 223–37.

Tocqueville, Alexis de. "Author's Preface to the Twelfth Edition." In *Democracy in America.* Trans. George W. Lawrence. Ed. J. P. Mayer. Garden City, N.Y.: Doubleday, 1969.

——. *Democracy in America.* Ed. and trans. Harvey C. Mansfield and Delba Winthrop. Chicago: University of Chicago Press, 2000.

——. *Democracy in America.* New York: Everyman's Library, 1994.

"Tocqueville and the Mullah." *New Republic* 333, no. 4 (February 2, 1998): 7–8.

Tomkins, Silvan S. *The Positive Affects*, vol. 1 of *Affect, Imagery, Consciousness*. New York: Springer Publishing Company, 1962.

———. *Shame and Its Sisters: A Silvan Tomkins Reader*. Ed. Eve Kosofsky Sedgwick and Adam Frank. Durham: Duke University Press, 1995.

Tompkins, Jane. *A Life in School: What the Teacher Learned*. Reading, Mass.: Addison-Wesley, 1996.

———. "Pedagogy of the Distressed." *College English* 52 (October 1990): 653–60.

Touraine, Alaine. *Return of the Actor: Social Theory in Postindustrial Society*. Trans. Myrna Godzich. Minneapolis: University of Minnesota Press, 1988.

Tribe, Laurence. "The Curvature of Constitutional Space: What Lawyers Can Learn from Modern Physics." *Harvard Law Review* 103 (1989): 1–39.

Turborg-Penn, Rosalind. *African American Women in the Struggle for the Vote, 1850–1920*. Bloomington: Indiana University Press, 1998.

Tuck, Richard. *Natural Rights Theories*. Cambridge: Cambridge University Press, 1979.

Tucker, Robert, ed. *The Marx-Engels Reader*. New York: Norton, 1972.

Tushnet, Mark V. *The American Law of Slavery, 1810–1860: Considerations of Humanity and Interest*. Princeton, NJ: Princeton University Press, 1981.

———. "An Essay on Rights." *Texas Law Review* 62 (1984): 1363–1403.

Tuska, Jon. *The Filming of the West*. Garden City, N.Y.: Doubleday, 1976.

Tyson, Tim. *Radio Free Dixie: Robert Williams and the Roots of Black Power*. Chapel Hill: University of North Carolina Press, 1999.

Unger, Roberto. *Democracy Realized: The Progressive Alternative*. London: Verso, 1998.

———. *False Necessity: Anti-Necessitarian Social Theory in the Service of Radical Democracy*, part 1 of *Politics: A Work in Constructive Social Theory*. Cambridge: Cambridge University Press, 1987.

U.S. Army Studies in Citizenship for Recruits. Washington, D.C.: Government Printing Office, 1922.

Vaid, Urvashi. *Virtual Equality: The Mainstreaming of Gay and Lesbian Liberation*. New York: Doubleday, 1995.

Vaux, Roberts. *Letter on the Penitentiary System of Pennsylvania, addressed to William Roscoe, Esquire*. Philadelphia: Printed by Jesper Harding, 1827.

Vlachou, Andriana, ed. *Contemporary Economic Theory: Radical Critiques of Neoliberalism*. New York: St. Martin's Press, 1999.

Vladislav, Jan, ed. *Vaclav Havel, or Living in Truth*. Boston: Faber & Faber, 1986.

Wald, Priscilla. *Constituting Americans: Cultural Anxiety and Narrative Form*. Durham: Duke University Press, 1995.

Walker, Alice. *In Search of Our Mothers' Gardens: Womanist Prose*. San Diego: Harcourt Brace Jovanovich, 1983.

Wallis, Michael. *The Real Wild West: The 101 Ranch and the Creation of the American West*. New York: St. Martin's Press, 1999.

Walzer, Michael. "The Civil Society Argument." In *Dimensions of Radical Democracy: Pluralism, Citizenship, Community*, ed. Chantal Mouffe. New York: Verso, 1992.

Ward, Peter. *Colonias and Public Policy: Urbanization by Stealth.* Austin: University of Texas Press, 1999.

Warner, Marina. *Monuments and Maidens: The Allegory of The Female Form.* New York: Atheneum, 1985.

Warner, Michael. "The Mass Public and the Mass Subject." *The Phantom Public Sphere,* ed. Bruce Robbins. Minneapolis: University of Minnesota Press, 1993. 234–56.

———. "Media Gays: A New Stone Wall." *Nation* 265 (July 14, 1997): 15–19.

———. *The Trouble with Normal: Sex, Politics, and the Ethics of Queer Life.* New York: The Free Press, 1999.

Washington, Mary Helen. "'The Darkened Eye Restored': Notes Toward a Literary History of Black Women." *Reading Black, Reading Feminist,* ed. Henry Louis Gates Jr. New York: Meridian, 1990.

Watkins, Mel. *On the Real Side: A History of African American Comedy.* New York: Simon & Schuster, 1994.

Weaver, Jace. *That the People Might Live: Native American Literatures and Native American Community.* New York: Oxford University Press, 1997.

Weems, Mason Locke. *The Life of Washington.* Ed. Marcus Cunliffe. Cambridge: The Belknap Press of Harvard University Press, 1962.

Weschler, Lawrence. *Solidarity: Poland in the Season of Its Passions.* New York: Simon and Schuster, 1982.

Westfall, Robert. *Never at Rest: A Biography of Isaac Newton.* New York: Cambridge University Press, 1980.

White, E. Frances. "Africa on My Mind: Gender, Counter Discourse and African-American Nationalism." *Journal of Women's History* 2 (1990): 73–97.

White, Hayden. "The Value of Narrativity in the Representation of Reality." *Critical Inquiry* 7 (1980): 5–27.

Wiebe, Robert. *Self-Rule: A Cultural History of American Democracy.* Chicago: University of Chicago Press, 1995.

Williams, Patricia. "Alchemical Notes: Reconstructing Ideals from Deconstructed Rights." *Harvard Civil Rights–Civil Liberties Law Review* 22 (1987): 401–34.

Williams, Raymond. *Marxism and Literature.* Oxford: Oxford University Press, 1977.

Willis, Ellen. *Beginning to See the Light: Sex, Hope, and Rock-and-Roll.* 2nd ed. Hanover, N.H.: Wesleyan University Press, 1992.

Wills, David. *Prosthesis.* Stanford: Stanford University Press, 1995.

Wills, Garry. *John Wayne's America: The Politics of Celebrity.* New York: Simon and Schuster, 1997.

Wilson, Harold F. *The Hill Country of Northern New England.* New York: Columbia University Press, 1936.

Wilson, Justina Leavitt. *Woman Suffrage: A Study Outline.* White Plains, N.Y.: The H. W. Wilson Co., 1916.

Wilson, Meredith. *The Music Man.* New York: G. P. Putnam's Sons, 1958.

Wolin, Sheldon S. *The Presence of the Past: Essays on the State and the Constitution.* Baltimore: Johns Hopkins University Press, 1989.

Womack, Craig S. *Red on Red: Native American Literary Separatism.* Minneapolis: University of Minnesota Press, 1999.

Wood, Gordon S. *Creation of the American Republic, 1776–1787.* New York: Norton, 1981.

——. "Democracy in America: Toqueville's Lesson." *New York Review of Books* 48, no. 8 (May 17, 2001): 46–50.

——. *The Radicalism of the American Revolution.* New York: Vintage, 1991.

Yagoda, Ben. *Will Rogers: A Biography.* New York: Knopf, 1993.

Yellin, Jean Fagan. "Introduction." In Harriet A. Jacobs, *Incidents in the Life of a Slave Girl,* ed. Jean Fagan Yellin. Cambridge: Harvard University Press, 1987.

Young, Robert B. *No Neutral Ground: Standing by the Values We Prize in Higher Education.* San Francisco: Jossey-Bass, 1997.

Zetterbaum, Marvin. *Tocqueville and the Problem of Democracy.* Stanford: Stanford University Press: 1967.

Žižek, Slavoj. "Eastern Europe's Republics of Gilead." *New Left Review* 183 (September/October 1990): 50–62.

CONTRIBUTORS

LAUREN BERLANT teaches in the English department at the University of Chicago. She is author of the national sentimentality trilogy *The Anatomy of National Fantasy* (1991), *The Queen of America Goes to Washington City: Essays in Sex and Citizenship* (1997), and the forthcoming *The Female Complaint: The Unfinished Business of Sentimentality in American Culture*, from which this essay comes. She is also editor of *Intimacy* (2000) and coeditor, with Lisa Duggan, of *Our Monica, Ourselves: The Clinton Affair and National Interest* (2001).

WENDY BROWN is Professor of Political Science and Women's Studies at the University of California, Berkeley. Her recent books include *States of Injury: Power and Freedom in Late Modernity* (1995) and *Politics Out of History* (2001). *Left Legalism/Left Critique*, coedited with Janet Halley is forthcoming in 2001.

CHRIS CASTIGLIA is Associate Professor of English at Loyola University, Chicago. He is author of *Bound and Determined: Captivity, Culture-Crossing, and White Womanhood from Mary Rowlandson to Patty Hearst* (1996) and *Interior States: The Romance of Reform and the Inner Life of the Nation* (forthcoming).

RUSS CASTRONOVO is Associate Professor of English and Director of American Studies at the University of Miami. He is author of *Necro Citizenship: Death, Eroticism, and the Public Sphere in the Nineteenth-Century United States* (2001) and *Fathering the Nation: American Genealogies of Slavery and Freedom* (1995). He is currently working on political aesthetics, formalism, and democracy in U.S. culture after the 1890s.

JOAN DAYAN, Professor of English at the University of Pennsylvania, whose works include *Fables of Mind: An Inquiry into Poe's Fiction* (1987) and *Haiti, History, and the Gods* (1995), is currently completing *Held in the Body of the State*, a book on prisons and the law, and *The Law Is a White Dog*, a series of essays on the mechanisms of law, spiritual belief, and the supernatural.

WAI CHEE DIMOCK is Professor of English at Yale University. She is author of two books, *Empire for Liberty: Melville and the Poetics of Individualism* (1989) and *Residues of Justice: Literature, Law, Philosophy* (1996), and coeditor of a volume of essays, *Rethinking Class* (1994). She is now at work on a new book project, "Literature for the Planet."

LISA DUGGAN is Associate Professor of American Studies at New York University. She is coauthor, with Nan D. Hunter, of *Sex Wars: Sexual Dissent and Political Culture* (1995), author of *Sapphic Slashers: Sex, Violence, and American Modernity* (2000), and coeditor, with Lauren Berlant, of *Our Monica, Ourselves: The Clinton Affair and National Interest* (2001). She is currently at work on a book about Jesse Helms and U.S. political culture.

RICHARD R. FLORES is Associate Professor of Anthropology and Mexican American Studies and Director of the Américo Paredes Center for Cultural Studies at the University of Texas at Austin. He works in the areas of critical theory, performance studies, semiotics, and historical anthropology. He is author of *Los Pastores: History and Performance in the Mexican Shepherd's Play of South Texas* (1995) and editor of Adina De Zavala's *History and Legends of the Alamo* (1996), and he has published essays in *American Ethnologist, Cultural Anthropology, American Literary History, Radical History Review,* and in the edited volume *Latino Cultural Citizenship.* His book *Remembering the Alamo: Memory, Modernity, and the Master Symbol* is forthcoming in 2002.

KEVIN GAINES teaches in the history department and the Center for Afro-American and African Studies at the University of Michigan, Ann Arbor. He is author of *Uplifting the Race: Black Leadership, Politics, and Culture during the Twentieth Century* (1996). He is currently writing a book on African American and African Caribbean expatriates in postindependence Ghana.

JEFFREY C. GOLDFARB, Michael E. Gellert Professor of Sociology at the New School for Social Research, is the author of numerous books and articles on the politics of culture and the culture of politics, including, most recently, *Civility and Subversion: The Intellectual in Democratic Society* (1998). He is presently working on a new project on media and micropolitics.

MICHAEL MOON is Professor of English at Johns Hopkins University. Author of *Disseminating Whitman: Revision and Corporeality in Leaves of Grass* (1991) and *A Small Boy and Others: Imitation and Initiation in American Culture from Henry James to Andy Warhol* (1998), he is completing *Shattered Territories: Oklahoma's Places in the National Imaginary.* He is coeditor of *Subjects and Citizens: Nation, Race, and Gender from* Oroonoko *to Anita Hill* (1995) and *Displacing Homophobia: Gay Male Perspectives on Literature and Culture* (1990).

DANA D. NELSON is Professor of English and Social Theory at the University of Kentucky. Author of *The Word in Black and White: Reading "Race" in American Literature, 1638–1867* (1993) and *National Manhood: Capitalist Citizenship and the Imagined Fraternity of White Men* (1998), she's currently working on a book-length project titled "Representative/Democracy."

CHRISTOPHER NEWFIELD is Professor of English at the University of California, Santa Barbara. He teaches and writes about American culture after 1830, with particular attention to fiction since 1920, race, sexuality, affect, California, and corporate culture. He is author of *Criticism, Inc.: The Humanities and Modern Management* (forthcoming) and *The Emerson Effect: Individualism and Submission in America*

(1996). He is also coeditor of *Mapping Multiculturalism* (1996) and *After Political Correctness: The Humanities and Society in the 1990s* (1995). He is currently working on two projects: "The Empowerment Wars," which explores the literature, management theory, and everyday life of cubicle dwellers in corporate America; and "Starting Up, Starting Over," a chronicle of the underside of the "New Economy" in Southern California.

DONALD E. PEASE is Avalon Professor of Humanities and Professor of English at Dartmouth College. He is editor of *National Identities and Post-Americanist Narratives* (1994) and coeditor, with Amy Kaplan, of *Cultures of United States Imperialism* (1993) and, with Walter Benn Michaels, of *The American Renaissance Reconsidered: Selected Papers of the English Institute* (1985). He is author of *Visionary Compacts: American Renaissance Writings in Cultural Context* (1987) and the coeditor, with Robyn Wiegman, of *The Futures of American Studies* (forthcoming in 2002).

INDEX

Affect: and "bare life," 165–79; and democratic practice, 7, 9, 110; as emotional literacy, 163; and exchange, 19; and governance, 197; as "national sentimentality," 156–65; and neoliberal privatization, 190; and pedagogy, 161, 164; and political representation, 218. *See also* Governance; Sentiment: and education

African Americans: diaspora identity, 294; expatriates in Ghana, 294, 303–6

Agamben, Giorgio, 158, 159–60, 166

Alamo, the: Battle of (1836), 97; as master symbol, 97; story, 98

Arendt, Hannah, 2, 221, 227, 228–29, 235, 236–40, 356, 364

Articles of Confederation, 222, 223

Artists: and free oppositional culture, 355

Bambara, Toni Cade, 296, 301, 306, 307, 310, 337; *The Black Woman*, 296, 301–3, 304, 306–10; *The Black Woman* and the Black Panther Party, 308; *The Black Woman* as critique of U.S. domestic nationalism, 303, 307, 308–9

Battle of the Little Bighorn (1876), 280

Bawer, Bruce, 176, 189

Beaumont, Gustave, 44, 69; as coauthor of *On the Penitentiary System in the United States*, 54, 69–70

Black Arts movement, 295

Black feminism, 294–310; as comprehensive democratic perspective, 296; critique of sexism, 296, 302–3, 305–6, 307–10; relation to white, middle-class women's movement in

the United States, 295–96; vision of radical democracy, 295, 307–10

Black Power movement: black feminist critique of, 294; and gender polarization, 296–97, 310

Blackstone, William, 54–55, 61

Blanchard, Rob, 183

Blood: and race, 62. *See also* Law

Boaz, David, 176, 189

Boone, Sylvia Arden, 305–6

Boston Tea Party, 317

Boudinot, Elias. See *Cherokee Phoenix*

Bracero Program, 96–103

Brooks, Gwendolyn, 296, 297–98, 301, 306, 309; "Maud Martha," 297–98

Butler, Judith, 120–22, 185–86, 236

Carnegie, Andrew, 4

Cherokee Phoenix: and Elias Boudinot, 279, 291 n.24

Cherokees: newspaper-writing traditions, 279–85, 288–90; and slavery, 288; syllabary, 276–77

Childress, Alice, 296, 298–99, 301, 309; *Like One of the Family*, 298–99

Citizenship: abstract versus local, 144–45, 149, 164, 166, 168–70, 211, 221; celebrity, 157–61; counterimaginary of, 139, 164, 165–67, 168–69, 196; as death, 118; and democratic subjectivity, 117–18, 120, 150–52; and desire, 30–31; governance versus participation, 240, 327; and heteronormativity, 154–56, 165; individual agency and system complexity, 327–30; liberal, and new formalism, 157; and market

353; as political guardianship, 345; as reproductive of socio-political order, 365; "teaching the conflicts" versus ignoring them, 353,
361; theories of liberal education, 118, 136–39;
and training students to be politically independent, 346, 353–54, 360–61, 363–65. *See
also* Liberal arts education; Pedagogy

Einstein, Albert, 250–51, 255–56, 263; ethics
and the challenge of empiricism, 256; relativity, 255

El Cenizo (Texas), 95, 106–10

Ellison, Ralph: *Invisible Man*, 298

Embodiment: and democracy theory, 116, 120–
25, 170; politics of materiality, 121–25, 128–30,
165–70; sacred, 148

Emerson, Ralph Waldo: *Representative Men*,
220–22, 225–30, 233, 234, 236, 238, 239

Esperanza Peace and Justice Center, 183

Ethics: and disagreement, 261; empirical, 258–
63; and formal absolutism, 251–58; physics
and metaphysics, 251, 255–58, 260–63; relativity, 255–63. *See also* Moralism; Morality

"False necessity," 222, 231, 238

Fanon, Frantz, 133

Felons (United States): and civil death, 68–70,
78–85; as intermediate category, 67; as "slave
of the state," 68–72, 86

Flirtation, 208–13; and democratic governance,
209; and ethical becoming, 209. *See also*
Governance

Freedom: as function of complexity, 321; political Left and nonmarket ideals of individual,
316, 329–38

Free market ideal: as illusion, 315. *See also* Market ideology

Freeman, Mary Wilkins: "A Far-Away Melody,"
260–61; "New England Nun," 259–60; "A Village Singer," 261; and phenomenology of
sound, 260

Gandhi, 373

Gay liberation activism, 177, 180–81; and privatization, 181; and publicity, 181–82

Geronimo, Don. See *Don and Mike Radio Show*

Glendon, Mary Ann, 249–50

Governance: versus government, 196; versus

self-culture, 225. *See also* Affect; "Unburdened agency"

Great Depression, 268, 271

Guess, George/Sequoyah (Cherokee), 267, 275,
276–78, 279; and invention of syllabary, 276;
and treaty process, 277; and vanishing act,
277, 279, 281

Guiliani, Rudolph (New York City mayor), 175,
332

Haage, Ghassan, 29–30

Haiti, 53

Hansberry, Lorraine, 296, 299–301, 309; *A Raisin in the Sun*, 300

Havel, Vaclav, 348–51, 352, 355, 257

Hertz, Neil, 41–42

Identity politics: confusing cynicism for critical
understanding, 361; and politics of "difference," 386–87; susceptibility to moralizing,
385; as symptom of the fragmentation of suffering, 386. *See also* Sarco-political

Ideology: definitions, 346–48; as a powerful
twentieth-century political force, 347; as a
special kind of thinking, 347

Ince, Thomas (movie director): and employment of Indian performers, 286–87

Independent Gay Forum, 175–76, 179, 182, 184,
189, 190

Intellectuals in democracy, 11–13, 348–53, 354; as
anti-ideological, 358; as facilitators and civi-
lizers of political dialogue, 349, 352, 357–58;
361; felt-impotence, 384; ideology and political disorientation, 378; and imperative for
political action, 377–78; independence and
ability to address general public, 357; and
moralism, 384; as providers of alternative
models and practices, 348–52, 354–56, 358–
60; as special kind of strangers, 357; as sub-
verters of conventional wisdom, 349–51, 358;
as undemocratic agents, 354, 357–58. *See also*
Left, the; Moralism

Interiority: and confession, 196; democratic,
195; insurgent countercitizenship, 202, 204;
interiorizing discourses, 196; relation to publicity, 195, 214 n.4; and world of tenderness,
203. *See also* Affect; Publicity

Library of Congress Cataloging-in-Publication Data
Materializing democracy: toward to revitalized cultural politics /
edited by Russ Castronovo and Dana D. Nelson.
p. cm. — (New Americanists)
Includes bibliographical references and index.
ISBN 0-8223-2910-7 (cloth)
ISBN 0-8223-2938-7 (pbk.)
1. Democracy—United States. I. Castronovo, Russ II. Nelson,
Dana D. III. Series.
JK1726 .M38 2002   321.8—dc21   2001008514

www.ingramcontent.com/pod-product-compliance
Lightning Source LLC
Chambersburg PA
CBHW051947270326
41929CB00015B/2560